Educational Research, the National Agenda, and Educational Reform

A History

A volume in
Studies in the History of Education

Series Editor:
Karen L. Riley, *Auburn University at Montgomery*

Studies in the History of Education

Karen L. Riley, Series Editor

Social Reconstruction: People, Politics, Perceptions (2006)
edited by Karen L. Riley

Language of the Land Policy, Politics, Identity (2007)
edited by Katherine Schuster and David Witkosky

*This Happened in America: Harold Rugg and
the Censure of Social Studies* (2007)
By Ronald W. Evans,

Educational Research, the National Agenda, and Educational Reform

A History

by

Erwin V. Johanningmeier
University of South Florida

and

Theresa Richardson
Ball State University

Information Age Publishing, Inc.
Charlotte, North Carolina • www.infoagepub.com

Library of Congress Cataloging-in-Publication Data

Johanningmeier, Erwin V.
 Educational research, the national agenda, and educational reform a history / by Erwin V. Johanningmeier and Theresa Richardson.
    p. cm. -- (Studies in the history of education)
  Includes bibliographical references and index.
   ISBN 978-1-59311-730-6 (pbk.) -- ISBN 978-1-59311-731-3 (hardcover) 1. Education--Research--United States. 2. Educational change--United States. I. Richardson, Theresa R., 1945- II. Title.
  LB1028.25.U6J64 2007
  370.7'2--dc22

                                                                          2007033618

ISBN 13: 978-1-59311-730-6 (paperback)
ISBN 13: 978-1-59311-731-3 (hardcover)

Printed in the United States of America

CONTENTS

PREFACE

This book is the result of our mutual interests in the history and dynamics of public education, childhood, and the standards of knowledge that guide policies and practices related to schooling and the treatment of children. E. V. Johanningmeier has for years been interested in the history of educational research and has taught the graduate course "Classics in Educational Research," for over twenty years, coming to the realization that what was taught, how it was taught, and the expectations for students to demonstrate knowledge on how to conduct research has changed dramatically. Teaching that course also led to the realization that educational research as well as education in general is fundamentally political. Theresa Richardson has been interested in the organization, support, and dissemination of social science research in the twentieth century, especially as applied to the needs, nature, and nurture of children. Her work focuses on the role of large-scale philanthropies, especially the Rockefeller philanthropies, that funded the expansion of education at all levels as well as research that directly contributed to the knowledge base of professionals concerned with children, education, public health, and social welfare fields. Through many discussions and exchanges over the years, we came to realize that we were pursuing the same interests, albeit from different vantage points.

Our complementary interests and discussions over the years also made it clear that the significance and meaning of educational research can only be appreciated if it is recognized that social scientists' research agendas are significantly shaped by the politics of the nation and what is called in this volume, the national agenda. Schools not only reflect the national agenda but also are part of the agenda. Since the end of the nineteenth century public education has been expected to solve the nation's problems. The public school has been an agency designed to carry out the social, economic, and political agenda of the nation state and its leadership. Educational researchers' agenda has tended to reflect and to conform to the national agenda. Researchers whose interests have conformed to the national agenda have often been funded either by the state or by private agencies acting in what they believe to be the public interest.

Researching, thinking about, and writing this volume have taken place over the course of both of our careers. This work is a synthesis of being participants and observers of our profession, researchers, and students. We have used primary and secondary sources and documents to tell a story we consider important. We would like to thank our colleagues in the social foundations of education area who have contributed to our thinking processes at professional meetings and through their work. Once again Sol Cohen's excellent five-volume, *Education in the United States: A Documentary History* (originally published 1974) was especially useful. We offer special thanks to our colleagues and students at the University of South Florida and Ball State University for their many conversations on all things educational. Theresa Richardson would especially like to thank and to acknowledge Director Darwin Stapleton and the staff at the Rockefeller Archive Center in Sleepy Hollow, New York. This magnificent collection and its faithful custodians provide many lifetimes of materials for historians in multiple fields. The book is dedicated to our five daughters: Christina Johanningmeier Cieslewiez, Genevieve L. Richardson, Anne Y. Richardson, Nicole Richardson Lemke and Elizabeth V. Johanningmeier.

Erwin V. Johanningmeier
University of South Florida
Theresa R. Richardson
Ball State University
January 2007

INTRODUCTION

While education is an agency of the nation-state used to promote the nation's social, political, and economic agenda, at the same time it is also a major agency for the expression of the public philosophy. In the United States, education, usually in the form of public schooling, is the agency historically selected as the instrument for social reform. The dominant view focuses on the individual as opposed to the social and economic structures that do so much either to enable or to restrict individuals as they try to exercise their talents.

Public education is not independent of the nation's agenda. Indeed, public education has been the agency called upon to address the nation's economic, political, and social problems and goals, and its need for human resources. At times the dominant classes of society and its leadership recognize either a challenge or an opportunity they believe must be either met or seized, and that challenge or opportunity is placed high on the national agenda. Charles Burgess and Merle Borrowman observed that when the nation has clear and specific human resource requirements, educational ideology emphasizes "social productivity" values. When human resource requirements are not readily identifiable, educational ideology stresses "consummatory values." At times, both the school and society, usually through the media, emphasize what students need to secure positions with significant social and economic rewards. In that way, a sufficient supply of properly trained personnel is assured to accomplish whatever is identified as being in the national interest. At other times, when there is less certainty about the kinds of skills and interests that are needed, schools emphasize how students can develop and enjoy their own interests.[1] At times, traditional school subjects and achievement are encouraged; at other times electives and enjoyment are encouraged. As the nation's agenda and its projected needs for human resources change so do the school's curricula and the researchers' agenda.

If there is any doubt about the relationship among educational research, educational reform and the national agenda, one only has to review the directives of the No Child Left Behind Act (NCLB) passed in 2002. NCLB basically legislates what is and is not good science and the research methods that are claimed to produce good science. The emphasis that NCLB has placed on eliminating the achievement gap between students from the mainstream dominant classes and students from minority groups can be explained by estimates of the future size and characteristics of the prime-age workforce (25 to 54 year olds). Between 1980 and 2000 the prime-age workforce grew by 35.1 million. It is projected that between 2000 and 2020 the prime-age workforce will increase by only 3.1 million. In an era when success in the global economy appears to be related to a highly qualified and highly educated workforce, the projections about the size and the characteristics of the prime-age workforce are significant and offer some explanations as to whey educators are responding to the imperative of NCLB to eliminate the achievement gap between majority and minority students. Approximately 30% of the prime-age workforce between 2000 and 2020 is expected to be classified as either African American or Hispanic, students who most likely either will not enter college or if they enter are not likely to graduate.[2] Another account suggests that college enrollment rates and graduation rates are not great enough to replace the college-educated workers who will retire in the coming decades. For example, it has been estimated that "the share of workers with at least some college will increase by only 3 percent between 2000 and 2020." Some projections show "that by 2012, we will have a surplus of more than three million workers with high-school degrees or less, and a shortage of about seven million workers with at least some college education."[3] Closing the achievement gap is a purpose endorsed by a majority of Americans. A survey in 2006 showed that the achievement gap was high on the national agenda. Sixty-seven percent of Americans believed it was "very important" to eliminate the achievement gap between white and minority (Black and Hispanic) students, and an additional twenty-one percent agreed that it was "somewhat important" to do so.[4]

There are three eras during which public education can be seen as especially responsive to the national agenda: (1) the Progressive Era when our modern professions and modern educational institutions were formed (2) the Post-World War II Era when developments led to intense criticism of education that took a significant turn when the Soviet Union successfully launched *Sputnik*; and, (3) the Post-World War II Civil Rights

Era that led to the *Equality of Educational Opportunity* (commonly known as the *Coleman Report* (1964). Consideration of developments in these eras shows that educational research did not develop in a vacuum. Since the focus of educational research has been so clearly related to public education, it has responded to demands and problems originating in the economic, social and political contexts in which schools are located. While the interaction between the educational enterprise and the many facets of society is in fact continuous, it has been more pronounced in some periods rather than others.

In each era, public education was seen as a major part of the problem as well as the solution, and more and improved research was seen as a necessity. Indeed, "most educators and lawmakers still believe that good research produces good policy and that good policy produces good education in the schools."[5] Proposed solutions typically entail the reform or restructuring of education based on more and better research as well as the establishment of measures, also grounded in research methods, to ensure accountability. Significantly, solutions are often seen as either instructional or perhaps curricular. Rarely, are problems and solutions conceptualized as involving the social and economic structures of society and how those structures disadvantage some and privilege others. Traditional educational research exacerbates the problem. Due to the ahistorical, universalistic, and individualistic assumptions upon which traditional educational research is based, the failure of marginalized populations to perform, that causes achievement gaps between minority and majority populations, is explained by factors internal to the group such as special negative qualities or deficiencies rather than by anything in the social context. Sometimes, the group is described as being deprived of some basic socialization process such as the failure of parents to minister to their children in the ways experts believe they should. Such students are often labeled as "disadvantaged," "at-risk," or "special."

The Progressive Era is particularly important, for it is the era during which the modern public school and modern educational research were firmly established. Education as the field of study now found in universities as well as the present institutional configuration of public education began to emerge simultaneously with the beginning of the Progressive Era. By the end of the Progressive Era, the urban school bureaucracy was in place, education as a field of study was fairly well organized, and what is now recognized as educational research had already begun. As public schools were asked to be cost effective, to identify talent, to produce good citizens and able and willing workers, educational researchers responded to these demands as did other educators.

Social, political, and economic developments also affect school enrollments and in turn what is expected of public schools, teachers, and the students who are required to attend school. Increased enrollments and new demands invariably affect the researchers' agenda as well. After World War II, "research and public affairs became more entangled."[6] The nation's leaders realized that education and educational research were instrumental in and explicitly linked to many of the items on the national agenda: national defense, civil rights, elimination of poverty, and even economic recovery and development. The Supreme Court's *Brown v. The Board of Education of Topeka Kansas* decision (1954) proved to have an enduring influence on researchers. For example, the authors of "Research on Early Childhood and Elementary Childhood and Elementary School Teaching Programs" in the third edition of the *Handbook of Research on Teaching* (1986) clearly recognized that those who had conducted studies on children had been responding to the national priorities. They pointed out that the first *Handbook* (1963) focused on mathematics and science programs that were funded during the *Sputnik* era. The *Second Handbook* (1973), it was noticed, focused on federally supported studies designed for low-income children during the Civil Rights era. Similarly, *A Nation at Risk* (1983) "challenged educators to provide quality education for high and low achievers so that all students might reach their potential."[7]

As political establishments at the state as well as the national level have demanded accountability, maintenance of high standards, and have agreed that no child should ever be left behind, schools and children are often assigned passing or failing marks based on a test constructed by an agency other than the classroom teacher. Policymakers, especially at the state and national levels, believe that tests are appropriate for monitoring and enforcing legislated accountability standards. Tests provide the data that allow officials to determine whether demands for accountability are being met and whether the achievement gap is being closed. There are many tests from which they can choose, and it was during the Progressive Era that educational researchers began stocking the shelves.

The history of educational research is more than an account of the many discussions and debates about whether education is or can be a science or discipline and more than an account of the topics and methods that have fallen in and out of favor with educational researchers and the agencies that have supported their efforts. The history of educational research is an avenue into how and why public education is organized how it is, how schooling has been conducted, how curricula have been conceptualized, and the various attempts to reform public education—to make it more effective, efficient and relevant to the interests and aspirations of students and, at the same time, to make it responsive to the social, political, and economic demands of the nation state.

While educational research or the science of education may be, as has been suggested, "an elusive science,"[8] review of what others have seen as its beginning demonstrates that it is certainly complex. While what others have seen as the beginnings are not overlooked, it is useful to ask what the necessary conditions for educational research are. In some views, what is classified as educational research must be focused on public schooling. To the extent that this is true, the founding and development of public education is one of those necessary conditions. The broader field of education, within which formal schools are situated, also implicates a range of topics on children, teaching, and subjects that have also attracted the attention of educational researchers. The purposes of public education and the problems encountered in attempts to realize them have also provided educational researchers with an agenda—an agenda that has changed as the purposes of public education and as the expectations placed on it have varied.

Discussions of what constitutes educational research are, in large measure, reflections of a magnificently rich, complex, confusing, and frustrating history.[9] Educators and researchers alike debate whether education is a field, discipline, science or something else.[10] There are many questions to which the answers are unclear. Can education be studied the same way as the natural sciences since it "is not a natural phenomenon" but a socially constructed institution? Why haven't educational reforms that question the dominant approaches to research been particularly successful?[11] Similarly, can newer research methods such as symbolic interaction, or ethno-methodology productively replace the social assumptions and significance of the dominant research paradigms that are empirical-analytical?[12] Will education advance like engineering, which "progressively incorporates more and more of science into itself?"[13] How much attention should be devoted to "conclusion-oriented" inquiry and how much to "decision-oriented" inquiry?[14] Have educational researchers served the managers of educational bureaucracies while neglecting the interests and needs of students and teachers? Do educational researchers fail to "inquire in any fundamental or open-minded way into the conflicting goals of education," but rather "tend to take purposes for granted?"[15] Has educational research been "the instrument of conservative leaders, and not the tool through which education can be radically transformed" as has been claimed?[16] Has educational research, in fact, made any difference;[17] does it needs to be rethought;[18] or strengthened since "research claims in education," some critics believe, "tend to be mushy, highly contingent, and heavily qualified?"[19] Does education have its own knowledge base and methods, or are "the conceptual and methodological problems of educational research ... very similar to (or indistinguishable from) the problems of psychological and sociological research?"[20] Should ahistorical educational research become historical?[21] Other critics argue that the focus on variables in classrooms should be abandoned altogether for a focus on matters of policy.[22]

The direction educational researchers should take remains open for discussion.[23] It has even been suggested that "educational research would do well to regard itself not as a science seeking theory to explain such phenomena as classroom learning, teaching, aptitude and the like, but as a technology designing and evaluating lessons, programs, and systems."[24] It has even been suggested that: "Educational research ... is not so much *about* education as it is research *for* education."[25] It has further been suggested that: "what should count as educational research is investigation into ways of developing power and resources in low-income communities."[26] Whatever one's position on the state of educational research or the direction it should take, there is no denying that the field is now marked by new levels of diversity and fragmentation that have resulted "in numerous and conflicting ideas of what constitutes scientific inquiry, evidence, and interpretation."[27]

The history of educational research in the United States is neither a record of continual progress nor a record of promises and expectations not fulfilled. At its worst, it is an attempt to apologize for or to explain why it has an "awful reputation."[28] Perhaps this is basically due to a history of undue worry about the status of educational research and its relationship to the social and behavioral sciences that presumably have more prestige attached to them than research internal to education. While it has been suggested that education schools where most educational researchers are trained and practice constitute the "Rodney Dangerfield of higher education" and thus command little or "no respect,"[29] the concern with status seems curious, for education as a university subject is about the same age as those areas of study often considered to be its foundational disciplines: sociology, psychology, philosophy and sometimes history. Philosophy, as a classic discipline, does have a history longer than that of the social and behavioral science disciplines but modern philosophy in its contemporary institutional configuration appeared at the same time that psychology and pedagogy became independent fields rather than branches of philosophy.

The history of educational research is a history of the attempts to understand and to solve the problems that challenged teachers and school administrators on a daily basis. Educational research was looked to at those times when schools were confronted with students who were previously not served, or not well served by public education, or when the nation saw an opportunity or a challenge to be seized or met. Early in the twentieth century some of those challenges were avoided through segregation, various forms of tracking, and by relying on the workplace to complete the education and the socialization of the young.

This book as a history of educational research in the United States seeks to accomplish three tasks. The first task is to show that the origins of so much of what is believed about public education today can be found in the dynamics of the Progressive Era. Educational research, however, would not have taken its modern form without prior events that came together at the end of the nineteenth century. The second task is to show that it is virtually impossible to consider educational research apart from psychology and educational psychology, that have provided educators with domain assumptions on: normal development; the stages of child-hood that they identified and constructed; the validity of measuring instruments developed within those disciplines; and the methods for interpreting the meaning and the significance of the measurements. Even though there are other forms of educational research, the dominance of these disciplines has lasting consequences for the way that education is organized in the United States and the way that educators and policy makers respond to external events and pressures. The third task is to show that all aspects of public education are influenced by and responds to events that reflect the national agenda.

The three chapters in Part I, Framing the Problem, set up the issues involved in the origins and nature of educational research including the debates and controversies. It is argued that no matter how the origin is determined or how educational research is defined, it can not be seen as independent of the larger political, economic, and social conditions that made public education possible and research desirable. Chapter 1, "The Progressives, Public Education, and Educational Research" argues that many critical elements came together in the dynamic period known as the Progressive Era. It was also a defining period for the enrollment expansion and growth of twentieth century systems of public schooling. Chapter 2, "Controversies Over the Origins of Educational Research," is an account of the various ways in which the origins of educational research can be dated and the extenuating arguments for periods and events that were played out in the Progressive Era. Chapter 3, "Defining Status and Privilege in Educational Research," is related to Chapter 2, for it explores how educational research has been defined and is defined. Clearly, what is accepted as a definition largely determines what is considered to be the origins and purpose of educational research. Similarly, there have been efforts to advance the status of some forms of research, such as quantitative approaches to psychological research, as more valid or useful than others, such as qualitative sociology or historical research. A dominant view has been that educational research to have a privileged status must be applicable to practice and grounded in clinical or experimental psychology.

Part II, Origins and Originating Myths, explore the necessary conditions for educational research that came together in the nineteenth century. Chapter 4, "Origins of Public Education and Educational Research: The Common School," is devoted to the formal origin of free, public education controlled and paid for by the state. Education could not become a focus of research until it took on an objective form as an institution with a mission. The Common School movement is the beginning of the public systems of education that eventually became compulsory for all children and the object of attention for the vast majority of educational research. Chapter 5, "Education as a Conscious Business: Herbart and the Herbartians," examines the German philosopher Johann Friedrich Herbart who died in 1841, and the educators in Germany and the United States who adapted his ideas and called themselves Herbartians. Johann Friedrich Herbart is important because he demonstrated that the process of education could and should be an object of inquiry. The American Herbartians in the Progressive Era contributed to the professionalization of psychology and its experimental approach to research in the social sciences as distinct from its origins in philosophy. Herbartians stressed teacher training and research on teaching in laboratory school settings. Chapter 6, "Darwinism in the United States," specifically looks at Charles Darwin's impact on research methods as applied to educational research through his work on evolution and speciation stemming from his four year voyage aboard the HMS Beagle as a naturalist. He proved the necessity for observation and the realization that the possibility of chance and error are ever present. This was essential for the development of quantitative and qualitative educational research based on the study of real subjects with careful attention to measuring variations in observations. The misuse of Darwin's research in the Eugenics and Social Darwinism movements also impacted educational policy and research. Minor human differences were classified and reified with Anglo-Saxons identified as superior to other groups. This was used to justify segregation, tracking, and other exclusionary policies. These chapters outline the three prior conditions necessary for the emergence of modern educational research in the Progressive Era as well as some of the problems addressed in the Post-World War II and Civil Rights Eras.

Part III, Psychologists and Testers, looks at the movements and actors who formalized educational research in the twentieth century. The major figures in these chapters used or applied psychology to provide modern conceptions of children and adolescents as school age students; conceptions of what learning is; and ways to measure and assess school practices and student achievement. Chapter 7, "Child-Study, G. Stanley Hall, Arnold Gesell, and Lewis Terman," looks at Hall and his students, who can be credited with inventing developmental stages, the notion of readiness, and the capacity to learn. Chapter 8, "Educational Efficiency and Tests: Daniel Starch and Stuart A. Courtis," examine two seminal figures who are not well known nor often given credit for getting the testing movement underway. For a time Starch had the most popular text in educational psychology. He demonstrated the efficiency of standardized letter grading. Courtis successfully developed and sold tests. He is of particular interest because he also questioned the efficacy of the testing and measurement movement. Chapter 9, "The Laws of Learning: The Legacy of Edward L. Thorndike," examines a figure who dominated educational psychology for decades and effectively defined learning for educators. He had considerable influence over how arithmetic was taught and developed with Barnhart a dictionary for children.

Part IV, Institutionalization of the Progressive Agenda, focuses on an underlying medical model for educational research with its individualistic focus, its claims to universality, and its tendency to concentrate on psychological and biological factors in learning and development. Medicine, as a model for professional development and research, predated the Progressive Era. Many of the primary figures in educational research were directly or indirectly influenced by the transition to modern medicine and medical research in a laboratory setting that developed with the financial and ideological support of large-scale U.S. philanthropies. Chapter 10, "The Mental Hygiene Movement: Psychiatry, Rockefeller, Philanthropy, and the Promotion of a Medical Model in Educational Research," looks at how this Progressive Era movement contributed to research on education and its psychobiological orientation. Chapter 11, "Nature-Nurture Controversies: Institutionalizing Intelligence as a Variable in Educational Research," focuses on how philanthropic support for educational research took up the banner of advancing standardized testing and the controversies that followed. Chapter 12, "Cultural Lag: The Laura Spelman Rockefeller Memorial and Educational Research," addresses the institutionalization of the progressive agenda in child study and developmental research that created a foundation for age-grade determination of competency. These chapters address how the support provided to selected researchers by Rockefeller related philanthropies privileged some conceptions of educational research. The fear of aberrant populations, who lag behind other groups in cultural conformity or educational attainment, served as an underlying motivation for educational research throughout much of the twentieth century. The concern follows historically from the earliest studies considered to be educational research in the late nineteenth century and is part of the achievement gap crisis that fueled the No Child Left Behind legislation in 2002.

The final section, Part V, The Post-World War II Era, brings this study up to date. In the years immediately subsequent to World War II it was generally accepted that the security and prosperity of the nation were directly linked to the efficacy of its public schools. There was great concern with the teaching of the traditional school subjects in the nation's public schools and a parallel concern with how the academic disciplines typically found in arts and sciences colleges related to the study of education and the training of teachers. Chapter 13, "Educational Reform and Educational Research in the Post-World War II Era," examines the new mandates for public education and the response of educators and educational researchers to the challenges of full enrollment. The national agenda becomes even more important in the Cold War period where education is challenged as inadequate to meet the needs of the times. Chapter 14, "The Achievement Gap: *The Coleman Report* and its Legacy in No Child Left Behind," looks at the Civil Rights Era and its impact on education. The educational research behind *The Coleman Report* dating from 1966 and its conclusions are examined in light of the most recent educational legislation, No Child Left Behind passed in 2002. Chapter 15, "The History of Education as Educational Research: The National Agenda and a Discipline," examines selected works of historians of education to show how education as a field of inquiry and research into education was transformed in the post-World War II era as educators responded to criticisms of public education and attempted to meet the demands of the national agenda.

NOTES

1. Charles Burgess and Merle L. Borrowman. *What Doctrines to Embrace: Studies in the History of American Education*. (Glenview, Illinois: Scott, Foresman and Co., 1969), pp. 126-135.
2. Charles E. M. Kolb. "The Cracks in Our Education Pipeline," *Education Week*. Vol. 25, No. 42 (July 12, 2006), pp. 54,45.
3. Anthony O. Carnevale, "Discounting Education's Value," *The Chronicle of Higher Education* Section B (The Chronicle Review), Vol. LIII, No. 5 (September 22, 2006), p. B7.
4. Lowell C. Rose and Alec M. Gallup. "The 38th Annual Phi Delta Kappan/ Gallup Poll of the Public's Attitudes Toward the Public Schools," *Phi Delta Kappan*, Vol. 88, No. 1 (September 2006), p. 46.
5. Tom Loveless. "The Use and Misuse of Research in Educational Reform" in Diane Ravitch (ed.). *Brookings Papers on Education 1998* (Washington, D. C.: Brookings Institution Press), p. 279.

6. David K. Cohen and Carol A. Barnes. "Research and the Purposes of Education" in Ellen Condliffe Lagemann and Lee S. Shulman (eds.). *Issues in Educational Research: Problems and Possibilities* (San Francisco: Jossey-Bass Publishers, 1999), p. 20.

7. Jane A. Stallings and Deborah Stipek. "Research on Early Childhood and Elementary School Teaching Programs" in Merlin C. Wittrock (ed.). *Handbook of Research on Teaching*. 3rd ed. (New York: Macmillan Publishing Co. 1986), p. 727.

8. Ellen Condliffe Lagemann. *An Elusive Science: The Troubling History of Educational Research: The Troubling History of Education Research* (Chicago: University of Chicago Press, 2000).

9. How to define educational research has been a longstanding problem. For an early discussion of the problem see: Walter Scott Monroe. *Ten Years of Educational Research, 1919-1927*, University *of Illinois Bureau of Educational Research Bulletin No. 42, University of Illinois Bulletin*, Vol. 25, No. 51 (1928), pp. 15-29. This issue receives further attention in this work.

10. For an extensive bibliography of the literature on these questions see: Bird T. Baldwin, "Principles of Education, The Present Status of Education as a Science," Papers presented for discussion at the meeting of the National Society of College Teachers of Education in St. Louis, Missouri, February 27-29, 1912. *School Review Monographs Number II* (Chicago: University of Chicago Press, 1912), pp. 129-134. Baldwin's bibliography contains over one hundred entries and includes works form Europe as well as the United States. Also see: Walter S. Monroe and Max D. Englehart. *The Scientific Study of Educational Problems* (New York: The Macmillan Co., 1936), p. 452.

11. For example, see: Ernest R. House. "Three Perspectives on Innovation" in Rolf Lehming and Michael Kane (eds.). *Improving Schools: Using What We Know* (Beverly Hills, California: Sage Publications, 1981).

12. See: Thomas K. Popkewitz. *Paradigm and Ideology in Educational Research: The Social Function of the Intellectual* (London: The Falmer Press, 1984),

13. John Dewey. *The Sources of a Science of Education* (New York: Horace Liveright, 1929), p. 13.

14. Lee J. Cronbach, Patrick Suppes, *et. al.* (eds.). *Research for Tomorrow's Schools* (New York: The Macmillan Co., 1969).

15. David Tyack and Elizabeth Hansot. *Managers of Virtue: Public School Leadership in America, 1820-1980* (New York: Basic Books, Inc., 1982), p. 153.

16. Robert M. W. Travers. *How Research Has Changed American Schools: A History from 1840 to the Present* (Kalamazoo, Michigan: Mythos Press, 1983), p. 125.

17. An early attempt to assess the influence of research on teaching is Geraldine Joncich Clifford. "A History of the Impact of Research on Teaching" in Robert M. W. Travers (ed.). *Second Handbook of Research on Teaching* (Chicago: Rand McNally, 1973). Also see: Patrick Suppes (ed.). *Impact of Research on Education: Some Case Studies* (Washington, D. C.: National Academy of Education, 1973); William J. Reese. "What History Teaches About the Impact of Educational Research on Practice" in Asghar Iran-Nejad and P. David Pearson (eds.). *Review of Research in Education 24* (Washington, D. C.: American Educational Research Association, 1999); and Bruce J. Biddle and Lawrence J. Saha. *The Untested Accusation: Principals, Research*

Knowledge, and Policy Making in Schools (Westport, Connecticut: Ablex Publishing, 2002).

18.   W. B. Dockrell and David Hamilton (eds.). *Rethinking Educational Research* (London: Hodder and Stoughton, 1980).

19.   David F. Labaree. "The Peculiar Problems of Preparing Educational Researchers," *Educational Researcher*, Vol. 32, No. 4 (May 2003), p. 14.

20.   Fred M. Kerlinger. "Research in Education, " in Robert L. Ebel (ed.). *Encyclopedia of Educational Research*, 4th ed. (Toronto: Collier-Macmillan, 1960), p. 1127.

21.   *Ibid.*

22.   Lee J. Cronbach. "Beyond the Two Disciplines of Scientific Psychology,"*American Psychologist*, Vol. 30, No. 2 (February 1975).

23.   For an interesting and unusually optimistic series of statements about possible directions for educational research in the 1980s and beyond see: Frank H. Farley. "The Future of Educational Research." *Educational Researcher*, Vol. 11, No. 8 (October 1982), pp. 11-19 and Vol. 11, No. 9 (November 1982), pp. 12-18. It is an edited version of a panel earlier organized for an American Education Research Association meeting and includes statements from N. L. Gage, Benjamin S. Bloom, David R. Kratwohl, Robert M. Gagne, Robert Glaser, Robert Ebel, Robert L. Thorndike, Fred M, Kerlinger, W. James Popham, and Maxine Greene.

24.   "An Interview with Gene V. Glass conducted by Daniel H. Robinson," *Educational Researcher*, Vol. 33, No. 33 (April 2004), p. 29.

25.   Gert J. J. Biesta and Nicholas C. Burbules. *Pragmatism and Educational Research* (Lanham, Maryland: Rowman & Littlefield Publishers, Inc. 2003), p. 1.

26.   Jean Anyon. "What Should Count as Educational Research: Notes Toward a New Paradigm" in Gloria Ladson-Billings and William F. Tate (eds.). *Education Research in the Public Interest: Social Justice, Action, and Policy* (New York: Teachers College Press, 2006), p. 17.

27.   B. Schneider. "Sociology of Education: An Overview of the Field at the Turn of the Twenty-First Century" in M. T. Hallinan, A. Garmoran, A. Kubitschek and T. Loveless (eds.). *Stability and Change in American Education* (New York: Werner Publications, 2003), p. 1472 quoted in Brian V. Carolan and Gary Natriello. "Data-Mining Journals and Books: Using the Science of Networks to Uncover the Structure of the Educational Research Community," *Educational Researcher*, Vol. 34, No. 3 (April 2005), p. 25.

28.   Carl Kaestle. "The Awful Reputation of Educational Research," *Educational Researcher*, Vol. 22 (January-February 1993).

29.   Labaree. "The Peculiar Problems of Preparing Educational Researchers," p. 13.

PART I

FRAMING THE PROBLEM

CHAPTER 1

THE PROGRESSIVES, PUBLIC EDUCATION, AND EDUCATIONAL RESEARCH

The late nineteenth and early twentieth century progressives were confronting problems and issues that began to emerge after Appomattox at the end of the Civil War. The first generation of progressives, born between 1854 and 1874, grew up in a Protestant-rural milieu, in homes that endorsed Protestant values, the Union, the values of Abraham Lincoln, and the Republican Party.[1] As adults, they had to invent ways to realize the values of their childhood in a nation that had been transformed by the processes of modernization: immigration, urbanization and industrialization. In the United States, as in England and Europe, industrialization produced a new group of powerful elites, the stratification of the workforce into owner capitalists, managers and bureaucrats in the middle, and working class wage earners at the bottom who competed with internal migrants and new immigrants. It was the period during which the frontier was closed and the United States was completing its transformation from an agrarian society of small towns to an industrialized society with large urban centers and even the beginnings of metropolitan areas. A new cultural-economic order was emerging. The first rags to riches billionaire, founder of the Standard Oil Company John D. Rockefeller Sr. had more resources than the U.S. government at the time. The first Rockefeller phi-

Educational Research, the National Agenda, and Educational Reform:
A History, pp. 3–27

lanthropy, the General Education Board (GEB) founded in 1903, had a mandate to establish a system of public schools in the Southern States under a charter approved by the U.S. Congress. How and where people worked and how and where they lived as well as how they played and worshipped were radically transformed. Their traditional ways of thinking and what they valued were challenged. Those in the midst of the transformation frequently saw not the emergence of a new cultural order but disorder. Public education was not unaffected by the transformation. The public school was the institution designed and designated to effect some measure of domestic tranquility, economic prosperity and political stability. Schooling was to create educated citizens prepared for life in a democracy. Some, John Dewey for example, further believed the school could assume the duties and functions of displaced and transformed institutions and even serve as an instrument for the creation of the great society. The school, however, became the institution assigned the task of fitting the individual to the new social-economic order. These contrasting purposes of public education are evident today. This chapter sets the stage for the twentieth century national agenda in changes in the late nineteenth century that produced the Progressive Movement, which among other reform initiatives sought the expansion and universalization of public education as well as the need to create a science to guide educators and make them efficient producers of workers and citizens in a stable social order.

THE PROGRESSIVE MOVEMENT AND EDUCATIONAL RESEARCH

In the 1890s when public school bureaucracies and educational research were beginning to take their now familiar configurations, the United States was beginning to recognize and to exercise its power. As the frontier closed, the Progressive Era (an era bracketed by two wars—the Spanish-American War and World War I) opened. The United States expanded its horizons and dominion and set out for Cuba, the Philippines, Hawaii, and Samoa. The nation's power in the international arena grew, and the nation attempted to spread the American Dream to other peoples.[2] Social Darwinism, which maintained that some peoples were more advanced than others, was used to explain and to defend oppressive and exclusionary practices and policies in matters of domestic policy as well as foreign policy. While the nation was exercising its power in other parts of the world, school enrollments grew due to the arrival of immigrants in unprecedented numbers. Many were then concerned with the characteristics and abilities of those who were classified as not white and those defined as not normal. Often overlooked is the close relationship between the attempt to render schools efficient agents of Americanization and the attempts to certify those immigrants fit to pass through Ellis Island and enter American society. Those judged fit, after having been examined and tested often by psychologists, to enter were to be Americanized in the public schools.

The social consequences of changes in manufacturing processes are probably best symbolized by the introduction in 1914 of "progressive line production" of automobiles by Henry Ford. No part of American life escaped the effects of the new economic and manufacturing processes. Samuel P. Hays observed that: "Whether one had sought to enhance his social prestige, to preserve his pattern of culture, to express his religious beliefs, or to gain material success, he had been forced to contend with the vast changes swirling about him."[3] Traditional values were challenged and social institutions were called upon to provide new services. Americans had to adjust their modes of thought, play, worship, and work to a new set of social and economic arrangements. One such set was set in motion in 1896 when the United States Supreme Court in its *Plessy v. Ferguson* decision allowed government to assign people to the social construction called race and then either to discriminate against people or to privilege them based on that assignment. Those patterns of privilege and discrimination persisted throughout and beyond the twentieth century. Consequently, a great deal of what was supposedly learned about schools and students did not apply to the entire population. Instruments, school structures, and school practices tested on and developed for a privileged population continue to privilege that population and discriminate against those who had for so long been ignored and excluded.

The same changes that required Americans to adjust their modes of thought, play, and work to a new setting also required an adjustment in their modes of schooling. As Walter Lippman observed in 1914:

> In former times you could make some effort to teach people what they needed to know. It was done badly, but at least it could be attempted. Men knew the kind of problems their children would have to face. But to-day education means a radically different thing. We have to prepare children to meet the unexpected, for their problems will not be the same as their fathers. To prepare them for the unexpected means to train them to methods instead of filling them with facts and rules. They will have to find their facts and make their own rules, and if schools can't give them that power then schools no longer educate for the modern world.[4]

As was the case with other social institutions, the scale and the character of the public school were dramatically changed. As the cities increased their numbers, housed a more diverse population, were required to provide more services, and called for more tax dollars, a steadily increasing percentage of school-age youth was attending school, the school term was lengthened, and attendance became more regular. The percentage of school-age youth (from five to seventeen years) attending school rose from fifty-seven in 1870 to seventy-eight in 1920. By 1890 the public high school was the most common kind of secondary school and between 1890 and 1910 its number increased by over 300%.

Schools, like factories, were larger in number and in size. Eventually, school architecture resembled factory architecture, and educators saw fit to view students as raw material, teachers as workers on the line who needed continual supervision, and graduates as finished products. The practice of viewing teachers as workers who were to follow orders persisted far into the twentieth century. For example, in 1975 John Goodlad offered his views on effective school reform. In his system, the superintendent of a public school system was compared to the general manager of a shipping company, the principal to a ship's captain, and the administrative and supervisory staff of the school to the support personnel who tends "to the care of ships carrying the freight—educating children in their care." The principal, he suggested, should be well schooled in modern management skills."[5] In his system, teachers become the crew.

Public education was fast becoming the nation's growth industry. In the early decades of the twentieth century, the expenditure of public funds for public education was greater than the combined expenditures for public welfare and national defense.[6] Increased support brought increased responsibility. The public school was to satisfy new social obligations as well as the obligation to serve new and different populations. It sought help from educational research that was believed to have the power to offer answers and solutions rooted in science.

PUBLIC EDUCATION, SCIENCE, AND EFFICIENCY

Science, as Karl Pearson advised in *The Grammar of Science* (1892), was believed to have the power to render human and social affairs orderly, efficient and ever more productive. Pearson's claim that not only were the methods of science applicable to all fields or disciplines but also that the processes and causal mechanisms were the same for all fields was accepted either tacitly or explicitly by those who were creating the new science of the mind, psychology. The scientific method, according to Pearson and those who accepted his claims, was the best way to solve social problems "because it provides standards of knowing that are independent of all individual interests and biases."[7] Thus, what was scientifically so was morally so.

Science was, as Herbert Spencer also had instructed and as Americans believed even before he so instructed, the knowledge of most worth. Science often meant counting and measuring, operations that produced numerical designations. By the early twentieth century, Americans accepted that they belonged "to certain 'sizes'—in shoes, shirts, trousers, and hats."[8] Just as it was accepted that one person wore a size 9 shoe and another a size 7 so Americans soon accepted that one person had an IQ of 102 and another had an IQ of 104 or that a sixth grader's understanding of scientific concepts placed him or her in the seventy-ninth percentile while his neighbor's placed him or her in the eighty-first percentile. Americans accepted and continue to accept what appear to be seemingly neutral numerical designations for their abilities and accomplishments. They accepted and continue to accept that a difference between two numerical designations is real and somehow meaningful. Few knew or cared about the standard error of measurement for the tests and scales they accepted. They accepted that the standards used to evaluate, place, and admit students were fair and objective and could be universally applied to all individuals without any consideration of the social context from which an individual hailed. Only when their own offspring fail to have the desired numerical designation assigned to them do they question the designation. Then, however, it is more often than not not the practice but the specific numerical designation that is typically questioned. How the social context was created and used, often by the privileged dominant group in society, to construct individuals as members of a designated racial or ethnic group, that holds the values and world views associated with those racial or ethnic groups is typically much less important that what tests purport to demonstrate.

While educators had to contend with the problems associated with the growth of the schools, they also had to contend with those who demanded that the schools contribute to social reform. The attempts to reform public education and to effect social reform were inextricably related. "Proponents of virtually every progressive cause from the 1890s through World I," as Lawrence A. Cremin observed, "had their programs for the school."[9] While American educational researchers were finding a place for themselves in the American university and beginning to develop their methods, a revolution in American secondary education was occurring. "The heart of this revolution was," according to Cremin, "a shift in the conception of the school, of what could and should be its primary goals and responsibilities."[10] The contrast between two major NEA reports—one coming at the beginning of the era and the other at its end—The Report of the Committee of Ten (1893) and the Report of the Commission on the Reorganization of Secondary Education (1918) that presented the *Seven Cardinal Principles of Education*, illustrates the changes that had occurred. The Committee of Ten was viewed as conceiving of the high school as a school for the few while the Commission was believed to have made a proposal for a school for all American youth up to age eighteen. The Commission saw the high school not as an adjunct to the college but as a "pivotal point in the public school system, one that carried forward objectives yet unfinished by the elementary school and opened new vistas leading on to the colleges."[11] From an institution concerned primarily with the cultivation of the intellect, the high school, some believed, could become a vehicle for "progressive amelioration of every individual and social need."[12] The new conception of the school was spelled out in the seven cardinal principles: health, command of fundamental processes, worthy home membership, vocation, citizenship, worthy use of leisure, and ethical character.

Some saw the public school as a vehicle for the reformation of society; others saw it as the place where youth could be prepared for a return to a time that was less unsettled; and still others saw it as the agency that would prepare the nation for a new social order. Some wanted a school that would produce social order; others wanted a school that would enhance freedom and individual choice. Educational researchers not only were expected to assist those who wanted to use the schools to effect social and educational reform but also were expected to provide information that would aid those charged with supervising and administering the schools effectively and efficiently.

The interests of the progressive reformers varied. Some attacked big business, political corruption, and the relationship between the two. Others believed the school could and therefore had an obligation to rid society of the evils associated with tobacco, alcohol, and popular music. Still others blamed the schools for creating society's ills and wanted the schools to remedy them. Edward A. Krug reported: "Every phase of reform was represented by a league, a committee, an association, a congress, a society, or by a department of the NEA."[13] The reformer's causes, recommendations, and complaints were given full discussion in the popular media, the educational journals, and educators' meetings, and provided, either directly or indirectly, educational researchers their agenda.

EDUCATIONAL RESEARCH FOR A NEW ERA

As modern social science was being developed, progressives turned away from speculation and turned to "empirical research and accurate description." They were committed to employing science and professionalism to create an efficient and ordered society. Research was expected to provide ways to increase the efficiency of public education and to supply the knowledge base for a newly developing education profession. Unlike their immediate predecessors, the Social Darwinists, they sought not to defend and to maintain the existing social order but "to describe it with accuracy, to understand it in new terms, and to improve it."[14] However, the social order educational researchers studied was not a social order that included all Americans. The Progressive Era was also the era of Jim Crow. African Americans were restricted from participating fully in American society. In the North as well as in the South African Americans were allowed, if allowed to attend, to attend only racially segregated and poorly supported schools. Native Americans had already been confined to reservations. Newly arrived immigrants were often confined to a ghetto. As Luis M. Laosa has observed: "By the last quarter of the nineteenth century, the United States had established policies that socially, politically, educationally, and economically isolated and excluded Blacks, Hispanics, and American Indians and that limited and often denied them the opportunity to become integrated."[15] Consequently, whatever educational researchers learned about American education and about students was necessarily incomplete. They developed surveys to assess facilities, practices and conditions and instruments to measure student progress and achievement. The norms they established for their instruments may have been appropriate for some Americans and for some schools but not all Americans and not all schools.

After Appomattox academics in almost all those areas now considered disciplines or scholarly fields wanted their pursuits to be recognized as scientific, for that which was scientific was invested with status and authority. When Charles W. Eliot, soon to become president of Harvard, presented his views on "The New Education" in 1869, he observed: "Fortunately for the country, education is getting to be a profession itself."[16] To achieve professional status educators sought to develop a science of education. To do so they had to acknowledge the importance of research and justify their recommendations for educational practices on a knowledge base supplied either by educational researchers or researchers in disciplines believed to be closely related to education. The discipline that was most successful in making the case for its utility was psychology. Consequently, educational researchers emphasized research design, hypothesis construction, measurement of one's ability to learn, measurement of changes in performance or learning, and statistical analysis of experimental results, and procedures for determining the probabilities of error and chance. Consequently, a major portion of the history of educational research is essentially a history of how the assumptions and methods of psychology and educational psychology have since the early twentieth century almost entirely "eclipsed older methods, notably those

associated with history and philosophy." The use of "ethnographic methods of anthropology, the discourse procedures of linguistics and sociolin-
guistics, and the 'think-aloud" and other forms of protocol analysis of
cognitive science" to supplement the "older [psychological] methods"
comprise a recent development.[17]

What is generally accepted and recognized as educational research has
two obvious but important characteristics. First, from a historical standpoint, it is a relatively new enterprise. Second, it is chiefly a practical
enterprise focused on processes mostly located in state-supported institutions known as public schools. Virtually all of educational research is
focused on schooling, on what is done in the name of education in
schools, especially public schools in the United States. Educational
research is firmly rooted in public education, the form and substance of
which were defined in and for a society committed to democratic capitalism and industrialism. It may not always be on the forefront of the
researcher's consciousness, but educational researchers were then and
they continue to be social reformers in the Progressive tradition. They
came into being when, as the muckraking magazines emphasized, society
was concerned with efficiency. They work to make schools more productive, more effective, more efficient, and sometimes even more humane.
Even when educational researchers focus on how individuals learn, often
individuals who share either a talent or a deficiency, they either directly or
indirectly urge that schools act on their findings so that more learning can
be achieved and achieved in less time so that the special needs of special
populations can be satisfied.

Modern educational research is one of the many developments that
comprise the Progressive Era. Americans were then working out their
response to the new industrial society, searching for ways to find order,
and worrying about the great number of immigrants whom they feared
would undermine the American way.[18] In the South, they worried about
the role of former slaves but more importantly they were concerned
about the illiterate poor white population. The public school was
selected as the venue where children could be brought up in a way that
would ensure that there would be adults who would maintain the American way and prevent what was then termed "race suicide." In order to
do this new knowledge had to be established that could inform leaders
of the future, new institutions had to be established to produce the
knowledge based on reliable standards, and to train professionals for
the field. School expansion included the primary and secondary sector
but it also had to provide for differentiated learning at the upper levels
to produce research and to teach those who would teach others.

PROFESSIONALIZING DISCIPLINES IN
RESEARCH BASED ON SCIENCE

In the late nineteenth century Johns Hopkins University emerged as a pivotal model. Opened in 1876, Johns Hopkins became the first true university in a modern sense with differentiated undergraduate, graduate, and post-graduate professional training. Medicine became the model for the advanced professional with a post-graduate education that combined the most advanced scientific research with clinical experience in a university setting. The first prominent leaders at Johns Hopkins including William Welsh, William Osler, and Adolf Meyer played central roles in institutionalizing the application of methods in the natural sciences (biology in particular) and medicine to solve problems in society including preventive public health measures, the efficient provision of education, and effective ways to socialize immigrants and children. They also were instrumental in directing both public and private philanthropic funds toward the support of scientific research and its accompanying ideology. It is not accidental that Johns Hopkins provided an early setting that nurtured the scientific study of children in the formative years of individuals who became major influences on twentieth century thought about children, schools, and educational research such as G. Stanley Hall, John Dewey, and John B. Watson. American behaviorism and clinical or experimental psychology as influential in educational psychology and research was initiated at Johns Hopkins in the work of Watson and Hall. Adolf Meyer in particular encouraged the emerging discipline of psychology to move away from philosophy toward clinical research.[19]

While it will be argued in this volume that a psychobiological medical model played an important underlying role in the history of educational research, it is in the form of the discipline of psychology that the influence was most prominent. By the turn of the century popular thought had bought into the idea that science could produce public good. Psychology proclaimed itself to be the new science of the mind. Americans then believed that properly applied science would solve human and social problems. While this assumption has been and continues to be challenged, it has survived surprisingly unchanged to this day even though there is in the view among some, that educators "backed the wrong horse" when they placed their faith in "experimental psychology."[20]

Modern educational research, as an identifiable and distinctive activity, has many of its origins in progressive education. Progressive education was part of progressivism "writ large."[21] As part of progressivism "writ large," progressive education was part of a movement that sought to democratize society and improve the lives of the people. The participants in the movement argued from their studies in history, philosophy and the social sciences. After World War I, so the story goes, progressive educators were no longer connected to the disciplines and focused on fitting the individual to the existing social structure. The work of Lewis M. Terman, a student of G. Stanley Hall, was the kind of work that allowed educators to place students where psychologists believed, based on the results of tests they constructed and administered, they would best fit.

The development of educational research, especially during the Progressive Era, is part of a story that includes the development of psychology as a discipline separate from philosophy and the development of educational psychology out of clinical psychology. Educational research was rarely a disinterested undertaking. Those who conducted it and those who used it expected it to improve the schools and even society. When the public raises questions about the efficacy and efficiency of its public schools, educational researchers ask for more support for their inquiries, and educators seek ways to use what is known about effective practice.[22]

THE REIFICATION OF TESTS AND TESTING

One of the outcomes of the application of scientific methods was the production of tests. During the Progressive Era, reformers and researchers introduced "objective" tests[23] of various sorts designed not only to measure what students have achieved or acquired but also to assess their experimental methods and materials. By 1918, Walter S. Monroe was able to report that: "During the past decade and especially during the past five years, the number of tests available for measuring the abilities of children in school subjects has grown very rapidly." For those responsible for students in elementary schools, there were eighty-four "standardized tests" covering ten different subjects: Arithmetic (Fundamental Operations as well as Arithmetic Reasoning); Drawing; Geography; Handwriting; History; Language; Music; Silent Reading; Oral Reading and Spelling. For those responsible for students in high schools, there were twenty-five standardized tests covering seven areas: Algebra; Drawing; Foreign Languages; Geometry; History; Physical Training and Physics.[24] They had already developed instruments—tests, scales and checklists—to diagnose students' abilities, progress and deficiencies; to assess school and student performance; to rate teachers, principals and school plants; and surveys to assess conditions and to determine future needs.

By the end of the Progressive Era, "the battle for educational measurement by means of objective tests had been won."[25] Educators were clearly convinced that virtually every aspect of education could be measured and they had already assembled a significant literature and battery of instruments. For the *Seventeenth Yearbook of the National Society for the Study of Education: Part II, The Measurement of Educational Products*, Edna Bryner of the Russell Sage Foundation assembled "A Selected Bibliography of Certain Phases of Educational Measurement." Her 606-item bibliography had nine divisions: Theory of Educational Measurement and Development of the Movement; Tests and Scales in Various School Subjects; General Reports on the Use of Tests and Scales in Schools; Lists of Tests and Scales; Correlations between Abilities; Teachers' Measurement; articles About Surveys and Lists of Surveys; City Surveys; and State, County and other Surveys. The Division on the Various School Subjects presented tests and scales for virtually every school subject: Algebra; Arithmetic; Drawing; English Composition, Language, and Vocabulary; English Grammar; French; Geography; Geometry; German; Handwriting; History; Latin; Physics; Reading; Spanish; and Spelling.[26]

Many tests designed to measure either mental ability or achievement have had a very long shelf life, and others have been revised for a new generation.[27] Some procedures developed for the administration of "performance" tests developed during the Progressive Era have "continued to be used by practitioners and researchers throughout the 20th century."[28] Still, new tests are being made. Each state, it seems, wants to have its own. That makes comparisons between and among states difficult. While each state wants to be able to be claim that it is number one, all agree on a way that will ensure that no state can be shown to rank fiftieth in education. Giving up the possibility of being first ensures that one will not be fiftieth.

NEW PURPOSES FOR EXPANDING SCHOOL SYSTEMS

During the great expansion of public education in the Progressive Era— the period during which elementary education achieved universal enrollment and high schools were being built at the rate of more than one day to accommodate an enrollment that was growing more than ten times as fast as the nation's entire population—educational research was developed to render the growing enterprise efficient and democratic. The obligations of public education were then many and complex. It had to attend to how students learned, what students were to learn, how to ascertain and measure what was learned, the training and education of teachers, the management not of a few schools but of large school systems, and the training of school administrators. Educational research was expected to provide a sound scientific base for the management and administration of a new institution and a new profession. Educational research eventually acquired its own identity and became a specialty within a profession but it was and is rooted in the development of public education.

As educators debated the propriety of new purposes and new methods, they turned to educational research, research conducted according to the dictates of the paradigm and protocols used by psychologists and educational psychologists, to support either their opposition or their endorsements. Those who were investigating educational problems scientifically either became partisans or saw others use the conclusions of their inquiries for partisan purposes. Questions about how children learn and questions about what should be taught in the schools became interwoven and confused one for the other. Educational researchers were from their very beginnings expected to answer not only questions about what was possible but also questions of value, of what ought to be. The many psychological discussions and the many editorial discussions about transfer of training illustrate that Americans wanted to use the findings of what they believed to be scientific inquiries to resolve what were essentially questions of value, to decide what should be taught and to whom it was to be taught. Eventually, educational researchers were expected to provide the means to enable educators to determine who was educable and who was not. Once they developed their intelligence tests they believed they were able to comply with that expectation.

INVENTING THE SCIENCES OF SOCIETY AND SOCIALIZATION

The commitment to the social and behavioral sciences and their protocols are also relatively new. The belief that it is possible to discover how society and its institutions work and that knowledge can be used to direct or to engineer society in order to perfect it are Enlightenment notions. However, it was not until the Progressive Era that liberal reformers maintained that the state had the power to use such knowledge, and that since such knowledge was available and since the state had the power, the state should exercise its power to use what was known. The bases and justification for inquiries into education developed subsequent to the introduction of public education. The academic disciplines and the sciences educational researchers regularly employ in their inquiries were developed and assumed their modern forms both as sciences and as professions after Appomattox, a full generation after the founding of the common school. In part, their developments were shaped by acting on the belief that the application of science to human and social problems would bring order to a culture that seemed to be growing ever more disorderly and expensive. However, it must be recognized that public schooling had and has characteristics that predate the intellectual apparatus subsequently used to analyze and improve it.

As educators turned to or accepted psychology as the foundation for a science of education and as a way to support practice with scientific authority, they were committed to measurement. Even before psychology moved away from exploring consciousness through introspection in favor of observing behavior, psychologists maintained that "the introspective data of conscious experience could ... be experimentally and mathematically measured." Once psychologists found a home in universities they began to employ "statistical methods for correlating individual differences and anthropometric techniques for measuring them [and] questionnaire methods for compiling data on child development."[29]

The arrival of behavioral psychology based on its universalistic assumptions and scientific management's procedures for maximizing efficiency and quality enabled the researchers to conduct countless studies of educational institutions and the abilities and characteristics of students and teachers. Psychology and educational psychology have served as authoritative advisers on child development and child rearing not only to parents but also to teachers. Educators solicit and receive recommendations from these experts and accept that those recommendations are based on and confirmed by the application of rigorous standards of scientific inquiry. Sometimes the recommendations are so based. At times they are based on elegantly crafted expressions of long held beliefs about children, their nature, and what is good for them.

THE SCIENCE OF ESTABLISHING NORMS FOR HUMAN DEVELOPMENT AND LEARNING

For years there have been norms for children that have been widely accepted. By the middle of the twentieth century and even earlier Americans accepted that the growth and development of children progressed through identifiable stages that can be distinguished from one another. They accepted that what was normal could be ascertained. What has been accepted or considered to be normal has changed from time to time, but the notion of normal has persisted. Arnold Gesell did more to popularize and extend the notion of stages and normality than did G. Stanley Hall his teacher who introduced the stages to Americans. Hall who is usually given credit for beginning the child study movement applied evolutionary theory to child development and identified distinctive stages. Each stage had its specific needs and abilities. Hall argued that any interference with the child's natural development would not only have deleterious effects on the growth of the child but also have negative arresting effects on the evolution of society. Hall and his student, Arnold Gesell, essentially gave legitimacy to the views and prescriptions of late eighteenth and nineteenth century reformers by making their claims and observations the objects of their scientific study. Rockefeller philanthropy supported Gesell's work at the Institute for Human Relations at Yale University.[30] The romantic beliefs of one era became the scientific knowledge of the next.

From the experts teachers, like parents, have developed expectations about what is normal growth and development of the children in their charge. The expectations have changed from time to time, but the framework—age-stage psychology—into which these expectations have been cast remained constant throughout the twentieth century. It has proved to be a useful framework, for it allows those responsible for children to explain their failures as well as their successes. When the child cannot be persuaded to cease the behavior in which he/she has been persisting, there is no reason for concern. It is simply a stage that the child will soon outgrow. Those who are not performing as the parent or teacher desires present no problem. The parent or teacher simply needs some patience, for clearly the child is not yet ready to perform in the desired manner. It is simply a matter of time before the child grows out of one stage and enters another. At times those responsible for children are held accountable for not effecting normal growth and development. Because children in school are expected to be taught in a way that will enable them to learn, educators accepted that they also needed to have knowledge of the laws of learning. Knowing those laws would somehow lead to effective teaching. For most of the twentieth century the views of Edward L. Thorndike were those accepted by educators.[31]

As educators sought scientific status and respectability, they emphasized research design, hypothesis construction, measurement of ability and changes in performance, and statistical analysis of various measurements to determine the probabilities of error and chance. That essentially entailed collecting data in systematic ways, preferably data that could be numerically displayed, and placing pedagogy or teaching methods on a scientific foundation. Placing pedagogy on a scientific foundation did not necessarily mean that a given pedagogy was tested scientifically. Often that simply meant showing through discourse that a given approach to pedagogy was consistent with or appeared to be a logical implication of a given psychology. Discourse, however, is often not supported by the observation of the results of experiments.

Psychology provided and continues to provide educational researchers with many speculations, hypotheses, theories, models, investigative techniques, and paradigms. For example, the National Institute of Education (NIE) let a contract in 1974 that resulted in a volume published in 1978 under the auspices of the National Academy of Education.[32] Of the nine case studies included in the volume four were clearly studies of psychologists or educational psychologists: "On the Theory-Practice Interface in the Measurement of Intellectual Abilities"; "Words for Schools: the Applications in Education of the Vocabulary Researches of Edward L. Thorndike"; "The Contributions of B. F. Skinner and Some Counter-Influences"; "The Theoretical Ideas of Piaget and Educational Practice." Some may claim that "Psychoanalysis and American Elementary Education" in the same volume was also a psychological study or a study very close related to such. Nearly a quarter of a century later, Ellen Condliffe Lagemann argued that one of the major difficulties with the development of educational research, or its failure to develop as many would have liked, was that the field was dominated by Thorndike whom she described as a behaviorist (though he is properly classified as a connectionist). She further claimed that the future for educational research, given the development of cognitive psychology, (a development that had its origins a quarter of century before the NIE sponsored volume appeared) was promising.[33] Whether the abandonment of one psychology in favor of another will in fact lead to better educational research, a robust science of education and improved practices in public schools that will eliminate the achievement gap remains to be seen. What is clear, however, is that the history of educational research and the attempts to improve educational practice have and continue to entail consideration of psychology and educational psychology. Interestingly, it was in 1948, the same year that marked the beginning of the cognitive revolution, when Ernest R. Hilgard advised in what proved to be an extraordinarily successful text that "the understanding of learning is central to the problems of teaching and of training, in school and out" and further advised that "it is very natural for psychologists to feel that the study of learning belongs to them."[34]

Hilgard's territorial claim may have been recognition of what Edward L. Thorndike had achieved. Whatever the case, that claim has not been successfully challenged. Consequently, an understanding of educational research and an understanding depends upon knowledge of the history of educational psychology, especially those who defined the field early in the century. As David F. Labaree observed: "Since the turn of the century, educational psychology has been one area within education schools that has been able to establish itself as a credible producer of academic knowledge and thus, its faculty as legitimate members of the university professoriate."[35] Educators want their students to learn and they have accepted how psychologists define and measure learning. For nearly a century, Edward L. Thorndike's learning theory dominated in education.[36] Indeed, it has been observed "that one cannot understand the history of education in the United States during the twentieth century unless one realizes that Edward L. Thorndike won and John Dewey lost."[37] Moreover, as education secured standing in universities, those trained in psychology not only dominated educational research but also quickly rose to prominent and influential positions in the newly created field. For example, when the National Society for the Study of Education presented material on eleven early leaders in American education, it reported that five of the eleven were trained in either psychology or educational psychology.[38] More recently, Shirley Brice Heath has observed that the reliance on psychology has had a limiting influence on educational research:

> Not surprisingly, within education research, especially research on human behavior, categories and research methods from psychology remain dominant, although occasionally they receive support from sociology, historically grounded in the study of mainstream middle-class groups and their institutions. A focus on individual subject with particular labels such as socioeconomic status, national origin, and family type still prevails in descriptions of research subjects. Behind these terms rests a host of assumptions about what is and is not normative. Experimental control groups remain highly desired, as do procedures or trials that can produce reliability. One legacy of the reliance on given and largely unexamined categories and research methods is the difficulty scholars have in legitimizing their studies of non-mainstream groups and of learning environments beyond the control of adults. The field of psychology has only recently begun to address the issue of its own culture boundedness within Euro-American contexts. [39]

THE DOMAIN BELIEFS SUPPORTING EDUCATIONAL RESEARCH

More important than any research study or collection of studies are the beliefs and assumptions that support those studies, for those beliefs and assumptions in subtle and ineffable ways guide practice and inform expectations. What is important is one's worldview, a view often not clearly and explicitly articulated. Those who are perceived, even though the perception may be at the tacit level, to be working in a tradition consistent with one's worldview are those whose work and recommendations are accepted and employed in practice. Educational research with its grounding in Progressive Era social reform movements exhibits multiple and sometimes contradictory tendencies as two facets of Enlightenment ideas that helped shaped the ideological framework of the United States as a nation. It has an orientation toward science, a positivistic rationalism directed toward controlling social change from positions of authority according to ideals of order and efficiency. Educational research also is informed by a broad based humanism directed toward perfecting the human condition by providing and improving education. As influenced by the ideal of a medical model applied to the professionalization of psychology, educational research focuses on the individual as a psychobiological entity that develops in specified patterns and stages that are universal.

The essence of universalism is the claim and belief that science is neutral, if not good, and to be followed because it yields objective results. Objectivity is achieved by studying animal or human interactions and animal or human behavior in the same way that a physicist studies the movement of objects and the interaction of objects. In this tradition the investigator is seen as separate from that which he or she is studying and as having no influence on what is being studied. Those who do not subscribe to this view and tradition often call those who do positivists. They tend to reject and question studies that produce data that is subjected to a variety of analyses the results of which are expressed numerically. They claim that context should not be overlooked and question whether the investigator can be separated from whatever it is that is being studied or observed.

Educational research, like more precisely defined areas of inquiry, is an activity that builds upon itself. As D. C. Phillips observed, "research usually is inspired by a theoretical position, and is part of an ongoing process or loosely defined movement."[40] Educational research has a history and rarely, if ever do educational researchers escape the "climate of opinion"[41] that prevails when and where they work. Those who argue for the variety of activities subsumed under qualitative as opposed to quantitative research are dealing with conceptualizations and disciplinary boundaries framed by their predecessors even when they are rejecting them. When educational researchers find it necessary to refute what has been bequeathed to them, their predecessors are participating in the definition of their inquiries just as those who are now conducting research are framing the questions for their critics and successors. There is little doubt that educational researchers will continue to work with and in the traditions established by their predecessors and there is little doubt that they will face problems and opportunities their predecessors did not confront. The society and the schools to which educators now attend also present new problems. Other problems and issues are generated by the researchers' inquiries as well as the new purposes society establishes for itself and its educators. As the priorities on the nation's agenda are rearranged so are the interests of educational researchers.

THE IMPORTANCE OF THE HISTORY OF EDUCATIONAL RESEARCH

To understand what considerations, assumptions, and purposes shaped the beginnings of educational research is to gain some insight into why educational researchers select and define problems as they do, why they seek to be located in some departments of some institutions and not in others, the alliances they seek to establish and maintain, the allegiances they form, the associations they maintain, and how they train their successors. An understanding of the history of educational research may explain why so much attention has been paid to learning and its measurement, to the development of instruments designed either to determine who could and could not learn or instruments designed to measure how much has been learned, and why so little attention, until relatively recently, has been paid to teaching.[42] As Jurgen Herbst observed, the history of education in the United States reveals that while education was professionalized teaching was not.[43] The first *Handbook on Research on Teaching*[44] did not appear until 1963. As Lee S. Shulman later observed, when N. L. Gage wrote his chapter, "Paradigms for Research on Teaching," for the first *Handbook*, the field—research on teaching—was in its "infancy." He reported that: "Gage drew most of his models from psychology or other behavioral sciences, rather than from the study of teaching itself."[45] Ellen Condliffe Lagemann and Lee S. Shulman later confirmed that assessment of how Gage approached the topic:

> For a long time many of the core problems or topics for education research were defined by the fundamental psychological processes of learning, such as memory, transfer, and problem solving. The research problems were expected to be general—How does learning occur?—rather than focused on the subjects of the school curriculum—How do students' prior conceptions of conservation affect their learning of physics? Even those who opted to study basic general process looked almost exclusively at the nature of learning, not considering teaching as a proper topic of investigation.[46]

A history of educational research must necessarily recognize the discussions about whether education could or should be an independent science or discipline, for those discussions occurred at a time in the nation's intellectual and professional life when church, state and science were being separated from one another. Then, natural philosophy and moral philosophy were being transformed as new disciplines were being constructed. The natural or physical sciences took the place of natural philosophy. The social sciences—economics, sociology, political science and psychology—took the place of moral philosophy. As researchers moved from the study to the laboratory or to the field to conduct their work, they were sometimes accused of abandoning theory. They were, to be sure, placing more emphasis on observation, experimentation and measurement and less on speculation. At that time, "some university scholars began to argue that *education*—the study of human development, the learning process, and man's educational institutions—was a legitimate enterprise within the older framework of liberal studies."[47] As Merle Borrowman observed, many "respected university scholars"—James McKeen Cattell, John Dewey, G. Stanley Hall, William James, Paul Monroe, Albion Small, Edward L. Thorndike, Thorstein Veblen and Lester Frank Ward, for example—turned their attention to education. In *Dynamic Sociology* (1883) Ward indicated that study of education was possible and would lead to an improved and orderly society, and his disciple, Small agreed.[48] As pedagogy was separated from moral philosophy, there was the belief that the new science of the mind, psychology, would form the foundation for a science of education. John Dewey, it may be recalled, described his laboratory school at the University of Chicago as "a laboratory of applied psychology."[49] At the same time, practitioners of the new science of the mind saw those assigned to school—children—as appropriate subjects of study. At the end of the nineteenth century, "one-quarter of all the experimental studies in the United States were explicitly concerned with the application of practical concerns; one-quarter of all experimental subjects were children or adolescents."[50] By 1910 three-fourths of the psychologists who turned to applied work turned to educational psychology and a third of the psychologists demonstrated an interest in education. Those who found educational psychology a fertile field focused on learning theory, tests, measurement of ability and performance, and they developed tests and scales for virtually every school subject.[51] A review of the *Psychological Index* shows that "by 1930, 'educational' studies accounted for the highest percentage—about 25%—of 25,472 articles in psychology."[52]

Most educational researchers and those who supported their inquiries were and are progressives in that they believed in the utility of science for the improvement of society. However, more often than not their focus was not on the structure of society—its institutions, practices and policies— but on individuals. They either sought to find ways to classify individuals so they could be prepared for and assigned to an appropriate place and role in the existing social structure or sought to discover the laws of learn- ing so that teachers could be trained and directed to apply those laws so that students would acquire the knowledge and skills needed in the exist- ing social-economic configuration. Educational researchers, often trained as psychologists or educational psychologists, successfully convinced those responsible for the training of teachers to teach their charges how to observe the laws of learning and developed scores of tests so students' abilities and achievements could be documented. Almost as soon as instruments were available for determining the ability of children in the primary grades, teachers were advised of their availability and encouraged to use them.[53]

CONCLUSION: LEGACIES OF PROGRESSIVISM

The history of educational research is important because the processes are not over but continue to be exhibited in educational policy and practices. Just as the designers of industrial processes used science to design their processes and products so the educators turned to the science of psychology and a medical model to enable them to convert their raw material into properly performing finished products. Psychology was a perfect expression of the industrial society. Its use by educators gave their enterprise respectability and authority and allowed them to claim they were employing science to render educational processes as efficient as possible. Quality control engineers taught industrialists how to make products "just good enough." If processes could be designed to accept wide rather than narrow variations in the treatment of the raw material and in the quality of the finished product, efficiency and productivity were maintained. The objective was to ensure that as many differences as possible would make no difference. Psychologists accepted and used the normal curve to show that a performance within a standard deviation from the mean in either direction was just as good as any other performance that fell into the same range. That was no small achievement, for plus or minus one standard deviation is a full two thirds of the population. Hence, two-thirds are "good enough" Because all could not be taught to perform, to be "just good enough," instruments that would enable identification of those not able to perform had to be devised. After World War I it was clear that the instrument of choice was the intelligence test. Those identified as not able to perform, often labeled as defective, tended to be not white or those who had very recently arrived form Eastern or Southern Europe. Such identification was consistent with longstanding misconceptions and prejudices. Significantly, those who were identified as being somehow intellectually inferior were also seen as morally defective.

In 1948 the Educational Testing Service[54] was founded to develop the tests and thus to foster the creation of a meritocracy, an aristocracy of talent.[55] Whether one agrees that standardized tests have and systematically continue to discriminate against specific minority populations[56] or whether one agrees that they are in fact fair and objective measures of ability, achievement, and reliable predictors of future performance, there is no denying that development of standardized tests, scales, checklists and scorecards that began in the Progressive Era are more important and more relevant than ever before.[57] Defenders of testing with standardized and objective instruments argue that system-wide use of standardized tests provides normative data that can be used to determine whether all populations are performing at comparable levels and whether some populations are better served than others. How "objective" came to be the adjective that is so often placed before "tests" and "instruments" is a study that clearly needs to be undertaken. Presumably, it is because the grader or scorer (human, mechanical or electronic) does not judge the respondent's answers but only records them. Somehow that takes a great deal of attention away from the author of the question and its answer. Teachers, as Dickson and Terman advised in 1927, who had access to "the standard mental tests and subject-matter tests" were able to make "impersonal" observations, "refine" their thinking, and make "safer" judgments.[58] The next chapter turns to controversies over the timing of the origins of educational research. Interpretations of when educational research began determine the definition and purpose of educational research in significant ways. Some interpretations obscure the sources of the ideas employed in educational research and thus its purposes in terms of pursuing the national agenda.

NOTES

1. Robert M. Crunden. *Ministers of Reform: The Progressives' Achievement in American Civilization, 1899-1920* (New York: Basic Books, 1982).
2. Emily S. Rosenberg. *Spreading the American Dream: American Economic and Cultural Expansion, 1890-1945* (New York: Hill and Wang, 1982).
3. Samuel P. Hays. *The Response to Industrialism, 1885-1914* (Chicago: University of Chicago Press, 1963), pp. 2-3.
4. Walter Lippman. *Drift and Mastery* (Englewood Cliffs, New Jersey: Spectrum Books, 1962), p. 92.
5. John I. Goodlad. *The Dynamics of Educational Change* (New York: McGraw-Hill, 1975), pp. 185-186.
6. John M. O'Donnell. *The Origins of Behaviorism: American Psychology, 1870-1920* (New York: New York University Press, 1985), p. 229.
7. Theodore M. Porter. *Karl Pearson: The Scientific Life in a Statistical Age* (Princeton, New Jersey: Princeton University Press. 2004), p. 7.
8. Daniel J. Boorstin. *The Americans: The Democratic Experience* (New York: Vintage Books, 1973), p. 189.
9. Lawrence A. Cremin. *The Transformation of the School: Progressivism in American Education, 1876-1957* (New York: Knopf, 1962), p. 85.
10. Lawrence A. Cremin, "The Revolution in American Secondary Education, 1893-1918," *Teachers College Record* , Vol. LVI, No. 6 (March 1955), p. 296.
11. *Ibid.*, p. 307.
12. *Ibid.*

13. Edward A. Krug. *The Shaping of the American High School* (New York: Harper and Row, 1964), p. 271.

14. Richard Hofstadter. *Social Darwinism in American Thought.* rev. ed. (Boston: The Beacon Press, 1955), p. 169.

15. Luis M. Laosa. "Social Policies toward Children of Diverse Ethnic, Racial, and Language Groups in the United States" in Harold W. Stevenson and Alberta E. Siegel (eds.). *Child Development Research and Social Policy* (Chicago: University of Chicago Press, 1984), p. 18.

16. Quoted in John M. O'Donnell. *The Origins of Behaviorism*, p. 100.

17. Ellen Condliffe Lagemann and Lee S. Shulman, "Introduction: The Improvement of Education Research: A Complex, Continuing Quest" in Lagemann and Shulman (eds.). *Issues in Education Research.* (San Francisco: Josey-Bass Publishers, 1999), p. xvi.

18. Hays. *The Response to Industrialism, 1885-1914* and Robert H. Wiebe. *The Search for Order, 1877-1920* (New York: Hill and Wang, 1967).

19. Theresa M. Richardson, *The Century of the Child: The Mental Hygiene Movement and Social Policy in the U.S. and Canada* (Albany, N.Y.: State University of New York, 1989), pp. 17-18.

20. Frank Smith. *Further Essays into Education* (Portsmouth, New Hampshire: Heineman, 1988), p. 111.

21. A. Cremin. *The Transformation of the School*, p. viii.

22. For what is entailed in actually introducing research findings in school settings see: Rolf Lehming and Michael Kane (eds.). *Improving Schools: Using What We Know* (Beverly Hills: Sage Publications, 1981).

23. For nearly all Americans an "objective test" has come to mean a "multiple-choice test." Frederick J. Kelly appears to have been the inventor of the multiple-choice test, and its first appearance was in the Kansas Silent Reading Test in 1914-1915. See: Vernon C. Hall. "Educational Psychology from 1890 to 1920" in Barry J. Zimmerman and Dale H. Schunk (eds.). *Educational Psychology: A Century of Contributions* (Mahwah, New Jersey: Lawrence Erlbaum Associates, 2003), pp. 29-30.

24. Walter S. Monroe. "Existing Tests and Standards" in Guy M. Whipple (ed.). *Seventeenth Yearbook of the National Society for the Study of Education: Part II, The Measurement of Educational Products* (Bloomington, Illinois: Public School Publishing Co., 1918), p. 71.

25. Walter S. Monroe. "Educational Measurement in 1920 and 1945," *Journal of Educational Measurement*, Vol. 38, No. 5 (January 1945), p. 334.

26. Edna Bryner. "A Selected Bibliography of Certain Phases of Educational Measurement" in Whipple (ed.). *The Seventeenth Yearbook of the National Society for the Study of Education*, pp. 161-190.

27. For example, the Weschler Preschool and Primary Scale of Intelligence— revised, often referred to as the "Wippsie R" that appeared in 1989 was a revision of the original test that appeared in 1967. The "Wippsie R" "contained mostly cosmetic changes to make it more colorful and appealing because the original test was criticized as overly long and tedious." See: Peter Sacks. *Standardized Minds: The High Price of America's Testing Culture and What We Can Do to Change It* (Cambridge, Massachusetts: Perseus Publishing, 1999), pp. 36-37.

28. John T. E. Richardson. "Howard Andrew Knox and the Origins of Performance Testing on Ellis Island, 1912-1916," *History of Psychology*, Vol. 6, No. 2 (May 2003), p. 143.

29. O'Donnell. *The Origins of Behaviorism*, pp. 1, and 88.

30. Minutes of the Meeting of the Committee on Child Growth and Development," December 1936, General Education Board (GEB) Archives 930, 1, 3, 369, 3849, Rockefeller Archive Center (RAC), Sleepy Hollow, New York.

31. Richard E. Mayer. "E. L. Thorndike's Enduring Contributions to Educational Psychology" in Zimmerman and Schunk (eds.). *Educational Psychology: A Century of Contributions*, p. 113.

32. Patrick Suppes (ed.). *Impact of Research on Education: Some Case Studies* (Washington, D. C.: National Academy of Education, 1978).

33. What Howard Gardner described as "the cognitive revolution" began in 1948 at "a rather dramatic meeting called the Hixon Symposium at the California Institute of Technology in 1948." At that meeting Karl Lashley broke with John B. Watson who had trained him and abandoned behaviorism. See: Ellen Condliffe Lagemann. *An Elusive Science: The Troubling History of Education Research* (Chicago: University of Chicago Press, 2000), p. 215.

34. Ernest R. Hilgard. *Theories of Learning* (New York: Appleton-Century-Crofts, Inc. 1949), p. 2.

35. David F. Labaree. "Power, Knowledge, and the Rationalization of Teaching: A Genealogy of the Movement to Professionalize Teaching," *Harvard Educational Review*, Vol. 62, No. 2 (Summer 1992), p. 137.

36. Richard E. Mayer. "E. L. Thorndike's Enduring Contributions to Educational Psychology" in Zimmerman and Schunk (eds.). *Educational Psychology: A Century of Contributions*, p. 113.

37. Ellen Condliffe Lagemann. "The Plural Worlds of Educational Research," *History of Education Quarterly*, Vol. 29, No. 2 (Summer 1989), p. 185. When Lagemann repeated this observation in *An Elusive Science*, she added: "Thorndike's triumph was not complete, p. xi.

38. See Robert J. Havighurst (ed.). *The Seventieth Yearbook of the National Society for the Study of Education: Part II Leaders in American Education* (Chicago: University of Chicago Press, 1971).

39. Shirley Brice Heath. "Discipline and Disciplines in Education Research: Elusive Goals?" in Lagemann and Shulman (eds.). *Issues in Education Research: Problems and Possibilities*, p. 215.

40. D. C. Phillips. "Post-Kuhnian Reflections of Educational Research" in Jonas F. Soltis (ed.). *Eightieth Yearbook of the National Society for the Study of Education: Part I, Philosophy and Education* (Chicago: University of Chicago Press, 1981), p. 257.

41. "Climate of opinion" is here used in the sense that Carl Becker used it in *The Heavenly City of the Eighteenth-Century Philosophers* (New Haven, Connecticut: Yale University Press, 1932): "...those instinctively held preconceptions in the broad sense, that Weltanschauung or world pattern . . . that imposes a peculiar use of the intelligence and a special type of logic" (p. 5).

42. The United States is not the only nation in which educational researchers tended to ignore teachers and teaching. In a discussion of the development of educational research in Great Britain, David Hamilton "Bread and

Circuses: Some Challenges to Educational Research in the 1980s:" Presidential address delivered at the Conference of the British Educational Research Association, Lancaster, 30th August-2nd September, 1984) observed that there "the Academy selectively nurtured the social sciences in the interests of what have been called the regulative functions of the state" (p. 10). He further pointed out that in a review of F. W. Taylor's *Principles of Scientific Management*, John Adams (Professor of Education at the University of London) pinpointed the issue at stake: "Perhaps the most important problem in educational theory of the future," he wrote, "is the place the teacher is to occupy" (pp. 9-10).

43.   Jurgen Herbst. *And Sadly Teach: Teacher Education and Professionalization in American Culture* (Madison: Wisconsin: University of Wisconsin Press, 1989), pp. 8 and 11.

44.   N. L. Gage (ed.). *Handbook of Research on Teaching* (Chicago: Rand McNally, 1963).

45.   Lee S. Shulman. "Paradigms and Research Programs in the Study of Teaching: A Contemporary Perspective" in Merlin C. Wittrock. (ed.). *Handbook of Research on Teaching*, 3rd. ed. (New York: Macmillan, 1986), p. 3.

46.   Lagemann and Schulman. "Introduction," *Issues in Education Research: Problems and Possibilities*, p. xv.

47.   Merle L. Borrownman. "Liberal Education and Professional Preparation of Teachers" in Merle L. Borrowman (ed.), Teacher Education in America: A Documentary History (New York; Teachers College Press, 1965), p. 11.

48.   *Ibid.*, pp. 12-13.

49.   John Dewey. *The School and Society and The Child and the Curriculum* (Chicago: University of Chicago Press ([1900,1902] 1990), p. 96.

50.   O'Donnell. *Origins of Behaviorism*, p. 157.

51.   *Ibid.*, pp. 226-227, 231.

52.   Stephen Petrina. "Luella Cole, Sidney Pressey, and Educational Psychoanalysis, 1921-1931," *History of Education Quarterly*, Vol. 44, No. 4 (Winter 2004), p. 524.

53.   For example, before the 1920s were over Virgil E. Dickson and Lewis M. Terman advised teachers: "There are many group mental tests on the market designed for first, second, or third grade, and some even for kindergarten pupils." Three tests they described as "now available" were: *Detroit First Grade Intelligence Test, Towne Picture Game,* and *Pintner-Cunningham Primary Mental Test.* See: "Tests and Classification in the Primary Grades" in The Classroom Teacher, Vol. II (Chicago: *The Classroom Teacher,* Inc., 1927-28), p. 13.

54.   ETS is well known for the admissions tests it has developed for college and graduate study: The College Board's SAT, the Test of English as a Foreign Language (TOEFL), the Graduate Record Examinations (GRE), and the Graduate Management Admission Test (GMAT). It is the world's largest nonprofit institution devoted to research and measurement in education.

55.   Nicholas Lemann. *The Big Test: The Secret History of the American Meritocracy* (New York: Farrar, Straus and Giroux, 1999).

56.   When Lewis Terman, often described as a test pioneer, found in 1916 that nearly 8% of the immigrants he tested appeared to be feeble-minded, he

did not question his test or testing procedures but concluded: "Their dullness seems to be racial, or at least in the family stocks from which they come. The fact that one meets this type with such extraordinary frequency among Indians, Mexicans, and Negroes suggests quite forcibly that the whole question of racial differences in mental traits will have to be taken up anew. . . . there will be discovered enormously significant racial differences . . . which cannot be wiped out by any schemes of mental culture." Quoted in Jeannie Oakes. *Keeping Track: How Schools Structure Equality* (New Haven: Yale University Press, 1985), p. 36.

57. See, for example: Alfie Kohn. *The Case Against Standardized Testing: Raising the Scores, Ruining the Schools* (Portsmouth, New Hampshire: Heinemann, 2000); Gary Orfield and Mindy L. Kornhaber (eds.). *Raising Standards or Raising Barriers? Inequality and High-Stakes Testing in Public Education* (New York: The Century Foundation Press, 2001) and Sacks. *Standardized Minds.*

58. Dickson and Terman. "Tests and Classification in the Primary Grades," p. 12.

CHAPTER 2

CONTROVERSIES OVER THE ORIGINS OF EDUCATIONAL RESEARCH

On July 26, 1954, President Eisenhower signed the 83rd Congress' legislation that created the Cooperative Research Act (Public Law 83-531) that authorized the United States Commissioner of Education "to enter into financial agreements with colleges, universities, and State educational agencies for research, surveys, and demonstrations in the field of education." In the same year Congress authorized the National Science Foundation to provide founds for "course content improvement."[1] While it can be argued that these developments in 1954 constituted recognition that educational research in academic settings was essential for the national welfare and that education was one of the means selected and used for realization of the national agenda, there still exists confusion about the beginnings of modern educational research. From the existing literature relevant to the history of educational research a simple multiple-choice question can be framed: "When did modern educational research begin?" The possible answers are: a) It began in the 1890s when Joseph Mayer Rice began his studies of education and his campaign to reform public education in the United States; b) It began in 1918 when a great variety of standardized tests were available; c) It began when modern psychology made its appearance; or d) It began with the founders of the common

Educational Research, the National Agenda, and Educational Reform:
A History, pp. 29–52

school, Horace Mann and Henry Barnard, and their successor William Torrey Harris.

Consideration and exploration of these possible answers show that there are many conceptions of educational research and that, not surprisingly, the different conceptions result in different views about the origins. Furthermore, exploration of these origins and conceptions begins to show what the interests of educational researchers were when they made the field and what they used to fashion their responses. They were responding to the problems and opportunities rapid expansion of schooling created, the need to fulfill the requirements of an increasingly democratic social order by ensuring that each and every student received his or her fair share of services, the desire to professionalize education, or a progressive agenda that demanded efficient and expert management of public institutions, the amelioration of social ills, and consideration of the needs and nature of children.

JOSEPH MAYER RICE'S STUDIES AND CAMPAIGN AS THE ORIGIN OF EDUCATIONAL RESEARCH

Joseph Mayer Rice has been identified as an "educational muckraker,"[2] the founder of progressive education,[3] "one of the founders of the American testing movement," "the real inventor of the comparative test,"[4] "a pioneer educational researcher,"[5] and, as Rice himself claimed in testimony prepared for the United States Congress in 1920s, the "father of educational research."[6] While some may want to dispute the founder and father claims, there is no denying that he wanted to reform public education by ridding it of the "old" or "mechanical education" and placing the "new education" in its stead and that he wanted to place knowledge or facts—what was known and what was determined possible to accomplish—in place of opinions. He claimed that educational discourse was characterized by opinions about opinions and few, if any, facts. His insistence that "the school system must be absolutely divorced from politics in every sense of the word" so that all "official acts" would "best serve the interests of the child"[7] certainly qualifies him to be counted among the progressive reformers.

In 1888, Rice gave up his practice as a pediatrician to study pedagogy and psychology in Europe, chiefly Germany. He attended the pedagogical seminar conducted by the Herbartian Wilhelm Rein at Jena, visited Wilhelm Wundt's psychological laboratory, and spent time visiting schools and observing teachers in Europe. Upon his return from Europe, Rice, encouraged by Walter Hines Page the editor of the *Forum* that was published by his brother Isaac Rice, began to investigate the condition of public education in the United States and can be said to have undertaken an early, if not the first, national survey of public education in the United States. To ascertain why the degree of excellence in schools varied from school to school and from city to city Rice spent from January 7 to June 25, 1892 visiting schools in thirty-six cities. After his reports were published in a series of articles in the *Forum*, thirteen of his reports were subsequently published in *The Public-School System of the United States* (1893).

In contemporary terms, Rice can be said to have conducted what many would now describe as a naturalistic study. Because experience had taught him "to place no reliance whatever on reports published by school officials regarding the condition of their schools" and because "such reports being frequently no more than purely political documents, and consequently as a rule, entirely misleading," he "relied, in studying the condition of the schools, only on personal observation of class-room instruction," and was careful not to base his assessment of a school system based on a visit to only one school. During his six-month study, he observed more than twelve hundred teachers. In addition, he interviewed superintendents, principals, and teachers and attended school board meetings and teachers' meetings.[8]

There is no doubt that Rice had an agenda. He argued that the school existed "for the benefit of the child and not for the benefit of the boards of education, superintendents, or teachers."[9] He clearly favored one form of pedagogy over another. He was opposed to the "old education" and favored the "new education" that "recognizes that there are elements aside from measurable results that require consideration in educating the child." The "old education" forgot the child while the "new education" was "guided by the fact that the child is a frail and tender, loving and lovable human being."[10] The difference between the two was clear. According to Rice:

> When natural methods are philosophically applied by the teacher, the child becomes interested in his work, and the school is converted into a house of pleasure. When, on the other hand, the child is taught by mechanical methods, his mental food is given to him in the most indigestible and unpalatable form, in consequence of which he takes no interest in his work, learning becomes a source of drudgery, and the school a house of bondage.[11]

In *The Public School-System of the United States* and his subsequent works Rice demonstrated that he was a reformer. He was responding to and perhaps even shaping the national educational agenda, for he was urging the use of the scientific method to settle questions about education and wanted scientific management of the schools. Like other progressives, he was committed to efficiency and to eliminating waste, especially the waste of time. Rice was committed to facts, to what could be known and focused on how time could be used more efficiently.

In 1896 in "Obstacles to Rational Educational Reform" Rice related that he no longer believed that the "obstacles to educational progress" could be rightfully "attributed to public indifference and its consequences—politics in school boards, incompetent supervision, insufficient preparation on the part of teachers, etc." The difficulty was with the educators themselves, for they could not agree on "what changes, if any, are desirable of feasible." Among educators there were a variety of opinions about what was possible, and there were "no proofs to offer as to who is right and who is wrong." Rice's assessment was that: "Everything is speculative: nothing is positive. 'I think' and 'I believe' are the stereotyped expressions of the educational world: "I know" has not yet been admitted."[12]

Educators agreed on the general aims of education: to produce good citizens, to produce graduates who could write a letter free from grammatical errors. However, there was no agreement on "practical questions." For Rice "practical questions" could be answered, and there was no reason not to answer them. Rice was not willing to settle "practical questions" by reasoning from psychological laws. He argued:

> That general psychology, in itself, should fail to be of direct assistance in determining the question of economy of effort is due to the fact that this subject is purely a qualitative science, treating of the qualities of the mind, while economy of effort in teaching is strictly a quantitative problem. Psychology teaches us the laws in accordance with which the mind digests ideas but gives us no information whatever in regard to the number of ideas that can be digested within a given period, or how much time is required to complete the digestion of given number of ideas.[13]

From psychology educators could learn that the abstract followed the concrete and that in teaching arithmetic children needed to spend time handling concrete objects. However, psychology could not tell educators how much time children should spend handling concrete objects. Only experience, could tell how much time was needed.

After having spent two years administering examinations to approximately 100,000 students, Rice concluded that it was possible to overcome the obstacles to rational educational reform.[14] The difficulty was that there were no established standards by which teachers could determine when their work was done. Even when there was a standard that could be identified, for example, the ability to write a letter without any grammatical mistakes, there was no way to determine how much time should be devoted to teaching grammar. Rice maintained:

That, at present we are absolutely unable to form an intelligent judgment in regard to how much time ought to be consumed in completing a piece of work is proved by what has already been stated; namely, that educators are not even agreed as to whether better spellers will be produced by devoting forty minutes daily to spelling than by devoting not more than five or ten minutes daily to that subject; or whether results secured by a five-year course in technical grammar are superior to those obtained by a one-year course.[15]

Determining the optimum time that should be devoted to a school subject was important. If it could be determined that the customary time given to a school subject was more than necessary to achieve a given standard, there would then be time to introduce new subjects into the curriculum that reformers wanted to introduce. The claim that there was not enough time for new subjects would be refuted not by opinion but by the facts.

The most noted of Rice's work is the attention he gave to spelling. His publication in 1897 of his study of how much time was devoted to spelling and how well students could spell was later described "as the first general survey of a particular educational field."[16] That work shows that he was a careful researcher who endeavored to secure valid and uniform measurements. After examining the results of the pilot test, he concluded that the unusually favorable results in certain classrooms did not represent the natural conditions, but were due to the peculiar manner in which the examinations had been conducted.[17] To remedy the variability in how various teachers administered the test, Rice abandoned the results of the pilot tests, and decided that he would administer the tests himself so there would be no variation in their administration. Rice's results revealed that students' performance in spelling could not be related to their attendance in either schools that adhered to the methods of the old education or to those that employed the new methods. Rice discovered that in the upper grades differences in students' spelling ability were small and that there were no significant relationships between spelling ability and the time devoted to spelling. That prompted him to ask: "Do these results not indicate that, in learning to spell, maturity is the leading factor, while method plays a subordinate part?"[18]

In a review of the progress of research in educational administration, published in 1945, Douglas E. Scates concluded: "It becomes clear that we should mislead ourselves should we entertain the notion that there was nothing of importance in educational research prior to 1920."[19] For him, Rice's "The Futility of the Spelling Grind" was "the beginning of the modern movement for the objective study of education."[20] While Rice did not have access to the subsequently developed sophisticated methods for test construction and for collecting and analyzing data, he did develop methods to gather "objective data and considered an array of variables that have been consistently addressed by educational researchers." According to Scates:

> [Rice] had a number of factors to dispose of before he could come to his point. Naturally the school people would argue that differences in spelling ability were the result of factors over which they had no control. Heredity? Environment? Age? As best one might without refined measures of socio-economic status, he analyzed his data with respect to these factors.[21]

As Julian Stanley later observed, Rice's analyses were tabular, without significance tests and the full-classification neatness of Fisherian ANOVA, of course, but his care and thoroughness were commendable for that day or this [1966].[22] In addition, it was also later observed that Rice's study of spelling showed "rudimentary concepts of test validity and reliability and some concern about variability."[23]

UNIVERSITIES' INTEREST IN EDUCATION AND THEIR CONTRIBUTION TO RESEARCH

That the occupational and academic structures in which so many educational researchers study, work, and conduct their inquiries were being built in the 1890s is another reason to agree that modern educational research began at the end of the nineteenth century. As the high school's popularity grew, especially after 1890, so grew the interest of universities in the art and science of education. During the 1870s, several state universities began to work our certificate systems with the high schools to facilitate the process of determining which high school graduates were qualified to enter the university. By 1890, "firm well-developed systems of certification had been adopted in Michigan, Minnesota, Iowa, Wisconsin, Indiana, Illinois, Ohio, Texas, Missouri, and California." By 1900, "42 other state universities and land-grant colleges and at least 150 of the private institutions had adopted some form of certification or accrediting.[24] As the universities attempted to determine what constituted a satisfactory high school curriculum, there soon developed professors who specialized in such determinations. Eventually, the position of high school visitor grew, and departments, colleges, or schools of education were established. The education profession was on its way.

By the turn of the century, high school enrollment had increased to nearly 520,000 from a mere 72,000 in 1870. Between 1890 and 1918, new high school enrollment increased by 711% while the nation's population increased by only 68%. New high schools were being built and opened at the rate of one a day.[25] Public education had become a growth industry in the United States by the end of the century. In the first decades of the twentieth century, the expenditure of public funds for education was greater than the combined expenditures for public welfare and defense.[26] As financial support for public education increased during this era, psychologists found an interest in pedagogy.[27] Universities quickly recognized their obligations to serve the public as well as the opportunities the growing school enrollments presented. The universities' interest in accrediting high schools and even preparing teachers for the high school grew with the growing high school enrollments.

As the popularity of the high school grew in the last decades of the nineteenth century, so did the interest of the universities in pedagogy and the science of education. In 1878, four years after the Kalamazoo decision, the University of Michigan announced that its newly created and filled chair of the "the Science and the Art of Teaching" would prepare students "for higher positions in the public school service," "promote the study of educational science," and render "a more perfect unity to our state educational system by bringing the secondary schools into closer relations with the university."[28] Training teachers was not, it should be observed, among the chief purposes of the new chair. Taking advantage of new opportunities was. The growth of public education created not only opportunities for careers that earlier did not exist—managerial and supervisory positions for males—but also the need for systematic studies conducted by experts so the new institutions could be managed professionally and efficiently. The requirements of public schools effectively created new graduate and professional programs. Graduate programs in education were developed almost as quickly as the enrollment in public schools increased.

Between the founding of the Michigan chair in 1878 and 1890, seven other universities established chairs, departments, or schools of education: Wisconsin (1881); Johns Hopkins, Missouri, and North Carolina (1884); Cornell and Indiana (1886); and Clark University (1899).[29] In 1890, professorships of education were reported in thirty-one institutions, chairs of pedagogy attached to another discipline in forty-five more, and seven universities reported lectureships in education.[30] The University of California at Berkley and Teachers College, Columbia University began awarding the doctorate in education in 1898. The University of Chicago added the Ph.D. degree in education to its program in 1901. The University of Michigan did the same in 1902, and in 1906 the Catholic University of America began its doctoral program in education. By 1915, there were eight universities offering the Ph.D. degree in education. Between 1915 and 1919 seven more institutions began similar programs.[31]

MEASUREMENT AND OBJECTIVE TESTS AS THE ORIGIN OF EDUCATIONAL RESEARCH

To agree that educational research began about 1918 is to agree with Walter Scott Monroe who wrote in 1928 that 1918 was the beginning of the modern period in educational research. All that occurred in the two or three decades before then belonged to the "pioneer period."[32] His reason for specifying 1918 as the beginning of the modern period in educational research is consistent with the belief that there can be no educational research without instruments—objective tests—with which measurements can be made. Those who hold to that position effectively claim that a reliable method for measuring ability and performance and a method for systematically making and recording observations that can be recorded as seemingly neutral numerical designations is essential. The assumption that events can be manipulated in the same way that the numerical designations assigned to them can may be implicit in this view.

According to Monroe, there was no measurement until standardized objective tests were developed: "The facts that there were only very limited formal provisions for educational research until near the close of this period, that practically no achievement tests were available until 1915, and that group intelligence tests were not available until after 1918 probably suggest that relatively little significant research was completed before 1918."[33] While there may be some question about how far advanced measurement techniques were, there was little question about how necessary they were. For example, In 1917 Daniel Starch wrote: "It is undoubtedly premature to write a book on educational measurements, because most of the measurements are in the experimental stage." However, according to Starch, the need for "definite, objective measures of educational products" was sufficiently "great" to justify making the existing tests and scales "accessible."[34]

It should also be noted that by 1918 the psychologists, the designers and authors of the achievement tests and the intelligence tests, had established their field in the universities, and many departments of psychology had already been established. After 1910 psychologists who sought to apply the findings of psychology to educational and social problems began to study tests brought back from France by way of Belgium by H. H. Goddard, a former student of G. Stanley Hall and Director of Vineland Training School for the Feebleminded in New Jersey.

Alfred Binet and Theophile Simon developed scaled tests for the French government to see why children differed in their progress in school. They did not intend for them to become a measure of some absolute characteristic that later became known as intelligence.[35] World War I presented psychologists with the opportunity to develop instruments for mass intelligence testing—Army Alpha and Army Beta—an opportunity they quickly seized. Still, there was some question as to how developed the practice of educational measurement was. According to Monroe, educational research did not mature quickly. He later observed: "From the vantage point of 1945 it appears that although the development of educational measurement had passed beyond the period of infancy by 1920, it can not be described as having passed beyond the period of adolescence."[36] By 1945, it had, he claimed, "developed to perhaps the status of early adulthood."[37]

Writing in England just after World War II, Charlotte M. Fleming observed: "Fifty years ago many procedures which are now familiar were quite unknown; and much current discussion would have been unintelligible to teachers skilled in the methods of the eighteen-nineties."[38] The traditional notion of education as "primarily the conquest of illiteracy" had been replaced by a new conception. Adherents of the new conception maintained that learning was "an active, complex process" and that the learner was "an active organism that developed by reacting and adjusting itself to concrete situations—perceiving, weighing alternatives, and discrimination."[39] Among those whom Fleming cited as responsible for providing "generalizations drawn from the findings of experimental study" that supported the new conception of education that attended to "the part played by pupils' physical, emotional, and social experiences" are many who contributed to the development of psychology and educational psychology: William James, Edward L. Thorndike, William McDougall, Sigmund Freud, Alfed Binet, Theophile Simon, G. Stanley Hall, Charles E. Spearman, and Max Wertheimer.

THE ESTABLISHMENT OF DISCIPLINES IN EDUCATION AND PSYCHOLOGY AS THE ORIGIN OF EDUCATIONAL RESEARCH

During the Progressive Era, a period of educational expansion, political science, sociology, economics, and psychology were being established as legitimate and distinct fields of scholarly inquiry and were becoming the disciplines they now are. Some educators then believed that "if the study of education were scholarly, and if it yielded insights for a more rational direction of human affairs, it too could demand a place in the circle of liberal arts and sciences."[40] How psychology related to inquiry into educational processes was at the center of the debate about the status of education as a science.[41]

As Americans embraced the "high machine age" and as ever greater numbers of immigrants arrived to work in the nation's factories and mines, it seemed necessary that citizens and prospective citizens be taught how to behave at their stations in the new social-economic order. The new order required people to perform in specified ways at specified times in specified places. Public schools through their organization, rules, routines, schedules, and content of instruction prepared the young to take their assigned stations. Psychologists provided educators "a model that proposed to raise the pupils' performance to meet pre-established norms."[42] They gave education a definition of learning that addressed what could be observed and measured. It was soon accepted that that which could not be measured either did not exist or was not important. As Edward L. Thorndike proclaimed in 1914, "If a thing exists, it exists in some amount; and if it exists in some amount, it can be measured."[43] Daniel Starch was among those who agreed with Thorndike. In 1916 he instructed his readers in a statement very much like the one Thorndike made in 1914 that "any quality of ability of human nature that is detectable is also measurable."[44] Starch earlier observed that "the [then] current movement for measuring school products is one of the three or four most important fields of investigation in the scientific study of educational 'programs'." He appeared confident that the old pedagogy was to be replaced with "quantitative studies, objective measurements, and carefully observed facts."[45]

To agree that educational research began with the appearance of modern psychology and psychometrics is to agree that modern psychology and measurement of ability or aptitude and performance constitute indispensable foundations for modern educational research. Those two areas began to assume their present form in the 1870s. 1870 was the year the American edition of Sir Francis Galton's *Hereditary Genius: An Inquiry into its Laws and Consequences* appeared. In 1878, Harvard awarded the first American Ph.D. in psychology to G. Stanley Hall and James opened his psychological laboratory for demonstrations at Harvard and began work on his *Principles of Psychology* (eventually published in 1890). Wilhelm Wundt opened his laboratory for psychological experimentation in 1879 where students were given assignments that committed [them] to psychology as an empirical science by linking theories to experimental data testing them and by substituting measurement for vagueness."[46] Soon after Wundt's laboratory was opened, according to Robert M. W. Travers, "everyone, across the world, who had aspirations of becoming a psychologist and the money to spend a year in Europe, came to work with Wundt."[47] Even if Travers' estimate of Wundt's early popularity is overstated, there is no denying Wundt's early importance. Among those who studied at his laboratory are G. Stanley Hall who was an important contributor and popularizer, if not the founder, of the child-study movement; Charles H. Judd, an early promoter of a science of education that left little or no room for either the history or the philosophy of education, who was responsible for a series of important research studies at the University of Chicago; James McKeen Cattell who influenced many American psychologists, including Thorndike; and Edward Bradford Titchener who, devoted his career to the psychological laboratory at Cornell University where he taught several who contributed greatly to American psychology and to American education, including William Chandler Bagley and Guy Montrose Whipple.

By the early 1880s an American edition of Alexander Bain's *Education as a Science* (1881) appeared and G. Stanley Hall published *The Contents of the Child's Mind* (1883), using the questionnaire.[48] Shortly thereafter, James Rowland Angell, John Dewey, and George Herbert Mead began work that led to the development of functional psychology and pragmatism at the University of Chicago where Dewey founded his laboratory school. In France Alfred Binet and Theophile Simon introduced their work on the diagnosis of inferior states of intelligence and intelligence scales, work that Lewis Terman would use to develop ways to measure intelligence and to identify gifted students.

THE COMMON SCHOOL ORIGIN OF EDUCATIONAL RESEARCH: BARNARD, MANN, AND HARRIS

To agree that educational research began with Henry Barnard, Horace Mann and William Torrey Harris is to agree with Travers who located its origins several decades before serious attempts were made to free psychology from philosophy, so it could become "scientific," several decades before measurement and statistics became part of the educational researcher's repertoire, and even before the growth in the popularity of the high school. Twentieth century education and twentieth century educational research, he maintained, were built on the foundations laid by Barnard, Mann, and Harris. "Both Barnard and Mann," he wrote, "must be credited with the social invention of using empirical data for the management and development of the schools."[49] Harris built on what Barnard and Mann developed and "was attempting to bring together the scientist and educator a full decade before Thorndike began to bring his new experimental psychology to bear on the problems of education and two decades before Judd began to develop a psychology of school subjects."[50]

The National Academy of Education

Still another approach to determining the origins of the history of American educational research is that suggested in the Report of the Committee on Educational Research of the National Academy of Education. The authors of the Committee's report then suggested that the development of educational research could be seen as having progressed through four periods: 1855-1895; 1895-1938; 1938-1955; and 1955-1969 (1969 is the year the report was published). The first period is seen as having begun with Henry Barnard's *American Journal of Education*, a period they characterized as "prescientific." During the first period, research was based on "the German ideal of *Wissenschaft* or systematized assembly of knowledge." The "prescientific stage, according to his view, gave way to the beginning of the scientific stage thirty-five years later when James' *Principles of Psychology* appeared, when John Dewey established his laboratory school at the University of Chicago, and when Joseph Mayer Rice and Edward L. Thorndike began to make their contributions to what they described as "a period of vigorous empiricism, with emphasis on the quantitative measurement of educational effectiveness"[51] The Eight-Year Study, the beginning of the *Social Frontier*, and the publication of the NSSE Yearbook on *The Scientific Movement in Education* (1938) signal the beginning of the third period. The third period is seen as the beginning of a decline in educational research, a period during which "writings on education were more often works of contention than of scholarship." The fourth period began when "the federal government began to assume a more central role in education, and there was a resurgence of interest in educational problems among scholars outside the ranks of educational specialists."[52]

Charles Brauner offered still another approach to the periodization of educational research in his discussion of Paul Monroe's *Cyclopedia of Education* (1909-1911). For Brauner the publication of the *Cyclopedia* marked the beginning of one era and the end of another in how educators thought of their field and work. "Coming at the close of the long epoch of conceptual gains," he wrote, "and at the beginning of the new era of fact-gathering worker-bees, Monroe's *Cyclopedia* crystallized the most important ideas of educational giants in their purest form at the moment of their richest maturity." The *Cyclopedia*, he concluded, served as "a key to the educational significance of the major ideas active through the nineteenth century."[53] Brauner was pointing out that a new conception of investigation and of science had emerged early in the twentieth century and that those new conceptions were embraced by educators.

ADVANTAGES AND DISADVANTAGES OF
INTERPRETATIONS OF THE ORIGINS OF
EDUCATIONAL RESEARCH: ROBERT M. W. TRAVERS

The difficulty with the approach of the National Academy of Education is twofold. First, it comes too close to limiting or equating science to either measurement or the collection of data that is easily quantifiable. Second, it is easy to be overly sanguine about the benefits that scholars from outside education may bring to education. For example, there is a difference between educational sociology and doing sociology in an educational setting.[54] Educational researchers try, or should try, to answer educational questions. Sociologists, for example, typically try to answer questions their colleagues in sociology find either interesting or useful, not necessarily the questions that interest educators. While fresh insights, new perspectives, and new methods should always be sought and welcomed once found, it is also necessary to insure that scholars inside education are not tempted to do work that meets the standards of other areas and in the process neglect the needs and standards of their own area. The significance or utility of a finding or an answer ultimately depends on the question with which the research began. Practitioners of the various disciplines ask questions according to the rules and conventions of their disciplines. Their questions may or may not be relevant to the needs and interests of those who have responsibility for public education.

Each answer to the multiple-choice question draws attention to important developments and traditions; each also excludes some. By placing the beginning of educational research in an era prior to the beginning of modern psychology and the modern high school, Travers suggests that the history of educational research may be something other than a history of educational psychology or a history of some applications and misapplications of psychology to education. Travers' position indicates that the history of educational research does not need to be bogged down in the is-education-a-science question and the is-education-one-or-several-disciplines questions. That the origins of the educational researchers' problems, the manner, and the site where conclusions must be verified may all be different from those in the social and the behavioral sciences are possibilities that should not be ignored.

To the extent that Travers' claim that modern educational research began before the development of modern psychology and modern measurement instruments is true, efforts to understand the origin, nature, and logic of educational beliefs and practices must include more than the subsequent scientific justifications that have been attached to them. By locating the origins of educational research in the development of the public school system, he makes it difficult to divorce considerations of the social, economic, and political purposes of public education from the purposes of educational research. Placing the beginning here is also tacit recognition that teachers were being trained in normal schools for a generation or two before universities turned either to the study of education or the education of teachers. What is often overlooked is that the normal school tradition did in a variety of subtle ways influence how the study of education was organized and conceptualized once universities assumed an interest and responsibility for public education. Indeed, many of the first professors of education in universities came with considerable experience in the normal schools.

If Travers is used as a guide for constructing a history of educational research, it is possible that insufficient attention would be paid to what others deem very important. While Monroe and Scates emphasized "objective measurement" as essential in educational research, Travers insisted: "Measurement and statistics cannot form the core of a vigorous educational enterprise any more than a course on the design of meters could constitute the core of engineering."[55] Educational research that has "involved massive testing programs," he claimed, "seems to have been the least productive and also the most expensive."[56] No matter how one assesses the utility of testing and measurement there is no denying their importance. Since the 1970s testing and concerns about uses of tests have received considerable attention.[57] The school survey—a term borrowed from the land surveys made by civil engineers[58]—that more often than not entailed mass testing programs has also received significant attention.[59] The school survey may have been not only the mechanism whereby new ideas and practices were introduced into the school but also the means by which educational researchers created the opportunity to gather data and to assess the extent to which new developments were being successfully introduced into the schools.[60]

Travers' claim that educational research began with the founding of the public schools has merit and utility. The requirements of public school leaders who were building the "one best system" and professionalizing education greatly influenced what researchers investigated. The researcher's agenda was often set by the public school administrators who were either assembling, organizing, or reforming their school systems. Tyack and Hansot claim that "although there was some basic research in education in the years from 1890 to 1930—the investigations of John Dewey, Edward L. Thorndike, and Lewis Terman, for example—the great bulk of investigation was applied, especially in the field of administration."[61] Even Monroe observed that:

> Many educators, including those superintendents and principals appear to
> think of educational research as consisting of the activities of collecting,

organizing, and disseminating information about schools. According to this point of view, the research worker is primarily a combination of a high-grade accountant and publicity agent.[62]

Use of Monroe as a guide for constructing a history of educational research would allow neither tests and measurement nor the many "decision-oriented" inquiries to be overlooked. Tyack and Hansot observed that Monroe's *Ten Years of Educational Research* which they described as "an extraordinarily complete bibliography" shows that for the period covered, 1918-1927, "the great mass of research studies in education were addressed to practical administrative and pedagogical concerns, frequently employing quantitative techniques."[63] While the requirements of educational leaders did undoubtedly shape much educational research, Fleming and Travers provide reason to believe that not all of what can be identified or accepted as educational research originated within the confines of either public schools or departments and schools of education. Educational leaders also selected work that was frequently not specifically designed to solve specific school problems simply because they shared in the widely held belief that the application of science to human affairs would improve how social institutions functioned and thereby benefit humanity. Travers did point out that Harris "was attempting to bring together the scientist and the educator" at least a full decade before the techniques of experimental psychology were applied to educational problems but did not point out that Harris' notion of good science was not the science that was to prevail in the late nineteenth and early twentieth centuries.[64] Harris' conception of the scientific method was not the method that Karl Pearson had articulated. Charlotte Fleming maintained that the difference between school practices of the 1890s and the 1940s was the result of a new conception of the learner provided by researchers whose attention was not restricted to learning and development as they occurred in schools.

OTHER VENUES FOR RESEARCH ON CHILDREN AND THE IMPLICATIONS FOR EDUCATIONAL RESEARCH

Researchers may have responded to school leaders but school leaders also responded to researchers. Some Progressive Era movements were compatible and concurrent with the development of educational research, contributing especially domain assumptions about children. The child-study movement serves as a good example. Some participants in the child-study movement—a movement that began in the 1880s and was very popular by the mid 1890s—were quite interested in improving the lives of children. Child-study workers focused on children in school not primarily or necessarily because they were trying to effect pedagogical reforms but because the school was where children were to be found. As Elizabeth M. R. Lomax reported: "it [school] also provided a potential laboratory for the observation and study of children and an environment in which children 'at-risk' could be identified."[65] Some were advocates of child welfare and were arguing that children were either so important or so valuable that society needed to know more about its valuable resource.

For others, however, developments in nineteenth century science, especially Darwin's work and the attempts to apply Darwinian principles to the study of humankind, made possible new conceptions of children. Those new conceptions made the study of children a subject worthy of investigation apart from any desire to improve schooling or even child welfare. As George H. Daniels observed:

> The biological concepts of continuity and inheritance had made the child distinctive—worth studying for his own sake—in marked contrast to the older associationist psychology, which held that the child was merely an adult in miniature. The child was thought to be closer to the origins of the human mind, for the mind of the adult is too much overlaid by experiences to reflect the basic forces of biological inheritance. It was primarily this belief that the child was more attuned to the primeval mind, rather than a concern for improvements in education that provided the critical push toward the systematic study of children that was developing concurrently with Dewey's New Pedagogy.[66]

The attempts to develop a new pedagogy and to improve the efficiency and efficacy of schooling certainly benefited from the systematic study of children, but the study and the reform movements issued from different concerns.

If one agrees that the child-study movement and the attempts to reform schooling intersected and complemented each other, that educators used the findings of the child-study movement to realize their own purposes, and that some child-study activists urged reforms and programs for schools based on their findings, then a complete history of educational research would have to attend to the child-study literature that can be said to have begun in 1882, if not earlier, when William Preyer published *The Mind of the Child* and ended in 1914 when William Stern reviewed nearly all the significant studies on childhood in his *Psychology of Early Childhood*.[67] Stern's work can be viewed as the final major statement of a movement that had then lost its identity as a distinct movement. By then the concerns of the child study movement had been appropriated by the educational psychologists who later claimed that the child-study movement was the beginning of educational psychology.[68]

While the claim that educational research began before the development of modern psychology can be supported, it would be a mistake not to examine how the development of experimental psychology and especially the tradition begun by the creator of nonsense syllables, Ebbinghaus, contributed to what was once called experimental pedagogy, or experimental education. By the time the *Cyclopedia of Education* (*c.* 1909) was published, there was an identifiable effort to distinguish between the old and the new experimental pedagogy. The distinction issued from how psychology was conceived to be related to experimental pedagogy. Practices based on the Herbartians' methods of observing classroom events were viewed as the "old," or sometimes not the truly experimental pedagogy, for they entailed only observation.[69] A good starting point for consideration of experimental pedagogy is the work of Ernst Meumann who began to outline a plan for experimental pedagogy in 1901. By 1908, he had produced a three-volume work on the psychological foundations of experimental pedagogy. Experimental pedagogy, he maintained, was built on the foundations provided by researchers and teachers who worked in classrooms as well as by those who worked in traditional academic psychological laboratories.[70] Wilhelm Lay who jointly founded the *Die Experimentelle Pädagogik* with Meumann insisted that experimental pedagogy be founded exclusively on the basis of classroom experiments.[71] Americans clearly did not side with Lay. They surrendered or closed their laboratory schools. Laboratory work was to be done by psychologists in their own laboratories and educators were to apply their findings.

THREE MORE ISSUES

There is reason to accept the claim that there is merit and utility in each of the possible answers to the question, "When did modern educational research begin?" To accept that claim diminishes the possibility of neglecting other important developments and contributions. The weaving together of all possible beginnings offers the possibility of a rich, if complicated, history. The climate of opinion that has sustained the belief that educational research, rooted in the principles of science, will somehow eventually provide useful, efficient, and just direction for the nation's educational enterprises merits examination. By the end of the nineteenth century, as Daniels observed:

> Science was coming more and more to supply American social thought with its vocabulary and its supply of images. It served as a major source of metaphor and, like figures borrowed from any area, the analogies drawn from

science variously suggested, explained, and justified social categories and values. This reflects the changing position of science in the hierarchy of American values; for since that time it has had a growing role as an absolute, able to justify and expected to motivate individual behavior.[72]

The lesson the early twentieth century progressives learned from the nineteenth century was that science was "the mainspring of inevitable progress."[73] From Karl Pearson's widely read *The Grammar of Science* (1892), American progressives derived the notion that "the successes of science were based upon a known technique termed 'the scientific method,' and this method could be applied to all human problems."[74] Progressives believed "research," "another magic word of the period, would allow the expert to solve problems—in government, in industry, in social enterprises of every sort."[75]

The origins of the modern frame of mind, the origins of science, and notions about the applicability of science to human affairs cannot be ignored. The origins of the modern frame of mind may be pushed backed to the scientific revolution of the sixteenth and seventeenth centuries when Bacon, Descartes, and Newton were disassembling the medieval *Weltanschauung*. While Descartes refined the notion of method by showing how complex phenomena could be reduced to simple parts, Bacon explained that science was important because it would allow for public control and that profit could be extracted from nature. Newton further demonstrated how powerful science was by showing that events could be predicted. According to David Hamilton:

> The excitement generated by these ideas, and the analogic thinking that they prompted, ran rapidly through the whole realm of natural philosophy. Could Newtonian notions account for the behavior of living as well as inanimate bodies? Was there a moral force, akin to gravity, that held together the disparate parts of civil society? Could complex social phenomena be reduced to a small number of basic human faculties? And did the motive forces furnished by such dispositions interact together in comparable causal patterns?[76]

The Influence of Charles Darwin and Evolutionary Theory

If the sixteenth and seventeenth centuries are too far back, it is possible to stop at Darwin who "presented to the world one of the first examples of the long, tightly reasoned hypothetical method that has come to be characteristic of modern science."[77] Darwin demonstrated that theories did not automatically flow from collections of facts. There is little doubt that educational research and the assumptions on which it was built were greatly influenced by how early investigators read and interpreted

Darwin. That Dewey, Thorndike and others found it necessary to acknowledge Darwin's influence is indeed important.[78] Darwin redefined science and gave researchers a new focus for their inquiries.

Beginning with what B. J. Lowenberg called Darwinism may be an appropriate beginning, for it encompasses the salient points suggested in the many choices already presented as well as focuses attention on the important economic, social, institutional, and intellectual transformations Americans suffered after Appomattox.[79] Beginning with Darwin's *Origin* (1859) does seem to exclude those whom Travers identifies as the founders of modern educational research—the founders of the common school. While it may be possible to exclude the founders, what they founded cannot be excluded. Clearly, Travers reminded us of an essential point: Modern educational research is devoted to understanding schooling and to finding ways of rendering it more effective. The *education* that is the focus of most educational research is schooling. Even when the focus is on extra-school activities, the purpose of the inquiry is still usually directed to rendering schools more effective and efficient or to explaining why the power of schooling is necessarily limited. The sources and methods of modern educational research are largely post-Darwinian but the objects of inquiry issue from public schooling that is devoted to the regulation and control of groups in schools through, notwithstanding the rhetoric about individual differences and satisfying the needs and interests of all children, a process of mass instruction. The origins of contemporary bureaucratic public educational systems are found in the common schools of the early nineteenth century. With the common school came a new definition of education. It is that new definition of education to which educational researchers address themselves. In the United States the school, especially the public school, is the institution assigned the primary responsibility for education. Hence, even though schooling and education are not quite the same, they are often taken to be the same.

As the public school was selected as the venue for education, learning, whether students could learn and how much they learned at a given age or in a given amount of time, became increasingly important objects of the researcher's agenda. Instruction, how material was presented and delivered, and the material—curriculum—became fields within a field. The school has been the arena where instruction and education have done battle, and instruction appears to have won. To determine whether instruction and education are necessarily mutually exclusive it may be necessary to examine the work of Johann Friedrich Herbart who showed us, as Dewey observed, that it was possible "to take the work of teaching out of the region of routine and accident, and make it into a conscious business with a definite aim and procedure, instead of being a compound of casual inspiration and subservience to tradition."[80] Schooling is a deliberate process. Education may certainly include deliberate processes but certainly is not limited to such. Educational research is nearly always an attempt to understand and improve schooling.

Controversies over the value of basic or applied research may not shed insight into the history and character of educational research in the twentieth century as connected to the national agenda. In fact these distinctions may obscure vital insights into the continuity of the history of educational research with the knowledge base used for contemporary policy making. The next chapter examines definitions of educational research in relation to the status of research on education versus the perceived value of research in the other social and behavioral sciences.

NOTES

1. Office of Education, U. S. Department of Health, Education, and Welfare. *Educational Research and Development in the United States* (Washington, D. C.: U. S. Government Printing Office, 1970), p. 44.

2. David B. Tyack. *The One Best System: A History of American Urban Education.* (Cambridge, Massachusetts: Harvard University Press, 1974), p. 133.

3. Lawrence A. Cremin. *The Transformation of the School: Progressivism in American Education, 1876-1962* (New York: Alfred A. Knopf, 1962), pp. 22, 358.

4. Leonard P. Ayres, "History and Present Status of Educational Measurements" in Guy Montrose Whipple (ed.). *The Seventeenth Yearbook of the National Society of Education, Part II, The Measurement of Educational Products* (Bloomington, Illinois: Public School Publishing Co., 1918), p. 11.

5. Julian C. Stanley, "Rice as a Pioneer Educational Researcher," *Journal of Educational Measurement*, Vol. 3, No. 2 (Summer 1966).

6. Reported in Patricia Albjerg Graham, "Joseph Mayer Rice as a Founder of the Progressive Education Movement, *Journal of Educational Measurement*, Vol. 3, No. 2 (Summer 1966), p. 132.

7. Joseph Mayer Rice. *The Public-School System of the United States* [1893] (New York: Arno Press and New York Times, 1969, p. 17

8. *Ibid.*, pp. 2-3.

9. *Ibid.*, p. 4

10. *Ibid.*, p. 22-23.

11. *Ibid.*, p. 23.

12. Joseph Mayer Rice, "Obstacles to Rational Educational Reform" first appeared in the *Forum* (December 1896) and was included in *Scientific Management in Education* [1913] (New York: Arno Press and New York Times, 1969), pp. 20, 22.

13. *Ibid.*, pp. 32-33.

14. *Ibid.*, p. 35.

15. *Ibid.*, p. 31.

16. Charles H. Judd. "Contributions of School Surveys," in Guy Montrose Whipple (ed.). *The Thirty-seventh Yearbook of he National Society for the Study of*

Education: Part II, The Scientific Movement in Education (Bloomington, Illinois: The Public School Publishing Co., 1938), p. 10.

17. Joseph Mayer Rice, "The Futility of the Spelling Grind" first appeared in the *Forum* (April 1897) and was included in *Scientific Management in Education*, pp. 68-69.

18. *Ibid.*, p. 78.

19. Douglas E. Scates. "Research and Progress in Educational Administration," *Journal of Educational Research*, Vol. 38, No. 5 (January 1945), p. 351.

20. Douglas E. Scates. "Fifty Years of Objective Measurement and Research in Education, *Journal of Educational Research*, Vol. 41, No. 4 (December 1947), p. 241.

21. *Ibid.*, p. 244.

22. Stanley, "Rice as a Pioneer Educational Researcher," pp. 136-137.

23. Max D. Engelhart and Macklin Thomas, "Rice as the Inventor of the Comparative Test," *Journal of Educational Measurement*. Vol. 3, No. 2 (Summer 1966), p. 143.

24. Frederick Rudolph. *The American College and University* (New York: Alfred A. Knopf, 1962), p. 284.

25. David B. Tyack. *The One Best System: A History of American Urban Education* (Cambridge, Massachusetts: Harvard University Press, 1974), p. 183.

26. John M. O'Donnell. *The Origins of Behaviorism: American Psychology, 1870-1920* (New York: New York University Press, 1985), p. 229.

27. *Ibid.*, p. 153.

28. B. A. Hinsdale. *History of the University of Michigan* (Ann Arbor, Michigan: University of Michigan, 1906) in Edgar W. Knight and Clifton L. Hall (eds.). *Readings in American Educational History* (New York: Appleton-Century-Crofts, 1951), p. 423.

29. Newton Edwards and Herman G. Richey. *The School in the American Social Order*, 2nd ed. (Boston: Houghton Mifflin, 1963), p. 605.

30. *Ibid.*

31. Harold E. Moore, John Russell, and Donald G. Ferguson. *The Doctorate in Education: Volume II--The Institutions* (Washington, D. C.: The American Association of Colleges for Teacher Education, 1969), p. 5.

32. Walter Scott Monroe. *Ten Years of Educational Research, 1919-1927. University of Illinois Bureau of Educational Research Bulletin No. 42, University of Illinois Bulletin* (Urbana, Illinois: University of Illinois),Vol. 25, No. 51 (1928), p. 44.

33. *Ibid.*, p. 41.

34. Daniel Starch. *Educational Measurements* (New York: the Macmillan Co., 1917), p. 1.

35. O'Donnell. *Origins of Behaviorism*, p. 184.

36. Walter Scott Monroe. "Educational Measurement in 1920 and 1945," *Journal of Educational Measurement*, Vol. 38, No. 5 (January 1945), p. 334.

37. *Ibid.*, p. 340.

38. Charlotte M. Fleming. *Research and the Basic Curriculum*. (London: University of London Press, 1946), p. 1.

39. *Ibid.*, p. 2.

40.   Merle L. Borrowman. "Liberal Education and the Professional Preparation of Teachers" in Borrowman (ed.). *Teacher Education in America: A Documentary History* (New York: Teachers College Press, 1965), p. 12.

41.   *Ibid.*, pp. 11-14 and Arthur G. Powell. *The Uncertain Profession: Harvard and the Search for Educational Authority* (Cambridge, Massachusetts: Harvard University Press, 1980), pp. 84-107. For an extensive bibliography of the literature on these questions see: Bird T. Baldwin. "Principles of Education," The Present Status of Education as a Science, Papers presented for discussion at the meeting of the National Society of College Teachers of Education in St. Louis, Missouri, February 27-29, 1912. *School Review Monographs Number II* (Chicago: University of Chicago Press, 1912), pp. 129-134. Baldwin's bibliography contains over one hundred entries and includes works form Europe as well as the United States. Also see: Walter S. Monroe and Max D. Englehart. *The Scientific Study of Educational Problems* (New York: The Macmillan Co., 1936), p. 452.

42.   O'Donnel. *Origins of Behaviorism*, p. 229.

43.   According to Douglas E. Scates, Thorndike made this statement at the First Annual Conference on Educational Measurements at Indiana University in the Spring of 1914. It was published in the *Bulletin of the Extension Division*, Indiana University, Vol. XII, No. 10 (September 1914), p. 37. In 1918, Thorndike gave the statement in a different form: "Whatever exists at all exists in some amount." It appeared in the *Seventeenth Yearbook of the National Society for the Study of Education: Part II, The Measurement of Educational Products* (1918), p. 16. See: Douglas E. Scates. "Fifty Years of Objective Measurement and Research in Education," *Journal of Educational Research*, Vol. XLI, No. 4 (December 1947), p. 247.

44.   Starch. *Educational Measurements*, p. 2.

45.   Daniel Starch. "The Measurement of Efficiency in Reading," *Journal of Educational Psychology*, Vol. VI, No. 1 (January 1915), p. 1.

46.   Ernest R. Hilgard. *Psychology in America: A Historical Survey* (San Diego: Harcourt Brace Jovanovich, 1987), p. 30.

47.   Robert M. W. Travers. *How Research Has Changed American Schools* (Kalamazoo, Michigan: Mythos Press, 1983), pp. 33-34.

48.   After Hall published his article in the *Princeton Review* the questionnaire became a very popular means of collecting data for educational research in the United States. It was not, however, a completely new instrument. The *Journal of the Statistical Society of London* (October 1841) reported a study on the condition of education in Bristol that was conducted with a "circular." Henry Barnard gathered information about education in Connecticut with the use of a questionnaire about fifteen years after the Bristol Study (*American Journal of Education* (May 1856)). In *Kind und Welt* (1856) B. Sigismund reported that he had tried to add to his own observations of children by sending out inquiries to others. The study that served as a model for Hall was conducted in Berlin in 1870 (F. Bartholomai und Schwabe. "Der Vorstellungskreis der Berliner Kinder beim Eintritt in die Schule," *Berlin Statistisches Jarhrbuch*, 1870).

49.   Travers. *How Research Has Changed American Schools*, p. 47.

50.   *Ibid.*, p. 46

51. Lee J. Cronbach and Patrick Suppes (eds.). *Research for Tomorrow's Schools: Disciplined Inquiry for Education* (Toronto: The Macmillan Co., 1969), pp. 33-34.

52. *Ibid.*

53. Charles J. Brauner. *American Educational Theory* (Englewood Cliffs, New Jersey: Prentice-Hall, Inc., 1964), pp. 139-140.

54. For a discussion of the difference between sociology of education and education sociology see: Florian Znaniecki. "The Scientific Function of Sociology of Education," *Educational Theory*, Vol. 1, No. 2 (August 1951), pp. 69-78, 86.

55. Travers. *How Research Has Changed American Schools*, p. 157.

56. *Ibid.*, p. 154.

57. See, for example: Ned Block and Gerald Dworkin (eds.). *The IQ Controversy* (London: Quartet Books, 1977); Lee J. Cronbach. "Five Decades of Public Controversy Over Mental Testing." *American Psychologist*, Vol. 30, No. 1 (January 1975); Clarence J. Karier (ed.). *Shaping the American Educational State* (New York: The Free Press, 1975); Brian Simon. *Intelligence, Psychology and Education* (London: Lawrence and Wishart, 1971); and James V. Smith and David Hamilton (eds.). *The Meritocratic Intellect: Studies in the History of Educational Research* (Aberdeen: Aberdeen University Press, 1980). More recent works include: Alfie Kohn. *The Case Against Standardized Testing: Raising the Scores, Ruining the Schools.* (Portsmouth, New Hampshire: Heinemann. 2000); Nicholas Lehman. *The Big Test: The Secret History of the American Meritocracy* (New York: Farrar, Straus and Giroux. 1999); Peter Sacks. *Standardized Minds: The High Price of America's Testing Culture and What We Can Do to Change It* (Cambridge, Massachusetts: Perseus Publishing. 1999); and Gary Orfield and Mindy L. Korbhaber (eds.). *Raising Standards or Raising Barriers? Inequality and High-Stakes Testing in Public Education* (New York: The Century Foundation Press. 1901).

58. Judd. "Contributions of School Surveys," p. 11.

59. The work that brought the survey to the attention of educational historians is Raymond E. Callahan. *Education and the Cult of Efficiency* (Chicago: The University of Chicago Press, 1962).

60. Nancy E. Adelman. "Sphere of Influence: Factors in the Educational Development of Three New Jersey Communities in the Progressive Era" in Ronald K. Goodenow and Diane Ravitch (eds.). *Schools in Cities* (New York: Holmes and Meier, 1983).

61. David Tyack and Elisabeth Hansot. *Managers of Virtue: Public School Leadership in America, 1820-1980* (New York: Basic Books, 1982), p. 154.

62. Monroe. *Ten Years of Educational Research*, p. 21.

63. Tyack and Hansot. *Managers of Virtue*, p. 154.

64. Harris had serious reservations about the new methods in inquiry that were emerging after Appomattox. In the first issue of his *Journal of Speculative Philosophy*, he not only promised "detailed criticisms of the 'Positive Philosophy'" but also promised that "the exposition of Hegel's Phenomenology of Spirit will furnish pertinent thoughts related to method." See: Preface to *Journal of Speculative Philosophy*, Vol. 1, No. 1 (1867), p. 1.

65. Elizabeth M. R. Lomax. *Science and Patterns of Child Care* (San Francisco: W. H. Freeman and Co., 1978), p. 13.

66. George H. Daniels. *Science in American Society: A Social History* (New York: Alfred A. Knopf, 1971), p. 250.

67. Significant works between those of Preyer and Stern are: James Sully. *Studies in Childhood* (London: Longmans Green, 1895); Karl Groos. *Die Spiele der Tiere* (Jena: Fischer, 1896); and *Die Spiele des Menschen* (Jena: Eischer, 1899); Ellen K. S. Key. *Barnets rhundrade* Paris: Schleicher Freres, 1900); and *Les Idees Modernes sur l'Enfants* (Paris: Flammarion, 1909); Antonia Marro. La Puberta (Toriono: Bocca, 1897); and G. Stanley Hall. *Adolescence* (New York: Appleton, 1904).

68. Gordon Hendrickson. "Educational Psychology" in Walter S. Monroe (ed.). *Encyclopedia of Educational Research* (New York: Macmillan, 1941), p. 417.

69. Edward H. Cameron. "Experimental Pedagogy" in Paul Monroe (ed.). A *Cyclopedia of Education*, Vol. 2 (New York: Macmillan, 1911), pp. 551-552.

70. Ernst Meumann. *Vorlesungen zur Einfurung in die experimentelle Pedagogie* (Leipzig: Engleman, 1907-08). Meumann's *Ekonomie und technik des Gedachtnisses* (1908) was translated by J. W. Baird. *The Psychology of Learning* (New York: Appleton, 1913).

71. Wilheim Lay's major works include: *Experimentelle Didaktik* (Wiesbaden, 1903); *Experimentelle Padagogik* (Leipzig: Teubner, 1908); A. Weil and E. K. Schawartz, trans., and appeared as *Experimental Pedagogy* (New York: Prentice-Hall, 1936); and *Die Tatschule* (Leipzig: Zickfeldt, 1911).

72. Daniels. *Science in American Society*, p. 264.

73. *Ibid.*, p. 290.

74. *Ibid.*, p. 296.

75. Ibid., p. 303

76. David Hamilton. "Bread and Circuses: Some Challenges to Educational Research in the 1980s." Presidential address delivered at the Conference of the British Educational Research Association, Lancaster, U.K. 30 August-02 September 1984, p. 4.

77. Daniels. *Science in American Society*, pp. 240-241.

78. See: John Dewey, "The Influence of Darwinism on Philosophy," *Popular Science Monthly* (July 1909), in John Dewey. *The Influence of Darwinism on Philosophy and Other Essays in Contemporary Thought* (New York: Peter Smith, 1951). According to Dewey, "the 'Origin of Species' introduced a mode of thinking that in the end was bound to transform the logic of knowledge, and hence the treatment of morals, politics and religion," p. 2; Edward L. Thorndike. "Darwin's Contribution to Psychology," *University of California Chronicle* Vol. 12 (1909), edited version in Geraldine M. Joncich. *Psychology and the Science of Education: Selected Writings of Edward L. Thorndike* (New York: Teachers College Press, 1962).

79. Bert James Loweneberg. "Darwinism Comes to America, 1859-1900," *Mississippi Valley Historical Review*, Vol. 28 (June 1941 to March 1942).

80. John Dewey. *Democracy and Education* (New York: Macmillan, 1916), p. 83.

CHAPTER 3

DEFINING STATUS AND PRIVILEGE IN EDUCATIONAL RESEARCH

While discussions that attempt to determine whether educational research falls into either the basic research or applied research category are sometimes quite engaging, it is more important to realize that educational researchers do respond to the national agenda. For example, since the enactment of No Child Left Behind and even before, educators accepted that they were working in era when the focus was on accountability. The title of a prominent educational researcher's most recent book—*Educational Research in an Age of Accountability*—clearly shows that educational researchers are aware of and responsive to the national agenda.[1] There is no denying that: "It is widely expected that educational research should generate knowledge that is relevant for the day-to-day practice of educators."[2] As reported in a popular text for prospective educational researchers, "the usual defense of educational research is that it develops new knowledge, which then is applied to the improvement of educational practice."[3] Consequently, it must be recognized that from its very beginning education research was a form of "applied science" and that early in the Progressive Era, "the term 'applied science' itself had taken on invidious connotations—something not quite worthy of the highest intellect."[4] Some question how useful

Educational Research, the National Agenda, and Educational Reform:
A History, pp. 53–85

educational research has been, but the dominant view is that it should have some utility.

The focus is on how educational research has been defined, what educational researchers thought it should be, and actions taken to privilege some forms of research and to disadvantage others. Those who have written about educational research usually believed it was an important and even necessary undertaking. Educational researchers, past and present, have agreed that it is better to know than not to know. Educators advocate for arrangements to support research even though such arrangements may be complex and expensive. Developing an organization within a public school system to conduct educational research could, if one followed the recommendations of Stuart A. Courtis and P. C. Packer, prove to be complex, if not cumbersome, and certainly costly. They maintained that: "In a fully developed school system, educational research would be carried on by some fourteen departments or divisions, each with a responsible head and each with research or clerical assistants." Some departments would even require "a large staff of specialists."[5]

INTERESTING AND USEFUL RESEARCH

For centuries, philosophers have tried to define knowledge and establish procedures for distinguishing between what is and is not knowledge, but if their work is temporarily overlooked, it can be seen that knowledge is, in many respects, like those collections of washers, springs, nuts, bolts, and screws in those little jars and tins scattered about countless workbenches. Some maintain those collections because they believe it is better to have those spare parts than not to have them. Why they believe it is better to have them than not to have them is to raise another set of questions: Why is knowledge good? Why should educational research be conducted? Why is it an activity worthy of special support? There appears to be fairly widespread agreement that there should be more educational research, that it should be better than it is, and that there should be more support for it. However, the support has not been substantial. At the end of the twentieth century less than one cent of every dollar spent on education is devoted to educational research, to securing knowledge.[6] Subsequently, support for educational research has been "remarkably thin" as "Large foundations, with the exception of Spencer, Smith Richardson, and a very few others, have virtually forsaken the field and instead pursue various forms of advocacy, usually without being encumbered by empirical evidence."[7]

Why do so many educators and educational researchers periodically make long journeys (usually at about the same time of the year—a time often tied to a religious holiday) to give and receive rewards and to engage in rituals and ceremonies to reaffirm their faith in it? Why are there so many books that carefully pass down from generation to generation the rules and procedures for doing educational research? Why do educational researchers maintain elaborate rites of passage and credentialing procedures to enable them to certify and identify who is and is not qualified to participate in this important, necessary, or good activity? Why do some researchers maintain that they should be seen as having special skills others cannot be expected to have. For example, in the first issue of the *Journal of Educational Research* (1920), the authors of the first article maintained that: "The technic [*sic*] of research demands special training and undivided attention, both of which are seldom possible for the average superintendent." They even wanted "research functions" to "be delegated to a special department."[8]

There appear to be only two reasonable ways to explain why educational research is done. It must be either useful or interesting. Some may claim that it is done because it has always, or nearly always, been done, because tradition somehow requires it. That may be so, but that is not a reasonable explanation for doing anything. Biddle and Saha who claim that research "is a costly enterprise that appears only in literate societies" appear to indicate that the desire for that which is useful is what supports the research enterprise. In response to the question—"Why then is research conducted?"—they replied:

> Investigators conduct research because they are curious, want to contribute to disciplinary knowledge, desire to solve practical problems, and because they earn rewards in the form of salaries, rank and tenure, and kudos for doing so. However, research is popular in the society at large because of its ability to create useful "knowledge." Thus, research projects in physics, chemistry, genetics, horticulture, astronomy, geology, bioengineering—and yes, the social sciences—are all supported, funded, and indeed, tolerated because of their unique abilities to generate knowledge of potential value to users.[9]

R. A. Beecher who questioned whether educational research has "any noticeable impact on the ordinary teacher and his [*sic*] work" maintained that if educational research was "not to be seen as an expensive self-indulgence, there must be a payoff of some kind."[10]

The distinction made here between interesting research and useful research is not unrelated to the distinction the members of the National Academy of Education made between "conclusion-oriented inquiry" and "decision-oriented inquiry." The "aim" of those who undertake conclusion oriented inquiries "is to conceptualize and understand the chosen phenomenon." Decision-oriented inquiries are designed "to provide information wanted by a decision-maker."[11] Decision-makers, it must be emphasized, have responsibilities that require them to act in a timely manner. They do not have the luxury of waiting for conclusive evidence. They must act on the basis of whatever information or evidence is at hand no matter how tentative or incomplete. While it can be argued that these categories are akin to what is ordinarily thought of as basic research as opposed to applied research, the members of the Academy concluded that the basic-applied distinction was "was hard to employ precisely."

Other distinctions or rubrics, as observed by Harold Dunkel, include "the 'hard' and the 'soft,' the 'pure' and the 'applied,' and the 'social,' and the 'humanistic.' "[12] According to Courtis and Packer, "pure, scientific research" entailed "the development of new technical methods of measurement, new tests, new devices, and new organization of existing science." It also included "the search for the natural laws underlying the teaching-learning process."[13] By the end of the nineteenth century, the academic community clearly favored pure science as opposed to applied science, but the border between the two was faintly drawn. Some even argued that pure science or "science for science's sake" ultimately had more utility than applied science. While claiming that theirs was a pure science, psychologists also claimed that they could do for education what the physical scientists did for engineers.[14]

People who engage in useful research like to fix things. They believe that there must be a better way to do whatever it is that is being done. They want to improve situations, to make things better. They save washers, springs, nuts, bolts, and screws because they just know that someday there will be good use for them. Their collections will enable them to offer to help, to fix one thing or another. Others maintain those collections because they simply find it interesting to see just how many different kinds of screws and nuts there are in an industrial society. What others do with the parts and the ways in which they can be used are not their concerns. Utility is not their concern. There is interesting research and there is useful research. Interesting research sometimes turns out to be useful, but there is no way to tell whether, when, where, or how it may be useful. Useful research may never by interesting.

Useful research is fueled by a desire for balance, harmony, and efficiency. Its quest is like that of Goldilocks who wanted her porridge to be neither too hot nor too cold. Goldilocks had no interest in determining just how hot or how cold porridge could or should be. Useful research seeks ways to save time or to increase yield. It seeks to minimize input and maximize output. It seeks those ways of instruction that will increase academic achievement. For example, consider the attention once given to process-product research. There the emphasis was on effecting increased levels of efficiency—to identifying those teachers whose behaviors were demonstrated to be associated with increased student learning. Useful researchers are usually on the side of reform. For them, reform means improvement, modification, increased efficiency, and increased yield. They are typically committed to the system in which they are working and usually do not question either its purpose or its legitimacy. Useful researchers typically seek to get their colleagues, patrons, and clients to support reform efforts. In their review of educational research conducted between 1890 and 1920 David Tyack and Elisabeth Hansot reported that: "The great mass of research studies in education were addressed to practical administrative and pedagogical concerns, frequently employing quantitative techniques." During this era, future school officials were "taught techniques of research that were directed toward the immediate decisions that school leaders needed to make." Such research was apparently useful as well as profitable. It "provided vulnerable school administrators with a defense against challenges by lay people, cloaking them with the expertise of science." The products—standardized tests—the researchers produced to create the scientific cloak proved to be a "profitable business."[15]

Useful researchers either accept or establish clearly expressed objectives. An objective is or is not achieved. The goal line is or is not crossed. When objectives are not met, it can be said that one came close, fell way short, or fell somewhere between the two extremes. Measurement—"the assignment of numerals to objects and events according to rules"[16]—is often employed to determine how close a method or curriculum came to meeting the objective. It is also possible to estimate within certain confidence intervals how accurate measurements are. There are even ways of expressing with varying degrees of confidence the significance of such measurements. Such measurements allow researchers to proclaim success or failure. Even failure of a new way of trying to achieve an objective has some utility, for it verifies that a current practice may not be the least effective practice. Useful researchers prefer hard data as opposed to other kinds, are careful with their data, and try to protect them from contamination. Useful researchers subject their data to objective, valid, and reliable tests. They seek high measures of reliability and validity.

Useful research has prevailed not because of any inherent deficiencies or preferences among those who conduct educational research but because public education is a *political* enterprise. It is political because it is an enterprise that attempts to realize values in action and because educators are not allowed to wait for final answers. The reading teacher cannot wait for conclusive research on the best way to teach reading just as the mathematics teacher cannot wait for the conclusive research on the best way to teach place value. School officials cannot tell students to return home for a year or two until they have the final answers. They must make the best possible decisions with whatever information is available. Useful researchers rightfully try to provide teachers and school administrators with useful, answers, answers that will support the decisions they must make.

Because public education is a *political* enterprise, educational purposes and objectives change as the nation's agenda changes, for the school is an agency for the expression of the public philosophy. Since the time of the progressives, "political reform" has been conceived "essentially in educational terms."[17] From time to time the public exercises its right to change its mind about the public philosophy and priorities on the nation's agenda are rearranged. What public schools offer and emphasize and what the public expects of them invariably adjust to the economy as it traverses its cycles and to changes in the national agenda. As educational priorities and emphases change so do the expectations placed on educational researchers. Educators and educational researchers do not always fully realize that there are no final answers, for as the public philosophy changes so do the questions they address, Answers, however, are only as good as the questions they answer. Rarely, is it realized, as John Dewey observed when considering the influence of Darwinism on philosophy that progress is made not by answering questions but by asking new questions.[18]

Researchers on Research

During a period when there is uncertainty about what educational research is, its effectiveness, and the direction it should take;[19] when researchers are questioning the utility of traditional perspectives[20] and trying to figure out how what is known can be used;[21] when some proclaim or celebrate the demise of positivism and others proclaim its death;[22] when the social assumptions and significance of traditional research paradigms (empirical-analytical) as well as newer ones (symbolic interaction and ethnomethodological) are being analyzed and debated;[23] when there is legitimate concern about the level at which the research enterprise will be supported; and when there are many competing and conflicting calls for school improvement and reform, it is appropriate—and perhaps interesting and maybe even useful—to examine what educational researchers have believed educational research to be. Such examinations contribute to an understanding of its purposes, assumptions and effects, intended and unintended, as well as how those have been transformed as public education has been assigned additional responsibilities to meet the requirements of a new social-economic order, the requirements of the post-industrial society, the requirements of a global economy, or the requirements of the new world order.

For nearly a century, the texts prepared for teachers have urged them to adopt a scientific viewpoint and to attend to the findings of educational research. Science, writers of such texts seemed to believe, makes clear the workings of nature and allows humankind to be more effective, empowering those so informed to control and direct human learning. For nearly a century, if not even longer, teachers have been told that educational research is important, and for nearly as long educational research texts have been available for teachers.[24] Many teachers are required to study such texts in the courses required for their certificates and degrees. Some even urged that the teachers themselves work as educational researchers as they perform their daily routines. For, example, B. R. Buckingham believed that "as long as learning experiments are handled by psychologists alone, we shall make slow progress as far as education is concerned." He further believed that "the only persons who can supply the need in this respect are the teachers."[25] William Chandler Bagley had earlier arrived at a similar conclusion when he wrote: "It is out of the question to solve satisfactorily the problems of education by deductive inferences from the principles that have been worked out in what we call the 'pure' sciences." It was not possible, he argued, to deduce solutions to educational problems from psychological principles that will "unerringly 'work.' " Education, he argued, needed to declare its independence and to apply the scientific method to its own problems.[26]

Researchers' Definitions of Educational Research

Walter Scott Monroe's early work (1928) is as good place to begin a search for definitions of educational research. Monroe was aware of the need for a definition and attempted to make some sense of the definitions that then obtained. He began his comprehensive review of a decade of educational research—1918 to 1927—with a candid admission that "an authoritative definition" of educational research was "wanting."[27] His review of the then extant definitions as well as his review of work identified as educational research showed:

> ...that the meaning associated with the term "educational research" is vague. Lack of agreement is undoubtedly due to the ready acceptance of the phrase "educational research" without a systematic attempt to define it. In fact, many persons use the term without seeming to have given much if any consideration to its meaning. It is applied as a label to several types of activity. Even writers who give explicit descriptions of educational research do not appear to have a clear and comprehensive concept of it.[28]

Monroe's review shows that while clear and precise definitions of education research were scarce early in the century, educational researchers tried to maintain that educational research was very much like other kinds of research and attended to the "essence" of educational research. They wanted the "facts" and were mindful of how "facts" were acquired. Method—how to collect facts and how to handle them once collected— was and continues to be important to educational researchers.

T. H. Briggs maintained that whether educational research was defined "narrowly" or "broadly," "its essence is careful firsthand inquiry directed to the discovery of facts."[29] A. J. Jones identified the "essence of educational research" as "a method that takes nothing for granted, that subjects every fact, every step to careful scrutiny before its acceptance, and absolutely rejects any substitute for the best fact, the best data obtainable." According to Jones, educational researchers tried to keep their distance from "a priori reasoning," "subjective judgments," and "speculation based upon insecure and unproved data." Educational researchers clearly preferred "inductive methods" but they did allow that:

> ... reflective studies that result in new applications of established principles may be included under the term educational research. Any testing of educational beliefs or theories by their consistency with ascertainable facts is research.[30]

Carter Alexander agreed that method was important and he was also concerned with facts. When he wrote about educational research in the field of educational administration, he early emphasized that researchers in that field used "the methods common to all fields of scientific inquiry" and tested their results "to determine whether they are consistent with all of the facts pertinent to the administrative procedure or principle under investigation."[31]

For H. B. Chapman, the "educational research movement" was "an attempt to get at the real facts at all cost, to learn their true significance, and to construct a new educational program in the light of the facts discovered."[32] Charles H. Judd strongly believed that many educational facts had been secured and that they had to be faced. In 1918, he wrote that "there is ... a very respectable body of fact which has been clearly enough defined so that it can in no wise be set aside."[33] Chapman and Judd were clearly interested in finding facts that would be useful.

Educational researchers continued to be interested in facts and the proper ways of acquiring them. In the widely used text, *The Methodology of Educational Research*, by Carter V. Good, A. S. Barr, and Douglas E. Scates, prospective educational researchers were given no clear definition of educational research but were immediately given a chapter on "The Nature of Scientific Thinking" in which they were instructed that "*science is based on facts*" and that "one of the distinguishing characteristics of the scientific method is its appeal to facts." Too often, they maintained, educators argued about possible answers to questions rather than apply "the simple principle of 'look and see.' "[34] In a *Review of Research Methods in Education*, written a generation after the Good-Barr-Scates text, M. Clemens Johnson related that:

> Researchers believe educators should speak from facts rather than from unfounded opinion. Researchers look at specific facts. These facts are obtained through measurement and observation, even though the procedures may be called evaluation, experimentation, research and development, systematic studies, planning and evaluation, systems analysis, or something else.[35]

Texts devoted to educational research pay great attention to how facts are to be observed and how observations are to be recorded.

FOUR VIEWS OF EDUCATIONAL RESEARCH

While Monroe was not able to offer a clear and succinct definition of educational research, he was able to identify and describe four views of it. What constituted educational research could, he maintained, be classified under one of four headings: 1. Educational research as high-grade accounting and publicity; 2. Educational research as objective methods; 3. Educational research as a means of arriving at final answers to questions about education; and 4. Educational research as critical reflective thinking.[36] Educational research as critical, reflective thinking was, he related, the "ascendant view" and the view he endorsed. It was also a view that endured. In 1972 Max D. Engelhart advised that: "The questions with which educational research should be concerned are questions requiring critical thinking."[37]

Accounting and Publicity

Those who could properly be placed under the accounting and publicity category tended to be those who worked in the educational research bureaus of large city school systems. Their chief activities were the collection, sorting and distribution of information. They gathered facts to assist budget officers, school administrators, and sometimes even teachers. They conducted surveys, organized and tabulated the facts they collected, checked checklists, made and distributed questionnaires, and administered and scored tests. They devoted their time and energy to answering questions, simple as well complex questions.

Not all agreed that data collection and question answering constituted educational research. J. H. Newlon clearly stated an opposing view: "Strictly speaking the gathering, compiling and distribution of statistical information regarding schools is not research."[38] The difficulty with accepting that such functions constituted educational research was that there was no "definite answer" to the question: "How complex must a question be before the answering of it qualifies as educational research?"[39] For Monroe, the question had to "require real reflective thinking." Gathering facts was insufficient. Charles H. Judd believed in "tests as a means of finding out where a pupil stands in his work." He also believed in "tests as valuable devices for the inspection and direction of school work by administrative officers," but using tests was far from "satisfying the demand for research" or far from what Judd called "true research."[40]

Objective Methods

To hold to the view that educational research entailed the use of "objective methods" was to agree that data, how data were collected, and how they were interpreted were all "independent of the one making the investigation." Methods had to be designed to insure the elimination of "opinion" and "prejudice." Subjectivity was the enemy of "objective methods." The difficulties with this position were that it eliminated the legitimacy of philosophical and historical research in education and not all were willing to accept the alleged purity of the objective-subjective dichotomy. Not all agreed that data could be completely objective. Not all agreed that subjective data had no utility. A National Committee on Research in Secondary Education recognized in 1926 "that all data, even those called objective, have their subjective responses." That committee was also prepared to admit "that purely subjective data based upon the judgments of teachers are valuable, often of even greater value than data that seem to be more objective, since education involves many elements not yet capable of objective determination; that opinions of people are legitimate objects of investigation and are admissible as data." The committee further claimed that philosophical research was "one of the greatest needs of education today."[41] The committee reported that: "Analysis and hypothesis are in themselves research."

Arriving at Final Answers

Those who believed that educational research was the "means of arriving at final answers to questions about education" believed that there were answers and that they could be found. Adherents of this view rejected tradition as a guide for making educational decisions just as they rejected debate. They believed in facts and usually agreed that "objective methods" were the best way to secure them. Although Monroe did not so indicate, adherents of this view were essentially agreeing with Joseph Mayer Rice who insisted that educators needed fewer opinions and more facts. As early as 1902 Rice argued that:

> Although many of the problems concerned in elementary education have confronted the world for centuries, and many great thinkers and practical educators have endeavored to aid in their solution, the entire field is still involved in uncertainty and indefiniteness. We have opinions innumerable, but no facts are at hand in support of our opinions.
>
> It may be said, therefore, without any exaggeration, that up to the present time the science of pedagogy has been in its entirety a structure based on no stronger foundation than one of opinions. In this regard pedagogy represents a remarkable anomalous condition; for, as the department that points the way to the development of the sciences, it has failed to adopt what it has long been recommending to other scientific pursuits, namely the inductive method of study. Its works consist of opinions, of reviews of opinions, and of opinions based on opinions, and therefore a mass of contradictory material; and no really sustained forward movement may be expected until the conflicting views are subjected to analysis in the light of clear and unmistakable facts.[42]

There was, according to Monroe, "a growing recognition that to obtain a final answer to some questions is very difficult if not impossible."[43] Educators were frequently discovering that what appeared to be a relatively simple problem often turned out to be quite complex.

Critical Reflective Thinking

Those who viewed educational research as critical, reflective thinking accepted the other views as well as their limitations. They avoided the objective-subjective-data debate by emphasizing the importance of securing only those data that were "the best obtainable." For them, "objective methods" were "desirable but not necessary." They expected inquiry to produce a "dependable, but not necessarily final" conclusion. It was however, essential "that the thinking be critical at all points."[44]

One reason why Monroe may have opted for the view of educational research as critical, reflective thinking is that it allowed him to make the claim that educational research was basically indistinguishable from any other kind of research. He wanted to support the contention that "educational research is but a special phase of research in general."[45] The position he endorsed came from the *Report of a Survey Conducted for the American Council of Learned Societies* in 1928. Significantly, that report included no description and no discussion of what would ordinarily, either then or now, be recognized as educational research. Educational research was neither recognized nor mentioned in the report. Still, Monroe used what Frederic A. Ogg had to say about the nature of research and tried to relate educational research to it. Ogg maintained that:

> There is no need of laboring over a definition of research. The term obviously excludes (although there is much popular confusion on the point) that which is only a search by one man for what another already knows, or the mere rearranging of facts and materials. But the name is worthily bestowed on any investigative effort—in library, laboratory, field, or ship—which has for its object an increase of the sum total of human knowledge, either by additions to the stock of actual present knowledge or by the discovery of new bases of knowledge, which for the research worker, and ultimately for the future of intellectual life, is of course far more important. Research may or may not come to success; it may or may add not anything to what is already known. It is sufficient that its objective be new knowledge, or at least a new mode or orientation of knowledge.[46]

Monroe's discussion of educational research shows that by the end of the 1920s, there was agreement on four points. First, educational research was, to use a phrase Monroe borrowed from Ogg, a "process of conscious premeditated inquiry."[47] It was a purposeful activity. One had to do it on purpose. Second, educational research was difficult to define and there was no point in trying to define it precisely. Third, educational research was somehow related to other disciplines and other areas of inquiry. Fourth, whatever educational research was, method was of paramount importance. How problems were investigated, how data were collected, and how data were treated were as important if not more important than the problems themselves. Educational research was not defined by specifying what was and was not an appropriate object of inquiry. It could be defined neither in terms of its purpose nor in terms of its unique methods.

THE BOUNDARY BETWEEN EDUCATIONAL RESEARCH AND OTHER RESEARCH

To the question—"What is the boundary beyond which research is not educational but belongs in another field?—Monroe answered: "It is not easy to answer this question." He did assert that education was "essentially an applied science" and noted that what was accepted as educational research bordered on "other fields of study, such as psychology, sociology, and theology."[48] His attention was ultimately focused on how similar educational research was to other scientific endeavors rather than on what the educational researcher's object of inquiry was. His attempt to relate educational research to research in other disciplines, especially the social and behavioral sciences, can be said to be the beginning, or at least an early stage, in a tradition among educational researchers that has long endured and reached a high point in the late 1950s and early 1960s.

The views reported and expressed by Monroe endured. A generation after Monroe's work, A. S. Barr reported in the third edition of the *Encyclopedia of Educational Research* (1960) that:

> The term *educational research* means different things to different people. This is what one might expect, however, in an area like education which finds its foundations distributed so generally among various fields such as history, philosophy, mathematics, sociology, psychology, and the biological sciences. Although education is in the process of developing methods of research especially adapted to its own unique needs, it has drawn heavily upon the methods of other fields of study. Thus the character of educational research will depend upon the aspect of education under consideration and how it is approached.[49]

Barr did not use Monroe's words, "critical, reflective thinking," but he did report that "research appeals to reason, employs evidence, and is based upon the principles of sound thinking." He did not indicate that it had to be "premeditated" but he did record that it issued from "sensed difficulties" and was "systematic rather than incidental and casual."[50] Even though there were a variety of definitions, all educational research had "common concerns" including "the manner in which problems are formulated, the definition of terms, the choice of subjects for investigation, the validation of data-gathering devices, the formulation of hypotheses, the analysis and the interpretation of data, and the processes of inference and generalization."[51] "Care" was the characteristic by which good research was distinguished from bad research. If "care" or "careful attention" was paid to each concern, the research was "good."[52] The object of inquiry seemed less important than the manner in which the inquiry was conducted.

Subsequent to Monroe and Barr, the border between educational research and research in the social and behavioral sciences was recognized; and once it was recognized, educational researchers tried to destroy it. Educational researchers clearly wanted to disguise themselves in others' garments. During the 1960s, educational researchers seemed

prepared to define educational research out of existence. The colonization was virtually complete. There was an attempt to minimize the differences between educational research and research in the social and
behavioral science disciplines. In the fourth edition of the *Encyclopedia of
Educational Research*, Fred N. Kerlinger defined educational research in a
way that emphasized how similar educational research was to that conducted by practitioners of those disciplines. Educational research, he
claimed:

> ... is social scientific research for a simple reason: an overwhelming majority
> of its variables are psychological, sociological, or social-psychological. Con-
> sider some of them: achievement, aptitude, motivation, intelligence,
> teacher characteristics, reinforcement, level of aspiration, class atmosphere,
> discipline, social class, race. All of these but he last two are psychological
> constructs. If the large portion of the variables are psychological, then the
> conceptual and methodological problems of educational research are very
> similar to the problems of psychological and sociological research.[53]

For Kerlinger, educational research that was neither historical nor social
scientific was simply "not as important as" that which was.

Kerlinger's focus was on how problems were conceptualized and how
methods were selected and employed. That purpose was not considered is
important. To the extent that he accepted that scientific or even philosophical (speculative) constructs constitute an adequate reconstruction of
processes that in fact occur in the time and space people actually inhabit,
it was a mistake and a denial of the purpose of the educator. He effectively
denied or overlooked that the purpose of the educator is different from
that of the psychologist. An earlier observation that the difference
between the two is still relevant:

> An educational theorist is interested in distinguishing true belief from false
> belief, or in distinguishing learning which accords with reality from learning
> which does not, and this is a kind of interest which a psychologist cannot
> share. For many psychologists at the present time, the process of learning
> what is in fact true is no different from the process of learning what is in fact
> false. And the construction of the standards by which truth is distinguished
> from its opposite is not the psychologist's business. But it is the business of
> an educational theorist and very close to the heart of his concern.[54]

Psychologists are interested in how people perform. Educators are
interested in determining what is worth learning and how that learning
can enlighten and inform choices people make. In a variety of ways public
school teachers and their supervisors are told that student performance,
as measured by a variety of tests, is still not good enough. Some challenge
the measures; others look for ways to enhance student performance.

While acknowledging that many believed and continued to believe that "educational research should be primarily, even exclusively a practical enterprise," Kerlinger maintained that using "practicality as the sole criterion of research" was "to restrict research unduly."[55] His position was different from earlier conceptions in that it was not one that emphasized the gathering and care of facts. For him, the object of science was not to collect facts but "to discover or invent general explanations of natural events."[56] That, of course, assumes that deliberately organized educational activities are natural events.

In his 1972 text, Max D. Engelhart offered a statement that effectively subscribed to what Monroe had earlier endorsed as well as to what Kerlinger was arguing. He then claimed that "educational research is the total procedure employed in collecting, organizing, summarizing, and interpreting data for the purpose of arriving at dependable answers to questions about education."[57] He further indicated that if one accepted philosophical and historical inquiries, his statement needed some modification so that it would be recognized that there were "three general types of scholarly inquiry in education: (1) scientific inquiry, (2) philosophical inquiry, and (3) historical inquiry." Each type shared common attributes: "*critical thinking*, collection and interpretation of data, and the quest for generalizations."[58] Like Kerlinger, he was especially interested in generalizations. Generalizations had a threefold utility. They helped to explain, predict, and control educational processes.

The claim that educational research is social scientific research may be a deceptively simple definition of educational research. It is, as D. Bob Gowin effectively pointed out, a position that requires acceptance of the claim that "educational phenomena" and the "natural events" studied in the sciences can both be studied profitably in the same manner.[59] Gowin's point is especially relevant for those who insist that formal education "is not a natural phenomena [*sic*]."[60]

Origins of the Quantitative-Qualitative Distinction

That one must adhere to positivistic metaphysical and epistemological beliefs if one is dealing with data and observations that have numerical designations assigned to them and that if one is a phenomenonologist, post-modernist, or constructivist of some sort and thus must use qualitative methods is essentially a claim that overlooks that the selection of research methods is, or should be, driven by the problem that is being investigated. Use of qualitative methods usually means offering observations and conclusions free of any numerical designations. The commitment to qualitative methods is often based on a desire to be sensitive to cultural, racial, and gender issues and respectful of differing worldviews, but conflating cultural, racial, and gender differences with epistemologies can lead to unnecessary skepticism and relativism.[61] Moreover, a case can be made that the now "familiar polarization" between quantitative research and qualitative research is neither "meaningful" nor "productive."[62]

While discussions of the relative merits of quantitative and qualitative research may seem relatively recent, the distinction can be traced back to December, 1896 when Joseph Mayer Rice explained in an article in the *Forum*, "Obstacles to Rational Educational Reform": "That general psychology, in itself, should fail to be of direct assistance in determining the question of economy of effort is due to the fact that this subject is purely a qualitative science, treating of the qualities of the mind, while economy of effort in teaching is strictly a quantitative problem."[63] In 1904 in his acknowledgement of receipt of Edward L. Thondikes' *An Introduction to the Theory of Mental and Social Measurements*, William James wrote that he had hoped for such a book when he was teaching psychology and went on to report: "I shall stick to "qualitative" work as more congruous with old age."[64] In 1918 in his discussion of the origins of educational measurement Leonard P. Ayres also acknowledged the distinction when he wrote: "It was he [Sir Francis Galton] who developed the statistical methods necessary for the quantitative study of material which seemed at the outset entirely qualitative and not at all numerical in nature."[65] In the same *NSSE Yearbook*, Thorndike came close to expressing the quantitative-qualitative distinction when he wrote: "Whatever exists at all exists in some amount. To know it thoroughly involves knowing its quantity as well as its quality."[66]

The belief that the origins of qualitative research are to be found in or are at least closely associated with the social unrest and political reform of the 1960s and 1970s is a belief that ignores the Post-World War II philosophers of science who began to question positivism and shows some lack of acquaintance with the history of educational research and education science. In the Post-World War II Era while philosophers of science were considering the conclusions of the Vienna Circle, there was widespread belief, especially among those who claimed an interest in public education, educational research, and educational science that a strong connection to the academic disciplines was absolutely necessary. Consequently, in the Post-World War II Era, there was widespread acceptance of the proposition that education research was or should be social scientific research and that social scientific research would gain the power and status of the natural sciences. The 1960s "began with the relatively clear dominance of a methodological paradigm in which the social sciences were seen as best modeled after the natural sciences, at least as these were understood in terms of logical positivism." Educational researchers were then urged to be concerned with "logical and methodological rigor," "greater mathematical sophistication and better experimental or correlational control."[67]

By the late 1960s those who advocated qualitative research no longer accepted that their approach, however useful it was for some issues, was subordinate to the dominant positivistic approach. They tended to align themselves with the social movements of the era and viewed the dominant approach "as either irrelevant to concrete issues and sentiments or as actually manipulative and repressive."[68] As recognition and concern with the sorting function of schools grew, it was recognized that schools did more to reproduce the social order than to create a meritocracy and that equality of educational opportunity did not obtain in the United States.

By the mid-1970s "disillusionment with the social and behavioral sciences grew." Those who had advocated the application of the research methods of the social science disciplines to social and educational problems began to realize "the inherent limitations of their disciplines in solving societal problems," and some policy makers viewed their work as "irrelevant while others attacked it for subverting American values."[69] Standardized tests were singled out as the instruments used to sort students and reproduce the social order. Subsequently and perhaps consequently, there developed in some quarters a rejection of testing. Traditional educational research came to be labeled quantitative, presumably because it employed tests to secure measurements and expressed its observations and conclusions numerically. The alternative, as though it is truly and either-or proposition, for those who believed that the schools should and could promote true equality of educational opportunity was qualitative research. How to determine whether equality of educational opportunity exists without specifying a standard and a means to assess it, dare we say "measure," is, of course, beyond the scope of this work.

David F. Labaree has observed: "After a quarter century of debate in the pages of *Educational Researcher*, the consensus seems to be that both methodologies are useful and valid approaches to educational research."[70] That consensus, however, may not be as solid and as widespread as he suggests, for not all in the community of educational researchers were convinced that their traditional ways and convictions were to be cast aside. Clearly, many are still not convinced. While the qualitative approach has achieved some recognition and some respect in the research community, it may be too soon to claim that the debate has been settled. As Paul Smeyers has observed: "There is still the general suspicion among academics that, in one way or another, social science research, including qualitative research, cannot adequately satisfy the need for knowledge. The consensus that "both methodologies [quantitative and qualitative] are useful and valid approaches to educational research"[71] may not be shared by the United States Congress, as indicated by its passage of the No Child Left Behind Act (Public Law 107-110) and its approval of the reorganization of the Office of Educational Research and Improvement (OERI) into the Institute for Educational Sciences that has opted for "scientifically-based research" that most seem to agree is "a code word for [large scale] randomized experiments."[72] The No Child Left Behind Act and the Education Sciences Reform Act of 2002 clearly favor those who conduct and espouse "experiments, meta-analyses, and randomized trials." Consequently, "some researchers have worried, with good reason, given the current political climate, that important ways of knowing, sometimes referred to as 'nonscientific,' (e.g. philosophical, historical, cultural, affective, postmodern, and practice-oriented,), will be forgotten in the rush to achieve scientifically based research." Those who so worry "point out that decades of widely accepted critiques of positivism and 'science modeled on physics' [will be] ignored if scientifically based research is conceived primarily in terms of experimental design."[73]

PRIVILEGED METHODS

The enactment of NCLB and the creation of the Institute of Education Sciences in 2002 was a clear attempt to privilege traditional research methods at the expense of others, but actions to privilege some methods over others began earlier. While traditional methods were challenged in the 1960s, and while the movement for alternative methods was growing, the challenge was answered by the established research community. For example, in the fourth edition of the *Encyclopedia of Educational Research*, (A Project of the American Educational Research Association), published in 1969, Fred N. Kerlinger defined educational research in a way that emphasized how similar educational research was to that conducted by practitioners of the social scientific disciplines: sociology and psychology. Education research, he claimed:

> ... is social scientific research for a simple reason: an overwhelming majority of its variables are psychological, sociological, or social-psychological. Consider some of them: achievement, aptitude, motivation, intelligence, teacher characteristics, reinforcement, level of aspiration, class atmosphere, discipline, social class, race. All of these but the last two are psychological constructs. If the large portion of the variables are psychological, then the conceptual and methodological problems of educational research are very similar to the problems of psychological and sociological research.[74]

For Kerlinger, educational research that was neither historical nor social scientific was simply "not as important as" that which was. That clearly was an assertion that privileged some forms of education research and marginalized others.

The Role of the Federal Government

Throughout the nineteenth and the first half of the twentieth century power—authority and responsibility—over public education, that was and remains a state responsibility, was mostly exercised at the local level. In the Post-World War II Era the federal government through the courts, legislation, and funding, began to use its power to direct how states and local communities would administer their responsibility and authority and even began to provide some support for education research. While the Education Research Act (Public Law 83-531) that authorized the United States Commissioner of Education "to enter into financial agreements with colleges, universities, and State educational agencies for research, surveys, and demonstrations in the field of education," there was no explicit attempt to favor some research methods over others. However, the areas of research that were favored were specified: "conservation and development of … human resources," "staffing and housing [the] Nation's schools and colleges," and "expanding technology and economy."[75] That "many educational psychologists, such as Ralph Tyler, Dewey Stuit, H. H. Remmers, and Chester Harris, served on advisory committees appointed by the U. S. Commissioner of Education"[76] may be taken as evidence that some approaches were favored over others. That most of the reviewers were psychologists may be evidence either that some methods were favored over others or that practitioners of some methods had achieved a hegemonic position. However, there is no indication that any deliberate or explicit attempt was made to define education science at this time. Rather the key role psychologists played is best seen as an instance of their successful colonization of education, but that is another story.

When Congress enacted the No Child Left Behind Act (Public Law 107-110) and its approval of the reorganization of the Office of Educational Research and Improvement (OERI) into the Institute for Educational Sciences, the "slow turn toward medical-style randomized studies" that began in the Clinton administration was "greatly accelerated."[78] The No Child Left Behind Act basically defined scientifically based research as research that used experimental or quasi-experimental designs to test hypotheses. Federal legislation—the No Child Left Behind Act and the Education Sciences Reform Act of 2002—favors those who espouse "experiments, meta-analyses, and randomized trials." Some may have reason to worry that scientifically based may also mean politically based, for President Bush issued a "signing statement" when he signed into law the bill that created the Institute of Education Sciences (IES). While the law states that the director of IES has the authority to publish research "without the approval" of the Secretary of Education, President "Bush's signing statement appears to flatly contradict that language, saying the IES director will be subject to 'the supervision and direction' of the secretary." The signing statement "also appears to assert the president's authority over the IES director's ability to set priorities for research."[80]

No Child Left Behind was designed to resolve what some view as a social justice issue—the strong relationship that is consistently found between social class and school success—that has been an issue on the nation's agenda ever since, if not before, the appearance of *Equality of Educational Opportunity* (commonly known as *The Coleman Report*) in 1966. It must be recognized that the No Child Left Behind Act requires that test scores must be disaggregated by race and ethnicity. The desired political outcome determined how test results were to be analyzed and reported. There is some belief that pursuit of what No Child Left Behind requires has effectively "reshaped much of the conscious paradigm regarding American education research." According to James W. Guthrie, the federal "Institute of Education Sciences, along with the National Institute for Child Health and Development and the National Science Foundation, is supporting research initiatives using rigorous randomized experiments to evaluate educational products and practices."[81] Presumably, such research will identify "what works" and enable schools to eliminate what has come to be known as the "achievement gap." The way to find "what works," it seems, is to encourage and to support educational research that is conducted in the same way that medical research is conducted. As Valerie Reyna of the Office of Educational Research and Improvement explained:

> The bottom line here is these same rules about what works and how to make inferences about what works, they are exactly the same for educational practice as the would be for medical practice. Same rules, exactly the same logic, whether you are talking about a treatment for cancer or whether talking about an intervention to help children learn.... When we teach students we really are engaging in kind of brain surgery.[82]

The What Works Clearinghouse received significant funding ($15 million) in 2002 from the Institute of Education Sciences. Scholars in the What Works Clearinghouse are attempting to identify effective instructional interventions by "using meta-analysis to aggregate the finings of different studies of the effectiveness of different instructional interventions."[83] The What Works Clearinghouse apparently found or had so little that actually worked, that met its rigorous criteria, that there was concern that its Web site would not be useful to policymakers and practitioners in education. To enhance its usefulness the What Works Clearinghouse changed the format it uses and introduced a new category, "potentially positive," to report on studies.[84] The emphasis on "what works" is so seductive that it merits more attention than can be given here. Clearly, the philosophers of education need to go to work and unpack the meaning of "what works."

The Society for Research on Educational Effectiveness

On January 27, 2006 the Society for Research on Educational Effectiveness (SREE) was "officially opened for business." The new Society's opening was made possible by a three-year $760,000 grant from the Institute for Education Sciences. The founders of the new Society clearly support "rigorous research designs" and studies that "randomly assign research subjects to control or experimental groups." That is a view thoroughly consistent with how the No Child Left Behind Act defined scientifically based research. The director of the Institute of Education Sciences, Grover J. Whitehurst, indicated that the new society "fits in with his agency's 'dissemination responsibilities'."[85] The Society plans not only to hold professional meetings but also plans to publish a journal and "a three-volume handbook compiling education studies that the group considers exemplary."[86]

Cause and Effect Relations

A press release, found on the Society for Research on Educational Effectiveness' WEB page (www.sree-net.org), reports that the Society was "established to help support a growing community of researchers committed to examining cause-and effect relations important for educational practice"—one might say that it is interested in "what works"—and that it will "provide a forum for investigators who are concerned with cause-and-effect relations important for education." The Society's mission statement, written by its advisory board at its first meeting in May 2005 and available on its Web page (www.sree-net.org) indicates that its purpose "is to advance and disseminate research on the causal effects of education interventions, practices, programs, and policies." The premise for the formation of the Society and the mission statement were based "on the idea that the education community would be well served by a research organization that has a focused interest on cause-and-effect relations important for education."

The Society's Web page indicated that it plans three publications: the *Journal of Research on Educational Effectiveness* that will "publish full-length research articles focused on research advances focused on cause-and-effect relations important for education; *The Handbook of Research on Educational Effectiveness* that will be a three-volume work that "will contain both seminal works and reports of recent developments related to the study of cause-and effect relations important for education;" and *Research Notes on Educational Effectiveness* that is scheduled to appear in the fall of 2007. *Research Notes* is to "serve as a rapid turnaround, peer-reviewed electronic outlet designed to disseminate recent research findings in the form of accessible research briefs." For those who may have overlooked the point, that page relates that each publication will provide "the research community, policy makers, and educational professionals with a reliable source of information on advances in research on cause-and-effect relations important for educational practice." Those interested in joining the Society have been told that it "will bring together members of various research communities who study cause-and-effect relations important for education."

The relationship between the co-chairs and the advisory board of the Society and the U. S. Department of Education merits some attention. The co-chairs are Mark A. Constas of Cornell where the Society's office will be located and Larry V. Hedges of Northwestern University. Constas, described as the Society's "architect" related that: "he began to see the need for a new professional group while working in the U. S. Department of Education." He left the Department in 2003 and subsequently submitted a proposal through the Department's "unsolicited-grants competition." The advisory-board members were described as "prominent research methodologists, a special education researcher, [and] foundation and think tank researchers."

THE SCHOLARS' RESPONSE

Debra Viadero, author of the *Education Week* article reported: "The creation of the new society is stirring criticism because its leaders, some of whom include prominent members of the AERA, struck out on their own rather than form a special-interest group or division under the larger group's umbrella."[87] However, those who may be strongly opposed or even mildly opposed are difficult to identify. Ellen Condliffe Lagemann was quoted as saying: "We need organizations and forces that pull everybody working on education research together, and that don't fragment our efforts." Apparently, she was "not sure creating a society around one method is sensible."[88] Michael J. Feuer, executive director of the National Academies division of behavioral and social sciences and education related: "People are very busy, and they're going to have to make choices as to which meetings they attend, which projects to get involved in." He also observed that: "Too much choice doesn't bring the kind of synergy one would hope for."

There is no indication that the founders of SREE see the new organization as a competitor to AERA. While they hope to attract researchers from "other disciplines, such as economics or social science, who might be reluctant to join a general-interest education group," they do not believe their new society will have a membership of more than 3,000, considerably less than AERA's membership of 22,000. Catherine E. Snow, a past president of AERA and a member of the SREE's advisory board, reported that she would also maintain her membership in AERA and in other professional societies.[89]

The American Educational Research Associations's Position

While it is difficult to comprehend how AERA, a 22,000-member organization with twelve divisions, and, according to its 2006 program, one hundred and fifty-five Special Interest Groups (SIGs as they are commonly called), could have a position on "scientifically based research" that would satisfy all its members, there is some evidence that it is sensitive to its critics and to what the federal government is now supporting. However, it should be first noted that the very structure of AERA—the distinction between divisions and special interest groups—may favor those whose research topics, designs, and methods are more traditional, that is scientifically based, than those whose topics, designs, and methods are not necessarily experimental or quasi-experimental. However, given the diversity of interests found in the SIGs, it seems unlikely that AERA could now take a Kerlinger-like position. At is 2006 annual meeting AERA did elicit "feedback from members on a set of draft standards for reporting research results" in AERA journals. The draft standards designed to cover "qualitative as well as quantitative designs call upon scholars to be clear about the study's purpose and the contribution its findings make to the field, to make sure the conclusions follow from the evidence, and to describe the methods used, among other conventions." Larry V. Hedges, a member of the panel that wrote the standards, reported: "We believe that many studies are actually not used as well as they could be, because they are not reported as well as they could be."[90] In August 2006 AERA announced that its "Standards for Reporting on Empirical Social Science

Research in AERA Publications" was available on its Web site (http://www.aera.net/?id=1480) and would be published in the August-September issue of the *Educational Researcher*."[91]

Given its many and varied Special Interest Groups, AERA can be said to be a great umbrella organization. Given the size of its membership, it is difficult to conclude that it is in danger of being dismantled. However, it may not be the only agency giving voice to the direction education research should take. It has been criticized, ridiculed may be the better word, for not focusing on what those in power deem important. For example, an April 10, 2006 blog[92] written by Frederick M. Hess, director of education policy studies at the American Enterprise Institute and Laura LoGerfo who earned a Ph.D. in educational psychology from the University of Michigan, gave an account of AERA's 2006 annual meeting. Their review began with a reminder that the nation's schools "are only graduating two-thirds of eighteen-year olds, are failing to produce the scientists and engineers we need," and that the nation "must address stubborn racial achievement gaps." After that introduction, they gave an account of meetings and topics that would surely confuse most ordinary citizens, and topics that did not fit the agenda they laid out in their opening paragraph. They found it appropriate to report that David C. Berliner, a past AERA president, claimed that education science was harder than "splitting either atoms or genes." Here, Berliner, an education researcher of some note, is being taken to task for equating education to the hard sciences. Interestingly, Mano Singham a physicist has written: "I come from the world of physics, in which tightly controlled experimentation is possible because it deals with inanimate objects that behave with predictable regularity, so that if you set up the same initial conditions, you end up with the same result.... The situation is vastly more complicated in education since we cannot completely specify the conditions under which we operate."[93] Hess and LoGerfo seemed not favorably impressed by "the Presidential Session that featured a compelling new paper: "Miami, What Did Nana Say" Public School and the Politics of Linguistic Genocide'." That, they claimed, was a presentation "beckoning any researcher truly concerned about teaching and learning" and reminded them of a paper presented at an earlier AERA meeting, "Chicanas From Outer Space—Chupacabras, Selena as Marian Image, and Other Tales from the Border." The following paragraph clearly indicates what the reviewers want to support and what they want to dismiss:

> In San Francisco, it quickly became evident that the scholars had buckled down to the crucial, serious work at hand. Professors had unflinchingly tackled each of the five major fields of educational inquiry: imperialism; ghetto culture; hegemonic oppression and right-thinking multiculturalism, cyber-

jargon; and the utterly incomprehensible. Sure, here was also some boring work on questions like student achievement and policy evaluation, but you only had to follow the crowds to see where the action was.

Hess and LoGerfo indicated that there was perhaps no reason to be surprised by what they saw as dominating the AERA meeting, for Nel Noddings, president of the National Academy of Education, is to said to have complained: "Why the emphasis on experimental and quasi-experimental research, when there's so much other good stuff out there, I don't know." Those associated with the American Enterprise Institute have a view of what is in the interest of the national agenda and certainly are not supportive of those who have held prominent positions in education research organizations and those who participate in the major organizations that have been traditionally concerned with education, education research, and educational policy, but they are supportive of the current administration in Washington, D.C.—the administration that has supported the What Works Clearinghouse and the founding of the Society for Research on Educational Effectiveness.

That AERA announced that it was accepting proposals for two handbooks—a Research Handbook of Cumulative Research Programs and a Handbook of Research on Achievement—may be taken as a sign that AERA is well aware of the Department of Education's priorities.[94]

The concern with what constitutes scientifically based research is important because it shows what kind of research is being privileged and by whom and what kind of research is disadvantaged, if not silenced or ridiculed out of existence. Those who have successfully secured the funding and the political support are winning and have framed the debate. They are all but controlling the questions asked, effectively eliminating others. As Catherine Cornbleth has observed:

> The most harmful threat to the public interest stemming from the current push for scientific research in education and the scientific research procedures debate ... lies in the diversion of attention and other resources from issues and research questions that simply do not fit the preferred procedures and the "what works (best)" question. How, for example, does school culture shape students' understanding of themselves, individually and collectively? In what ways do racism and sexism appear to limit or enhance some students' opportunities to learn in school? With such knowledge, interventions could be devised, tried, and evaluated to alleviate documented ill effects and not only support equity and social justice but also likely increase the achievement of students previously disadvantaged by school culture and practices. But if we do not even ask these kinds of questions and receive at least encouragement if not tangible support for pursuing them, the social-pedagogical status quo is maintained and too many students "fall through the (expanding) cracks."[95]

The questions that Cornbleth believes should be asked are clearly not the questions that the Institute of Education Sciences intends to ask. The research priorities the Department of Education published in the June 16, 2005 *Federal Register*, according to a report in *Education Week*, concentrated "on studying conditions that are under the control of the education system: curriculum, instruction, assessment, the quality of teachers ad administrators, accountability systems, and school choice."[96]

The move to support only education research that promises to demonstrate "what works" began with Congress' reauthorization of Title I of the Elementary and Secondary Education Action, now known as the No Child Left Behind Act. The essence of NCLB is that the school and teachers are solely responsible for student achievement. Now, of course, educators wish to emphasize the social context. They are returning to what *Equality of Educational Opportunity* (1966) was generally believed to demonstrate, that student achievement is more closely related to socioeconomic factors than to the quality of schools. In their discussion of the "Relation of achievement to school characteristics," the authors of *Equality of Educational Opportunity* reported:

> The first finding is that the schools are remarkably similar in the way they relate to the achievement of their pupils when the socioeconomic background of the students is taken into account. It is known that socioeconomic factors bear a strong relation to academic achievement. When these factors are statistically controlled, however, it appears that differences between schools account for only a small fraction of differences in pupil achievement.[97]

It was clearly stated in *Equality of Educational Opportunity* that "it should be noted that many characteristics of teachers were not measured in this survey; therefore, the results are not at all conclusive regarding the specific characteristics of teachers that are important."[98] Yet, *Equality of Educational Opportunity* was generally interpreted to mean that neither schools nor teachers were strongly related to student achievement.

In 1986 when the third *Handbook of Research on Teaching* appeared, it was clear that education researchers were still dealing with issues framed by *Equality of Educational Opportunity* and trying to show that schools and teachers, especially teachers, were important, that they did make a difference. Some believed there just had to be good teachers and good schools, and they needed to be identified so others could see "what works." In other words, the education establishment was not very happy with a report that "in effect declared that professional practice in a major social institution was not nearly so efficacious as had been thought."[99] In the 1970s, especially the period between 1972 and 1978, "research on teaching simply took on new meaning and emphasis as classroom researchers scrambled to refute overinterpretations and overreactions to the negative findings from the school effects research exemplified by *The Coleman Report.*"[100] There may have been overinterpretations and overreactions, but there is no denying that *Equality of Educational Opportunity* and other input-output research gave many good reason to argue that that schooling had minimal effect on student achievement.[101] Some argued that: "Much research in the late 1960s and early 1970s suggests that differences in school resources and practices do not relate to variations in student achievement as measured by standardized achievement tests." Others argued that "there could be some unusually effective individual schools" and that some unusually *ineffective schools* can also be masked when data are reported only in *group averages.*"[102] By the mid-1980s, it was claimed that research on school effectiveness that focused on school processes demonstrated that schools could make a difference. That research showed some schools employed processes that produced more student achievement (output) than comparable schools with similar resources (inputs) and that "some [school] processes consistently characterize more and less successful schools."[103]

Clearly, those who want to place all responsibility for student achievement on schools and teachers only need to return to what came to be known as the process-product research or continue to look for cause-and-effect relationships so they can tell teachers "what works." They do indeed want to ignore that "studies of school practices have consistently discovered powerful effects of family background on educational outcomes, much more powerful than the influence of schooling resources."[104] There is little doubt that "the current debate about paradigms can be viewed as emerging from a variety of historical, social and intellectual sources."[105] At the end of the nineteenth century when church, state, and science were being separated from one another and when natural philosophy was giving way to the physical and biological sciences and moral philosophy was giving way to the newly socially constructed behavioral and social sciences, there was considerable belief that a science of education was indeed possible. Since then, the science of education, the scientific movement in education, and educational research were frequently used synonymously and conflated with one another. At times, discussions of educational research spilled over into questions that philosophers of education have addressed: Is there, or can there be, a science of education? Such questions and discussions were can be traced back to the founding of the nation's common schools.[106] Is education a discipline? Is it a field of study? Is education a basic or an applied science? Even if the literature on such questions is overlooked, there still remains a large body of literature that claims that educational research is of the utmost importance.

NOTES

1. Robert E. Slavin, *Educational Research in an Age of Accountability* (Baltimore: Johns Hopkins University Press, 2007).

2. Gert J. J. Biesta and Nicholas C. Burbules. *Pragmatism and Educational Research* (Lanham, Maryland: Rowman & Littlefield Publishers, Inc. 2003), p. 1.

3. Walter R. Borg and Meredith D. Gall. *Educational Research: An Introduction.* 4th ed. (New York: Longman, 1983. p. 5. The first edition of their text appeared in 1963.

4. George H. Daniels. *Science in American Society: A Social History* (New York: Alfred A. Knopf, 1971), p. 288.

5. Stuart A. Courtis and P. C. Packer. "Educational Research," *Journal of Educational Research*, Vol. 1, No. 1 (January 1920), p11.

6. Ellen Condliffe Lagemann. *An Elusive Science: The Troubling History of Education Research* (Chicago: University of Chicago Press, 2000), p. 212.

7. James W. Guthrie. "'For Want of a Nail....'" *Education Week*, Vol. 24, No. 34 (May 4, 2005), p. 48.

8. Courtis and Packer. "Educational Research," p. 9.

9. Bruce J. Biddle and Lawrence J. Saha. *The Untested Accusation: Principals, Research Knowledge, and Policy Making in Schools* (Westport, Connecticut: Ablex Publishing, 2002), p. 9.

10. R. A. Beecher. "Research into Practice" in W. B. Dockrell and David Hamilton (eds.). *Rethinking Educational Research* (London: Hodder and Stoughton, 1980), p. 65.

11. Lee J. Cronbach and Patrick Suppes (eds.). *Research for Tomorrow's Schools: Disciplined Inquiry for Education* (New York: The Macmillan Co., 1969), pp. 19-21.

12. Harold Dunkle. "Wanted: New Paradigms and a Normative Base for Research," in Lawrence G. Thomas (ed.). *Philosophical Redirection of Educational Research: The Seventy-first Yearbook of the National Society for the Study of Education* (Chicago: University of Chicago Press, 1972), p. 77.

13. Courtis and Packer. "Educational Research," pp. 16-17.

14. John M. O'Donnell. *The Origins of Behaviorism: American Psychology, 1870-1920* (New York: New York University Press. 1985), pp.125-127, 139.

15. David Tyack and Elisabeth Hansot. *Managers of Virtue: Public School Leadership in American, 1820-1980* (New York: Basic Books, 1982), p. 154.

16. S. S. Stevens. *Mathematics, Measurement, and Psychophysics, Handbook of Experimental Psychology* (New York: John Wiley & Sons), pp. 1-49) quoted in D. Bob Gowin. "Is Educational Research Distinctive?" in Thomas (ed.). *Philosophical Redirection of Educational Research*, p. 19.

17. Lawrence A. Cremin. *The Genius of American Education* (New York: Vintage Books, 1965), p. 10.

18. John Dewey. *The Influence of Darwin on Philosophy and Other Essays in Contemporary Thought* (New York: Peter Smith, 1910), p. 19.

19. For an interesting and unusually optimistic series of statements about the possible directions for educational research see Frank H. Farley's." The Future of Educational Research, *Educational Researcher*, Vol. 11, No. 8

(October 1982), pp. 11-19 for part 1 and Vol. 11, No. 9 (November 1982), pp. 12-18 for part 2. It is an edited version of a panel earlier organized for an AERA meeting and included statements from N. L. Gage, Benjamin S. Bloom, David R. Kratwohl, Robert M. Gagne, Robert Glaser, Robert Ebel, Robert L. Thorndike, Fred M. Kerlinger, W. James Popham and Maxine Greene. Virtually all—Maxine Greene being the notable exception—of these participants, it should be noted work in a research tradition laid down by Edward Lee Thorndike early in the twentieth century.

20. See, for example: Ernest R. House. "Three Perspectives on Innovation" in Rolf Lehming and Michael Kane (eds.). *Improving Schools: Using What We Know* (Beverly Hills, California: Sage Publications, 1981).

21. See: Lehming and Kane. *Improving Schools.*

22. D. C. Phillips. *Philosophy, Science, and Social Inquiry: Contemporary Methodological Controversies in Social Science and Related Applied Fields of Research* (Oxford: Pergamon Press. 1987), pp. 36-45.

23. See, for example: Thomas S. Popkewitz. *Paradigm and Ideology in Educational Research: The Social Function of the Intellectual* (London: The Falmer Press, 1984).

24. Edward L. Thorndike's *Introduction to the Theory of Mental and Social Measurements* (1904) is generally accepted to signal the beginning of the application of statistical methods to educational problems in the United States--an application that generally means "scientific methods"—even the work of Jams McKeen Cattell and Sir Francis Galton was already known and even though there was already some teaching of statistics in some American universities--and was widely used in schools, colleges, and departments of education. However, Harold O. Rugg's *Statistical Methods Applied to Education* (1917) was the book that was widely used in teacher training courses. According to Walter S. Monroe, Rugg's text "which dealt with tabulation, averages, variability, rectilinear correlation, the normal frequency curve, and so forth, in easily understood language, began at once to receive wide use ... and served to give thousands of workers in the field of education an elementary but practical knowledge of statistical methods." See: Walter S. Monroe. *Ten Years of Educational Research, 1918-1927* (Urbana, Illinois: University of Illinois Press, 1928), p. 36

25. B. R. Buckingham. *Research for Teachers* (New York: Silver, Burdett and Co., 1923), p. 369. Buckingham's plea was very different from the advice William James offered teachers at the end of the nineteenth century: "Least of all need you, merely as teachers, deem it part of your duty to become contributors to psychological science or to make psychological observations in a methodical or responsible manner." William James. *Talks to Teachers* (New York: Dover Publications, 1962), p. 5.

26. William Chandler Bagley. "A Plea for the Scientific Study of Educational Problems," *Kansas School Magazine*, Vol. 1, No. 2 (February 1912), p. 54.

27. Monroe. *Ten Years of Educational Research*, p. 15.

28. *Ibid.*, pp. 18-19.

29. T. H. Briggs. "Needed Research in Secondary Education," *Fifteenth Yearbook of the National Society of College Teachers of Education* (Chicago: University of Chicago Press, 1926), p. 67 quoted in Monroe. *Ten Years of Educational Research*, p. 15.

30. A. J. Jones. *An Outline of Methods of Research with Suggestions for High School Principals and Teachers, United States Bureau of Education Bulletin*, 1926, No. 24 (Washington, D.C.: Government Printing Office, 1927), pp. 5 & 8 quoted in Monroe. *Ten Years of Educational Research*, p. 15.

31. Carter Alexander. *Educational Research: Suggestions and Sources of Data with Specific Reference to Administration* (New York: Bureau of Publications, Teachers College, Columbia University, 1927), p. 1 quoted in Monroe. *Ten Years of Educational Research*, p. 15.

32. H. B. Chapman. *Organized Research in Education*, Ohio State University Studies, Bureau of Educational Research Monographs No. 7 (Columbus, Ohio: The Ohio State University Press, 1927), p. 221 quoted in Monroe. *Ten Years of Educational Research*, p. 24.

33. Charles H. Judd. *Introduction to the Scientific Study of Education* (Boston: Ginn and Co., 1918), p. 3

34. Carter V. Good, A. S. Barr, and Douglas E. Scates. *The Methodology of Educational Research* (New York: Appleton-Century-Crofts, 1941), p. 11.

35. M. Clemens Johnson. *A Review of Research Methods in Education* (Chicago: Rand McNally and Co., 1972), p. 2.

36. Monroe. *Ten Years of Educational Research*, pp. 21-26.

37. Max D. Engelhart. *Methods of Educational Research* (Chicago, Illinois: Rand McNally and Co., 1972), p. 2.

38. J. H. Newlon. "What Research Can Do for the Superintendent." *Journal of Educational Research*, Vol. 8 (September 1923) quoted in Monroe. *Ten Years of Educational Research*, p. 25.

39. Monroe. *Ten Years of Educational Research*, p. 21.

40. Charles H. Judd. "Needed Research in Elementary Education," *Fifteenth Yearbook of the National Society of College Teachers of Education*, pp. 57-58.

41. Jones. *Outline of Methods of Research with Suggestions for High School Principals and Teachers*, pp. 6 & 18 quoted in Monroe. *Ten Years of Educational Research*, p. 25.

42. Joseph Mayer Rice. *Scientific Management in Education* (New York: Hinds, Noble & Eldredge, 1914), pp. 1-2. Rice's views on educational research originally appeared in The Forum (July-September 1902) and were reprinted in *Scientific Management in Education*.

43. Monroe. *Ten Years of Educational Research*, p. 26.

44. *Ibid.*, p. 24.

45. *Ibid.*, p. 19.

46. F. A. Ogg. *Research in the Humanistic and Social Sciences* (New York: The Century Co., 1928), p. 13 quoted in Monroe. *Ten Years of Educational Research*, p. 19.

47. *Ibid.*

48. Monroe. *Ten Years of Educational Research*, pp. 27-28.

49. A. S. Barr. "Research Methods" in Chester W. Harris (ed.). *Encyclopedia of Educational Research*, 3rd. ed. (New York: The Macmillan Co., 1960), p. 1160.

50. *Ibid.*

51. *Ibid.*, p. 1161.

52. *Ibid.*

53. Fred N. Kerlinger. "Research in Education" in Robert L. Ebel (ed.) *Encyclopedia of Educational Research*, 4th ed. (Toronto: Collier-Macmillan, 1969), p. 1127.

54. Foster McMurray. "Preface to an Autonomous Discipline of Education," *Educational Theory* Vol. 3, No. 1 (1955) p. 140.

55. Kerlinger. "Research in Education," p. 1127.

56. *Ibid.*, p. 1128.

57. Engelhart. *Methods of Educational Research*, p. 2.

58. *Ibid.*, p. 8. Emphasis added.

59. Gowin. "Is Educational Research Distinctive?" p. 18.

60. Robert L. Ebel."Some Limitations of Basic Research in Education." *Phi Delta Kappan* (October 1967) reprinted in Harry S. Broudy, Robert H. Ennis and Leonard I. Krimerman (eds.). *Philosophy of Educational Research* (New York: John Wiley & Sons, Inc., 1973), p. 126.

61. Harvey Siegel. "Epistemological Diversity and Education Research: Much Ado About Nothing Much?" *Educational Researcher*, Vol. 35, No. 2 (March 2006), p. 10.

62. Kadriye Ercikan and Wolff-Michael Roth,"What Good Is Polarizing Research Into Qualitative and Quantitative?" *Educational Researcher*, Vol. 35, No. 5 (June/July 2006), p. 14.

63. Reproduced in Rice's *Scientific Management in Education* [1913], pp. 32-33.

64. Quoted in Geraldine Jonçich Clifford. *Edward L. Thorndike: The Sane Positivist* (Middletown, Connecticut: Wesleyan University Press. 1984), 290.

65. Leonard P. Ayres, "History and Present Status of Educational Measurements, in Guy M. Whipple (ed.) *The Seventeenth Yearbook of the National Society for the Study of Education: Part II, The Measurement of Educational Products* (Bloomington, Illinois: Public School Publishing Company, 1918), 11.

66. Edward L. Thorndike. "The Nature, Purposes, and General Methods of Measurements of Educational Products," in Whipple (ed.) *The Seventeenth Yearbook of the National Society for the Study of Education*, p. 16.

67. Eric Bredo and Walter Feinberg "Introduction: Competing Modes of Social and Educational Research," in Eric Bredo and Walter Feinberg (eds). *Knowledge and Values in Social and Educational Research* (Philadelphia: Temple University Press, 1982), p. 3.

68. Bredo and Feinberg. "Introduction," 4.

69. Maris A. Vinovskis, "The Changing Role of the Federal Government in Educational Research and Statistics," *History of Education Quarterly*, Vol. 36, No. 2 (Summer 1996), p. 119.

70. David F. Labaree. "The Peculiar Problems of Preparing Educational Researchers," *Educational Researcher*. Vol. 32, No. 4 (May 2003), p. 14.

71. *Ibid.*

72. Joseph A. Maxwell. "Causal Explanation, Qualitative Research, and Scientific Inquiry in Education," *Educational Researcher*, Vol. 33, No. 2 (March 2004), p. 3. Actually, there is little doubt that the federal government has opted to accelerate and fund studies that employ large-scale randomized trials.

73. Margaret Eisenhart and Lisa Towne. "Contestation and Change in National Policy on 'Scientifically Based' Education Research," *Educational Researcher*, Vol. 32, No. 7 (October 2003), p. 31.

74. Kerlinger, "Research in Education," p. 1127.

75. For an early discussion of this act see: Herold C. Hunt. "Educational Research and National Education Policy," *Journal of Educational Research* XLIX, No. 9 (May 1956), p. 643. Hunt was then the Under Secretary of Health, Education, and Welfare.

76. J. William Asher. "The Rise to Prominence: Educational Psychology 1920-1960," in Barry J. Zimmerman and Dale H. Schunk (eds.) *Educational Psychology: A Century of Contributors* (Mahwah, New Jersey: Lawrence Erlbaum Associates, 2003), p. 199.

77. David Glenn. "No Classroom Left Unstudied," *The Chronicle of Higher Education*, (May 28, 2004), p. A12.

78. Sean Cavanagh "Some Conditions May Apply" Education Week, Vol. 25n No. 44, (August 9, 2006), p. 25.

79. James W. Guthrie. "For Want of a Nail…," *Education Week*, Vol. 24, No. 34 (May 4, 2005), p. 48.

80. U. S. Department of Education. "What is scientifically based evidence? What is its logic?" http://www.ed.gov/offices/OESE/esea/research/reyna.html quoted in Daniel A. Laitsch, Elizabeth E. Heilman, and Paul Shaker. "Teacher Education, Pro-Market Policy and Advocacy Research," *Teaching Education*, Vol. 13, No. 3 (2002), p. 255.

81. Ellen Condliffe Lagemann. "Does History Matter in Education Research? A Brief for the Humanities in an Age of Science," *Harvard Educational Review*, Vol. 75, No. 1 (2005), p. 18.

82. Debra Viadero. "'What Works' Rates Programs' Effectiveness," *Education Week*, Vol. 25, No. 37 (May 17, 2006), pp. 24, 26.

83. Debra Viadero. "New Group of Researchers Focuses on Scientific Study," *Education Week*, Vol. 25, No. 1 (February 1, 2006), pp. 1 and 16.

84. *Ibid.*, p. 16.

85. *Ibid.*

86. *Ibid.*

87. *Ibid.*

88. Debra Viadero. "AERA Sessions Run Gamut From NCLB To Instant Messages," *Education Week*, Vol. 25, No. 32 (April 19, 2006), p. 14.

89. From the E-Mail Box of the [AERA] Executive Director. Summer News Update. See: American Educational Research Association. "Standards for Reporting on Empirical Social Science Research in AERA Publications, *Educational Researcher*, Vol. 35, No. 6 (August/September 2006), pp. 33-40.

90. Retrieved from http://hesslo.blogspot.com/.

91. Mano Singham. *The Achievement Gap in U. S. Education: Canaries in the Mine* (Lanham, Maryland: Rowman & Littlefield, 2005), pp. 1-2.

92. From the E-Mail Box of the [AERA] Executive Director. Summer News Update.

93. Catherine Cornbleth. "Curriculum and Students: Diverting the Public Interest" in Gloria Ladson-Billings and William F. Tate (eds.). *Education*

Research in the Public Interest: Social Justice, Action, and Policy. (New York: Teachers College Press, 2006), p. 202.

94. Debraa Viadero. Learning by At-Risk Students Tops List of Proposed Research Priotiries. *Education Week*. Vol. 24, No. 42 (July 13, 2005), p. 30.

95. James S. Coleman, Ernest Q. Campbell, Carol J. Hobson, James McPart-land, Alexander M. Mood, Frederic D. Weinfeld and Robert L. York. *Equality of Educational Opportunity* (Washington, D. C.: U. S. Government Printing Office, 1966), pp. 20-21

96. *Ibid.*, p. 22.

97. Daniel P. Moynihan. "Sources of Resistance to the Coleman Report," *Harvard Educational Review*. Vol. 38, No. 1 (Winter 1968), p. 25.

98. Richard J. Shavelson, Noreen M. Webb, and Leigh Burstein. "Measurement of Teaching" in Merlin C. Wittrock (ed.). *Handbook of Research on Teaching, 3rd ed.* (New York: Macmillan,1 986), p. 51.

99. Thomas L. Good and Jere E. Brophy. "School Effects" in Wittrock (ed.) *Handbook of Research on Teaching*, p. 571.

100. *Ibid.*, p. 572.

101. *Ibid.*, p. 598.

102. William F. Tate. "In the Public Interest" in Ladson-Billings and Tate (eds.). *Education Research in the Public Interest*, p. 251.

103. *Ibid.*, p. 88.

104. James R. Robarts. "The Rise of Educational Science in America." Unpublished Ph. D. dissertation, University of Illinois, 1963.

PART II

ORIGINS AND ORIGINATING MYTHS

CHAPTER 4

ORIGINS OF PUBLIC EDUCATION AND EDUCATIONAL RESEARCH

THE COMMON SCHOOL

Educational research is clearly intimately connected to public education as the object of study and would not exist without the development of public school systems, the children who attend them, teachers and administrators who teach in and guide their progress, and parents and tax payers who somehow believe in the efficacy of providing a formal education to "children of school age." We took the position in chapter two that Robert M. W. Traver's argument that educational research therefore begins with the establishment of public education. Modern educational research was not grounded in the religious education or family laws of the founding colonies. Its modern form had its origin in the common school movement of the 1820s and 1930s that predated the disciplines that have defined and guided their progress in the twentieth century. Both modern disciplines and modern public schools were associated with the institutional growth of systems of public education that expanded in attendance from a selected few to the majority of children. This began with the common school movement in an era that began to create a rationale for a

Educational Research, the National Agenda, and Educational Reform:
A History, pp. 89–122

variety of public institutions including schools but also insane asylums, hospitals, and jails for juveniles. The unique character and early history of public schooling in the United States, as well as the myths of the origin of not only the nation state but also its institutions including public schools, figures into beliefs about and uses of research to inform public policies and practices. The emergent belief in the responsibility of the state to educate children and youth followed from the dynamics of U.S. society in times of great changes in the Antebellum and Post-Civil War Era when compulsory attendance laws were argued for and enacted. Research became necessary and useful once the state instead of the family became responsible for schooling. Those in charge of schooling had to develop and use objective methods in the socialization of the children in their charge and they had to be held accountable for their progress. Educational researchers filled this role in the regulation of both children and eventually, through related research, their families. This chapter addresses these dynamics

HISTORICAL FOUNDING MYTHS AND EDUCATIONAL RESEARCH

Many believe, for it is often written and taught, that the history of public education in the United States began with the Puritans in the Massachusetts Bay Colony.[1] While it is true that the General Court (the legislative body) of the Bay Colony enacted laws in 1642, 1645, 1647, and 1648 that have been described as school laws,[2] these laws, enacted more than one hundred and thirty years before the colonists decided to declare their independence from the English Crown, are more appropriately interpreted as education or, more specifically, as family laws.

In 1642 the General Court of the Massachusetts Bay Colony took note of "the great neglect of many parents and masters in training up their children in learning, and labor, and other employments which may be profitable to the common wealth." The Court then indicated that it was the responsibility of the family and masters to ensure that their children had the "ability to read and understand the principles of religion and the capitall lawes of this country."[3] Officials of each town were required to ensure that parents and masters were satisfying their responsibilities. In 1645 the Court's observation and order created what is perhaps the first military school in colonial America. Then, it observed that "the training of youth to the art and practice of arms will be of great use in the country" and ordered that "all youth ... from ten years old to the age of sixteen years, shall be instructed by some one of the officers ... or some other experienced soldier ... in the exercise of arms, as small guns, half pikes, bows and arrows, etc."[4]

The 1647 law, commonly known as the "Old Deluder Satan Act," required that towns of fifty or more households appoint one of themselves to teach all children to read and write if the children were available for instruction. The wages of the teacher, who was to teach "all such children as shall resort to him to write and reade," were to be paid either by the parents or master of the children, or by the inhabitants in general. Parents who sent their children to the town school were not to "be oppressed by paying much more than they can have them taught for in other townes."[5] The Act further required that once a town had grown to one hundred or more households, a grammar school be established to prepare youth for the university. In 1648 the Court observed that "the good education of children is of singular behoof and benefit to any Commonwealth" and that "many parents and masters are too indulgent and negligent of their duty in that kinde" To correct the situation brought about by parental neglect the Court ordered that "the Select men of everie town, in the severall precincts and quarters where they dwell, shall have a vigilant eye over their brethren and neighbors, to see, first that none of them shall suffer so much barbarism in any of their families as not to indeavour to teach by themselves or others, their children and apprentices so much learning as may inable them perfectly to read the English tongue, and knowledge of the Captial lawes; upon penaltie of twentie shillings for each neglect therein." In addition, all heads of families were ordered to "catechize their children and servants in the grounds and principles of religion" at least once a week."[6] While these laws required and reminded the family of its responsibility to educate all children and even servants, none required compulsory school attendance. Schools had to be available, but children were not required to attend them. Except for Massachusetts, which enacted a compulsory school attendance law in 1852, other states did not begin to enact compulsory school attendance laws until after Appomattox,[7] over two centuries after the enactment of the "school laws" in the Bay Colony.

The Origin of Modern Schooling

The system of public education so familiar to virtually all in the United States had its beginnings not in the first half of the seventeenth century but in the early nineteenth century. An American system of public education required Americans, and there were no Americans (members of a new nation, the United States of America) until the end of the eighteenth century. Its intellectual foundation is to be found more in Enlightenment principles than in the religious beliefs held by early seventeenth century Puritan colonists.

Public education in the United States is a social invention of a new society, a society that had recently created a new nation, invented a new political order and one that was preparing to embrace an industrial economy. The public school was designed to serve the political requirements articulated by the founders of the newly created American Republic at the end of the eighteenth century and the requirements of the nineteenth century industrial nation-state. The significance of this new social invention, the public school, is that once it was invented the primary responsibility for the education of children and youth was assigned to the school; that responsibility was no longer, as it was in seventeenth century New England, the family's.

THE ENLIGHTENMENT AND THE ORIGINS OF PUBLIC EDUCATION

During the Age of the Enlightenment many people were breaking away from traditional ways and beliefs and were trying to build new social, intellectual, and political orders. As Peter Gay emphasized, "there were many philosophies in the eighteenth century, but there was only one Enlightenment." The proponents of those many philosophies, the *philosophes*, constituted an "informal, wholly unorganized coalition of cultural critics, religious skeptics, and political reformers from Edinburgh to Naples, Paris to Berlin, Boston to Philadelphia." The *philosophes* did not agree on all matters. They were, however, "united on a vastly ambitious program of secularism, humanity, cosmopolitanism, and freedom, above all freedom in its many forms—freedom from arbitrary power, freedom of speech, freedom of trade, freedom to realize one's talents, freedom of aesthetic response, freedom in a word, of moral man to make his own way in the world."[8]

Besides their strong belief in freedom, the *philosophes* believed in the power of reason, that there was a discernible hierarchical order to nature, that nature operated according to laws, that such laws also operated in society, and that discovery, adherence, and use of those laws made possible social progress and the perfectibility of humankind. Adherence to those laws provided the means to organize society and to educate its members to create an orderly, harmonious, and just society. Accordingly, the Renaissance belief that organized schooling could serve as the agency for the shaping and ordering of society and its members was extensively explored during the Enlightenment and acted upon in the nineteenth century. While freedom was important to the *philosophes*, so was order. Adam Smith, for example, saw no conflict between the interests of the individual and those of society. Just as nature was well ordered, Smith believed, so was, or so must be, society. The hierarchical arrangement of society and a division of labor—different places and different functions for different individuals—were viewed as natural and hence lawful.

Subscription to the ideals and analytical principles of the Enlightenment did not necessarily mean that all agreed on all matters "even when the thinking started from identical principles and used the same methods of reasoning."[9] American *philosophes* generally objected to the imposition of traditional controls on human thought and behavior. They sought freedom to create their own controls and their own traditions. They placed more emphasis on creating institutions and their rational management than on individual freedom. They did, however, create the *Bill of Rights*.

During the last quarter of the eighteenth century, American *philosophes* directed their efforts not toward systematic expositions on the new principles that promised to ensure the perfectibility of humankind but to the justification for their recent Declaration of Independence and to the winning of that independence. Once independence was won, they directed their attention to the problems attendant to establishing a secure and a stable nation. They were trying to protect what had so recently been achieved, for they quickly realized how fragile their new nation and their new society were. For example, in his *History of the American Revolution* (1789), David Ramsay offered an appraisal of "the influence of the Revolution on the minds and morals of the citizens." He concluded that "the literary, political, and military talents of the citizens of the United States have been improved by the revolution, but their moral character is inferior to what it formerly was." He feared that the ability to overthrow a government that Americans had developed could be used continuously by "factious demagogues." He warned that "a long time and much prudence will be necessary to reproduce a spirit of union and that reverence for government, without which society is a rope of sand."[10]

Critics and Warnings

For a full generation many Americans and observers of the new nation examined the social and economic order of the United States and warned that a harsh class system was emerging. The social critic Parke Godwin argued that the philosophies of the American and the French revolutions could be realized only in a society organized in the communal pattern set down by Fourier. He maintained that while the modern democratic revolutions had accomplished much, equality was still more an abstraction than a reality. Privileged classes no longer had constitutional protection and status, but the people were still governed by the privileged. He warned that the *laissez-faire* economic system, uncontrolled, was "anarchical." It lowered workers' wages; promoted "an endless warfare between human arms, and machinery and capital"; created uncontrollable economic recession and depressions; and was reducing the "middling and lower classes to a precarious and miserable existence."[11] When Alexis de Tocqueville toured the United States in the 1830s he observed that a new aristocracy was emerging. He warned that the new aristocracy could become the mechanism whereby "permanent inequality of conditions" could again penetrate into the world." While claiming that the new aristocracy was one of the world's "least dangerous," he also maintained that it was "one of the harshest which ever existed.[12]

While de Tocqueville was touring the new nation, common school advocates were beginning to argue that the establishment of common schools would serve to ameliorate the harsh conditions, teach patriotism, and maintain social harmony. For example, in 1848 the year of the *Communist Manifesto* and social upheaval and revolution in Europe, Horace Mann wrote in his *Twelfth Report* about the European and the American systems of social classes. Dissociating America from Europe, he maintained that in the United States, education had the power "to obliterate factious distinctions in society." The common school was to serve as "the balance-wheel of the social machinery."[13] By teaching all people how to create new wealth the common school would prevent revolution and even the necessity of redistributing wealth. That was effectively a reply to those inclined to side with Parke Godwin.

Determining the Meaning of the American Revolution

The leading intellects of the new republic investigated the meaning of the American Revolution, worked to ensure that what had been won would not be lost, and concluded that a system of education to train citizens for the new nation was imperative. Americans accepted those Enlightenment ideas that suited their purposes and ignored others. Many accepted the claim of Helevtius that anything could be accomplished through education and the faith of Condorcet that reason would triumph and allow humankind to reach a state of perfectibility. They were not inclined to accept the observation of Hollbach that the majority had neither the ability nor the time to read and to reason. Most believed that humankind was malleable. All the Lockean tablets were not uniformly impressionable but all were impressionable. Accordingly, several proposed to transform the nation's children into good citizens through carefully planned systems of education, education that would occur not in the home but in schools. When they directed their attention to designing such systems, they were usually more interested in forging unity than in encouraging diversity. Believing that education was the solution to nearly all problems, they developed plans designed to create the perfect and free American, an American who would embrace the new social-political order.

THOMAS JEFFERSON'S PROPOSALS FOR
THE ESTABLISHMENT OF SCHOOLS

As early as 1779, as governor of Virginia one of America's notable repre- sentatives of the Enlightenment, Thomas Jefferson, proposed his *Bill for the More General Diffusion of Knowledge* to the Virginia legislature. His *Bill* is appropriately characterized as an Enlightenment document, for it was primarily concerned with freedom, especially political freedom, political freedom for those designated as citizens with the privilege of suffrage. Jefferson maintained that the only certain way to protect freedom and to prevent the rise of tyranny was "to illuminate as far as practicable, the minds of the people at large." By teaching all to read and write and by directing all in the study of history, all would "be enabled to know ambi- tion under all its shapes," and thus be empowered to defeat all forces opposed to liberty.[14]

Jefferson's claim that the state had an obligation to ensure that all had an opportunity for three years of schooling was based on his belief that the Creator and nature were separable and that each had different rela- tionships with humankind. The Creator had endowed all with certain rights: life, liberty, and the pursuit of happiness. Because all had been so endowed, all were equal. However, nature had not endowed all with the same abilities. Because nature did not necessarily bestow more "genius and virtue" upon the offspring of the wealthy than upon the poor, it was necessary to devise special means to identify and prepare all who might benefit from a liberal education. That poverty prohibited so many from properly educating their children was unfortunate and wasteful. Those poor but able children could, if educated, "become useful instruments for the public." As Jefferson explained in his *Notes on the State of Virginia* (1781), it was necessary to establish a system of schooling to ensure that "the best geniuses will be raked from rubbish annually, and be instructed at the public expense."[15] The alternative was to leave the happiness and freedom of the people in the hands of the "weak and wicked." The Vir- ginia legislature did not enact Jefferson's bill. When he presented another bill for a system of public education in 1817, the legislature once again demurred. The legislature was not then prepared to amend the state's constitution to allow taxation for schools.

The process to identify the "best geniuses" was rigorous. It was to begin in the early years of the hundred schools. The supervisor was to make an annual selection of boys (not girls) who showed outstanding ability but whose parents were too poor to pay for their schooling so they could continue in school at the public's expense. Those who wished to remain longer could do so at their parent's expense. The supervisors were also to be charged with selecting boys who showed promise for the grammar schools. Those who were selected were known as "public foundationers." One third of the "public foundationers" were to be eliminated at the end of the first year. All but one of the "public foundationers" was to be eliminated at the end of the second year. The survivor of the process was free to remain in the grammar school for four or more years at the public's expense. Jefferson expected that the grammar schools would graduate twenty "public foundationers" each year. Ten were to enroll in the College of William and Mary at the public's expense. The other ten, he suggested, could become teachers.

THE NATIONAL PLANS

On May 1, 1795, the American Philosophical Society for Promoting Useful Knowledge (a society originating in the educational efforts of Benjamin Franklin) offered a $100 prize for the best essay "on a system of liberal education and literary instruction, adapted to the genius of the government and best calculated to promote the general welfare of the United States: comprehending also a plan for instruction and conducting public schools in this country on principles of the most extensive utility."[16] On December 15, 1797, the Society decided that the prize should be divided between two contestants the Reverend Samuel Knox and Samuel Harrison Smith.

Samuel Knox and Samuel Harrison Smith

When his prize-winning essay was published in 1799, Knox was headmaster of the Frederick Academy in Maryland. Although he had been pastor of a Presbyterian church in Bladensburg, Maryland, Knox endorsed what is now expressed as "the separation of church and state" in his essay: "It is a happy circumstance peculiarly favorable to an uniform plan of public education that this country hath excluded ecclesiastical from civil policy and emancipated the human mind from the tyranny of church authority and church establishments." He further suggested that each religious denomination could open its own school for the study of theology and the preparation of clergy. Those who wanted to prepare for the ministry would do better in such specialized schools, for the "licentious habits" and "domestic indulgences" of nondenominational public schools would be "little suited to the pious examples and virtuous dignity of the sacred function."[17]

Knox noted that in public schools there were students of all sorts. The public school gave "youth an opportunity to form such friendships and connections as often in a literary and interested view contribute eminently to their future prosperity and happiness."[18] Knox reminded his readers of the size and diversity of the United States, observing that the nation was populated with people from various places with different customs and manners. Their morals and literary attainments were uneven, varying from one place to another. The nation's tremendous diversity could, he maintained, be harmonized with a "uniform system of national education." The most important reason for public education, was that it provided a way "for distinguishing literary genius and merit and consequently pointing out to public view such talents as are best fitted to fill the various stations and offices which the different exigencies of the state and the many departments of society require."[19] Like Jefferson, he believed schooling could be used to promote a meritocracy.

Knox recommended that students begin their schooling in local primary schools large enough to accommodate thirty-five students conducted in a "proper house" located on a few acres of land. He did not want compulsory attendance for all students at the public's expense but he did urge that each school enroll "at least three promising boys, whose parents could not afford to educate them." These "public foundationers" were to become teachers when they completed their schooling. At age twelve the boys were to move on to the county schools where they would reside with two hundred or two hundred and fifty other boys until they reached age fifteen. Between ages fifteen and eighteen the boys were to attend college, continuing the studies begun in the county schools until they earned a Bachelor of Arts degree. From the colleges the young men could go on to the national university, where they could earn a Master of Arts degree. Some scholarships were to be available for the colleges and the national university. The entire system was to be uniform throughout the nation. To ensure the uniformity, Knox proposed common textbooks, licensed printers in each state, and federal supervisors.

Samuel Harrison Smith, a graduate of the University of Pennsylvania and a Philadelphia journalist demonstrated his familiarity with classical and modern authors: Lucretius, Quintilian, Bacon, Montesquieu, Rousseau and Locke. Siding with the adherents of the Enlightenment, he argued that education was the key to social progress and the improvement of humanity. He maintained that "under a republic, duly constructed, man feels as strong a bias to improvement as under a despotism he feels an impulse to ignorance and depression." In a republic the ways to happiness were available to all, but happiness could not be achieved unless people had ways to improve their minds and interact with others who had taken the opportunity to improve theirs. People needed to live in a land where there was a "general diffusion of knowledge" and where there was opportunity to develop the "capacity to think and speak correctly."[20]

Smith strongly agreed with those (for example, Aristotle and Quintilian) who believed the state had the right to insist that all children be educated by the public. He believed that the effects of compulsory education were so obviously beneficial that the state could expect "a general acquiescence" from the people should it exercise this duty."[21] To support this claim he cited Jean Jacques Regis de Cambacères who had participated in the writing of the Napoleonic civil code and who had declared: "It is proper to remind parents that their children belong to the state and that in their education they ought to conform to the rules which it prescribes."[22] It was, according to Smith, "the duty of a nation to superintend and even to coerce the education of children."

Smith also urged the establishment of colleges and a national university. His plan called for each college to enroll two hundred students and to accept scholarship students from each of the primary schools in its district. The preceptor of each primary school was to select one boy each year whose "industry and talents" made him worthy of education at "public expense." College students were to continue the studies of the upper division of the primary school as well as begin the study of "polite literature." The faculty of the colleges was to select annually one out of every ten students for promotion to the national university, where the "highest branches of science and literature" would be taught.

Benjamin Rush

Knox and Smith were but two of several who wrote about education and its importance for the new republic.[23] Most believed education was the means whereby people could improve their own circumstances and their society and that through education Americans would be able to transcend regional peculiarities and consider the needs of the new nation. Most were considering how education—education conducted in a school—was related to the requirements of the new nation. For example, when Benjamin Rush whose commitment to the new republic was as strong as his commitment to Christianity offered his "Thoughts upon the Mode of Education Proper in a Republic in 1786," he had no doubts about what was necessary. Traditional methods of schooling had to be examined carefully and adapted to the new form of government brought about by independence. The citizens of the new nation had come from not one but from many different places. Schools would have to create unity out of the extant diversity. If properly conducted, schools could "render the mass of the people more homogenous and thereby fit them for uniform and peaceable government."[24] Schools were to convert men into "republican machines," teaching the student that nothing except this duty to God was more important than the republic, and that he did not belong to himself, but was public property. Above all, Rush's model student was to be transformed into the perfect citizen, setting aside amusement for work. The good citizen was to love all humanity but have a special regard and affection for his fellow citizen.

Like many others of his era, Rush wanted a system of education that would include elementary schools in every township of one hundred families, academies in each of the counties, colleges and a university. All members of the community were to be taxed for the schools, even "the estates of orphans, bachelors, and persons who have no children." To those who objected that there were already too many taxes to pay, he answered that taxes for schools would lead ultimately to a reduction of taxes. Schooling would increase the knowledge and therefore the productivity of manufactories and agriculture as well as lead to a significant reduction in crime. An educated people would constitute an efficient, safe and moral community where all would benefit. According to Rush, the following catalogue of benefits could be derived from a system of universal schooling:

> The bachelor will in time save his tax for this purpose by being able to sleep with fewer bolts and locks on his doors, the estates of orphans will in time be benefited by being protected from the ravages of unprincipled and idle boys, and the children of the wealthy parents will be less tempted, by bad company, to extravagance. Fewer pillories and whipping posts and smaller jails, with their usual expenses and taxes, will be necessary when our youth are properly educated than at present. I believe it could be proved that the expenses of confining, trying, and executing criminals amount every year, in most of the counties, to more money than would be sufficient to maintain all the schools that would be necessary.[25]

Rush was not the last to argue that an investment in education would serve as a deterrent to crime and that schools are less expensive to maintain than jails.

The leaders of the new nation and the American *philosophes* failed to convince the majority of Americans that the federal government should tend to their education. Americans seem to have understood that the those who founded the new republic and even their early nineteenth-century successors were so interested in protecting the new government that they devised plans designed to teach people to conform to authority rather than encourage them to heed Kant's imperative and "dare to know." It may not have been totally arbitrary authority but it was still authority. As Rush Welter observed, "alongside a theoretical belief in the right of revolution and in social progress, in fact, many of the national plans for education emphasized the importance of instruction in common obligations to government and to the established institutions of society."[26] Some plans, Jefferson's is a good example, were designed not to provide education for all as long as they wanted to pursue their individual interests but to select those who promised to be good "instruments" for the preservation of the new government. Such plans may have been well designed to protect all from the possible oppression of church, monarch, or the mob, but they were not designed to protect freedom in all its forms. The advocates of national systems of education did provide the arguments and expressed the beliefs that were to be accepted and used, frequently and successfully, by common school crusaders in the 1830s and 1840s: that people were educable; that people could improve themselves and their society through deliberate educational efforts; that the investment in schooling would more than pay for itself in the form of reduced crime, reduced poverty and increased economic productivity; and that the strength, security and reputation of the nation depended on its educational strength.

The Principles of Republican Government

The various national plans for education represent a significant transformation in how education was viewed. By the beginning of the nineteenth century, the institution selected for education was not the family but the school, and the emphasis on the principles of the Christian religion, though not completely eliminated, gave way to an emphasis on the principles of republican government. Early twentieth-century progressives basically agreed with Samuel Harrison Smith's claim that the state had a right and duty to insist upon the education of children. When Ellwood P. Cubberley was promoting the further expansion of public education and reviewing the significance of the educational legislation of the Massachusetts Bay Colony in the seventeenth century, he quoted, with approval, a passage from George Martin, an earlier historian of education in Massachusetts. Martin clearly endorsed the right of the state to insist upon the education of children:

> It is important to note here that the idea underlying all this legislation was neither paternalistic nor socialistic. The child is to be educated, not to advance his personal interests, *but because the State will suffer if he is not educated*. The State does not provide schools to relieve the parent, nor because it can educate better than the parent can, but because it can thereby better enforce the obligation which it imposes.[27]

At about the same time Cubberley was writing, Ella Arvilla Merritt a member of the Children's Bureau Staff effectively rejected the notion that "the care of our children was entirely an affair of the home." For her, "it was a great step forward when, after much opposition, the idea that it is the duty of the State to furnish schools for its children and to see that they attend those schools, gradually found expression in our compulsory education laws."[28] The school, however, was neither solely responsible nor completely capable of tending to children. According to Lawrence A. Cremin, Merritt's "most fundamental point" was:

> Little by little we have been forced to recognize that neither the home nor the school, unaided, can properly guard the welfare of the child. We need the strength of the State to protect him from carelessness and selfishness, for the child is weak, and his natural protectors, individually are weak also.

Merritt claimed that "government was better equipped than any other agency" to assume responsibility for determining what constituted good care.[29]

While many believe that the education of children is the right of the family, the reality is that the state while allowing many to so believe has maintained that it is its right. Progressives basically agreed. As Cremin observed, "Though progressives asserted the primacy of familial education, they advanced the pre-eminence of schooling."[30] Parents were quietly, subtly and effectively excluded from decisions about school processes. The citizenry was expected to be trusting and compliant and rely on the professional educators, the experts.

Once it was decided that the requirements of the modern state needed an educated citizenry and that the necessary education should be provided and received in schools, conditions (institutional arrangements and beliefs in the efficacy of scientifically-based processes for effecting or predicting desired human performance) that would in all likelihood, if not inevitably, lead to the ascendancy of instruction and the demise of education were accepted and set in motion. The public school, built within what Ernest R. House described as the "technological perspective"[31] became the arena in which instruction came to take the place of education.

Before the American Revolution *education* and *teaching* had been related almost exclusively to an individual ideal, the growth in private wisdom and piety of the unique individual being educated. Many who wrote on education wrote about, as Robert McClintock observed, "study" and "self-culture." Montaigne and Erasmus, for example, preferred "a theory of study to a theory of teaching."[32] Even vocational education was a private and individual affair. The master did not have a class of apprentices. He usually had one, maybe a few; and the master's obligation extended beyond teaching his charge the technical aspects of a trade. The commitment to schooling eventually created teaching or instruction as an object of concern and inquiry and allowed the eventual professionalization of education.

SELECTING AND INVENTING THE COMMON SCHOOL

As the new American society was establishing itself, the explosive expansion of knowledge, especially during the later half of the nineteenth century, made universal participation all the more necessary. Neither the new state nor the new economy could function without an educated, or literate, citizenry. Eventually, some citizens would need specific skills. Maintenance of the new political and economic orders required the rapid and widest possible extension of schooling and eventually the wholesale recasting of the traditional school curriculum. It required the deliberate teaching of subjects that had not needed to be taught except to those already prepared to undertake them—reading and writing, for example. The common school—a new, universal institution created to assume responsibility for mass instruction—was the invention selected to satisfy the new requirements. It was to teach those personal and civic virtues that would incline people not to riot and thereby insure preservation of domestic tranquility.

The first suggestions that science could be profitably applied to human endeavors created social, economic, political and cultural conditions that required that the problem of education be approached in a new manner. *Education* and *teaching* had to be examined systematically, critically and institutionally. The word *education* continued to be used but it increasingly meant *schooling*. The relationship between student and teacher changed. Discussions about whether education should be an individual process whereby students were privately tutored or a group process conducted in public—in view of all other students—gave way to questions about how to establish and administer the public group process, schooling. As Americans accepted the idea of the common school, they accepted new conceptions of *education* and *teaching*. Before they entered the twentieth century, most believed a national system of education had been built. For example, when Richard Grant White wrote near the end of the nineteenth century about the failure of the nation's school and the need for reform, he related: "There is probably not one of those various social contrivances, political engines, or modes of common action called institutions which are regarded as characteristic of the United States, if not peculiar to them, in which the people of this country have placed more confidence, or felt greater pride, than its public-school system."[33]

Before the adoption of the common school, the consideration of educational theory and practice was a widespread but largely amateur endeavor. Their origins were not scientific—not based on systematic and tested observations—but traditional and metaphysical. The development of educational theory was a speculative undertaking. Educational theory and prescriptions for educational practice were often founded on advice from one whose authority in some other field was transferred to his or her pronouncements on education, a topic upon which any learned and accomplished person was supposed to be an expert. Informed opinion ruled. Those who offered advice on education were often more concerned with the character of the teacher, often the tutor, than with his or her other accomplishments. The eloquence and the status of the writer were the criteria by which educational theories were selected. Milton, Locke, Kant, and Wollstonecraft are examples of such writers. Late eighteenth and early nineteenth century developments undermined the rule of amateurs. The rise of the nation-state committed to an industrial economy required a new conception of education. Once the common school was accepted as the agency for education, the utility of traditional educational theory was severely limited: "Whether we like it or not, many former educators considered education to consist of neither teaching nor learning; instead, they found the diverse forms of study to be the driving force of education."[34] The common school required the invention, management, and evaluation of instruction.

The Common School

By the middle of the nineteenth century education was clearly becoming a public institution, a universal social, political and cultural instrumentality. As such, it was conceptualized as a process of general schooling rather than as an essentially tutorial relationship. Serialized individualized instruction gave way to mass instruction. For Horace Mann, for example, mass, or group instruction, was "not merely a practical necessity but a social desideratum." He believed "that the tutorial relationship could never serve the social ends of education, that only with a heterogeneous group of students could the unifying goals of the common school be achieved."[35] The new educational institution devoted to mass, or group, instruction eventually created new vocations, the *professional* teacher and then the *professional* school administrator.

Once the notion of the common school was invented, it was recognized that no merely accidental definition of teaching and keeping school would suffice for the new public schools that were being spread across the land. Social agencies—school board members—had to do more than select and supervise teachers. They had to tend to their preparation; they had to teach them how to teach and what to teach. Preparation of teachers became a special concern, and that social concern became part of higher education's responsibility once college and university presidents decided to seize the opportunities the expansion of public education offered them and to demonstrate the social utility of higher education to their patrons and trustees. Universities eventually organized themselves to serve society's institutions and its commercial and industrial needs by preparing personnel to work in them. Universities established specialized departments, institutes, schools and colleges to train and to certify all the specialists who were to tend to people in their assigned spaces and roles. They opened schools of agriculture and engineering to assist the farmers and the railroads. Now there are schools or colleges for business, library science, social work, education, journalism, art and even physical education. Now it is generally believed that whatever personnel society needs it can presumably secure properly trained professionals from the appropriate department of the nearby university, personnel who know how to administer or deliver approved treatments to clients. Students are prepared for specific economic roles and functions in schools. Program and curriculum development are driven by the economic and political requirements of the nation, not by any commitment to the tradition of the liberal arts or any conception of what constitutes an educated person. Teachers are expected to deliver instruction, and educational researchers are expected to develop, evaluate, and to improve delivery systems.

Teacher Education

James G. Carter early recognized the need for a new kind of institution to serve the common schools. He asked for a school specifically devoted to the preparation of teachers. Recognizing that the new kind of school could be described neither as a school of science nor a school of literature, he described it in this way:

> The institution from its peculiar purpose must necessarily be both literary and scientific in its character. And although, with its design constantly in view, we could not reasonably expect it to add, directly, much to the stock of what is now called literature, or to enlarge much the boundaries of what is now called science; yet, from the very nature of the subject to which it would be devoted, and upon which it would be employed, it must in its progress create a kind of literature of its own, and open a new science somewhat peculiar to itself—*the science of communicating knowledge from one mind to another while at a different state of maturity.*[36]

Carter understood that the common school was a new invention, that it required a new process—teaching, and that attention had to be paid to the administration of that process. Like Johann Friedrich Herbart, he understood that teaching—instruction—was a necessary object of study and inquiry. He not only identified the activity that is now the object to which professional educators and some professional researchers claim to attend but also clearly showed that it was indeed a new undertaking. Subsequently, educators allowed their new territory to be colonized by psychologists who cast the educators' concerns to fit the interests and requirements of their own field. For the most part, educators welcomed the colonization. Few questioned it.[37]

Teachers are increasingly directed to *train* students in the basic skills. It is widely believed that it is possible to find a process that teachers can be trained to administer so that teachers and students will perform according to predetermined standards. Consequently, there is little recognition that the choices teachers must make are often ethical choices. Carter believed that something was communicated in the process of teaching. Later, many either acted as though the process could be easily and cleanly separated from subject matter[38] or claim that the nature of the process can be ignored if the teacher has mastery of the subject. The commitment to a universal process has prevailed. One side invests in the *delivery* process (instruction); the other invests in the goods that are to be delivered (subject matter). Each has subscribed to the same conception; each has succumbed to the notion that education is simply the transportation of information from one place to another, from one who allegedly has it to one who allegedly needs it. It is a conception that tacitly assumes that the student is passive. Students are seen as recipients of instruction who will perform as expected or predicted provided the instruction is properly delivered.

AFTER APPOMATTOX

Eighteenth century developments did not reach their full strength until after the Civil War. The nation was then neither fully industrialized nor fully urbanized but it was well on its way. As Bert James Lowenberg observed, "the end of the Civil War closed an era and ushered in an epoch."[39] The modernization processes changed the face of the nation, and Americans required a new *Weltanschauung* to make sense out of and to adjust to what was happening to them and about them. Like their counterparts in Europe, Americans were entering the "high machine age" and doing so with enthusiasm, "for the late nineteenth century, the cradle of modernism, did not feel the uncertainties about the machine age that we do." Then "no statistics on pollution, no prospect of melt-downs or core explosions lay on the horizon."[40]

World Fairs: Education Writ Large

To celebrate the new age, nation after nation hosted World's Fairs, what Robert Hughes called "those festivals of high-machine age capitalism" where they displayed their manufactured goods, and spectators could marvel at new inventions: the telephone, the typewriter, the duplex telegraph, and the Singer sewing machine in 1876 at the *Philadelphia Centennial Exposition*; Edison's phonograph in 1889 at *L'Exposition de Paris*; electricity in 1893 at the *World Columbian Exposition* in what is now Chicago's Jackson Park; and television in 1939 at the New York World's Fair. Then, as now, monuments were built for those celebrations. The precedent began at mid-century when in 1851 Victoria's Prince Albert gave the world Paxton's Crystal Palace—a "cathedral of the machine age" "with its vaults of glittering glass and nearly invisible iron tracery in London's Hyde Park. It was the forerunner of the mirror faced towers that now reflect each other in American Cities."[41] The greatest of these monuments was, of course, built for the 1889 Paris fair. Significantly, Gustav Eifel was not an architect but an engineer. Accordingly, he used iron to build the great gothic spire of the high machine age. The Americans built no iron tower but they did bind their nation together with steel tracks, iron bridges and telegraph wire. Rationality, efficiency and utility were as important, if not more important, than beauty. How to realize a vision was becoming more important than the vision itself. Method was often separated from content and purpose and made an object of study. There was widespread belief, as Karl Pearson maintained, that an efficacious universal method, the scientific method, could be found and then applied to virtually any undertaking, political, social, economic, industrial or educational. John Dewey was, of course, among those who believed in the importance of the scientific method and devoted his long career to applying the method of inquiry to all human interests and institutions.

The pattern of what was beginning to be viewed as a national system of education had emerged by the time the nation celebrated its centennial. As Americans were preparing to celebrate the centennial of their independence, they were, according to Daniel Calhoun, "becoming confident that they had a genuine 'system' of education." The United States Bureau of Education, under the direction of William Torrey Harris acknowledged the differences among the states, but "the very sureness with which he described regional or other differences among schools only underscored the sureness of the system he felt."[42] The national system may not have been *de jure* but it was becoming *de facto*. Most states had exercised their authority to establish school systems, and about half the nation's children were attending school. The National Education Association was beginning to assume its modern form and by the 1890s was issuing reports that created a national agenda for educational discussions. As the scope, power and importance of the public school increased, it increasingly mirrored the industrial society of which it was a part. The industrial system strove for universal standards, and the schools did not lag too far behind as professional educators competed with each other to build the "one best system."

With other industrialized nations, the Americans participated in "those festivals of high machine-age capitalism." When they did so, they displayed not only examples of their industrial prowess but also evidence of their cultural development, especially their public school systems, the instrumentality for the development of the modern nation-state that was supporting its development. The American educational exhibits were more impressive than their industrial exhibits. The manufactured goods the Americans exhibited in Vienna in 1873 were not especially impressive, but, Merle Curti reported: "The exhibit of an American school, with its maps, charts, textbooks, and other equipment, helped dispel the prevailing critical European view of American education. The educational exhibits the Americans presented at the 1867 Paris and the 1873 Vienna fairs "prepared Europeans for what was accomplished at Paris in 1878."[43]

The 1878 exhibition of educational accomplishments included private as well as public education and every level of education. "The international jury awarded the American educational exhibitors twenty-eight more honors than those of any country save France; and although the educational exhibits comprised only one one/hundredth of the American section, they took nearly one sixth of the prizes given American participants." The educational exhibit was so impressive that "both Paris and London bid for the permanent possession of the American educational display." The 1878 exhibition, "with its illustrations of educational buildings, furniture, fittings, appliances, with the 2,500 volumes of educational literature, including reports of city superintendents, state boards of education, regents, and trustees, and the 400 volumes containing specimens of the work of American school and college students, won merited praise in many circles." "American superiority in textbooks the backbone of the American school curriculum was generally admitted."[44]

In just half a century the Americans had built the foundations of an impressive school system, and there was a textbook industry that supported it. That the textbooks received such recognition at the 1878 fair is significant, for the textbook is the means used to standardize and reduce, if not eliminate, variability from class to class and from school to school.

The curriculum is the course set out to control students and teachers, and the textbook, especially the graded text or reader, is designed to keep teachers and students on course. The textbook soon became an instructional material built according to what were believed to be scientifically determined specifications. Psychologists produced word lists that specified the words authors were to use when preparing text materials for specific ages or grade levels.

The Americans' greatest "festival of high machine-age capitalism" was, of course, the *Philadelphia Centennial Exposition* in 1876. Nearly ten million celebrants viewed the machines then proudly displayed and now enshrined at the Smithsonian in Washington, D. C. Americans spent over five years and over $11 million not only to celebrate its centennial but also to show that it too was a major competitor in the western world's quest for industrial supremacy.[45] Functional relationships and processes were becoming more powerful in holding people together than were shared beliefs and values. Even the view Americans had of the space they inhabited was being transformed by the time the centennial was celebrated. The fairs celebrated, sanctioned, and perhaps even legitimized the transformation of how people worked, where they worked, how and where they lived, and how they viewed their world.

At the *Centennial Exposition* Americans were inspired by the work of Della Vos of the Moscow Imperial Technical School. From him they learned about an instructional process that broke down tasks and trades into their specific components or skills. Pedagogy now mirrored the industrial process. Schools became the sites designated for teaching people how to function in the new and the transformed spaces. Schools took children from the home and prepared them for the work place, a function the family was, it was claimed by professional educators, not prepared to fulfill. The home was the place where children were prepared for school, prepared for what was accepted as education.

New Spaces, New Functions, and New Institutions

Once the frontier, what Frederick Jackson Turner called "the meeting point between savagery and civilization"[46] was closed, the west became a vast space to be exploited, settled and transformed—filled with people and the artifacts of the industrial society, not just a place where soldiers and native Americans engaged and enraged each other. The wilderness was connected to the settled areas by iron and steam and was divided into specific spaces for specific purposes. The pattern that began to emerge after Appomattox was clear by 1890. Some of the west had been given to the railroads, and the railroads and the telegraph did bind the land together.

Some of the west was reserved for Native Americans; some for play; and some was to be wilderness forever. As Burton J. Bledstein observed, "in the newly founded national parks—Yellowstone in 1872, Sequoia and Yosemite in 1890—spatial boundaries now protected wild nature itself."[47] Nature had become a cultural artifact. Natural became a special, if not manufactured, quality. Curiously, *natural* became a contrivance.[48] Educators and psychologists invented conceptions of the *natural* child, then *adolescence* and notions of what was *normal* development and *normal* behavior on which they based their instructional programs. Education became a regularized and prescribed process. It became a series of treatments applied to children after their abilities and learning styles were properly identified with the aid of norms and measures constructed by psychologists.

America's mid-Victorians not only tamed the wilderness but also organized all the time and space about them. The world of their youth was, depending on one's perspective, either being transformed into something new or was being disassembled. Whether they saw destruction or new possibilities, they did see the demise of what they had known. They responded by giving to virtually everything and everybody a time and a space. They took the simplest, the most fundamental categories—time and space—and applied them relentlessly to create a new and seemingly orderly world. "Mid-Victorians turned their interest toward identifying every category of person who naturally belonged in a specific ground-space: the woman in the residential home, the child in the school, the man in his place of work, the dying person in the hospital, and the body in the funeral parlor; the immigrant in the ghetto, the criminal in the prison, the insane in the asylum, the Indian on the reservation, the Negro in his segregated area, the Irishman in the saloon, the prostitute and the pimp in the red-light district."[49] Even animals were given special places— zoos. The newly crated space for little children—the *Kindergarten*—was another social invention of this era. To help people adjust to their spaces and learn the behaviors appropriate for those spaces there developed specialists of all sorts. Nurses helped people in sickness. Social workers helped people learn how to be poor and to live in the slums. Teachers tended to students in schools. The specialists earned their credentials by completing professional courses controlled by colleges and universities.

Spaces could not be distinguished from each other unless they were marked off by boundaries. Those boundaries not only protected the spaces and the people in them but also regulated and controlled the behavior of those assigned to their allegedly appropriate spaces. The conviction that children and youth belong in school was so great by the middle of the twentieth century that since then enormous energy and effort have been spent trying to retain all in school and solve the dropout problem. Schools—elementary, middle, junior high, high—have been designed for specific age groups. Within schools students of specified ages, interest, or abilities are assigned to specific classes that have their assigned spaces, rooms. Students are evaluated and then assigned to spaces—rooms where appropriate specialized teachers either administer appropriate treatments or deliver instruction.

The instruments of the modernization process—industrialization, immigration and urbanization—transformed the social as well as the physical landscape. Cities gave people a new kind of independence and more opportunities than ever before but they also destroyed traditional notions of community as well as the sense of community. Some, John Dewey for example, called upon the schools to do what the community could no longer do. He wanted the school to tend to the process whereby humans become humans as well as teach subject matter, combat illiteracy, and realize the social, political and economic purposes of the nation-state. While Dewey wanted the public school to be an educational as well as a political instrumentality, others were tending to the improvement of instruction, instruction designed to teach students specific skills.

THE PROFESSIONALIZATION OF EDUCATORS

Progressives abandoned tradition and metaphysics and turned to science, bureaucracy and professionalism to manage the newly created spaces. Even the public school became a collection of specialized units. They were bureaucratically organized, and departmentalization was introduced. Professionals quickly developed ways to study and gather information to use in the rationalization and standardization of the complex system they were creating. By World War I, virtually every institution and every group had been surveyed and measured not once but many times. Professional educators were especially enthusiastic about surveys. Before World War I, Edward L. Thorndike claimed that "an educational survey of one state would seem to be at least as elaborate a task as a geological survey of a continent."[50] Schooling and the administration of schools became increasingly complex, important and regulated by two standards: science and democracy. Each standard required the application of public principles in uniform ways. Education was presumed to be equal for all as long as instruction was uniformly delivered. Eventually, researchers and evaluators accepted that it was appropriate and to the advantage of the profession to focus on how well a process was administered or how well a treatment was applied rather than on whether a process or treatment made any significant difference. That made it possible for a teacher to receive a high score for his or her performance if her or his teaching behaviors were seen to be those that have been documented to be associated with student learning. It is a system that does not necessarily require an examination of what the teacher's student may or may not have learned. Instruction is, it is claimed, related to learning but not necessarily to learning by a designated student at a designated time and place. Politicians' requirements for what has been described by educators and some critics as "high-stakes testing" has, of course, undermined that approach based on what was known as process-product research.

Public school administrative and supervisory positions grew significantly during the progressive era, for public education was being professionalized. Ironically, teaching, not withstanding the rhetoric of the professional educators, as Jurgen Herbst demonstrated, was not being professionalized.[51] The administration of schooling and the supervision of teachers, a workforce that was essentially not very well educated,[52] powerless and mostly female, were responsibilities that required new professional personnel. The new class of professional personnel were mostly male. For the year 1889, according to the United States Commissioner of Education, 484 cities reported an average of only four supervisors per city. Between 1890 and 1920, as David Tyack reported, the growth of supervisory positions in public school systems was phenomenal. It increased from nine to 144 in Baltimore, seven to 159 in Boston, thirty-one to 329 in Detroit, fifty-eight to 155 in St. Louis, 235 to 1310 in New York, ten to 159 in Cleveland and sixty to 268 in Philadelphia.[53] To support this cadre of professionals city school systems founded bureaus or departments of educational research, and universities did likewise. Before 1918 there were eighteen bureaus or departments of educational research in public school systems and only seven such organizations in teacher-training institutions. By 1925 there were sixty-nine bureaus in the school systems and twenty-nine in teacher-training institutions.[54] Special spaces had been created for new professionals, educational researchers. They filled time and space with studies designed to support the administration and supervision of the schools and their teachers.

The specialization of administrative and supervisory personnel extended down through the ranks of teachers. As the diversity of students and their needs increased with the growth of school populations, the viability of establishing special programs increased: programs for the retarded, physically handicapped, the delinquent, and the gifted as well as special programs with vocational emphases. States quickly revised and differentiated their certification standards and categories. "In 1900," Tyack reported, "only two states had specialized credentials; by 1930 almost all states had elaborate certification laws."[55] By 1916, for example, Teachers College, Columbia University, gave its students a choice of work leading to specialized diplomas for fifty-five different positions.[56] Specialization of teaching required more supervisors and administrators and the further professionalization of education.

Professionals were expected to be accountable. They were basically required to manage public institutions, including public schools, effectively and efficiently. Yet, educators were also obliged to attend to the desires of the public who created the public institutions as well as to the standards of their profession or discipline. What the public wanted was sometimes different from how professionals believed schools should be managed. By definition, professionals needed a knowledge base for what they did. They needed something other than tradition to justify their ways of doing what they did. Educational research became not only useful but also politically necessary. It provided a knowledge base for the new social functionary—the public school administrator. Research that was claimed to be scientific was a source of authority different from the authority that resided in the community.

Professional educators and educational researchers focused not on education but on schooling. Education always entails the possibility of controversy about fundamental values that cannot be clearly and definitively resolved. In principle, instructional questions seem to have answers. Effectiveness of methods can be assessed, even, within certain confidence intervals, measured. Values cannot be measured. Educational administrators, as Tyack and Hansot recorded, "tried to turn political issues into administrative ones."[57] The educators', especially the professional administrators', use of science and practices claimed to be based on science turned out to be a way to exercise power while not assuming responsibility. It also turned out to be a way to limit choice and avoid discussions of purpose. As Thomas B. Greenfield observed:

> A commitment to science in organizational affairs is not simply a commitment to rationality; it is, rather, a commitment to a restricted framework of rationality. Such a framework, called science, eases the sense of responsibility for powerful actors in organizational administrative settings. It denies both responsibility and personal choice in the making of everyday decisions and in the making of decisions in a powerful world of organized reality. Such science takes sides in conflicts about the rightness of organizational purposes and about appropriate means for achieving them, but it denies it takes sides and claims to look dispassionately at such reality … obedience to a truncated concept of rationality has become a cover for the powerful administrator: science and rationality provide the ultimately persuasive and irrefutable excuse for the abdication of personal choice and responsibility.[58]

It is believed to be a fair and impersonal system.

ACHIEVING FULL ENROLLMENT IN PUBLIC EDUCATION

By the 1930s, it was generally accepted that high school attendance was desirable for all American youth. After World War II, the public schools began to experience full enrollment. By 1950, nearly 90% of American youth between ages fourteen and seventeen were attending secondary schools, 80% more than in 1900. The long-held goal of professional educators earlier expressed by the Commission on the Reorganization of Secondary Education was being realized. However, full enrollment had its price. It required schools to carry out two seemingly contradictory functions: a sorting function and a custodial function. They had to sort—to identify those who showed promise of becoming "useful instruments for the public"—and to tend to students who were frequently there because they had no place else to go and could not find or were not eligible for gainful employment. What was once choice had become compulsory. When choice became compulsion, the social dynamics of schooling were radically transformed. The difference in the deportment of those who wanted to attend school and those who were compelled was quite often quite impressive. As Cremin observed, "the dreams of democratic idealists may have resided in compulsory-attendance laws, but so did the makings of the blackboard jungle."[59]

Compulsory Education for the Masses

As long as school attendance was voluntary, school authorities could easily manage the behavior of students by threatening them with expulsion. Compulsory attendance laws and their enforcement eliminated that threat. School officials had to find new ways to manage and to control students. As students openly rebelled in school or resisted by becoming passively aggressive in the classroom, educators invested their efforts in the application of psychologically derived behavior management and behavior modification techniques. They did not confront the new situation by examining the curriculum.[60] They looked not so much at content but at the process of delivering the content and at ways of modifying behavior. Frequently, they discarded content. Required courses gave way to electives that promised to be relevant. Not surprisingly, indices of student performance—for example, SAT scores—subsequently showed declines. Few observed that students tend not to do very well on tests that assess or measure their mastery of material they have not studied.

It was once recognized that compulsory attendance required development of a variety of programs and even different kinds of schools. As early as 1910, some understood that compulsory attendance required school systems to organize different kinds of schools:

> (a) Those pupils who have become quite incorrigible, and whose parents have lost control of them, must be sent to an institutional school, committed for a term of years. Only thoroughgoing reform is adequate. (b) A day truant school, where hours are long and manual work abundant. This school, while allowing pupils to sleep at home, should aim primarily to keep them off the street and away from the contagion of bad company. Such schools do not exist in America, but are found in English cities. (c) Special classes should be provided for pupils who cannot easily be brought under the ordinary school discipline. These classes may have the same programs as the ordinary classes, but should be under charge of teachers of sufficient maturity, experience, and personal character to cope with this type of child. (d) Possibly a fourth type of class should be for those who by irregular attendance have fallen away from the regular class attainments.[61]

Compulsory attendance clearly required more of teachers and of schools than did voluntary attendance. Once compulsory attendance was instituted, teachers had to know more than what they were assigned to teach. They needed to know how to handle their students, how to interest and motivate them, and how to control their behavior. Once compulsory attendance was instituted, schools had to develop not only a variety of curricula but also a variety of ways to present it in a variety of settings to a variety of students. According to Cremin:

> compulsory attendance marked a new era in the history of American education. The crippled, the blind, the deaf, the sick, the slow-witted, and the needy arrived in growing numbers. Thousands of recalcitrants and incorrigibles who in former times might have dropped out of school now become public charges for a minimum period. And as the school-leaving age moved progressively upward, every problem was aggravated as youngsters, became bigger, stronger, and more resourceful.[62]

Compulsory attendance was the beginning of the differentiated curriculum, or the beginning of what some describe as course proliferation or the abandonment of standards. The differentiated curriculum is the device that allows the school to perform both its sorting and its custodial functions. It necessarily entails differentiation of the student body—the separation of some students from others. As early as 1861, John Philbrick of the Boston Schools argued for the establishment of industrial schools for "a class of children, or less numerous, which is too low down in the depths of vice, crime, and poverty, to be reached by the benefits of a system of public education."[63] A generation later, California's superintendent urged that compulsory attendance legislation be supported so that

the people would be saved "from the rapidly increasing herd of non-producers ... from the wretches who prey upon society like wild beasts." The
"non-producers," or "wild beasts," were not to be placed in schools, for
they needed "labor schools, ships, industrial and technical schools"—
schools where they would be taught "how to work" as well as how to
read.[64] Before compulsory education, schools did some sorting of students. Some failed and a few were expelled. After compulsory schooling
was instituted, schools had to do more sorting.

Following World War II, schools had to find ways to sort and to retain
students in school. They had to solve what became the dropout problem.
After World War II youth had little choice but to remain in school—at
least through high school. As Morris Janowitz observed, "the transformation and organization of the labor market under advanced industrialization restricted opportunities for youth and assigned a new role to the
public schools." Before the depression of the 1930s, "the socialization of
youngsters from European immigrant families and of migrants from rural
areas was in good measure accomplished through work experiences—part
time and full time."[65] Then, "high school graduation or its equivalent—
not only in terms of social attitude, interpersonal competence, and maturity—[was] defined as a desirable and required goal, even for the lowest
income groups."[66] During this era, "actual work requirements, changed
standards of employment and trade unions, and new legislation about
minimum wages" required the public schools to "accept responsibility for
all youngsters who [were] not college bound until they develop[ed] levels
of personal maturity sufficient for them to enter the labor market."[67]
Educators welcomed the consequent expansion of public education, for it
seemed a true extension of equality of educational opportunity. The difficulty was that the public schools, especially the high schools, attempted to
do mainly what they had been accustomed to doing, but for a population
that was in many instances and in many respects very different from any
they had previously served. Those who had previously dropped out of
school to take jobs began to remain in school because there was no place
else for them. What had once been a population seeking and exercising
an opportunity became, in large measure, a captive population.

THE COLONIZATION OF EDUCATION

After Appomattox higher education was being reorganized so it could supply the new social-economic order with a cadre of experts to tend to the
specialized functions in the newly defined spaces. Charles W. Eliot who had
been appointed to the presidency of Harvard in 1869 was making Harvard
into a modern university by attending to science and the professional

schools. He also worked on shaping the public high schools so they would serve the purposes of his new vision of a university. To guide and to motivate him, there was Johns Hopkins, that became an important model for advanced graduate education in the late nineteenth and early twentieth centuries. When the opening exercises were conducted at Johns Hopkins in 1876, a new era in higher education was effectively announced. Denominational exercises and even prayer were conspicuous by their absence and among the speakers was Darwin's "bulldog," Thomas Huxley.

Darwin was largely accepted in the academy and was being used to establish a new scholarship and new scientific disciplines that would presumably assist the new cultural order. Psychology was one of the new disciplines that constituted the seedbed out of which educational research and instructional methods based on scientific principles grew. Educators charged with maintaining public education allowed social scientists, especially psychologists, to colonize their own newly developing field.[68]

The expectation that the imposition of the colonists' conceptions of mind and human learning and their investigative techniques and protocols would be productive and useful was founded on the assumption that education was not an independent enterprise but only a collection of applications form a variety of other disciplines. However, the colonists could not give effective direction to education. As Foster McMurray explained:

> What is important to recognize is that the empirical findings of research conducted in or concerning the schools, when problems and procedures are those of the recognized social sciences, do not tell us how to teach nor what to teach. In the same way that application of pure science to the industrial process is not found by simple deduction from basic knowledge, but is rather the product of creative invention, so also the "meaning" of the social sciences for education must be discovered by activities of a higher intellectual order than following suggestions, analogies, or supposed "implications" from foundational sciences.[69]

McMurray was making a point that William James had made a half century earlier. In *Talks to Teachers*, originally delivered as a series of lectures to Massachusetts's teachers, James instructed:

> you make a great, a very great mistake if you think that psychology, being the science of the mind's laws is something from which you can deduce definite programs and schemes and methods of instruction for immediate schoolroom use. Psychology is a science, and teaching is an art; and sciences never generate arts directly out of themselves.[70]

James' admonition was not heeded. Since he offered it, the practice of education and educational research have been closely tied to psychology.

Educators continued to pursue the educational implications of psychological theories and speculations, not realizing that the number of possible implications is limited only by the number of those looking for implications or the imaginations of those who are looking for the implications. The irony is that those who have been trying to build "the one best system" have made commitments that can give choice but not *the* answer.

While James was expressing his doubts about the utility of psychology for education, an entire generation of prospective school administrators, educational leaders, and educational researchers who were to determine how the problems of public education would be conceptualized and how research questions would be framed were preparing for their careers by studying psychology and how it might be applied to the newly and rapidly developing field of education. Psychologists saw the opportunities the new field offered and quickly made their "new science" available to education. Almost as soon as psychologists were graduated from American universities they found opportunities in the recently developed departments, schools, and colleges of education. For example, John M. O'Donnell reported that "[G. Stanley] Hall granted twenty-seven doctorates in the 1890s; nearly three-quarters of these recipients found positions in teachers college, training schools, or child-study departments. Others, even though nominally appointed to departments of philosophy, continued to cultivate their educational concerns."[71] Colonization was apace with a vengeance.

By 1920 American psychologists had rejected introspection, were more interested in human performance than the nature and quality of human experience, and were keenly interested in becoming useful to society. They generally agreed that human behavior was thoroughly observable and therefore, in principle, predictable and even subject to modification and control. They believed their usefulness to society was their ability to predict and to control how humans would perform in given situations at given tasks.

For many, there was no question that the application of science, as defined by psychologists, to the problems of public education was the only way to render the means and the newly defined ends of public education— specific performances and skills—more efficient than they had been. Inquiry into child development, learning, how to assess and measure learning and development, and how to predict who would and would not learn were high on the researchers' agenda. Study of Monroe's *Teaching-Learning Theory and Teacher Education, 1890 to 1950* (1952) shows not only how convinced so many were that psychology had to be the basis for the study of education but also how long that belief endured. Monroe showed that teaching became not a problem to be studied directly but rather was conceived as practices that were believed to be consistent with what was known about learning. Research on teaching often became little more than the attempt to derive pedagogical principles from one of the many learning theories psychology offered, to do what James argued could not be done. Monroe accepted the notion that education was essentially defined by learning theory and that there could be no educational research without measures of learning and measures of one's ability to learn.

Educators are interested in determining what is worth learning and how that learning can enlighten and inform choices people make. In variety of ways public school teachers and their supervisors are told that student performance, as measured by a variety of tests, is still not good enough. Some challenge the measures; others look for ways to enhance student performance. The next chapter addresses the origins of the idea that human consciousness is a fundamental consideration in education as first addressed by Johann Friedrich Herbart in Germany in the eighteenth century and his advocates in the late nineteenth century in the U.S. American Herbartians put their own interpretations on the psychology of learning in relationship to pedagogy.

NOTES

1. See, for example: Ellwood P. Cubberley. *Public Education in the United States* (Boston: Houghton Mifflin, Co., 1919), p. 18 and Samuel Eliot Morison. *The Oxford History of the American People*, Vol. 1 (New York: New American Library), 1972), p. 113.

2. These laws have been reproduced in Sol Cohen (ed.). *Education in the United States: A Documentary History*, Vol. 1 (New York: Random House, 1974), pp. 393-395. Cohen did label each of these laws a "school law."

3. *Ibid.*, p. 393.

4. *Ibid.*, pp. 393-394.

5. *Ibid.*

6. *Ibid.*, pp. 394-395.

7. The District of Columbia enacted a compulsory school attendance law in 1864. The next such law was enacted by Vermont in 1867. During the 1870s, fourteen other states enacted such laws. Seventeen states waited until the twentieth century to enact compulsory school attendance laws. See: Nelda Umbeck. *State Legislation on School Attendance* (Washington, D.C.: U. S. Government Printing Office, 1960).

8. Peter Gay. *The Enlightenment: The Rise of Modern Paganism* (New York: Alfred A. Knopf, 1966), p. 1.

9. Joseph L. Blau. *Men and Movements in American Philosophy* (New York: Prentice-Hall, Inc., 1952), p. 37.

10. David Ramsay. *The History of the American Revolution*, Vol. II. 1789, Lester H. Cohen (ed.), (Indianapolis: Liberty Fund. 1989), pp. 637-638.

11. Parke Godwin. *Democracy, Constructive and Pacific* (New York: J. Winchester, 1844), pp. 10, 21.

12. Alexis de Tocqueville. *Democracy in America* in Willard Thorp, Merle Curti and Carlos Baker (eds.). *American Issues: The Social Record* Vol. I, rev. ed. (New York: Lippincott, 1955), p. 408.

13. Horace Mann. *Twelfth Annual Report* in Lawrence A. Cremin (ed.). *The Republic and the School: Horace Mann on the Education of Free Men* (New York: Teachers College Press, 1957), p. 87

14. Thomas Jefferson. "A Bill for the More General Diffusion of Knowledge" in Gordon C. Lee (ed.). *Crusade Against Ignorance* (New York: Teachers College Press, 1961), p. 83.

15. Thomas Jefferson. *Notes on the State of Virginia* in Lee (ed.). *Crusade Against Ignorance*, p. 94.

16. Minutes of the American Philosophical Society, March 6, 1795, quoted in Merle M. Odgers. "Education and the American Philosophical Society," *Proceedings of the American Philosophical Society*, Vol. 87, No. 1 (July 1943), p. 13.

17. Samuel Knox. "An Essay on the Best System of Liberal Education, Adapted to the Genius of the Government of the United States. Comprehending also, an Uniform General Plan for Instituting and Conducting Public Schools, in This County on Principles of the Most Extensive Utility" reprinted in Frederick Rudolph (ed.). *Essays on Education in the Early Republic* (Cambridge, Massachusetts: Harvard University Press, 1965), pp. 315-316.

18. *Ibid.*, p. 306.

19. *Ibid.*, p. 308.

20. Samuel Harrison Smith. "Remarks on Education: Illustrating the Close Connection Between Virtue and Wisdom. To Which is Annexed a System of Liberal Education...." reprinted in Rudolph (ed.). *Essays on Education in the Early Republic*, pp. 188-189.

21. *Ibid.*, p. 190.

22. *Ibid.*

23. The prize-winning essays written by Knox and Smith were published and so have been available for study by several generations of Americans. Frederick Rudolph identified five others who wrote and published essays on education between 1786 and 1799. The five others he has made available are: Robert Coram, Simeon Doggett, Amable-Louis-Rose de Lafitte du Corteil, Benjamin Rush, and Noah Webster. In Allen Oscar Hansen. *Liberalism and American Education in the Eighteenth Century* (New York: The Macmillan Co., 1926) are discussions of eighteenth-century educational theorists: Nathaniel Chipman, Robert Coram, Amable-Louis-Rose de Lafitte du Corteil, Pierre Samuel DuPont de Nemour, Samuel Knox, Benjamin Rush, Samuel Harrison Smith, James Sullivan and Noah Webster.

24. Benjamin Rush. "Thoughts upon the Mode of Education Proper in a Republic" reprinted in Rudolph. *Essays on Education*, p. 10.

25. Benjamin Rush. "Plan for the Establishment of Public Schools" reprinted in Rudolph. *Essays on Education*, pp. 6-7.

26. Rush Welter. *Popular Education and Democratic Thought in America* (New York: Columbia University Press, 1965), pp. 26-27.

27. Cubberley. *Public Education in the United States*, p. 19.

28.   Quoted in Lawrence A. Cremin. *American Education: The Metropolitan Experience, 1876-1980* (New York: Harper and Row, 1988), pp. 297.

29.   Cremin. *American Education: The Metropolitan Experience*, pp. 297-298.

30.   *Ibid.*, p. 295.

31.   Ernest R. House. "Three Perspectives on Innovation: Technological, Political and Cultural" in Rolf Lehming and Michael Kane (eds.). *Improving Schools: Using What We Know* (Beverly Hills, California: Sage, 1981).

32.   Robert McClintock. "Toward a Place for Study in a World of Instruction," *Teachers College Record*, Vol. 73 (1971), p. 162.

33.   Richard Grant White. "The Public-School Failure." *North American Review*. Vol. CXXXI. (1880) reproduced in Daniel Calhoun (ed.). *The Educating of Americans: A Documentary History* (Boston: Houghton Mifflin Co., 1969), p. 304.

34.   McClintock. "Toward a Place for Study in a World of Instruction," p. 167.

35.   Lawrence A. Cremin. *The Transformation of the School: Progressivism in American Education, 1876-1957* (New York: Alfred A. Knopf, 1962), p. 11.

36.   James G. Carter. *Essays Upon Education Containing a Particular Examination of the Schools of Massachusetts, and an Outline of an Institution for the Education of Teachers* (Boston: Bowles and Darborn, 1826), p. 47.

37.   William Chandler Bagley who was a trained psychology was one of the few who questioned how much education should rely on psychology. In 1912 he wrote: "It is out of the question to solve satisfactorily the problems of education by deductive inferences from the principles that have been worked out in what we call the 'pure' sciences. We cannot for example, take the principles of psychology and deduce from these conclusions regarding educational problems that will unerringly 'work'.... We must, in a sense, declare our independence, take the scientific method which is our most precious heritage from the basic sciences, and with its aid work out our own salvation." See: William Chandler Bagley. "A Plea for the Scientific Study of Educational Problems," *Kansas School Magazine*, Vol. 1, No. 2 (February 1912), p. 54.

38.   Lee S. Schulman. "Knowledge and Teaching: Foundations of the New Reform." *Harvard Educational Review*, Vol. 57, No. 1 (February 1987), pp. 6-7.

39.   Bert James Lowenberg. "Darwinism Comes to America," *Mississippi Valley Historical Review*, Vol. 28 (1941-42), p. 341.

40.   Robert Hughes. *The Shock of the New* (New York: Alfred A. Knopf, 1981), p. 11.

41.   *Ibid.*, pp. 9-10.

42.   Daniel Calhoun (ed.). *Educating the Americans: A Documentary History* (Boston: Houghton Mifflin, 1969), p. 295.

43.   Merle Curti. "America at the World's Fairs, 1851-1893," *American Historical Review*, Vol. 55 (1950), p. 842.

44.   *Ibid.*, p. 852.

45.   Cremin. *Transformation of the School*, p. 23.

46.   Frederick Jackson Turner. *The Frontier in American History* (New York: Holt, Rinehart and Winston, 1962), p. 3.

47.   Burton J. Bledstein. *The Culture of Professionalism: The Middle Class and the Development of Higher Education in America* (New York: W. W. Norton & Co., 1976), p. 7.

48.   Daniel Boorstin. *The Image: A Guide to Pseudo-Events in America* (New York: Atheneum, 1977), p. 288.

49.   Bledstein. *Culture of Professionalism*, p. 56.

50.   Edward L. Thorndike. "Quantitative Investigations in Education: With Special Reference to Co-operation Within this Association." *School Review Monograph No. 2: National Society of College Teachers of Education Yearbook* (Chicago: University of Chicago Press, 1912), pp. 34-35.

51.   Jurgen Herbst. *And Sadly Teach: Teacher Education and Professionalization in American Culture* (Madison, Wisconsin: University of Wisconsin Press, 1989), p. 11.

52.   For a description of the qualifications and demographic characteristics of teachers at this time see: Lotus Delta Coffman. *The Social Composition of the Teaching Population* (New York: Teachers College, Columbia University, 1911).

53.   David B. Tyack. *The One Best System: A History of American Urban Education* (Cambridge, Massachusetts: Harvard University Press, 1974), p. 56.

54.   Walter Scott Monroe. *Ten years of Educational Research, 1918-1927. University of Illinois Bulletin. 25* (Urbana, Illinois: Bureau of Educational Research, College of Education, University of Illinois, 1928), p. 58; B. Liu. *Educational Research in Major American Cities* (New York: Kings Crown Press, 1945); Douglas Scates. "Organized Research in Education: National, State, City, and University Bureaus of Educational Research," *Review of Educational Research*, Vol. 9 (1939).

55.   Tyack. *One Best System*, p. 185.

56.   Michael Katz. "From Theory to Survey in Graduate Schools of Education," *Journal of Higher Education*, Vol. 37 (1966), p. 328.

57.   David B. Tyack and Elisabeth Hansot. "From Social Movement to Professional Management: An Inquiry into the Changing Character of Leadership in Public Education." *American Journal of Education* (1980), p. 295.

58.   Thomas B. Greenfield in D. Griffths, R. Stout. and P. Forsyth (eds.). *Leaders for America's Schools* (Berkeley, California: McCutchan, 1988), p. 139.

59.   Cremin. *Transformation of the School*, p. 128.

60.   J. Ruchin. "Does School Crime Need the Attention of Policemen or Educators?" *Teachers College Record*, Vol. 79 (1977), p. 238.

61.   "Attendance" in Paul Monroe (ed.). *Cyclopedia of Education*, Vol. 1 (New York: The Macmillan Co., 1911), p. 294.

62.   Cremin. *Transformation of the School*, pp. 127-128.

63.   Quoted in Tyack. *One Best System*, pp. 69-70.

64.   Quoted in Tyack. *One Best System*, pp. 68-69.

65.   Morris Janowitz. *Institution Building in Urban Education* (Russell Sage Foundation, 1969), pp. 8-9.

66.   *Ibid.*, p. 9.

67.   *Ibid.*

68. David Hamilton. *Towards a Theory of Schooling* (London: Falmer Press, 1989), p. 152.

69. Foster McMurray. "Preface to an Autonomous Discipline of Education." *Educational Theory*, Vol. 5. No. e (July 1955), p. 134.

70. William James. *Talks to Teachers* (New York: Dover, 1962), p. 3.

71. John M. O'Donnell. *The Origins of Behaviorism: American Psychology, 1870-1920* (New York: New York University Press, 1985), p. 154.

CHAPTER 5

EDUCATION AS A CONSCIOUS BUSINESS

HERBART AND THE HERBARTIANS

Johann Friedrich Herbart was a German philosopher who succeeded Immanuel Kant at Königsberg two hundred years before psychology and education (pedagogy) were organized and conceptualized as disciplines different from philosophy. However, Herbart's interest in instruction, education, and psychology were precursors to the modern fields of psychology and education, especially education. He identified education as an object of systematic study and created a laboratory school for the study of education. A generation after his death other German philosophers who were committed to the study of education and the training of teachers adapted his work and created a movement now known as Herbartianism. The German Herbartians influenced a generation of American Herbartians who further adapted Herbartian principles for their own purposes. American Herbartians in the Progressive Era did not accept Herbart's philososphical system, but they found Herbartianism useful as they addressed the needs of an expanding public school system in the United States. This chapter examines Herbart's ideas in the early nineteenth century and his contributions to the movement that took his name in the late nineteenth and early twentieth centuries.

Educational Research, the National Agenda, and Educational Reform:
A History, pp. 123–151

HERBART: EDUCATION AS A SUBJECT OF RESEARCH

Johann Friedrich Herbart, born in 1776 in Oldenburg, Germany a few months before the beginning of the American War of Independence, has been identified with Johann Heinrich Pestalozzi and Friedrich Schleiermacher as one of the "founding fathers of modern educational theory."[1] He is of special interest to theoreticians of education and educational researchers, for he was, as John Dewey observed, the first to demonstrate that education was an activity that could be studied directly.[2] For Herbart's predecessors as well as his contemporaries, the consideration of educational theory and practice was a widespread but largely amateur endeavor. Its origins were metaphysical, not scientific, not based on observation. The development of educational theory was a speculative undertaking. Educational theory and prescriptions for educational practice were founded on advice from an authority in some field other than education, a topic open to the opinion of any learned and accomplished person. Herbart believed that order and deliberation had to be introduced into how education was conceptualized. He maintained that: "the more education appears in the daily round of experience, the more necessary it is to bring our thoughts about it into more definite order and to fix them lest they be lost in the stream of opinion."[3]

Herbart's contribution was to change how educational questions were framed and addressed. John Dewey clearly recognized that when in 1916 he wrote: "Herbart's great service was to take the work of teaching out of the region of routine and accident, and make it into a conscious business with a definite aim and procedure, instead of being a compound of casual inspiration and subservience to tradition."[4] Herbart's approach to pedagogy, psychology, and philosophy as well as how he saw the relationship among them are different from today's perspective and debates. Exploration of Herbart's work on education in relationship to his work in philosophy and psychology constitutes an exploration of questions about the proper and the useful relationships among these three areas that are now separate from one another as exemplified by institutional arrangements and professional organizations. The clear distinctions that now exist among philosophy, psychology, and education had not yet been made when Herbart was developing his philosophical system and educational theory.

While Herbart can be said to have shown that education is an activity that can be an object of inquiry, he also maintained that his philosophy and psychology were related to his inquiries into education. It is still the custom to ask whether educational prescriptions and recommendations have a sound psychological foundation just as similar questions are asked about the philosophical foundation for educational programs and practices. How educational research is conceptualized depends on whether one maintains that education is or must be supported by either psychology or philosophy. Education or pedagogy can be interpreted as applied psychology. Education was once a branch of philosophy, and departmental arrangements and appointments reflected that conception. For example, when Dewey accepted his appointment at the University of Chicago in 1894, it was an appointment as chair of the combined department of philosophy, psychology and pedagogy.

To examine Herbart is to examine the possibility that education: 1) is an activity that is deduced from philosophy or psychology; 2) should be informed by philosophy or psychology; 3) has no necessary and logical relationship to philosophy or psychology; or 4) is indistinguishable from philosophy or psychology. For Herbart, as for John Dewey, the attention given to education may have been a philosophical inquiry into how humans became intelligent, moral, and social beings. For Herbart, the study of education was the study of the development of mind, for mind was defined by its contents; and mind does distinguish humans from other beings.

Herbartians accepted Herbart's position that education was a necessary object of inquiry, but they had little interest in or use for Herbart's metaphysics. Their interest was practical and political. They attended to education as it was carried out in schools. They endeavored to develop a science of education and to develop instructional practices and school curricula for students who were required to attend stated-supported and state-managed schools.

Herbart's Early Interest in Education

Percival R. Cole suggested that Herbart's theory of education may have been "based ... as much upon the results of his own experience as the logical implications of his philosophy and psychology."[5] The beginning of his interest and his subsequently developed theory of education may have been Herbart's experience as a teacher, in this case as a tutor. In 1796, Herbart accepted a position as tutor to the sons of Herr von Steiger, Interlaken's governor. Tutoring the Steiger children gave him the opportunity to observe and interact with children in a context that raised questions he pursued throughout his professional career. Harold Dunkel also suggested that Herbart probably "developed his psychology out of his pedagogy rather than basing his pedagogy on psychology as he insisted he did."[6] The five letters Herbart wrote to Herr von Steiger[7] indicate not only that he took his work as tutor seriously but also that he had already begun to organize his thoughts on education. This suggests that Herbart had identified education as a subject of inquiry and that his approach was through direct observation of the subject rather than speculation.

In 1799, Herbart took leave of his position as tutor but he gave up neither his interest in education nor his use of observation. He visited Johann Heinrich Pestalozzi at Burgdorf to examine his educational work with children.[8] He began to write on pedagogy and Pestalozzi's methods in 1801.[9] In 1802, he began to study philosophy at Göttingen where he was awarded a doctorate in 1805. He remained there and taught education and philosophy and completed three more works on education. His work at Göttingen was sufficiently noteworthy to earn him a call to succeed Immanuel Kant at Königsberg in 1809.

While at Königsberg, Herbart wrote five books on education and four on psychology as well as a text to accompany his lectures.[10] He grew dissatisfied with only teaching the theory of pedagogy. He wanted to establish a laboratory where educational principles could be demonstrated and practiced. As Herbart maintained:

> But education cannot merely be taught; it must be demonstrated and practiced. Besides, I wish to extend my ten years' experience in it. So I long ago conceived the idea of teaching a small number of selected boys myself for an hour daily, in the presence of some young men acquainted with my pedagogy, who will afterwards attempt in my place and under my eye, to carry on what I have begun. Gradually in this way teachers may be trained, whose methods must be perfected by mutual observation and exchange of experience. Since a plan of instruction is worthless without teachers, and moreover such teachers as are inspired by the spirit of the plan, and skilled in the use of the method, perhaps a small experimental school such as I propose will be the best preparation for future and more extended movements.[11]

The school Herbart founded was designed to accompany his lectures on pedagogy creating a laboratory-like situation. The school's existence was initially announced on the university's 1810 summer calendar. That first announcement indicated that the seminar was to consist of "teaching exercises practiced by ten to twelve competent students under my [Herbart's] direction and with my collaboration."[12] Herbart participated in the school as a mathematics teacher. The authorities that authorized the founding of the school saw it as a "training college" for teachers but Herbart failed to develop his "training college" as quickly and as extensively as his superiors had wished.[13] He was primarily interested in studying the educative process; training teachers was not his chief interest. However, for Herbart's followers, the Herbartians in Germany as well as in the United States, the existence of a laboratory school proved to be very important, for they were interested in training teachers. In 1833, Herbart accepted an invitation to return to Göttingen where he continued his work on education and philosophy until his death in 1841. From the beginning to the end of his career, Herbart maintained his inquiries and writings on educational subjects.[14]

HERBART'S PHILOSOPHY

Herbart acknowledged that his professor Fichte, who was also an admirer of Pestalozzi's achievements[15] and a philosophical idealist, stimulated him greatly, but Herbart adopted neither the views of Fichte nor those of his predecessor at Königsberg, Kant. He was a realist when the fashion was idealism. For Herbart, neither soul nor matter could be defined; and, he claimed, they could not be separated. That was a notion that could serve as precursor to a psychobiological approach to educational inquiry. Soul/mind and matter/body were aspects of a common substance. The soul had no parts; it was indivisible. It was an essence, not a *tabula rasa* on which impressions were made. It had neither innate talents nor faculties. It consisted of neither feelings nor concepts and possessed no forms of perception.

The apparent difference between soul and matter was not to be found in the nature of either but in how they were approached. Matter was a reality of the natural world. In its contact with the natural world the soul, he maintained, built mind by building a manifold of self-preserving ideas or concepts that were representations of the impressions made upon people by the natural world. They were copies in consciousness of the objects of the physical world that resulted from the soul's contact with natural objects.

The mind was not an active agent that produced changes in the world but a depository, an assemblage of the impressions that issued from the soul's contact with the world. Mind was thus a product of experience. Its characteristics and how it functioned depended on its contents and how those contents were assembled. Education, as a deliberate undertaking, was the process whereby the right content was selected and organized into the proper configuration as well as the process that allowed teachers to control the human relationships under their charge and to present appropriate content. Experience was essential to the development of the individual. Herbart found a way to discuss mind and morality not in the abstract extra-experiential realm but within the realm of experience. Interest led to learning. There were two kinds of interest. In addition to primary interest, that which the child shows on his or her own without any prompting or encouragement from others, there was secondary interest, that which was created by others, for example, the teacher.

Axiology was particularly important to Herbart. From ethics he derived his aim of education. He repeatedly claimed that the end of education was to be determined by ethics; that the whole problem of education could be defined by the concept of morality;[16] that the purpose of education could be expressed in the term virtue; and that the ultimate purpose of instruction was to be found in the notion of virtue. Aesthetics was even more important to Herbart than ethics. The aesthetic judgment was subordinate to the ethical judgment. Morality was not absolute, for that which determined what was either right or wrong was to be found in the existing social order. However, the aesthetic judgment was absolute and unconditional. Harmony either existed or it did not.

How Herbart Thought About Education

Herbart did not believe that the state should direct schools. His focus was more on the tutorial relationship than on anything approaching modern classroom instruction. He was interested in how the individual became a moral person as opposed to producing citizens for the modern nation state. According to Dunkel: "His first and true love was education within the family through the private tutor—at a time when state and national systems of education with large schools and large classes were first coming into their full strength."[17] The psychology he developed was one that focused not on groups but on the individual.[18] That his emphasis was on the individual was clearly recognized and articulated by A. E. Winship in 1888 when he announced that the *Journal of Education* would soon publish a series of articles on Herbart by Margaret K. Smith who had recently completed a translation of Herbart's *Teacher's Manual of Psychology*. According to Winship: "Herbart's centralizing of his psychology and pedagogy in the individual, protesting against all theories which place as the aim of education, the family, the church, the state, or humanity, has captured not a few."[19] The Herbartian philosophy, Winship maintained, was an alternative to the philosophies of Hegel and Rosenkranz[20] who drew "away from the individual through the home and church to the state."

So that the individual could be fully developed and empowered, it was necessary that ethics, aesthetics and truth determine education. Intellectual inquiry and religious reverence, Herbart maintained, were natural to humankind. They had to be acknowledged and cultivated just as ethics and aesthetics had to be observed so the individual could develop fully. One became a moral person through an educative process, an educative process that required teachers to pay particular attention not only to how they instructed their charges but also to the content they presented to them. Herbart's chief interest was the nature and the development of the moral person. Dunkel observed that ultimately "the only kind of education in which Herbart was interested was moral education."[21] Education was the activity on which he focused to get at his chief interest.

The interest Herbart developed in pedagogy as a tutor as well as the time he spent with the wives of his friends discussing the development of their children were philosophical inquiries and observations into the nature of the process whereby humankind acquires its distinctive characteristics and the process whereby each individual becomes a moral agent. Herbart observed children and concluded that morality, the essence of humankind, depended upon the contents of mind; and the contents depended on the child's experiences—experiences that could be, in significant measure, controlled.

IDENTIFYING PEDAGOGY AND CURRICULUM AS SUBJECTS IN EDUCATIONAL INQUIRY

Herbart's conception of apperception was consistent with the earlier observations of others, for example, Comenius and Rousseau, that learning was best achieved by connecting the new or the unknown to what was already known. For the Herbartians of the nineteenth and early twentieth century, Herbart's conception of apperception and his four steps of thought (clearness, association, system, and method) that they elaborated into five teaching steps (preparation, presentation, association, generalization, and application) constituted a method that was to be used to teach any subject. The reports of the activities in his school at Königsberg emphasized the progress he was making in working out the instructional processes and their proper sequence.[22] For Herbart instruction was not a process that could be separated from content; and content was important. He emphasized that the purpose of education was embedded in the instructional process. Herbart sought to work out how the right contents were to be acquired, taught and built into the right configuration. His psychology was instrumental in that process. It was to provide the laws for the force with which contents were to be presented and the way the contents were to be assembled. Content was to be deliberately selected and organized. It had to be related to the content children brought to the educational situation, for, as Herbart insisted, the will was "not a faculty to be trained but a structure to be built."[23] Educators were to begin with what children knew upon entering school, but they were not to allow them to remain where they were. Herbart effectively demonstrated to his successors that there was a difference between school subjects and the academic disciplines just, as Dewey would later explain when he described the methods and purpose of his laboratory school at the University of Chicago.[24] An early manifestation of Herbart's and others' concern with content can be seen in the study conducted in 1870 that reported what Berlin children knew—specifically what the contents of their minds were—upon entering school.[25] After Herbart the curriculum, assumed a new importance for educators. Consider, for example, the topics the American Herbartian Charles DeGarmo discussed in his "Introductory Discussion" to *The First Year Book of the Herbart Society for the Scientific Study of Teaching*: "The Ethical Function of Studies;" "Correlation, Co-ordination, Concentration of Studies;" "The Educational Value of Studies—The Demands of Civilization vs. Mental Discipline as the Basis of Selection;" "The Equivalence of Studies;" "The Scope of Psychological Correlation;" "The Principle of Sequence for Culture Studies;" "Concentration—The Subordination of Secondary to Primary Studies;" "The Subordination of 'Form' to Thought Studies;" and "Correlation within Departments of Study."[26]

THE LEGACY OF HERBART'S SYSTEM OF THOUGHT ON EDUCATION

Herbart created a system that allowed his successors to accept that education constituted a field of study. He effectively maintained that observation and experience were more important than opinion. For those who would later build upon Herbart and develop Herbartian principles that meant that children and teaching had to be studied through observation. Herbartians and others would eventually claim that to observe children properly, laboratory schools were necessary.[27] His work and career show that to learn about education, education must be the object of inquiry. They may also show, certainly in the case of Herbart, that pedagogy was the practice of philosophy.

To understand what Herbart was trying to accomplish it may be necessary to move back beyond the effects of what he may have accomplished and examine what he was trying to achieve. Herbart's early and enduring interests were philosophical. He was a professional philosopher. As a professional philosopher, he taught philosophy, wrote philosophical works, tried to develop his own philosophical system, and like many other philosophers who worked before the invention of modern psychology and its clear and distinct separation from philosophy, he wrote about psychology and education. The possibility of education as a field of study and inquiry separate from psychology and from philosophy was not being considered when Herbart began his work. However, it is something that Herbart, as Dewey recognized, made possible. Education was extremely important to him. Its conceptualization as an activity that can be identified and studied appears to have been the result of his primary philosophical interests.

Education may have been the major instrumentality Herbart used to realize his primary interest, the development of the moral individual. He may have used education just as Dewey would later use it. "Education," Dewey wrote, "is the laboratory in which philosophic distinctions become concrete and are tested."[28] To focus on how Herbart's philosophy and his psychology are related to his educational notions is to focus on the effect and the uses of his work and reflects the belief that the study of education must be based on one of the disciplines or that education is only something to which disciplines are to be applied. To maintain such a focus may be to neglect Herbart's own purposes, purposes that were different from those of the Herbartians who found utility and inspiration in his works a generation after his death. Herbartians responded to the agenda of their own era. They were primarily interested in universal compulsory schooling and the establishment of either laboratory schools or practice schools for the training of teachers and the study of teaching.

For Herbart, metaphysics became involved in education mainly through its application, psychology as it relates to the nature of the soul and mind and the origin and nature of presentations. In his educational works Herbart did not make much of these metaphysical foundations. As a result, educators following him paid little or no attention to them. They took "mind" as somehow furnished with "ideas" through sense impressions, without trying to define what the mind was, why it had ideas, or why ideas became associated or otherwise reacted with each other.

Because Herbart did not make strong connections between his metaphysics and his educational works, it was possible for Herbartians to create a science of education without being required to either solve or take positions on longstanding philosophical differences and puzzles. Like Herbart, his followers could work in the world of naive realism.[29] That was an important contribution to those who were trying to assemble systems of schooling and who were concerned with the preparation of teachers in the late nineteenth and early twentieth centuries as well as to those who would later want to free psychology from philosophy.

Herbart appears to have begun with philosophy, psychology and pedagogy simultaneously. Philosophy and pedagogy appear to be two aspects of the same activity just as soul and mind were conceived as two aspects of the same essence. If philosophy and pedagogy are two aspects of the same undertaking, then relationships between them probably cannot be found. If the notion of relationships is surrendered, it may be possible to see that they were two aspects of the same undertaking. To look for links between Herbart's philosophy and pedagogy and Herbart's psychology and education is to assume divisions that may not have been there for Herbart. Herbart was working before the development of modern psychology, a generation before Wilhelm Wundt opened his psychological laboratory at Leipzig and began the modern science of psychology, a science based on experimentation and observation.

It may be appropriate to criticize Herbart for developing his psychology subsequent to his pedagogical and educational ideas only if there is good reason to believe that pedagogical deductions can be made from psychological principles or findings. It is possible to make such deductions, but there is no reason to believe that one set of deductions will necessarily be better than or worse than any other set. Everything or anything can be derived from any given premise. Several different philosophical positions can be used to justify a given educational position. Knowing one's pedagogical position is not necessarily the key to knowing one's philosophical position. A given philosophical position or psychological principle does not necessarily support one and only one pedagogical position. To search for the implications that any given psychological finding or philosophical doctrine may have for educational theory or practice is to set out on an interesting search that will prove inconclusive, for there is no limit to what can be deduced.

A half century after Herbart's death, William James recognized the futility of trying to deduce pedagogical principles from psychology, for he was very much aware that human purpose could not be cleansed from human endeavors. James warned:

> I say moreover that you make a great, a very great mistake, if you think that psychology, being the science of the mind's laws, is something from which you can deduce definite programmes and schemes and methods of instruction for immediate schoolroom use. Psychology is a science, and teaching is an art; and sciences never generate arts directly out of themselves.[30]

James did not deny that psychology might have some utility for teachers. He even agreed that psychology ought to help teachers, but he doubted that psychology could provide as much direction for pedagogical practice as teachers desired. Knowledge of psychology would not ensure pedagogical prowess. To derive rules for the art of pedagogical practice from the science of psychology one needed the requisite for any technology that attempts to translate theory into practice—what James called an "inventive mind."[31] James wanted teachers to be mindful of psychological laws, laws that could indicate what was potentially harmful to students. Psychology may be an important "auxiliary science" of pedagogy but it is not the foundation upon which educational programs and pedagogy must necessarily be constructed.

It is possible to argue that Herbart did not clearly and directly derive his pedagogical principles from either psychology or philosophy.

Psychology and philosophy did not provide him major premises from which he deduced his pedagogical principles. He developed his pedagogical principles from the phenomenon itself—his experience as a tutor and a teacher—and then used psychology to support the means for realizing his end, morality. That Herbart effectively fitted his psychology to this pedagogy demonstrates that one can learn about pedagogy and education by attending to them, by observing the process. For Herbart, the individual was always more important than any generalizations about individuals: "It [psychology] can never substitute for observation of the pupil; the individual can only be discovered, not deduced."[32]

Herbart began with observation, experience. However, he did more than repeat the experience and wisdom of "countless generations of schoolmasters." He sought to support pedagogy with a psychology. In doing so, he became one of the first to formulate psychology as a science. It was not an experimental science but for Herbartians and others at the end of the nineteenth century it proved to be an acceptable alternative to faculty psychology and mental discipline. In building a science of education, he gave education a technical vocabulary and a procedure. To his successors, to those who used him as justification for their own pursuits, Herbart gave education status and independence, especially independence.

THE HERBARTIAN MOVEMENT

The Herbartian movement, especially in the United States, shows that often the time between one's accomplishments and their recognition and use by others is often considerable. Herbart's work and its eventual use by those later identified as Herbartians, in and out of Germany, provide such an example. When Herbart died in 1841, the system of public education now long established in the United States was just beginning to be established. Horace Mann was then approaching the half way mark in his tenure as Secretary to the Massachusetts Board of Education. At the time, there was little or no interest in Herbart's work. It appears that the first notice of Herbart's work in the United States appeared a full century after his birth.[33] American Herbartians were influenced by the European movement that was also slow to materialize.

Herbart's work remained virtually unnoticed in Europe until 1865 when Tuiskon Ziller, a professor at Leipzig, published what the American Herbartian Charles DeGarmo later described as an "epoch-making work,"[34] *Grundlegung zur Lehre vom erziehenden Unterricht* (*Basis of the Doctrine of Instruction as a Moral Force*) that set forth Herbart's conception of instruction as a moral force. In 1868, the *Verein für Wissenschaftliche*

Pädagogik, a confederation of local clubs devoted to studying educational problems from the Herbartian standpoint was founded with Ziller as its leader. "By the late eighteen-eighties, Herbartian principles as interpreted by Karl Volkmar Stoy, Tuiskon Ziller, Wilhelm Rein, and Otto Frick were being widely discussed and talked about and practiced in Germany." L. R. Klemm reported that the "labyrinth of conflicting interpretations of the Herbart-Ziller movement" was then "stirring up the pedagogical world of Germany as a leviathan does the quiet depths of the sea."[35] By 1894, *die Vereinen* (clubs) boasted over 800 members.

Half a century after Herbart's death, interest in his work was great in and out of Germany. There were German Herbartians, and there were significant Herbartian influences and movements in other countries.[36] There were Herbartians in Great Britain,[37] and there were of course American Herbartians. Like other students traveling abroad in this period to study at German universities, the Americans carried Herbartianism back to their homeland. The Americans learned their Herbartian principles from Karl Volkmar Stoy and his collaborators Otto Frick, Tuiskon Ziller, and Wilhelm Rein. By the time the Americans encountered Herbartian ideas they were part of a more general and sometimes conflicting dialogue. Fidelity to Herbart was not a major issue.[38]

German Herbartians' Influence on Americans

The major German Herbartians from whom American Herbartians learned about Herbartianism were Karl Volkmar Stoy, and Tuiskon Ziller who were contemporaries, and the younger Wilhelm Rein, their successor. When Americans Charles DeGarmo and the brothers, Charles and Frank McMurry arrived in Germany to study, the two major chairs of pedagogy were held by Herbartians. Stoy held the chair at Jena, and Ziller occupied the pedagogical chair at Leipzig. Ziller's student, Rein, succeeded Stoy at Jena in 1886. Herbart held a university position in philosophy, but the Herbartians were educators with positions in pedagogy.

Ziller began to lecture at Leipzig in 1853. By 1862 he had opened his pedagogical seminary and practice school modeled after the school Herbart had established at Königsberg. Ziller built upon Herbart's system, developing new principles and practices that he thought to be natural outgrowths of Herbart's work. The chief notions that Ziller developed that came to be accepted by nearly all Herbartians except Stoy and his followers were: 1) the historical stages or the culture epoch theory of child development; 2) the theory of concentration in studies; and 3) the five formal steps of instruction. Herbart did not elaborate the culture epoch theory, but Ziller developed it to the point where it was subsequently accepted and used by Herbert Spencer and G. Stanley Hall. Ziller's first Herbartian works were *Introduction to General Pedagogy* (1856) and *The Government of Children* (1857), but it was his *Basis of the Doctrine of Instruction as a Moral Force* (1865) that created the most popular interest in Herbart.

Stoy went to Leipzig in 1833 to study theology, philosophy and philology. He was introduced to Herbart's work by Mortiz Wilhelm Drobisch. He proceeded to Göttingen where he established a relationship with Herbart. From Herbart he acquired the belief that practice was an important dimension of pedagogy and that the theoretical side had to be complemented with practice. He took a post at a boarding school in Winheim in Baden in 1839 to learn about the practical side of pedagogy. When he returned to Jena where he succeeded H. G. Brzoska who had been Herbart's assistant,[39] he lectured as a *privatdocent* and organized a pedagogical seminary similar to the one Herbart had established at Königsberg. It later became the pedagogical seminary that received widespread attention under the direction of Rein. Stoy also founded a normal school at Bielitz. and later a higher school for girls. Stoy applied his understanding of Herbart to the elementary schools while his collaborator, Otto Frick, focused on the *gymnasia*. Stoy was conservative in his interpretation of Herbart's work.[40]

Ziller and Stoy died a few years apart in the early and mid-1880s. Rein took the leadership in the promulgation and interpretation of Herbartian pedagogy. Rein was not as conservative as Stoy. Like Ziller, he promoted the culture epoch theory, concentration, and the five formal steps as the essence of Herbartian pedagogy. He developed a practice school with a detailed course of study filling two large volumes. Practice lessons thoroughly planned and the methods employed in the practice school were subjected to critiques and analysis.

American Herbartianism

Between 1885 and 1890, "no less than nine" American students studied in Jena, "the fountainhead of American Herbartianism." By the beginning of the twentieth century about fifty Americans had studied Herbartianism at Jena, Leipzig, or Halle.[41] The most popular and the most influential American Herbartians were Charles DeGarmo, and Charles and Frank McMurry. Like other American Herbartians, they were not so much students of Herbart as they were students of the German Herbartians who themselves were not strict followers of Herbart. American students did not pursue training in Herbartianism rather they found Herbartianism part of the intellectual climate of the era in German academcis.[42] When the McMurry brothers and DeGarmo arrived in Germany "none of the three expected to make a career of importing and advocating Herbartianism."[43] DeGarmo saw education as a field of new opportunities "and went to prepare for a career in it by studying the history and philosophy of education."[44] American Herbartians fundamentally were educators like their German teachers not philosophers like Herbart.

Upon their return to the United States, DeGarmo and the McMurry's introduced their versions of Herbartian practices and ideas. In 1892, Charles McMurry published his *General Methods* and in 1897 with his brother Frank published *Method in the Recitation*. In 1895, DeGarmo published *Herbart and the Herbartians*. These three works probably did more to popularize Herbartian educational ideas and to introduce them into the normal schools and colleges of the United States than all other influences combined. The American Herbartians "demolished the preeminence of both a tired Hegelianism and a desiccated Pestalozzian classicism,[45] and provided an alternative to philosophy such as Rosenkranz's *Philosophy of Education*.

Professionalizing Teacher Training: Setting the Stage for Research on Teaching

Besides serving as president of the National Herbart Society from 1892 to 1897 Charles DeGarmo began a program of publishing works devoted to Herbartian notions. In 1891 he published *Essentials of Method*. He served as editor of the Herbart Club's translation of Karl Lange's *Apperception* (1893) and the Club's translation of Christian Ufer's *Pedagogics of Herbart* (1894). His most well known work, *Herbart and the Herbartians* (1895),was followed by other works on Herbartian pedagogy: *Language Lessons* (1897); *Outlines of Educational Doctrine* (1901); *Interest and Education* (1902); and *Principles of Secondary Education* (1907).

DeGarmo was interested in the training of teachers before he decided to pursue his studies in Germany. He believed "teaching teachers meant having children for them to teach ... because teaching was an action. Learned by doing it—at least in part."[46] In 1883 his views on the "The Importance of Model Schools to Normals [Schools]," were "given wide distribution in the influential journal, *Education*." In 1884, he urged the National Education Association to consider "The Place and Function of the Model School." "A model school was central to [DeGarmo's] every notion about pedagogical training and research."[47] Upon returning from Germany he applied Herbartian principles to upgrading teacher training. Westfall in his study of the adaptation of German ideas to the United States cites DeGarmo's "most Herbartian article as "The German System of Normal Schools," first delivered as a speech before the 1887 annual meeting of the National Education Association. Other publications and presentations followed including "What Constitutes Professional Work in the State Normal Schools" (1891); and "Co-ordination of the Normal School and the University in the Training of Teachers" (1892).[48] DeGarmo advocated teacher education within the context of or in connection with the university so that a laboratory or model school would be available for research on pedagogy and curriculum.

DeGarmo used Jena as a model and described in detail the practice school and its relationship to the university-based professor of pedagogy. Although the practice school had a headmaster who presided in the absence of the professor, the professor of pedagogy was "the real head of both seminary and practice school."[49] The work of the students in the pedagogical seminary was organized into three weekly meetings: The Practicum, The Theoretikum and The Conference. Each meeting had a different form and purpose. The Pratikum consisted of a model recitation performed by one of the student teachers of the practice school. The recitation, observed by each member of the seminary, was not an examination but "a typical illustration of the art of instruction."[50] Each member made notes on his observations and one member was usually appointed to prepare a written critique of the recitation. The Theoretikum was a meeting conducted by the professor in a university classroom. It was usually "devoted to the discussion and elucidation of such technical or special questions" that presented themselves during the week's work in the practice school.[51] DeGarmo who had spent some time at Jena while Stoy was still alive reported: "Many of these concern[ed] the principles of methods, the treatment of special difficulties in discipline, the mental condition of individual pupils; further, the examination of special books on methods, or school textbooks, and the laying out of programs of study."[52] Frequently, a student presented a written paper on an "assigned topic." The Conference occurred immediately after the Theoretikum. In DeGarmo's time at Jena the Theoretikum was held from 7:00 to 8:00 p.m. on Fridays. Upon its adjournment, the seminary moved to a nearby hotel where a room was held in reserve. DeGarmo provided a detailed description of the Conference:

> In Dr. Stoy's time, some twenty persons were usually assembled at that hour, seated about long tables arranged in the form of the capital letter T. Behind the cross-table at the head of the room sat Dr. Stoy upon the inevitable German sofa. The purpose of the Conference was to hear the reports of the

critics upon the recitations that had been conducted on the previous Wednesday at the Pratikum. After a few preliminaries the person who presented the model recitation read a written self-criticism of the effort, telling what he had tried to do, his methods of procedure, and his own judgment as to the degree of success he had obtained. This was followed immediately by the report of the appointed critic, who usually went into details, fortifying his conclusions by facts and arguments. As soon as the reading of this critique had been concluded, the person whose work was under examination replied to his critic, either acknowledging the justice of his criticisms, or showing reasons why he did not regard them as valid. At this point, the discussion was thrown open to students and teachers alike, each speaking upon whatever point seemed to him most worthy of comment. The Conference lasted until 11 o'clock, when it was closed by Professor Stoy himself with a masterly review of the whole discussion.[53]

According to DeGarmo, the seminary directed by Stoy and then Rein was "an organic part of the university" and received "a yearly stipend from the state" and constituted its unique and important feature.[54] DeGarmo was effectively arguing that American universities needed to support the study of education and the training of teachers.

Charles and Frank McMurry are reported to have been the first Americans to study with Rein.[55] Frank later reported that his encounter with Ufer's *Formalen Stufen* and Lange's *Apperception* led to his "educational conversion."[56] He was awarded a doctorate in Education from Jena in 1889. Like his brother and Charles DeGarmo, Frank McMurry's interest was in applying Herbartian principles to teaching. In 1898, he accepted a position at Teachers College, Columbia University. Frank McMurry is not recognized as one of the great theoreticians of the American Herbartian movement but was "regarded as perhaps the greatest classroom teacher of the Herbartian cadre."[57]

Upon returning from Germany, Charles McMurry like the others participated in creating an Herbartian movement in the United States by serving as secretary of the Herbart Club and as editor of its first three yearbooks. Like his brother and DeGarmo his chief interest was in the training of teachers and in applying Herbartian principles to the public school curriculum and instructional methods. His most significant work on the training of teachers was *Conflicting Principles in Education* (1919). Other works that demonstrate his interest in the work of the normal schools where most teachers were trained, if they received any training, were his contributions to the *Proceedings and Addresses* of the NEA: "Requirements for the Degree Doctor of Pedagogy" (1893) and "Influence of Herbart's Doctrine on the Course of Study in the Common School" (1895). Charles followed his brother Frank as principal of the University Practice Schools and as a model school teacher at the Illinois State

Normal University. In 1899, he took a position at the new normal school in DeKalb, Illinois where he remained until 1915 when he was appointed Professor of Elementary Education at the George Peabody School for Teachers. He published extensively on elementary school methods and the social studies curriculum. His most significant works were *Elements of General Method* (1892) and *The Method of Recitation* (1898) that he co-authored with is brother Frank.

THE HERBARTIAN WAVE

American Herbartianism got its start as a formal movement in 1892 and again in 1895, a half-century after Herbart's death. At the 1892 meeting of the National Education Association (NEA) in Saratoga, the meeting at which the Committee of Ten was appointed, Charles DeGarmo and the McMurry brothers founded the Herbart Club, an imitation of Tuiskon Ziller's *Verein für wissenschaftliche Pädagogik*. Its purpose was to show how Herbartianism could be applied to American schools. By the end of its first year the newly founded Club had 700 members.[58] In 1895 it was reorganized to emphasize the members' interest in the "scientific" study of education and given a new name, The National Herbart Society for the Scientific Study of Education. The members of the first executive council constituted a veritable "Who's Who in Education": DeGarmo, Nicholas Murray Butler, John Dewey. Wilbur S. Jackman, Elmer E. Brown, the McMurry brothers, Levi Seeley and C. C. Van Liew. By 1896, the National Herbart Society's membership was nearly a thousand. Most members were classroom teachers but "practically every noted educator in the country" was a member.[59] The society's first yearbooks were devoted to rigorous discussion of problems of interest to American Herbartians: interest, apperception, correlation, recitation methods, moral education, the culture epoch theory, training for citizenship, the social functions of history and geography and similar subjects. That not all members of the society were devoted to the application of Herbartianism to American schools was soon reflected in the society's yearbooks. The fourth yearbook was not totally devoted to Herbartian topics, and the main topic of the fifth was Fredrick Jackson Turner's newly announced "Frontier Thesis."

During this time, Herbartianism had good press. *School and Home Education* under the editorship of George P. Brown nearly became the official organ of the Herbartians in the 1890s. *The Educational Review*, edited by Nicholas Murray Butler, and A. E. Winship's *Journal of Education* were usually sympathetic to the Herbartians. Herbartian ideas spread quickly over the United States, particularly in the normal schools of the Upper Mississippi Valley where educators had been introduced to German philosophy and pedagogy by William Torrey Harris.[60] Methods of instruction in history and in literature and a new psychology were then being added to the course of study in the normal schools. New courses of study for training teachers were being worked out in which the elementary school subjects were divided into drill subjects, content subjects and motor-activity subjects. Educational discourse was then framed in Herbartian terms: apperception, correlation, social purpose, moral education, recitation methods and the five steps. From the normal schools these ideas spread rapidly to the better city school systems and soon found their way into the courses of study. Practice schools and the model lessons in dozens of normal schools were remodeled after the pattern of those the Herbartians found in Germany, particularly what they had seen at Halle, Jena, and Leipzig.

The Herbartian wave of the 1890s resembled the Pestalozzian wave of the 1860s. Each, for a time, furnished new ideas in education. Each reminded educators of the importance of instruction. Pestalozzianism contributed to the elementary school and Herbartianism to the secondary as well as the elementary school. Each influenced the training of teachers in the normal schools by giving instruction a new importance and by providing a new way to consider instruction. Each gradually settled down into its proper place in educational practice and history. For a decade Herbartian ideas and child study vied with each other for the place of first importance in educational thinking. Each eventually lost the spotlight to educational psychology, which incorporated much of the work of the workers in the child-study movement. Somehow educational psychology managed to hold on to first place. However, the Herbartians' rejection of the long-dominant faculty psychology did serve as a bridge to a new psychology, a psychology that was soon dominated by Edward L. Thorndike.

Initially, the American Herbartians undertook to explain to American educators the different principles enunciated by the German proponents of Herbart. They discussed the whole range of theories developed by Herbart, Stoy, Ziller and Rein. In the process they developed an American Herbartian pedagogy. In doing so, they soon adapted the terms and ideas they had learned in Germany to American conditions. They were more interested in developing a theory and practice of pedagogy than in fidelity to any creed. As an early student of the Herbartian movement in the United States observed: "The Americans who were first instrumental in introducing Herbartianism recognized that in Germany it was a collective term which included exponents of quite varied opinions." It did not, "find unquestioned acceptance without a change."[61] DeGarmo made his own view quite clear in the introduction to *Herbart and the Herbartians*. He was interested in Herbartianism and bold to recommend it to teachers, not as a set of metaphysical niceties but as offering "an intelligent answer" to the

problems posed by mass education: the need to order the schools purposes and methods in some consistent system.[62] Herbart, DeGarmo
claimed, more than any other, provided "a series of fine observations giving clearness and certainty to the procedure of instruction."[63] It was Herbart's psychology that was important for DeGarmo, for it provided a
rational defense for getting content to the center of the educational process. Herbart's psychology and his legitimatization of the necessity of
developing the student's interest—a factor crucial in dealing with mass
education—provided both a rationale for an educational revolution and
was capable of generating the classroom technique that DeGarmo took to
be the educational theorists' prime objective.[64] His first chapter posed
the question of "What Pestalozzi left for Herbart to do." The answer, the
weightiest chapter in the volume, was Herbart's psychology.[65] DeGarmo
focused on the practice school that came to be the center both of the educational theorist's activity and the regimen for preparing teachers.

Herbartian Pedagogy in the United States

In Herbart the Herbartians found hints for what they soon elaborated
as the culture epoch theory. The culture epoch theory held that the civil
and religious history of a people was characterized by a succession of ever-
more complex and sophisticated periods that were distinguishable from
one another and that the study of children revealed a parallel development. The theory essentially held that history is a record of progress from
the primitive to the civilized state and that individual abilities, mental as
well as physical, progress from the simple to the complex. As children
grew, their interests and abilities were analogous to those their people
passed through as they progressed from early savagery to their present
highly civilized state. Herbartians believed the relationship between the
historical periods and the developmental stages of the individual called
for a curriculum that included ordered historical content that would
interest children as they grew from one stage to the next.

At the center of the Herbartian pedagogy were the five formal steps
that Americans learned from Rein. Herbart had identified four factors in
thinking: clearness, association, system, and method. Clearness entailed
analysis and comprehension of every fact. Association was the process of
connecting newly presented facts with each other and with previous
knowledge. System entailed the arrangement of ideas into a logical or
coherent system. Method was the process of applying the newly acquired
material. Rein elaborated these into five steps[66] that teachers were taught
to follow in preparing and presenting their lessons: Preparation,
Presentation, Association (sometimes called Comparison and

Abstraction[67]), Generalization and Application. Teachers were to "prepare" students for new lessons by reminding them of what they already knew. Sometimes this is called review, and it is a practice that has endured in classrooms and in textbooks. After being prepared, students were to be "presented" with new material, material that would be added to that already known, to that which had just been brought up to their consciousness. Thus, the first two steps were devoted to the presenting and assembling of new materials or facts. After the new material was presented, the teacher was to show how the old and new were "associated" with each other and how they were related to another fact or principle. Once the association was made, it was possible to create a "generalization." Thus, the third and fourth steps were devoted to establishing generalizations. Finally, the generalization was "applied' to explain further principles or facts. DeGarmo's estimation of the steps was clear. He claimed that educators were "indebted to Herbart, perhaps more than to any other man, for a series of fine observations giving clearness and certainty to the procedure of instruction."[67] Prospective teachers were taught that these steps were to be followed in order and were appropriate for all subjects.[69] For example, the McMurry brothers claimed that the five steps constituted the right order of instruction and were to be applied to all school subjects:

> If the leading thoughts thus far presented are true, there are certain steps in instruction that are universal. No matter what the study be, whether Latin, mathematics, science, or some other, there is a certain order that the mind must follow in acquiring knowledge. Through the old related experiences (first step, preparation) new individual notions are reached (second step), presentation); these are compared and their essential characteristics abstracted (third step, comparison), and the resulting general truth is worded (forth step, generalization); this generalization finally receives application (fifth step, application). Since these steps are passed through in this order without reference to the nature of the subject-matter presented, they are rightly called the Formal Steps of Instruction. They indicate the order of the movements of the mind, or of the forms through which thought must pass in reaching full maturity.[70]

As William Chandler Bagley reported in 1911, "institutions for the training of teachers have come to lay strong emphasis upon the well-known 'formal steps' of development."[70] In time some debated whether these five steps constituted an account of how children learned or were only the instructional regimen that teachers were to follow. Instruction was important to Herbart and to the Herbartians because it was what teachers could control. Through instruction mind could be filed or built with content, for mind was its contents. Mind's contents were important because they believed that mind was what controlled behavior.

The Herbartian Wave faded quickly. By 1899 the Herbartian Society had perished. In 1902 it was reorganized as the National Society for the Scientific Study of Education. Harold Dunkel concluded: "As a theoretical movement producing publications, speeches, and general excitement, American Herbartianism was dead by 1905."[72] However, its direct influence on teachers and their practice seems to have lasted at least into the 1920s.[73] Herbartian ideas exercised a significant influence on the American curriculum long after the movement faded and lost its vitality.

Herbartian thought enabled Americans to organize the newly developing field of education. The Herbartians were among the first to mark off the modern field of education and to identify the component parts of pedagogy and curriculum opening up the possibility of studying each in relationship to teaching and learning.

The Focus on Schools

Those who came to be known as Herbartians, German and American, did not overlook the seminar Herbart established at Königsberg. It was the existence of the school, not the precise activities that occurred there that became important to the Herbartians. According to Harold Dunkel:

> ... the Herbartians, of whatever kind, will pay relatively little attention to the procedures of the pedagogical seminar except to use the existence of the seminar as proof that the master was no mere cloistered theorists but actually a practical and practicing pedagogue. Beyond performing this function, the work of Herbart's seminar will be of slight use or interest to the Herbartians.[74]

Subsequently, nearly all Herbartians agreed that some sort of school was necessary for the study of education, the training of teachers or both. Pedagogy, Herbartians believed, had a theoretical and a practical side. However, their attempts to establish schools for the study and practice of pedagogy were frequently confusing and not always successful.

During the nineteenth century, many universities maintained academies where applicants to the university were sent to complete their preparation for admission to the university. At the end of the nineteenth century and during the early years of the twentieth century, when high schools were improved, became standardized and conformed to standards set by regional accrediting agencies that the universities supported and accepted, the academies seemed to many, no longer necessary. However, at the same time, universities were beginning to, or had just begun, to pay more attention to education as a field of study, and professors of education frequently desired to use and maintain the academies as their laboratories or practice schools. A laboratory was then seen as essential for scientific inquiry, and educators often aware of developments in psychology wanted to create a science of education. Some saw the academies already attached to or part of the university as a school that could easily be used as a laboratory. When the professors of education indicated how they would make use of the academies, they used many terms and specified many specialized functions. Consequently, laboratory school, practice school, model school, demonstration school and experimental school sometimes had distinctive meanings and sometimes meant the same thing.[75] Often the academy was seen as a venue for the training of teachers, a responsibility some in the university were beginning to assume.

There was a time when there was a choice. Either education could be studied directly or it could be studied indirectly through psychology, history and philosophy. The decisions made within the university typically did not favor the direct study of education. Many professors objected to any activity on the campus that was not truly university work. Education was placed on a psychological foundation, and psychology already had, so it seemed its laboratories and experimental methods.

In Herbart and especially in their Herbartian teachers, American Herbartians found justification for their conviction that teaching was a process worthy of deliberate and sustained investigation. They wanted to study teaching. In Herbartianism, there was a model and a justification for what they wanted to do. In Herbart there was a rationale for that. Herbart had conducted a school, and "Herbartian theory had the further advantage of being developed from the outset in contact with children."[76] The study of education in the universities was not developed along the lines the Herbartians advocated. Professors of education had difficulty establishing or maintaining their practice schools. Eventually, most had only the public schools to use as practice schools for those who wanted to be teachers. The model the Herbartians would have had established was not the one adopted. Professors of education had little or no control over what occurred in the classrooms of the public school. Consequently their views on the training of teachers and on educational research were limited by what public school officials could or would allow.

CONCLUSIONS: HERBART VERSUS HERBARTIANS

By the early 1890s Herbartism was of sufficient interest in the United States that it merited a 145-item "Bibliography of Herbartianism" in the 1892-93 *Report* of the United States Commissioner of Education. The

Herbartians, like Herbart, may belong to the past, but the issues they raised, defined and addressed endure. Herbart did effectively show, as Dewey observed, that education could be conceived of as an activity worthy of study, and Herbart's successors built upon what he accomplished. There are, however, differences between Herbart and the Herbartians. To consider the differences is to consider the difference between education and schooling, the difference between education as an individual process and education as a social-political process, to the difference between creating a moral human, the process whereby one acquires those qualities that define one as human, and the means whereby citizens are created for the modern nation-state. How to educate a person and how to manage schooling are different processes. Herbartians were very much committed to schooling and to creating good citizens. Public schools are political institutions, for their purposes are largely defined and assigned by the state.

The American Herbartians, especially Charles DeGarmo and the brothers McMurry, Charles and Frank, were interested in teaching, in how to prepare teachers so they would be effective in the classroom.[77] DeGarmo was quite cognizant of the status of universal compulsory schooling in the United States. In his contribution to the first yearbook of the Herbart Society (1895), DeGarmo noted that the commitment to universal schooling began forty or fifty years earlier. During that half century, he explained, "it is not to be wondered at that our chief efforts in the past have been directed to the perfection of the external machinery necessary for its successful prosecution." Now, he indicated, "One of the problems that has already forced itself upon us, is therefore: What shall the public school teach?" The American Herbartians were now asking researchable questions about curriculum and instruction as part of a national agenda.[78]

The utility the Herbartians found in Herbart seemed neither to require nor to inspire strict adherence to the principles and purpose he had articulated. Herbart's framework, views, and methods were appropriated for applications to problems and purposes different from those Herbart addressed. That he created a system that could so easily be sacked may have been one of his chief contributions. American Herbartians were typically interested in how to conduct the process of schooling for what was then the still-developing modern industrial nation state. Even in Germany educators were interested in using Herbart's work to address their own interests and problems. As the following report from L. R. Klemm indicates, Herbartians used Herbart to organize their discussions even when they did not accept Herbart:

I asked Dr. Otto Frick, the director of the "Francke Stiftungen," to what extent Herbart's principles and Ziller's interpretations were adopted in the different schools of the "Stiftungen." He replied: "We have absolutely no compulsion with regard to the methods of teaching. I am not autocratically inclined, and like to leave to each teacher the choice of methods. Of course, I advocate Herbart, and in our own teachers' methods we discuss his works thoroughly. His ideas have found their way into our schools with the impressibility of truth. There is still opposition among my numerous teachers against Herbart, and that will perhaps not end so long as there exists a peg to hang an argument on; but, while I am happy to say Herbart is gaining ground, I am rejoiced also in noticing that the wholesome opposition (which, of course, never turns into hostility) acts like a clarifying element in the Herbart camp.[79]

"There are good grounds for suggesting that Herbart's educational theory was largely independent of his metaphysics and his psychology, or at least can be treated as if it were," as Dunkel concluded.[80] That independence is what made Herbart the originator of the modern science of education. Herbart's successors—the Herbartians—were able to adopt his educational views without paying any metaphysical tribute.

NOTES

1. Gert J. J. Biesta and Nicholas C. Burbules. *Pragmatism and Educational Research* (Lanham, Maryland: Rowman & Littlefield, 2003), p. 1.

2. John Dewey. *Democracy and Education* (New York: The Macmillan Co., 1916), p. 83.

3. Quoted in Charles DeGarmo. *Herbart and the Herbartians* (New York: Charles Scribner's Sons, 1895), p. 181.

4. Dewey. *Democracy and Education*, p. 83.

5. Percival R. Cole. "Herbart" in Paul Monore (ed.). *Cyclopedia of Education*, Vol. 3 (New York: The Macmillan Co., 1909), p. 253. Cole had earlier completed a doctoral dissertation, half of which was devoted to Herbart: *Herbart and Froebel: an Attempt at Synthesis*. Columbia University Contributions to Education, Teachers College Series No. 14 (New York: Teachers College, Columbia University, 1907).

6. Harold Dunkel. *Herbart and Herbartianism: An Educational Ghost Story* (Chicago: University of Chicago Press, 1979). p. 140.

7. Herbart's letters to Herr von Steiger were translated by H. M. and E. Felkin in *Letters and Lectures on Education* (London, 1894).

8. H. M. Knox. "The Progressive Development of J. F. Herbart's Educational Thought." *British Journal of Educational Studies*, Vol. XXIII, No. 3 (October 1975), p. 275.

9. He wrote *Idee zu einem pädagogischen Lehrplan für höhere Studien* (1801) as well as critiques of Pestalozzi's *Wie Gertud ihre Kinder lehrt* (*How Gertrude*

Teaches Her Children) (1802) and Pestalozzi's *Idee eines ABC der Anschauung* (*Idea of an ABC of Sense Perception*) (1802).

10. The educational works he completed at Königsberg included: *Erziehung unter öffentlicher Mitwirkung* (1810); *Über die dunkel seite der Pädagogik* (1812); *Das Verhaltniss der Schule zum Leben* (1818); *Briefe über Anwendungen der Psychologie und die Pädagogik* (1831); and *Das Verhaltniss des Idealismus zur Pädagogik* (1831). The works on psychology that supported his educational notions included: *Psychologschen Bemerkungen zur Tonlehre* (1811) and *Psychologisch Untersuchung über die Starke einer gegenbeneu Vorstellung als Funktion ihrer Dauer Betrachtet.* His most important psychological work, *Psychologie als Wissenschaft neu gegrundet auf Erfarhung, Metaphysic, und Mathematick (Manual of Psychology as Science, Founded According to a New Metod on Experience, Metaphysics and Mathematics)* appeared in two parts (1824 and 1825), although it was actually completed about a decade earlier. As a text for those who attended his lectures, he prepared *Lehrbuch zur Psychologie.*

11. Quoted in "Translators' introduction" in Johann Friedrich Herbart. *The Science of Education: Its General Principles Deduced from its aims and the Aesthetic Revelation of the World* tr. Henry M. and Emmie Felkin (Boston: D. C. Heath and Co., 1896), p. 17.

12. Friedrich Bartholomai. Johann Friedrich Herbart's Leben in E. Von Sallwürk (ed.). *J. F. Herbarts pädagogische Schriften*, 7th ed. (Langensalze: H. Beyer und Söhne, 1903), p. 78 quoted in Ursula Stendel Hendon. Herbart's Concept of Morality in Education and Its Role in America, Ph. D. Dissertation, University of Alabama, 1980, p. 34.

13. Harold Dunkel. *Herbart and Herbartianism: An Educational Ghost Story* (Chicago: University of Chicago, 1970), pp, 66-72.

14. After his return to Göttingen, Herbart completed *Umriss pädagogischer Vorlesungen (Outlines of Educational Doctrine)* (1835) and *Umriss der allgemeinen Pädagogik* (1841); *Ideen zu einem pädagogischen Lehrplan fur höhre Studien* (1801),; *Umriss der allgemeinen Pädagogik* (1841); and eleven others: *Wie Getrud iher Kinder lehrt* (1801), *Idee eines A B C der Anschauung* (1802), *Die aestheische Darstellung der Welt als das Haupgeschaft der Erziehung* (1804), *Standpunkt der Beurteilung der Pestalozzischen Unterrichtsmethode* (1804), *Allgemeine Pädagogik* (1806), *Erziehung unter offentlicher Mitwirkung* (1810), *Über die dunkel Seite der Pädagogik* (1812), *Das Verhaltniss der Schule zum Leben (1818)*, *Briefe uber Anwendung der Psychologie auf die Pädagogik* (1813), *Das Verhaltniss des Idealismus zur Pädagogik* (1831), *Das Verhaltniss des Idealismus zur Pädagogik* (1831) and *Umriss pädagogischer Vorlesungen* (1835).

15. Knox. "The Progressive Development of J. F. Herbart's Educational Thought," p. 266.

16. Even as a teenager, Herbart was interested in morality, having written an essay, "Commonest Causes that Affect the Growth and Decay of Morality in the various States." See: Adolphe E. Meyer. *Am Educational History of the Western World* (New York: McGraw-Hill. 1965), p. 359.

17. Dunkel. *Herbart and Herbartianism*, p. 286.

18. *Ibid.*, p. 154.

19. A. E. Winship. "The Herbartian System," *Journal of Education*, Vol. XXVIII, No. 7 (August 23, 1888), p. 128.

20.   Johann Karl Friedrich Rosenkranz was a German Hegelian philosopher, whose one book on the philosophy of education, *Pädagogik als System: Ein Grundiss* (1848) was introduced to American readers in translation by Anna C. Brackett in William Torrey Harris' *Journal of Speculative Philosophy* (1872-74). Harris edited Brackett's translation for Appleton's International Education series in 1886 under the title *The Philosophy of Education*. In 1833 he was called to Königsberg to succeed Herbart to the chair of philosophy and pedagogy.

21.   Harold Dunkel. *Herbart and Education* (New York: Random House, 1969), p. 65. Also see *Herbart and Herbartianism*, pp. 30, 83-84, 98, 151 and 159-160.

22.   Dunkel. *Herbart and the Herbartians*, pp. 180, 183-194.

23.   *Ibid.*, p. 151.

24.   John Dewey. *The Child and the Curriculum* [1902] in *The School and Society and The Child and the Curriculum* ed. Philip W. Jackson (Chicago: University of Chicago Press, 1990, pp. 189-190.

25.   See: F. Bartholomai und Schwabe. "Der Vorstellungskreis der Berliner Kinder beim Eintritt in die Schule," *Berlin Statistisches Jarhbuch*, 1870. G. Stanley Hall's "The Contents of the Children's Mind," *Princeton Review* (1883) was modeled after the Berlin study.

26.   *The National Herbart Society Yearbooks 1-5* (New York: Arno Press and New York Times, 1969), pp. 1-26.

27.   Alfred Binet was another who earlier claimed that laboratories and schools were necessary for observation and that careful observation of the results of experimental pedagogy were essential. See: Linda Jarvin and Robert J. Sternberg. "Alfred Binet's Contribution to Educational Psychology" in Barry J. Zimmerman and Dale H. Schunk (eds.). *Educational Psychology: A Century of Contributions* (Mahwah, New Jersey: Lawrence Erlbaum Associates, 2003), p. 68.

28.   Dewey. *Democracy and Education*, p. 384.

29.   Dunkel. *Herbart and Education*, p. 97.

30.   William James. *Talks to Teachers on Psychology* (New York: W. W. Norton and Co., 1958), pp. 23-24.

31.   *Ibid.*, p. 24.

32.   Quoted in Dunkel. *Herbart and the Herbartians*, p. 154.

33.   A sketch of Herbart's pedagogy—"Herbart's Ideas on Education"—by Karl Schmidt appeared in William Torrey Harris' *Journal of Speculative Philosophy*, Vol. 10 (April 1876).

34.   Charles DeGarmo. *Herbart and the Herbartians* (New York: Charles Scribner's Sons, 1895). p. 104.

35.   L. R. Klemm. *European Schools, or What I Saw in the Schools of German, France, Austria and Switzerland* (New York: D. Appleton and Co., 1897), p. 185.

36.   Klemm. *European Schools*; Laszo Felkai. "The Influence of Herbart's and Ziiller's Theory in Hungary" in Sandor Komlosi (ed.). *Conference Papers for the 9th Session of the International Standing Conference for the History of Education: History of International Relations*. Vol. 1 (Pecs, Hungary: Jannus Pannonous University, 1987), pp. 159-168.

37. Early in the twentieth century, Alexander Darroch, Lecturer on Educational Method and Psychology in the Church of Scotland Training College, Edinburgh related that while Herbartianism was neither as severe nor as extensive in his country as it was in the United States, it had nonetheless "found a footing." Herbartian theory, he acknowledged, "underlies a good deal of our educational thought, and pervades a good deal of our educational literature." See: *Herbart and the Herbartian Theory of Education: A Criticism* (London: Longmans, Green and Co., 1903), pp. 1-2.

38. Klemm. *European Schools*, p. 192.

39. The practice school that Herbart had organized at Königsberg was abandoned by the authorities when he returned to Göttingen in 1833. However, Brzoska remained committed to the necessity of a practice school. In 1836 he published *Die Notwendigkeit pädaagogischer Seminare auf der Universität und ihre zweckmässige Einrichtung (The Necessity of Pedagogical Seminaries in Universities).*

40. Dorothy McMurry. *Herbartian Contributions to History Instruction in American Elementary Schools.* Columbia University Contributions to Education, Teachers College Series, *No. 920* (New York: Bureau of Publications, Teachers College, Columbia University, 1946), p. 40.

41. George Basis Randels. "The Doctrines of Herbart in the United States." A Ph.D. thesis presented to the Graduate School of the University of Pennsylvania, 1911, p. 17; Barry H. Westfall. "German Educational Thought Adapted to American Schools: Herbartian Influence on American Teacher Education Through Selected Publications of Charles DeGarmo, and Charles and Frank McMurry." Ph. Dissertation, Northern Illinois University. 1987, p. 15.

42. In the 1880s and 1890s, many of the Americans who went to study in Europe, especially Germany, would later form "the nucleus of the Herbart Club" (that became the National Herbart Society in 1895) in 1892 at Saratoga. They included: "Nicholas Murray Butler, who attended Berlin and Paris in 1884-1885; Charles DeGarmo, who received the degree of doctor of philosophy from Halle in 1886; Levi Seeley, Leipzig, 1886; Charles McMurry who received his doctorate from Halle in 1887; Frank McMurry, Ph.D., Jena, 1889; Elmer Ellsworth Brown, Halle-Wittenberg, 1889; Herman T. Luckens, Jena, 1891; C. C. Van Liew, Ph.D. Jena, 1893; John Hall, Jena, 1892-1895; and James E. Russell, Ph.D. Leipzig, 1894, and student at Jena, Leipzig, and Berlin, 1893-1895. See: Clinton R. Prewett. "The Development of the Unit method of Teaching from the Herbartian Movement to the Present." Ph. D. Dissertation, University of North Carolina at Chapel Hill, 1950, p. 157.

43. Dunkel. *Herbart and Herbartianism*, p. 247.

44. *Ibid.*

45. Henry C. Johnson and Erwin V. Johanningmeier. *Teachers for the Prairie: The University of Illinois and the Schools, 1868-1945* (Urbana, Illinois: University of Illinois Press, 1972), pp. 68-69.

46. *Ibid.*, p. 72; Erwin V. Johanningmeier and Henry C. Johnson. "Charles DeGarmo, Where Are You—Now That We Need You? *Philosophy of Education 1969: Proceedings of the Twenty-fifth Annual Meeting of the Philosophy of Education Society* (Carbondale, Illinois, 1969), pp. 190-199.

47. Johnson and Johanningmeier. *Teachers for the Prairie*, pp. 72-73.

48. Westfall. "German Educational Thought Adapted to American Schools," pp. 20-21.
49. *Ibid.*, p. 181.
50. *Ibid.*
51. *Ibid.*, p. 182.
52. *Ibid.*, p. 181.
53. *Ibid.*, pp. 182-183.
54. DeGarmo. *Herbart and the Herbartians*, p. 181.
55. Westfall. "German Educational Thought Adapted to American Schools," p. 77.
56. *Ibid.*
57. Johnson and Johanningmeier, *Teachers for the Prairie*, p. 75.
58. Westfall. "German Educational Thought Adapted to American Schools," p. 80.
59. *Ibid.*, p. 16. Westfall's source for this claim is an unpublished paper by Henry Hugh Edmunds, "The History of the Herbartian Movement in the United States" (1929) located in the Archives of the Illinois State University in Bloomington.
60. While William Torrey Harris was certainly no supporter of either Herbart or Herbartianism and cannot be assigned responsibility for the Herbartian wave, he did publish some of Herbart's works in his *Journal of Speculative Philosophy* before Herbartianism gained its popularity in the United States. In 1874, Harris published a selection from Herbart's *Rational Psychology* translated by Hugo Haanel. In 1877 he published Haanel's translation of Herbart's "Possibility and Necessity of Applying Mathematics in Psychology." In 1876, "Herbart's Ideas on Education"—Haanel's translation of a selection from Karl Schmidt's *Geschichte der Pädagogik*—appeared in Harris' journal.
61. Randels. "Doctrines of Herbart," p. 5.
62. DeGarmo. *Herbart and the Herbartians*, pp. v and 215.
63. *Ibid.*, pp. 74-75.
64. *Ibid.*, pp. 209, 225, 235.
65. *Ibid.*, pp. 23-56.
66. Many have incorrectly attributed the five Herbartian steps to Herbart. For example, in *How We Think* (Boston: D. C. Heath & Co. Publishers, 1910) John Dewey discussed "the analysis by Herbart of a recitation into five successive steps." p. 202.
67. See, for example: Boyd Henry Bode. *How We Learn* (Boston: D. C. Heath and Co., 1940), p. 148.
68. DeGarmo. *Herbart and the Herbartians*, pp. 74-75. For DeGarmo's description of Herbart's four steps, see pp. 79-81.
69. *Ibid.*, p. 149.
70. Charles A. McMurry and Frank M. McMurry. *The Method of the Recitation* (New York: The Macmillan Co., 1987), p. 288.
71. William Chandler Bagley. *Educational Values* (New York: The Macmillan Co., 1911), pp. 50-51.

72. Harold Dunkel. *Herbart and Education*, p. 123. Also see Dunkel's *Herbart and Herbartianism*, pp. 277-278.

73. Paul Monroe. *A Brief Course in the History of Education* (New York: The Macmillan Co., 1927), p. 345.

74. Harold Dunkel. *Herbart and Herbartianism*, p. 194.

75. One of the clearest statements on how such academies could be used by professors of education remains unpublished. It was written in 1909 by Charles M. McConn, the principal of the Academy at the University of Illinois. For a discussion of the distinctions McConn made and citations to other relevant literature see: Johnson, Jr. and Johanningmeier. *Teachers for the Prairie*, pp. 164-175.

76. Randels. "Doctrines of Herbart," p. 23.

77. It has been observed that when one considers the "quantity of materials published" on Herbartianism, the "length of time" they participated in the Herbartian movement, and their leadership positions, Charles DeGarmo, Charles McMurry and Frank McMurry "were the most active in the movement." See: Westfall. "German Educational Thought Adapted to American Schools, p. 4.

78. Charles DeGarmo. "Most Pressing Problems: Concerning the Elementary Course of Study" in Charles A. Mcurry (ed.) *The First Yearbook of the Herbart Society for the Scientific Study of Teaching* [1895] (New York: Arno Press and the New York Times, 1969), pp.3-4.

79. Klemm. *European Schools*, p. 193.

80. Dunkel. *Herbart and Education*, p. 97.

CHAPTER 6

DARWINISM IN
THE UNITED STATES

In order for a systematic approach to research on education to develop in
the Progressive Era, there had to be three extenuating circumstances.
First, the invention of the object of attention, the school, which we saw
evolved out of the Common School Movement of the early and mid-
nineteenth century and experienced increased enrollments in the
Progressive Era. Second, the school had to be identified as an object of
study, a process begun with Johann Friedrich Herbart's theories of
education and completed by his followers the Herbartians. Herbart and
the Herbartians also began to outline a method of inquiry based in
observation in controlled settings in model and laboratory schools. While
Herbart and Herbartianism moved away from metaphysical speculation, a
scientific approach to obtaining data and its analysis had to become
legitimated on a broad scale. Third, the popularity and controversies
surrounding British naturalist Charles Robert Darwin (1809-1882), the
world's first evolutionary biologist, set the stage for a new epoch in
academic inquiry that was especially influential in the United States. This
chapter examines the influence of Darwinism as a foundation of
educational research methods.

Educational Research, the National Agenda, and Educational Reform:
A History, pp. 153–173
Copyright © 2008 by Information Age Publishing
All rights of reproduction in any form reserved.

THE IMPACT OF DARWIN ON SCIENTIFIC METHODS OF INQUIRY

Darwin studied medicine at Edinburgh but found it unsuitable and left to study theology at Cambridge (Christ's Church) where he took up an interest in zoology and geography due to an association with a biology professor John Stevens Henslow. Henslow recommended Darwin for a position as a naturalist and gentleman's companion to Captain Robert FitzRoy of the HMS Beagle on a voyage to chart the coast of South America. This fortuitous circumstance set Darwin off on a five-year (1831-1836) adventure; launched his career as a scientist; created a hands on environment that evoked his theory of evolution; made him popular, famous, and controversial. The attention attracted by his journal of the voyage published as *Zoology of the Voyage of the HMS Beagle* (1839, 1843) in five volumes, and *The Origin of the Species By Means of Natural Selection or The Preservation of Favoured Races in the Struggle for Life* (1859), not only catapulted a scientific and popular debate over the ideas put forth but also legitimated Darwin's approach to proving what was true and untrue in the orderly fashion and method of inquiry that he popularized, which we now call the scientific method.

It was not just the idea of natural selection or survival of the fittest that was unique to Darwin's contribution to his times. Alfred Russell Wallace came up with similar ideas in a contemporary essay. Wallace and Darwin were scheduled to do a joint presentation on June 18, 1858. That encouraged each to publish his material in spite of the fact that the ideas faced a furiously critical scientific community. Darwin had been struggling with finding credible ways to present his ideas to his colleagues. While Wallace and Darwin's theories came out at the same time, it was Darwin whose name and work attracted both positive and negative attention at the time and historically. It is not surprising that theories that directly questioned Bibical explanations of the origins of the earth's geography, plants, animals, and humankind created heated opposition. Without concrete specific evidence the version of creation in the King James Bible described in Genesis held sway even for well-educated populations. The difference with Darwin was that his evidence was difficult to refute or ignore.

The Darwinian Approach to Scientific Research

The Beagle's voyage presented Darwin with a massive interlocking data set, of which he took full advantage. He spent five years, two-thirds of it on land, daily, hourly scrutinizing every variation that he observed in geological features, fossils, and living organisms both plant and animal along the

South American coast that revealed millions of years of slow, continuous change. He collected extensive specimens and produced extensive detailed sketches and recorded them and his observations in his journal. In keeping with the scientific method, Darwin conducted careful, disciplined, logical research by observing and examining the best possible evidence he could find, evaluating and comparing each piece of information for its validity and usefulness. Through the variations he observed from an overwhelming array of sources, he concluded that the earth and all that is on it could not have been created whole in a short time. He wrote in the *Origin of the Species*: "I have called this principle, by which each slight variation, if useful, is preserved by the term Natural Selection."

The methods Darwin brought before the popular public and academy were not new but he demonstrated that systematic investigation could be used to study any aspect of the universe to uncover new knowledge. It concretely demonstrated that arguments alone in metaphysics could not determine whether a statement is correct. Proof is required. First and foremost, research that produces proof is based on careful observation or experimentation. Second, a hypothesis is formed explaining what has been observed. Third, the hypothesis is used to predict what should be observed under similar circumstances. The hypothesis is tested and, if warranted by new or additional evidence modified. Fourth, when there are no discrepancies between the hypothesis and the observation and consistency is obtained, the hypothesis becomes a theory, or a law of nature, a coherent set of propositions that explain a class of observed phenomenon. Theories or laws of nature provide a framework within which observations are explained and predictions made.

The advantage of the scientific method is that it is unprejudiced. Skeptics can reproduce the data irrespective of their belief system. Theories are not based on the prestige or power of the investigator but on the results obtained through the method. Further, theories so derived have to be repeatable and falsifiable. Theories can be shown to be untrue by the introduction of new evidence. Darwin found evidence that the earth and everything on it was produced by blind, automatic, natural causes. Darwin's ideas of natural and sexual selection in his theory of evolution, and that species develop over time from a common origin, had huge implications for many areas in social thought unrelated to the natural sciences. Like Herbart's, Darwin's ideas took on a trajectory of their own when translated into philosophy and the social and behavioral sciences such as anthropology, psychology, and education. Darwin's theories and writing in combination with Gregor Mendel's genetics created the so-called "modern synthesis," which is the basis for modern biology. However, the fame and popularity of Darwin's name became associated with ideas and

popular movements that had no direct relation to his writings and sometimes even contradicted his views.

The Eugenics Movement, for example, was based on Darwin's cousin,
Francis Galton's publication, *Hereditary Genius*, which argued that
human talent and genius were inherited (1869) and Darwin's own work.
Neither advocated intervention by any state or government agency
much less the compulsory sterilization campaigns pursued in the
United States and the Holocaust pursued by the Nazis in Germany to
eliminate those deemed less desirable. The Social Darwinism Movement combined the population studies of Thomas Malthus, *An Essay on
the Principle of Population* (1826) and Herbert Spencer's application of
evolution to society, nations, and other human populations in the late
nineteenth and early twentieth centuries. Social Darwinism supported
contradictory ideological perspectives such as *laissez faire* economics,
colonialism, racism, and imperialism. These perspectives actually predate *The Origin of the Species* (1859). Malthus, for example, died in 1834
and Spencer published his major works on economics in 1851 and on
evolution in 1855. These applications of unscientific perspectives for
social purposes represent a pseudo science used for political purposes
to drive an agenda that is neither objective nor disinterested science.
They did, however, have an influence on educational research and the
effort to make it scientific.

CONTROVERSY OVER THE IMPLICATIONS OF NATURAL SELECTION

Just as Copernicus and then Newton required some to adjust their
worldviews into harmony with the new theories, and allowed still others
to use the new theories to "support their own views on subjects quite
remote from science" so did Darwinism. Here it is necessary to distinguish between what Darwinism meant to practitioners in the social and
behavioral sciences as well as the biological sciences and what it meant
to "those [for example, Herbert Spencer and William Graham Sumner]
who wished to defend the political status quo, above all the *laissez-faire*
conservatives" who came to be known as Social Darwinists. As Charles
Coulston Gillispie observed, Social Darwinism may be defined "as the
re-exportation into social science of a language quite speciously forti-
fied with the deterministic vigor of natural science—opinions converted into truths through having traversed science."[1] Here the focus is
less on the "Social Darwinists" or "Social Darwinism" and more on how
"Darwinism established a new approach to nature and gave fresh impe-
tus to the conception of development."[2]

Darwinism in the United States

To explore Darwinism in the United States is to explore a controversy that was remarkably timely, remarkably intense, and perhaps remarkably short-lived. Its outcome, however, was decisive. It transformed how scholars and scientists conceived of humankind and how they conducted their inquiries. Darwin's *Origin of Species* arrived in the United States on the eve of the Civil War. It received immediate attention but was not fully accepted in the American academy until after Appomattox. After Appomattox, Darwin was even more difficult to ignore. In 1869 the American Philosophical Society recognized Darwin by granting him honorary membership in its society.

After Appomattox, Darwin's theory of evolution had to be recognized in one way or another. By then the majority of American scientists had accepted evolution, for those "committed to empirical methods of argument" had to acknowledge the "massive empirical compilation of evidence" that Darwin presented in the *Origin*.[3] For the Social Darwinists the notion of natural selection meant for some that the strong or society in general had no responsibility for those perceived as weak or somehow deficient or defective. However, for those interested in human growth and development the observation that the characteristics of human infants differed greatly from those of animals was noted and seen as significant. The prolonged dependence of human infants, as compared to other animals, made that dependent period especially important. As Alexander Francis Chamberlain observed, "The whole period of growth in man, adolescence (if we interpret the term literally), seems to form a considerably larger portion of this life than the corresponding epoch in the existence of other mammals."[4]

While it was perhaps all but inevitable that it would be claimed that the characteristics and abilities a child displayed at the end of the period of dependency was due to heredity and that others would assign more power to the environment, there was no denying that experience was important. While there was and continues to be some debate about the relative importance of nature as opposed to nurture, there was no denying that how children interacted with their environment and that the nature of their environment—how it was furnished—was important. The environment was, in principle, capable of being controlled and studied. How a subject related to or interacted with its environment could also be an object of inquiry. Social reformers and those concerned with the health and stability of society saw that infancy and its relatively prolonged dependency, created the family as a necessity. Humankind was seen as having a function or ability commonly known as a mind that, if properly nurtured, would appear and function at the appropriate time. Child growth, both physical and mental, was an evolutionary process. Growth was not instantaneous. It was a process that occurred through time. The time at which changes appeared to begin and to end could be observed and recorded. Those observations or records came to designate the beginning and the end of stages, and each stage was seen to be characterized by abilities and capacities not seen in earlier stages.

In the *Descent of Man and Selection in Relation to Sex* (1871) Darwin made explicit what was not so explicit in the *Origin*. There it was made clear that humankind was no longer exempted from nature's laws. After Darwin the scientists' methods and assumptions changed. In the *Origin*, "Darwin had presented to the world one of the first examples of the long, tightly reasoned hypothetical method that has come to be characteristic of modern science."[5] Even more important than the changes in the scientists' methods were the changes in how scientists defined the purposes and the objects of their inquiries. Certainty gave way to probability. Permanence gave way to change. Darwin recognized and did not deny the importance of chance and novelty. Subsequently, investigators had to accept the ever-present possibility of chance. Eventually, they would develop ways to estimate the probability that events and relationships were either chance events or chance relationships.

The Acceptance of Darwin

According to Bert James Lowenberg, the Darwinian controversy can be divided into two nearly equal periods. The first began in 1859 and ended in 1880. While the first stage was marked by "acrid polemics," its "real significance" was "the conversion of men of science."[6] The second stage ended at the turn of the century. According to Lowenberg:

> It was characterized by the influx of testimony and the infiltration of evolutionism into every division of scholarship, but it was also distinguished by the popularization of evolution and the fact of its acceptance. A profusion of books inducted neophytes into biological sanctums and explained evolution in language unadorned by technicalities. Periodicals multiplied and expanded, offering readers expert synopses as well as generalized discussions. Numerous public speakers, liberal, conservative, and radical; clerical, scientific, and lay broadcast Darwin's message within reach of every literature stratum. Evolution took its place in the universities, and scientists aired its implications from the rostrum. Denominational journals conveyed Darwinism to the clergy who, in turn, carried it into church and vestry, while theologians brought science into the classrooms of the seminary. The linotype, the library, and the mansions of learning united to produce a basic uniformity and a milieu favorable to acceptance. The endorsement of the

educated when added to the verdict of science brought the debate to a close. Moreover, the deepening of social change which had formerly intensified opposition now smoothed the path of assent.[7]

For the historian Merle Curti, it was understandable that Americans accepted popular conceptions of evolution. According to Curti:

> Notwithstanding orthodox scruples against it, evolution as popularly inter-preted fitted admirably into the dominant mood of America. It was an opti-mistic concept, and Americans believed in the future, their future. Everything was moving fast. America had long subscribed to the doctrine of progress, and evolution gave that doctrine scientific standing. Moreover, the doctrine of evolution, while it might upset ecclesiastic authority, tended to make many who accepted it more rather than less satisfied with the existing social and economic order. Whatever ought to be, will be, ultimately. The process of change is slow, and nature has it in her keeping. Whatever is, that is a step in the process.[8]

As John Herman Randall observed, "Darwin's ideas came into an intel-lectual world admirably prepared to welcome them."[9] They appeared at the right time and the right place, certainly a time and place suitable for an intense reaction and sustained attention. It offered an explanation of change. "The fact is," Cynthia Eagle Russett observed, "that the times were ripe for a reorientation of intellect, and Darwinism offered itself as symbol and mechanism of such a reorientation."[10] Darwinism and the American condition had a synergistic effect on each other. "Darwinism intensified the uncertainties which succeeded rapid social change, while rapid social change exaggerated the threat of Darwinism."[11]

Some who objected to Darwinism, such as Harvard's Louis Aggasiz, did have serious scientific objections. Others saw Darwin's notion of evolu-tion, variation and natural selection as direct challenges not only to their search for a cosmic law but also to the preservation of their ways of living, working, believing, thinking and interpreting their world and their expe-riences. Many Americans wanted the certainty that can only be underwrit-ten by absolutes. It mattered little to them "whether the law which rules the cosmos was initially revealed, intuitively apprehended, or rationally deduced,"[12] but there had to be a fundamental law. There had to be some certainty. There had to be a design that could be easily apprehended. Even Asa Gray, Darwin's most important and most effective defender in the United States, emphasized that "the concept of evolution by natural selection did not exclude design from nature."[13] Yet, Darwinism did effec-tively erode traditional assumptions about absolutes—not necessarily any particular absolute but absolutes *qua* absolutes. This erosion occurred while economic revolutions were eroding traditional assumptions about the nature of social reality and the efficacy of traditional values.[14] Darwinism "attacked absolutisms whether of species or thought systems" and gave "change, emergence, and becoming" a "scientific dignity" they previously did not enjoy as well as a "new importance."[15] Darwinism undermined what an earlier generation—the generation to which the founders of the common school belonged—conceived of as science as well as what they believed knowledge was. Darwinism did not challenge the structure of American thought; it undermined its foundation.

THE DARWINIAN VIEW

The founders of the common school valued learning, information, and knowledge, but their "science" was not Darwinian science. While it is true that they sought to make decisions based on information, or "empirical data" and deliberately set out to gather what they believed the relevant information was on an issue before making a decision, their assumptions were basically Enlightenment assumptions. Eighteenth-century philosophers tended to view nature as a mechanism governed by complicated but perfectly functioning designs. Nature was, to use William Paley's metaphor, a complex clock. Like most American intellectuals between the American Revolution and the Civil War, they believed in Paley's watchmaker[16] and in common sense. There was, they maintained, a discernible design in the universe and the design, they reasoned, must have had a designer, the Creator. As the Common Sense Realists of the Scottish Enlightenment argued, humankind's perception was basically veridical. Nature was orderly and did basically function as humankind perceived it to function. The order and design of nature were discernible. Nature's design and order gave regularity to the world, to one's experience, and even provided a justification for an ethical system. It was generally believed that if one acted in accordance with the discernible "intelligible and purposeful scheme of things," one could find "moral meaning and value."[17] At times, Americans may have been Baconian, believing that nature did not readily give up its secrets, that they had to be painfully and laboriously extracted, but the secrets were there and the design was discernible. The Darwinian view was that nature was undergoing a continuous dynamic process whereby some species and some characteristics survived and some did not. Newtonian mechanics and fixed truth gave way to Darwinian biology and probable truth, to what pragmatists would later call warranted assertions.

The generation—James G. Carter, Horace Mann and Henry Barnard, for example—that founded the common school believed in extracting, collecting and using information. Investigation basically allowed assembly of a picture of what was, and what always had been and always would be. The object of attention was fundamentally on what was fixed, on what was permanent. What was once science became prescience. For example, a Committee on Educational Research of the National Academy of Education, indicated that Henry Barnard's *American Journal of Education* (1855) marked the beginning of the "prescientific" period of educational research—a period of research based on "the German ideal of *Wissenschaft* or systematized assembly of knowledge."[18] Then the object of science was to discern what was and to record its order. Change had not yet become the object of the scientists' investigations, but the revolution was not far away.

Statistics and the Laws of Nature

For Darwin "the laws of nature were statistical rather than mechanical, that is [they] were approximations concerning probabilities rather than fixed rules from which one could deduce certain consequences."[19] After Darwin, scientific laws were not seen as governing or exposing the workings of nature but as "leading principles of scientific investigation, instruments to guide inquiry."[20] In the Darwinian wake psychologists eventually turned away from introspective methods and turned to observation and controlled experiments.

Darwinism was revolutionary and unsettling because it challenged a conventional wisdom that worked for centuries. Since the beginning of western civilization, humankind's sages tried to distinguish between the real and that which only appeared to be real, between what was permanent and what was transitory, between the immutable and the mutable. After Darwin, scientists had to surrender their traditional object of inquiry. As Randall reported:

> Knowledge and science [could] no longer aim at realities lying behind and beyond the processes of nature, but rather at mutual interactions of changing things; not an Order of Nature, as XVIIth and XVIII-century science had aimed, but at events situations, processes. This shift involved a fundamental temporalizing of all our thinking.[21]

Without the immutable, it seemed to many people that there was no way to control and to govern social relationships. Americans were in the habit of "seeing" an order in nature and believing that a similar order had to obtain in social affairs. The mutable was inferior to the immutable. Change was seen as decay. However, Darwinism turned that conventional wisdom inside out. After Darwin, "Change [was] no longer a sign of defect and unreality, but fundamental in all that exists."[22] Darwin piled uncertainty upon uncertainty, for he questioned the notion of permanence itself. Darwin's supposition that variable as well as permanent characteristics were inheritable meant that characteristics were not immutable. That supposition also gave a radically new meaning to the notion of species. Because species were not immutable, they were obviously not something to be discovered in nature. Species were neither discerned nor discovered by the investigator but products of the investigation. They were found at a particular time and represented a stage of development at a particular time. They were identifiable points in a process. Such points were pauses, perhaps long pauses, but they were neither cessations nor culminations of a process, for there was no necessary end to the process. Moreover, chance could not be ignored; it was an ever-present factor. Since fortuitous variation was inheritable, the range of possible forms and characteristics was seemingly infinite—certainly, not easily predictable.

"By crashing the conceptual barricades surrounding species—plant, animal, and human—Darwin exposed mind, morals and therefore the whole scope of social relations to change, and ultimately to naturalism."[23] Naturalism meant that humankind was not apart from nature but a part of nature. The relationship between humankind and nature "was fundamentally altered." Humankind no longer held a privileged position "halfway between beast and angel."[24] Humankinds' relationship to nature was conceptualized anew. The individual "was no linger a fallen angel, but a great ape trying to make good, the last and best-born of nature's children.[25]

Darwin forged a link between humankind and animals that was to remain fixed.[26] Darwin did not explicitly state that conclusion in the *Origin of Species*. However, in 1871 in the *Descent of Man* he did explicitly apply his account of evolution to humankind when he wrote that humankind had descended from "a hairy quadruped, of arboreal habits, furnished with a tail and pointed ears."[27] The application of the theory of evolution to humankind opened new areas of inquiry for social and behavioral scientists. As Robert Scoon reported:

> Until Darwin made this evolutionary naturalism plausible to scientists and a large following of generally intelligent persons, modern science had extended its sway over the material world, including the physiological processes of man's body, but had left untouched the distinctively human activities of mind; these were still regarded as the region of purpose, will, mind, spirit, and the clear evidence of a divine Creator. Now Darwin, particularly in his later works, *The Descent of Man* and *Expression of the Emotions in Man and Animals*, showed that in his fully developed theory man could not be said to have any more distinctive a position than any other terrestrial species and that even his most cherished sentiments were but the

product of an evolutionary process which linked him with the other animals.[28]

Darwin's German follower, Ernst Haeckel, welcomed a view that eliminated distinctions between the physical and the metaphysical and that conceived of life "not as a mystic eccentricity in an orderly nature, but plainly as a higher form of the great cosmic mechanism."[29] Followers and users of Darwin clearly saw that eliminating the radical difference between humankind and the remainder of nature gave humankind a new place and required a new method of inquiry in the social and behavioral sciences. Darwin's argument forced scientists to attend "to beginnings and to the processes by which things come to be what they are." The "genetic method" became the dominant method in the humanities and the social sciences. For example, by the turn of the century, John Dewey recognized genetic psychology as an already established area of inquiry.[30]

By the beginning of the twentieth century, investigators accepted that the qualitative difference between animal and human had effectively been eliminated or simply reduced to differences that one could, in principle, count and measure. Edward L. Thorndike, for example, believed that and clearly stated the point. For him, mind, whatever it was, was not peculiar to humans. As he related in article in the *Popular Science Monthly*:

> ... among the minds of animals that of man is the chief, but also kinsman; ruler but also brother.... Among the minds of animals that of man leads, not as a demigod from another planet, but as a king from the same race.[31]

Differences were not differences of kind but of degree, and, as Thorndike would later maintain, those differences could be measured.

Thorndike's view was not exceptional. A year later, Michael Lane wrote that "in discussing social groups we must ... place man where he belongs under the general laws of life." It was no longer possible to "set apart" humankind "as something unique among the social groups." For Lane, "a political group of men does not evolve into a form different from that evolved by a bee-group because of any fundamental difference in the laws by which both groups are carried forward." Laws were laws. They applied to all living creatures without discrimination. "Social development is essentially an identical process wherever it is to be found."[32] For researchers, differences were basically differences in degree, or amount. Some subjects were bigger or smaller, more or less complex than others. Thus, Thorndike, for example, conducted "a somewhat extended series of studies of the intelligent behavior of fishes, reptiles, birds and mammals, including the monkeys."[33] The subjects of his doctoral dissertation were cats, dogs, and chicks.

Humans as Subjects

The ability to argue effectively that humankind was a part of nature and not apart from it was of no small consequence. "With man now one animal, one biological organism among others, his experience became fundamentally that of any animal, an interaction between an organism and its environment."[34] Once a rationale was established for so viewing humankind, it became possible to study it in the same manner as any other part or dimension of nature. Basically, the investigator had two choices: First, the object of investigation—humankind, whether it was a collection of factory workers or supermarket patrons, children on a playground or in a classroom, or infants in cribs under Arnold Gesell's movie cameras—could be observed. Second, the subjects of investigation could be disturbed, stimulated or have some sort of treatment administered to them. The subjects' reactions to the disturbance or treatment could not only be observed and recorded but also measured. Some call the first choice descriptive or sometimes survey research; the second choice is known as experimental research. While either choice presents interesting methodological problems, those who choose to disturb—sometimes described as either administering a treatment or as the delivery of instruction—and observe the effects of the disturbance are confronted with special problems. They usually want to be certain that the effects they see are the effects of the disturbance they created and administered and not the effects of some other factor. One way to achieve that kind of certainty is to create highly controlled settings. Those settings are frequently called laboratories where extraneous factors can be eliminated or controlled. When disturbances are administered in a laboratory, investigators can be fairly confident that what they are observing is, in fact, what they are observing, that it is a consequence of the treatments they administered. Another way to simplify matters so that precise observations of disturbances can be documented is to simplify the subject—use a surrogate. One approach to the surrogate solution is to select typical or representative subjects so one can avoid the responsibility of disturbing the entire population. That, of course, entails determining what an appropriate sample size is as well as developing methods that have a high probability of producing a representative sample. Another approach is to follow the example of Thorndike and choose a surrogate that is the same but different, the same but simpler: a primate, a cat, a dog, a rat, a fish, a bird or chick. After all, so the argument goes, behavior is behavior and learning is learning. There are differences but differences differ and they can be measured.

There are, of course, arguments about how far one can generalize from a representative or from a surrogate. However, those arguments accept that humankind is part of nature. Even if an attempt is made to argue that humankind is a special case worthy of and requiring special methods, it is an argument that has been effectively framed by Darwin.

After Darwin, mind, life, and society were seen as not fixed but subject to change. The climate in which scholarship was conducted and the objects of inquiry were different after Darwin. Psychologists, for example, especially the American functionalists, turned their attention to Darwin's interests: function, growth and development, individual differences, adaptation and adjustment.[35] Post-Darwinian scholarship "made function the criterion and emergence the norm."[36] Time and change, objects of modern educational inquiries, received a new found attention. As Horace Kallen recorded, Darwinian ideas shifted "the conception of 'scientific thinking' into a temporal perspective." The application of Darwinian ideas prompted investigators "to stress relations and activities as against terms and substances, genesis and development as against intrinsic character, transformation as against continuing form, dynamic pattern as against static organization, processes of conflict and integration as against formal composition out of unchanging elements."[37] Change, the conditions under which it occurs, whether, how it can be controlled, and how much time is needed to effect the change all became objects of inquiry, basic and applied. In education, the purpose of the inquiry frequently was, and continues to be, learning how to effect maximum change in exchange for minimum effort in the shortest possible time. In education, there is a special term, borrowed from psychologists, for change. It is called learning. Significantly, educational researchers as well as educational practitioners have accepted the psychologists' definitions and their criteria for ascertaining whether learning has occurred and how much learning has occurred. For some it became either interesting or useful to determine whether "something learned" was in fact learned or whether it was a characteristic of a developmental stage. It is, it should be noted, inefficient to attempt to teach that which will typically manifest itself as a characteristic of a subsequent stage in the growth process. Determining when, at which stage in the developmental process change or learning can be efficiently effected became an important research question.

Naturalism, Evidence, and Hypothesis

As important as the attention Darwin directed toward time and change was the influence he had on methods of inquiry in virtually all fields. After Darwin, "naturalism ... permeated intellectual activity in all its aspects" and "experimental methodology" became the favored way to investigate.[38] Darwin offered not assertions but hypotheses, not conclusions based solely on rational methods but hypotheses that could be demonstrated to be true or false only in light of evidence. His method eventually demonstrated to researchers that nature does not always conform to the logical deductions of the investigator. He showed, as Daniels observed, that "empirical science and logic are two different things."[39] The Darwinian method was not speculative; it was experimental. It relied on data gathered from observations and experiments made either in the field or in the laboratory. It set aside logically self-evident axioms in favor of inductive generalizations founded on observations. Facts were important but not in the Baconian sense. Facts were not examined to see what theory naturally flowed from them but were collected so that hypotheses could be denied or supported. After Darwin, "evolutionary relativism" took the place of certainty and absolutes. In principle, conclusions were not only subject to empirical verification but also subject to subsequent revisions. To use Deweyean language, it is possible to set forth warranted assertions but not certainty. After Darwin, there was to be an ever present need for more research. Frequently, finding facts is often seen as research, but the gathering of facts is but a step in the scientific method.

As American progressive reformers turned to social science to solve social problems and to render social institutions efficient, it became clear that Darwinism had been used to shape the social sciences. As Daniels reported, "each of the social sciences, for example, eagerly adopted the approach of the social evolutionists, who looked upon human institutions as organic things adapting themselves to an every changing environment."[40] At the newly founded Johns Hopkins University the historian Herbert Baxter Adams used his "germ theory of politics" to argue that the nation's democratic institutions evolved from earlier primitive German forests. The then professor and future president of the United States, Woodrow Wilson, maintained government was "accountable to Darwin, not to Newton." For Wilson, "Living political constitutions must be Darwinian in structure and in practice."[41]

DARWIN AND AMERICAN BELIEF SYSTEMS

In retrospect, it seems not terribly surprising that Darwinism was accepted in the Untied States by the end of the nineteenth century. Its acceptance did require abandonment of common sense realism, but experience was no longer supporting that view of the world as it did in the late eighteenth and early nineteenth centuries. Darwin's work was scientific, and Americans were long interested in science. Science was not yet the profession it now is. It did not make its way into school curricula until the last quarter of the nineteenth century, but science did have its following in the United States. The model of the universe Americans had used was a Newtonian model. Newton's discoveries had been "transmuted into a cosmic world view that set the pattern for every intellectual endeavor." After Darwin, "the ruling model remained scientific, though the dominance passed from physics to biology."[42] One scientific metaphor gave want to another. As John Fiske observed, "Paley's simile of the watch" had to give way to "the simile of the flower." The universe was no longer to be seen as a "machine" but as an "organism." It was to be seen not as having been "made" but as having "grown."[43]

Darwin's theory of evolution did challenge traditional beliefs, but they were also challenged by the forceful modernization processes. Darwin enabled Americans to construct a *Weltanschauung* that allowed for expansion, progress and optimism. As Scoon observed:

> When the scientific theory of evolution won acceptance in the last century, its significance ... was manifold; but certainly one fundamental significance was its suggestion of a process of upbuilding and creativity in the universe, quite the reverse of the repetitiousness of mechanism, the gradual disintegration implied in the Second Law of Thermodynamics, and even the tight logical determinism of rationalistic monisms such as those of Spinoza and Hegel. Against all these interpretations of nature as essentially a dead hand of law squeezing every activity into some pre-existent groove, evolution pointed to new species of living things, a continuous process of organic invention (adaptation), and a cosmological organization loose enough to permit a real freedom to human endeavor.[44]

Darwinism was popular, fertile and seminal. It was applied and even misapplied by many to many areas. It was "transmuted into a sanction for progress" and "employed as a footnote to the doctrine of pessimism."[45] However, in Darwinism many Americans found justification for their beliefs in progress, expansion and optimism. Those who wanted the promise of perfection could find it in Darwin. Darwin did suggest that perfection was possible when he wrote:

> We may look with some confidence to a secure future of great length. And as natural selection works solely by and for the good of each being, all corporal and mental endowments will tend to progress toward perfection.[46]

Those who did not read Darwin received assurances of progress and perfection from Herbert Spencer and Thomas Huxley.

Darwinism and Social Control

While Darwinism eventually touched all areas of human life and tran-
sormed the American *Weltanschauung*, it clearly and directly influenced
the sciences, natural and social. The pre-Civil War *Weltanschauung* gave
Americans a sense of certainty and the kind of comfort that issues from
the assurance that there is a rational design in nature. Darwin did take
away certainty, but after Americans recovered from the shock, they began
to comprehend that the new *Weltanschauung* based on science, specifically
Darwinism, certainly had its advantages. It seemed to offer a universal
method. As Scoon recorded, Darwin seemed not to adhere to any "clear
line of demarcation between biology and other closely allied sciences, or
between science and morality." Moreover, Darwin's "theory of evolution
ranged into psychology and ethics."[47] Darwinian science allowed for the
possibility of control. Relationships were temporal and a function of the
environment. It appeared to promise the power to manage society. The
new experimental method could be applied to any area of interest, to any
object of inquiry that humankind wanted to control or improve. It was
reasoned that if humankind was part of nature and subject to nature's universal laws, so were the works, customs, mores and institutions of humankind. Nothing was permanent. Everything was subject to change.
Through investigation the conditions of change could be ascertained and
power to control human behavior and social relations could thus be
secured.

Before Darwin, scientific laws were seen as fixed. They were prescriptions. After Darwin, scientific laws are not prescriptions that precede
experience but are descriptions of a reality already experienced. Scientific
laws become histories. They are statements of what occurred when, where,
why and how. While scientific laws are not prescriptions, they can, and
indeed often do allow, with some considerable confidence but not absolute certainty, predictions. Their predictive power is contingent upon the
similarities between the conditions at two different times, but a similar
condition is not an identical condition. Darwinian science may tell that
best single predictor of future performance is past performance, but the
best is not necessarily perfect. By believing they could establish identical
conditions in the past, present and future scientists frequently convinced
themselves that they could escape the ravages of time.

Late nineteenth and early twentieth century social and behavioral scientists were not generally concerned with methodological niceties or with
the conditions that limited how far their generalizations could be
extended. They had a new metaphor and wanted to see just how far they
could take it. Darwinism became a defense for whatever the investigator
or proponent wanted. For some it was a defense for the *status quo* and an

explanation as to why any attempts to make matters different were bound to be futile. For others it was a rationale for deliberately trying to effect progress, social perfection.

AMERICAN PSYCHOLOGY AND MEASUREMENT

The foundations of an American psychology were being prepared in 1878 when William James promised Henry Holt that he would produce a psychology text for Holt's American Science Series. In 1890—five years after the agreed upon date for the completion of the text—James' two-volume *Principles of Psychology* appeared. James accepted Darwin and made evolution acceptable to Americans. He presented a grand synthesis of psychology and liberated American psychologists from the European origins of psychology. It was the beginning of an American psychology that was to emphasize the functional and adaptive behavior of humankind. His interest was not on introspection as means of ascertaining the contents of consciousness but on how consciousness enabled individuals to adapt to their environment by making decisions, by making choices. James had successfully taken two traditions—brass instrument psychology practiced in German laboratories and the English theories of evolution and associationism—and incorporated them into his own evolutionary point of view. His view was acceptable because he left the future course of evolution uncharted. He insisted that the human mind acted on the environment as the environment was acting on it. Mind worked; it was not passive. To be able to accept evolution and still have a choice in how humanity would be affected by it was an inviting position. It was widely accepted.

By 1883, Lester Frank Ward, a paleobotanist for the United States Geological Survey published *Dynamic Sociology* in which he challenged the claims of the "Social Darwinists" Herbert Spencer and William G. Sumner. According to Ward, humankind did not need to accept whatever was as the irrevocable effect of blind natural laws but could use a product of evolution—human intelligence—to intervene and control society and social relationships. Progress was possible as was social control.

By the turn of the century many reformers were not only accepting the school as a mediating institution between a traditional and besieged family and an ever more complex society but were also beginning to argue that the school could be deliberately used as an instrument of social progress. Few objected, and many turned their attention to an institution that was growing in size and social importance. William James, John Dewey, Edward L. Thorndike, G. Stanley Hall, Albion Small and many others turned their attention to public education and used, in one way or another, Darwin to define the issues and problems of modern educational research. Even when they did not explicitly invoke Darwin but only turned to "science," they were applying Darwinian notions, for Darwin had effectively reconceptualized the object of scientific attention. Change, the conditions that retard or promote change and control of change became the major foci of inquiry. The possibility of controlling and even causing change in a desired direction was as exciting as the sciental apple was tempting.

As change and adjustment were becoming the objects of inquiry, there was developing a "technology" for their measurement, especially changes in human behavior. Child study workers spent countless hours measuring, weighing, and observing children so that norms could be established to enable researchers and other interested parties to assess whether change—usually called growth and development—was occurring on schedule. Nearly every imaginable aspect of a child's ability or growth was measured. A report of that to which children in the Chicago University Primary School were subjected indicates just how much measuring was occurring by the end of the nineteenth century:

- Measurements were taken in sight, ascertaining the visual acuity, testing also for astigmatism, color discrimination, sensitiveness to light, power of coordinating the eyes, and judgment of division of length of sight.
- In hearing, the auditory range and discrimination of pitch were tested.
- In feeling, tests were made determining the minimum of discernible pressure, the span of double touch, discrimination of weights, using active lifting and passive pressure, and the ability to discriminate different temperatures.
- Smell and taste were tested by determining the pupils' ability to detect different solutions.
- Besides these sensory tests, motor measurements were made of the strength of grip, and also tests in reaction time.
- In addition to the above tests, anthropometrical measurements were taken in connection with the gymnasium.[48]

So many measurements of children were taken that "one gentlemen was led to remark that the children were in danger of becoming shop-worn through so much handling."[49]

As American investigators accepted the new object of inquiry—change, they accepted the new technology. Measurements and new ways of measuring the reliability and the validity of measurements as well as a way of estimating error and the probability of chance results and relationships became all but indispensable to most educational researchers. Darwin's cousin, Sir Francis Galton, Karl Pearson, and Ronald A. Fischer were the sources for these indispensable statistical skills and applications of probability theory to assessment, measurement and prediction of human performance. That technology was so necessary because the psychologists were in the process of making changes in performance and behavior—what they typically call learning—the dominant behavioral science. Educators did not successfully resist the introduction of their conceptions into their own field. Indeed, they welcomed what Harold O. Rugg described as "one long orgy of tabulation" where "the air was full of normal curves, standard deviations, coefficients of correlation, [and] regression equations."[50]

As the theory of evolution was accepted by Americans, its acceptance was to be seen in the nation's schools. According to Merle E. Curti, it "pushed biology into the schools, stimulated the cult of child study, and virtually refashioned the psychology which had conditioned so much that was done in the classroom." It also supported those who maintained that "a changing society necessitated more attention to the social studies."[51] In addition, acceptance of the theory of evolution was one of the factors that "helped to emancipate the child from the old Calvinistic dogma of original sin, an idea which had condemned the young in school to a blind and brutal discipline." Its emphasis on individual differences served to challenge "the lock-step organization, the stereotyped recitation, and the demand for rigid conformity" and "demanded revolutionary changes in the technique of teaching."[52]

NOTES

1. Charles Coulston Gillispie. *The Edge of Objectivity: An Essay in the History of Scientific Ideas* (Princeton, New Jersey: Princeton University Press, 1960), p. 343.

2. Richard Hofstadter. *Social Darwinism in American Thought.* rev. ed. (Boston: The Beacon Press. 1955), pp. 3, 5.

3. John M. O'Donnell. *The Origins of Behaviorism: American Psychology, 1870-1920* (New York: New York University Press, 1985), pp. 56-57.

4. Alexander Francis Chamberlain. *The Child: A Study in the Evolution of Man* (New York: Charles Scribner's Sons, 1900), Chapter 1 reproduced in Robert E. Grinder. *A History of Genetic Psychology: The First Science of Human Development* (New York: John Wiley and Sons, Inc. 1967), p. 208.

5. George H. Daniels. *Science in American Society: A Social History.* (New York: Alfred A. Knopf. 1971), pp. 240-241.

6. Bert James Lowenberg. "Darwinism Comes to America, 1859-1900," *The Mississippi Valley Historical Review* Volume XXVIII (June, 1941 to March, 1942), p. 340.

7. *Ibid.*, p. 341.

8. Merle E. Curti. *The Social Ideas of American Educators*, rev. ed. (Totowa, New Jersey: Littlefield, Adams & Co., 1971), p. 402.

9. John Herman Randall. "The Changing Impact of Darwin on Philosophy," *Journal of the History of Ideas*, Vol. XXII, No. 4 (October-December 1961), p. 439.

10. Cynthia Eagle Russett. *Darwin in America: The Intellectual Response, 1865-1912*, (San Francisco: W. H. Freeman and Co., 1976), p. 217.

11. Lowenberg. "Darwinism Comes to America," p. 343.

12. *Ibid.*, p. 368.

13. Bert James Lowenberg. "The Reaction of American Scientists to Darwinism." *American Historical Review*, Vol. 38 (1938), p. 695.

14. Russett. *Darwin in America*, pp. 215-217.

15. Lowenberg. "Darwinism Comes to America," p. 358.

16. William Paley introduced the metaphor of the watchmaker in 1802 in *Natural Theology; or, Evidences of the Existence and Attributes of the Deity, Collected from the Appearances of Nature*. It became one of the most well known metaphors in the philosophy of science.

17. R. J. Wilson (ed.). *Darwinism and the American Intellectual* (Homewood, Illinois: The Dorsey Press, 1967), p. 3.

18. Lee J. Cronbach and Patrick Suppes (eds.). *Research for Tomorrow's Schools: Disciplined Inquiry for Education* (London: Collier-Macmillan Limited, 1969), pp. 33-34.

19. Robert C. Bannister. *Social Darwinism: Science and Myth in Anglo-American Social Thought* (Philadelphia, Pennsylvania: Temple University Press, 1979), p. 18.

20. Randall. "The Changing Impact of Darwin on Philosophy," p. 440.

21. *Ibid.*," p. 451.

22. *Ibid.*

23. Lowenberg. "Darwinism Comes to America," pp. 366-367.

24. O'Donnell. *The Origins of Behaviorism*, p. 58.

25. Randall. "The Changing Impact of Darwin on philosophy," p. 453.

26. Robert J. Richards. "Why Darwin Delayed, or Interesting Problems and Models in the History of Science," *Journal of the History of the Behavioral Sciences*, Vol. 19 (1983) reproduced in Ludy T. Benjamin, Jr. (ed.). *A History of Psychology: Original Sources and Contemporary Research* (New York: McGraw-Hill Book Co., 1998), p. 255.

27. Quoted in Russett. *Darwin in America*, pp. 12-13.

28. Robert Scoon. "The Rise and Impact of Evolutionary Ideas" in Stow Persons (ed.). *Evolutionary Thought in America* (New Haven, Connecticut: Yale University Press, 1950), pp. 39-40.

29. Quoted in Cynthia Eagle Russett. *The Concept of Equilibrium in American Social Thought* (New Haven: Yale University Press, 1966), p. 24.

30. In Appendix B of the third edition of his *Psychology,* John Dewey directed his readers attention to several works on genetic psychology. The included: Preyer, *Die Seele des Kindes;* Perez, *First Three Years of Childhood,* and *La Psychologie de Enfant;* Kussmaul, *Untersuchungen über das Seelenoleben des neugeborenen Menschen;* Egger, *Sur le Developpement de Intelligence et du Langage;* Lobisch, *Die Seele des Kindes;* Schultze, *Die Sprache des Kindes;* Taine, in *Revue Philosophique,* for Jan., 1876; Darwin, in *Mind,* Vol. II, p. 285 ff.; Pollock, in *Mind* for July, 1878; Genzmer, "Die Sinneswahrnehmungen des neugeborenen Menschen." See: John Dewey. *Psychology* 3rd rev. ed. (New York: Harper and Brothers, 1894), p. 366.

31. Edward L. Thorndike. "The Evolution of the Human Intellect." *Popular Science Monthly.* Vol. 69 (November 1901), p. 65.

32. Michael A. Lane. *The Level of Social Motion: An Inquiry into the Future Conditions of Human Society* (New York: Macmillan, 1902), p. 193.

33. Thorndike. "Evolution of the Human Intellect," p. 58.

34. Randall. "The Changing Impact of Darwin on Philosophy," p. 459.

35. Consider, for example, how often psychologists use adaptation and adjustment in their definitions of learning.

36. Lowenberg. "Darwinism Comes to America," p. 367.

37. Horace Kallen. "Functionalism," *Encyclopedia of the Social Sciences,* Vol. 6 (New York: Macmillan, 1931), p. 523.

38. Lowenberg. "Darwinism Comes to America," p. 362.

39. Daniels. *Science in American Society,* p. 241.

40. *Ibid.,* p. 249.

41. Quoted in Daniels. *Science in American Society,* p. 249.

42. Russett. *Darwin in America,* pp. 18-19.

43. Quoted in Daniels. *Science in American Society,* p. 248.

44. Scoon. "Rise and Impact of Evolutionary Ideas," pp. 39-40.

45. Lowenberg. "Darwinism Comes to America," p. 363.

46. Charles Darwin. *The Origin of Species* 6th ed. Quoted in Scoon. "Rise and Impact of Evolutionary Ideas," 24-25.

47. Scoon. "Rise and Impact of Evolutionary Ideas," p. 24.

48. Frederick W. Smedley. "A Report on the Measurement of the Sensory and Motor Abilities of the Pupils of the Chicago University Primary School and the Pedagogical Value of Such Measurements," *Transactions of the Illinois Society for Child Study.* Vol. II, No. 2 (1896-97). pp. 85-86.

49. *Ibid.,* p. 86.

50. Harold O. Rugg. *That Men May Understand* (New York, 1941), p. 182 quoted in Lawrence A. Cremin. *The Transformation of the School: Progressivism in American Education, 1876-1950* (New York: Alfred A. Knopf, 1962), p. 181.

51. Curti. *Social Ideas of American Educators,* p. 207.

52. *Ibid.,* p. 208.

PART III

CHAPTER 7

CHILD STUDY, G. STANLEY HALL, ARNOLD GESELL, AND LEWIS M. TERMAN

Progressives' acceptance of Ellen Key's assertion that the twentieth century was to be the century of the child is one indicator that children were high on the nation's agenda during the Progressive Era. Her widely accepted claim meant that science was to be applied to the care and the rearing of children. To save and to know children it was necessary to apply science to their care and rearing. As the century progressed, the science that was selected and applied was psychology. Child-study advocates and educational reformers turned to psychology just as the psychologists and other scientists considered children ideal subjects for the study of growth, development, learning, and disease. Child study was more than the acting out of a generous and romantic impulse made possible by an increasingly productive and prosperous society. It was also a cultural and an economic imperative. Proper care and education of children was to preserve the American way of life and protect the nation from the beliefs and practices of the many immigrants who were arriving in great numbers. Children had to be properly nurtured and educated, for they were the nation's most valuable resource. If protected from child labor and properly educated, they would become productive American citizens.

Educational Research, the National Agenda, and Educational Reform:
A History, pp. 177–213

HISTORY OF CHILDHOOD AND THE CHILD AS SUBJECT

Given that children and adolescents constitute the populations that are assigned to school in the expectation that they and society will benefit from their having been schooled, it is understandable that they have been the subject of social and behavioral scientists' investigations. Those responsible for schooling have been interested in understanding the characteristics and the nature of those designated as students, for there has been established a long-held belief that the content and the method of instruction must be conducted in accordance with the child's nature or his/her developmental stage. The results of experiments and studies of children have been used by parents and educators who are responsible for how children are taught at home and while in school. Children and adolescents become the objects of inquiry as researchers seek to learn how various methods of caring for and instructing children affect their development and their ability to learn. In such studies, the behavior or the responses of children are observed and recorded as their performance as the result of the administration of a treatment of some sort is compared to that of another to determine its efficacy.

Indicative of the interests of those interested in understanding children is the list of topics provided by the founding editors of the *Journal of Educational Psychology*. In the first issue of their new journal they promised to include "not only the well-known field covered by the average text-book ... but also problems of mental development—heredity, adolescence and the inexhaustible of child-study—the study of individual differences, of retarded and precocious development, the psychology of the 'special class,' the nature of mental endowments, the measurement of mental capacity, the psychology of mental tests, the correlation of mental abilities, the psychology of special methods in the several school branches [and] the important problems of mental hygiene."[1] They intended to include works that covered "all those phases of mental life that concern education." What the editors of the new journal did not announce was that the systematic and scientific study of children grew out of the interests and recommendations of eighteenth and nineteenth century reformers who maintained that children were not miniature adults and thus required nurturing and education based on their nature.

Consideration of how children have been defined and studied requires recognition of interests and developments that cannot easily be disentangled from one another. Interest in and the study of children near the end of the nineteenth century was concurrent with increased school enrollments at the end of the nineteenth century and with the concerns of progressive reformers in the early twentieth century. Knowledge of children was to enable teachers to be more effective and efficient. Interest in the study of children also coincided with progressive reformers' questions about the long tradition of using child labor in the United States. Americans then began to question earlier claims that child labor was economically and ethically beneficial. Progressive reformers very much wanted to protect childhood and even prolong it, for they believed that the exploitation of children as laborers "undermined their biological potential as parents." That was particularly important when many of the dominant class mindful of the influx of immigrants feared the loss of their dominance or what was then cast as "race suicide."[2]

Some studied children not because they were interested in how students might perform in school but because they were primarily interested in studying other topics: disease, growth and development, or some other topic of interest to physicians, public health officials and psychologists. For example, the physician Abraham Jacobi maintained that children were good subjects to study to learn about disease. He also maintained that observation of children allowed investigators to determine what normal growth was and provided "for the generation of scientific hypotheses that would aid medicine to provide adequate and effective treatment of the sick."[3] Studying children was not necessarily aimed at effecting pedagogical reforms even though the two were often concurrent and complimentary. As George H. Daniels observed:

> The biological concepts of continuity and inheritance had made the child distinctive—worth studying for his own sake—in marked contrast to the older associationist psychology, which held that the child was merely an adult in miniature. The child was thought to be closer to the origins of the human mind, for the mind of the adult is too much overlaid by experience to reflect the basic forces of biological inheritance. It was primarily this belief that the child was more attuned to the primeval mind, rather than a concern for improvements in education, that provided the critical push toward the systematic study of children that was developing concurrently with Dewey's New Pedagogy.[4]

Interest in the care of children and interest in their nature were sometimes closely related. The early aims of The Bureau of Educational Experiments, founded by Lucy Sprague Mitchell, Caroline Pratt, and Harriet Johnson in 1915, were "to conduct research which will lead to further and fuller data concerning children's growth" and "to bring schools and specialists dealing with various aspects of children into intimate and working contact with one another."[5] Two decades after its founding, the Bureau's early years were described as a time when the Bureau was interested in "child research" and having a "psychological attitude toward research" that was "educational as well as scientific."[6] Even after World War II, as Ethel Kawin emphasized, how the results of the observations, tests, and measurements of children were recorded was important, for those results served one of two purposes: "service objectives and research objectives." Those interested in "service objectives" focused on "all efforts to facilitate the understanding and wise handling of children through knowledge of the children and their environments and experiences." Those interested in "research objectives" made "carefully planned and controlled studies of young children in order to gather facts and data which may be used in various ways to increase scientific knowledge." At times, the objectives were "combined." Combined efforts contributed to "the development of a science of education."[7]

Reformers and researchers emphasized that children could not be neglected, for they were different from the issue of other species. They were biologically and socially dependent on their parents, other adults, or even older children for a longer period than were the issue of other species. They were much less mature at birth and developed toward maturity more slowly than other species. Without adult care they had little, if any, chance for survival and full development. Those concerned with the health and stability of society saw that that dependency created the family as a necessity. New organizations were formed to promote the interests of children and by providing education for their caregivers. In 1897 Alice McLellan Birney, taken with the ideas of Friedrich Froebel and G. Stanley Hall, and Phoebe Apperson Hearst organized the National Congress of Mothers (renamed in 1907 as the National Congress of Mothers and Parent-Teachers Associations and again in 1924 when in became The National Congress of Parents and Teachers). Its founders who represented "the philanthropic, religious, social and political interests of the nation" "realized that while mothers have ever been the leading factor in determining the character of young children have failed, lacking guidance and means of cooperation, to exert the influence upon the race which might be possible were conditions beyond the home brought under at least partial control." The Congress focused on the home and the school, "the two social institutions exercising the most direct influence upon children."[8] The school was important not only because it contributed to the socialization of children but also because it "provided a potential laboratory for the observation and study of children and an environment in which children 'at risk' could be identified."[9]

The scientific study of children, the family, parenting, and child labor was clearly underway by the end of the nineteenth century when reformers saw investment in the welfare of children as the way either to improve society or to save it from perceived evils. By 1900, G. Stanley Hall was able to report that the relatively new child-study movement was "already represented by a bibliography of some two thousand titles, including only the books and articles worth reading ... by two journals in this country devoted exclusively to it, and by several more which make it a department; by three journals in Germany, two in France, one each in England, Italy, Japan, Russia, and Spain."[10]

Child Study

Wilhelm Preyer's *Mind of the Child* (1882) has been identified as the cornerstone of the child-study movement,[11] but the conventional way to begin a discussion of child study in the United States is to note that G. Stanley Hall is more often than not credited with beginning the child-study movement.[12] Robert E. Grinder claimed that the publication of Hall's "The Contents of Children's Minds" (1883) and "Henry P. Bowditch's 1879 study of the physical measurements of Boston schoolchildren mark the beginning of the child study movement in the United States."[13] If not the founder, Hall certainly was the "bellwether"[14] or the "high priest of scientific child study."[15] Hall was a leader in the movement and was unquestionably successful in popularizing the movement. However, it is useful to note that "foundings are rarely unequivocal and child-study is no exception; the continuity of ideas that is the intellectual history of child study began long before the writings of Hall."[16] To begin with Hall is to overlook the context in which he worked, what preceded his work, and what others were contributing at approximately the same time. For example, when the United States Commissioner of Education devoted a chapter of his *1897-1898 Report* to child study in the United States, Arthur MacDonald a specialist in the U.S. Bureau of Education and the author of the chapter acknowledged that "it is often difficult to trace the origin of any movement" but admitted that "the initiatory impulse to child-study was from the Continent of Europe." He also claimed that: "more perhaps has done in America in the study of children than in all the rest of the world" and indicated that those who had contributed to the movement did so "under the inspiration of Dr. Hall."[17]

Rousseau's Legacy: Baesdow, Pestallozi, and Sheldon

The attention given at the turn of the century to the study of children and their nature, growth, and development can be seen not only as the emergence of new interests but also as a continuation of interests that began in the eighteenth century with the appearance of Jean-Jacques Rousseau's *Julie ou la novelle Héloïe* in 1761, his *Emile* in 1762 and in 1787 when Dietrich Tiedemann's *Beobachtungen über die Entwicklung der Seelenfähigkeiten bei Kindern* (*Observations on the Mental Development of a Child*) appeared, the first of what Wayne Dennis identified as the "baby biographies."[18]

Rousseau's *Emile* was seen as recommending that children should never be forced to learn anything, that direct experience with objects in nature was preferable to structured lessons in a classroom, and that education was to be directed not by the teacher but by the interests and nature of the child. Rousseau maintained that education should be a natural process based on the native instincts and capacities of the child. It was a claim G. Stanley Hall and his student Arnold Gesell popularized and supported with the results of their psychological investigations. Hall and Gesell, especially Gesell, gave legitimacy to views and prescriptions of late eighteenth and nineteenth century reformers by making their claims and observations the objects of their scientific study. The romantic views of one era became the scientific knowledge of the next.

Among those who were inspired to design new approaches to schooling based on the belief that children were basically good and only needed the right setting to develop were the German educator Johann Bernhard Basedow and the Swiss educator Johann Heinrich Pestalozzi. Baesdow's *An Address to the Friends of Humanity and to Persons in Power, on Schools, on Education, and its Influence on Public Happiness* (1768) included a plan for reforming existing systems of elementary education. He subsequently produced *Book of Method for Fathers and Mothers of Families and of Nations* and *Elementary Work* (1774). In these works Baesdow argued that children were different from adults and that education should be a natural rather than a formal process. That meant teaching languages not through study of grammar but through conversation, using games and exercises, and making use of the reality children knew so that ideas and words were connected to their concrete experiences. Making use of what children already knew was later emphasized by Herbart and then by a succession of educators. These were practices that would later be given a psychological justification and described as progressive.

An interpretation of Pestalozzi's accomplishments began to make its way to the United States in 1859 when while on a holiday in Toronto, Canada, Edward A. Sheldon visited a museum where he saw a display of an English version of Pestalozzian materials. He brought his discovery back to Oswego, acquired materials from London and the services of two experienced assistants, Margaret Jones and Herman Krusi, Jr. whose father had served as one of Pestalozzi's assistants. Krusi, Jr. had become a specialist in teaching teachers how to use object lessons in the classroom. By 1861 it was reported that in those schools where the teachers had "caught the spirit of the plan" and applied it properly, students displayed an interest and enthusiasm for school that had not been previously experienced in Oswego.[19]

In an account of object teaching in Oswego that appeared in Henry Barnard's *American Journal of Education*, Sheldon explained that the new approach to pedagogy began with the nature of the child. The moral, physical, and intellectual development of children was more important than mastery of subject matter. Children were to be viewed as having "certain marked and distinctive characteristics," the most important of which were "activity, love of sympathy, and a desire for constant variety." In place of logically ordered lessons and drills, teachers were to provide lessons that would "quicken the perceptions [of children], and give them accuracy, awaken thought, and cultivate language." Children were to be allowed to observe objects so that they could learn to observe, describe, and define what they had seen. There was a natural order of development in children, and it was to be observed.[20]

Baby Biogaphies

Dietrich Tiedemann, a historian of philosophy recorded his observations of his first child, a son, from birth to about age two and a half. It has been described as the first "naturalistic description" of "the behavioral development of a normal child." Wayne Dennis maintained that: "many aspects of child behavior mentioned by Tiedemann have become areas of research for present-day [1972] workers." If translated into "current psychologese," Tiedemann would sound "most modern."[21]

Charles Darwin, known for *The Origin of Species* (1859), wrote a baby biography of his son. While written in 1840, Darwin did not publish it until 1877. His explanation for "looking over" what he had done thirty-seven years earlier and publishing it was that he had recently read "[Hippolyte Adolphe] Taine's very interesting account of the mental development of an infant."[22] Taine had observed how a little girl acquired language. He focused on how the mental capacity of the little girl he studied compared to that of animals. As future psychologists would, he saw the differences between humans and animals to be not qualitative but quantitative. Lomax reported that: "Taine ended his sketch with a brief reference to recapitulation theory, which was then finding extensive theoretical biologic application."[23] According to Taine, "the child presents in a passing state the mental characteristics that are found in a fixed state in primitive civilizations, very much as the human embryo presents in a passing state the physical characteristics that are found in a fixed state in the classes of inferior animals."[24] Within a few years G. Stanley Hall would find recapitulation theory inviting and useful.

When Darwin published his baby biography, he indicated that his "chief object was emotional expression, and my notes were used in my book [*The Expression of the Emotions in Man and Animals* (1872)] on this subject."[25] In *Expressions* Darwin indicated that while it was "easy to observe infants whilst screaming," he "found photographs made by the instantaneous process the best means for observation, as allowing more deliberation."[26] Subsequently, Arnold Gesell would use movie cameras to develop a record of infant behavior. Darwin collected twelve photographs. Gesell eventually accumulated fifty-seven miles of film showing the behavior of 12,000 children.

By the end of the 1880s there were ten more baby biographies, two in the 1870s and eight in the 1880s. In each of the following three decades (1881-1890, 1891-1900 and 1901-1910) there were eleven baby biographies. Of the sixty-four baby biographies in Dennis' list, twenty-one appeared in Germany, one in Italy, one France, and one in Portugal. The others appeared either in England or the United States. In retrospect in can be said that sustained interest in the study of children began in the 1880s, was clearly underway in the 1890s and was not confined to the United States. Among the significant works that appeared in the 1880s were those of Wilhelm Preyer, James Sully, and G. Stanley Hall. In 1881 Sully's "Babies and Science" appeared in the *Cornhill Magazine*. In 1882 the German physiologist and biologist Preyer published *Die Seele des Kindes* (*The Mind of the Child*) "the first full empirical treatise on child development." While Preyer made use of the already existing work on child development, he supplemented the earlier work with "continuous observations of his son."[27]

During the next two decades (1891-1910), interest in systematic and scientific study of children was clearly increasing. In 1893 Millicent W. Shinn at the University of California-Berkeley began publishing her accounts of the sensory and motor development of a child from birth to age three.[28] In England Sully published his widely read *Studies in Childhood* (1895);[29] and Karl Groos presented two books on play, one on the play of animals in 1896 and one the play of humans in 1899.[30] In Italy Antonia Marro presented the first significant and substantive study of adolescents.[31] In 1900, the Swedish reformer Ellen Key argued that the individual needs of children deserved and required attention.[32] In France, Alfred Binet produced a work on suggestibility in children that was an account of ten years' work on the subject; a work on the evolution of intelligence; and his account of the child study movement.[33] In 1907 the Sterns showed that the study of children's speech was a key to the development of their thought processes.[34] In 1914 Stern provided a thorough review of all the work that had been accomplished in child-study during the previous three decades.[35]

Measuring and Counting Children

By the middle of the nineteenth century and thereafter, children were studied in ways that produced data that could be expressed numerically. Then, "Children began to be measured, weighed, observed, and described, in the hope that the collected information could be used to facilitate understanding of their growth."[36] In 1875, Henry Pickering Bowditch who taught physiology at the Harvard Medical School weighed and measured over 24,000 Boston school children for the Massachusetts Board of Health. In his 1877 report he related that children born of American parents were usually taller and heavier than their counterparts whose parents were Irish. He attributed the difference to environmental conditions. American children enjoyed a diet and living conditions superior to what was available to Irish immigrant children. Bowditch concluded that social class or "mode of life" was "at least equal to, and possibly even greater than, that of race [here race should be read to mean nationality]" and accounted for the differences among children.[37] That was a comment on what later became known as the nature-nurture controversy. In 1897, the physician in charge of "the medical inspection of Boston schoolchildren" reported that there were 98,000 children and 1,500 teachers and that the schools provided "the best opportunity for the exercise of professional observation and sanitary precautions against the diseases of childhood incident to school attendance."[38]

William Porter, a physiologist, examined school children in St. Louis and concluded that there was a "physical basis of precocity and dullness,"[39] thereby providing support for the belief that a sound body and a sound mind are indicative of one another. Franz Boas challenged Porter's conclusion, arguing that correlation was not causation. For Boas there were three factors that influenced the growth rates of children: "hereditary influences, the preceding life story of the individual and the average conditions during the period under consideration."[40] Boas further reasoned that healthy children were probably brighter than children who were less physically fit because they likely spent more time in school. Boas' response to Porter, like Bowditch's observation, is a precursor of the nature-nurture debates that would later provoke a great deal of interest in the 1920s and thereafter. Advocates of child-study not only "emphasized the importance of hereditary and early environmental influences" but also "reinforced the significance of the teacher and school to child saving in the relative plasticity of childhood."[41] However, for the first quarter of the twentieth century, hereditarianism was the view that dominated.

Measurement of infants and children proved to be a practice carried well into the twentieth century. As the United States was entering World War I, Bird T. Baldwin had already begun his investigation of the physical, physiological and mental growth of a thousand normal boys and a thousand normal girls. From these normal boys and girls he collected 43,840 physical measurements and 21,683 academic marks."[42] Normal, it must be emphasized, more likely than not, meant white and middle class; and certainly did not include those children classified as belonging to a minority group. As late as 1956, it was reported that a third of the nation' children belonged to a minority group: "These include approximately 4,000,000 Negro children, over 1,000,000 Jewish children, 140,000 Indians, 15,000 Chinese, 56,000 Japanese, 600,000 Mexican children, and about 8,000,000 other children who were either born abroad or have foreign-born or mixed parents." It was further reported that virtually nothing was known about the children who were assigned to "minority groups." "Social and psychological studies of these children are limited to a few excellent studies of Negroes and the familiar studies of racial prejudice." Nothing was known about "the experience of growing up as a member of a minority group."[43] Even as late as 1973, it was acknowledged that historians of education knew "little" "about the education of American minority groups, particularly blacks and Indians."[44]

"Normal children" continue to be seen as white middle class children. Carol D. Lee has reported that "scientifically determined normative development continues to be the purview of communities of people of European descent, as can be seen in the most recent *Handbook of Child Psychology*. Only one chapter in this volume has an explicit focus on African-American and Latino populations. Across other chapters in the volume, research that includes these populations as exemplars of the range of normative psychosocial and cognitive development is difficult to locate. In the chapter "The Cultural Psychology of Development" "the European-American middle class is consistently used as the point of reference from which to compare cultural practices with other national and international ethnic groups."[45]

In 1933 Mary M. Shirley who conducted a longitudinal study of twenty-five infants reported not only on the measurements that were taken but also provided an account of the "irritability" expressed by the infants when measured. The measurements taken in Shirley's study included: "head measurements, trunk and arm circumferences, trunk bilateral diameters, leg and foot measurements, Babinski reflexes, and trunk anterior-posterior diameters." In addition, "The number of items at which screaming or fussing occurred was counted for each group of measures on each examination."[46]

G. Stanley Hall

Hall was unquestionably the dominant figure in American psychology in the 1880s and early 1890s, having awarded over half the earned doctorates in psychology in the United States during this period.[47] He was responsible for the founding of the American Psychological Association (APA), founded the *American Journal of Psychology* and the *Pedagogical Seminary*, made Clark University into an important center for the study of psychology and pedagogy, and helped to forge the link between psychology and pedagogy.

In June 1878, Hall completed his doctoral dissertation, "The Muscular Perception of Space," and was examined by William James and four other Harvard professors. He answered their questions satisfactorily and was awarded a doctorate in psychology. It was an historic occasion, for Hall's was the first Ph.D. in psychology to be awarded by any university in the United States. Still, he was unable to find a suitable position in an American university. He postponed the problem of finding a position by returning to Germany to study with Wilhelm Wundt at Leipzig. He also spent time acquainting himself with the latest developments in pedagogical theory and practice in Europe. Upon his return, Charles W. Eliot, president of Harvard, invited him to offer two series of lectures: one on the history of philosophy and one on pedagogy.

Each series was successful, and according to Dorothy Ross, there were several reasons for his success. First, Hall gave his lectures on pedagogy not in Cambridge but in Boston on Saturday mornings, a convenient time and place for teachers. Second, many people in the Boston area were already interested in pedagogy, for in nearby Quincy, Col. Francis W. Parker had already generated interest in educational reform. Third, teachers desired whatever help they could find in managing their classrooms more efficiently and professionally. Most teachers were women, poorly trained and poorly paid; and their task was becoming increasingly troublesome because of the growing diversity of the students. Fourth, Hall's lectures seemed "scientific," and in the last quarter of the nineteenth century there was widespread belief that science would solve all social problems and restore some semblance of order to society that was being transformed by the arrival of immigrants in ever increasing numbers. Finally, Hall's lectures, contained elements that appealed to reformers as well as to traditional or conservative thinkers. While he demonstrated that psychology supported the new ideas on teaching set forth by Pestalozzi and Froebel, he also maintained that physical punishment was often necessary to help children conform to the rules of school and society.[48]

Encouraged by the success of his lectures on pedagogy, Hall submitted two articles to the *Princeton Review* in 1882: "The Moral and Religious Training of Children" and "The Education of the Will." In each of these articles he artfully combined new theories and old values. He advised against forcing religious training at too early an age. He believed that children would naturally acquire the proper religious outlook as they approached adolescence. In these early articles he was already expressing his belief in recapitulation, the notion earlier articulated by the German evolutionist Ernst Haeckel that "ontogeny recapitulates phylogeny."[49] Based on evolution and embryology, recapitulation suggested that the child's mental growth was parallel to or a repetition of the race's phylogenetic development. It served as the basis for his genetic psychology. When applied to education, it dictated that pedagogy had to be directly related to the child's developmental stage. Education was to be pediocentric. Accordingly, it was incumbent upon educators to provide the curricular materials that would enable children to express those feelings and impulses that corresponded to their stage or culture epoch they were then recapitulating. He concluded that children should not receive any instruction in the doctrines of a religion until they had attained adolescence.

Hall also openly discussed adolescents' preoccupation with the problems that puberty presented. Adolescents needed some independence from their parents while sex and religion were their chief concerns. Those who believed that the "new education" (interpretations and applications of ideas from Pestalozzi and Froebel) was too permissive could find in Hall assurance that it was still proper to insist that children learn to obey adults. As children had a natural inclination to abide by the direction given to them by those in authority, that inclination should be used to train the young to obey. Hall used his version of psychology and evolutionary theory to support traditional values. For Hall pedagogy was applied psychology.

"The Contents of Children's Minds"

In 1882 in an address given to school superintendents at the National Education Association (NEA) meeting Hall urged the adoption of a new approach to education that would place the child at its center. The next year he published "The Contents of the Children's Minds."[50] Hall and his supporters urged the NEA to organize a Department of Child-Study, and it did so in 1894. By 1900 he was able to report that many women's clubs, summer schools, and Sunday-school teachers' organizations were devoting their attention to child-study. He had "received some two thousand letters—either unacknowledged or inadequately answered—from all parts of the world, asking how to organize local work, requesting suggestions for reading, or very often seeking advice concerning children."[51]

Hall began the "Contents" by relating that the model for his study was one that had been conducted a decade earlier in Berlin. He used his knowledge of studies conducted earlier in Germany to explore just what children did and did not know as they entered school. He investigated how many boys, how many girls, how many American children, how many Irish children, and how many children who had been to Kindergarten knew what he believed children of their age should know. With the help of assistants from a nearby Kindergarten, he assembled lists of concepts and objects. They included: beehive, frog, butterfly, ribs, ankles, the origin of butter, the source of milk, growing of dandelions, growing of apples, the number five, right from left, sunset, rivers and many other items.

No one child was completely ignorant of the questions asked, but no children knew all the answers. Knowing that every child had some misconceptions or ignorance of common objects was especially important for teachers. Every idea had to be presented in a way that would ensure its connection with an idea the child already had incorporated into his or her Herbartian "apperceptive mass." A mistaken assumption about what the child knew could "make utter nonsense or mere verbal cram of the most careful instruction."[52] For example, many children could explain what a cow was, how it provided people with milk and leather, and yet believe "that it was no bigger than a small mouse." What children learned from their picture books was not always what adults thought they learned.

Hall's study suggested that "country children" knew more and were better prepared for schoolwork than "city children." He explained the difference by noting that the content of the primers used in the schools was based on life in the country rather than the city. Curiously, Hall did not recommend that the texts be changed to relate to what children already knew, but rather, warned that the difference demonstrated that "the danger of unwarranted presupposition is considerable." Hall advised his readers that:

> As our methods of teaching grow natural we realize that city life is unnatural, and that those who grow up without knowing the country are defrauded of that without which childhood can never be completed or normal. On the whole the material of the city is no doubt inferior in pedagogic value to country experience.[53]

To remedy the difference between "country children" and "city children," Hall urged that the "city children" be taken to the country for a few days so their intelligence could be improved.

When Hall spoke to the Young Men's Christian Association in 1901, he told his audience that only in the country could humanity be natural and offered a catalogue of ills brought on by life in the city. City life restricted "the eye, which normally roves freely far and near, to the monotonous zigzag of he printed page." Other ills that could be attributed to the city were "the pallid, muddy or choloritic complexions, stoop, decaying teeth, premature grayness and baldness" as well as "the great increase of nervous disorders."[54] Hall's fear of the evils of an urban industrial society and his romantic invocations of the worthiness of nature were not unlike those of many Americans who came after him. For example, President Franklin D. Roosevelt recommend the founding of the Civilian Conservation Corps (CCC) during the Great Depression in part because he believed young men would benefit from a stay in the country. Subsequently, many Head Start teachers made special efforts to plan visits to the country for children from inner cities, and yearly thousands of middle-class Americans send their children to summer camps in the country because, they, like Hall, believe that children benefit from being near nature in the great outdoors.

After publication of "The Contents of Children's Minds" the questionnaire became a popular means of collecting data for educational research in the United States. It was not, as Hall admitted, a new instrument.[55] The *Journal of the Statistical Society of London* (October 1841) reported a study on the condition of education in Bristol that was conducted with a "circular." Henry Barnard gathered information about education in Connecticut with the use of a questionnaire about fifteen years after the Bristol Study (*American Journal of Education* (May 1856)). In *Kind und Welt* (1856) B. Sigismund reported that he had tried to add to his own observations of children by sending out inquiries to others. In October 1869 R. Schobert, president of the *Berliner pädagogische Verein* sent a letter to Berlin *Volkschulen* principals. Attached to the letter was a seventy-five item questionnaire designed to "discover the contents of the minds of children just entering the schools of the city of Berlin."[56] Hall developed considerable faith in the questionnaire as an instrument for gathering information on virtually every aspect of children, their traits, and their behavior. Between 1894 and 1915 Hall and his associates at Clark University constructed and distributed 195 questionnaires.[57]

Stages

Hall applied evolutionary theory to child development and identified what was appropriate for each stage and what could be expected of each stage. The Kindergarten stage—age two or three to six or seven—was the stage when the body needed the "most attention, and the soul the least." During this stage, children needed "more mother, and less teacher." Children of the rich were different from children of the poor, and Hall wanted appropriate treatments for the rich and the poor based on how they had been reared. "The children of the rich, generally prematurely individualized or over-individualized, especially when they are only children, must be disciplined and subordinated; while the children of the poor, usually under-individualized, should be indulged." Age seven or eight was a transitional period of great interest to science. At this stage, "there is a year or more of increased danger to the heart; the breath is shorter and fatigue easier; lassitude, nervousness, visual disorders, and cough are somewhat more imminent; and the blood is more often impoverished." At this stage, the child's brain had completed its growth. Yet, it was necessary to reduce "work and strain," for there was a yet to be understood turning point in its development. Children were not yet developmentally ready for reading and writing at this stage, and such instruction was "wasteful."[58]

Age eight or nine marked the beginning of a four-year period that ended with the beginning of puberty. During this stage, "the age of reason is only dawning," "Discipline" was to be the "watchword" and the emphasis was to be on "drill, habituation, and mechanism." This was the stage during which children were to be introduced to reading and writing for "verbal memory" was "at its very best." Arithmetic, a subject "greatly overdone in American schools" was to be taught "with plenty of mental exercises" and "with only little attempt at explanation." This was also the stage during which foreign languages were to be introduced, for this stage in the child's life represented "the stage when human speech evolved fastest."[59]

Hall's *Adolescence*

After ten years of work, Hall's two volume work—*Adolescence: Its Psychology, and Its Relations to Physiology, Anthropology, Sociology, Sex, Crime, Religion, and Education* (1904) appeared. It was the first major work on the subject, and "sold over 25,000 copies, an astonishing figure for a work of this length [over 1,300 pages], especially at a time when relatively few Americans received even a high school education." It inaugurated "the scientific study of adolescent psychology."[60] Its treatment of the topic was indeed comprehensive. E. G. Boring reported that it "had tremendous vogue," for it appeared "at the time when psychology was supposed to be about to unlock the door to scientific education."[61] In developing his notions on adolescence, Hall used the recapitulation theory to revive notions set forth in Rousseau's *Émile*. Like Rousseau, Hall emphasized the dramatic changes youth experienced when they reached puberty. The change was so great that it clearly marked the great difference between the "savage" child and the "civilized" adolescent. Puberty was nothing less than a "new birth," a time of great "storm and stress" comparable to significant upheavals in the development of the race. During adolescence, Hall wrote, "development is less gradual and more salutatory, suggestive of some ancient period of storm and stress when old moorings were broken and a higher level achieved."[62]

For adolescents, teachers could safely abandon the drill and regimentation administered to younger children and emphasize content. Adolescents were sensitive, idealistic, and ready to respond sympathetically and properly to the requirements of the adult world. In adolescents, Hall found all the noble qualities that, if properly nurtured and protected from the corrupt influences of the modern world, would save humanity. The adolescent sought "more knowledge of body and mind," was "more objective than subjective," and was interested "in adult life and in vocations."[63] Adolescence was nothing less than "a marvelous new birth, and those who believe that nothing is so worthy of love, reverence, and service as the body and soul of youth, and who hold that the best test of every human institution is how much it contributes to bring youth to the ever fullest possible development, may well review themselves and the civilization in which we live to see how far it is satisfied this supreme test."[64]

Hall was willing to broach "the relations between sex and psychology at a time when Victorian strictures on the subject had not yet given way to the relative freedom of discussion that marked the 1920s."[65] He advocated deliberate and systematic sex instruction for students. While he advocated that boys and girls be separated from each other for sex instruction, he also indicated that "where it is not practical this should not prevent teaching the subject, even to mixed classes just before puberty."[66] For girls, "the chief need" was for "hygienic instruction concerning their monthly regimen at an age when folly and ignorance are most dangerous."[67] Boys needed more instruction than girls. They needed "to know the harmfulness of self-abuse, which is very grave, although it has been the fashion to exaggerate it," and "some plain talk about the dangers of infection, both by the black plague and gonorrhea and the enormous evils of the latter, which are only lately adequately understood." They also needed to be "disabused of their morbid fears of being lost because of the spontaneous nocturnal experiences which quacks know so well how to prey upon."[68] The responsibility of educators was to promote and encourage whatever would "sublimate, spiritualize and normalize sex."[69] The best way to normalize sexual curiosity and sexual desires, Hall maintained, was through the strenuous life, not through denial of the body but through its proper development.

Hall's claim that sound mental development depended on physical development was one others would attempt to demonstrate. Related to that claim was Hall's concern with normality. In fact, he has been credited for helping "to invent the 'normal' child.[70] He and others were eager to establish what normal rates of development were. Normal development was seen as proceeding through stages that are distinguishable from one another. Hall and his students were responsible for giving age-stage psychology widespread currency. Each stage had its characteristics, and there were norms for those stages. Hall's claim that children progressed through a series of stages was early accepted. Hall's model was used by the United Census Bureau when it classified child laborers.[71] What has been accepted or considered normal has changed but the belief that there are stages and that there are norms for the stages has endured. Hall's research was used to support those who wanted to reform public education by adopting curriculum and methods that were appropriate for the child's nature and developmental stage.

Hall's Critics

Some believed that the process of studying children would destroy their natural naiveté. Hall, however, explained that data could be collected without children even knowing that they were being observed. The tasks required of the children to tap their fingers, press down on a dynamometer, count objects, insert a needle into a small hole, read, or name their favorite storydid not seem to bother or strain them. At other times children were subjected to simple examinations of their sight, hearing, speech, or height and weight. It was beneficial to ask children about their fears, for the "very calling of attention to these psychoses, which have often secretly haunted adolescence for years, has, in itself, helped toward their dissipation and control."[72]

Hall's introduction of the questionnaire into child-study in the United States was the beginning of a movement. As the questionnaires flowed out of Clark University so did the criticism. Among those who raised questions about the practice of using teachers to administer questionnaires was William James who argued that teachers did not need to be active participants in the child-study movement:

> Least of all need you, merely as *teachers*, deem it part of your duty to become contributors to psychological science or to make psychological observations in a methodical or responsible manner. I fear that some of the enthusiasts for child-study have thrown a certain burden on you in this way. Buy all means let child-study go on—it is refreshing all our sense of the child's life. There are teachers who take a spontaneous delight in filling syllabuses, inscribing observations, compiling statistics, and computing the per cent. Child-study will certainly enrich their lives. And, if its results, as treated statistically, would seem on the whole to have but trifling values, yet the anecdotes and observations of which it in part consists do certainly acquaint us more intimately with our pupils.... But, for Heaven's sake, let the rank and file of teachers be passive readers if they so prefer, and feel free not to contribute to the accumulation.[73]

James believed that the teachers were "overworked already." He agreed with his colleague Professor Munsterberg who maintained that: "the teacher's attitude toward the child, being concrete and ethical, is positively opposed to the psychological observer's, which is abstract and analytic."[74]

Psychologists have tried to move away from Hall by employing different and more precise research methods and by constructing theories on carefully collected data, but they have had to acknowledge his views on adolescence. Even as others attempted to study and to define adolescence in a manner different from Hall, the attempt to be different has turned out to be recognition that Hall continued to be an influence. In 1925, when Leta S. Hollingsworth tried to replace what Robert E. Grinder described as "Hall's superficially plausible theory with an outlook based on clinical diagnoses,"[75] she made a point in her preface to warn Hall's students that they would "miss extensive reference to his voluminous pioneer work on adolescence." The ways psychologists approached the topic, as well as social conditions, had changed so much that references to Hall would be of "historic value primarily, rather than of scientific or practical value today."[76] Twenty years later, George D. Stoddard was still trying to show that the study of adolescence had gone beyond Hall, that it was no longer "the happy hunting ground of sentimentalists and fanatics." He acknowledged that "G. Stanley Hall knew that adolescence was important, and knew why" but also suggested that Hall's "followers were tainted with a sense of vicarious sin." Consequently, "they wallowed in subscience and sermons; the adolescent veered from evil to saintliness, without enough good, rational explorable territory in between."[77] Those interested in adolescence continue to turn to Hall's work as evidenced by the Symposium on G. Stanley held at the 2004 meeting of the Society of Research on Adolescence and its publication in the August 2006 issue of *History of Psychology*.

Arnold Gesell and Stages of Development

Through Arnold Gesell, one of Hall's outstanding students, child-study became an enduring feature of American culture and education. Gesell may have done more to popularize and extend the notions of stages and normality than even his teacher. After attending the normal school in Stevens Point, Wisconsin, Gesell earned a Bachelor of Philosophy degree from the University of Wisconsin in 1903. He accepted the advice of Wisconsin's professor of psychology, Joseph Jastrow and enrolled in Clark University to study with Hall, and was awarded a Ph.D. in 1906. He went to Los Angeles to become principal and assistant professor of psychology at the Los Angeles State Normal School. After two years in Los Angeles, he returned to the University of Wisconsin to prepare for medical school, because he had decided he needed knowledge of medicine to better understand children with special needs. He was soon invited to Yale University as a part-time assistant professor of psychology. He accepted because that position enabled him to earn a medical degree, a necessity for the kind of work he wanted to undertake. In 1915, with his M.D., Gesell began to map the entire course of child development from infancy to age five. He had begun the work earlier in the New Haven dispensary; later it was conducted through the Yale Clinic of Child Development.

Like his teacher Hall, Gesell accepted an interpretation of Darwinian theory of evolution that held that heredity was a more powerful determinant of ability than was environment. His model of development was biological; the child's genetic blueprint directed his/her development. Maturation could not be ignored. There was a fixed sequence of development, but the rate of development varied from child to child. That basically meant that the child should not be unduly restricted. Given appropriate care, children would grow through a series of stages and reach adulthood. Education had to be child-centered. A child's personality could only develop properly when "his emotions are stirred in vital accompaniment to his intellectual work." That was, Gesell maintained, "a natural law."[78]

Even before Gesell completed his map, he recommended how parents and teachers should respond to and treat children based on what he claimed was normal. In *The Normal Child and Primary Education* published in 1912, only one year after the establishment of the Clinic for Child Development at Yale, Gesell began not only to define normal but also to warn that parents and teachers had an obligation to understand the growth and needs of children and not interfere with normal growth. Children, he advised, did not want to be "impressed"; they want to "express" themselves. In school, "promising" children were "thwarted in [their] growth by the incessant inhibition and prescription of early grades." Even before he had completed all his studies, Gesell was convinced that schools were organized to work against the interests and nature of children:

It is the bias of schools that everything goes like clockwork. Such formalistic uniformity and concerted action are foreign to the grace, spontaneity, and individuality of childhood. Children who grow up under such systematized direction are denied the very essence of mental growth, which depends upon original, constructive effort. The child mind loses its power to organize, and becomes as inconsequent as an atrophied muscle. Nature endowed the six-year-old with an impulse to investigate, pry into, and discover. Some primary schools are veritable tombs of deadened curiosity and initiative.[79]

Gesell advised against any early emphasis on reading instruction. Children, he claimed, were more interested in being active:

> What does the six-year-old child care for print? His fingers are itching for contact with things, and his legs are set for chasing butterflies. Too much formalism in childhood kills spontaneity and interest. Education cannot, by formulating courses of study, force intellectual functions. The laws which govern the growth of mind are as immediate and irresistible in their operation as those which govern the growth of the body. If we force either the one or the other, personality is foiled. Let us, by putting faith in instinctive impulse, conserve more of childhood to the race.[80]

Adults who forced their "motives and standards" on children risked "arresting a natural process of growth."

When and how to teach reading were and continue to be unresolved issues. One answer was provided in 1931 when Mabel V. Morphett and Carleton Washburn reported on studies conducted in Winnetka in two successive school years, 1928-29 and 1929-30. The researchers administered two intelligence tests—The Detroit First-Grade Intelligence Test and the Stanford Revision of the Binet-Simon Scale—to first grade students. Subsequently, they sought to determine whether there was an optimum age for introducing reading and concluded that: "When the Detroit test was used as a basis for determining mental age groups, the children who had a mental age of six years and six months made far better progress than did the less mature children and practically as satisfactory progress as did the children of a higher mental age." When the Stanford-Binet was used to measure intelligence, it was found that "the children with a mental age of six years and six months again made very much better progress in reading than did those of less maturity, but they made less satisfactory progress than did those whose mental age was six months greater." Those who were introduced to reading at too early an age, had difficulty, experienced discouragement or a "mental set against reading" that "lasted for years" and "hampered all their school work."[81] The federal government, as expressed in No Child Left Behind wants all children to be reading at grade level. How the norms for the various grades are being established is a question deserving an answer, for it is not clear whether there is a universal norm or different norms for different communities. What is clear is that the vast majority of students are assigned to grades based not on mental age but on chronological age.

In 1918, Gesell and his staff undertook a complete mental survey of the children in New Haven's elementary schools. The results of that survey led to the recommendations he offered in *Exceptional Children and Public School Policy* (1921). He then insisted that the school had to be constantly aware of the principles of mental hygiene, deal with each child as an individual, and have as its primary objective each child's healthy psychological and physical development.

Gesell found a way to gather data that was more reliable than Hall's use of teachers' observations and the distribution and collection of questionnaires. He developed "cinemanalyis." For the study of infants he developed a dome encased by a one-way-vision screen. On the quadrants of the dome, silent movie cameras moved back and forth to record the behavior of the infants. Before his career ended, he had accumulated nearly fifty-seven miles of film, showing the behavior of 12,000 children. Many of his books were illustrated with photographs of the specific behavior he discussed. *An Atlas of Infant Behavior: A Systematic Delineation of the Forms and Early Growth of Human Behavior Patters* (1934) contained 3,200 photographs The data he collected enabled him to map the entirety of child development.

Hall, Gesell and those who followed their lead introduced a new way to discuss schooling. In place of discourse about student's accomplishments in traditional school subjects there developed a language that emphasized the need for healthy self-concepts and the well-adjusted child, For example, in *The First Five Years of Life*, Gesell maintained what he urged some thirty years earlier: that "early reading difficulties would vanish if the natural processes of maturation were given a chance to assert themselves."[82] The problem of reading could be easily corrected by attending to the child's development. When cultural pressures and psychological processes conflicted, the best course, he urged, was to follow the psychological course:

> When culture and child come into conflict it is time to be mindful of growth factors. Reading is a major cultural goal set up by society in an age which is strongly eye-minded. Important as the goal may be, it cannot be realized through sheer drill and direct pressure. Concessions must be made to the nascent needs and to the pattern of individual development.[83]

Some used the norms Gesell developed to allow children to do what they wanted to do. They believed all children would learn what they needed to know when they were *ready* to learn it. For others, Gesel's norms were a source of concern when the children in their charge did not seem to measure up to what Gesell had laid out. Subsequently, Gesell's theories on maturation had some impact on Head Start programs in the 1960s.[84]

Lewis M. Terman

Lewis M. Terman has been described as one of the few along with John Dewey and Edward L. Thorndkie who conducted basic research in education between 1890 and 1930.[85] Equally significant is the observation that Terman was among those who "worked more directly with teachers to structure and develop the mainstream of thinking and practice in American public education."[86] At age fifteen, two years after completing the eighth grade, Terman resumed his education by enrolling in the Central Normal College in Danville, Indiana. By 1898 he had earned three degrees from Central Normal: for completing the scientific course he was warded a B.S.; a B.Pd. for completing the pedagogical course; and an A.B. for completing the classical course. While studying at Danville, he encountered Hegelian and Herbartian thought, John Dewey's *Psychology*, and works by William James, Herbert Spencer, and Ernst Haeckel. In between completing those three "courses," he served as a teacher for two years. He then accepted the position of principal of a township high school in Smiths Valley, Indiana where he is said to have taught the entire curriculum to the school's forty students.[87] In 1901, he enrolled in Indiana University where his normal school credits allowed him to enter as a junior. In June of 1903, he was graduated with a bachelor's degree and a master's degree. His master's thesis, later revised and published in 1904 in *Pedagogical Seminary*—"A Preliminary Study in the Psychology and Pedagogy of Leadership"—was based on Alfred Binet's recent work on suggestibility and works from the field of child-study conducted by Hall and Hall's students. He attempted to determine the leadership skills of a hundred white children and sixteen "colored" children by assessing their responses to questions about pictures and objects.[88]

Several of Terman's professors at Indiana were graduates of Clark University and they, especially Ernest H. Lindley, recommended that he study for the doctorate at Clark where Hall was its president and professor who offered several lecture courses and conducted a seminar very much like the one Karl Volkmar Stoy had held in Jena. While in Indiana, Terman developed an interested in gifted children and defective children. At Clark he pursued that interest for his doctoral dissertation: "Genius and Stupidity: A Study of Some of the Intellectual Processes of Seven 'Bright' and Seven 'Stupid' Boys."[89] He determined who was "bright" and who was not by administering several tests to each of the fourteen boys: a test designed to assess how inventive and creative the subject was; a test of logic; mathematical tests; mastery of language; their interpretation of fables; how well they learned chess; tests of memory; and motor skill tests. He was awarded his doctorate in 1905, the same year that the Binet-Simon scale appeared. Terman was not then aware of the Binet-Simon scale, but his use of a variety of tests to arrive at an estimate of one's "brightness" was consistent with the approach taken by Binet and Simon.[90]

Wanting to live in a warm climate because of his health (tuberculosis), Terman accepted a principalship in San Bernardino, California. In 1906 he secured a position of professor of child-study and pedagogy at the Los Angeles State Normal School, that later became the University of California at Los Angeles (UCLA). In 1910 Terman happily accepted Ellwood P. Cubberley's invitation to serve as an assistant professor of education at Stanford University. At Stanford, Terman devoted his professorial career to topics he worked on while at Clark: the study of gifted children or the psychology of genius and the measurement of intelligence. He accepted Hall's evolutionary outlook and accepted that nature was a greater determinant of intelligence than was nurture or one's environment. He had little faith in Hall's questionnaire method and opted for the empirical method—testing—earlier begun by Sir Francis Galton.

In the years before this appointment to Stanford, Terman's writings in popular magazine as well as educational journals showed that he, like many other progressives, was interested not only in child-study but also the elimination of waste. As Henry L. Minton reported, "Terman pointed out that it was the purpose of child study to scientifically investigate the sources of educational waste and to prescribe corrective messages." He maintained that regimented drill was a waste of time and argued that teachers should focus on building moral character.[91] He would, as others of his era would, soon maintain that intelligence and character were very closely related to one another. "It is well known that," he maintained, "in general, a high correlation obtains between favorable mental traits of all kinds; that for example, children superior in intelligence also tend to be superior in moral qualities."[92]

Between 1910 and 1914, Terman worked on school hygiene and mental tests. In 1914 he published two books directed to those who had direct responsibility for children. *The Hygiene of the School Child* (1914), a text aimed at those preparing to become teachers as well as parents, demonstrated that he was aware of and supportive of progressive interests and concerns. The introduction of health work in the schools was more than an educational reform. It was a way to eliminate waste; and Terman recognized that: "The prevention of waste has become, in fact, the dominant issue of our entire political, industrial, and educational situation."[93] He accepted that society was "utilizing the school as an instrument for the accomplishment of its ends" and that it was "legitimate" for society to assign the school responsibility for making "any contribution" it could make to "human welfare."[94] *Health Work in the Schools*, coauthored with Ernest Bryant and also in the series edited by Elwood P. Cubberley, was directed toward teachers and other school officials. The basic claim was that the high incidence of health difficulties found in children was evidence that the parental role was not as effective as it should be. The claim that school had to provide services for children because parents were either not capable or not willing was not peculiar to the progressives but was one the progressives did clearly embrace.

Henry H. Goddard and the Binet-Simon Tests

Henry H. Goddard, another of Hall's students, became the first psychologist to secure a post outside a university when he was appointed to the post of director of psychological research at the Vineland Training School in 1906.[95] According to Goddard, the problem of measuring intelligence first appeared in 1905 when Binet and Simon published an article ("Upon the Necessity of Establishing a Scientific Diagnosis of Inferior States of Intellintence") in *L' Année Psychologique*. That volume arrived in the United States in early 1906, but Goddard's search for literature on the problem of measuring intelligence bore no fruit, not even a reference to the work of Binet and Simon. In the Spring of 1908 he visited Dr. Decroly in Brussels and learned that Decroly and Mlle. Degand had recently completed a "try-out" of the Binet-Simon tests. He subsequently secured the 1905 article and in 1908 published a brief account of the tests, thereby introducing the Binet-Simon tests to America."[96] In 1916 when Goddard published translations of five Binet-Simon articles that constituted "a complete history and exposition of the Measuring Scale as Binet left it, he claimed it was no "exaggeration . . . to say that the world is talking of the Binet-Simon scale."[97] By 1914 he had identified a 254-item bibliography devoted to the Scale and it was being used in at least a dozen countries. His laboratory "without effort or advertisement" had "distributed 22,000 copies of the pamphlet describing the tests, and 88,000 record blanks."[98] Americans were clearly interested in ways to arrive at seemingly numerical designations.

Terman and the Binet-Simon Tests and Scales

By 1911, just after Terman's arrival at Stanford, several translations of the Binet-Simon tests and scales were available. Terman's first revision of the Binet-Simon tests appeared in 1912. He gathered normative data for each of the original tests, and based on the data he collected assigned different age levels to many of the original tests. He also used other tests that had been developed by others and even developed some of his own. In 1915 he published what came to be known as the Stanford-Binet. It and other such tests came to be known as IQ tests because Terman adopted and modified William Stern's earlier suggestion that one's mental quotient could be expressed by dividing one's mental age by one's chronological age. For example, a ten-year old with a mental age of eight would have a mental quotient of .8. Terman decided to do away with the decimal point by multiplying Stern's mental quotient by 100. Thus, in this example the person's IQ was to be expressed as 80, a whole number.

In 1916 Terman published an account of the work that led up to his revision of the Binet-Simon Scale as well as instructions on how to use it. Terman agreed that the Binet-Simon Scale has "value as an instrument for the classification of mentally-retarded children and otherwise exceptional children," but "there was a dearth of tests at the higher mental levels."[99] His revision was the product of several years of work and entailed "the examination of approximately 2,300 subjects, 1,700 of whom were "normal children," "200 defective and superior children, and more than 400 adults." To secure a representative sample he selected "a school in a community of average social status, a school attended by all or practically all the children in the district where it was located." Because he wanted to ascertain what differences there were among different children of different ages, tests were administered to all children who were "within two months of a birthday, without any consideration of the grade in which they were enrolled. He wanted a scale that would show an average child of age five to have a mental age of five, that is, an IQ of 100. Terman reported that "in the treatment of results" the "tests of foreign-born children ... were eliminated," but did not explain why they were eliminated.[100]

When Terman presented his revision of the Binet-Simon Scale with an argument for its use, he showed that he was, like other progressives, wanting to eliminate waste and to promote efficiency. There was no question, he claimed, that "between a third and a half of school children fail to progress through the grades at the expected rate." Children were being re-taught what they had already been taught at a cost of "10 per cent of the $400,000,000" that was spent for public education in the United States.[101] Administration of intelligence tests to children would guarantee proper placement and eliminate the waste.

Terman's purpose was different from Binet's. In the early years of the twentieth century in France there was considerable interest in the care and education of retarded children. In the fall of 1905, Binet was appointed to the Ministerial Commission for the Study of Retarded Children. He soon concluded that the Commission's members were "unconcerned with any objective means of selecting retardates from among normal children" and realized that "an effective test must be oriented to "tasks or behavior" rather than to so-called faculties" was needed.[102] Binet saw the tests as an instrument for diagnosis so that methods could be devised to improve children's ability to learn. Terman wanted to measure one's innate ability, an ability that, he maintained, remained fixed throughout one's life. Just as Thomas Jefferson proposed an educational plan for identifying and educating those endowed with "genius and virtue" who, if educated, would become "useful instruments for the public," so Terman proposed using his test to identify the gifted or the geniuses. There were, he claimed, a relatively small number of superior children, and it was necessary for the national welfare that they become the leaders:

> The future welfare of the country hinges, in no small degree, upon the right education of these superior children. Whether civilization moves on and up depends most on the advances made by creative thinkers and leaders in science, politics, art, morality, and religion. Moderate ability can follow, or imitate, but genius must show the way.[103]

Army Alpha and Army Beta and the National Intelligence Tests

During World War I, Terman was among a handful of psychologists led by Robert M. Yerkes who developed the now infamous Army Alpha and Army Beta tests, tests that were ultimately administered to 1.7 million men.[104] The work of that committee was greatly facilitated by the earlier work of Terman's student, Arthur S. Otis. Otis had already been developed paper-and-pencil tests for children in grades four through eight that could be administered not just to an individual as was the case with the kind of test developed by Binet and Simon and revised by Terman but to an entire group. Otis' tests served as the basis for what came to be known as Army Alpha. Army Alpha was developed for draftees and recruits who knew English and were literate. Army Beta was developed for those who either did not understand English or who were illiterate. The group tests and the group testing methods the psychologists developed during World War I while serving as officers in the Sanitary Corps were soon extended to the public schools, and Terman played a major role in that extension.

After the war the General Education Board, a Rockefeller philanthropy, agreed to awarded $25,000 to Terman and Yerkes so that they could develop group tests that could be used in schools provided that their work would be sponsored by an appropriate research agency. The National Research Council agreed to sponsor their work, and the Committee on Intelligence Tests for Elementary Schools was formed. Besides Terman and Yerkes, who agreed to serve as its chair, it included M. E. Haggerty, Edward L. Thorndike, and Guy M. Whipple. The result of the committee's work was the National Intelligence Tests. Like the Army tests, there were verbal and nonverbal forms. Norms for the National Tests were based on the performance of children from the dominant class. Others—minority children, rural children, children from the lower classes—were not included in the group on which norms were based, and the test developers knew they were establishing norms on a select group. However, they then believed their tests measured native ability and that differences between members of a minority group and those from the dominant group reflected true differences in native ability and certainly were not due to any cultural differences. The World Book Co. agreed to publish the test, and by the summer of 1920 it was ready for distribution.[105] During its first year of availability 575,000 copies were sold; two years later 800,000 copies were sold.[106] That so many were so soon sold is not really surprising, for after the war Terman and Yerkes received many requests from public school officials who wanted to administer the Army tests to schoolchildren. Advertisements for the National Intelllligence Tests clearly indicated that the tests were "the direct result of the application of the army testing methods to school needs."[107]

Terman followed his work on the National Intelligence by developing a test for students in grades seven through twelve, the Terman Group Test of Mental Ability. Like the National Intelligence Test, its test items were drawn from the Army tests. It was also published by the World Book Co., and was soon selling over 500,000 copies annually.[108] It was now, given Terman's view of the world, possible to administer easily and inexpensively an intelligence test to all students so that all would be assigned to a proper place in school and guided toward an appropriate vocation.[109]

During the Progressive Era, educators were aware of and trying to come to terms with those identified as laggards or retardates. The prevailing or "common" opinion, as reported by Terman, was that "nearly all children are capable of satisfactorily accomplishing eight grades of school work in eight years, and that if they fail to do so it is because of faulty school management."[110] That opinion is, of course, very much like the belief system embedded in the No Child Left Behind legislation that has as a major objective every child reading at grade level. No Child Left Behind basically holds the school and the teacher responsible for students' performance and maintains that virtually all should be performing (testing) at grade level. If the research conducted by Terman and others is accepted, then reforms in school management and holding teachers responsible for students' performance can not be expected to result in solving the problem of laggards, of students not performing at grade level.

If one accepts the claim of those who hold that intelligence is innate and fixed and that not all have the same amount, then the requirement of

No Child Left Behind that all children should be reading or performing at grade level poses some interesting challenges. Because there were "innate differences in intelligence," it was not reasonable or, according to Terman, possible for all, to use current language, to perform or achieve at grade-level. Terman was not willing to hold all to the same standard: "Instead of a single curriculum for all, merely divided into eight successive levels, it would be better to arrange parallel courses of study for children of different grades of ability."[111] Since enactment of No Child Left Behind and even before, it has been documented that there exists what has come to be known as the "achievement gap." Scores of minority groups on standardized tests of achievement tend to be lower than those of the majority or dominant groups. For those who hold to Terman's research and conclusions, that "gap" is not likely to be closed, for Terman clearly accepted that there were difference among races. He believed that there were "enormously significant racial differences in general intelligence" and held that those differences "cannot be wiped out by any scheme of mental culture." Children who belonged to those racial groups were to be "segregated in special classes" where the instruction would be "concrete and practical."[112]

The Dissemination of Terman's Research

The results of Terman's research on intelligence were effectively endorsed and widely disseminated by Ellwood P. Cubberley who had earlier invited Terman to join the Stanford faculty. *The Measurement of Intelligence* appeared in the Houghton Mifflin series that was edited by Cubberley who began his editor's introduction by relating that Terman's book was "one of the most significant books, viewed from the standpoint of the future of our educational theory and practice, that has been issued in years." He went on to relate how useful and important the measurement of intelligence was:

> The educational significance of the results to be obtained from careful measurements of the intelligence of children can be hardly overestimated. Questions relating to the choice of studies, vocational guidance, schoolroom procedure, the grading of pupils, promotional schemes, the study of the retardation of children in the schools, juvenile delinquency, and the proper handling of subnormals on the one hand and gifted children on the other,—all alike acquire new meaning and significance when viewed in the light of the measurement of intelligence as outlined in this volume.[113]

Cubberley's assessment held. Cubberley not only disseminated Terman's views and research but also popularized them among those who were preparing to be teachers. He did so not in professional journals but in widely used textbooks. What he wrote in 1916, was also to be found in his widely used 1919 text, *Public Education in the United States*. There he related that the "significance" of the newly "perfected" way—Terman's revision of the 1911 Binet-Simon test—to measure intelligence was "very large."[114] Educators had a way to determine what a child of six or eight years intelligence was and could be confident that the measurement then made would be a measurement that would remain constant throughout the child's adult life. Children were not born "free and equal" but were "free and unequal." The ability to measure accurately students' intelligence allowed educators to answer effectively and efficiently questions related to "proper classification in school, grading, promotion, choice of studies, schoolroom procedure, vocational guidance, and the proper handling of subnormal children on the one hand and gifted children on the other." Prospective teachers who were assigned Cubberley's "introductory textbook" were told that the school could only make useful the intelligence the student brought to the school. What the student brought to the school came from his/her "racial and family inheritance."[115] They were also told that about 2% of the students could never be expected to reach "a grade of intelligence above that normal for a twelve-year-old child." Being able to identify those with "low mentality" was important, for "low mentality, retardation in school, truancy, immorality, and criminal tendencies are all tied up closely together." A boy with low mentality was a "potential criminal; a girl with low mentality was a "potential prostitute."[116]

In his 1925 text, *An Introduction to the Study of Education and to Teaching*, Cubberley informed prospective teachers that after World War I "group intelligence tests have been perfected for use with school children of different ages, by means of which a whole class may be tested at one time."[117] As in the 1919 text, he outlined the significance and uses of intelligence tests and emphasized that heredity was more important and more powerful than environment. As he then expressed the point: "Brains tend to breed brains, and feeble-mindedness to breed feeble-mindedness." Education could only develop the mental capacity of students; it could not create it. In discussing the results of the Army tests, he related that: "The larger proportion of very inferior men was largely accounted for by the large number of South Europeans of inferior racial stock brought in by the draft."[118]

When Cubberley's revised and enlarged edition of *Public Education in the United States* appeared in 1934 (and the copyright was renewed in 1962), he continued his support for intelligence testing, relying once again on Terman's research. He acknowledged that there had been a nature-nurture debate that had "raged rather fiercely." He did acknowledge the *Twenty-Seventh Yearbook of the National Society for the Study of Education* that was devoted to a discussion of the nature-nurture controversy but did not acknowledge the symposium that appeared in 1921 in the *Journal of Educational Psychology* that revealed that there was not one but many definitions of intelligence.[119] Cubberley held to the position he articulated in 1919 and continued to support Terman's research and Terman's views. Once again he instructed prospective teachers that the school could not create intelligence. He admitted that "environment is undoubtedly a factor in mental development," but emphasized that environment "is a factor largely limited in turn by native mental capacity." One's "mental capacity" came from one's "racial and family inheritance."[120]

Cubberley not only supported the use of intelligence tests to render the work of the schools scientific and efficient, but also, as indicated in his 1925 text, recommended the use of "educational tests and measures of accomplishment" (now commonly known as achievement tests) to give supervision of classrooms and their teachers "scientific accuracy." There were then approximately three hundred such tests, and "at least twenty-five to thirty are of enough importance for the work of the school that a teacher should know something about them and their use, and a principal should be able to use at least this number accurately." If "statistical or charted results" were maintained, principals would be able to tell "almost at a glance" all they needed to know to ensure what is now known as "accountability." From such results, principals would be able to discern:

> ... whether pupils or rooms are making progress; when any group has made all desirable progress and should advance; how well a working group is suited to continue working together; whether instruction is being directed to what are the weak points; the location of teachers who are carrying a heavy load or who need help; in what rooms the load of the teacher is not properly adjusted; and whether the teachers are getting out of the pupils as much as they are capable of doing.[121]

In his 1934 revision of his 1919 text, Cubberley again related that standardized tests were important tools that would enable teachers, principals, and school superintendents to do eliminate waste and achieve "scientific accuracy" in their work.[122] All the instruments and procedures needed to ensure the kind of accountability supported by proponents of No Child Left Behind were developed during the Progressive Era.

In 1917, as the Progressive Era was coming to a close, John Dewey attached "considerable importance ... to the movement for introducing scales, standards, and methods of measurement into teaching and administration, not so much because of the amount of attention they are now receiving" but "because they represent ... a seeping on education of 'efficiency' concepts and methods which modern life is making inevitable."[123] The "tendency" Dewey then identified was one that persisted and one that has not yet abated. In 1922, Guy M. Whipple provided a list of forty-five group intelligence tests that he admitted was an incomplete list. By the end of the twentieth century, over 100 million standardized tests were administered yearly, and 44% of those were intelligence tests.[124]

NOTES

1. W. C. Bagley, W. C. Bell, C. E. Seashore and G. M. Whipple. "Editorial," *Journal of Educational Psychology*, Vol. 1, No. 1 (1910), pp. 2-3.

2. Robert H. Bremner, John Barnard, Tamara K. Hareven and Robert M. Mennel (eds.). *Children and Youth in America: A Documentary History, Volume II: 1866-1932* (Cambridge, Massachusetts: Harvard University Press, 1971), p. 602.

3. *Ibid.*, p. 15.

4. George H. Daniels. *Science in American Society: A Social History.* (New York: Alfred A. Knopf, 1971), p. 250.

5. Charlotte B. Winsor, ed. *Experimental Schools Revisited: Bulletins of the Bureau of Educational Experiments*, p. 9 quoted in V. Celia Lascardies and Blythe F. Hinitz. *History of Early Childhood Education* (New York: Falmer Press, 2000), p. 299.

6. Barbara Bibler. *School Begins at Two: A Book for Teachers and Parents* (New York: Agathon Press, Inc., 1936 reprinted 1970), p. xiii quoted in Lascardies and Hinitz, *History of Early Childhood Education*, p.300.

7. Ethel Kawin. "Records and Reports; Observations, Tests, and Measurements" in Nelson B. Henry (ed.). *The Forty-Sixth Yearbook of the National Society for the Study of Education: Part II, Early Childhood Education* (Chicago, Illinois: The University of Chicago Press, 1956), pp. 281-282.

8. "History of the Movement in Preschool and Parental Education" in Guy M. Whipple (ed). *The Twenty-Eighth Yearbook of the National Society for the Study of Education: Part I, Preschool and Parental Education: Organization and Development* (Bloomington, Illinois, 1929), p. 24.

9. Elizabeth M. R. Lomax. *Science and Patterns of Child Care* (San Francisco: W. H. Freeman and Company, 1978), p. 13

10. G. Stanley Hall. "Child-Study and Its Relation to Education," *The Forum.* Vol. XXIX (1901) in Sol Cohen. (ed.). *Education In The United States: A Documentary History*, vol. 3 (New York: Random House, 1974), p. 1842.

11. John M. O'Donnell. *The Origins of Behaviorism: American Psychology, 1870-1920* (New York: New York University Press. 1985), p. 27.

12. Emily S. Davidson and Ludy T. Benjamin, Jr. "A History of the Child Study Movement in America" in John A. Glover and Royce R. Ronning (eds.). *Historical Foundations of Educational Psychology* (New York: Plenum Press, 1987), p. 46.

13. Robert E. Grinder. *A History of Genetic Psychology: The First Science of Human Development* (New York: John Wiley and Sons, Inc. 1967), p. 205.

14. Thomas K. Fagan. "Compulsory Schooling, Child Study, Clinical Psychology, and Special Education," *American Psychologist*, Vol. 47, No. 2 (February 1992), p. 238.

15. Hamilton Cravens. *Before Head Start: The Iowa Station and America's Children* (Chapel Hill: University of North Carolina Press, 1993), p. 7.

16. Davidson and Benjamin, Jr. "A History of the Child Study Movement in America," p. 41.

17. Arthur MacDonald. "Child Study in the United States," *Report of the Commissioner of Education for the Year 1897-98*, Vol. 2, Whole Number 258 (Washington: Government Printing Office, 1899), p. 1281.

18. Dennis' bibliography of sixty-four baby biographies first appeared in *Child Development*, Vol, 7 (1934), pp. 70-74. It was reproduced in Wayne Dennis (ed.). *Readings in Child Psychology* (Englewood Cliffs, New Jersey: Prentice-Hall, Inc., 1951), pp. 64-67. A translated portion of Tiedmann's *Beobachtungen* is included in Wayne Dennis (ed.). *Historical Readings in Developmental Psychology* (New York: Appleton-Century Crofts, 1972), pp. 11-31.

19. *Eighth Annual Report of the Board of Education, of the City of Oswego* (1861) in Cohen (ed.). *Education in the United States*, Vol. 3, p. 1781.

20. Edward A. Sheldon. "Object Teaching" in Cohen (ed.). *Education in the United States*, pp. 1782-1783.

21. Dennis (ed.). *Historical Readings in Developmental Psychology*, p. 11.

22. Charles Darwin. "A Biographical Sketch of an Infant" in Dennis (ed.). *Readings in Child Psychology*, p. 55. The original appeared in *Mind*, Vol. 2 (1871), pp. 285-294. It was later reprinted in *Popular Science Monthly*, Vol. 57 (1900), pp. 197-205. Darwin was referring to Hippolyte Taine's "The Acquisition of Language by Children" that appeared in *Mind*, Vol. 2 (1877). What appeared in *Mind* was a translation of Taine's work that originally appeared in 1876 in *Revue Philosophique*.

23. Lomax. *Science and Patterns of Child Care*, p. 25.

24. Taine "The Acquisition of Language" quoted in Lomax. *Science and Patterns of Child Care*, p. 25.

25. Darwin. "A Biographical Sketch of an Infant" in Dennis (ed.). *Readings in Child Psychology*, p. 55.

26. Charles Darwin. *The Expression of the Emotions in Man and Animals* in Dennis (ed.). *Historical Readings in Developmental Psychology*, p. 75.

27. Dennis (ed.). *Historical Readings in Developmental Psychology*, p. 106.

28. See, for example: Millicent W. Shinn. *Notes on the Development of a Child. I. University of California Publications in Education*, Vol. 1 (Berkeley: University of California Press, 1893-1899); Millicent W. Shinn. *The Biography of a Baby* (Boston: Houghton Mifflin Co., 1900); and Millicent W. Shinn. *Notes on the Development of a Child. II. The Development of the Senses in the First Three Years of Childhood. University of California Publications in Education*, Vol. 4 (Berkeley: University of California Press, 1904. Dennis included these in his list.

29. In 1905 an American edition, *Studies of Childhood* published by D. Appleton & Co. appeared. The English edition was published by Longmans Green.

30. Karl Groos. *Die Spiele der Tiere* (Jena: Fischer, 1899) and Karl Groos. *Die Spile des Menschen* (Jena: Fischer, 1899).

31. Antonia Marro. *La Puberta* (Torino: Bocca, 1897).

32. Ellen K. S. Key. *Barnets århundrade* (Stockholm: A. Bonnier, 1900). An English translation of Key's work, *The Century of the Child*, (New York: G. Putnam's Sons) appeared in 1909. The English translation was, in fact, a translation of a German translation: *Das Jahrhundert Des Kindes* (Berlin: S. Fischer, 1905).

33. Alfred Binet. *La Suggestibilité* (Paris: Schleicher Frères, 1900); Alfred Binet. *Les Idées Modernes sur lEnfants* (Paris: Flammarion, 1909).

34. Clara and L. W. Stern. *Die Kindersprache* (Leipzig: Barth, 1907).

35. W. Stern. *Psychologie der Frühen Kindheit* (Leipzig: Quelle and Mayer, 1914).

36. Lomax. *Science and Patterns of Child Care*, p. 19.

37. Quoted in Lomax. *Science and Patterns of Child Care*, pp. 21-22.

38. Quoted in Lomax. *Science and Patterns of Child Care*, p. 15.

39. Quoted in Lomax, *Science and Patterns of Child Care*, p. 22.

40. Quoted in Lomax, *Science and Patterns of Child Care*, p. 23.

41. Fagan. "Compulsory Schooling, Child Study, Clinical Psychology, and Special Education," p. 238.

42. Cravens. *Before Head Start*, p. 28.

43. Leah Levinger and Lois Barclay Murphy. "Implications of the Social Scene for the Education of Young Children" in Nelson B. Henry (ed). *The Forty-Sixth Yearbook of the National Society for the Study of Education: Part II, Early Childhood Education* (Chicago, Illinois: University of Chicago Press, 1956). P. 16.

44. Douglas Sloan. "Historiography and the History of Education" in Fred N. Kerlinger (ed.). *Review of Research in Education 1* (Itasca, Illinois: F. E. Peacock Publishers, Inc., 1973), p. 261.

45. Carol D. Lee. "Why We Need to Re-Think Race and Ethnicity in Educational Research," *Educational Researcher*, Vol. 32, No. 5 (June/July 2003), p. 3

46. Mary M. Shirley. *The First Two Years*, Vol. 3 (Minneapolis: University of Minneapolis Press, 1933) reproduced in Dennis. *Readings in Child Psychology*, p. 97.

47. O'Donnell. *The Origins of Behaviorism*, p. 141.

48. Dorothy Ross. *G. Stanley Hall: The Psychologist as Prophet* (Chicago: University of Chicago Press, 1972), pp. 113-117.

49. Ernst H. Haeckel (1834-1919) a German biologist and Darwinist maintained that natural law made progress inevitable. He also maintained that developing organisms relived their evolutionary history as they traveled through stages that recapitulated those of their predecessors.

50. Hall's "Contents" article originally appeared in the *Princeton Review* (1883). It was reproduced in its entirety in Dennis (ed.). *Readings in the History of Psychology*, pp. 255-276.

51. G. Stanley Hall, "Child-Study and its Relation to Education," *The Forum*, Vol. 29 (August 1900) in Charles E. Strickland and Charles Burgess (eds.).

Health, Growth, and Heredity: G. Stanley Hall on Natural Education (New York: Teachers College Press, 1965), p. 75.

52.   G. Stanley Hall. "The Contents of Children's Minds," *Princeton Review*, (1883) in Dennis ed. *Readings in the History of Psychology*, p. 260.

53.   *Ibid.*, p. 261.

54.   G. Stanley Hall. "Christianity and Physical Culture," *The Pedagogical Seminary*, Vol. 9 (September 1902) in Strickland and Burgess (eds.). *Health Growth, and Heredity*, p. 157.

55.   For an early account of the use of the questionnaire see: Robert H. Gault. "A History of the Questionnaire Method of Research in Psychology," *Pedagogical Seminary*, Vol. 14, No. 3 (September 1907), pp. 366-383.

56.   See: Gault. "A History of the Questionnaire," p. 375 and F. Bartholomai and Schwabe. "*Der Vorstellungskreis der Berliner Kinder, beim Eintritt in die Schule*," *Städtisches Jahrbuch, Berlin und seine Entwicklung*, Vol. 4, (1870). A translation, "The Contents of Children's Minds on Entering School at the Age of 6 Years," appeared in the *Report of the Commissioner of Education for the Year 1900-1901*, Vol. 1 (Washington, D. C.: Government Printing Office, 1902), pp. 710-727.

57.   These are listed in Lomax. *Science and Patterns of Child Care*, pp. 222-230.

58.   G. Stanley Hall, "The Ideal School as Based on Child Study," National Education Association, *Journal of Addresses and Proceedings, 1901* (Washington, D. C., 1901) in Cohen (ed.). *Education in the United States*, Vol. 3, pp. 1845-1848.

59.   *Ibid.*, pp.. 1847-1848.

60.   Jeffrey Jensen Arnett and Hamilton Cravens, "G. Stanley Hall's *Adolescence*: A Centennial Reappraisal," *History of Psychology*, Vol. 9, No. 3 (August 2006), p. 165.

61.   Edwin G. Boring. *A History of Experimental Psychology*, 2nd ed. (New York: Appleton-Century-Crofts, 1950, p. 522.

62.   G. Stanley Hall. *Adolescence* in Strickland and Burgess (eds.). *Health, Growth and Heredity*, p. 106.

63.   *Ibid.*, p. 108.

64.   *Ibid.*, p. 109.

65.   Strickland and Burgess. *Health, Growth, and Heredity*, p. 161.

66.   G. Stanley Hall. "The Needs and Methods of Educating Young People in the Hygiene of Sex," *The Pedagogical Seminary*, Vol. 15 (March 1908) in Strickland and Burgess (eds.). *Health, Growth, and Heredity*, p. 170.

67.   *Ibid.*, pp. 170-171.

68.   *Ibid.*

69.   *Ibid.*, p. 174.

70.   Fagan. "Compulsory Schooling, Child Study, Clinical Psychology, and Special Education," p. 238.

71.   United States Department of Commerce and Labor, Bureau of the Census. *Bulletin 69* (Washington, D. C., 1907) in Bremner. Vol. II, p. 602.

72.   G. Stanley Hall. "Child-Study and Its Relation to Education," *The Forum*, Vol. 29 (August 1900) in Strickland and Burgess (ed.). *Health, Growth and Heredity*, p. 79.

73. William James. *Talks to Teachers on Psychology* (New York: Henry Holt and Co., 1901), pp. 12-13.

74. *Ibid.*, p. 13.

75. Robert E. Grinder. "Epilogue: Two Models for the Study of Youth—1944 versus 1975" in Robert J. Havighurst and Philip H. Dreyer (eds.). *The Seventy-Fourth Yearbook of the National Society for the Study of Education: Part I, Youth* (Chicago: University of Chicago Press, 1975), p. 435.

76. Leta S. Hollingsworth. *The Psychology of the Adolescent* (New York: D. Appleton Century, 1925), p. ix.

77. George D. Stoddard. "An Evaluation of the Yearbook" in Nelson B. Henry (ed.). *The Forty-Third Yearbook of the National Society for the Study of Education: Part I, Adolescence* (Chicago: University of Chicago Press, 1944), p. 347.

78. Arnold Gesell. *The Normal Child and Primary Education* (Boston, 1912) reproduced in Robert H. Bremner *et al.* (eds). *Children and Youth in America: A Documentary History*, Vol. 11, 1866-1932, Parts 7-8 (Cambridge, Massachusetts, 1971) p. 1124.

79. *Ibid.*, pp. 1123-1124.

80. *Ibid.*, p. 1125.

81. Mabel V. Morphett and Carleton Washburn, "When Should Children Begin to Read? *Elementary School Journal*, Vol. 31 (1931) in Dennis (ed.). *Readings in Child Psychology*, pp. 601-602, 595.

82. Arnold Gesell, *et. al. The First Five Years of Life* (New York: Harper and Brothers, 1940), p. 313.

83. *Ibid.*, pp. 313-314.

84. Lascarides and F. Hinitz. *History of Early Childhood Education*, p. 401.

85. David Tyack and Elisabeth Hansot. *Mangers of Virtue: Public School Leadership in American Education* (New York: Basic Books, 1982), p. 154.

86. Clarence J. Karrier. *Scientists of the Mind: Intellectual Founders of Modern Psychology* (Urbana, Illinois: University of Illinois Press, 1986), p. 93.

87. Henry L. Minton, *Lewis M. Terman: Pioneer in Psychological Testing* (New York: New York University Press, 1988), pp. 10-13.

88. *Ibid.*, p. 20.

89. It was published in 1906 in the *Pedagogical Seminary*.

90. Minton. *Lewis M. Terman*, p. 27.

91. *Ibid.*, p, 34.

92. Lewis M. Terman. "The Intelligence Quotient of Francis Galton in Childhood," *American Journal of Psychology*, Vol. 28 (1917) in Dennis (ed.). *Readings in Child Psychology*, pp. 375-376.

93. Lewis M. Terman. *The Hygiene of the School Child* (Boston: Houghton Mifflin Co. 1914), pp. 1-2 in Minton. *Lewis M. Terman*, p. 43.

94. Terman. *Hygiene of the School Child*, pp. 10-11.

95. O'Donnell. *The Origins of Behaviorism*, p. 222.

96. Henry H. Goddard, "Editor's Introduction] in Henry H. Goddard (ed.). *The Development of Intelligence in Children*, tr. By Elizaabeth S. Kite. Publications of the Training School at Vineland, New Jersey, Department of Research, No. 11, May 1916 (Baltimore: Williams and Wilkins Co., 1916), p. 5.

97. *Ibid.*, pp. 6-7. . The five Binet-Simon articles that made up *The Development of Intelligence in Children* were: "Upon the Necessity of Establishing a Scientific Diagnosis of Inferior States of Intelligence," *LAnné Psychologique* (1905); "New Methods for the Diagnosis of the Intellectual level of Subnormals," *LAnné Psychologique* (1905); "Application of the New Methods to the Diagnois of the Intellectual Level Among Normal and Subnormal Children in Institutions and in the Primary Grades;" "The Development of Intelligence in the Child," *LAnné Psychologique* (1908); and "New Investigation Upon the Measure of the Intellectual Level Among School Children," *LAnné Psychologique* (1911).

98. *Ibid.*, p. 6.

99. Lewis M. Terman. *The Measurement of Intelligence: An Explanation of and a Complete Guide for the Use of the Stanford Revision and the Extension of The Binet-Simon Intelligence Scale* (Boston: Houghton Mifflin Co., 1916), p. 51.

100. *Ibid.*, pp.52- 53.

101. *Ibid.*, p. 3.

102. Theta H. Wolf. *Alfred Binet* (Chicago: University of Chicago Press, 1973), p. 29.

103. Terman. *Measurement of Intelligence*, p. 12.

104. For accounts of the development of the Army tests see: Stephen Jay Gould. *The Mismeasure of Man* (New York: W. Norton & Co., 1981), pp. 192-232 and Franz Samelson. "World War I Intelligence Testing and the Development of Psychology, *Journal of History of the Behavioral Sciences*, Vol. 13, No. 3 (July 1977).

105. Minton. *Lewis M. Terman*, pp. 91-92,. .

106. Ellwood P. Cubberley. *Public Education in the United States: A Study and Interpretation of American Educational History* rev. ed. (Boston: Houghton Mifflin Co., 1934), p. 700.

107. From a World Book Company advertisement reproduced in Gould. *The Mismeasure of Man*, p. 503.

108. Minton. *Lewis M. Terman*, p. 94.

109. Lewis M. Terman. *The Intelligence of School Children* (Boston: Houghton Mifflin, 1919) in Robert H. Bremner, et al. (eds). *Children and Youth in America: Volume II*, p. 1450.

110. *Ibid.*, p. 1448.

111. *Ibid.*, pp. 1448-1449.

112. Terman. *Measurement of Intelligence*, p. 92.

113. Ellwood P. Cuberley. "Editors Introduction" to Terman. *Measurement of Intelligence*, pp. vii-viii.

114. Ellwood P. Cubberley. *Public Education in the United States: A Study and Interpretation of American Educational History* (Boston: Houghton Mifflin Co., 1919), p. 452.

115. *Ibid.*, p. 451.

116. *Ibid.*, p. 453.

117. Ellwood P. Cubberley. *An Introduction to the Study of Education and to Teaching* (Boston: Houghton Mifflin Co., 1925), p. 196.

118. *Ibid.*, p. 198.

119. For a discussion of the 1921 symposium in the *Journal of Educational Psychology* see: Paul L. Boynton. "Intelligence and Intelligence Testing" in Walter S. Monroe (ed.). *Encyclopedia of Educational Research* (New York: The Macmillan Co., 1941), pp. 622-623.

120. Ellwood P. Cubberley. *Public Education in the United States: A Study and Interprettion of American Educational History* rev. ed. (Boston: Houghton Mifflin Co., 1934), P. 700.

121. Cubberley. *An Introduction to the Study of Education and to Teaching*, pp. 258-259.

122. Cubberley. *Public Education in the United States*, rev. ed., pp. 697-698.

123. John Dewey, "Current Tendencies in Education," *The Dial*, Vol. LXII, No. 739 (April 5, 1917), p. 288.

124. Theresa Richardson and Erwin V. Johanningmeier. "Intelligence Testing: The Legitimation of a Meritocratic Educational Science," *International Journal of Educational Research*, Vol. 37, No. 8 (1997), p. 700.

CHAPTER 8

EDUCATIONAL EFFICIENCY AND TESTS

Daniel Starch and Stuart A. Courtis

Many professional educators in the first half of the twentieth century got caught up in what Raymond E. Callahan called the "cult of efficiency."[1] This was true of two representative and influential educators who contributed to the spread of the cult of efficiency, Daniel Starch and Stuart A. Courtis. Efficiency and accountability were as much a part of the language of the Progressive Era as discussions on the nature of children and fitting pedagogy and curriculum to their special needs at various stages of development. Starch and Courtis were clearly interested in "efficiency" and the elimination of "waste." They pioneered in making educational institutions accountable through quantifiable assessment. Progressives concerned with accountability talked about educational "products," bringing to mind the factory. Factory and military metaphors permeated educational discourse at the turn of the century.[2] Starch and Courtis were representatives of this era. They believed in science, believed psychology was a science, and believed in measurement. This chapter examines the American fascination with accountability through testing and measurement with special attention to the role of Daniel Starch and Stuart A. Courtis in the first half of the twentieth century.

Educational Research, the National Agenda, and Educational Reform:
A History, pp. 215–247
Copyright © 2008 by Information Age Publishing
All rights of reproduction in any form reserved.

215

AMERICANS, MEASUREMENT, AND STATISTICAL KNOWLEDGE

In considering Starch and Courtis as representatives of Progressive Era accountability and its influence, still a prominent if not dominant part of educational policy and practice, it may be fruitful to recall that Americans have always been fascinated by statistical knowledge. For example, when Francis Grund related his observations on American life and education in 1837, he noted that the Americans were "great admirers of statistics." He reported that "the rage for statistical tables, as a means of obtaining knowledge in a quick and easy manner, exists in the United States to a still greater degree than in England or France."[3] Daniel Boorstin observed that the "distinctive fact" about Americans' use of statistics "was not their rise as a learned specialty," but their "unprecedented popular diffusion." Boorstin also suggested that in "the twentieth century a new kind of number consciousness captured the public mind."[4]

It is also useful to follow the lead suggested by David Hamilton in his "Educational Research and the Shadows of Francis Galton and Ronald Fisher."[5] It did not take long for Galton's work to reach the United States. In the 1870s Galton was promoting the study of anthropometry and urging that anthropmetric records be made and stored. Galton opened a laboratory in London in 1882 at the South Kensington Museum where in exchange for a fee any person could have his physical measurements taken and be given a vision test, hearing tests, and have his reaction times measured. In 1893 Joseph Jastrow of the University of Wisconsin found many at the World's Columbian Exposition in Chicago who were willing to have psychological tests administered to them. James McKeen Cattell who was to become Edward L. Thorndike's mentor and who had described Galton as the greatest man he had ever known was probably the first to use the term "mental tests" when he administered a battery of tests to one hundred University of Pennsylvania freshmen.[6] At Clark University Franz Boas was teaching courses in statistics in 1889.[7] In 1891 Boaz with encouragement from G. Stanley Hall began measuring fifteen hundred Worcester school children.[8] Hall had already surveyed "The Contents of Children's Minds" (1883).

The use of statistics has not been limited to educators. Indeed, it has been applied to the administration of nearly all affairs of the state and to nearly all social service institutions. William H. Allen, the general agent for the New York Association for Improving the Condition of the Poor, suggested what the origin and the meaning of the word, statistics, may be. Allen related that "this much hated word [statistics]" began life in 1648 as the name for facts "which concern obviously the prosperity of the state, either in obstructing it or contributing to it." Statistics, as a word, he indicated came from a German word—*Staatsmerkwürdigkeiten*—the literal translation of which is: "Of the state—note—worthy—things."[9]

The United States as a state appears to have realized the use it could make of statistics early in the twentieth century. The statistics gathered by psychologists turned army officers during the administration of Army Alpha and Army Beta is but one example. An examination of the careers of those who received doctorates in the social sciences in the early years of the twentieth century is instructive. Social scientists, armed with statistical procedures, aided several branches of government adopt the new science. Two who did so are Leonard P. Ayers and Edmund Alonzo Day.

Ayers employed his knowledge of social science methods to the problems of school dropouts and retardation in *Laggards in Our Schools* (1909). While holding several important public positions between 1917 and 1920, Ayers applied the techniques of social science research to national defense, war and peace-making. In April, 1917 Ayers and eight members of his staff from the Russell Sage Foundation volunteered to organize the Division of Statistics of the Council of National Defense. After six months, Ayers was also responsible for statistical reporting and analysis for the War Industries Board, the Priorities Committee and the Allies' Purchasing Committee. In addition to these duties, Ayers provided services to the United States Army that had no facility for statistics until Ayers was made a lieutenant colonel and assigned that responsibility. Soon he had a staff of fifty and was directing the statistical summary of the war, *The War With Germany* (1919) that brought him considerable public attention. He returned to France as the chief statistical officer to the American Commission to Negotiate Peace. Upon returning from Versailles in 1920, he became vice-president and chief economist of the Cleveland Trust Company. He was in charge of statistics at the bank.

Edmund Ezra Day, who was awarded a PhD in economics from Harvard in 1910, also used his statistical skills in the war effort. From September to December, 1918 he served as a statistician for the Central Bureau of Planning and Statistics for the War Industries Board. For seven months during 1918-19, he served as a statistician for the Division of Planning and Statistics of the United States Shipping Board and from June to August 1919, he served as director of that Division. Subsequently, he served as a Director of the Rockefeller Foundation, as a representative on the Preparatory Commission of Experts for the World Monetary and Economic Conference in London in 1933, and as President of Cornell University. He was also a member of the National Education Association's Educational Policies Commission.

Those equipped with statistical skills were able to assist government conduct its affairs efficiently. How this introduction and residence has influenced public education policy remains to be thoroughly investigated.

During the Progressive Era, as William Allan, observed "the modern Diogenes does not go about with a lantern seeking goodness; he looks for efficiency and expects goodness to be thrown in."[10] The modern Diogenes still roams all the halls of that social enterprise known as public education.

DANIEL STARCH, EFFICIENCY AND ACHIEVEMENT

Daniel Starch[11] is an example of a late nineteenth century farm boy who met with academic and professional success in the first half of the twentieth century. He may even be one of those whom Daniel Boorstin described as "Go-Getters."[12] He attended the Morningside College in Sioux City, Iowa where he majored in psychology and mathematics, subjects that prepared him to pursue the new field of experimental psychology. After being graduated from Morningside in 1903 at age nineteen, the youngest in his graduating class, he secured a fellowship from the State University of Iowa in Iowa City where Carl Emil Seashore had been recently appointed professor of psychology. In 1904 he was awarded an M.A. degree and elected to remain in Iowa to continue his work in psychology. He received his Ph.D. in 1906 after completing his dissertation, "Localization of Sound."

After earning his doctorate, Starch remained at Iowa for a year to serve as an instructor in experimental psychology. He then moved to Massachusetts to serve as an instructor in experimental psychology at Wellesley College and to study experimental psychology at Harvard. In 1908 he began his twelve-year tenure at the University of Wisconsin where he applied the conclusions of the new science to education and to advertising. That work enabled him to publish several books: *Principles of Advertising—A Systematic Syllabus* (1910); *Experiments in Educational Psychology* (1911); *Advertising: Its Principles, Practices and Technique* (1914); and *Educational Psychology* (1919).[13]

Starch's applications of psychology to practical affairs, advertising and education met with success. His growing reputation in the psychology of advertising led to his appointment as a lecturer at the Harvard Graduate School of Business in 1919. From then on, most, though not all, of his professional efforts were in the field of advertising. While at Harvard, he took an assignment from the Liberty Mutual Insurance Company that was looking for an effective way to advertise automobile liability insurance. The company submitted half-a-dozen layouts, and Starch evaluated them. His "findings showed that the ad using a picture of an automobile collision received first attention and reading." In 1962 it was reported that "although the agencies handling its account have changed over the years,

Liberty Mutual still uses the theme recommended by Starch, and "reader-ship reports over the years have shown consistently that ads with this theme are high in both 'noted' and 'read most' scores."[14]

Starch devoted considerable attention to the problem of measuring readership of advertisements even though he was told it could not be done. In 1922 he completed his work on his readership-scoring method. He reported his method in *Principles of Advertising* (1923) that became a standard text in the field for several years. He reported that the book's "royalties were more than my year's salary as a teacher." In 1923, he founded his own research company, "Daniel Starch and Staff." Starch left Harvard in 1927 to devote full time to his company. In 1963 his company had offices in Chicago, Toronto, Montreal and Sydney besides the home office in Mamaroneck, New York. Within the United States Starch's com-pany employed nearly 900 people.[15]

It appears that Starch will be best known for two accomplishments: first, for formulating Netapps in 1958—a method for determining what portion of a product's sales can be attributed to advertising in any media;[16] and second for determining how many families had a radio in 1928. When the National Broadcasting Company (NBC) asked him the question, Starch, in order to answer it, designed a probability-sample technique to determine how well a random sample of a given area would be representative of the whole. His methods were successful, for the sur-vey taken by the Bureau of the Census in 1930 showed that Starch's esti-mate was within 4% of that established by the Census.

While Starch did publish work on human behavior and on human behavior and education with Hazel Stanton and Wilhelmine Koenth in 1936 and 1941 (*Controlling Human Behavior* (1936) and *Psychology in Edu-cation* (1941)) his career in educational psychology is basically limited to the period before his tenure at Harvard. His work in educational psychol-ogy may be examined under two headings: first, his attempts to deter-mine how to measure the educational product—the measurement of pupil achievement; the reliability of grading practices; and his attempt to determine the worth of school subjects; and second, his text *Educational Psychology* (1919).

In a review of Starch's *Experiments in Educational Psychology*, Frank N. Freeman of the University of Chicago observed that Starch's work repre-sented "one type of educational psychology." Freeman maintained "that there is also another, and at least equally productive, type, which consists in the experimental analysis of specific educational processes, such for example, as reading, writing, spelling, and counting."[17] According to Freeman, statistical studies that were psychological in nature could be profitably applied to educational problems. Examination of Starch's works subsequent to Freeman's review suggests that he may have followed

Freeman's advice. Starch soon produced a series of articles that dealt with the measurement of ability or efficiency in various school subjects. During 1912-13, he collaborated with E. C. Elliott in the publication of grading practices in high school English, history, and mathematics.[18]

The Starch-Elliott studies were among the first of their kind. Before them, there were only a few similar studies; one by Edgeworth in 1890; Max Meyer's "Grading of Students" in 1908; Walter F. Dearborn's "The Relative Standings of Pupils in High School and in the University" in 1909 and his *School and University Grades* in 1910, and Franklin W. Johnson's "A Study of High School Grades" in 1911.[19]

Starch and Elliott set out to determine how widely grading practices varied. Their findings consistently revealed that marks assigned to a given paper by different readers varied widely. The wide ranges of variation led Starch to write *Educational Measurements* (1916). He admitted that most educational measurements were still in the experimental stage but also observed that "the need of definite, objective measures of educational products" was sufficiently "great" to proceed with the task.[20] A year earlier Starch had offered the judgment that "the current movement for measuring school products is one of the three or four most important fields of investigation in the scientific study of educational 'problems.'"[21] The tests and scales that were available could be further refined through more use and serve as "tools for evaluating quantitatively the results of methods and factors in teaching and learning, and for examining various aspects of efficiency of instruction and administration of school systems. About the principle of educational measurement Starch had no doubts. The old time pedagogy was giving way to the new. In its place were "quantitative studies, objective measurements, and carefully observed facts." In a statement consistent with Thorndike's views, Starch wrote: "Any quality of ability in human nature that is detectable is also measurable."[22] The task of education was "to discover more and more accurate means of measurement."

Educational Measurement: Assigning Grades Systematically

The practice of educational measurement only needed to be improved. It did not need to be defended. It was part of the day-to-day work of the school. It was either used or misused each time a grade or mark was assigned. There were "numerous and momentous problems" in the working of a school that depended upon those marks. Decisions about "promotion, retardation, elimination, honors, eligibility for contests and societies, graduation, admission to higher institutions, recommendations for future positions" all depended upon the grades assigned to students. In all aspects of educational activity and human activity measurements were made. Better than or worse than was commonly ascribed to a person or a situation just as judgments were made about what was more or less useful. All sorts of comparative judgments about all sorts of matters were made on a daily basis. In place of rough comparative judgments Starch wanted people, especially in school matters, to be more precise. Educational measurement would allow refinement of judgments and enable school officials to "express them in terms of known units of a definable character, so that we may be able to say, for example, that a pupil can read three words per second of a certain passage and to report so and so much of it, that he knows the English meaning of 2,000 Latin words and can translate without error sentences of specified difficulty. If there were educational "products or by-products" that could not be judged to exist in some quantity, then, Starch advised," we may be suspicious of their actual existence."[23]

Although educators were generally so confident of their marking procedures that they often used fractions even when they had a scale of a hundred points, there was, Starch maintained, no reason to believe that the grades assigned to students were reliable. Numerous studies had shown that there were wide ranges or differences in grading practices from school to school and even from teacher to teacher within a department. The percent of "excellent" grades and percent of "failures" in the same subject in the same department varied too widely too frequently. Even the folk wisdom about grades was in error: "Contrary to current belief, grades in mathematics are as unreliable as grades in language or in history." Investigations had shown that "the mathematics instructors did not agree any more closely with their own marks than the language or science instructors."[24] It was found that the marks assigned to a set of papers in plane geometry by 116 teachers ranged from twenty-eight to ninety two.

To remedy the wide diversity of practices in marking, Starch advised adoption of appropriate marking scales and standards for the distribution of marks. Those scales employing 100, 99, 98, 97...0 were not appropriate, for they had no "objective validity." The divisions on a marking scale had to be large enough to allow 75% of all measurements of a student's paper to fall within that division in order to insure validity.

Starch's own calculations recommended that a scale with five marks be used. The scale and the distribution he recommended resembles a bell curve:

A or Excellent, approximately 7% of the pupils.
B or Superior, approximately 24% of he pupils.

C or Average, approximately 38% of he pupils.

D or Inferior, approximately 24% of the pupils.

E or Unsatisfactory, approximately 7% of the pupils.[25]

Starch further advised that letters and symbols were preferable to words such as "good" or "fair" or "poor." Words had "moral implications" that Starch wanted to avoid, though in his text on educational psychology he observed that students with high marks are usually of superior character.[26]

Starch recommended that "marks on the whole and for large groups of pupils of usual ability should be distributed with a reasonably close conformity to the normal, bell-shaped, probability curve."[27] He observed that since human physical traits and psychological traits to the extent that they had been measured conformed to the probability curve, there was no reason why all marks should not be normally distributed. While there were factors that tended to skew the curve in one direction or the other, they ultimately counterbalanced each other. For, example, elimination of poor students from schools, especially in the upper grades, and the improved performance of students because of good teaching were often offset by the lower performance of students who did not always employ maximum effort.[28] The elimination of poor students was "not a cutting off at a definite point of the curve, but rather a smooth shaving off along the entire range." Starch maintained that marks would "be assigned much more justly if they are assigned with reasonably close conformity to the probability distribution."[29] During the same period that Starch was working, Harold O. Rugg presented data that showed "that the normal distribution did not hold in some cases and that many factors affecting marks were not susceptible to an assumption of normality,"[30] but Starch and others continued to maintain that all measurements and all performances involving students invariably fit the normal curve.

Ability, Performance and Experimentation

To assist school personnel Starch provided several chapters on the testing of ability and school performance. He devoted a chapter to testing in each of the following school subjects: Reading, writing, spelling, grammar, arithmetic, composition, drawing, Latin, German, French and physics. Teachers were told how tests could be secured, how they were scored, and what they tested. Teachers of a given subject were effectively provided a convenient recipe for testing and grading in the subjects they taught. Starch devoted some two hundred pages to these same topics in his educational psychology text. In fact, the account he provided on "the results of experimental studies in school subjects" had "never before been attempted in a text on educational psychology."[31]

In the last chapter of *Educational Measurements* Starch explained how standardized tests could be used in school experiments. Psychologists had collected "a very considerable body of facts about the learning of more or less artificial material such as syllables, words, poetry, prose and symbols of various sorts," but there was "not a single school subject regarding which we have anything more than a fragmentary psychology of the factors and conditions that affect the progress of learning in that particular subject."[32] Teachers could, he explained, use standardized tests in educational experiments in their classrooms. They could divide students into groups using "the equal squad method" (now often called a control group and an experimental group), administer the tests before instruction, and compare results after instruction. Such experiments could be conducted without interrupting the normal day-to-day routines of the classroom. Starch indicated that the equal squad method "has been used in a limited way in various types of investigations, not so much with human beings as with animals and plants in agricultural experiment stations."[33] It was a method that would be extensively used in the future by educational researchers in their attempts to eliminate wasted time and to increase yield, that is, student achievement.

Starch's recommendation that the "equal squad" method be used in educational research is a reminder that the methods used in educational measurement are rooted in agriculture. If it is remembered that the method came from agriculture, it may be possible to view schools and how they function and the culture in which they exist in different ways. For example, Brian Simon argued that the tradition of applying statistical concepts to psychological phenomena started by Sir Francis Galton and extended by Karl Pearson and Ronald A. Fisher can be challenged. As early as 1975, Simon indicated that: "It can be argued that these methods are not strictly applicable to spheres other than agricultural botany, but they so enhanced procedural rigor as to prove irresistible."[34]

Texts in Educational Psychology

Starch's *Educational Psychology* was the most widely used text in the field for about ten years.[35] It was reprinted thirteen times, and a revised edition appeared in 1927. In 1922 H. H. Remmers and R. B. Knight set out to answer the following question: "To what extent do the beginning courses in educational psychology—which represent the sum total of the training in psychology that all but a negligible part of young teachers in training receive—attempt to give the prospective young teachers a mastery of the subject through an experimental approach?"[36] They observed that a comparison of texts in the field showed "a decided divergence in point of view, organization, and content." They further observed "that there are some fundamental differences in viewpoint may further be seen by comparing that of Starch and Thorndike, who as indicated by the returns are the leaders in educational psychology."[37]

In 1925, O. B. Douglas surveyed seventy-three institutions to assess the status of introductory courses in educational psychology. Douglas also reported some of the findings of the Remmers and Knight study. Remmers and Knight had forty-one usable replies to their survey. They revealed that Starch's text was mentioned eleven times as the text used in the introductory educational psychology course. Thorndike's text was mentioned ten times. There were thirty-two other texts mentioned, but only four of them were named five or more times. Douglas found that in March, 1924, Starch's text was still the most frequently used text. Thorndike's had fallen to sixth place. Starch's text was most popular in courses offered at the sophomore and junior levels. Twenty of the twenty-eight schools that used Starch's text used it at either the sophomore or junior level.[38]

Remmers and Knight reported that they had wanted to provide an analysis of the various texts but found so much diversity that they had to abandon the analysis. They reported that there were significant and fundamental differences between Thorndike and Starch but did not observe that Thorndike as well as Starch agreed on the need for definite measures and their agreement that whatever existed could be measured. Rather, they noted that while Thorndike devoted all of Volume I of his three-volume *Educational Psychology* to instinct under the rubric of "original tendencies," "Starch definitely belittles the place of instincts in educational practice."[39] The 1920 review of Starch's text in the *Journal of Educational Psychology* noted that Starch "points out that instincts as such have very little significance for education, and that the chief educational doctrines based upon instincts (dynamic theory of instincts, transitoriness, and recapitulation) have very little justification in verified fact." The review also went on to offer the judgment that Starch's was a "sane view" and expressed "hope that it will tend to neutralize the overemphasis of instincts that has been prevalent in educational discussion since James."[40]

Starch did reproduce Thorndike's list of forty-two instincts, but he had little use for it. According to Starch, the true number of instincts as well as how much learning was involved in their activity was a matter of opinion. When it came to the relationship between the forty-two instincts and the learning of a given school subject, Starch was even more definite. Early in his text he instructed his readers to examine each instinct and attempt to determine "to what extent each one may be appealed to or used in teaching the various subjects." He was confident that "two-thirds or three-fourths of them are probably never immediately but only indirectly concerned in school exercises, and most of the remaining ones, such as rivalry, cooperation, collecting, and hoarding, are serviceable chiefly as general motives." While Starch maintained that "the most important role of instinct in education lies in motivating and energizing the learning process," he basically reduced them to responses in a stimulus-response model. "The instinctive elements in learning any school subject are," he argued, "for the most part simple reflex actions or undeveloped connections."[41]

Starch's position on the relative insignificance of instincts in education was basically a rejection of William James' position and a dismissal of much of G. Stanley Hall. As such it was a departure from the prevailing point of view. For example, in 1911 Bird T. Baldwin claimed that after James brought instinct into educational discussions, there was no "reputable book in educational psychology" that did not devote "several pages of chapters to instinct." According to Baldwin, James successfully shifted the basis and aim of education as "the organization or acquired habits of conduct and tendencies to behavior." That was very different from Plato's moral aim, Socrates' quest for truth, Luther's service to the state and church, or even Spencer's preparation for complete living. James' emphasis on native tendencies or instincts "directed attention to the native resources of the child and the place these native tendencies to reaction must necessarily have in any scheme of education in which children are concerned."[42] The emphasis on native tendencies, or instincts, provided an alternative to the Herbartian pedagogy and psychology that emphasized the organization of subject matter. Starch rejected instinct as an important concept and emphasized testing, measurement, and reliable grading of students' performances in the various school subjects. In opting for measurement of the educational product and emphasis on testing, he moved the emphasis back to subject matter, at least to the measurement of how students respond to the subject matter presented to them. The requirements of a good test shaped the organization of teaching and subject mater. A good test met four conditions:

1. The test or scale for a given subject should measure the knowledge or skill acquired wherever proper instruction or training in the field is provided. The material of the test should be based upon the material that has actually been covered or should be covered in the subject.
2. The test ought to permit of accurate, impersonal evaluation.
3. It ought to permit of duplication or repeated application almost indefinitely.

    4.   It ought to measure adequately the knowledge, skill or ability for which it is designed.[43]

Effective use of standardized tests, as Starch recommended, was a way to effectively minimize the teacher's role. Specification of the product or outcome leads to specification of the materials and the processes to be used. Outcomes are invariably specified in a manner that allows their easy detection and measurement. That practice allows educators to report whether students have learned or achieved and how much they have achieved.

Dean A. Worcester's 1927 analysis of several educational psychology texts clearly shows what Starch's emphases were. Worcester reported that while Gates' text that was the second most widely used text in 1924 devoted 12% of its space "to a discussion of the receiving, connecting and reacting mechanisms" and 4% "to a description of conscious states and processes."[44] Starch did not even deal with these topics—topics that purport to deal with how individuals learn and how they make use of their experiences. Starch devoted over half of his text to the psychology of various school subjects and to tests in the school subjects. While Gates devoted 4% of his text to the transfer of training, Starch devoted 14% of his text to transfer. In his treatment of transfer, Starch used approximately thirty tables and three graphs. About 5% of Starch's work was devoted to individual differences—differences that could be measured.

For Starch education was "the production of useful changes in human beings." He cautioned that "useful" should not be narrowly defined so as to exclude "all changes which will broaden and enrich the life of the individual," but his emphasis was on finding whatever "exact information" there was and in determining which methods of education were "most economical."[45] The problems of educational psychology that were in accordance with the definition of education as production useful changes were four:

1.   What changes are made in human beings?
2.   What are the agencies by which the changes may be brought about?
3.   What are the capacities which human beings possess for acquiring changes?
4.   What are the most economical methods by which these changes may be brought about?[46]

Problems 2 and 4 were basically psychological problems. The first was a philosophical and sociological problem, for its answer depended not on psychological findings but on "our ideals of life and our views of society." The second problem was partly sociological because the agencies that a society selected for education depended on its physical and social content. The second problem was also a psychological problem because it required study of how various school subjects—Latin, physics, grammar, or whatever—might bring about changes in mental processes. How to test a student's performance in a school subject and how performance in one subjected related to performance in another subject were topics to which Starch gave considerable attention. For him education was effectively reduced to school subjects. How much of a school subject a student learned could be measured.

ELIMINATING WASTE AND SAVING TIME

Waste in education was for Starch, as it was for many others of his era, a problem that presumably had a solution. Early in his text Starch presented a passage that indicated how waste could be eliminated or how time could be saved:

> For example, we do not know with any definite assurance what is the most economical amount of time to devote to any one of the school subjects. From such investigations as have been made, we may infer that there is an enormous waste in our educational practices which is indicated by such facts as the following: It has been found by recent tests and measurements that some schools obtain just as good results by devoting only one-half as much time to writing as other schools do. Similar facts have brought out in the case of reading, arithmetic, and other school subjects. Schools which have devoted as much as 100 minutes a week, or 20 minutes a day, have obtained no better results than other schools devoting 50 minutes a week, or 10 minutes a day, to the same subject. If these facts actually represent the real possibilities, it seems quite obvious hat thee is an enormous waste in our schools and this waste is far greater than we realize until we make definite calculations of the possible saving of time. If by some means it were possible to save one minute a day for every school day during the eight years of a child's school life, we would be able to save one entire week of school time. If we could save four minutes a day for the same length of time, we would be able to save one month; if we were able to save 18 minutes a day, we would be able to save one-half a school year; and if by more economical methods of learning and distribution of time we wee able to save 36 minutes a day for eight years, we would be able to save an entire school year. Such a saving is not impossible; indeed, by a better use of time and more effective methods of learning, it is highly probable. Eighteen minutes a day would mean a reduction of only 4½ minutes in each of four subjects; 36 minutes a day would mean a reduction of only 9 minutes a day in each of four subjects.[47]

Not enough was known about learning to enable a shortening of the school day and the school year for all, but it was possible to do so for some. That was so because the "differences among human beings are quantitative rather than qualitative."[48] All had reflexes, instincts, and the capacity to perceive, discriminate, to attend, to retain, and to reason but they did son to varying degrees. However, differences among people were differences in the strength or the amount of their abilities. Differences were "qualitative only in the sense that combinations of varying amounts of diverse traits occur."[49] The range of differences among people was great, but it was quantitative and could be measured. As Starch explained, "We find that on the average the best pupil is able to do from two to twenty-five times as much as the poorest pupil, or is able to do the same task from two to twenty-five times as well as he poorest pupil."[50] All facets of human performance could be reduced to either time or amount. They could be measured.

To explain the nature of human variation Starch employed the normal curve. That the normal curve may only represent how widely distributed variations were and not what they meant to either an individual or a society was not a question Starch addressed. To know that human abilities varied in accordance with the normal curve was to know the nature of human variation. To illustrate the nature of human variation he presented in graphic form a number of distributions. They included: the memory ability of 173 university students, the ability of 164 university students to cancel "A's" in one minute, ability of 164 persons to cancel a specified geometrical figure in a page of figures in one minute, the ability of 135 persons in giving associations to a stimulus word in fifteen seconds, chest measurement of English soldiers, the height of 1, 052 women, the head girth of 1,071 boys 16 to 19 years of age, and he number of heads up in tossing ten pennies 1,000 times. For Starch, all distributions of human traits and abilities approximated a normal distribution.

Just as improved methods of teaching based on scientific knowledge about learning might result in the savings of minutes and perhaps even years so did the variability in human ability make possible the savings of school time. For Starch, measurement of students' abilities in the various school subjects showed that "the differences in abilities in school subjects are fully as wide as in special psychological capacities."[51] Since the wide range of differences was "probably due primarily to native ability rather than to differences in opportunity, training, or environment," a wide range of ability could be expected in every class and in every school. Even after the abilities of the students in the various school subjects were averaged, there was a range such that the superior second and third grade students were nearly equal to the poorest students in the eighth grade. According to Starch, "*this enormous range of ability and the resulting overlapping of successive grades, is probably the most important single fact discovered with reference to education in the last decade.*"[52]

Proper promotion and classification of students would, Starch maintained, would allow 33% of the students to complete eight grades of school in less than eight years; 33% would finish in eight years and 33% would need more than eight years to complete eight grades satisfactorily. Not to separate students according to their abilities was wasteful. As Starch expressed it, "to keep an ordinary class of pupils together is no doubt very wasteful in time both for the gifted as well as for the stupid pupils."[53] Each group would suffer as proper attention was directed at the other.

There were, Starch observed, two ways to meet the needs of the superior, industrious students. One was to "attempt to keep the pupils of a given class together but vary the manner of instruction for the pupils of different capacities;" the other was to "keep the manner of instruction uniform but promote or retard pupils according to their achievements."[54] While various plans for varying the methods of instruction had been in use for the past thirty years, they were not always reliable. They seemed to work best "when carried out under the immediate supervision of those who devised them." However, when others attempted to employ the plans for individualizing or varying instruction, "they have not been so satisfactory." Starch warned that plans that relied on individualization of instruction may neglect the necessary "social stimulus" that all students needed. He opted for those plans that allowed for rapid acceleration. A practical program that allowed for acceleration was the St. Louis Promotion Plan as described by W. J. Stevens in 1914.[55] In the St. Louis Schools each grade was divided into four ten-week quarters. At the end of each quarter, average students moved on according to schedule. Superior students were allowed to move on to the "next higher class." Stevens' study of 1,439 students in four elementary schools in St. Louis showed that "about 1% of the pupils required approximately four years, 6.3% five years, 22.8% six years, 34.6% seven years, 24.9% eight years, 7.6% nine years, 1.7% ten yeas and 1.3% eleven to thirteen years to complete the eight grades."[56] Stevens' findings agreed quite closely with Starch's own calculations on how many students needed more or less time to complete successfully eight grades.

That the schools seemed to give more attention to children at the left end of the normal curve than to the right end concerned Starch. He related that "the schools have given special attention to the backward pupils by organizing separate classes for them and by giving them extra help, but they have given little or no attention to the advanced pupils."[57] When he revised his text in 1927, he expanded his chapter on "Variation in Human Capacities" and gave even more attention to the need of special provision for students at either end of the normal curve. Children at either end required special attention. Fully 5% of those who enrolled in the public schools were "so inferior physically, mentally, educationally, and socially that they may properly be identified as 'special class children.' "[58] These were the students who needed instruction that emphasized the concrete and who should be trained for useful jobs. Teaching special-class children jobs to make them economically independent would make life happier for them and allow savings of "thousands of dollars of tax money which would otherwise be spent for law enforcement and institutional care."[59] Starch recommended that children at the other end of the normal curve be allowed to move through school quickly. In the first edition of his text he complained that: "School progress is determined too much by the calendar and not enough by capacity." To free schools from the calendar would benefit society: "Society would be compensated far more for paying at least equal attention to the gifted pupils since they primarily will determine the future progress of mankind."[60] In the revised edition of his text he also argued that the superior students should enjoy the benefits their superiority would bring them as adults. Presumably, these were the students who would benefit rather than tax society.

Starch wanted to promote and to reward achievement. Achievement and character were, for Starch, closely related. He described the relationship as follows:

> Considerable information concerning the character traits of a child may be inferred from his mental and educational test data. If in educational attainment a child is one quartile position above that customary for children of his intelligence quotient, excellent character traits are likely to be present; if his educational attainment accords with that customary for children of his intelligence quotient, average character traits may be inferred; if, however, his educational attainment is one quartile position below that customary for children of his intelligence quotient, poor character traits are probable.[61]

It may be that the science of psychology and its instruments for measuring human traits and accomplishments helped Starch to discover a not very new form of early American Calvinism in which the able take the place of the selected or the saved. The able are good because they achieve and because they have achieved they are good. In place of the selector is nature, operating through heredity. On the nature-nurture question Starch was on the side of nature.

Starch warned that it was necessary to consider the social and physical status of the student in acceleration programs, but they were preferable to enrichment programs. Acceleration programs typically required students to accomplish more than normal students proceeding through eight grades in eight years. Enrichment programs that varied requirements so as to occupy the time of the superior student were not completely satisfactory. While the student did receive the benefit of accomplishing additional work, the student did not receive the full benefit of his/her ability. Outside the school, what he called "practical life," "the capable man performs several times as much work or makes several times as rapid progress in the same period of time as the incapable man, both having equal opportunities." Starch asked: "Why should not the schools permit progress according to ability and achievement?"[62] The possibility of moving through school more quickly than the normal rate would probably disincline students from dawdling and motivate them to do as much as they could as quickly as they could in school. He clearly wanted to organize schools to benefit the gifted. To do so "would make for maximum progress based upon ability and performance, not upon birth or social caste."[63]

STUART APPLETON COURTIS AND THE DEVELOPMENT OF TESTS

As a teacher, a developer of tests in a variety of subjects, a member of several school surveys, a founding member of the John Dewey Society, a student of educational measurement, and a director of a bureau of educational research, Stuart Appleton Courtis participated in the twentieth-century transformation of public education. His birthday—May 15, 1874—places him in the company of others whose careers in education began during the early years of the Progressive Era: for example, Charles H. Judd, 1873; William C. Bagley, 1874; Edward L. Thorndike, 1874; and Guy Montrose Whippple, 1876. His place of birth in the upper Midwest—Wyandotte, Michigan—places him in the company of still others who worked in the Progressive Era: Daniel Starch, LaCrosse, Wisconsin in 1883; Arnold Gesell, Alama, Wisconsin in 1880; and William C. Bagley who grew up and was educated in Michigan. Like others of his era, he entered the field of education not because he had prepared himself for such a position but simply because he needed a job, and jobs were available in that era of educational expansion. In 1898 Courtis abandoned his studies in electrical engineering at the Massachusetts Institute of Technology and became a teacher at the Liggett School for Girls in Detroit because he wanted to remain near the woman with whom he had fallen in love.

Courtis, like others of his era, began his teaching career without a college degree. He eventually earned a degree, a B.S. at Teachers College in 1919. His other degrees—a M.A. from Teachers College (1921) and a Ph.D. from the University of Michigan (1925) were earned after he set the course for his career. In 1914 Courtis left the Liggett School to become the Director of Educational Research in the Detroit Public Schools (1914-1919). There he "was turned loose among two thousand teachers and seventy thousand students to attempt to improve the efficiency of teaching of the fundamental subjects."[64] From then on his efforts were nearly evenly divided between work in school systems and higher education: Director of Instruction and Dean at the Detroit Teachers College from 1920 to 1924; educational consultant to the Detroit Public Schools from 1924 to 1931; and educational consultant to the Hamtramack Public Schools from 1926 to 1930. From 1931 to 1944 he taught at Wayne University and from 1924 to 1944 at the University of Michigan where he was appointed Professor Emeritus upon his retirement.[65]

Courtis' positions were mostly confined to Michigan, but his work and influence extended beyond his home state. Besides serving on the Hanus Committee on School Inquiry, New York City, 1911, he participated in the resurvey of the New York City Public Schools in 1924 and in the Gary, Indiana Survey in 1916, and was in charge of testing in the Boston Public Schools in 1916. He served as president of the American Association for the Advancement of Science (1918-19) and was a contributing member of the National Society for the Study of Education and the National Society of College Teachers of Education. He was a member of the National Association of Directors of Educational Research (the organization that led to the formation of the American Educational Research Association) and contributed to the first issue of the *Journal of Educational Research* in 1920.

Courtis' first significant work—the publication of his arithmetic test in 1909, his positions, and his publications demonstrate that he was devoted to the development and practice of educational measurement. Like others in the Progressive Era, he believed education could be improved through educational measurement. However, during the course of his career, he changed some of his beliefs about educational measurement, criticized the educational measurement movement and some of its practices but did not completely abandon his belief in the utility of measurement. Like other progressives, he questioned traditional conceptions and practices. As educators turned to psychology either to defend earlier changes in educational practices or to improve the efficiency of public education, some developed a new perspective. As Courtis observed about his first year as a teacher:

> We who began to teach in the last century, before there were any tests, never realized that children differed so greatly in their achievements. We had no conception of the divergent tastes, talents, and developments which prevailed in our classes, and which still prevail after forty years of measurement. We supposed that if any child could learn, all the children in the class could be made to learn if they and the teacher would only try.[66]

For some, documentation of individual differences led to a focus on the "individual child"; for others, it led to a romantic celebration of the value of the differences among children. Courtis was no romantic but he did value those differences and came to believe that a *"revolution* in education is long overdue." He acknowledged that philosophy deserved "credit for directing attention to the importance of the personality and social elements in education," but also maintained that the testing movement had shown "that the subject matter aims and objectives of education are not being achieved." Tests, he maintained as late as 1946, had "helped focus teachers' attention on the individual child" and would eventually be seen as having prepared the way for the revolution.[67]

By 1906 Courtis had been appointed head of the Science and Mathematics Department at the Liggett School. Soon thereafter C. W. Stone published his arithmetic tests, and Courtis administered them to the students under his charge. As Arthur B. Moehlman related, "they revealed, as tests always do, an enormous range of individual differences in every grade."[68] After his examination of the students' performances on the tests, Courtis concluded that he was not a very good teacher and offered his resignation to his principal, Emma Liggett. Rather than accept his resignation, she urged him to find out why the range of differences existed. He studied the works of Charles H. Judd and Edward L. Thorndike and developed his own tests—the Courtis Arithmetic Tests, Series A. They were published in 1909. The development of those tests placed him in the company of Thorndike, Hillegas, Buckingham and Ayers—those who "pioneered the movement toward development of instruments for measuring pupil achievement."[69]

The Courtis Arithmetic Tests, Series A were used in the 1911 New York City Survey and thus became the first "objective" tests to be used in any such survey. They were then administered to thirty thousand New York City students. They were "objective" in that the students' answers were either right or wrong. They were designed to be easily scored, but they were not multiple-choice tests.

While Courtis and others—Stone, Thorndike, Ayers, Starch, Hillegas, Buckingham—were developing their instruments, there was widespread belief in the utility of measurement. Measurement was becoming an essential ingredient in the science of education. Courtis believed that measurement was "a method of proved worth in education." Those who declared that measurements were a "failure" were confessing their "own lack of confidence" or their "own incompetence."[70]

Administration of tests to assess the quality or efficiency of teaching constituted a new form of evaluation. It was consistent with the tradition of superintendents who evaluated their teachers by examining a set of students' papers but was very different from the practice of offering judgments after a few casual observations. Leonard P. Ayers later observed that the use of Courtis' tests "which had by that time attracted a good deal of attention" not only "settled all doubts as to the availability of the tests themselves for the measurement of educational attainment" but also "established the principle that in conducting school surveys scientific tests must be utilized where they are available."[71]

The thirty thousand New York City students proved to be but a fraction of the students who would have Courtis' tests administered to them. Between August 1914 and August 1915, 455,007 of Courtis' tests had been sent to educators in 42 states.[72] He soon developed tests for several other areas: Composition Tests (1916); Series R, Reading Tests (1917); Series S, Spelling Tests (1918); Series W, Writing Tests (1918); Test A, Geography, Supervisory with B. A. Barnes (1918); Standard Samples of Handwriting (1919); Standard Samples of Compositions (1919); Test B, Geography, Supervisory with B. A. Barnes (1919); *Courtis Standard Practice Tests in Arithmetic* published by the World Book Company (1920); *Courtis Standard Practice Tests in Handwriting* with Lena M. Shaw also published by the World Book Company (1922); Teacher Rating (1922); Series M, Music Tests (1922) and the Courtis Standard Research Tests (1920-1934).[73]

Courtis' arithmetic tests (Series A and Series B) were found to be unsatisfactory for the Cleveland Survey, but, as George S. Counts reported in his dissertation, Courtis' help was secured in the construction of an appropriate test. Between Series A and Series B there was a gap between "the very simple type of example in the first series and the highly complex type in the second series." Courtis helped to develop "tests representing types of intermediate complexity"—a development described by Counts as "the logical evolution of Mr. Courtis' own system." According to Counts, "whatever merit" the new test had was due to Courtis' contributions.[74] Counts used the data from the administration of the tests in Cleveland and Grand Rapids to complete his dissertation.

When Walter S. Monroe presented his account of then existing "tests and standards," in 1918, he included several of Courtis' tests. Courtis' Arithmetic Tests, Series A, he reported, had been replaced by Series B in 1914. Series A was an eight part test that included one test for each of the four fundamental operations for the number combinations 0 to 9 as well as tests on copying figures, speed reasoning, fundamental operations, and reasoning. Series B was "used extensively" and "proved reliable in 79 to 90% of the cases." Abbreviated forms of the Series B tests were used in the National Business Ability Tests. However, according to Monroe, the Series B tests did not allow as detailed an analysis as did the Cleveland Survey Tests developed under the supervision of Judd and did not offer "carefully graded" examples "arranged in order of difficulty."[75]

Courtis later commented on Stone's Arithmetic Reasoning Test (1908) test and those who opposed his kind of tests. Stone "under Thorndike's guidance utilized the idea of [Joseph Mayer] Rice's controlled examination, but added to it the careful standardization of the questions." Courtis' tests were "rate tests composed of material made uniform in terms of objective criteria." However, the prevailing climate of opinion opposed rate tests. Thorndike "threw the weight of his influence against rate tests: and ridiculed them out of court for many persons." Yet, as late as 1942 even after he withdrew his tests from the market, Courtis maintained that rate tests represented "an avenue of development largely unexplored and held that his efforts "at least resulted in the widespread use of educational tests."[76]

Courtis' Handwriting, Series W Test was "an untimed 'maximum performance' test, designed to secure samples of the children's best writing after practice." It employed the scale developed by Ayers to measure the quality of the work and used material that allowed "an analysis of the defects in the writing of a particular child."[77] Courtis' Standard Research Tests in English were designed to measure both speed and comprehension in silent reading but were discontinued because the test "was so complex that the marking of the test papers was a laborious task.[78] His Silent Reading Test measured reading ability in grades II, III, and IV, and afforded measures for rate and comprehension. Scoring was easy, for students answered questions by simply marking either yes or no. Teachers, it was believed, were able to determine easily how much progress students made between the beginning and the end of the school term by administering one form of the test at the beginning of the year and the other form at its end. Courtis' Spelling test used words from Ayers' Scale that were placed in sentences, "and the sentences [were] arranged so that they [could] be dictated at specified rates, which correspond to the rate of writing in several grades." The standards for this test were "slightly lower" than those set for the Ayres Scale.[79]

Courtis sold more than thirteen million copies of his tests by 1925. By then, there were over a hundred discussions of his tests in the literature.[80] However, after completing his dissertation—"Why Children Succeed"— he concluded "that the mathematical assumptions underlying educational measurement, including his own, were wrong." He then "scrapped his tests and continued more extensive research in Detroit schools and in certain foreign countries."[81] Courtis himself reported "between 1909, when my first tests were published, and 1938, when I withdrew all my tests from the market because I had discovered that they did not measure what they were supposed to measure, I sold more than twenty million copies around the world."[82]

COURTIS RECONSIDERS

Courtis' views about educational measurement and the use of tests in education changed significantly while "on [his] way home from the Educational Measurements Conference at Indiana University in 1926." Then he realized that "the Gompertz formula, developed in 1825 in England for life insurance statistics, applies universally to all growth curves when growth takes place under controlled conditions." He believed that his discovery would eventually "revivify the whole measurement movement" because it "opened the door for adequate and consistent statistical treatment of growth data."[83] He presented his discovery of the applicability of the Gompertz formula to the Mental Tests Section of the Ninth International Congress of Psychology at Yale University in 1929. He began by specifying that growth was simply progress toward maturity and that it was produced by the action of nurture on nature. Growth that was the result of constant nurture acting uniformly upon constant nature could be expressed by a simplex curve. Growth that was the result of variations in either nature or nurture could be expressed as a complex curve. Complex curves could be viewed "as composed of two or more parts, each of which is a *portion* of some simplex curve."[84] The laws of growth and the influence of any factor on growth could all be properly described as "simplex situations" and thus could be expressed mathematically. Claims that conditions were never perfectly constant were unimportant because "the literature of growth is full of curves whose deviation from mathematically perfect simplex curves is, on average, not more than two or three percent." That small deviation made Courtis' discovery, so he believed, "practical."[85]

The Gompertz equation was an exponential equation. Like all exponential equations, computation of the Gompertz equation was cumbersome. To overcome that difficulty, Courtis transformed the exponential equation into a linear equation: $y_1 = r_1 t + s_1$ (t stands for units of time and y_1, s_1 and r_1 are the "isochrons." He claimed he was able to make this transformation because the only differences among growth curves was the time required for full maturation. Thus, he reasoned that the total time for any and every such growth curve could be divided into one hundred equal units that he called "isochrons." According to Courtis' "isochron theorem," it was possible to consider any developments or degrees of growth that occurred in equal time intervals to be equal. After applying the "isochron theorem" to the growth curve (a mathematically perfect curve, "the development from 0 percent. to 10 percent. is considered equal to the development from 10 percent. to 48 percent., from 48 percent. to 80 percent., etc., since each is made in ten isochrons."[86]

Even after his retirement, Courtis wrote about growth curves and employed his "discovery" in his assessments of the progress and status of educational measurement. He also tried to teach others how to employ the isochron theorem. In 1932 he prepared *The Measurement of Growth*, a text for a course with the same title he taught at the University of Michigan. He explained the Gompertz law to students, provided a series of exercises to teach students how to use isochrons, and even prepared tables of values for isochrones to facilitate computation. Even in his *Philosophy of Education*, he presented students with discussions of growth, the isochron theorem and exercises on how to compute with isochrons. He then emphasized that:

> Scores in *no tests* can be interpreted correctly except in terms of the individual's own curve of growth. All educational planning must be based on a comprehensive study of the development of the *child as a whole* because growth in one phase of development may vitally effect or condition growth in other phases.[87]

Courtis' assessment of educational measurement at the end of the 1930s was that it had just reached the point where it could begin to make significant progress. Its first half-century had been characterized by a series of fanciful conclusions based on incorrect assumptions:

> It is a fact that we have many instruments of measurement, but our assumptions that they measure intelligence, reading, personality, etc. can easily be proved to be gross superstitions. It is a fact that we have a number of scaling techniques, but it can readily be shown that these techniques are based on unwarranted assumptions and yield at best only units of performance, not units of ability. It is a fact that our libraries are filled with countless records of experimentation and statistical analyses, having all the forms and trappings of scientific procedure, but it is not difficult to show that all this fine appearance is appearance only, that all our experimentation likewise rests on untenable foundations and really does not yield enduring truth.[88]

Toward the end of his career, Courtis offered assessments of his work and the field with which he identified. Some criticisms were directed to his colleagues in measurement, others to educational practitioners—teachers and school administrators, and some were even aimed at parents. He admitted that the interests of engineers had influenced his own early inquiries and that the first educational measures were crude:

> At the time efficiency was an ideal widely accepted in the engineering world; for a period it also dominated the thinking of investigators in education. One school survey after another brought new 'deficiencies' to light and

emphasized the range of individual differences in achievements at all levels and subjects.[89]

Courtis even cited his own work on the New York Survey as an example of "crude comparative testings" that were used to show how inefficient teaching was. He constructed a table to display the range of scores in arithmetic and then advised the New York authorities that the table

> ... points out plainly facts of the largest significance both for education generally and for the local situation. It is the distributions of the individual scores that are stirringly—yes, sensationally significant. The real meaning is that, so far as any individual child is concerned, to say that he has completed the course in arithmetic in the public schools is to convey *no* information as to his ability in even the simplest work. He may be almost an absolute incompetent so far as practical work is concerned, or he may have acquired a degree of skill that would be adequate for any situation in which he is likely to find himself. As a whole, therefore, the table more than justifies the criticism that has yet been made by the 'man on the street.'[90]

In 1938 Courtis wrote that: "After thirty years of study my conclusion is that no single test and no battery of tests of any type or description yields unambiguous information about the quantities educationalists wished to measure." Current instruments were about as valuable as those of the ancient astrologers and alchemists. Interpretation was "intelligent guess work"—Courtis' words for "scientific deduction."[91] Progress in interpretation of tests could not be made until two important conditions had been satisfied. First, it was necessary to develop a measure of effort, for it was essential to know how hard an individual was trying in order to interpret his or her test scores. From time to time, Courtis brought this factor to his readers' attention by indicating that sickness may affect performance or by relating how students might be stimulated to work harder or faster by either the promise of a reward or an encouraging talk. Second, Courtis wanted to abandon age and/or grade norms and replace them with repeated measures of the individual's "progress in terms of *his own growth curve*."[92]

As Courtis had outlined at the Indiana Educational Measurements Conference in 1942, the various studies of child growth provided researchers with hundreds of growth curves. All they needed to do was to use them. His own analyses of these studies as well as his own studies convinced him that "the pattern of growth for an individual differs markedly from the pattern of growth derived from mass averages." Growth was "cyclic in character." Growth occurred at different times for different individuals.[93] Because each person was unique, each test score required a unique interpretation. Similar or identical scores on a test did not indicate that children were or would be identical or even similar. Two children who are equal in height at the same time do not necessarily grow to identical or even similar heights. Similarly, two children who achieve identical scores on a test administered at the same time may not have the same scores once each is fully grown or even on subsequent tests. Rates of growth varied and those variations made an important difference, especially to Courtis.

Courtis objected to what he considered the excessive dependence on deductive reasoning in educational research and measurement. Statistics, as a branch of mathematics, he claimed, was not an experimental discipline but a deductive one. He observed an increasing tendency toward using "logical mathematical reasoning" rather than using "concrete experimental evidence" in the educational measurement literature. That tendency was widening the gap between those who constructed tests and scales and the teachers who used them. Mathematical reasoning about educational matters needed to be checked by objective experimentation, but that was not being done. Moreover, teachers, he warned, "cannot read and understand discussions of item analysis, factor loadings, correlational pathways, and the host of statistical methods and proofs to be found in measurement articles, but they do sense the contrast between the promises of educational measurement and the actual inadequacies of tests in the classroom."[94] Courtis practiced what he advocated. He provided examples taken from tests administered to students or measurements from students taken in school settings. Frequently, they were tests he himself had administered.

Courtis objected to "mass statistics" and called for "personalized statistics." He argued that "research in psychology and education is stymied by the domination of mass statistics in analyses of results of tests and experiments." He reminded his readers that, according to Ronald A. Fischer, any statistical value that was derived from an observed or measured sample was calculated to make a characterization about the group. The difficulty was that education was concerned "not with groups, small or large, but with individual children." Because no two were alike, it made no sense to assume that they were and use "mass statistics."[95] To do so was to make false assumptions and was not unlike grouping a potato, an apple and an onion, and then performing a series of measurements to determine their characteristics.

Courtis had specific recommendations for how statistics were to be used:

Statistical methods must be used in which averaging correlation, factorial analysis, etc. will not occur until the utmost has been done to render original measurements homogeneous by separation into groups as alike as it is possible to make them. Similarly, the actual measurements must be converted into homogenous groups.[96]

To illustrate what he meant he suggested that while it did not make sense to add the weights of the apple, potato and onion, and then compute averages, standard deviations, etc., it did make sense to report that "the potato weighted 2.3 times the onion, and the apple, 1.3 times the onion." Such a procedure would provide comparable units that could be named. They would also provide "elements" that would have more meaning than "intelligence, ability, attitudes, etc., upon whose definitions psychologists cannot agree." As matters stood, the "elements" used by psychologists and educational researchers were comparable to the fire, water, air and earth of the alchemists.

All growth, Courtis firmly believed, could be expressed with the same mathematical formula Teachers only needed to know that the rate of growth of an individual child made a difference. The formula itself was "of value to statisticians, not to most teachers." All that teachers needed to know about the growth pattern was that:

> ... learning in its early stages proceeds very slowly, but gradually the process speeds up and for a time seems to move forward at a fairly uniform rate. But in the end it inevitably rounds off to a maximum that differs for each individual. Teachers should know, also, that the change from speed-up to slow-down takes place at about a third of the total period of development ... and that the last stages of mastery are acquired very slowly.[97]

If teachers knew about the rates of growth and the pattern of the growth, there were practical applications they could make to their own work. For example, since the typical passing mark (75%) was achieved at the point where an individual had achieved 42% of his or her total growth, there was little advantage in pushing for mastery, say 95%. To achieve mastery it would take longer to gain the additional 20% than it did to achieve the 75% level (58% vs. 42%), because the ability to attain mastery came after the point where growth had slowed. That explained why student performance so frequently fell once drill was curtailed. Rather than invest energy in trying to achieve mastery it would be better to wait and allow nature to take its course.

Teachers, Courtis urged, should study the growth of their students and surrender the notion that they had something to teach. Ideally, teachers' efforts should be devoted "to helping them achieve *their* purposes to answering *their* questions, to rewarding effort sympathetically, to enjoying the dynamic vitality of the children and cooperating with them." Courtis told teachers that: "In the garden where children grow, you, like the farmer, can prepare the soil, water the ground, but you simply cannot 'learn' children at will."[98] Teachers did not do the growing; children did. It was not even likely that teachers could serve as guides, for the requirements for effective guidance were not easily attained: "A perquisite for true guidance is at least several years of developmental measures of growth in many distinct aspects of personality—physical, mental, emotional, social and spiritual as well as educational—and the intimate confidences of the individual."[99] The best that teachers could do was to stop worshipping tests and scales and opt for the "sympathetic understanding" of the student rather than the "test score" whenever there was a conflict between the two.

Even as late as 1950, Courtis was arguing for a new way to interpret test scores. He then claimed that true comprehension of learning as "primarily a maturation process" worked "havoc with many of the commonly accepted ideas in education." IQ scores, he once again argued, were not indicators of ability but were merely an indication of the "developmental status of the child." More important than what any test could determine was "some major factor in the maturation process." Whatever that factor that Courtis could not yet identify was it accounted for the various differences that testing revealed. This unidentified factor was so powerful that "a child's score in a test increases from year to year *whether he* learns anything or not, just because he is larger, stronger, more mature."[100] Intelligence tests and all other tests could be stripped of their "specific factors." That stripping revealed that one's performance on all tests tended "to approach common values." Because teachers and school administrators generally did not know how to make the detailed analyses necessary for proper interpretations of tests, they were "of little practical value."

Courtis wanted to curtail, if not eliminate, the use of tests. He claimed that "most of the conclusions drawn from the results of measurements made with educational and mental tests are either false or misleading, especially as they relate to evaluation of individuals, teachers or methods of teaching." The belief that intelligence tests actually measured intelligence and that spelling tests measured spelling ability was "false" and stood in the way "of an appraisal of factual data from the point of view of maturation."[101] Courtis had concluded that "the conventional teacher's mind is cluttered with a false ideology" and he was seeking to remove the clutter.

CONCLUSION

While Starch firmly believed in the efficacy of educational measurement and Courtis questioned the use and fairness of tests, especially intelligence tests, both advanced the use and availability of tests and their use.

They were not alone. The appetite for tests seemed insatiable. For example, Henry Chauncey wanted "to mount a vast scientific project that [would] categorize, sort, and route the entire population...by administering a series of multiple-choice mental tests to everyone, and then by suggesting, on the basis of the scores, what each person's role in society should be—suggestions everyone [would] surely accept gratefully."[102] In 1945, Chauncey agreed to become head of the College Board. An organization that was set up to organize testing for the whole country. Chauncey had led the charge to administer the Scholastic Aptitude Test (SAT) to many more students than had taken it prior to World War II. James Bryant Conant, President of Harvard, was then in a position to "revive his old idea of combining all the testing agencies in America into one."[103] On January 1, 1948, "the one big testing organization of the whole country"—the Educational Testing Service (ETS), with Chauncey as its head, opened for business. Competitors, such as the American Council on Education's Psychological Examination, "were immediately discontinued."[104] The SAT—an examination that was designed to test not achievement but aptitude (some would say intelligence)—and other ETS examinations began a path that would come to touch the lives of virtually all Americans. Now, "TestLink, a service of ETS, is a database of over 20,000 tests, measurement instruments, and devices." However, more is never enough. In an advertisement placed in the *Educational Researcher*, the ETS called for "more." The service wants you to put "yours," that is your test, in their data bank.[105]

Courtis was not the only educational researcher to call for Americans to stop reifying the IQ and to point out the dangers of worshipping other tests and scales. However, the persistence and popularity of tests may be built into Americans long-held faith in science as associated with statistics, measurement, and other methods of investigation that produce seeming neutral numerical designations in the search for objective truths and opportunities based on personal ability and achievement. In the United States the fascination with statistics and the use of statistics has not been confined to matters educational. By the early twentieth century most Americans accepted that they had numbers assigned to them that described their identity. Each individual carries a set of numeral designations that define his/her physical, mental, and social status at school and at work. Americans accepted—and to continue to accept—what appear to be seemingly neutral designations for their abilities and accomplishments. We accept that differences between two designations are somehow real and meaningful. The belief in the truth revealed in numbers allows them to shape reality and opportunity sometimes in ways that free us of traditional categories of class, race, or gender and at other times in ways that justify one's proper place in the social order.

NOTES

1. Raymond E. Calllahan. *Education and the Cult of Efficiency: A Study of the Social Forces That Have Shaped the Administration of Public Schools* (Chicago: University of Chicago Press, 1962.

2. Erwin V. Johanningmeier. *Americans and Their Schools* (Boston: Houghton Mifflin, 1980), pp. 230-237.

3. Francis Grund. *The Americans, In Their Moral Social, and Political Relations* (Boston, 1837) in Sol Cohen (ed.). *Education in the United States: A Documentary History* (New York: Random House, 19745), Vol. 2, p. 943.

4. Daniel J. Boorstin. *The Americans: The Democratic Experience* (New York: Vintage Books, 1974) p. 188.

5. David Hamilton. "Educational Research and the Shadows of Francis Galton and Ronald Fisher" in W. B. Dockrell and David Hamilton (eds.). *Rethinking Educational Research* (London: Hodder and Stoughton, 1980).

6. A. A. Roback. *History of American Psychology* (New York: Library Publishers, 1952), pp. 176-177; Boorstin. *The Americans*, p. 219.

7. Boorstin. *The Americans*, p. 189.

8. *Ibid.*, p. 220.

9. William H. Allen. *Efficient Democracy* (New York: Dodd, Mead and Co., 1908), p. 18.

10. *Ibid.*, p. 6.

11. For biographical sketches of Daniel Starch see: Neil H. Borden. "Daniel Starch," *The Journal of Marketing*, Vol. XXI, No. 3 (January, 1952), pp. 265-267; *Current Biography*, (1963), pp. 393-395; *National Cyclopedia of America Biography*, Vol. F (1939-42), pp. 183-184; and "Starch: The Man Behind the Name," *Printer's Ink* (February 16, 1962), pp. 54-58.

12. Boorstin. *The Americans*, p. 3

13. Starch was not the only psychologist-educator interested in advertising. See, for example: Edward R. Strong, Jr. "Psychological Methods as Applied to Advertising," *Journal of Educational Psychology*, Vol. IV, No. 7 (September 1913).

14. "Starch," *Printer's Ink*, p. 56

15. *Ibid*, pp. 56, 58.

16. *Harvard Business Review* (May-June, 1958).

17. Frank N. Freeman. Review of *Experiments in Educational Psychology*, *School Review*, Vol. XX, No. 3 (March 1912), p. 204.

18. Daniel Starch and E. C. Elliott. "The Reliability of Grading High School Work in English," *School Review*, Vol. XX, (1912), pp. 442-457; "The Reliability of Grading Work in Mathematics," *School Review*, Vol. XXI, (1913), pp. 254-269; and "Reliability of Grading Work in History," *School Review*, Vol. XXI, (1913), pp. 676-681.

19. Max D. Engelhart. "Examinations" in Walter S. Monroe (ed.). *Encyclopedia of Educational Research* (New York: The Macmillan Co., 1941), pp. 471-472; Ann Z. Smith and John E. Dobbin. "Marks and Marking Systems" in Chester W. Harris (ed.). *Encyclopedia of Educational Research*, 3rd. ed. (New York: The Macmillan Co., 1960), pp. 783-784 and Walter S. Monroe and Max D.

444444444

Engelhart. *The Scientific Study of Educational Problems* (New York: The Macmillan Co., 1936), pp. 454-455.

20. Daniel Starch. *Educational Measurements* (New York: The Macmillan Co., 1916), p. 1.

21. Daniel Starch. "The Measurement of Efficiency in Reading," *Journal of Educational Psychology*, Vol. VI, No. 1 (January, 1915), p. 1.

22. Starch. *Educational Measurements*, p. 2.

23. *Ibid.*, pp. 2-3

24. *Ibid.*, pp. 8-9.

25. *Ibid.*, p. 15.

26. Daniel Starch. *Educational Psychology*, rev. ed. (New York: The Macmillan Co., 1927), pp. 45-46. Starch's observation that students with high marks was not reported in the first edition of his text (1919). It should be noted that Lewis M. Terman earlier related that "It is well known that, in general, a high correlation obtains between favorable mental traits of all kinds; that for example, children superior in intelligence also end to be superior in moral qualities." See: "Six—The Intelligence Quotient of Francis Galton in Childhood," *American Journal of Psychology*, Vol. 28 (1917) in Wayne Dennis (ed.). *Readings in Child Psychology* (Englewood Cliffs, New Jersey, Prentice-Hall, Inc.,), pp. 375-376.

27. Starch. *Educational Measurements*, p. 12.

28. *Ibid.*

29. *Ibid.*,

30. Smith and Dobbin, "Marks and Marking Systems," p. 484.

31. "Review (unsigned) of *Educational Psychology* by Daniel Starch," *Journal of Educational Psychology* (1920), p. 536.

32. Starch. *Educational Measurements*, p. 194.

33. *Ibid.*, p. 195.

34. Brian Simon. "Education and Social Change," paper delivered at meeting of American Educational Research Association, Washington, D. C. (April 2, 1975), p. 11.

35. "Daniel Starch." *National Cyclopedia of American Biography*, p. 183; Stephen Petrina. "Luella Cole, Sidney Pressey, and Educational Psychoanalysis, 1921-1931," *History of Education Quarterly*, Vol. 44, No. 4 (Winter 2004).

36. H. H. Remmers and F. B. Knight. The Teaching of Educational Psychology in the United States," *Journal of Educational Psychology*, Vol. 13 (1922), p. 399.

37. *Ibid.*, p. 406.

38. O. B. Douglas. "The Present Status of the Introductory Course in Educational Psychology in American Institutions of Learning," *Journal of Educational Psychology*, Vol. 16 (1925), pp. 403-407.

39. Remmers and Knight. "The Teaching of Educational Psychology, p. 406.

40. "Starch's *Educational Psychology*," p. 535.

41. Daniel Starch. *Educational Psychology* (New York: The Macmillan Co., 1919), p. 12.

42. Bird T. Baldwin. "William James' Contributions to Educational Psychology," *Journal of Educational Psychology*, Vol. II (1911), p. 376.

43. Daniel Starch. "A Test in Latin," *Journal of Educational Psychology*, Vol. X, No. 10 (December 1919), p. 489.

44. Dean A. Worcester. "The Wide Diversities of Practice in First Courses in Educational Psychology," *Journal of Educational Psychology*, Vol. XXVIII (1927), pp. 13-14.

45. Starch. *Educational Psychology*, pp. 1-3.

46. *Ibid.*, p. 2.

47. *Ibid.*, pp. 3-4.

48. *Ibid.*, p. 26.

49. *Ibid.*, p. 28.

50. *Ibid.*, p. 29.

51. *Ibid.*, p. 33.

52. *Ibid.*, p. 39. Starch's emphasis.

53. *Ibid.*, p. 41.

54. *Ibid.*, p. 42.

55. *Ibid.*, pp. 44- 45.

56. *Ibid.*, pp. 45-46.

57. *Ibid.*, p. 47.

58. Starch. *Educational Psychology* (1927), p.p. 45-46.

59. *Ibid.*, p. 51.

60. Starch. *Educational Psychology* (1919), p. 47.

61. *Ibid.*, pp. 45-46.

62. *Ibid.*, p. 51.

63. *Ibid.*, p. 48.

64. Stuart A. Courtis. "Research Work in Arithmetic," *Educational Administration and Supervision*, Vol. 3, No. 2 (February 1917), p. 61.

65. Arthur B. Moehlman. "Stuart Appleton Courtis: Master Teacher." *The Nation's Schools*, Vol. 33, No. 2 (June 1944) and John F. Ohles. "Courtis, Stuart A." in John F. Ohles (ed.). *Biographical Dictionary of American Educators* (Westport, Connecticut: Greenwood Press, 1978).

66. Stuart A. Courtis. "Forty Years of Educational Measurement: An Appraisal and a Prophecy." *National Elementary Principal*. (1946). p. 21.

67. *Ibid.*

68. Moehlman. "Stuart Appleton Courtis," p. 19.

69. Carter V. Good, A. S. Barr and Douglas E. Scates. *The Methodology of Educational Research* (New York: Appleton-Century-Crofts, Inc., 1941), p. 484.

70. Stuart A. Courtis. "Courtis Tests in Arithmetic: Value to Superintendents and Teachers" in Guy M. Whipple (ed.). *Fifteenth Yearbook of the National Society for the Study of Education: Part I, Standards and Tests for the Measurement of the Efficiency of Schools and School Systems* (Bloomington, Illinois: Public School Publishing Co., 1916), p. 91.

71. Leonard P. Ayers. "History and Present Status of Educational Measurements" in Guy M. Whipple (ed.). *Seventeenth Yearbook of the National Society of Education: Part II, The Measurement of Educational Products* (Bloomington, Illinois: Public School Publishing Co., 1918). p. 13.

72.   Courtis. "Courtis Tests in Arithmetic: Value to Superintendents and Teachers" p. 91.

73.   Detroit Public Schools, University of Michigan and Wayne University. *Educational Contributions of Stuart A. Courtis: Listings and Summaries of Published Articles, Books and Tests through June 1944* (Detroit, Michigan: Detroit Public Schools, University of Michigan and Wayne University, 1944), p. 45.

74.   George S. Counts. *Arithmetic Tests and Studies in the Psychology of Arithmetic. Supplementary Educational Monographs*, Vol. 1. (Chicago: University of Chicago Press, 1917), pp. 4-6,

75.   Walter S. Monroe. "Existing Tests and Standards" in Whipple (ed.). *Seventeenth Yearbook*, pp. 73-75.

76.   Stuart A. Courtis. "Fact and Fancy in Educational Measurement," *Bulletin of the University of Indiana School of Education*, Vol. XVIII (Bloomington, Indiana, September 1942), p. 9.

77.   *Ibid.*, p. 81.

78.   *Ibid.*, p. 89.

79.   *Ibid.*, p. 95.

80.   B. R. Buckingham, Margaret Doherty and Josephine MacLatchy. *Bibliography of Educational and Psychological Tests and Measurements.* U. S. Bureau of Education Bulletin, No. 55 (Washington, D. C., 1924),

81.   Moehlman. "Stuart Appleton Courtis," p. 19.

82.   Courtis. "Forty Years of Educational Measurement, p. 19.

83.   Courtis. "Fact and Fancy in Educational Measurement," pp. 10-11.

84.   Stuart A. Courtis. "Maturation Units for the Measurement of Growth," *School and Society*, Vol. XXX (November 16, 1929), p. 685.

85.   *Ibid.*

86.   *Ibid.*, p. 690.

87.   Stuart A. Courtis. *Philosophy of Education* (Ann Arbor, Michigan: Brumfield and Brumfield, 1939), p. 177.

88.   Courtis. "Fact and Fancy in Educational Measurement," p. 11.

89.   Stuart A. Courtis. "Contributions of Research to the Individualization of Instruction" in Guy M. Whipple. *Thirty-Seventh Yearbook of the National Society of Education: Part II, The Scientific Movement in Education* (Bloomington, Illinois: Public School Publishing Co., 1938), p. 205.

90.   Courtis. "Fact and Fancy in Educational Measurement," pp. 12-13.

91.   Courtis. "Contributions of Research to the Individualization of Instruction," p. 638.

92.   *Ibid.*, p. 648. Courtis' emphasis.

93.   Courtis. "Fact and Fancy in Educational Measurement," p. 15.

94.   Courtis. "Contributions of Research to the Individualization of Instruction," p. 549.

95.   Stuart A. Courtis, "Personalized Statistics in Education." *School and Society.* Vol. LXXX (May 1955), p. 170.

96.   *Ibid.*, p. 171.

97.   Stuart A. Courtis. "The Rate of Growth Makes a Difference," *Phi Delta Kappan*, Vol. 30 (April 1949), p. 320.

98. *Ibid.*, pp. 320-321.
99. Stuart A. Courtis. "Let's Stop This Worship of Tests and Scales." *The Nation's Schools*, Vol. 31, No. 3 (March 1943), p. 17.
100. Stuart A. Courtis. "Debunking the I.Q." *The Nation's Schools*, Vol. 45, No. 2 (February 1950), p.p. 57-58.
101. *Ibid.*, pp. 58-59.
102. Nicholas Lemann. *The Big Test: The Secret History of the American Meritocracy* (New York: Farrar, Straus and Giroux, 2000), p. 5.
103. *Ibid.*, p. 58.
104. *Ibid.*, p. 65.
105. *Educational Researcher*, Vol. 32, No. 5 (June/July 2003), p. 53.

CHAPTER 9

THE LAWS OF LEARNING

The Legacy of Edward L. Thorndike

Edward L. Thorndike like his contemporary psychologists in the early twentieth century, Lewis Terman and Daniel Starch, believed there to be a strong relationship among intelligence, morality and success. Stuart A. Courtis may have questioned these conclusions as over estimating the validity of IQ as a measurement, but other psychologists and the public were willing to be convinced if statistics could provide evidence. Thorndike claimed that they did. He argued that "history records no career, war or revolution that can compare in significance with the fact that the correlation between intellect and morality is approximately .3, a fact to which perhaps a fourth of the world's progress is due."[1] For Thorndike there was no question that "the correlation between the divergences of an individual from the average in desirable traits are positive, that the man [sic] who is above the average of his race [sic] in intellect is above rather than below it in decency, sanity, even bodily health."[2] Good health and success in school and in one's career (indications of middle to upper class status) were indicators of a person's moral integrity and superior intellect. Poverty, in this view, indicated the opposite. The value and effectiveness of educating all children equally was at stake. Clearly, an objective science of education was on controversial grounds. The national agenda included commitments that had the potential for undermining

---

Educational Research, the National Agenda, and Educational Reform:
A History, pp. 249–268

one another. The commitment to employing instruments to measure educational progress and efficiency as well as one's ability and then to assign him or her to a course in school appropriate for one's measured ability very often undermined the commitment to provide equality of educational opportunity for all the nation's children and youth in the nation's public schools. Given Thorndike's influence and success, it appears that the former trumped the later.

Educators often claim that they wish to empower students, to make them active and creative participants in the social, economic, and political lives of their communities. In varying configurations professional educators have agreed that public schooling should contribute to the productivity, well-being, and efficiency of society; enhance the individual's chances for success (social and economic mobility); and teach individuals how to participate in the political life of their communities and nation. Schools are avenues for individual mobility. Social efficiency is a purpose of public education that has been and continues to be all but universally held by both the public and professional educators. It is also a purpose that provides psychologists with ample opportunities to employ their testing, measurement, and assessment technologies. Educational researchers had previously singled out pedagogy and curriculum as variables to study in the educational process. Schools and children were identified as subjects of educational research. As a psychologist interested in learning, more even than the ability to learn, Thorndike focused on learning through experimental research in a laboratory not a school setting. Under these circumstances the learner—for example, a cat, a dog, or a chick—was subjected to different interventions and was not seen as an active, purposeful agent. The irony was that once headed on this path, Thorndike did not really even need children for his research on learning. If there were universal laws underlying the learning process, they could be uncovered through the study of animals. He applied his findings to prescribe educational practices that were widely adopted.

That teaching has become a process of instruction that is *delivered* to the learner, how teaching strategies and materials are designed and evaluated, how teachers are supervised and evaluated, how the spaces for learning are designed and controlled, the approaches and methods that dominate inquiries into teaching and learning, and the assessment and evaluation of learning are based on how psychologists and educational psychologists have defined learning. Edward L. Thorndike was a central figure in establishing the laws of learning that have guided learning theory in educational psychology and educational research in the first half of the twentieth century and beyond. "Thorndike's views, his agenda for inquiry, and his graduate students" dominated and "defined" educational research and "education in education."[3] This chapter examines this development and its consequences for school policies today.

EDWARD L. THORNDIKE

No account of educational psychology would be complete without some discussion of Edward L. Thorndike, his work and legacy. The son of a New England clergyman, he was born in 1874, four years before William James opened his laboratory for psychological demonstrations at Harvard and five years before Wilhelm Wundt opened his psychological laboratory at Leipzig. Twenty years later in a required course in psychology at Wesleyan University he encountered William James' *Principles of Psychology*. Forty years later Thorndike reported that the chapters "were stimulating, more so than any book that I had read before, and possibly more so than any read since."[4] The two volumes of the *Principles* were the only two books outside his major field of study—literature—that he purchased during his four years at Wesleyan. He admonished his professor for not using James' work as the course text. When he completed his studies, he set out for Harvard to study under William James.

When Thorndike arrived at Harvard, he planned to study literature, philosophy, and psychology, but psychology soon consumed all his interest and effort. Thorndike described in his autobiography how he came to focus on learning itself rather than learning specifically with human subjects. Since he was not in the field of education at the time it did not matter. The convenience of using chickens and later cats, dogs, and chicks took precedence over humans as subjects due to circumstances at first beyond Thorndike's control. After arriving at Harvard he began a series of experiments on children's thinking processes in which children were to guess what he was thinking about. For guessing correctly the children were rewarded with a piece of candy. For reasons Thorndike did not report, the authorities at Harvard disapproved of his experiments and he was asked to discontinue them. Unable to work with children, he sought new subjects and in time turned to chickens as suitable subjects. As this often told story goes, Thorndike again ran into trouble. There wasn't any place to keep chickens at Harvard. Understandably, his landlady frowned on bringing them home and his keeping them in a closet in his room or elsewhere on the premises. William James came to Thorndike's rescue, delighting his young children in the process, by offering his cellar to Thorndike's experimental subjects.

In 1898, Thorndike received an offer from James McKeen Cattell to complete his work in psychology at Columbia University. He set out for

New York, carrying a basket with his "two most educated chickens." He had planned to breed them so he could "test the influences of acquired mental traits upon inherited capacity."[5] The breeding rate of chickens, he later reported, rendered that "a foolish plan." He abandoned his fowl and turned to cats, dogs (cats and dogs that he "picked up in the street at random"[6]), and chicks and completed his doctoral dissertation, *Animal Intelligence: An Experimental Study of Associative Processes in Animals* (1898).

After completing his dissertation Thorndike was offered a position at the College for Women of Western Reserve University in Cleveland. Thorndike's appointment required him to teach in a department of education, a field in which he had neither training nor experience. This introduction to the field proved fruitful for his career. In 1899, he was invited to teach psychology and child study at Teachers College, Columbia University where he soon became one of the twentieth century's leading figures in education and educational psychology. He quickly adapted his research on the psychology of learning to educational psychology and educational research.

The first edition of *Animal Intelligence* did not apply Thorndike's theory of animal learning to human subjects. However, in the 1911 revision he suggested that his work with animals had pedagogical relevance for children and schooling:

> At least some of our results possess considerable pedagogical interest. The fundamental form of intellection, the association-process in animals, is one ... which requires the personal experience of the animal in all its elements. The association cannot be taught by putting the animal through it or giving it a chance to imitate. Now every observant teacher realizes how often the cleverest explanation and the best models for imitation fail. Yet often, in such cases, a pupil if somehow enticed to do the thing, even without comprehension of what it means, even without any real knowledge of what he is dong, will finally get hold of it. So, also, in very many kinds of knowledge, the pupil who does anything from imitation, or who does anything from being put through it, fails to get a real and permanent mastery of the thing. I am sure that with a certain type of mind the only way to teach fractions in algebra, for example, is to get the pupil to do, do, do. I am inclined to think that in many individuals certain things cannot be learned save by actual performance. And I think it is often a fair question, when explanation, imitation and actual performance are all possible methods, which is the best. We are here alongside the foundations of mental life, and this hitherto unsuspected law of animal mind may prevail in human mind to an extent hitherto unknown. The best way with children may often be, in the pompous words of an animal trainer, "to arrange everything in connection with the trick so that the animal will be compelled by the laws of his own nature to perform it."[7]

Thorndike's discussion of the pedagogical applications of his work on animal learning, or animal intelligence, is important and merits some comment. Specifically, it should be noted that Thorndike *believed* that what was known about how animals learned was also applicable to how children learned. He did not offer experimental evidence for this foray into anthropomorphism. He applied this belief in his discovery of universal laws of learning applicable to all animal life in his subsequent works throughout his career. In spite of this unproved unscientific leap of faith, Thorndike's research quickly placed him at the center of major educational questions and controversies and gave him a reputation that has endured.

Clarence Karier observed that "William H. Kilpatrick was probably correct when he asserted, 'America believes as does no country, that education must be based on a study of psychology'." Kilpatrick attributed that belief "in no small degree to the influence of President [G. Stanley] Hall."[8] Given that Thorndike's bibliography contains more than 500 publications (approximately 250,000 pages) and that he probably did more than any other individual "to establish educational psychology as a scientific discipline" and "shaped the character of educational psychology for more than 100 years,"[9] it is indeed possible that had Kilpatrick offered such an observation at the end of the twentieth century rather than near its beginning, he would have remarked upon the influence of Edward L. Thorndike. Like others in the Progressive Era, Thorndike was committed to science and was among those who were devoted to efficiency in education. "Through his many disciples, and his textbooks, tests, achievement scales, and teachers' manuals" he contributed greatly to the structure and practices of public education in the twentieth century. He was among those who taught school officials "to regard their students objectively and quantitatively,"[10] much like Thorndike treated his own subjects.

EDUCATIONAL RESEARCH AS A PSYCHOLOGY OF LEARNING

In collaboration with Robert S. Woodworth, Thorndike published the first of three articles on transfer of training in the May, 1901 issue of the *Psychological Review*. The three Thorndike-Woodworth articles were significant. Their transfer experiments received almost immediate attention because they related directly to one of the major educational questions of the time, Herbert Spencer's question: "What knowledge is of most worth?" That the tasks subjects had to perform in the Thorndike-Woodworth experiments did not relate to the traditional or even new school subjects was neither noted nor seemed important to those who used the studies to support new school curricula. Thorndike and

Woodworth were seen as having dealt a fatal blow to the foundation of the traditional defense for school curricula, and that was enough for its critics. From then on, Thorndike was a major architect of the American classroom, doing for American public education in the twentieth century what Henry Barnard did in the nineteenth century. He gave specific instructions on what to teach and how to teach and provided the theoretical justifications for his instructions, and even developed instruments to enable educators to measure accurately what students had achieved.

Animal Intelligence that proved to be an important work in animal or comparative psychology and his work on transfer with Robert S. Woodworth in 1901 show how central his work and ideas were for so long in the twentieth century. *Animal Intelligence* was the basis for his laws of learning that were taught to teachers and used to structure his texts for student use in schools. The Thorndike-Woodworth studies not only related to questions about what should be taught in the nation's high schools but also served as a model for conducting studies in education.

Like others in the Progressive Era, he devoted his efforts to the measurement of educational products. Between 1911 and 1916, he developed scales for the measurement of writing, arithmetic, drawing, reading spelling, and even aesthetic appreciation. That Thorndike was committed to testing and to measurement is, of course, well known. Like the progressives of his era, he believed issues and problems could be solved not through philosophical speculation or consideration of popular opinions but through scientific investigation. For Thorndike science meant finding facts and the relationships among facts as precisely as possible. As a scientist, he was interested in observations and recording those observations consistently and uniformly, and the means for doing so were testing and measurement. His commitment to assigning numerical designations to events and statements was early expressed, even before his often quoted claim that "Whatever exists at all exists in some amount" and even before the publication of his *Introduction to the Theory of Mental and Social Measurements* (1904). He observed in *Notes on Child-Study* (1901) that statements could be made "more valuable and more exact" by expressing their "numerical probability" and "by giving with all averages numerical measurements of the extent of variation from that average."[11] In the preface to *Educational Psychology* (1903), he credited his knowledge of statistics to the teaching of James M. Cattell and Franz Boas and the writings of Sir Francis Galton and Karl Pearson.[12] In *An Introduction to the Theory of Mental and Social Measurements* he introduced many to the work of Galton, Cattell, Boas, and Pearson and showed how the methods of the physical and natural sciences could be applied to the problems educators were facing and were expected to solve. When Merle Curti assessed the social ideas of American educators in the 1930s, he concluded that Thorndike's "influence in establishing and popularizing fact-finding, statistical, and experimental technique in education has been immeasurable."[13]

THE TRANSFER STUDIES

Whether examined from the vantage point of psychology, educational psychology, educational theory, of considerations of what the high school curriculum should include, the three articles Thorndike and Woodworth published in 1901 on transfer of training[14] are unquestionably significant. They began a line of inquiry that has not yet reached its end. The purpose of the Thorndike-Woodworth studies was to determine as precisely as possible whether improvement in one activity would lead to improvement in another activity. Their use of a control group and an experimental group placed them among the first, if not the first, to investigate transfer in that manner.[15] They created carefully controlled experimental settings and tasks just as Thorndike created carefully controlled experimental situations for his dissertation. For example, the experimental group practiced estimating the area of rectangles of various sizes. Subsequently, that group was assigned the task of estimating the size of triangles, a task they had not practiced. Similar experiments were conducted in which the experimental group estimated lengths and weights. The performances of the experimental groups and the control groups were compared to determine whether the performance of the experimental group was better than that of the control group. The results of these experiments allowed the investigators to conclude that training in one activity resulted in either no or an insignificant amount of improvement in the subsequent activity. Improvement from one activity to another could only be expected when the two activities contained "identical elements." The activities subjects practiced in the Thorndike-Woodworth experiments were clearly very far removed from the subjects students studied in school. Still, the results of their experiments were used as evidence in debates about the high school curriculum that had been waging since the early 1890s and even earlier.

The Thorndike-Woodworth experiments received almost immediate attention. They appeared to relate to one of the major issues of the time—the high school and its curriculum. After the Kalamazoo decision (1874), it was generally accepted that a community had the right to tax itself to support a high school. By 1890 few questioned whether there would be tax-supported high schools just as there were already established tax-supported elementary schools. The high school was on a firm legal foundation and was growing at a rate that required construction of a new high school each day for the next twenty-five years. The questions were: What knowledge was of the most worth? Should the high school prepare its students for college or for life? Should training be specific and practical or should general education continue? Educators then had to decide whether to continue to offer a general education curriculum founded on adherence to faculty psychology and a belief in mental discipline or whether training should be specific and subjects selected for their practical value.

What the high school curriculum was to include and the psychological justification for what was included were questions answered (but not to the satisfaction of all) by the National Education Association's Committee of Ten in 1893. Before, during, and after the time of the Committee of Ten, its chair and the principal author of the Report, Harvard's president, Charles W. Eliot, argued that all school subjects should be training subjects.[16] By so arguing, Eliot was basically arguing for mental discipline and placing himself in a tradition as old, if not older than the 1828 Yale Report that maintained that the classics employed every faculty of the mind and that the "discipline" of the mind was more important than its "furniture." The Committee of Ten Report held to the doctrine of mental discipline, maintaining that those school subjects that best prepared one for college also best prepared the student for the tasks and problems that befall one in ordinary, everyday life. "Every youth who entered college," according to the Report, "would have spent four years in studying a few subjects thoroughly; and, on the theory that all subjects are to be considered equivalent in educational rank for the purposes of admission to college, it would make no difference which subjects he had chosen from the programme—he would have had four years of strong and effective mental training."[17] Students' choices were, however, confined to a restricted list of subjects. In the following years, there would be considerable debate about the most appropriate subjects for high school students. Eliot wanted students to be better prepared in science before entering college. Others would express similar desires or recommendations from time to time in the twentieth century.

When Thorndike and Woodworth created experimental situations to determine precisely the extent to which improvement in one activity would transfer to other activities, they embarked upon a course that was to change the character of future educational and psychological debates. Debates about faculty psychology and mental discipline would continue, but after Thorndike and Woodworth the concepts would fall under a new heading, either transfer of training or transfer of learning; and the participants would be required to have experimental evidence to support their claims. The Thorndike-Woodworth studies served as a model for over a hundred other such studies that were conducted in the following decade.[18] Most of those studies failed to support the traditional broad claims for transfer.[19]

The immediate effect of the Thorndike-Woodworth studies and those that soon followed was to support the position of those who were trying to discredit the old psychological doctrines and replace the classical curriculum with its emphasis on languages (usually Latin and Greek) with one that would be practical, useful, and relevant to students in the first years of the twentieth century. Thorndike and Woodworth appeared to offer not only theoretical doubt about transfer, mental discipline, and faculty psychology but also experimental proof. As James Rowland Angell, the Chicago functionalist proclaimed, there soon developed "the heretical creed of certain pedagogical radicals, who have dared to proclaim in high places that the formal discipline cult was founded upon a myth, and the educational value of a study is measured directly by its intrinsic worth and not by its indirect gymnastic qualities."[20]

Even those who wanted to hold on to traditional views and conceptions had to come to terms with the new experimental studies. For example, William C. Bagley had to admit in 1904 that "the doctrine of 'formal discipline" seems doomed."[21] He told the faculty of the University of Chicago College of Education, "Personally, I believe that those who still cling to the dogma in its original form cannot justify their position; I also believe that those who have entirely cast aside the idea of formal training have done so too hastily."[22] He had what he called the "ideal" as his own alternative to the "old doctrine." It was similar to a notion that Charles H. Judd called the "theory of conscious generalization" later classified as a theory of common elements."[23]

Thorndike's interest in transfer did not end with the 1901 studies. In the 1920s he and his associates conducted two studies of high school students that included the performances of nearly 14,000 students. At the beginning and at the end of the school year the *I.E.R. Tests of Selective and Relational Thinking* were administered to the students to determine whether their scores had changed. The purpose of the study was to determine whether students with equal abilities who had studied different subjects would show any transfer effect of any given subject they studied. Some transfer effects were found but they were small; and Thorndike concluded that the intelligence of the students was more important than the subjects they studied.[24]

Transfer studies were frequently used to support what educators wanted to believe. After Thorndike's 1924 study, Harold O. Rugg reported that no major curriculum committee attempted to determine through scientific investigation whether any school subject as then taught contributed to increasing the student's ability to think. The way to answer such a question—by careful measurement of the ability of large groups of students before and after instruction in a specified subject—had awaited Thorndike's 1924 study. According to Rugg, Thorndike "showed by measuring carefully the ability of 9,000 tenth-grade pupils before and after taking a year of Latin that one year's study of Latin as now organized does increase one's ability to reason—by a small amount—but that the gain is no larger than that due to the study of other school subjects as now organized." Rugg observed that "it is of great importance to find, for example, that bookkeeping, cooking, and sewing increases one's ability to generalize even more in some instances than does the study of the Classics!"[25] Rugg further reported that the Advisory Committee of the Classical League had devoted only two sentences to Thorndike's study. The League's Report recorded that: "The study shows that the amount of growth produced by certain school subjects in the ability measured by the test varies so slightly that no definite conclusions can be drawn therefrom."[26] Rather than accept the findings of a study based on careful measurement, the League's Advisory Committee solicited the judgments of seventy psychologists, psychologists who supported study of the classics.

Attempts to find an alternative to the conclusions of the Thorndike-Woodworth studies continued into the 1930s. Bagley then reported that Pedro Orata, a student at Ohio State University, had demonstrated "beyond a peradventure of a doubt" that "the 'transfer' evidence had not only been overworked but actually abused."[27] He later reported that Orata's "searching analysis" of ninety-nine transfer experiments conducted between 1890 and 1928 showed that "the total evidence of these experiments, far from demolishing the theory of mental discipline, actually supports it, although obviously not its earlier naïve form."[28] Orata's work[29] can rightfully be interpreted as an attempt to discredit Thorndike's work. However, it does demonstrate how much attention the transfer issue generated. Orata's bibliography on "transfer of training" included twenty-eight "laboratory experiments," fifteen "memory investigations," nine researches in "cross-education," four "experiments with animals," fifty-one "classroom experiments," twenty-two "correlational studies," twelve "questionnaire studies," fifty-seven "theoretical discussions based on experimental evidence," fifty-six "discussions that are largely theoretical," and fourteen other references.

Attempts to find or to deny transfer have continued. In 1941 Peter Sandiford reported that he had reviewed 810 articles on transfer. He found that transfer was a "real factor" in education, but the amount transfer that can be expected is usually small.[30] In 1953 C. E. Osgood concluded that it was not certain that the old doctrine of formal discipline was invalid.[31] In 1966 Lawrence M. Stolurow reviewed 1,700 articles on transfer and developed a taxonomy that showed over 200 principles of transfer.[32] As late as 2003, Richard E. Mayer was able to provide evidence—studies conducted in the 1990s—to support his observation that: "Modern researchers have continued to have difficulty in finding evidence of transfer, but the search of transfer continues."[33]

ANIMAL INTELLIGENCE

Thorndike, like his teacher William James and like so many other psychologists of his generation, accepted Charles Darwin's theory of evolution. Darwin had presented a theory that explained variations in and development of species in terms of their successful responses (adaptations) to threatening situations in their environments. In similar fashion, those who accepted Darwinian evolution accepted adaptation and adaptation became learning. Learning, more often than not, was a change of some sort, an adjustment or an adaptation. Thorndike subscribed to an "emergency" theory, claiming that organisms adapted and learned when they faced a critical situation. Through trial and error, subjects—be they animals or humans—learned which responses were successful and thus satisfying and which were not. The learning theory Thorndike developed came to be known as connectionism. Learning consisted of the formation of bonds, or connections, between stimuli in a situation and the learner's satisfying response to the stimuli. As people made connections or formed bonds, they were effectively changed, that is, they learned.

By the end of the nineteenth century, the physical scientists—chemists and physicists—had made important discoveries by studying simple phenomena under well-controlled conditions, the laboratory. Psychologists set out to do the same. They attempted to identify simple forms of behavior in the laboratory. The relatively simple forms of behavior that were best suited for experimentation under laboratory conditions were animal behaviors. Thorndike accepted that research based on lower animals could be applied to the understanding of human behavior. Darwin appeared to provide psychologists with a theoretical justification for using the behavior of lower species to generalize about human behavior.

Animal Intelligence: An Experimental Study of Associative Processes in Animals was a study of animal behavior designed to provide knowledge of human behavior. It proved to be significantly different from earlier studies. Earlier studies were based on observations of animals in their natural settings. Thorndike's observations and conclusions were based on his work with cats, dogs, and chicks in a controlled experimental setting. He created fifteen puzzle-boxes in which hungry cats were confined and from which they could free themselves "by some simple act, such as pulling at a loop of cord, pressing a lever, or stepping on a platform."[34] He also created nine puzzle-boxes for dogs and for chicks he made three mazes by standing books on end. Thorndike's experiments demonstrated that learning was a relatively slow continuous process in which the subject formed a link, bond, or connection between a situation and response. Thorndike's work with cats, dogs, and chicks served as the foundation for his learning theory. It is the study that allowed Thorndike to establish his "law of effect" that was the basis of his learning theory.

In Chapter II, of Volume II, "The Laws of Learning in Animals," of his *Educational Psychology* (1913)[35] Thorndike explained that: "The complexities of human learning will in the end be best understood if we avoid them, examining rather the behavior of the lower animals as they learn to meet certain situations in changed, and more remunerative, ways."[36] He then gave an account of how a chick learned to get from one point to another, an account in which he offered some assumptions about how chicks feel and what they want.

Thorndike explained that he removed a chick from a pen where it had been with other chicks. It was then "confronted by a situation which is, in essence, *Confining walls and the absence of the other chicks, food and familiar surroundings.*" The chick reacted to "the situation by running around, making loud sounds, and jumping at the walls." Jumping at the walls produced "the discomforts of thwarted effort." When the chick found its way out, it had "the satisfaction of being with the other chicks, of eating, and "of being in its usual habitat." After a number of such removals, the chick "learned the way out." After five trials, two chicks "learned" how to escape and return to the other chicks "within five or six seconds," considerably faster than the three to four minutes they needed on their first trial.[37] Thorndike related that the chicks' "dislike of loneliness acts as a uniform motive to get back to the other chicks."[38]

Thorndike's account of his experiments with chicks is instructive and merits some comment, for it tells a great deal about how Thorndike, and by extension, many other educational psychologists and educators, viewed learning. First it should be noted that Thorndike attributed "discomfort" to the chicks. He offered no evidence for that attribution. That the chicks suffered discomfort may or may not be true, but until evidence is provided it is only an assumption. Similarly, Thorndike's claim that the chick "has the satisfaction of being with the other chicks, of eating, and of being in its usual habitat" once "it gets out" is also an assumption for which there is no evidence. Yet, Thorndike did seem to profess that he knew a great deal about how various animals felt.

Not long after completing his dissertation he explained how animals thought and felt:

The essential thing about the thinking of the animals is that they feel things in gross. The kitten that learned to respond differently to the signals "I must feed those cats" and "I will not feed them," felt each signal as a vague total including the tone, the movements of my head, etc. It did not have an idea of the sound of *I*, another of the sound of *must*, another of the sound of *feed*, etc. It did not turn the complex impression into a lot of elements, but felt it, as I have said, in gross. The dog that learned to get out of a box by pulling a loop of wire did not feel the parts of the box separately, the loop as a definite circle of a certain size, did not feel his act as a sum of certain particular movements. The monkey that learned to know the letter K from the letter Y did not feel the separate lines of the letter, have definite ideas of the parts. He just felt one way when he saw one total impression and another way when he saw another.[39]

That a chick "is confronted by situation" when it is removed from one experimenter-made context to another experimenter-made context is unquestionably so, but either situation is unnatural and contrived. That the situation is experimenter-made, unnatural, and contrived is important, for it restricts what the experimenter, the psychologist, can accept as learning. The contrived situation effectively defines learning. When the chick moves itself with dispatch from one place to another, during a time interval and in a manner deemed acceptable to the experimenter, or the psychologist, "it has formed an association, or connection, or bond ... In common language, it has learned ... has learned the way out." Learning is thus "an association, or connection, or bond." Learning can also properly be seen as the performance of a behavior by a subject, be it a a cat, a dog, a chick or a student—a behavior the psychologist wants the subject to perform. In this instance moving itself from one place to another in an orderly manner, without loud noises, and without jumping at the walls. However, there is no evidence that the chick ever wanted to learn how to move itself from one place to another.

It takes little imagination and even less wit to see that there may be no significant difference between chicks that have been placed in an experimenter-made situation and students who have been placed in a classroom. Placement of the chick in the maze, in a strange setting, may be comparable to placing the child to an assigned seat in a classroom. Just as the chick is said to have learned once it does what the experimenter wants it to do so it can be said that the student has learned once it performs in the way that the teacher wants him or her to perform. The subject, sometimes it was called a learner but now it seems fashionable to call it a participant or a client, is not seen as a self-starting, purposeful agent. The subject, be it a student or a chick, is placed in a situation it did not make or choose and a situation over which it has little or no control. Once placed in that situation it is expected to form associations, connections, or make bonds that the experimenter, teacher, or psychologist wants it to make. If it does not learn, does not indicate that it has made the desired associations, connections, or bonds by performing or behaving in the manner desired by the experimenter, it is given a proper stimulus. It is deliberately annoyed. It is made to experience some sort of discomfort. When it alleviates its discomfort in a way that satisfies the experimenter, the psychologist, or the teacher, it can be said to have learned. When the subject, in this case the student, satisfies the teacher, it can be said to have learned. Learning is satisfaction; learning is satisfying the teacher. When the teacher is satisfied, so is the student. At least he or she is not deliberately disturbed.

Thorndike claimed that what was known about how animals learned was also applicable to how children learned, but he offered no experimental evidence for that claim. However, it was not a totally unreasonable claim given his claim expressed in "Evolution of the Human Intellect" that humans were part of and not apart of nature. The suggestion that Thorndike saw students as not significantly different from cats, dogs, chicks or whatever has some foundation. For Thorndike the similarities between humans and animals were more significant than the differences. The differences between humans and animals were basically quantitative. The ability to form associations and the number and the speed at which they could be made were the most important features of any animal. Even before he published *Educational Psychology* he related that:

> This growth in the number, speed of formation, permanence, delicacy and complexity of associations possible for an animal reaches its acme in the case of man. Even if we leave out of question the power of reasoning, the possession of a multitude of ideas and abstractions and the power of control over impulses, purposive action, man is still the intellectual leader of the animal kingdom by virtue of the superior development in him of the power of forming associations between situations or sense impressions and acts, by virtue of the degree to which the mere learning by selection possessed by all intelligent animals has advanced. In man the type of intellect common to the animal kingdom finds its fullest development, and with it is combined the hitherto non-existent power of thinking about things and rationally directing action in accord with thought.[40]

While Thorndike acknowledged that humans had "the power of thinking about things and rationally directing action in accord with thought," he also maintained that "this very reason, self-consciousness and self-control which seem to sever human intellect so sharply from that of all other animals are really but secondary results of the tremendous increase in the number, delicacy and complexity of associations which the human animal can form."[41] The ability of humans to associate, to make connections, to form bonds—that is, to learn—better than or faster than animals was easily explained by the complex cell structure of human brains.[42] Human brains were larger and more complex than those of other animals. For Thorndike the similarities between animals and humankind were important and were not to be overlooked. The differences that mattered were not differences in kind but differences of quantity. Humankind was a part of nature not apart from it: "Amongst the minds of animals that of man leads, not as a demigod from another planet, but as a king from the same race."[43] The "real continuity" of the evolutionary process that explained the development of mental capacities and mental processes that made humankind a part of rather than apart from nature justified the use of a universal method for the study of learning whether it be the learning of a human or the learning of an animal, and this view, or paradigm still dominates. If one wanted to try to disturb either an animal or a human, the method for disturbing was therefore essentially the same. Differences in either complexity or quantity could be admitted but not qualitative differences.

THORNDIKE'S LEARNING LAWS

By 1914 Thorndike had published *Educational Psychology* (1903), *The Principles of Teaching* (1906), and his three-volume *Educational Psychology* (Volume I of *Educational Psychology* was titled *The Original Nature of Man*; Volume II was titled *The Psychology of Learning*; and Volume II, originally published in 1903 as *Educational Psychology* was titled *Individual Differences*.). In these works he presented the law of effect, the theory of identical elements; the law of readiness; and the law of exercise. These laws, he maintained, were applicable to teaching. For Thorndike, "the art of teaching" was "the art of giving and withholding stimuli with the result of producing or preventing certain responses."[44]

Thorndike's "law of effect" held that bonds or connections between a stimulus or situation and a response were strengthened when the subject derived pleasure or satisfaction from making the appropriate response and that bonds were weakened when the required response was annoying. To use this law to good advantage in the classroom, teachers needed to structure students' work in a way that would allow them to derive satisfaction from their work and to avoid failure. It was not, however, necessary for the teacher to dispense rewards. The rewards were to be found in the work itself. Teachers did not need to implement token economies in their classrooms. The satisfaction or reward derived from success—from arriving at a correct answer to a problem—served as motivation for continuing the work. For example, in *The Psychology of Arithmetic*, he explained that:

... computation is not dull if the pupil can compute. He does not himself object to its barrenness of vital meaning, so long as the barrenness of failure is prevented. We must not forget that pupils like to learn. In teaching excessively dull individuals, who has not often observed the great interest which they display in anything they are enabled to master?[45]

The law of effect also required teachers to build their lessons in accordance with students' interests. That was a prescription consistent with those who had been promoting the "new education."

The "theory of identical elements" was based on the work he completed with Woodworth. It maintained that what students learned in one learning task would not transfer to another task unless each task contained identical, or very similar, elements. In 1917 Thorndike applied the theory of identical elements to *The Thorndike Arithmetics* a three-book series of texts that proved to be very successful. In *The Psychology of Arithmetic* (1920), he demonstrated how arithmetic content could be organized to secure maximum advantage of the theory of identical elements. Those two works significantly changed how arithmetic was taught by showing that teaching effectiveness could be increased if the subject matter was organized according to how students learned rather than organized according to the logic of the discipline.

The "law of readiness" maintained that when the student was in a state conductive to the formation of a bond, forming that bond would be satisfying. However, if the situation were not satisfying, attempts to form a bond would only serve to annoy the student. This law was consistent with the teachings of the "new education," for it accepted that there were a developmental stages in a student's life. It also reinforced earlier notions that held that learning should always be associated with pleasure rather than pain.

The "law of exercise" held that connections or bonds were strengthened by use and weakened by disuse. This law was directly applicable to the time-honored practice of drills. As Thorndike researched its practical application, he discovered that distributed practice, or drill, was more effective in many instances than concentrated practice. Consequently, countless students were required to practice their spelling words, penmanship, arithmetic, and other skills a few minutes a day rather than until they achieved mastery at one sitting.

By the end of the Progressive Era, Thorndike's learning theory was dominating educational psychology, was seen as bringing pedagogy nearer to being a science than ever before," and found to be useful by John Dewey and William Heard Kilkpatrick. Dewey's *How We Think* (1910) was tooled "with the concepts of connectionism," and Kilpatrick was "preparing to base his 'project method' of teaching upon the laws of learning of stimulus-response psychology."[46]

By the end of the Progressive Era, Thorndike's position was clear: "The task of education is to make changes in human beings." To accomplish that task educators needed "exact knowledge" of the changes they needed to effect and those they had achieved. Education was a "form of human engineering" and educators needed measurements comparable to "the foot-pound, calorie, volt, and ampere" used by mechanical and electrical engineers.[47] When Edna Bryner presented her "Selected Bibliography of Certain Phases of Educational Measurement" in 1918, it was clear that Thorndike had already offered a number of ways to measure changes or performances in a number of areas. Between 1911 and 1914 Thorndike had presented six publications that related to the "Theory of Educational Measurement and Development of the Movement." In 1914 he presented four publications related to assessment of the teaching and learning of arithmetic. Between 1911 and 1913 he had five publications related to securing measurements in English Composition, Language, and Vocabulary. Between 1910 and 1915, he published five items related to students' handwriting. In 1915 he published a work on how to measure student achievement in spelling.[48]

Even though Thorndike is so closely associated with connectionism and even though he devoted so much attention to connections, how they were formed, how they were weakened, and how they were strengthened, his notion of learning is fundamentally one that entails change. For Thorndike a change was a change. Ultimately it makes no difference what kind of change it was. Either the weakening or the strengthening of a bond between the S and the R was a change, and a change was learning. It made no difference how strong or how weak. Learning and what in ordinary language might be called "unlearning" are both learning. If schooling were a process thoroughly consistent with Thorndike's notion of learning, students who begin performing well and then proceed to do less well would be given credit for having learned.

To the extent that the Progressive Era was an era of reform, an era that called for standardization in public education, accountability, and the means for providing measures to demonstrate accountability, Thorndike was indeed a major contributor with his laws of learning. The next section explores a different but related paradigm in the history of educational research. An underlying medical model pervades the establishment of the "new" social sciences out of the classic disciplines of philosophy, natural science, and rhetoric. Modern medicine and medical schools were models for post-graduate education and academic research that produced theories that could be applied to real life and make a difference in health, education, and welfare. Major figures in psychology criss-crossed paths with medicine and psychiatry including William James, Thorndike's mentor, and G. Stanley Hall, his contemporary.

NOTES

1. Edward L. Thorndike. *Science*, n. s. Vol. XXXVII (January 24, 1913), p. 42, Quoted in Merele E. Curti. *The Social Ideas of American Educators*, rev. ed. (Totowa, New Jersey: Littlefield, Adams & Co., 1959), p. 482.
2. Edward L. Thorndike, "Eugenics: With Special Reference to Intellect and Character," *Popular Science Monthly*, Vol. LXXXIII (April 1913), pp. 131-132; also see: Robert L. Church and Michael W. Sedlack, *Education in the United States: An Interpretive History* (New York: The Free Press, 1976), p. 357.
3. David K. Cohen and Carol A. Barnes. "Research and the Purposes of Education," in Ellen Confliffe Lagemann and Lee S. Shullman (eds.). *Issues in Education Research: Problems and Possibilities* (San Francisco: Josey-Bass Publishers, 1999), p. 20.
4. Edward L. Thorndike. "Autobiography" in Geraldine M. Joncich (ed.). *Psychology and the Science of Education: Selected Writings of Edward L. Thorndike* (New York: Teachers College Press, 1962), p. 28.
5. *Ibid.*, pp. 29-30.
6. Edward L. Thorndike. "Do Animals Reason?" *Popular Science Monthly* (1899) in Wayne Dennis (ed.). *Readings in General Psychology* (New York: Prentice-Hall, Inc., 1949), p. 301.
7. Edward L. Thorndike. *Animal Intelligence* (Darien, Connecticut: Hafner Publishing Co., 1970), pp. 149-150.
8. Clarence J. Karier. *Scientists of the Mind: Intellectual Founders of Modern Psychology* (Urbana, Illinois: University of Illinois Press, 1986), p. 162.
9. Richard E. Mayer. "E. L. Thorndike's Enduring Contributions to Educational Psychology" in Barry Zimmerman and Dale H. Schunk (eds.). *Educational Psychology: A Century of Contributions* (Mahwah, New Jersey: Lawrence Erlbaum Associates, 2003), p. 113.
10. Karier. *Scientists of the Mind*, pp. 101-102.
11. Edward L. Thorndike. *Notes on Child Study* (New York: The Macmillan Co., 1901), pp. 19-20.
12. Geraldine Joncich Clifford. *Edward L. Thorndike: The Sane Positivist* (Middletown, Connecticut: Wesleyan University Press, 1984), pp. 290-291.
13. Curti. *The Social Ideas of American Educators*, rev. ed., p. 460.
14. Edward L. Thorndike and Robert S. Woodworth, "I. The Influence of Improvement in One Mental Function upon the Efficiency of other Functions;" "II. The Estimation of Magnitudes;" and "III. Functions Involving Attention, Observation and Discrimination." *Psychological Review*, Vol. VIII (May, July and November, 1901), pp. 247-261; 384-395; 553-564.
15. Richard L. Solomon. "An Extension of Control Group Design," *Psychological Bulletin*, Vol. XLIX (1949), pp. 137-138.

16. Edward A. Krug, *The Shaping of the American High School* (New York: Harper and Row, 1964), pp. 204-205.

17. *Report of the Committee on Secondary School Studies Appointed at the Meeting of the National Education Association, July 9, 1892 with the Reports of the Conference Arranged by the Committee and Held December 28-30, 1892* (Washington, D. C.: Government Printing Office, 1893), p. 53.

18. Walter B. Kolesnik. *Mental Discipline in Modern Education* (Madison, Wisconsin: University of Wisconsin Press, 1962), p. 32.

19. John S. Brubacher, *A History of the Problems of Education* (New York: The McGraw-Hill Book Co., 1966), p. 155.

20. James Rowland Angell. "The Doctrine of Formal Discipline in the Light of the Principles of General Psycholoy," *Educational Review*, Vol. XXXVI (June, 1908), p. 1.

21. William C. Bagley, "Ideals Versus Generalized Habits," *School and Home Education*, Vol. XXIV, No. 3 (November 1904), p. 102.

22. William C. Bagley, "The School's Responsibility for Developing the Controls of Conduct," *The Elementary School Teacher*, Vol. 8, No. 7 (March 1908), p. 356.

23. Peter Sandiford, "Transfer of Learning" in Walter S. Monroe (ed.). *Encyclopedia of Educational Research*. Rev. ed. (New York: The Macmillan Co., 1950), p. 1311.

24. Edward L. Thorndike, "Mental Discipline in High School Studies," *Journal of Educational Psychology*, Vol. 15 (1924), pp. 1-22 and 83-98; and C. R. Broyler, E. L. Thorndike, and Ella Woodward, "A Second Study of Mental Discipline in High School Studies," *Journal of Educational Psychology*, Vol. 18 (1927), pp. 377-401.

25. Harold O. Rugg, "Three Decades of Mental Discipline: Curriculum Making *via* National Committees" in Guy M. Whipple (ed.). *The Twenty-Sixth Yearbook of the National Society for the Study of Education: The Foundations and Technique of Curriculum-Construction* (Bloomington, Illinois, The Public School Publishing Co., 1926), p. 61.

26. Quoted in Rugg, "Three Decades of Mental Discipline," p. 62.

27. William C. Bagley. *Education, Crime and Social Progress* (New York: The Macmillan Co., 1931), p. 126.

28. William C. Bagley. *Education and Emergent Man* (New York: Thomas Nelson and Sons, 1934), p. 37.

29. Pedro Orata. *The Theory of Identical Elements* (Columbus, Ohio: The Ohio State University Press, 1928).

30. Peter Sandiford, "Transfer of Learning" in Walter S. Monroe (ed.). *Encyclopedia of Educational Research*, rev. ed. (New York: The Macmillan Co., 1950), p. 1312.

31. C. E. Osgood, *Method and Theory in Experimental Psychology* (New York: Oxford University Press, 1953).

32. Lawrence M. Stolurow, *Psychological and Educational Factors in Transfer of Training*, Section 1, Final Report. (Training Research Laboratory, Urbana, Illinois, 1966).

33.   Richard E. Mayer, "E. L. Thorndike's Enduring Contributions to Educational Psychology" in Zimmerman and Schunk (eds.). *Educational Psychology: A Century of Contributions*, p. 135.

34.   Edward L. Thorndike. *Animal Intelligence* from the *Psychological Review Monograph Supplements*, 1898, No. 8 reproduced in Wayne Dennis (ed.). *Readings in the History of Psychology* (New York: Appleton-Century-Crofts, Inc., 1948), p. 380. For another account of the study see: Edward L. Thorndike, "Do Animals Reason?" *Popular Science Monthly*, 1899 reproduced in Wayne Dennis (ed.). *Readings in General Psychology* (New York: Prentice-Hall, Inc., 1949), pp. 289-301.

35.   Volume I of *Educational Psychology* was titled *The Original Nature of Man*; Volume II was titled *The Psychology of Learning*; and Volume II, originally published in 1903 as *Educational Psychology* was titled *Individual Differences*. The edition used here is the edition printed in 1919 and published by Teachers College, Columbia University.

36.   Thorndike. *Psychology of Learning*, pp. 6-7.

37.   *Ibid.*, pp. 6-7.

38.   Thorndike. *Animal Intelligence* in Dennis, *Readings in the History of Psychology*, p. 381.

39.   Edward L. Thorndike, "The Evolution of the Human Intellect," *Popular Science Monthly*, Vol. 69, No. 5 (November, 1901), p. 62.

40.   Thorndike. "The Evolution of the Human Intellect," p. 60.

41.   *Ibid.*

42.   *Ibid.*, p. 61.

43.   *Ibid.*, p. 62.

44.   Edward L. Thorndike. *The Principles of Teaching Based on Psychology* (New York: A. G. Seller, 1906) in Geraldine M. Joncich (ed.). *Psychology and the Science of Education: Selected Writings of Edward L. Thorndike* (New York: Teachers College Press, 1967), p. 61.

45.   Edward L. Thorndike. *The Psychology of Arithmetic* (New York: The Macmillan Co., 1922) in Joncich (ed.). *Psychology and the Science of Education: Selected Writings of Edward L. Thorndike*, pp. 88-89.

46.   Geraldine Joncich Clifford. *Edward L. Thorndike: The Sane Positivist*, pp. 345-346.

47.   Edward L. Thorndike, "Measurement in Education" in Guy M. Whipple (ed.). *The Twenty-First Yearbook of the National Society for the Study of Education: Intelligence Tests and Their Use* (Bloomington, Illinois: Public School Publishing Co., 1922), p. 1.

48.   Edna Bryner. "Selected Bibliography of Certain Phases of Educational Measurement" in Guy Whipple (ed.). *The Seventeenth Yearbook of the National Society for the Study of Education: Part II, The Measurement of Educational Products* (Bloomington, Illinois: The Public School Publishing Co., 1918), pp. 161-190.

PART IV

INSTITUTIONALIZATION OF
THE PROGRESSIVE AGENDA

CHAPTER 10

THE MENTAL HYGIENE MOVEMENT

Rockefeller Philanthropy and the Promotion of a Medical Model in Educational Research

The twentieth century movement to establish and to organize educational research is not often understood within the tradition of the history of medical research. It is more commonly associated with the professionalization of experimental psychology in the social sciences.[1] Progressive Era surveys, from Joseph Mayer Rice's descriptions of school practices to Leonard P. Ayres' "laggards in the schools," supported a scientific foundation for the expansion of research in education that dealt with differences in children both mental and physical as well as their ability to learn. Edward L. Thorndike established a celebrated career by concentrating on learning and applying this findings and theories to pedagogy and the school curriculum.[2] Little attention has been paid to the underlying ideology and the faith in science that established a rationale for systematically studying individual growth in the Progressive Era and beyond. Preventive medicine and public health reform were founded on the belief that scientific methods

Educational Research, the National Agenda, and Educational Reform:
A History, pp. 271–298

should be used in research on human subjects. Medicine was one of the sciences used in research directed toward the establishment of a science of public policy in areas that included but were not exclusively concerned with public education.[3] The boundaries of educational research and the protocols for what came to be known as progressive education, as they were formulated in Progressive Era, were closely associated with public health reform. Close ties existed between the social and behavioral sciences and the medical sciences in the early stages of their development. This chapter examines this connection in the legacy of the mental hygiene movement in child guidance and child study as part of the ideology that sought to establish educational research as a scientific endeavor.

THE MENTAL HYGIENCE MOVEMENT

Mental hygiene was an idealistic movement rooted in Progressive Era preventive medicine and the "new" psychiatry associated with public health reform. Progressive doctors and asylum superintendents who conceptualized the mental hygiene perspective hoped to further the development of a science of conserving mental health and preventing mental illness.[4] During the Progressive Era, the medical sciences were considered by their promoters to combine the best of the natural and social sciences because they used the methods of pure research applied to the most fundamental human problem: disease.[5] It was believed that mental medicine of psychiatry "broadly defined" would become the apex of the medical sciences and would ensure not only health but also happiness. The medicalization of education was receiving increased attention in the 1920s and 1930s as indicated by Mandel Sherman's contribution to *The Thirty-Seventh Yearbook of the National Society for the Study of Education* (1938). Historians of education overlooked this movement until the 1980s when Sol Cohen addressed the significant roll of the mental hygiene movement in American Education.[6] The legacy of medicalization is most apparent in educational research as a domain assumption that postulates the inseparability of mental and physical well being, which, in turn, supports the efficacy of researching children as a corrective to the problems of adults and ultimately society.[7]

The Mental Hygiene Movement and Twentieth Century Psychiatry

Educators, such as Charles W. Eliot and John Dewey, who were influential in establishing a progressive orientation toward children and their institutions, were more concerned with health care in the schools than in formal classroom experiences. The attempt to establish child psychiatry in the 1920s and 1930s transformed traditional moral conceptualizations of the child toward a "true nature" of childhood as a psychobiological phenomenon. Mental hygiene ideas were firmly grounded in the secularization of social thought based on scientific research. Progressive education and mental hygiene were mutually supportive perspectives and were often advanced by the same organizations and individuals.[8]

Education was inescapably caught up in the activities of the National Committee for Mental Hygiene (NCMH), founded by Clifford Beers in 1909.[9] Those concerned with mental defects early turned to children as a part of the public health emphasis on school hygiene.[10] The attention paid to children was encouraged by Victorian sentimentalism and the progressive reformers' fascination with children as the future of the human race. Mental hygienists used the juvenile courts and school classrooms for research purposes. Schools, where children were a captive population, served as laboratories and clinics. Compulsory school attendance legislation ensured that schools would provide access to a major portion of the population at a critical point in life. In 1919, psychiatrist William White declared childhood to be the "golden age of mental hygiene."[11] The mental hygiene movement advanced the ideological position that schooling is essentially a psychotherapeutic enterprise and not a purely academic enterprise. Mental hygienists viewed what was taught in school as less important than to whom it was taught. They were concerned with whether practices fit the needs and abilities of the child. They argued that the objectives of schooling were synonymous with those of mental hygiene.[12]

Direct psychiatric input into educational research or policy-making was rare. A major reason was the slow development of psychiatry within the medical sciences. There simply were not enough medical doctors much less doctors who had completed a specialization in psychiatry to fill the demands of the ambitious mental hygiene agenda. As medical researchers sought ways to eliminate contagious diseases and to develop a body of knowledge that could be taught to medical students, basic research on mental illness lagged and the area remained speculative. Lack of definitive research on the causes and cure of adult mental illness made it difficult to perfect child psychiatry. The first English language textbook on child psychiatry was not published until 1935.[13] In addition, in the United States psychiatry developed in a way different from how it developed in Europe where psychoanalysis did not remain within the medical profession. In the United States psychoanalysis, psychiatry, and neurology remained identified with medical science.[14] The lack of a scientific cure

for mental illness also made preventive work more important and emphasized the need to understand how healthy children develop. Hence, perspectives for the study of children were provided by Arnold Gesell, who
provided a research-based template for understanding age-stage normal
development, and Edward L. Thorndike, who applied his studies of animal learning to the education of children in school. Adolf Meyer's psychobiology and Thomas W. Salmon's preventive psychiatry, which
dominated mental hygiene, were compatible with various interpretations
of psychoanalysis, developmental theory, as well as behavioral and educational psychology. At the same time, the slow integration of psychiatric
training into medical schools encouraged the infiltration of psychiatric
and psychoanalytic theories into other disciplines, including social work,
psychology, and education. Mental hygienists actively propagandized and
fostered that infiltration. The mixed influence of preventive psychiatry on
educational research is best understood as the process whereby ideas are
institutionalized.[15]

The mental hygiene movement had three dimensions: a method, a
subject orientation, and a theoretical perspective. The method was based
on a medical model where dysfunctional behavior was likened to a disease. Pathological conditions were identified according to their simplest
component parts, and attempts were made to treat patients in the earliest
stages of their illness. In keeping with the preventive focus, the subject
orientation was toward young subject-clients. Children were tested and
screened as early as possible in order to detect incipient mental or physical abnormalities.

While committed to prevention and grounded in the notion that mental and physical well being were linked, mental hygiene proved adaptable
in its therapeutic orientation as various mental hygiene research projects
reveal. The concept of mental hygiene evolved from the original perspectives of the of the National Committee for Mental Hygiene from its inception to the end of World War I as advocacy organization devoted to
drawing public attention to a social problem. It is not accidental that
mental hygienists and educational psychologists worked side by side to
develop the Army Alpha and Army Beta intelligence tests during World
War I. The inclination to test and regulate continued and even grew. In
1918, the NCMH was joined by the formation of the Canadian National
Committee for Mental Hygiene (CNCMH). Philanthropic support for the
development of research programs and the initiation of child guidance
and child-study projects in the 1920s and 1930s. The distribution and
legitimization of research supported by the use of psychiatric screening
during World War I and II witnessed the institutionalization of psychotherapeutic ideas in social and educational policy in the Post-World War II
Era.

Organizing Research for the Promotion of Mental Hygiene

Research conducted by the National Committee for Mental Hygiene that upgraded and professionalized psychiatric research directed toward children was supported by private philanthropy.[16] The Commonwealth Fund and the Rockefeller philanthropies supported the National Committee's efforts to establish a scientific approach to public health research and to provide opportunities to demonstrate the value of preventive practices involving mental health with a focus on children in juvenile courts, health clinics, and public school classrooms. Through the efforts of influential mental hygiene supporters and the work of Clifford Beers, the Rockefeller Foundation at the time of its inception in 1913 decided to incorporate mental hygiene into its agenda.[17] The Foundation's officers, for example, President George Vincent, interpreted mental hygiene within the Foundation's medical/public health orientation as "psychiatry broadly defined."[18] The Commonwealth Fund, founded in 1918, also looked to mental hygiene as part of a public health campaign in the 1920s and 1930s. In 1933, Rockefeller philanthropy embarked on a major campaign for the expansion of public schooling at the secondary level adapted to the personality and developmental needs of youth along with its continuing support of medical research and public health research.[19]

The first programs initiated by the National Committee for Mental Hygiene supported by philanthropic funds were developed at the Gedney Farms Conference of Rockefeller executive officers in January 1920 and at a Commonwealth Fund conference held at Lakewood, New Jersey in March 1921. Thomas W. Salmon, medical director of the National Committee for Mental Hygiene and a consultant for the Rockefeller Foundation, argued before the influential boards at each forum that: "The greatest hour of American psychiatry is at hand."[20] The Monmouth County Demonstration that resulted from the conferences illustrates the close ties and the divergent orientations in mental hygiene research as expressed in the child guidance and the child-study movements in the early 1920s. The first demonstration of applied research in child guidance was supported by Rockefeller philanthropy and conducted by the National Committee for Mental Health.[21] The Monmouth County Organization for Social Service, a local voluntary association, initiated the project. Its concerns reflected a common Progressive Era belief that the quality of life and mental development among rural children was dwindling.[22] These beliefs were expressed by President Theodore Roosevelt's Commission on Country Life (1907), the 1909 White House Conference on Dependent Children, and the National Committee's mental hygiene surveys and exhibits on the problems and dangers of dependent, delinquent, deranged, and mentally deficient populations.[23]

Popular child-study societies and their eugenic offshoots, such as the "better babies movement," encouraged public action against feeblemindedness through health education and the cultivation of normality.[24] The purpose of the Monmouth County project was to survey the mental and physical status of the county's school-age children.[25]

There were internal disagreements over the clinical orientation of the research. The disagreements were over the emphasis on case-based research directed toward the remediation of the numerous mentally abnormal children discovered by the initial school survey as opposed to a focus on preventive education directed toward the normal population.[26] The Commonwealth Fund favored psychiatric intervention though child guidance activities, a position supported by V. V. Anderson, the National Committee for Mental Hygiene psychiatrist. The leadership of the local organization of Monmouth County favored a preventive approach through education. Lawrence K. Frank, an officer and child development advocate with Rockefeller philanthropy, supported the latter view. Frank agreed to fund the project after the local organization broke with the Commonwealth Fund and the National Committee for Mental Hygiene.[27] The Rockefeller support for the Monmouth County project effectively served to support large-scale school surveys that screened the school-age population for potential mental, physical, and emotional defects. It further promoted the introduction of the mental hygiene curriculum into the public school agenda using a preventive model for public health advocacy.

With support from the Commonwealth Fund the National Committee for Mental Hygiene continued to pursue a multifaceted effort in mental hygiene research based on a therapeutic model that used child guidance as is framework. A five-year program devoted to the prevention of juvenile delinquency was developed. Delinquency was interpreted as a symptom of maladjustment that if prevented, would reduce the incidence of mental illness in adults. The program included research into the clinical use of psychiatry, the training of psychiatric field workers, and the application of mental hygiene to educational practice. Research was conducted by three divisions, and a joint steering committee worked to integrate the program's activities.

ELABORATING INSTITUTIONS AND
RESOURCES FOR CHILD GUIDANCE

The National Committee for Mental Hygiene conducted the Commonwealth Fund's Program for the Prevention of Delinquency. The Committee created two departments to administer the research: the Department of Experimentation and Demonstration and the Department of Psychiatric Field Services. These departments operated under Division III of the Commonwealth Fund Program. Field service, under V. V. Anderson, became the major vehicle for the adaptation of mental hygiene research for educational settings through clinical studies in child guidance. Ironically, child guidance advanced the professionalization of psychology and social work more than psychiatry as the dominant interpreter of psychiatric perspectives in the field due to the lack of suitable psychiatrists.[28]

The National Committee for Mental Hygiene conducted eight demonstration clinics designed to demonstrate the utility and value of psychiatry in preventive work with children. The child guidance clinics served as laboratories for the study of incipient mental illness in children and for the training of personnel in the use of psychiatric practices in therapy. Clinics were funded for a specified period. The hope was that local organizations would assume the cost of continuing the clinics at the end of the funded demonstration period. The demonstrations provided communities models for providing mental hygiene services for children. Psychiatric child guidance demonstrations were located in St. Louis, Missouri; Norfolk, Virginia; Dallas Texas; St. Paul and Minneapolis, Minnesota; Cleveland, Ohio; Los Angeles, California; and Philadelphia, Pennsylvania.[29] Locally supported clinics were established in all cities except Norfolk. Consulting services provided assistance to clinics in Pasadena, California; Richmond, Virginia; Memphis, Tennessee; Macon, Georgia; Milwaukee, Wisconsin; and Baltimore, Maryland. Clinics in Richmond and Baltimore received some funding. Clinics in Macon and Memphis were later discontinued.[30] By the end of the five-year demonstration period the focus of child guidance changed from a concern with delinquency to an emphasis on a well-child orientation. Child guidance changed its focus from a court-based project to interest in school and community research and services. The original child clients referred by public sources were replaced by family generated referrals characterized by a paying middle class clientele.[31]

The National Committee for Mental Hygiene and the Commonwealth Fund began the Program for the Prevention of Delinquency in St. Louis in 1922. The St. Louis demonstration project found it difficult to focus exclusively on delinquency.[32] The origins of child misconduct appeared to lie in the family and the school. Subsequent demonstrations turned away from the juvenile court as a source of clients. The needs of community agencies and the public schools assumed a gradually larger portion of child guidance research and work. This reorientation was attempted in a demonstration in Norfolk and it was successfully applied in a third demonstration in Dallas. In the fourth demonstration, held in the twin cities of St. Paul and Minneapolis, the University of Minnesota and the public schools were regarded as major resources for clinical demonstrations, professional education, and research in connection with child psychiatry. The Monmouth County practice of separating child guidance from child welfare research proved impractical. The University of Minnesota demonstration by the National Committee for Mental Hygiene in child guidance came back to back with the Laura Spelman Memorial's funding for child development research.

The University of Minnesota demonstration began in November 1923. Lawson Lowrey, who had participated in the Dallas demonstration, directed the project. A central child guidance clinic and nursery school at the university was coordinated with traveling clinics that operated out of Duluth and the Teachers College at Mankato. The demonstration coordinated an inter-disciplinary team of researchers from the university. The team included members from the medical school and faculty from the departments of psychology, sociology, and education. This demonstration was the first sustained attempt to establish professional standards for child guidance staff and to provide professional training for psychiatrists, social workers, and teachers. Trainees were selected from the New York School of Social Work and Smith College. Three psychiatrists, two psychologists, and thirty-seven social workers were trained during the demonstration.[33]

Lowrey also pioneered a school child guidance clinic in conjunction with the Minneapolis Public Schools. The school program was made possible by the sympathetic attitude of Superintendent William Frank Webster, a vocal and supportive mental hygiene advocate. In 1924 an extensive school survey was conducted. The survey experimented with different ways to rate a child's personality in relationship to his/her behavior and performance. The survey also included systematic physical and mental testing by the clinic's staff.[34] The Minnesota legislature failed to support a permanent child guidance clinic at the university, but a permanent clinic was organized with the help of the school district at the end of the demonstration. The child guidance clinic established under the demonstration in St, Paul was continued with funds from the Community Chest and support from a local philanthropy, the Amherst H. Wilder Charities.[35]

The research oriented nursery school laboratory at the University of Minnesota was continued under the auspices of he Laura Spelman Rockefeller Memorial that granted $245,000 toward the maintenance of the Institute for Child Welfare from April 1925 to June 1930 under its own program for the promotion of parent education and child-study research. During the 1928 restructuring of the Rockefeller philanthropic boards, the General Education Board agreed to continue to support the Minneapolis Institute for a ten-year period. For this purpose, $665,000 was granted with the eventual objective of having the university find ways to "absorb the program."[36]

The research initiated in the Commonwealth demonstrations began to be used with some success during the period of Rockefeller support. The Institute for Child Welfare continued to work closely with public schools and clinics, using their facilities to research and to train students. As a training center and forum for disseminating research on the mental and physical dynamics of young life applied to school practices, parent training, clinical therapy, and professional training, the demonstration was a success. Smiley Blanton, the director of the Institute for Child Welfare, published on one of the first college-level textbooks on child guidance. It was based case studies conducted in the Institute's school child guidance clinic and nursery school. Thomas Salmon, the first medical director for the National Committee for Mental Hygiene, wrote the introduction. In it he recorded that Blanton emphasized "keeping well children well" rather than "curing behavior disorders."[37] The Institute staff was influential in the field of early childhood through its research and its contributions to the testing movement. Florence Goodenough created and evaluated intelligence scales to measure the ability of young children. She also researched and wrote on developmental psychology from a mental hygiene perspective. John E. Anderson wrote on parent education and early childhood, applying the principles of psychoanalysis and psychiatry.[38] The Institute also produced a monograph series to disseminate its research findings.[39] The Minneapolis demonstration and its subsequent continuation that was conducted in the context of public school and involved research and professional training in a university contributed to making the connection between normal and abnormal psychology.

PSYCHIATRIC SOCIAL WORKERS AND VISITING TEACHERS

The extensive use of auxiliary personnel other than psychiatrists in child guidance was not accidental. The Commonwealth Fund Program for the Prevention of Delinquency was intended to foster the training of social workers to supplement and extend the impact of psychiatry in everyday practices. To further this end, a Bureau of Child Guidance was created in connection with the New York School of Social Work as Division I of the Program for the Prevention of Delinquency. Directed by psychiatrist Bernard Glueck and later by Marion Kenworthy with the assistance of Porter R. Lee, the Bureau trained psychiatric social workers and operated a clinic and demonstration services in connection with research on school-age children.

The Bureau's investigations took on an increasingly psychoanalytic view of child life. Therapy was based on the case-study method. The Bureau also conducted twelve international conferences on applied psychiatry in social casework with children. At the close of the demonstration in 1927, the Bureau was renamed the Institute for Child Guidance. Commonwealth Fund support was discontinued in 1933. The Fund's Barry Smith believed that social work had been successfully established and that philanthropy could better serve mental hygiene research elsewhere.[40] In 1938, of the eight schools of social work in the United States, the New York School of Social Work had the most consistent emphasis on psychiatry in its training of social workers and visiting teachers. It included instruction by psychiatrists rather than psychologists or social workers.[41]

The National Coalition of Visiting Teachers was established in association with the Progressive Education Association (PEA) of New York and supported through Division II of the Commonwealth Fund Program for the Prevention of Delinquency. The Coalition also operated in close connection with Division I of the Commonwealth Fund and the New York School of Social Work. The Coalition was coordinated by Harold Nudd and directed by Jane Culbert. The visiting teacher program actively promoted a whole child approach to healthy development that was based on a psychiatric model. Visiting teachers were trained in psychiatric social work with a focus on public schools and child guidance clinics. Visiting teachers brought psychiatric concepts of child health, stress, and behavior directly into the classroom through demonstrations and workshops.[42] The intention was to disseminate mental hygiene concepts in instances where teachers might not otherwise come into contact with these new ideas. Visiting teachers, as social workers, also tried to forge stronger ties between home experiences and school experiences.[43] The visiting teacher movement strongly supported the Progressive Education Association's contention that "less formal educational opportunities ... assured [a] happy, wholesome child" and that it could be brought about if in school "attention was given to the growth and development of children rather than to the acquisition of subject matter."[44]

The Progressive Education Association's demonstrations were not limited to New York. However, the first demonstration was conducted at Public School 64 in New York City. While cities such as Philadelphia and Rochester had prior visiting teacher movements, the demonstrations by the Progressive Education Association were unique.[45] Thirty visiting teacher demonstrations were carried out nationwide between 1922 and 1927. Twenty-four of the programs were taken over by local school districts or clinics after the demonstration ended. In most cases, those trained by the Progressive Education Association remained in the community.[46] In addition to local demonstrations, regional conferences were held in Richmond, Virginia and Omaha, Nebraska. There were ninety-one visiting teachers in twenty-eight communities in fifteen states in 1921. By 1927, there were 205 teachers in seventy-eight communities in thirty-four states.[47] The Commonwealth Fund held that the success of the visiting teacher program was due to the coordination between the program and the child guidance demonstrations.[48]

The Commonwealth Fund appropriated $41,000 in 1922 for the demonstration program in delinquency. In 1927 when the program ended, the Fund had been granting an annual appropriation of $140,000.[49] At the close of the demonstrations the two departments of the Nation Committee for Mental Hygiene in Psychiatric Field Services and Experimentation and Demonstration were combined to form a new Division on Community Clinics directed by George Stevenson. The name change reflected a change in the conceptualization of child-oriented mental hygiene as it contributed to the legitimation of child psychiatry as a specialty concerned with disturbed rather than delinquent children. It also reflected the seemingly inevitable use of psychiatric social workers and psychologists rather than psychiatrists to carry out clinical work in spite of the preferred model in which a psychiatrist served as the director of research who had assistants trained in social work and in psychology.

By the end of the demonstrations 102 child guidance clinics had opened. With the popularization of child guidance, the number increased to 300 by 1930 and 617 by 1935.[50] The National Committee was not pleased with the increase of clinics, for many did not have active psychiatrists on staff. In 1940, the National Committee for Mental Hygiene created the American Association of Psychiatric Clinics for Children as part of the Division on Community Clinics as an attempt to regulate and standardize procedures. However, the Association's criteria were so rigid that only fifty-five clinics qualified for membership and only eighteen qualified as training centers in community psychiatry. The lack of trained psychiatrists to serve as director, researcher, and teacher was at the heart of the problem.[51]

CALIFORNIA CHILD GUIDANCE AND
THE MENTAL HYGIENE RESEARCH CENTER

California presented a diverse field for mental hygiene demonstrations and practices for both child guidance and child welfare. The early research conducted on school-age children and in schools increasingly found its way into popular forums directed at school practices in the 1930s. The California experience illustrates the degree to which the intentions of the medical men and the psychiatrists in the mental hygiene movement were not fulfilled. The ideal was to have a psychiatrist oversee the mental well being of children's health and education as advocated by the National Committee for Mental Hygiene, under the umbrella of social work, educational psychology, education counseling, and teaching.

The Los Angeles Child Guidance Clinic was one of the rare instances that retained the National Committee for Mental Hygiene's model of a psychiatrist director assisted by social workers and psychologists. The Los Angeles demonstration opened in January 1924 with three psychiatrists, two psychologists, and six social workers. However, a precedent had already been set. Since 1915, clinical studies in Los Angeles dealt with delinquents in the juvenile court with Miriam Van Waters.[52] However, the child guidance clinic received only 10.7 percent of its clients from the court. The majority of clients were parent referrals. Ralph Truitt, its director and his chief psychiatrist, Christine Leonard, hoped to integrate the clinic's services with social and community services. That was the model for child guidance preferred in the Cleveland and the Minneapolis demonstrations. To achieve the integration, the clinic did consulting work for the Los Angeles Public Schools. It also served as a training center in psychiatry under a National Committee for Mental Hygiene fellowship program.[53] The clinic survived after the close of the demonstration with support from private sources and the Commonwealth Fund and continued during the Great Depression by consolidating funds and services.

Publicly funded imitations of the National Committee for Mental Hygiene demonstrations in child guidance changed the professional staff model. The Los Angeles County Health Department organized a publicly supported mental hygiene clinic in the 1930s. However, psychologists and social workers staffed the clinic. The school boards of Los Angeles and Long Beach supported part-time clinics with psychiatrists employed as consultants. The psychiatric work conducted in these clinics mostly dealt with "behavior problems" and health related "athletic needs" of the school districts.

From 1929 to 1931 the California Bureau of Juvenile Research operated a traveling child guidance clinic that worked out of the Whittier State School for Boys. This project used the services of a psychiatrist, a psychologist, and social workers. The financial crisis brought about by the Great Depression curtailed the work at about the same time that it curtailed Miriam Van Water's program with the Los Angeles Juvenile Court. The psychiatrist and social worker were laid off, but Norman Fenton, the psychologist, was retained as the director of the Bureau of Juvenile Research. Fenton later joined the faculty of Claremont College where he established summer training programs in mental hygiene directed toward teachers, school psychologists, and social workers. Fenton worked to introduce mental hygiene into public schools at a minimum cost through the use of lay personnel and professionals—teachers and principals—already employed in the schools. Fenton was less concerned with introducing psychiatrists or preventive therapy supervised by medical professional into school practices than with using psychiatry as applied knowledge. His approach to mental hygiene in school practices emphasized psychiatric case study methods with extensive record keeping and standardized testing procedures not unlike current practices.[54] When cases indicated, teachers and principals conducted home visits and wrote reports on standardized forms.[55]

Fenton began publishing practical "how to" materials in mental hygiene in 1928, but his major book on the topic did not appear until 1943 after he joined the Stanford University faculty.[56] *Mental Hygiene in School Practice* offered explicit instructions for organizing a mental hygiene program. It provided lessons, exercises in counseling and testing, and detailed illustrations of case studies that described how to conduct them. His directions were detailed enough so that the forms in the appendix could be copied and used. In addition, there were catalogues of testing and guidance materials that could be ordered from the Stanford University Press.[57] Fenton's texts proved to be popular and were reprinted annually throughout the 1940s.

The period of Fenton's popular work in child guidance and his active promotion of mental hygiene in California schools through Stanford University coincided with a massive research project, housed at the University of California in the East San Francisco Bay Area, supported by state funds and Rockefeller philanthropy. In 1923, the California legislature passed a bill that approved the creation of an Institute of Child Welfare at the University of California, Berkeley. Rockefeller philanthropies then began negotiations over the nature of the work and the possibilities for support for research, clinics, and demonstrations.[58]

Herbert Stoltz, a Stanford trained physician actively involved in public school health reform and parent education through the California state government, was appointed director of the Institute. Harold Jones, a psychologist from Columbia University was Stoltz' assistant in charge of research. Jean Walker MacFarlane, also a psychologist, was appointed director of the child guidance program. The departments of education, household science, hygiene, psychology, and zoology as well as the medical school were to collaborate with the Institute. State agencies, local school districts, community organizations, businesses, voluntary associations, and hundreds of families were drawn into direct contact with the Institute.

From the beginning, the research program in Berkeley was complex and ambitious. It involved longitudinal and clinical data collection as well as therapeutic child guidance services. A survey of infants in Berkeley in the mid-1920s was used as a data set to follow children throughout their school careers. A component of the project to study adolescence was introduced in 1930 in Oakland, Berkeley's southern municipal neighbor. The studies on Berkeley infants and Oakland adolescents provided data on children from birth through young adulthood. The close connection with Oakland Public Schools was forged, in part, when Herbert Stoltz left the directorship of the Institute to become assistant superintendent for the Oakland school district. Stoltz also remained close to the legislature and government officials in Sacramento.

In Oakland, laboratory classrooms and meeting rooms for project staff were provided in portable buildings at school sites. A nursery school and a clinic were created at the university. Jean MacFarlane opened the child guidance clinic in May 1928. She became director of the Institute in 1938. The child guidance project provided community family services and conducted clinical studies in conjunction with other longitudinal research into child and family life. Data was collected from experimental studies and with every research tool then available, including medical investigations on physical health, and clinical studies on mental well being. Studies were conducted with psychological apparatus to test sense perception and motor functions. Measurements from biological testing and mental testing were systematically taken from thousands of children.[59] All sites served as laboratories for data collection. The material from this research produced book length monographs on subjects never intended by the original plan of study but made possible because an enormous amount of varied and detailed data had been collected over an extended period.[60]

The Berkeley researchers tried unsuccessfully to integrate psychoanalysis into the program. At the urging of Rockefeller officials, refugee psychoanalyst Erik Erikson joined the faculty of the Institute for Child Welfare in 1939. He worked with the Institute's staff for three years, but his work was not considered successfully integrated into the Berkeley data either by Erikson or Jean MacFarlane, the Institute's Director. MacFarlane wanted Erikson to use psychoanalytic theory to interpret their data and to produce case studies. However, Erikson used his time to observe children's play in the clinics and the nursery school. He conducted ethnographic studies and cultural studies of children with other Berkeley faculty in anthropology. Robert J. Havighurst, Alan Gregg, and Flora Rhind, officers of the Rockefeller philanthropies, were equally disappointed by Erikson's refusal to conform to their model for the uses of psychiatry in education related research on children.[61] Erikson was neither unproductive nor did he fail to influence his field. He produced a working paper for the Mid-Century White House Conference on Children that was subsequently published as the now well-known *Childhood and Society*.[62]

Rockefeller philanthropy supported the Berkeley Institute for Child Welfare through the 1940s and into the 1950s.[63] The General Education Board's appropriations in the 1950s were directed to the dissemination of research findings.[64] The Berkeley projects were slow to materialize. However, by 1938 the longitudinal data proved useful. With Rockefeller help, four theses, two monograph series that included six publications, eleven articles, and seven other abstracts or papers were then published.[65]

A major yearbook on adolescence, *Somatic Development in Adolescent Boys*, by Herbert Stoltz and his wife Lois Meek Stoltz was published in 1943 the same year that Fenton's book on mental hygiene practices in schools appeared.[66] These works appeared to be different from each other but they complemented each other. The yearbook's main contribution was that it coordinated detailed longitudinal data on biological development from birth through puberty and on to adulthood that was correlated with behavior and emotional states. The adolescent studies appeared to validate and synthesize the educational and child development research that differentiated children from preteens and adolescents that had been conducted since the beginning of the twentieth century. The thesis proved enticing and seemed above reproach as a model of the systematic scientific method. Direct implications were drawn for curriculum development and school organization to accommodate the validated uniqueness of children at various stages of mental and physical development.

PSYCHIATRY AS A HIDDEN AGENDA

Psychiatric perspectives were legitimated in the popular arena and in relation to auxiliary personnel more than in the medical arena. Hundreds of monographs and articles serve as witness to the explosion of literature on the school related mental hygiene area in the 1930s and 1940s. Much of this literature was an outgrowth of the child guidance demonstrations, bulletins, and reports disseminated by the National Committee for Mental Hygiene, the Commonwealth Fund, and the Rockefeller related philanthropies. The Commonwealth Fund publications program, an early offshoot of the Program for the Prevention of Juvenile Delinquency, greatly contributed to the dissemination of mental hygiene literature. One early report cited 94,949 copies of mental hygiene reports and bulletins distributed from the child guidance demonstrations by May 1, 1928. The publication of texts, monographs, and compilations of studies increased in the years after the demonstrations.[67] The United States Office of Education, the National Education Association, the Children's Bureau, the American Council on Education, the Child Study Association of America, and the Progressive Education Association also contributed to the dissemination of mental hygiene material and research deemed appropriate for school use.[68] The National Committee for Mental Hygiene or one of its patrons supported many of the seventeen periodicals Fenton recommended to parents and teachers. Fenton's recommendations included: *Mental Hygiene, Parent's Magazine, Understanding the Child, American Journal of Orthopsychiatry, American Journal of Psychiatry, Child Development, Educational and Psychological Measurement, Journal of Consulting Psychology, Journal of Genetic Psychology* (formerly G. Stanley Hall's *Pedagogical Seminary*), *Journal of Social and Abnormal Psychology, Occupations, Psychological Abstracts, Smith College Studies on Social Work, Vocational Guidance Digest, Hygeia: The Health Magazine,* and the *National Parent-Teachers Association Magazine.*

The out-of-context popularization of mental hygiene research through clinics and demonstrations was seen as problematic by the Rockefeller Foundation as early as 1937. Edumd E. Day, director of its Division of Social Sciences, commented that "fact-finding" and "fact-using" were not well coordinated.[69] A participant in a Laura Spelman Rockefeller Memorial conference on mental hygiene research and its implications for practice wrote Beardsley Ruml that the application of psychiatry to school practices, in a specific reference to its "child oriented" focus amounted to "silly twaddle," and that there seemed to be a tendency to "get the cart before horse" where research and practice were concerned.[70]

The strategy for dealing with the problem was to monitor the quality of research, the dissemination of results, and to encourage professional organizations of publicly funded bodies to monitor information provided to the public. The establishment of the National Research Council Committee on Child Development and the monograph series on child development, *Child Development Abstracts*, represent the efforts that were undertaken. The creation of the University of Chicago's Center for Collaboration and Documentation in 1930 was a similar attempt to monitor the quality of research on child welfare before it was promoted and interpreted in public policies and institutions.

The General Education Board supported a series of mental hygiene related educational studies in the 1930s. The research and the dissemination of the findings were coordinated. The Commission on the Secondary School Curriculum, a subcommittee of the Progressive Education Association, began a study in 1932 that used a mental hygiene approach to solving the problems of youth exacerbated by the Great Depression. Findings and reports associated with the Eight-Year study promoted progressive mental hygiene approaches to the organization and expansion of secondary education.[71] In 1938, a Commission on Teacher Education was established under the American Council of Education with an appropriation of

$250,00 from the General Education Board.[72] Fifteen collaborators representing the major research centers supported by the Laura Spelman Rockefeller Memorial were called together to identify "scientifically validated generalizations or principles" from the "research findings in the biological, psychological, sociological, and medical sciences," including psychiatry. Robert J. Havighurst, who helped to oversee the Berkeley and Oakland research in the 1930s took a position at the University of Chicago as Secretary of the Committee on Human Development. A newly formed subcommittee on the standards of the American Association of Teachers Colleges was formed to cooperate with the collaborators by relaying their conclusions to the 175-member institutions directly concerned with the professional education of teachers. Information was also distributed to college administrators, curriculum committees, and professors in relevant disciplines such as psychology and child study.[73]

In 1938 the Commission on Human Relations produced a series of publications and later produced motion pictures to introduce adolescents and secondary school teachers to the current state of scientific research on emotional problems.[74] Other works in this series by Lois Hayden Meek emphasized that schools had a responsibility to reduce emotional tensions in children that are "expressed in fears, hatred, and compulsive behavior toward society."[75] A 1938 report by Daniel A. Prescott submitted to the American Council on Education dealt with the "relation of emotion to the educative process." Prescott suggested that teachers be called "personnel workers" and that they be selected "for their sympathetic insight into children's needs and behavior, and for their skill in getting along with children" rather than their academic qualifications.[76]

The difficulties that the National Committee for Mental Hygiene and their patrons faced in promoting sound research in psychiatry paralleled the difficulties experienced in keeping unscientific speculations based on unsound research from being popularized. From the time of the first International Congress on Mental Hygiene held in Washington, D. C. in 1930, psychiatric theory spread widely. However, the research consistently failed to produce results that led to remediation of mental illness or preventing its occurrence through intervention in childhood. The National Committee for Mental Hygiene created a Division on Psychiatric Education in 1930 to promote research and the training of psychiatrists in medical schools. The American Board of Psychiatry and Neurology was not formed until 1934.[77] The Rockefeller Foundation supported psychiatric research in the United States and even supported it in other countries. Yet, in the early 1940s the psychiatric profession had not provided everything others believed it should provide. It appeared to be in a formative or transformative stage.[78] The state of psychiatry provoked a considerable amount of painstaking self-reflection and frustration among the Rockefeller Foundation officers. In 1948, the Foundation's President Chester I. Barnard expressed the difficulties encountered in sorting through the research and its possible applications to psychiatry. He asked Alan Gregg director of the Rockefeller Foundation Medical Division: "Isn't there any way to blast this situation?"[79]

The National Committee for Mental Hygiene, the Rockefeller Foundation, and he Commonwealth Fund took advantage of the promotion of psychiatry in the United States Army during World War II. As the war drew to a close, they looked to post-war needs and established a new organization The Group for the Advancement of Psychiatry. It was supposed to "act as a mobile striking [force] for American psychiatry."[80] The Group was successful in that it proved to be influential in the American Psychiatric Association. Robert Felix, head of the federal Division of Mental Hygiene and an active member in the Group for the Advancement of Psychiatry, was appointed Director of the National Institute of Mental Health when it was created in 1949. However, Felix's major work on mental illness was not published until 1967.[81] A year before the formation of the National Institute of Mental Health, the Third International Congress was convened. A World Federation for Mental Health was established under the auspices of the United Nations' World Health Organization. English psychiatrist, John Bowlby became a consultant in 1950. His *Mental Health and Maternal Love* focused worldwide attention on the application of psychiatry to children in relation to parenting and the role of mothers in a psychoanalytic interpretation of normal and abnormal development.[82]

The Group for the Advancement of Psychiatry began an internal review of child psychiatry in 1951. In a major report published in 1957, *Diagnostic Processes in Child Psychiatry,* noted the backwardness of the field and the lack of standard classifications for children's mental disorders. The Group addressed the need for standard classifications in 1965 when in produced *Psychopathological Disorders in Children: Theoretical Considerations and a Proposed Classification.* The World Health Organization's third international seminar on the classification of mental disorders was held in Paris in 1967. The seminar's theme was "Psychiatric Disorders of Childhood."

Classifications of childhood disorders in the United States as well as internationally were only belatedly listed. After 1970, the manuals of the World Health Organization and the American Psychiatric Association devoted space to disorders experienced by children. By the late 1970s and early 1980s approximately one-third of the categories listed related to children. The World Health Organization currently distributes a free booklet, *Caring for Children and Adolescents with Mental Disorders,* to a worldwide audience. The current *Diagnostic and Statistical Manual of Mental Disorders (DSM-IV TR),* devotes ninety-six pages to childhood and youth disorders.[83] The elaboration of categories of differences since World War II contributed to the expansion of psychological testing and classification of students in schools in the 1970s. These practices continue to increase, and there is now no reason to believe they will abate. Special education classrooms now focus on treating and educating students identified with various disorders, abilities, and disabilities. Regular classroom teachers are required to work with "mainstreamed" special education students, fulfilling Fenton's ideal of the teacher serving as a mental hygienist. Specialized and differentiated curriculums proliferate as do the training programs and research in teacher training institutions.[84]

After World War II studies of soldiers with brain injuries received in combat created an interest in children who were hyperactive or behaved oddly due to the effects of a trauma or birth defects. World War II and subsequent international engagements have also drawn attention to the application of adult disorders to children based on an underlying medical-psychiatric model. These theories and classifications based on theories developed in the 1970s continue to be employed in research and practice. They are seen as useful in understanding the learning process in early life even though actual abnormality in the body or brain is not present and even though testing may prove inconclusive.[85] The therapeutic approach toward children and the search for cures for mental and emotional disorders, learning problems, and disruptive behaviors continue to use a medical model. Therapies of the past have followed the trends in medicine and psychiatry toward experimentation with pharmacology including psychotropic drugs.[86]

Research produced the first psychotropic drugs in the mid-1950s. Drug therapies were applied to institutionalized adult populations almost immediately, but such drugs did not become widespread or controversial with children until commercial products such as Ritalin were used increasingly with disruptive school-age children in the 1970s.[87]

Sociological and demographic research has questioned the medical orientation in education and has also questioned the expansion of special classes for children classified and labeled as mildly retarded.[88] The overrepresentation of minorities in special education classes occasioned revisions of the definitions and labels as well as the criteria for admission to special education classes. The fastest growing labels were associated with learning disabilities and conduct disorders. At the same time, there was a growing interest in services for children labeled as gifted and in multicultural education. These trends and developments culminated in and were elaborated by one of the most significant pieces of educational legislation in the twentieth century, the 1975 federal legislation that specified that all children had a legal right to a public school education regardless of any handicapping condition.[89] Affirming a therapeutic medical model in education, this legislation placed mental health and necessary support services and accommodation for individual differences into the mainstream of public education.

THE MORAL ORDER AND
MEDICAL PROGRESS IN EDUCATIONAL RESEARCH

Psychiatry and educational research have run on parallel tracks. While mental hygiene is not formally recognized as a foundation for systematically acquired educational knowledge, medical perspectives supported educational practices through mental hygiene research. Research transformed traditional beliefs and in turn became common sense. In some cases, it became law. Child guidance research and demonstrations as well as child welfare research institutes not only dealt peripherally with education in their use of schools as laboratories and children as subjects but also established paradigms for normality and abnormality as central for decisions about what was taught and to whom it was taught. The reach of mental hygiene research influenced how subjects should be taught to particular populations and how and what should be evaluated as the ultimate purpose of public education.

Mental hygiene research contributed to the institutionalization of systematic studies in education that used medical models of individual differences to define research questions. The premises of mental hygiene can be seen in current rationales for educational policy. The current emphasis on fitness and alarm over obesity demonstrate beliefs about the relationship between mental and physical abilities. Educators are generally concerned with the effects of emotional trauma and self-image on achievement for both teachers and students. Learning or behavioral problems continue to be likened to illnesses that need to be cured. In a skeptical post-modern world it still seems obvious that problems can be prevented and cured through early interventions and that school-based testing is central to identifying and diagnosing problems. The emphasis on the standardization of assessment and continual accountability requires continual collection of measurements. It also places pressures on students, educational researchers, school administrators, teachers, and schools to meet and to conform to prescribed achievement levels. Professional educators have suffered undue criticism because the common belief that the health and happiness of students are legitimate objectives of public education has been widely accepted by the public. That has been unfair to the public as well as to the professional educators.

World War II represented a significant break in the evolution of child directed mental hygiene. Research funds for the prevention and remediation of mental illness were then to be secured from government agencies and programs such as the National Institute of Mental Health. With the availability of federal funds for research and the withdrawal of philanthropic support, the National Committee for Mental Hygiene and the movement it spearheaded was significantly transformed. It became the National Association for Mental Health, a voluntary advocacy organization. It was no longer a partner of philanthropy in advocating innovation in social policy and supporting research. Psychiatric research became even more detached from educational research, but focused more directly on the disorders of childhood. However, psychiatric perspectives are still found in education, for mental hygiene perspectives continue to influence school practices.

The next chapter examines one of the major issues in educational research that was a product of a mental hygiene orientation toward the studying and the perfecting of humankind: the continuing nature-nurture debates as they relate to the development of children and their progress in school.

NOTES

1. Guy M. Whipple (ed.). *The Thirty-Seventh Yearbook of the National Society for the Study of Education: Part II, The Scientific Movement in Education* (Bloomington, Illinois: The Public School Publishing Co, 1938); Donald Ary, Lucy Cheser Jacobs, and Asghar Razavieh. *Introduction to Research in Education* (New York: Holt, Rinehart and Winston, 1979, 1966), pp. 30-35.

2. Joseph Mayer Rice, "The Futility of the Spelling Grind," *The Forum*, Vol. 23 (April 1897), pp. 167-172 and (June 1897), pp. 409-419; Leonard P. Ayres. *Laggards in Our Schools: A Study of Retardation and Elimination in City School Systems* (New York: Charities Publications Committees, Russell Sage Foundation, 1909); Edward L. Thorndike, *Notes on Child Study* (New York: Macmillan, 1901); Edward L. Thorndike, *Introduction to the Theory of Mental and Social Measurements* (New York: Science Press, 1904); and Charles H. Judd. "Contributions of School Surveys" in Whipple (ed.) *The Thirty-Seventh Yearbook of the National Education Society.*

3. John C. Burnham. *Paths to American Culture: Psychology, Medicine and Morals* (Philadelphia: Temple University Press, 1988; Charles E. Rosenberg. *No Other Gods: Science and American Thought* (Baltimore: Johns Hopkins University Press, 1988); James Leiby. *A History of Social Welfare and Social Work in the United States* (New York: Columbia University Press, 1978).

4. See: Theresa R. Richardson. *The Century of the Child: The Mental Hygiene Movement and Social Policy in the United States and Canada* (Albany, New York: State University of New York Press, 1989).

5. Simon Flexner and James Thomas Flexner, *William Henry Welch and the Heroic Age of American Medicine* (New York: Viking Press, 1941); Lloyd C. Taylor. *The Medical Profession and Social Reform, 1885-1945* (New York: St.

Martin's Press, 1974); and George Rosen. *Preventive Medicine in the United States, 1900-1975* (New York: Science History Publications, 1975).

6. Mandel Sherman. "Contributions to Education of Scientific Knowledge in Mental Hygiene," in Whipple (ed.). *Thirty-Seventh Yearbook of the National Society for the Study of Education*, pp. 435-443; Sol Cohen. "The Mental Hygiene Movement, the Development of Personality, and the School," *History of Education Quarterly*, Vol. 23, No. 2 (summer 1983), pp. 123-150; Sol Cohen, "The Mental Hygiene Movement: The Medicalization of American Education" in Gerald Benjamin (ed.). *Private Philanthropy and Public Elementary and Secondary Education: Proceedings of the Rockefeller Archive Center Conference Held on June 8, 1979* (Tarrytown, New York: Rockefeller Archive Center Publication, 1979), pp. 33-46; and Sol Cohen. "The School and Personality Development: Intellectual History" in John Best (ed.). *Historical Inquiry in Education: A Research Agenda* (Washington, D. C.: American Educational Research Association, 1983), pp. 109-137.

7. Robert Caste, Francoise Castel, Anne Lovell. *The Psychiatric Society* tr. Arthur Goldhammer (New York: Columbia University Press, (1982), pp. 33-42 and Jacques Donzelot. *The Policing of Families tr. Robert Hurley* (New York: Pantheon, 1979), pp. 188-212,

8. John Dewey. "The Body and Mind," *Mental Hygiene*, Vol. XII, No. 1 (1928), pp. 3-17; Lawrence A. Cremin. *The Transformation of the School: Progressivism in American Education, 1876-1957* (New York: Alfred A. Knopf, 1961), p. 273 and chapter 8.

9. Clifford Beers. *A Mind that Found Itself,* preface by Robert Coles (New York: Longmans Green, (1907); Pittsburg: University of Pittsburg Press, 1981) and Norman Dain, *Clifford Beers: Advocate for the Insane* (Pittsburg: University of Pittsburg Press, 1980).

10. W. B. Drummond. *An Introduction to Child Study* (London: Edward Arnold, 1908); Irving King. *Education for Social Efficiency: A Study in the Social Relations of Education* (New York: D. Appleton, 1913); William A. White. *The Mental Hygiene of Childhood* (Boston: Little, Brown and Co., 1919); S. Josephine Baker. *Child Hygiene* (New York: Harper and Bros., 1925); and C. W. Kimmins. *The Mental and Physical Welfare of the Child* (London: Partridge, 1927).

11. White. *The Mental Hygiene of Childhood.*

12. Barry C. Smith. "Report of the General Director, November 1921, Child Welfare Program for the Prevention of Delinquency," p. 35, Laura Spelman Rockefeller Memorial (LSRM), 3, 111, 1113, Rockefeller Archive Center (RAC), Sleepy Hollow, New York. Also see: V. V. Anderson. *Psychiatry in Education* (New York: Harper and Bros., 1932) and Lester D. Crow and Alice Crow. *Mental Hygiene in School and Home Life* (New York: McGraw-Hill, 1942).

13. Leo Kanner. *Child Psychiatry* (Springfield, Illinois: Charles C. Thomas, 1935, 1957).

14. Sander L. Gilman. "The Struggle of Psychiatry with Psychoanalysis. Who Won?" *Critical Inquiry*, Vol. 13, No. 2 (Winter 1987, pp. 293-313 and Castel *et al. The Psychiatric Society*, chapters 2 and 3.

15. Cohen. "The School and Personality," p. 109. Also see: Robert Wutnow. *Meaning and Moral Order: Explorations in Cultural Analysis* (Berkeley: University of California Press, 1987), p. 265.

16. National Committee for Mental Hygiene. "How and By Whom the Work of the National Committee for Mental Hygiene Had Been Financed, Covering the Organizing Period, 1907-1911 and the Period of Work to Date, 1918" January 29, 1918, pp. 1-6. Rockefeller Foundation Archives, RG, 1.1, 200, 33, 275. Rockefeller Archive Center, RF.

17. Rockefeller Foundation. *Annual Report, 1913-1914* (New York: Rockefeller Foundation, 1914), p. 1.

18. Rockefeller Foundation. *Annual Report, 1921* (New York: Rockefeller Foundation, 1922), p. 21; George Vincent. *President's Annual Review* (New York: Rockefeller Foundation, 1922), p. 8.

19. Raymond D. Fosdick. *The Story of the Rockefeller Foundation* (New York: Harper and Bros., 1952); E. Richard Brown. *Rockefeller Medicine Men* (Berkeley: University of California Press, 1960).

20. Thomas W. Salmon to Walter B. James, April 9, 1919; Thomas W. Salmon to George E. Vincent, April 9, 1919, Rockefeller Foundation, 1.1, 200, National Committee for Mental Health 1919; Rockefeller History 900-1, 6 pp. 1424-1426, Rockefeller Archive Center.

21. "Application to the LSRM for an Appropriation of $12,000 a year for a mobile mental hygiene clinic in Monmouth County, New Jersey," July 12, LSRM 3, 34, 558, Rockefeller Archive Center.

22. Katherine B. Davis. "Monmouth County Organization for Social Service, Inc., Application for Mrs. Lewis S. Thompson, "typed report, August 1, 1921; "A Supplemental Report on the Request of Mrs. Lewis S. Thompson," September 14, 1921, LSRM 3, 34, 358, Rockefeller Archive Center.

23. National Committee for Mental Hygiene and the Committee on Mental Hygiene of New York State Charities Aid Association, "Mental Hygiene Conference and Exhibit, College of the City of New York" November 8-15, 1912;" J. D. Greene. "Memo," November 15, 1912, RF 1.1 200, 32, 363 Rockefeller Archive Center; Paul H. Landis. *Rural Life in Process* (New York: McGraw-Hill, 1940.

24. "Entire Families May Enter Lists for Blue Ribbons," undated news clipping on Mary T. Watts of Audubon, Iowa and the "better babies" and "fitter families" movement a state fairs. LSRM 3, 43, 450, Rockefeller Archive Center. This movement contributed to the founding of the Iowa Child Welfare Research Station in 1917 that received Rockefeller support; Dorothy E. Bradbury. *Pioneering in Child Welfare Research Station, 1917-1933* (Iowa City: University of Iowa Press, 1933).

25. V. V. Anderson. "Clinic Conducted by the Division on the Prevention of Delinquency by the National committee for Mental Hygiene," pp. 9-10, 13, LSRM 3, 34, 364 Rockefeller Archive Center.

26. Geraldine Thompson to Lawrence K. Frank. February 25, 1924, LSRM 3, 34, 359, Rockefeller Archive Center.

27. Lawrence K. Frank. "Monmouth County Organization for Social Service, Memorandum. January 12, 1924; Lawrence K. Frank. "Memorandum: Monmouth County Organization Clinic," January 22 1924; John L. Montgomery to Barry Smith,. January 7, 1924 and January 16, 1924; Lawrence K. Frank to Kenneth Chorley. "Memorandum." April 7, 1925. LSRM 3,34, 359. Rockefeller Archive Center.

28. "Annual Report to the Commonwealth Fund on the Operation of the Bureau of Child Guidance by the New York School of Social Work as Section I of the Program for the Prevention of Delinquency Covering the Year 1924-1925." Commonwealth Fund Archives (CF) 65. Rockefelller Archive Center.

29. For an overview see: George S. Stevenson and Geddes Smith. *Child Guidance Clinics: A Quarter Century of Development* (New York: Commonwealth Fund, 1934); George S. Stevenson. "Child Guidance and the National Committee" in Lawson Lowrey and Victoria Sloan (eds). *Orthopsychiatry, 1923-1948: Retrospect and Prospect* (Menasha, Wisconsin: George Banta Publishing for American Ortthopsychiatric Association, 1948), p. 67.

30. Commonwealth Fund. *Annual Report* (New York: Commonwealth Fund, 1924, p. 27.

31. Margo Horne, "The Moral Message of Child Guidance, 1925-1945," *Journal of Social History* (September 1984). Pp. 23-36; Margo Horne. *Before It's Too Late: The Child Guidance Movement* (Philadelphia, Temple University Press, 1989).

32. V. V. Anderson and Thomas Salmon. "Address on the Work of the St. Louis Clinic" presented to the American Association for the Study of Feeble-mindedness, St. Louis; Commonwealth Fund. "Minutes," May 24, 1922, p. 27. Commonwealth Fund Archives 376, Rockefeller Archive Center.

33. Stevenson and Smith. *Child Guidance*, pp. 36-37.

34. "Case Reports, Longfellow School Survey, Minneapolis, Minnesota, 1924" and "Instructions for Using the Rating Scale." Commonwealth Fund Archives 66, Rockefeller Archive Center.

35. "Memorandum, Re: The Laura Spelman Rockefeller Memorial's Grant to Some of the Larger Child Welfare Centers in the United States." General Education Board (GEB) 930 1, 3, 372, 3887, Rockefeller Archive Center.

36. *Ibid.*

37. Smiley D. Blanton and M. G. Blanton. *Child Guidance* (New York: Century, 1927).

38. Florence Goodenough. *The Kuhlman-Binet Tests for Children of Preschool Age: A Critical Study and Evaluation* (Westport, Connecticut: Greewood, 1928, 1973); Florence Goodenough. *Developmental Psychology* (New York: D. Appleton, 1934); John E. Anderson. "The Clientele of a Parental Education Program," *School and Society*, Vol. 26 (August 26, 1927), p. 179; *and* John E. Anderson. "The Genesis of Social Relations in the Young Child" in *The Unconscious: A Symposium* (New York: Knopf, 1927).

39. For example, see: J.C. Foster and J. E. Anderson. *The Young Child and His Parents: A Study of One Hundred Cases* (Minneapolis: University of Minnesota Press, 1927).

40. "Preliminary Report to the Commonwealth Fund from the New York School of Social Work, December 1, 1921 to June 30, 1927." Commonwealth Fund 65. Rockefeller Archive Center; Louise C. Odencrantz. *The Social Worker: In Family, Medical and Psychiatric Social Work* (New York: Harper and Row, 1929); Roy Lubove. *The Professional Altruist: The Emergence of Social Work as a Career, 1880-1930* (Cambridge, Massachusetts: Harvard University Press, 1965), pp. 98-99.

41. Lois Meredith French. *Psychiatric Social Work* (New York: Commonwealth Fund, 1940), p. 262. In Table 16, New York is compared to Chicago, National Catholic, Simmons, Smith, Pennsylvania, Tulane, and Western Reserve.

42. Odencrantz. *The Social Worker,* pp. 326-333.

43. Progressive Education Association of the City of New York. *The Visiting Teacher in the United States.* 2nd. ed. (New York: Progressive Education Association, 1923); W. I. Thomas. *The Child in America: Behavior Problems and Programs* (New York: Alfred A. Knopf, 1926, Johnson Reprint Corporation, 1970), p. 229.

44. W. Carson Ryan. "History of Mental Hygiene in Schools," *American Journal of Insanity, Centenary Edition* (New York: American Psychiatric Association, 1944), pp. 144-145.

45. Thomas and Thomas. *The Child,* pp. 249, 253.

46. *Ibid.,* pp. 250-251; Commonwealth Fund. *Annual Report for 1923* (New York: Commonwealth Fund, 1923), pp. 44-46; J. J. Openheimer. *Teacher Movement* (New York: Progressive Education Association, 1924), p. 20; Sophia C. Gleim. "The Visiting Teacher," *United States Bureau of Education,* Bulletin No. 10 (1921), p. 8.

47. Reported by Ethel B. Allen, National Committee on Visiting Teachers of the Progressive Education Association in Thomas and Thomas. *The Child,* pp. 256-257; *The Visiting Teacher,* p. 23; Commonwealth Fund. *Annual Report for 1923* (New York: Commonwealth Fund, 1923, pp. 44-46.

48. Commonwealth Fund. *Annual Report for 1926* (New York: Commonwealth Fund, 1926).

49. Arthur H. Ruggles to Edward S. Harkness, June 7, 1924, Thomas W. Salmon Papers, 4, American Foundation for Mental Health (AFMH), Columbia Medical Center Archives, New York City.

50. Lawson Lowrey. "Psychiatry for Children," *American Journal of Psychiatry,* Vol. 101 (November 1044), pp. 375-388.

51. Jules V. Coleman to Mildred C. Scovillle, November 29, 1949; George S. Stevenson to Mildred C. Scoville, June 9, 1947. Commonwealth Fund Archive 67, Rockefeller Archive Center.

52. Miriam Van Waters. "The Socialization of Juvenile Court Procedures in Ernest B. Hoag and Edward H. Williams (ed.). *Crime, Abnormal Minds and the Law* (Indianapolis: Bobbs-Merrill Co., 1923); Katharine F. Lenroot and Emma O. Lundberg. *Juvenile Courts at Work: A Study of the Organization and Methods of Ten Courts.* U. S. Department of Labor, Children's Bureau Publication No. 141 (Washington, D. C.: U. S. Government Printing Office, 1925), pp. 12-13, 32, 97-99, 129.

53. Barry S. Smith to Mildred Scovillle. "Memorandun," February 12, 1929. Commonwealth Fund Archive 67. Rockefeller Archive Center.

54. Norman Fenton. "A Survey of Clinical and Descriptive Instructions in Child Guidance in Superior Medical Schools," *Journal of Juvenile Research,* Vol. 13 (1929), pp. 141-145.

55. Norman Fenton. *Organizing a Mental Hygiene Program Through the Child Guidance Conference.* Bulletin no. 9, New Series (Sacramento, California: State Printing Office, 1933); Norman Fenton. "Mental Hygiene and Its

Administration in High School," *Junior-Senior School Clearing House*, Vol. 6 (1932), pp. 63-68.

56.   Norman Fenton. *Mental Hygiene in School Practice* (Stanford: Stanford University Press, 1943, 1949); Norman Fenton. "Personality Guidance for Teachers," *Educational Review*, Vol. 75 (1928).

57.   Norman Fenton. *The Counselor's Interview with the Student, School Case Work Manuals* (Stanford: Stanford University Press, 1943, 1949); Norman Fenton. *The Counselor's Approach to the Home, School Case Work Manuals* (Stanford: Stanford University Press, 1943, 1949).

58.   Lawrence K. Frank to Faculty and Officers, University of California, Berkeley, March 6-12, 1925; Lawrence K. Frank to Ethel Richardson, April 15, 1927. Laura Spelman Rockefeller Memorial 3, 43, 452. Rockefeller Archive Center.

59.   "First Annual Report of the Institute of Child Welfare for the Year 1927-28: To the President of the University," October 15, 1928; "Progress Report, University of California," October 15, 1928;" "Progress Report, University of California," November 15, 1929;" "Progress Report, University of California," October 29, 1930." Laura Spelman Rockefeller Memorial 3, 43, Rockefeller Archive Center; Robert J. Havighurst to Prof. Edward Tolman, September 9, 1940. General Education Board 930, 1, 3, 374. 3912. Rockefeller Archive Center.

60.   Glen Eldler. *Children of the Great Depression* (Chicago: University of Chicago Press, 1974). Elder's book was based on data collected in Oakland in the 1930s.

61.   Robert J. Havighurst. "Interview with Erik Homburger Erikson, Guidance Study, University of California," December 20, 1940. General Education Board 930, 1, 3, 375, 3912. Rockefeller Archive Center; Jean MacFarlane to Alan Gregg, November 18, 1941; Alan Gregg to Jean MacFarlane, November 21, 1941; Flora Rhind, "interview with Erik Erikson," September 17, 1947. General Education Board 930, 1, 3, 374, 3914. Rockefeller Archive Center.

62.   Erik H. Erikson. *Childhood and Society* (New York: W. W. Norton, 1950, 1963, 1985).

63.   Robert J. Havighurst. "Memo Concerning the Guidance Study at the University of California," January 19, 1938; W. W. Brierly to Robert Sproul, December 16, 1938. General Education Board 930, 1, 3, 375, 3912. Rockefeller Archive Center.

64.   Robert J. Havighurst. "Publication Results of Research at the California Institute of Child Welfare," December 22, 1938. General Education Board 930, 1, 3, 374, 3911. Rockefeller Archive Center.

65.   Jean W. MacFarlane. "Statement of Objectives and Points of View," October 26, 1938. General Education Board 930 1, 3, 374, 3911. Rockefeller Archive Center.

66.   Grants in Aid to I 48049; Flora Rhind. "Interview with Harold Jones, Re: Publication *Yearbook*," May 4, 1943; "Outline of the Yearbook on Adolescence." General Education Board 930 1, 3, 374, 3911. Rockefeller Archive Center.

67.   "List of Publications Published by the National Committee for Mental Hygiene," November 1927. Laura Spelman Rockefeller Memorial 3, 35,

368 Rockefeller Archive Center; "The Mental Hygiene Program of the Commonwealth Fund and Some Evidence of its Value," undated, pp. 13-14. Commonwealth Fund Archive 66. Rockefeller Archive Center.

68. Fenton. *Mental Hygiene in School Practice*, p. 400.

69. Edmund E. Day to Beardsley Ruml. "Child Study and Parent Education," March 17, 1927. Laura Spelman Rockefeller Memorial 3, 31, 329. Rockefeller Archive Center.

70. L. B. D. to Beardslley Ruml." Your Memorandum of March 11 to the Memorial's Trustee Committee of Review of Child Study and Parent Education," March 15, 1927. Laura Spelman Rockefelller Memorial 3, 31, 329. Rockefeller Archive Center.

71. Caroline Zachry. "Emotion and Conduct in Adolescence;" Peter Blos. "The Adolescent Personality" in V. T. Thayer et al. (eds.). *Reorganizing the Secondary School Curriculum* (New York: Appleton-Century, 1940).

72. "Inter-University Collaboration to Further Research in Human Development and Behavior and to Extend the Use of Research Findings in the Education of Professional Persons," March 15, 1944. General Education Board 930 1, 3, 375, 3920. Rockefeller Archive Center.

73. "The University of Chicago Announcement of the Continuation of the Collaboration Center on Human Development and Education," October 6, 1943, p. 2. General Education Board 930 1, 3, 375, 3920. Rockefeller Archive Center.

74. Alice V. Keliher. *Life and Growth* (New York: Appleton-Century, 1938).

75. Lois Hayden Meek, *et al. The Personal Development of Boys and Girls* (New York: Progressive Education Association, 1940).

76. Daniel A. Prescott. *Emotion and the Educative Process* (Washington, D.C.: American Council on Education, 1938).

77. Note that the Association of Medical Superintendents of American Institutions for Insane had a much longer history, having been formed in 1844. Its name was changed to the American Psychiatric Association in 1921.

78. Fosdick. *The Story of the Rockefeller Foundation*, pp. 130-131.

79. Chester I. Barnard to Alan Gregg, August 5, 1948, RFA, RG 3, 906 18. Rockefeller Archive Center.

80. William C. Menninger to Mildred C. Scoville, April 20, 1948; "Conference on Psychiatric Needs in Post-War Situation and Plans to Meet Them," November 22, 1944 (typescript); "Appendix I Skeleton Report of the Hersey Conference, Presented to the Director at the Meeting of June 14, 1945." Commonwealth Fund Archives 64. Rockefeller Archive Center.

81. Robert Felix. *Mental Illness, Progress and Prospects* (New York: Columbia University Press, 1967).

82. John Bowlby. *Mental Health and Maternal Love* (New York: Columbia University Press, 1951); and the abridged summary: *Child Care and the Growth of Love* (ed.). Margery Fry (New York: Penguin, 1953).

83. World Health Organization. *Manual of the International Classification of Disease, Injuries, and Causes of Death*, 9th ed., 2 volumes (Geneva, Switzerland: World Health Organization, 1977); World Health Organization. *Caring for Children and Adolescents with Mental Disorders* (Geneva, Switzerland: Department of Mental Health and Substance Abuse, 2003); American Psychiatric

Association. *Diagnostic and Statistical Manual of Mental Disorders*, 4th ed. DSM-IV Text Revision (Washington, D. C.: American Psychiatric Association, 1994, 2000).

84. See: Nicholas Hobbes (ed.). *Issues in the Classification of Children*, 2 volumes (San Francisco: Jossey-Bass, 1975).

85. Paul H. Winder. *Minimal Brain Dysfunction in Children* (New York: John Wiley, 1971); Castel, Castel and Lovell. The Psychiatric Society, pp. 208-209.

86. "The Introduction of Chlorpromazine." *Hospital and Community Psychiatry* (July 1976); Castel, Castel andLovell. The Psychiatric Society.

87. *Ibid.*

88. Jane R. Mercer. *Labeling the Mentally Retarded* (Berkeley: The University of California Press, 1977); James Carrier, *Learning Disabilities, Social Class, and the Construction of Inequality in American Education* (Westport, Connecticut: Greenwood Press, 1986).

89. "The Education for All handicapped Children Act," Public Law 94-142, 20 U. S. C. Sec. 1401 et seq. (1975); Judith D. Singer and John A. Butler. "The Education for All Handicapped Children Act: Schools as Agents of Social Reform," *Harvard Educational Review*, Vol. 57, No. 2 (May 1987), pp. 125-152. In 1990, the U. S. Congress changed the name of the law to "Individuals with Disabilities Education Act," Public Law 101-476. This law retained all the provisions of Public Law 94-142 and added "autism" and "traumatic brain injury" to the list of disabilities and also provided for the adjustment of secondary education students to adult life.

CHAPTER 11

NATURE-NURTURE CONTROVERSIES

Institutionalizing Intelligence as a Variable in Educational Research

The mental hygienists' concern with the identification and prevention of mental illness fostered two tendencies in educational research. Child development advocates researched normality and how to identify ways to prevent a child from veering off the path of healthy development. Their focus on children and youth implied that the young could be molded, educated, and changed by their environment. Hence, this approach to educational research stressed nurture as the primary influence on the capacity of parents and teachers to make a difference in a child's life. On the other hand, child guidance fostered research on how to identify and reform children who were seen as veering from the path of normal development. The research conducted under the influence of mental hygiene in its effort to be scientific, systematic, empirical, and grounded in psychobiological concepts about the true nature of the child stressed the seemingly contradictory premise that biology preordained a child's capacity to learn and perform as an adult. Nature, from this view, determined or limited the potential of individuals. Some groups by virtue of their heredity were either superior or inferior to others. Given the premise of

Educational Research, the National Agenda, and Educational Reform:
A History, pp. 299–324
Copyright © 2008 by Information Age Publishing
All rights of reproduction in any form reserved.

innate potential or lack thereof, effective educational research was expected to identify which children had the inborn capacity to profit from being nurtured. While educational researchers in the twentieth century adopted one side or the other in these controversies, the differences in their beliefs were less divisive than immediately apparent in that the premises for the emphasis on either nurture or nature as they influenced the formation of research questions and the interpretation of data, developed from the same mental hygiene premises about the integration of mind and body. The research results were in many ways symbiotic. This chapter examines the origins and consequences for educational research of the nature-nurture debates that grew from changes in the knowledge systems and social organization of the nineteenth century as they were played out in the expansion of schooling and research on education in the twentieth century.

EDUCATIONAL RESEARCH AND HEREDITARIAN THOUGHT

Contrary to the underlying assumptions of the researchers examined in this chapter, this history of educational research identifies intelligence as a social rather than a biological construct. The biological realities of the potential of any individual or groups of individuals with common characteristics are interpreted by their social and cultural context. The interpretation of the skills required to meet standards of competence can vary enormously from context to context. The subject of study becomes how hereditarian thought based on a perceived biological predetermination of a person's status was constructed and the outcome of that construction. The rise of ideas about a fixed reality external from human subjectivity that can be tapped by systematic investigations was a product of the Enlightenment. The application of ideas from philosophers such as John Locke that empowered human beings to construct and study their own world supported the American Revolution. This innovation in social thought broke through the unquestioned acceptance of predetermination by higher religious powers of adult status by virtue of the inheritance of social class status within monarchial societies. In the nineteenth century with the rise of a class-based society reflecting the rise of a capitalist economy there was a move to affirm the superiority of the traditional upper classes as well as individuals who were successful in a competitive economy. Hereditarian ideas persisted as part of a common perception of reality in spite of the commonly held belief that individuals have the capacity to change the circumstances of their lives by the choices they make regardless of the conditions of their birth. The belief that constructs such as intelligence are a biological trait with implications for group classification has been of enormous significance in the twentieth century. The concept of intelligence as a psychobiological reality became part of the social fabric and cultural world view of advanced Western societies with special implications in the United States for educational research and for the classification of school-age children.

While racial and other biological and evolution-based theories of difference evolved in the mid-nineteenth century, they have really only been formalized in social institutions and public policy in the twentieth century. A major transition occurred when newly developed statistical methods were incorporated into simple-to-administer tests that isolated intelligence as a constant identifiable in a number, the intelligence quotient or IQ score. Adapted for public schools as a means to classify children by ability, the manufacture of standardized intelligence tests and their use have continued to expand exponentially since 1920. By 1956-1957 one hundred and eight million children were assessed.[1] Today, in the United States alone, one hundred million standardized tests are administered in schools as part of state or federal mandates such as No Child Left Behind.[2] Intelligence testing and other assessments have had widespread use in the sorting and classifying of children as public schooling expanded, became more complex, and more bureaucratic. Classification served as a means to the ends espoused by mental hygienists, eugenicists, and social efficiency advocates. The legitimacy of the classification schemes has been fostered by their claim to validity as the products of systematic research.[3]

The story of the construction of ideas such as intelligence as the underpinning of the nature side of the nature-nurture debates and the persistence of hereditarian thought in American educational research is part of the persistence of mental hygiene beliefs in the primacy of psychobiology as a medical approach to problem solving as therapy. This is the overt subject of this chapter but it is impossible to understand this perspective without examining the intersection of the development of modern disciplines in the social and behavioral sciences. Mental hygiene and psychiatric perspectives empowered psychology as the major discipline in educational research. Educational research on mental measurement and school administration were the academic vehicles for the testing movement. The testing movement flourished on the same wave that brought the formal study of social life and organization, as they were promoted in the United States, to international prominence. The characteristics of social science in the United States, as opposed to the more historical and theoretical European tradition, was critical. Social science in the United States as grounded in a medical model of scientific research was early focused on individual subjects. As positivistic, it is also ahistorical, empirically driven, and tends to universalize its findings.[4]

These characteristics are fundamental to the dynamics that provided support for the psychobiological claims that used the research on intelligence as a valid basis for the classification of children.

Similar to the discussion on the relationship between the history of psychiatry as an underlying premise driving educational research on children, examining the persistence of hereditarian thought in educational research and the dimensions of the nature-nurture debates is more than historical analysis. It is the examination of the temporal and special architecture of social thought as part of the domain assumptions that shape research and its application to practice. The history of the formation of paradigms, just as paradigms themselves, change in relationship to the way they are interpreted over time. The nature-nurture debates over the efficacy of creating and using standardized tests versus researching development or how children process material show the struggle for ideas and different emphases on opposite sides of the debates, that were different sides of the same coin.

Schooling and the Social Origin of Standardized Testing as Educational Research

Prior to the American Revolution, education and teaching were almost exclusively related to personal growth and an individual ideal. In the nation building process the emergent American political order and economic structures increasingly required literacy as a public developed around the institution of the nation state. The nation state had to find a balance between individual freedom won from the Revolution and the order required in the public interest for social continuity. Rational decision-making by an educated citizenry was to preserve individualism and freedom. Schooling was the instrumentality that was selected to preserve order and to train the young to fill productive and compliant adult roles. A reform movement to establish free, universal, public education spread rapidly between the American Revolution and the onset of the Civil War, 1780 to 1860.[5] Out of this grew a new social and cultural phenomenon, the common school.[6]

After Appomattox the modernization process accelerated, and the social, political, and economic structures of the nation experienced unsettling transformations. Industrialization, urbanization, and an ever-growing number of immigrants transformed American life at all levels.[7] The early tension between education for freedom and schooling for order increased. The organization of common schools could not now be left to chance. Expanded enrollment demanded a systematic approach to pedagogy, to the evaluation of students, and the administration of schools.

Teaching and administration had to be examined systematically. Teachers had to be taught how to teach, and administrators had to be taught to supervise instruction. As school practices became systemized, the differences in students' performances and behaviors became ever more apparent. As the cost of formal public education increased, it became important to differentiate between students who could profit from schooling and those who would not. Research was needed so that decisions could be made in a rational and efficient manner.

Public Schooling and Nativism

Public interest and concern about the character and cause of human differences and their possible effects on the progress of American society increased during the last half of the nineteenth century. The claim that physical, mental, and moral traits were inherited gained ascendancy over earlier beliefs grounded in the optimistic view that physical, mental, and moral traits were curable. The theory of nativism, that human differences were the result of irreversible pathologies, held by Pinel by the end of the eighteenth century seemed increasingly plausible. The rise of scientific medicine and specialties such as neurology after 1850 allowed researchers to investigate the possible biological basis for human differences. Charles Darwin's *Origin of the Species* (1859) provided a theoretical argument for evolution and the inheritance of disabilities as well as abilities. Herbert Spencer, who was more popular in the United States than in his native England, used Darwin's "survival of the fittest" to explain the workings of society. Evolution, progress, and competition fit well with American beliefs in freedom and just rewards associated with the Protestant work ethic and ideals of rugged individualism.[8] Darwin's cousin, Sir Francis Galton, took these ideas and laid the ground work for the testing movement in the *Hereditary Genius* in 1869. Galton provided the foundation for the eugenics movement by examining the connection between ability and family histories. Eugenicists believed that science should be used to promote the genetic advancement of the human race and its opposite, the elimination of populations and individuals who might introduce or perpetuate defects that would deteriorate the human population. Galton elaborated on the implications of biological inheritance for mental development, assuming the superiority of the upper classes and the superiority in general of the English over other populations. Galton used the work of Belgian statistician, Adolphe Quetelet to show that the laws of probability could be applied to the measurement of human differences.[9] His student, Karl Pearson, developed essential statistical methods that made quantitative educational research possible. He developed techniques for the study of contingency and probability, produced a formula for the correlation of factors, and the chi-square test for the "goodness of fit."

The growth of psychology as a discipline based on scientific research issued from the establishment of early primitive psychological laboratories that studied the senses and human differences in reaction times. Wilhem Wundt established the first psychological laboratory in Leipzig, Germany in 1879. Galton established a laboratory in 1882, where he explored mental differences by inventorying British abilities and showing how they fit with patterns of inheritance. Between Appomattox and World War I many Americans traveled to Europe for advanced study. Many future leaders in educational research studied under Wundt or Galton and returned to the United States to set up laboratories of their own.[10] James McKeen Cattell opened a laboratory modeled after Galton's. There he devised a set of fifty tests to measure college students' memories and reaction times, and published a paper in 1890 that introduced the term "mental test."[11] Joseph Jastrow established a laboratory at the University of Wisconsin in 1892 where he constructed a set of tests similar to Cattell's.[12] In 1896, Lightner Witmer, founder of the journal *Psychological Clinic,* opened what was probably the first laboratory for "clinical psychology," a field closely associated with school- based psychology.

G. Stanley Hall, as noted earlier is recognized as the founder of child-study in the United States. Hall also introduced hereditarian thought to the study of children and intelligence. He established a psychological laboratory at Johns Hopkins University in 1893. He left Johns Hopkins for Clark University to assume the presidency and to set up a graduate program in psychology and education. While Hall produced no intelligence tests, his eugenic theories and his emphasis on the use of clinical methods to study children influenced his students. Henry H. Goddard, who became director of research at Vineland Training School for the Feeble-minded, contributed to the introduction of intelligence tests to the United States and their dissemination. Lewis M. Terman, perhaps the most influential figure in the expansion of the intelligence testing movement in the United States, wrote the singularly most popular intelligence test used in the United States, the Stanford-Binet.[13]

RESEARCHING AND PRODUCING STANDARDIZED TESTS IN THE PROGRESSIVE ERA, 1890-1917

At the end of the nineteenth century the progressive reform movement raised public consciousness about corruption and inefficiency in government. Progressives turned to professionals and experts for answers. They advocated the application of methods of scientific inquiry to social problem solving. The use of statistics achieved widespread acceptance as an objective path to knowledge. Activists in the social settlement, social hygiene, and mental hygiene movements used surveys with various degrees of sophistication to collect data on the extent of social problems. The number and range of social vices in inner cities, the status of immigrants arriving at Ellis Island in seeming ever greater numbers, the mental condition of inmates in prisons, and the ethnic origins of patients in hospitals and asylums became subjects of inquiry. During the Progressive Era, hereditarian views and beliefs were widely accepted among a public that was increasing concerned about the effects on society of inherited incompetence and feared that it was increasing. Alarmist descriptions of new immigrants as inferior to earlier groups who settled the nation fueled nativistic beliefs.[14] On the one hand, progressive child savers sought to order and uplift the lower classes; on the other hand, progressives inclined toward efficiency and hereditarian beliefs saw great dangers for society that quite possibly consist of a citizenry that not only lacked a basic understanding of American institutions but also lacked the basic capacity to grasp what that citizenship meant. Attention shifted from adults, often considered not capable of remediation, to their children and to the school as an acculturation agency. Some believed that humans were malleable and that schooling was necessary for the creation of competent adults; others believed that human capacities were biologically predetermined and that portions of the lower classes would not benefit from public education. The socio-political climate was sympathetic to the creation of instruments and procedures that could resolve the issues that surrounded human differences and their implications for the public school. Educations and professionals were committed to conducting research in the social scientific disciplines to resolve these issues and to answer the questions they raised.

The First Intelligence Test in France: The Binet-Simon Scale

Up to 1905, mental tests were limited to the examination of individual traits based on faculty psychology that was under attack but not yet completely out of fashion. They were designed to test and compare differences among subjects' sensory discrimination, reaction times and memories. French psychologist, Alfred Binet, was interested in a child's capacity to learn. He wanted to assess overall mental functioning. In 1889, he joined Henri Beaunis to found the first French psychological laboratory at the Sorbonne where he studied children's ability to reason abstractly and to make intelligent judgments. In the fall of 1905, Binet was appointed to the Ministerial Commission for the Study of Retarded

Children. He soon concluded that the Commission's members were "unconcerned with any objective means of selecting retardates from among normal children" and realized that "an effective test must be oriented to "tasks or behavior" rather than to so-called faculties" was needed.[15] With his colleague Theophile Simon, Binet developed a test of general intellectual functioning that differed significantly from previous mental tests. They developed a series of tasks that were standardized on a select group of children in order to determine what a normal level of performance was for a given age group. Binet saw the tests as an instrument for diagnosis so that methods could be devised to improve children's ability to learn. The purpose was to develop a means by which maladapted and underdeveloped children could be identified and classified for school purposes. Test items were subsequently arranged according to their level of difficulty rather than by subject matter. Higher mental processes such as the ability to execute orders, to distinguish between objects, and to imitate certain gestures became items for testing a person's soundness of judgment. The Binet-Simon test did not address sensory, perceptual, or motor functions. When they published the work in 1905 Binet and Simon effectively accomplished the development of the first scaled test of intelligence that could classify and compare children as normal or average for their age with children who were subnormal or advanced for their age level. Revisions of the 1905 test appeared in 1908 and 1911, the year of Binet's death.[16]

In 1909, the same year that the Binet-Simon scales were brought to the United States, Leonard Ayres brought the problem of maladjusted and underdeveloped children in the classroom to public attention in his *Laggards in the Schools*. Ayres down played biological factors, but the problem contributed to debates over immigrants and the education of their children. This explained why while Binet's scale received a great deal of attention in France, Germany, Russia, and England, the most profound response was in the United States. Psychiatrist William Healy and G. Stanley Hall's student, Henry H. Goddard, introduced the Binet-Simon scale simultaneously with two different outcomes.[17] William Healy and his assistant, psychologist Grace Fernald, experimented with the Binet-Simon scales by testing children in a juvenile "psychopathic" clinic attached to the juvenile court in Chicago. The results did not show a strong correlation between those identified as subnormal and delinquency. Healy remained skeptical about of the usefulness of the test and recommended caution.[18] Henry H. Goddard, on the other hand, was a vocal advocate who increased the importance of the test as well as their public profile. Goddard published translations of Binet's French versions into English and used the scale to evaluate 400 students at Vineland Training School for the Feebleminded. As he expected, he found that the results substantiated that the population was subnormal. Goddard believed that the intelligence tests justified formerly unsubstantiated popular hereditarian beliefs about the poor and the underclass as inferior beings who posed a danger to moral and civic order. Following in the genre of Richard Dugdale's *The Jukes: A Study of Crime, Pauperism, Disease, and Heredity* (1877), Goddard provided a seemingly rational argument that the poor posed a threat to civilized society based on their biological inferiority. The intelligence test provided him with the evidence he needed to make his political convictions seem objective and scientific. He published *The Kallikak Family: A Study in the Heredity of Feeblemindedness* in 1912 and *Feeblemindedness: Its causes and Consequences* in 1914. These popular works considerably raised public fears about the mental functioning of vulnerable groups in society. Steven Jay Gould examined Goddard's work and found that the photographs that accompanied his text were doctored to make the subjects, inmates of Vineland, look crazed or abnormal.[19]

In the early twentieth century several developments combined to make intelligence tests easy to use on a mass basis and to make their use appear as scientific research in the natural sciences in ways that encouraged hereditarian conclusions. This connection was not with biology or laboratory science but with psychometry. Building on the work of Karl Pearson, a statistician and eugenicist, Charles Spearman and Cyril Burt argued that the correlation of scores on intelligence tests support the notion of a general "g" factor. The "g" factor, they argued was inheritable. This allowed the test score to be reified as representing intelligence as a thing-in-itself and as a generalizable biologically inheritable trait. Alfred Binet specifically warned that the scale should not be generalized in this manner. Wilhelm Stern added another important piece to the usability of intelligence testing. On his examination of the 1911 Binet-Simon scale, he noted that a "mental quotient" could easily be calculated by dividing one's mental age as measured on the intelligence scale by the individual's chronological age. Terman adopted and modified William Stern's earlier suggestion and decided to eliminate the decimal point by multiplying Stern's mental quotient by 100. That produced a score now commonly known as an IQ score.

Another student of G. Stanley Hall, Frederick Kuhlmann a psychologist who became superintendent of the Minnesota School for the Feebleminded and Colony for Epileptics in Faribault, also experimented with creating mental tests similar to Goddard's but with results that would have favored a nurturing perspective had they been widely adopted. Kuhlmann conducted early experimental studies in mental deficiency but he turned to mental testing in 1912 when he completed a revised version of the Binet-Simon scale. He was particularly interested in very young children. His conclusions on the meaning of scores was consistent with Binet's

conviction that they should not be generalized. Kuhlmann's tests produced a single score for the children being tested. He preferred to call the
score a personal constant or a PC. He looked for growth and development
and neither compared infants nor established an absolute fixed scale. He
compared the individual to his/her own record in order to find a pattern
of performance that could be used to assess readiness for school. His view
that all individuals do not reach uniform standards at precisely the same
age allowed for appropriate interventions and attention to a child's developmental characteristics as a key to advancement through education and
training.[20]

LEWIS M. TERMAN AND THE STANFORD-BINET: RESEARCH AND TESTING IN THE PUBLIC SCHOOL

Four years after Kuhlmann's revision of the Binet-Simon scale and shortly
before World War I, Lewis M. Terman reworked the Binet-Simon scale
and began experimental testing on school children.[21] The Stanford-Binet
consisted of ninety tests arranged by age level in sequential order. Most
important in the Terman revision was the incorporation of two ideas that
made administering and scoring the test very easy and adaptable for
school use. Terman's approach allowed the comparative use of scores by
designating different levels to intelligence score ranges. The top one percent of one thousand scores in the sample he used to standardize the tests
were assigned an IQ score of 130. This group was designated as one of
"very superior intelligence." A child with this score was designated as a
genius. Terman considered himself to be a genius and he closely identified with this group. He devoted his academic life to longitudinal research
on the child genius he uncovered and pioneered gifted education. He
called his research cohort "his children." In a revision of the tests three
levels of above average intelligence were specified by Terman as somewhat superior, decidedly superior, and extremely superior.[22]

   At the other end of the scale, the bottom one percent of one thousand
was assigned an IQ score of 70. Those who so scored were designated as
"feebleminded" or "mentally deficient" Goddard divided the lower group
into three subgroups: morons, idiots, and imbeciles. The early mental test
that was an imprecise measure of an individual's potential or capacity to
learn was now taken to be a precise measure of an individual's capacity to
learn and function. Whether accurate or inaccurate, testing could be used
to identify children who would profit from school, or from a rigorous
academic program; and those students who would not profit from
schooling and needed a practical program. Intelligence was further seen
as distributed unevenly in society and as class dependent. IQ became a

handy measure of a person's worth. Terman and other psychologists need a mass demonstration to prove the efficacy of testing. World War I provided the opportunity they needed.

From Experiments to Mass Production: The Army Alpha and Beta Tests

While the two decades surrounding the turn of the century mark what may be viewed as the experimental period in the development of intelligence testing, World War I marks a significant turning point. When war was declared by the United States, Robert M. Yerkes, president of the American Psychological Association and chair of the Psychology Committee of the National Research Council, met with a group of psychologists who agreed that the new profession should make a contribution to the war effort. A Committee on the Psychological Examination of the Recruits was formed. It included Henry Goddard and Lewis Terman. The committee wrote the Surgeon General that intelligence tests could assist in identifying individuals unfit for military service. The group met at Vineland and within two weeks prepared two versions of the Binet-Simon scale, the Army Alpha and the Army Beta tests. These tests were modeled on a new group test battery prepared by Arthur Otis. The testing program was implemented. By January 1919 when the program ended, over 1.7 million men had been administered intelligence tests and assigned duty based on their IQ scores.

The Army testing program produced not only tests but also a broad network of professional clinical psychologists that resulted in the formation of the American Association of Clinical Psychologists. Many officers who were trained to administer the tests in the Army's Psychological Division later pursued advanced degrees in psychology. This provided both leadership and researchers in the field.[23] Teachers and professors who had been loaned to the Army to assist in the testing program returned to their schools and universities convinced of the merit of the tests. They also disseminated the implications of the testing program for school policy. The Army test results identified the average intelligence of recruits as equivalent to a twelve year old. Scores showed variation among the intelligence of various ethnic groups. It was argued that this proved that certain ethnic and racial groups were not capable of benefiting from formal education.[24] There were clear implications for the efficiency of providing an equal public school education for populations who were not intellectually equal. It was argued that mass testing was needed in schools. Testing could easily be adapted for school use since the Army program demonstrated that thousands of tests could be given in a cost effective and time efficient way. Populations could effectively be classified on the basis of test results for administrative purposes. The point was not lost on Terman and the other psychologists attached to the Army program who turned to the civilian school population armed with the know-how and justification for a mass testing of children.[25]

One day after the Army dismantled its Psychological Division, Abraham Flexner, secretary of the General Education Board, a Rockefeller family related philanthropy established in 1903, received and granted a request for $25,000 to enable the Army psychologists to create intelligence tests for use in schools.[26] The Elementary School Intelligence Board was established to complete the revision and soon produced the National Intelligence Tests. After a series of trials, norms were established based on the performance of school children in New York City, Kansas, Pittsburgh, and Cincinnati. Early in 1920, the World Book Company agreed to publish the tests. By the Fall of 1920, 400,000 were distributed to school districts.[27] During this period Terman, revised his 1916 version of the Stanford-Binet. It was published in 1919. Since the National Intelligence Test concentrated on children in grades three through eight, he developed the Terman Group Test for children in grades seven through twelve. He also produced a battery of achievement tests and wrote extensively on testing, school reform, and the ability of children.[28]

The tests could not have been prepared at a more fortuitous time. During the war, immigration declined but after the war it increased. In 1920, the nation received half a million immigrants and a good number of them had children who enrolled in public schools. Internal migration from rural areas to urban centers placed added pressure on city schools. Between 1920 and 1930, elementary school enrollment increased by 22 percent, from 23.3 million to 28.3 million. During the same period, high school enrollment doubled, from 2.2 to 4.2 million. School administrators were receptive to testing. Educators had eagerly secured survey and census statistics since 1911. Virtually every major city school district was surveyed between 1911 and 1925.[29] At first the collection of data was primitive but it improved with administrative efforts to standardize practices. Researchers such as Ellwood Patterson Cubberly, a graduate of Teachers College, Columbia University, who became Dean of Education at Stanford University was a major leader in the professionalization of public school administration.[30] The new tests that established norms for performance made it possible for administrators to document the effects of increased enrollment and to identify populations that performed below the norm in a systematic and supposedly objective way.

From the early data returns, Lewis Terman concluded that the environmental or organizational factors that Leonard Ayres used to explain differential rates of progress among students, could not account for the number of students who appeared not to profit from school, did not attend regularly, or who simply progressed slower than their classmates. Using the argument of biological determinism, Terman took the position that his tests proved that such students were indeed mentally inferior, that such inferiority could be identified objectively through intelligence tests, and that the inferiority so identified could not be overcome.[31] He claimed that students should be classified by their IQ and schooled accordingly in order to foster their mental health and adjustment. Terman's conclusion satisfied both sides of the progressive debate over nature versus nurture. While Terman was a leader on the hereditarian side of the debate, he argued in terms acceptable to mental hygienists and those concerned with individual adjustment. The acceptance of biological determinism and belief in the validity of intelligence testing allowed educators to justify not only variation in the provision of universal school services but also legitimated different educational outcomes for different children and groups of children. Terman argued that intelligence tests should be administered to all children in order to identify the innate differences among them so they could be sorted into classes geared to their special needs and abilities. He recommended that schools be reformed to include five homogeneous tracks for students who were gifted, bright, average, slow or special. He also indicated what percent of the student population could be expected in each rank: 2.5% were gifted, 15% were bright, 65% were average; 15% were slow, and 2.5% special. Notice that Terman's calculations form a bell or normal curve, which he thought could be applied to the general population. In school the bottom 2.5% designated as special would be assigned to ungraded classes separate from the general school population. While Terman initially recognized that permanent placement of students into such tracks might be considered unjustifiable and un-American, he was soon able to tell the membership of the National Education Association: "I have no patience with those who condemn this plan as undemocratic. The abandonment of the single-track, pre-high school curriculum is the first necessary step toward educational democracy."[32] He staunchly defended testing in the highly publicized debates with Walter Lippman published in the *New Republic* in 1922 and 1923.[33]

TESTING, VOCATIONS, AND SCHOOL EFFICIENCY

Intelligence testing not only framed curricula and pedagogy but was also used to direct vocational outcomes. After completing the sixth grade the slow group was to be trained with a vocational skill. Those with low scores were deemed not capable of doing work beyond that of menial unskilled labor. The average were capable of skilled work. Bright individuals could be considered capable of entering business or the professions. The gifted were to be prepared for college and leadership roles in society. Determining students' probable usefulness to society early in life was cost effective in that it did not waste time and money on children who could not succeed according to the test. Organizing formal schooling so that it fit a child's supposedly innate abilities constituted a "conversion of talent" that would render both schools and the nation's economy efficient. At the same time, such reforms would assure competent leadership and reduce corruption, Terman maintained.[34]

Terman's recommendations were thoroughly consistent with the administrative emphasis on school efficiency, an interest begun as Frederick W. Taylor's system of scientific management captured the imagination of reformers earlier in the century. Taylor argued that the laws of management should be based on the laws of nature and that impartial judgments about the management of individuals in organizations should be made scientifically. A person's occupation and class standing as well as social stratification in general, according to this view, reflected biological facts. Sorting individuals according to their social origins was not considered prejudicial nor discriminatory; it was simply a prudent and efficient use of time and resources.[35] School administrators, at the urging of people like Ellwood Cubberley, quickly adopted Taylor's arguments and applied them to all facets of public education.[36] Cubberley, like Terman and Goddard, was taken with hereditarian theories of the deficiency of certain ethnic groups and supported the idea that talent or the lack thereof should be identified and acted on. Tracking was considered a welcome solution. Cubberley made Stanford University the West Coast leader in educational psychology and school administration in research and practice. Cubberley's promotion of educational research in the survey movement as used to professionalize school administration and organization was complementary with Lewis Terman's research and implementation of intelligence testing and the effort to track students.

The two major tenets of progressive education—child-centered school and curriculum and objective meritocratic administrative procedures—stood hand in hand. The Progressive Education Association, founded in 1919, promoted the classification of children, the child-centered school, and the bureaucratization of schooling, which was referred to as the professionalization of public education. In retrospect, it is clear that the call for child-centered pedagogy and curriculum remained rhetorical and that the tendency toward standardization, sorting, and bureaucracy became the school policy. Rational sorting made possible with standardized tests supported a socially and racially stratified system that was argued to be meritocratic.[37] A child-centered focus on individual differences justified the diversification of curriculum programs segregated on the basis of a supposedly natural distribution of talent and ability.

Terman rose to national prominence in the Post-World War II Era. He helped forge a national network of psychologists who promoted intelligence testing. As chair of the Department of Psychology at Stanford University, his program had the largest budget of the sixteen departments in the United States that offered advanced degrees in psychology. By 1924, Stanford rose from last to sixth behind Teachers College, Columbia; University of Chicago; Clark University; Harvard; and Cornell in awarding degrees.[38] He edited the World Book's series on Measurement and Adjustment—a series that included twenty textbooks on intelligence testing. The first book in the series, *Mental Tests and the Classroom Teacher*, favorably promoted mass intelligence testing programs, and bureaucratized models for school administration that could put the test scores to use. In Oakand, California in conjunction with the Berkeley studies, the public school district implemented a five-track curriculum based on intelligence tests.[39] Terman was in a strategic position to disseminate educational research driven by psychobiological determinism. He served as editor of six major journals: *Journal of Juvenile Research; Journal of Applied Psychology; Journal of Educational Research; Journal of Educational Psychology; Journal of Personnel Research* and *the Journal of Genetic Psychology*. The plethora of professional journals served as forums for the legitimation of research and testing based on the unscientific premise that nature dominated nurture in human development. Even though most qualified researchers in medical science and genetics in particular rejected extreme perspectives on biological determinism by 1915, the public continued to look at eugenics favorably. As the ideas of genetic predetermination lost scientific credibility, support for these ideas in educational research and policy continued to advance these ideas in the public mind and in educational research that drove school practices in the 1920s and 1930s.[40]

Terman became a founding director of the Psychological Corporation, a test publishing firm, in 1921. The Psychological Corporation was the idea of James McKeen Cattell. As president of the American Psychological Association, Terman estimated that 65% of the association's members were engaged in research that involved intelligence testing. During this period, one topic on Terman's research agenda included the correlation of intelligence with race. Given the assumption that the tests actually measured a universal reality, the correlation of the test results with social class status as well as cultural differences was ignored. Students who were not Anglo-European, middle to upper class and exposed to standard English, and enriched environments did not perform well. Research on intelligence contributed to the reification of the idea that there are different subspecies of human beings and that there is a hierarchical order with

Anglo-Europeans on the top. Such views supported the segregation of African American students or their relegation to ungraded classroom and the acquisition of menial skills associated with their "special" status. It also endangered other cultural and ethnic minorities as well as rural families, and the poor or working class population. Terman's other research interests associated with testing included an examination of the interrelationships among mental traits, and the connections among mental development, genius, and insanity.[41] The power of tests to sort among social classes was matched by their power to distinguish group differences between racial and ethnic groups. Findings were used to support eugenic views of superiority and inferiority: Due to the cultural biases built into the tests, "white" American students out performed "negroes" as well as southern and eastern Europeans. Only 36% of the Italians, 41% of the Poles, and 36% of the Germans exceeded the median of American groups."[42]

A great flood of new tests and revisions were produced in the 1920s and 1930s. In 1933, the U.S. Bureau of Education published *A Bibliography of Mental Tests and Rating Scales*. It offered educators information on 133 tests that could be used for classifying students according to various mental abilities. Four were published before 1910. Seventeen, including Binet's and revisions by others for use with adults and only three for children between the ages of three and fourteen, were published between 1910 and 1914. Seventeen additional tests, mostly for children of elementary school age or adults, were published between 1915 and 1919. Between 1920 and 1924, thirty-eight additional tests were published for all ages from preschool through adulthood. The United States was the world leader in test publishing. The combined efforts of Germany, Great Britain, Belgium, France, and other European countries did not match those of the United States. Germany, which had produced forty-one tests up to this time, was a distant second to the United States. The total number of standardized tests of all types available world wide in 1932 was 2,558. There were 218 tests designed exclusively for classifying students according to mental ability.[43] By the end of the 1920s ability grouping was already widespread, especially in cities with populations over 100,000. By the end of the 1930s nearly all, if not all, school systems across the nation were highly differentiated and frequently used intelligence and achievement tests to classify students. [44]

World War II may have had an even greater effect on extending and entrenching standardized testing than did World War I. Between 1941 and 1945 the American Armed Forces took advantage of the great number of test and the great number of professionals qualified to administer them to develop a sophisticated and complex testing program. The General Classification Test was used to sort recruits, assign them to training programs, and to determine their eligibility for officers candidate schools. Besides sitting for intelligence tests, recruits were given batteries of tests designed to determine aptitudes and eight different abilities. The program was so extensive that nineteen volumes were needed to record the Air Force's program. The Armed Forces' program to diagnose and treat psychiatric problems and mental illness served to legitimate mental disorders. The various brain damage syndromes, combat fatigue, and disorders due to shock or stress that were identified were eventually applied to children who were behavior problems or who had learning problems in school. World War II served not only to publicize intelligence and aptitude tests of various sorts; it also profiled the epidemiology of mental and emotional problems as a psychobiological phenomena that psychometry could identify. In the late 1940s and 1950s, industries, government agencies, social welfare agencies, hospitals and clinics, colleges, universities, and public school systems adapted tests to their specific needs and populations just as other war industries and technologies were adapted for domestic use. World War II assured that teachers and school administrators would be on the look out for children with mental and emotional problems; and, the Post-World War II baby boom insured that test publishers would have a market for their wares.

CONTROVERSIES QUESTIONING THE EFFICACY OF THE RESEARCH AND IMPLEMENTATION OF TESTING

The eugenics argument that defective populations should be identified, segregated, detained, and sterilized was fully developed, expressed, and accepted by many during the Progressive Era. The biological sciences were inconclusive and the state of eugenics research was primitive at that time. Research in neurology and genetics as it progressed did not support either the idea of a general intelligence factor, or "g." It also did not support the biological reality of inherited gene pools that differentiated human populations by race. The concept of race has no biological basis but rather is a social and historical term identifying individuals on the basis of extraneous physical features such as skin, hair, or eye color. IQ scores are, nonetheless, still used to support the argument that extraneous physical attributes and connected to mental attributes.[45] From the beginning to the present, arguments for the reification of IQ have been statistical and hypothetical. Terman's advocacy of intelligence testing and his fascination with genius was not unlike the earlier work of Francis Galton in that they were mostly based on statistical correlations among class, race, and intelligence. The relationship between race and IQ was argued from 1918 to 1963 with frequent reference to the "brute fact that negroes

[sic] earn on an average lower scores on intelligence tests than do whites [sic].[46] Terman reported in his 1919 study of school children that upper class children scored on the average seven points above the middle class student, who on average scored 100 and that working class students scored seven points below that mean. Yerkes' 1921 report of the differences revealed by the U.S. Army tests showed results that corresponded to Terman's earlier findings.[47] The populations on which the tests were originally normed and the nature of the test items measured ensured that there would be a relationship between scores and social class. Tests, such as the Stanford Binet, were constructed with little consideration of the factors that greatly influence an individual's performance: social class, educational opportunities, facility with the English language, cultural differences in experience.[48] It has been persistently argued by defenders of IQ that the "g" factor makes such consideration unnecessary and that intelligence scores represent psychobiological characteristics inherent in human biology, which reflects the stratified character of class, race, and gender differences.

Some psychologists continue to vigorously defend IQ tests and the validity of the "g" factor. In 1969, University of California-Berkeley psychologist Arthur Jensen published his now infamous, "How Much Can We Boost IQ and Scholastic Achievement?" He argued that African Americans and those from the lower classes were innately inferior. His return to overtly genetic arguments about the nature of intelligence and the reliable constancy of IQ scores as correlated with a generalizable estimate of overall mental ability dates back to the arguments extended by Galton, Goddard, and Terman. Jensen's article received widespread public attention and stimulated debate among educators and psychologists,[49] similar to the public debates between Walter Lippmann and Lewis Terman in the 1920s.[50] It also garnered support for racism. Psychologist Hans Eysenck strongly supported Jensen's conclusion that race and intelligence were correlated and that the low intelligence of certain ethnic groups and racial minorities warranted segregation. Low intelligence, he claimed, explained and justified the under representation of certain minority groups in advanced education programs. A similar position was taken by Richard J. Herrnstein and Charles Murray in the mid-1990s in *The Bell Shaped Curve*.[51] Defenses of testing as legitimate measures of innate inferiority correlated with class, race, and ethnicity continue to be argued almost exclusively in psychometric terms in spite of mounting scientific evidence that refutes this interpretation.[52]

Questions about the validity of intelligence tests and the research that supports them have been raised before and after their explosive growth in the 1920s. While agreeing with their potential utility, John Dewey in 1916 spoke out against the use of tests to limit students' opportunities. Beardsley Ruml, a psychologist who served as director of the Laura Spelman Rockefeller Memorial in the 1920s when the philanthropy became a major funding source for social science research on children, questioned the vagueness of Terman's definition of intelligence, his use of statistics, and his assertions about the constancy of IQ.[53] William C. Bagley of Teachers College, Columbia University became an outspoken critic of progressive education, directly attacking the deterministic assumptions inherent in the testing movement. He warned school superintendents to be cautious about using such unrefined concepts as intelligence as well as the unwarranted applications of pseudo science into school practices.[54] He was especially opposed to Terman's use of tests as an instrument in administrative tracking programs. Bagley emphasized the discrepancy between the American credo that professed the equality of humankind and the persistent suppression, discrimination, and inequality that was not only tolerated but supported in American institutions.

Standardized Testing, Civil Rights, and the Misrepresentation of Minority Groups

Some groups have been consistently harmed by the domination of standardized tests in public schooling. African Americans were deliberately excluded from public education or relegated to inferior schools in both the South and North. Between 1896 and 1954 "Jim Crow" legislation allowed separate facilities for white and black children. The lack of educational opportunity clearly sustained social, political, and economic inequalities. Special institutions also segregated individuals with hearing or sight problems as well as those deemed to have either mental or emotional problems. Intelligence and other standardized tests contributed to the fact that substantial proportions of the population of school age children have been denied schooling on the basis of educational research and the results of test scores. By 1960, a quarter of a million children were institutionalized with one quarter of the children in institutions for the mentally handicapped.[55] The movement from exclusion to inclusion of both minorities and individuals with disability has been slow. James Coleman and Christopher Jencks in separate studies demonstrated the impact of the court case that desegregated schools along racial lines, *Brown versus the Board of Education*, 1954, and the Civil Rights Act in 1964 and the strong relationship between poverty and school achievement.[56] These studies gave significant support to those who believed that equality of educational opportunity could only be achieved if all children were included on an equal basis in the public school. However, inclusion in common public schooling did not necessarily provide equal opportunity due to the internal segregation of children into ability related groups on the basis of intelligence and more recently on other standardized tests provided by state of federal mandates. While African American children were being integrated into public schools, special education classes were increased in order to accommodate children who were being deinstitutionalized from segregated residential facilities or who had not previously been in schools. Intelligence testing also selected children out of regular classrooms and placed them in special classes. These school populations became intertwined after the Civil Rights Act of 1964 with the assignment of minority children on the basis of IQ scores to classes for the mentally retarded.

The over representation of poor and minority children in special education became part of a major anti-testing debate. In 1968, Lloyd Dunn, a special educator, asked whether special education classes as segregated environments were educationally justifiable. He also pointed out that placement in special education tended to carry a stigma that was disproportionately applied to minority students. Intelligence testing was the primary means for identifying a child as eligible for placement in segregated classes and separate schools for profound handicapping conditions. Poor children and minority children—who more often than not were also poor—did not do as well on intelligence tests as children from the dominant culture. When sociologist and social psychologist, Jane Mercer, systematically surveyed special classes in southern California in the 1970s she found that students who were placed in special education based on IQ scores were typically students from non-middle class environments who did not speak standard English.[57] A report from the Washington Research Project revealed that many school children were not benefiting or benefiting very little from their school experience. In addition, two million school age children were not even enrolled in school. Three quarters of a million of the two million were under age thirteen. For the most part, these children were different by way of "their race, income, physical, mental, emotional 'handicaps' and age." They were excluded from school having been judged as uneducable by an intelligence test.[58]

Mercer's documentation of the over representation of African American and Latino children in classes for the "Educable Mentally Retarded" came to the attention of other researchers and educators. The Black Psychologists section of the American Psychological Association decided to become advocates for minority students mislabeled as handicapped and segregated in school. In the *Larry P. v. the Board of Education*, the court restricted the use of intelligence tests to classify and assign minorities to tracked programs of study that limited their educational opportunities. The return of many special education students to regular classrooms resulted in the proliferation of other labels such as learning disabilities, attention deficit disorders, emotionally handicapped, and severely emotionally disturbed. The list of different syndromes continues to grow. New special placements were followed by an effort to place children in the "least restrictive environment," which often meant placement in a regular classroom. This effort toward full inclusion gained support and momentum from court decisions such as *Miller v. the Board of Education* in 1972 *and PARC et. al. v. the Commonwealth of Pennsylvania* in 1979. Legislation followed the court decisions. The Free Appropriate Public Education Act eliminated the category "unable to benefit from education" as well as the legal identification of severely disabled children as "custodial cases" by simply identifying them as "students." It also deemed legally indefensible the placement of minority students as "trainable mentally retarded" and "educable mentally retarded" solely on the basis of intelligence tests. That legislation served as the cornerstone for the Education for All Handicapped Act in 1975, which clearly stated that every child in the United States has right to a public education and that regardless of the severity of an individual's condition everyone can profit from stimulation, and support though education.[59] This legislation steps away from hereditarian prescriptions in favor of the potential of all human beings to profit from being nurtured.

Unfortunately, the clear requirement to include in public education all children neither discouraged the use of tests nor did it disentangle the relationship among socio-economic status, ethnicity, perceived race, and the placement of children into ability groups including various forms of tracking. Special education continues to grow as it has since 1967. The growth of special education increases the need for research and the proliferation of testing. During the 1984-1985 school year, 4.1 million children were deemed eligible for testing. Six years later that number had increased to 4.8 million.[60] Recent legislation mandating universal achievement testing may in practice also increase other types of standardized testing on ability. The classification of students is still largely determined through testing based on educational research with its underlying assumptions about the prominence of biological predispositions to certain behaviors and manifestations of abilities. Testing remains a dominant feature of public schooling as it has since the 1920s supported by educational research.

CONCLUDING OBSERVATIONS ON MERIT AND MERITOCRACY

Intelligence tests were created as, and are, accurate and efficient sorting mechanisms that reinforce dominant values and contribute to social stability by justifying inequality of outcomes as a natural and objective process supported by scientific research. The colonization of schooling by psychology and measurement enabled the translation of the concept of the equality of humankind as a natural right that required equal access to education to equality of opportunity in a meritocracy where opportunity is qualified, or restricted, by the natural stratification of intelligence.[61] The focus of intelligence tests on individual differences originated within a humanitarian, progressive, child-centered framework, simultaneously fostered by eugenics and efficiency movements. Researchers framed their questions around the scientific debates that favored biological determinism and they justified their findings with the language of nurture. The transformative power of schooling was considerably weakened by the persistence of standardized testing in that tests of intelligence among others have built into them class, racial, gender, and cultural biases. The attempt to create culture free tests has been unsuccessful in that they eliminate the usefulness of the application of research to practice as classificatory device that are easy to administer.

The acceptance of and dependence on educational research grounded in biological determinism as well as the persistent faith in the efficacy of testing legitimated fundamental American values and served to aid the school in its mission to reproduce the social configuration, maintain social stability, and assure continuity in spite of demographic, political, and economic transformations. Intelligence tests were welcomed because they served very well the agenda of reformers of the Progressive Era, and because they were useful in organizing and rationalizing school practices based on research. Testing promised to increase administrative efficiency, to save time, and to save money for growing state and school bureaucracies. Testing promised to reduce error and waste that were inherent in the effort to meet individual needs while providing for universal education. Testing grew with the professionalization of the fields of psychology and education. It is a big business. In spite of the current scientific consensus that intelligence is considerably more complex than what can be expressed in a single score and in spite of mounting evidence that tests are biased against various cultural minorities, the research and testing remain, and the industry continues to grow.

The next chapter takes up an underlying problem in educational research on children that can be attributed to the impulse to establish criteria for normalcy and tests to measure and quantify conformity to a standard based on the performance of the dominant group. Rockefeller philanthropies took up the problem later identified as "cultural lag" to refer to the identification and remediation of those children and populations who fell below the standard.

NOTES

1.   Educational Testing Service. *Conference on Testing* (Princeton: Princeton University 1958), pp. 30-40, 56-59; W. Rudy. *Schools in an Age of Mass Culture: An Exploration of Selected Themes in the History of Twentieth Century American Education* (Englewood Cliffs, N.J.: Prentice Hall, 1965).

2.   Richard Brown. *Rockefeller Medicine Men: Medicine and Capital in America* (Berkeley: University of California, 1979); Kathleen B. deMarrais and Margaret LeComte. *The Way Schools Work: A Sociological Analysis* 2nd ed. (New York: Longmans, 1995).

3.   Theresa Richardson. *The Century of the Child: The Mental Hygiene Movement and Social Policy in the United States and Canada* (Albany, New York: State University of New York Press, 1989); Mark H. Haller. *Eugenics: Hereditarian Attitudes in American Thought* (New Brunswick, New Jersey: Rutgers University Press 1963); Raymond Callahan. *Education and the Cult of Efficiency* (Chicago: University of Chicago Press, 1962); Donald T. Pickens. *Eugenics and Progressives* (Nashville: Vanderbilt University Press, 1968); Daniel J. Kevles. *In the Name of Eugenics: Genetics and the Uses of Human Heredity* (New York: Knopf, 1985); Carl Degler. *In Search of Human Nature: The Decline and Revival of Darwinianism in American Social Thought* (New York: Oxford, 1991).

4.   Dan A. Chekki. *American Sociological Hegemony: Transnational Explorations* (New York: University Press of America, 1987); Dorothy Ross *The Origins of American Social Science* (New York: Cambridge, 1991); Raj P. Mohan and Arthur S. Wilke, eds. *International Handbook of Contemporary Developments in Sociology* (Westport, Connecticut: Greenwood, 1994); Thomas L. Haskell. *The Emergence of Professional Social Science: The American Social Science Association and the Nineteenth Century Crisis of Authority* (Baltimore: Johns Hopkins University Press, 2000).

5.   Carl Kaestle. *Pillars of the Republic* (New York: Hill & Wang, 1983); Horace Mann. *Twelfth Annual Report of the Board of Education. Together with the Twelfth Annual Report of the Secretary of the Board* (Boston: Board of Education, 1849).

6.   Erwin V. Johanningmeier. "It Was More that a Thirty Year's War but Instruction Finally Won: The Demise of Education in Industrial Society" in Kathryn M. Borman and Nancy P. Greenman eds. *Changing American Education: Recapturing the Past or Inventing the Future?* (Albany, New York: State University of New York Press, 1994).

7.   W. Licht. *Industrializing America in the Nineteenth Century* (Baltimore: Johns Hopkins University Press, 1995).

8.   James Mark Baldwin. *Darwin and the Humanities* (Baltimore: Review Publishing Co., 1909); Richard Hofstadter. *Social Darwinism in American Thought* (New York: George Braziller, 1955); Merle Curti. *The Social Ideas of American Educators* rev. ed. (Totowa, New Jersey: Littlefield, Adams & Co., 1971); Merle Curti. *Human Nature in American Thought* (Madison: University of Wisconsin Press, 1980).

9.   Willis Rudy. *Schools in an Age of Mass Culture: An Exploration of Selected Themes in the History of Twentieth Century* American Education (Englewood Cliffs, New Jersey.: Prentice Hall, 1965).

322   E. V. JOHANNINGMEIER and T. RICHARDSON

10. B. Hoffman. *The Tyranny of Testing* (New York: Crowell-Collier Press, 1962).

11. James M. Cattell. "Mental Tests and Measurement," *Mind*, Vol. 15 (1890), pp. 373-379.

12. Joseph Jastrow and G. W. Moorhouse. "Some Anthropometric and Psychologic Tests of College Students," *American Journal of Psychology*, Vol. 4 (April 1892), pp. 420-228.

13. Lewis M. Terman. *The Measurement of Intelligence* (Boston: Houghton Mifflin, 1916); Lewis M. Terman. *The Stanford Revision of the Binet-Simon* (Boston: Houghton Mifflin, 1916); E. G. Boring, *A History of Experimental Psychology* (New York: Appleton, 1950); Alfred Binet and Theophile Simon, *Mentally Defective Children* tr. B. Drummond (London: E. Arnold, 1907); Alfred Binet and Theophile Simon, *The Development of Intelligence in Children* tr. Elizabeth.S. Kite, Henry H. Goddard ed. (Baltimore: Williams and Wilkes, 1916).

14. J. Higham. *Strangers in the Land: Patterns of American Nativism, 1860-1925* (New York: Atheneum,1965).

15. Theta H. Wolf. *Alfred Binet* (Chicago: University of Chicago Press, 1973), p. 29.

16. Binet and Simon, *The Development of Intelligence in Children*.

17. Rudy. *Schools in an Age of Mass Culture*.

18. Richardson *Century of the Child*; Margo Horne. *Before It's Too Late: The Child Guidance Movement in the United States, 1922 to 1945* (Philadelphia: Temple University Press, 1989); R. I. Watson, "A Brief History of Clinical Psychology," in J. Brozek, R. B. Evans, eds., *R. I. Watson's Selected Papers on the History of Psychology* (New Hampshire: University Press of New England, 1977.

19. Stephen Jay Gould. *The Mismeasure of Man*, revised and expanded (New York: Norton, 1996).

20. Frederick Kuhlmann. *Experimental Studies in Mental Deficiency* (Worchester, Massachusetts: Clark University,1904); Frederick Kuhlmann, *A Revision of the Binet-Simon System for Measuring the Intelligence of Children* (Faribault: Minnesota School for Feebleminded and Colony for Epileptics, 1912); Frederick Kuhlman, *Tests of Mental Development: a Complete Scale for Individual Examination* (Minneapolis, Educational Test Bureau: Educational Publishers, 1939).

21. Terman. *The Measurement of Intelligence*; and Terman. *The Stanford Revision of the Binet-Simon*.

22. *Ibid.*

23. Franz Samelson, "World War I Intelligence Testing and the Development of Psychology," *Journal of the History of the Behavioral Sciences*, Vol. 13, No. 3 (July 1977), p. 277; Chapman. *Schools as Sorter;: Lewis M. Terman Applied Psychology and the Intelligence Testing Movement* (New York: New York University Press, 1988).

24. Robert M. Yerkes. *Psychological Examinations in the U.S. Army*, Vol. 15 (Washington D.C.: National Academy of Science).

25. *Ibid,*; Samelson. "World War I Intelligence Testing and the Development of Psychology;" Erwin V. Johanningmeier. *Americans and Their Schools* (Boston: Houghton: Mifflin, 1980).

26. Chapman. *Schools as Sorters*.

27. Lewis M. Terman. *National Intelligence Tests, With Manual of Directions* (Yonkers-on-Hudson, New York: World Publishing Co. 1920).

28. Lewis M. Terman. *The Intelligence of School Children: How Children Differ in Ability, the Use of Mental Tests in School Grading and the Proper Education of Exceptional Children* (Boston: Houghton Mifflin, 1919); Lewis M. Terman, *Intelligence Tests and School Reorganization* (Yonkers-On-Hudson, New York: World Book Publishing Co. 1922); Lewis M. Terman. "The Conservation of Talent," *School and Society* (March 1924), p. 363; Lewis M. Terman. "The Mental Test as a Psychological Method," *Psychological Review* Vol. 31 (March 1924), pp. 93-117.

29. Callahan, *Education and the Cult of Efficiency*.

30. Ellwood P. Cubberley. *Public School Administration* (Boston: Houghton Mifflin, 1916); Elwood P. Cubberley. *Public Education in the United States* (Boston: Houghton Mifflin, 1919); Lawrence Cremin, *The Wonderful World of Ellwood Patterson Cubberley: An Essay on the Historiography of American Education* (New York: Bureau of Publications, Teachers College, Columbia University, 1965).

31. Terman, 1919; Leonard P. Ayres. *Laggards in Our Schools: A Study of Retardation and Elimination in City School Systems* (New York: Charities Publications Committee, Russell Sage Foundation, 1909).

32. Lewis M. Terman. "The Conservation of Talent," *School and Society* (March 1924), p. 363; Lewis M. Terman. "The Mental Test as a Psychological Method," *Psychology Review* Vol. 31 (March 1924), pp. 93-117.

33. Ned Joel Block and Gerald Dworkin. eds. *The IQ Controversy: Critical Readings* (New York: Pantheon Books, 1976), pp. 4-73.

34. Terman. *Intelligence Tests and School Reorganization*.

35. Samuel Haber. *Efficiency and Uplift Scientific Manaagement in the Progressive Era, 1890-1920* (Chicago: University of Chicago Press, 1973).

36. Cubberley. *Public School Administration*; Cubberley. *Public Education in the United States*; Callahan. *Education and the Cult of Efficiency*.

37. Lawrence A. Cremin. *The Transformation of the School: Progressivism in American Education, 1876-1957* (New York: Alfred A. Knopf, 1961); Chapman. *Schools as Sorters: Lewis M. Terman. Applied Psychology and the Intelligence Testing Movement, 1890-1930* (New York: New York University Press, 1988).

38. Boring. *A History of Experimental Psychology*.

39. Virgil Dickenson. *Mental Tests and the Classroom Teacher* (Yonkers-On-Hudson, New York: World Book Co., 1923).

40. Angus McLaren. *Our Own Master Race: Eugenics in Canada, 1885-1945* (Toronto: McClelland and Stewart, 1990), p. 10.

41. Terman. "The Mental Test as a Psychological Method."

42. *Ibid*.

43. Chapman, *Schools as Sorters*; Gertrude Howell Hildreth. *A Bibliography of Mental Tests and Rating Scales* (New York: Psychological Corporation, 1933).

44. *Ibid*, Chapman. *Schools as Sorters*.

45. T. J. Bouchard "The Hereditarian Research Program: Triumphs and Tribulations," in S. Modgil and C. Modgil, eds. *Arthur Jensen: Consensus and Controversy* (New York: Falmer Press, 1987), pp 55-76.

46.   R. D. Tuddenham. "Intelligence Measurement," *Encyclopedia of Educational Research* 5th ed. Vol. 2 (New York: Macmillan, 1969); Richard Herrnstein and Charles Murray. *The Bell Curve: Intelligence and Class Structure in the United States* (New York: Free Press, 1996).

47.   Robert M. Yerkes. *Psychological Examinations in the U.S. Army* Vol. 15 (Washington D.C.: National Academy of Science, 1921); Terman, *The Intelligence of School Children*.

48.   Stephen Jay Gould. *The Mismeasure of Man* (New York: W. W. Norton, 1996); D. Bell. "On Meritocracy and Equality," in *The Coming of Post-Industrial Society* (New York: Basic Books, 1973).

49.   Guy M. Whipple. *Twenty-First Yearbook of the National Society for the Study of Education: Part II, The Administrative Use of Tests* (Bloomington, Illinois: Public School Publish Co., 1922); L. J. Kamin. *The Science and Politics of IQ* (Potomac Maruland: Erlbaum Associates, 1974); Modgil and Modgil. *Arthur Jensen*; Block and Dworkin, eds. *The IQ Controversy*.

50.   Block and Dworkin, eds. *The IQ Controversy*.

51.   Herrnstein and Murray. *The Bell Curve*; Arthur Jensen. *Straight Talk About Mental Tests: Their Uses and Abused in No-Nonsence Terms by the Worlds Foremost Authority* (New York: The Free Press, 1981).

52.   Gould, *The Mismeasure*; Modgil and Modgil. *Arthur Jensen*; Block and Dworkin eds. *The IQ Controversy*.

53.   Chapman. *Schools as Sorters*.

54.   William C. Bagley. "Professor Terman's Determinism," *Journal of Educational Research* (December 1922), 376-385; William C. Bagley. *Determinism in Education* (Baltimore: Warwick and York, 1925).

55.   P. L. Stafford and E. J. Stafford. *A History of Childhood and Disability* (New York: Teachers College, Columbia, 1996).

56.   James S Coleman. *et al. Equality of Educational Opportunity* (Washington D.C.: U.S. Government Printing Office, 1966); Christopher Jencks. *Inequality: A Reassessment of the Effects of Family and School in America* (New York: Basic Books, 1972).

57.   Jane Mercer. *Labeling the Mentally Retarded* (Berkeley: University of California Press, 1973).

58.   Washington Research Project. *Children Out of School in America* (Washington D.C.: Children's Defense Fund, 1974).

59.   Stafford and Stafford. *A History of Childhood and Disability*.

60.   *Ibid*.

61.   Michael D. Young. *The Rise of the Meritocracy* (New Brunswick, New Jersey.: Transaction, 1994).

CHAPTER 12

CULTURAL LAG

The Laura Spelman Rockefeller Memorial and Educational Research

In 1922, William Ogburn introduced the term "cultural lag" in *Social Change in Respect to Culture and Original Nature.* At the beginning of the Progressive Era, academics and political and social elites feared that backward populations of Southern and Eastern European, African Americans, Hispanics, Asians, and American Indians would slow or curtail the progress of Anglo-Saxon civilization. Progressives wanted to protect and strengthen the "good stock" and to pacify and civilize others so they would conform to the culture of the traditionally dominant groups that first settled New England. Philanthropy supported the effort to avoid the potentially destructive consequences of cultural lag.

John D. Rockefeller Sr., Standard Oil magnate and the world's first billionaire, began to address "cultural lag" before Ogburn coined the term. Rockefeller was born of modest circumstances in Ohio in 1839, when racial slavery was being legitimated by "scientific racism." The rising tide of racism was to be found in the South, the North, the Midwest, and even on the expanding frontier. His marriage to Laura Spelman introduced him to the abolitionists. Chief among them was his mother-in-law, Lucy Henry Spelman, who participated in the Underground

Educational Research, the National Agenda, and Educational Reform:
A History, pp. 325–355
325

Railroad. Thus, it seems not surprising that his first major philanthropic gift was to a seminary for African American women in Atlanta that was subsequently renamed the Spelman Seminary for Women.

At the beginning of the Progressive Era, as Rockefeller's riches grew, his devout, practical Baptist faith very early led him to charity and then to philanthropy. He did not personally participate in the building of the large-scale philanthropic organizations that carried his name, but his surrogates including his son, John D. Rockefeller Jr., looked after his and the family's interests. The agenda of Rockefeller philanthropy did not significantly differ from the other reformers' agenda during the Progressive Era. For example, Rockefeller support for the mental hygiene movement as well as its support for both either sides of the nature-nurture controversies was an expression of its belief that humanity should and could be perfected. Rockefeller philanthropy, like the progressive reformers, wanted to maintain social control and social order; each wanted a future that was rationally ordered and managed.

During the Progressive Era, social policies that emphasized social control clearly constituted a response to and were directed toward the millions of newly arriving immigrants from Southern and Eastern Europe as well as African American migrants fleeing the rural South and its repressive Black Code segregation laws. The newcomers, looking for a better life and economic opportunities, mostly settled in northern cities. They were mostly assigned to and confined to cities' slums.

This chapter examines the funding activities of the Laura Spelman Rockefeller Memorial (LSRM), the General Education Board (GEB), and Spelman Fund of New York (SF), as they supported educational research on children in the 1920s and 1930s. During this period, educational research supported by Rockefeller philanthropy was directed toward forestalling or avoiding cultural lag. The southern states were an early focus of northern philanthropists. In cooperation with southern elites, northerners helped to reorder the New South after Reconstruction failed and as industrialization and its benefits and opportunities grew in the North and bypassed the rural South. Poor folks of the South were considered to be a backward people, and the South was viewed as a backward region torn apart by the Civil War. Planter-class southerners struggled to regain a power and create a socio-political structure that would protect their interests while also establishing an economy supported by an inexpensive and compliant workforce. In the minds of both southern and northern elites, that agenda required acknowledgement that a portion of the population was characterized by its former status as slaves, a status that had been supported by "scientific racism." A distinction was made between the alleged "natural" inferiority of African Americans as laggards and the unnatural cultural lag of the "forgotten man," the poor white population.[1] This concern was also found in the North and Midwest where local agencies and early progressive reformist advocacy groups worried about "defective immigrants and their progeny."

THE LAURA SPELMAN ROCKEFELLER MEMORIAL, RESEARCH ON CULTURE AND HABITS

Between the two world wars, Rockefeller philanthropy actively facilitated and supported research on children. The Laura Spelman Rockefeller Memorial was founded in 1918 in memory of the family matriarch. As a reflection of Laura Spelman Rockefeller's charitable interests, the Memorials' original mandate was to better the lives of women and children. Supporting and advocating the study of children as well as the development of the social sciences was the way that mandate was carried out. The Memorial was used by its officers as a vehicle for the legitimation of the formal investigation of the patterns of normal development in children and young adults using the social sciences.

Psychologists Beardsley Ruml, director of the LSRM and his associate, Lawrence K. Frank, were influenced by behaviorism with its emphasis on the formation of "social habits." They concluded that cultural lag, if seen as a series of bad habits, could be offset and eliminated. It seemed logical that if research could determine the origin of habits and acquire the ability to change aberrant behaviors early in life, the dysfunction that such habits caused in human society could be avoided. The idea of habit breaking incorporated what was seen as a battle against family traditions and child rearing customs that had grown dysfunctional or lagged behind changing times. Rockefeller philanthropy, as guided by Ruml and Frank, strove to be anti-formalist. They opposed esoteric knowledge isolated in formal schooling and classic disciplines. The anti-formalist argument supported the use of science rather than academic tradition in the same way that traditional cultural practices were to be avoided. The old ways of rearing children were to be replaced by new proven ways. This orientation produced pressure to move toward the newer social and behavioral sciences and away from traditional studies in the humanities with their moral philosophies based on abstract and theoretical propositions. Science was seen as and accepted as the key to the future.

Behaviorist thought, as understood by Frank, dealt with the formation of habits and personality as they were developed in a social context. Because habits could be formed or developed, personal and social changes were possible. That was a possibility that psychologies that focused on innate instincts appeared not to allow. The behaviorist position was different from and contrary to the eugenic tendencies in the mental hygiene movement. The problem to be addressed was that modern culture had advanced while traditional educational institutions— the family and the school—continued with traditional educational and child rearing practices that produced habits and personalities that did not equip children and youth for the new and emerging social order characterized by rapid scientific and technological change. The failure to develop the necessary habits caused not only individual personality problems but also, as they were sustained and accumulated, ultimately contributed to poverty, delinquency, mental retardation, mental illness, crime, violence, labor unrest, and even war. As the pace of modern civilization accelerated, the problem of cultural lag among susceptible individuals and populations became ever acute. Because the problem was conceived of as a problem for individuals, it became imperative to address the problem on individual basis similar to how medicine approached the problems of individuals. Because the Memorial was committed to the welfare of children and because the future depended on children, the child became the focus of research. Proper attention to children would prevent future social problems. Thus, parent education was necessary as was the need to train professionals with the knowledge and techniques needed for successful training and intervention Research was sorely needed in order to specify what was normal and to identify habits parents should instill. Before such research could be undertaken, it had to be demonstrated that ill-formed habits could be undone.[2] Remediation was just as necessary as was prevention.

In 1922, the Laura Spelman Rockefeller Memorial initiated its program to support the development social science research. Its purpose, in Ruml's words, was to promote "a better understanding of the conditions and forces that affect the ability of people and peoples to live together happily on a shrinking planet, and that, as a result of this growing knowledge, ways and means of greater and less precision might be found that would contribute to improved social controls in the interests of all."[3] Ruml further noted "that none of the other foundations had addressed themselves systematically to this field," which made "all the more inviting the exploration of its possibilities."[4] The goal was to establish between twelve and twenty "effective research institutions." Ruml identified the London School of Economics as an important center of social science research and supported it so the School could further its work. The University of Chicago received its first major social science research grant in 1923. The Social Science Research Council (SSRC) was created Ruml in 1923. University of Chicago political science professor and president of the American Political Science Association, Charles E. Merriam, was appointed to serve as its chief officer. In 1924, the Memorial awarded

$425,000 to the Social Science Research Council and $490,000 to the Brookings Institute Graduate School. Columbia University and Harvard University each received awards of $250,000.[5] The interest in social science research was "in the last analysis an interest in the ultimate practical usefulness of increased knowledge." Rum's goal was to create through research a "social technology" as well as a cadre of professionals in "medicine, education, and home economics" who could guarantee effective results based on interventions.[6] Four propositions guided the Memorial's work in applied social science research directed toward the improvement of child socialization and welfare: (1) Research efforts were directed toward prevention rather than cures. (2) Attention was directed toward adults in positions to influence socialization patterns, for example, teachers and parents. (3) Parents were to be taught how to make children "wholesome," according to research that proved to influence children's "physical, mental, and moral" development. (4) Scientific investigation of a rigorous nature was to focus on increasing knowledge about the "growth and development of children."[7] Research in the area of social science technology was pursued in the belief that "in time [it would] result in substantial social control" provided that the research increased the "body of knowledge in the hands of competent technicians." Control was sought over "social organization and social processes" with contributions from a variety of areas: "economics, political science, sociology, psychology, ethnology, human geography (migration patterns), and history." These academic fields of research were to be applied to "technological subjects in business, public administration, social work, and the law." The distinctions among the subjects were not to follow the customary distinctions made among the "social science disciplines" but were to be made according to "the nature of the phenomena of which modern social life is compounded." The concern over modernization extended throughout American society as well as international settings where the sources of cultural lag produced "backward countries." The primary interest was to solve "*contemporary* social problems in *modern* society."[8]

CONTROLLING RESEARCH ON CHILD LIFE

Until the founding of the Laura Spelman Rockefeller Memorial, child study, by contemporary standards efforts was mostly an unscientific enterprise. The first study group among middle class parents was created in 1888. G. Stanley Hall formed child-study groups in the 1890s. He also encouraged his students at Clark University to pursue child oriented research. The Child Study Association of America (CSAA) was expanded as the Federation for Child Study (FCS) in 1909. In 1924, Sidonie

Gruenberg, the Federation's director, disseminated a series of publications to the general public. They included pamphlets on obedience, punishment, truth and falsehood, and money management. A monthly magazine was produced as well as reading lists on children and their habits. The Federation provided extension services to other child care agencies and organizations. Local lectures and radio addresses were directed toward mother's groups, clubs, and social settlements. Academic courses and professional training were carried out in cooperation with Teachers College, Columbia University.[9] Memorial grants supported these services for the general public and also supported academic research and training. In 1925, the Memorial supported conferences that explored research on children's curiosity, imagination, activities during the summer or on vacation, habit formation, concepts of truth and falsehood, and issues of heredity.[10]

Increased funding for social science research by large-scale philanthropies supported expansion of studies on socialization, education, and mental health. The National Research Council was established in 1916 by the National Academy of Sciences under a Congressional Charter in cooperation with the National Scientific and Technical Societies of the United States. A Child Welfare Committee was formed under the Division of Anthropology and Psychology but it remained inactive due to lack of funds. In 1924, Teachers College Columbia University psychologist, Robert S. Woodsworth, became chair of the division and Bird T. Baldwin, director of the Iowa Child Welfare Research Station, became the chair of the Committee on Child Development. Support was acquired from the Memorial through annual appropriations of $40,000.[11] Conferences supported by Rockefeller philanthropy coordinated and assessed the state of child research including the "subject matter, problems, technics, methods of coordination, and dissemination." Special committees were formed to deal with areas of research as diverse as "animal development in relation to child development; the physical growth and anatomy of the young child; nutrition of the young child; medical care of the young child; the psychology of the young child; the mental hygiene of the young child; the education of the young child in schools and laboratories; and the publication of research and abstracts."[12] The National Research Council also served as a "child study clearing house and laboratory." This endeavor was closely related to concerns over cultural lag and operated for funding purposes under the title "human migration" research. It also served as a distribution agency stationed between the philanthropy and universities in such areas as the distribution of fellowships, the funding of research, and distribution of research to academic and to popular audiences. Regular conferences, supported by the Memorial, were held to coordinate the committee's work and to exchange ideas and discuss the value of findings.[13]

Research projects addressed the specific needs of the areas and participants. They also conformed to the Memorials' agenda. Concern with cultural lag continued as an issue in the research proposals of Harold Odum at the University of North Carolina. Odum in a letter to Syndor H. Walker of the Memorial proposed "rural work" designed to gather preliminary knowledge in vital fields of interest: "genetic studies of marginal families; studies of leadership resources; school attendance and delinquency; mental tests of groups of children; and special studies of health and dietary conditions." Odum was interested in preschool children's quality of life and their relationships within the family that, he feared, would reflect the retarding effect of rural living and the rural lifestyle. Inquiries, he argued, should therefore be made "concerning home, school, and vocational adaptations and opportunities in rural places." The role of researchers and practical "technical" experts was to be examined in the "resources for voluntary social work and leadership." The local population's resistance to being reformed was to be studied by investigating the "attitudes toward social work and cooperation" among the rural poor. Rural southern families were to be compared with standard cases. The quality of leadership and potential for cooperation from local officials were to be assessed with reference to the superintendents of schools, superintendents of public welfare, county boards of public health, and local charities. The Memorial hoped not only to study the history and present state of rural groups but also to find the best way to intervene though visiting teachers, public health nurses, social workers, assistants to county officials, and county-wide home and farm demonstration agents. The family, and especially the mother, was identified as an important subject of interest. The purpose was to understand the relationship among undernourishment in the home, poor schoolwork, and misbehavior. Once understood, caregivers could be taught how to intervene to change the outcomes. County agents as well as school teachers were trained in counseling so that young people could be directed toward vocations that matched their mental health and aptitude in order to prevent juvenile delinquency and other types of "backward" behavior. The organization of activities was on a countywide basis. That offered the opportunity to use a casework approach to supervision with detailed record keeping for research purposes. The most "backward" regions were targeted. In some cases, county casework could be consolidated and special consideration paid to developing ways to "interpret public welfare to countywide groups and especially to county commissioners and members of the boards of education."[14]

These prescriptions for research and action paralleled and borrowed from Rockefeller work in the General Education Board, Bureau for the

Eradication of Hookworm Disease in the Southern States, Bureau of Social Hygiene, and other public health and mental hygiene projects of Rockefeller related philanthropy from the early decades of the twentieth century. The poor white population of tenant farmers was of special interest in the general education campaign. At the same time, African Americans were identified as a population that did not need general education as much as they needed vocational skill work, industrial social work, and adult teaching. The role of the state in relationship to county government was to be explored and the isolation of the special geographic settings was offset by demonstrations that catered to their needs in the "mountain areas" and "East Carolina sandhills."[15] Research and demonstrations were conducted in the 1920s and 1930s, and findings were disseminated through *Child Development Abstracts*.

The Society for the Study of Child Development (SSCD) was established as a subgroup of the National Research Council in 1934. In preparation for launching the SSCD the dissemination and control of research on children was rethought and made more accountable. The purpose of the *Abstracts* was to classify research and to eliminate unscientific studies or those that did not meet the social science standards imposed by members of the council.[16] This highly successful endeavor explains in part the consistency of the orientation of educational research. When the Memorial was folded into the Rockefeller Foundation and General Education Board in the 1929 reorganization of the Rockefeller philanthropies, funding sources had to be renegotiated. Given the pressure at the onset of the Great Depression, philanthropic support for research was essential for the continuance of programs supported by the Society for the Study of Child Development from 1934 to 1948 when it became an autonomous organization.[17]

Educational Research on Children: Social Efficiency and Social Control

As Viviana Zelizer observed, children went from being useful as laborers to being useless in terms of income contributions but also "priceless" in terms of their social value at the turn of the century.[18] Only after child labor was made legally irrelevant to the organization of society were children considered important enough to be insured by policies against their injury or loss.[19] The pricelessness was also a class phenomenon. Newly emergent professionals validated bourgeois class values as authoritative normative standards to be applied universally to the working classes and under classes as well as to immigrants. The enactment of laws that prohibited and regulated child labor coincided with enactment and enforcement of compulsory school attendance laws and specialized institutions associated with courts, schools, and clinics that were invented to shape, nurture and develop what was increasingly defined as the potential of the young and their value to society as a properly socialized adult-citizen and worker. As the child was viewed not as a child but also as a future adult, the view of the desired future adult influenced how the child was to be educated and socialized. Various disciplines in the social and behavioral sciences were professionalized through the application of scientific methods in building a knowledge base to guide the education and socialization of children. The effort to apply science to social problems was supported by liberal elites and social activists in a variety of social movements associated with progressivism, social efficiency, the social gospel, mental hygiene, and child study movements. Child development research and parent training received massive support from large-scale philanthropy in the formative stages of the welfare state's expansion,[20]

UNIVERSITY BASED RESEARCH IN THE INTER-WAR PERIOD

While the Laura Spelman Rockefeller Memorial supported a variety of university-based research projects associated with scientific child-study in the United States and Canada, two university-based programs represent models for intervention in addressing cultural lag: The Iowa Child Welfare Research Station and Teachers College, Columbia University, Child Study Institute. The problems of the rural child and the urban child were the focus of attention. As Memorial policy was being established in the 1920s, Ruml and Frank, especially Frank, began to investigate and support experiments with various models for applying research to interventions in the field. The Monmouth County Organization for Social Service was awarded $75,000 for three years to supplement the program it had initiated in 1912. It was originally supported by the Russell Sage Foundation and the Commonwealth Fund under the auspices of the National Committee for Mental Hygiene and other local voluntary groups. By the end of 1923, its work was extended with Memorial assistance. That allowed the addition to the staff of the child-study supervisor, visiting teacher, a parole officer, a family social work office, and a rural nurse's office. Activities for children were arranged through the Boy Scouts. Three clinics were established in baby welfare, child guidance, and for the treatment of tuberculosis. [21] When the Commonwealth Fund and National Committee for Mental Hygiene decided to continue to emphasize the child guidance aspect of the Monmouth County project, the Memorial decided to follow up on the healthy child development aspects that they preferred. Iowa was the site chosen to follow up on the work of the Monmouth County group with investigations of the degree to which the conditions of rural life lagged behind the general population and what could be done to provide for the improvement of environmental deficits. New York became the site to further the prospects of the largely urban constituency of the Federation for Child Study. The State University of Iowa was the first to receive Memorial funds, and Teachers College, Columbia University the second.

Iowa Child Welfare Research Station

After a sixteen-year statewide campaign lead by Cory Bussey Hillis, the Iowa Child Welfare Research Station was approved by the Iowa State legislature on 21 April 1917. The Station received widespread support from local and national groups that ranged from the progressive child-study movement, to segments of the eugenics movement that pressed for competitions at state fairs for the genetic classification of families in order to stock the future with "fitter families" and "better babies."[22] The legislative mandate for the Station sounded much like the policy the LSRM was to later follow. It included: "the investigation of the best scientific methods of conserving and developing the normal child, the dissemination of the information acquired by such investigations and the training of students for work in such fields.[23] Hillis' original rationale for the Station reflected progressive concern with reform and social improvement. The work was conceived as "on-going" rather than short term: "The very putting of anything into effect in child life is analogous to a great engineering project calling for up-to-date, unique information at every point." In a later assessment of the Station's work the second director, George D. Stoddard, concurred with Hillis that "child research, like medical research, cannot be envisaged as complete at any fixed future time." The result of not pursuing continuous improvement would be dire. "The optimum child in the best environment is something not attained, but pushed forward to. To relax the mighty controls over conditions, causes, and events which research can harness would be to risk another dark age."[24]

The Station's work was unique in that it did not focus on investigating "laggards" or "defective feebleminded" children. Its purpose was to "develop and to correlate the fundamental research material available on the problems centered around the conservation and development of normal and superior children." The original departments included research on heredity and human genetics, physical development, nutrition, preventive medicine, child psychology, child sociology, education, and morals. Bird T. Baldwin, a Harvard trained psychologist, the first director of the Station, measured the growth of children through anthropometry and mental testing. The Station from its origin sought to establish relationships with the medical and dental schools, public health nursing, the speech department, the law school, and the college of education.[25]

By 1920, Baldwin was seeking support for the Station from the Laura Spelman Rockefeller Memorial in order to expand the Station's research program. Baldwin wrote to the early officers of the Memorial to explain the Station's work and to request an "appropriation sufficient to make the work of this Research Station more effective as a national central laboratory which will furnish scientific data for various parts of the world." Baldwin argued that: "Little of permanent value for a dependable science of child rearing can be accomplished through the scattered efforts now in practice."[26] Three years later, when Beardsley Ruml became the Memorial's director, the University of Iowa was granted the first of several large grants for its pioneering program.[27] It can be argued that the Iowa Station also influenced Ruml's and Frank's views of what research devoted to the welfare of women and children could accomplish.

The first appropriation for $124,000 was to be used over two years for an experiment in using state educational institutions to carry out child study-parent training extension work similar to the Monmouth County program on the problems of rural children. In May 1923, plans were underway for "our new investigation of the rural child of Iowa."[28] A month later a group of educators, social workers, and State University of Iowa personnel set out to find appropriate research sites. The team was interested in systematically uncovering the factors that influenced the physical, mental, educational, and social development of children in rural settings.

The team's main question was: Were rural children's "endowments, ambitions and opportunities" limited by the physical conditions of their homes, communities, and schools? The team observed that conditions varied dramatically not only between urban and rural settings but also within the rural settings. Two representative districts fifty miles apart in East Central Iowa were chosen as ideal typical models of the variation among rural environments. The districts had similar characteristics: fertile land, a primary crop of corn with hay and grain secondary, and a great number of hogs and cattle. Railroads had gone through after the Civil War, but transportation remained difficult over country roads. Several additional districts with similar characteristics were selected in 1926 and compared with the findings gathered in the first two years of intensive research between 1923 and 1925. The first district, Homeland Township, represented the "average rural" community dominated by one-room schools. The second township, Cedar Creek, represented the more sophisticated type of community. It had consolidated its one-room schools into two-story modern schools.[29] The team collected historical data on the communities; did a geographical analysis; examined schooling, religion, and social life; and economic conditions. They also assessed the character of the interactions between family members and the community. They evaluated the nutrition of the children and assessed maternal and infant hygiene in the homes. Children were given medical and dental exams, and, if needed, treatment. Psychiatric and behavior problems were also recorded. Anthropomorphic measurements were taken and a battery of psychological tests and achievement tests were administered. The measurements were used to compare the development of rural and city children.

Rural Childhood in Homeland: A Study of Dysfunction

In the final report Homeland was portrayed as a dreadful example of the processes and outcomes of cultural lag. In spite of the rhetoric about producing a scientific and objective evaluation, the conclusions tended to bear out the researchers' hypothesis that fearful living conditions, low expectations, limited opportunities, and backward attitudes created a situation that was not only dangerous for the mental, physical, and social health of the children but also for the family unit and community. The tacit assumptions about cultural lag, social class, and cultural biases on the part of the researchers were evident in their analysis.[30]

Homeland was a community populated largely by the descendents of German immigrants from Wisconsin, Illinois, Indiana, and Ohio. Many had limited proficiency in English. Limited language skills and the isolated setting and poor roads cut off outside influences in the lives of parents especially the mothers. Mothers engaged in hard farm labor and had little time to spend with their children and tend to their basic needs. They fed their children what the researchers considered to be "inappropriate food" at "inappropriate times." Out of ignorance, they denied their children basic health.[31] Mothers had few opportunities to learn habits different from their German heritage or, due to their isolation, to profit from others' experiences. Researchers also found that the mothers rejected help even when it was offered, whether in the form of medical and dental care for their children or the opportunity to form child study groups to learn ways consistent with the ideals of the Child Welfare Station.[32] Most mothers, for example, did not provide their children with toys or learning materials that would stimulate their otherwise "hidden" talents or abilities. Mothers also typically did not tend to talk to their children in ways researchers thought appropriate or in ways that would stimulate language development. In the case of a fifteen-year old girl, Ida, this resulted in a "weak "s" lisp, nasality, general indistinctness of articulation, non-standard sound usage, and provincial, illiterate pronunciation." This could have been part of the child's German accent or a local dialect. Researchers found her mental abilities also suffered and her interests "lay in the practical rather than the academic fields." Her intelligence quotient and educational quotient were measured as 82, or low normal, on standardized tests. Her brother, Hans, was similarly described as having a "drab personality" that matched his "mediocrity of intelligence and educational ability."[33] This immigrant family, praised for its hard work and relative financial success, was criticized as "handicapped by a lack of appreciation of culture, ignorant of the need for the education of their children, and with instinctive but unintelligent interest in their children's health." The researchers asked: "whether the low rating of the children was the result of impoverished cultural opportunities, or whether these children and their parents had minds that were accustomed to functioning only in material realms."[34]

Houses and out buildings in Homeland were described as run down, unpainted, and gloomy. Homes were declared to be largely poorly or impractically furnished, and the yards as littered and uncared for. Homeland was the place to find dysfunctional families. Religious expression and the history of the community's churches experienced sectarian confrontations and schisms that caused the loss of religious fervor. Two isolated groups had formed as a result of quarreling that resulted in lingering bitterness among neighbors and that led to a "breach" between "maturity and youth." The "self-contained spirituality of the older generation" did not facilitate an understanding of the "ideals of adolescence." The adolescents appeared to be more advanced than their elders but they were held back by the collective mentality and their family's practices. Consequently, the "revolts of adolescent idealism were apt to languish into spiritual indifference." Sources of creativity and progress rather than being tapped as energy for regeneration became mechanisms that were psychologically damaging to personality development that led to further regression in the community. There were few active community organization—The Women's Christian Temperance Union and the Farm Bureau—but they were not strong enough to halt the regression. The Farm Bureau did provide a Boy's Club and a Girl's Club. The churches, described as poorly constructed and plain, provided Sunday Schools for young children. There were few community events to stimulate the intellect and imagination. The community lacked fairs, plays, parades, and other community celebrations. The "social attitudes" of the community members were marked by class biases and isolation. The researchers rated the community as indifferent to new arrivals rather than helpful. That was a reflection of how quarrelsome they were with each other.

There was little opportunity for an education in Homeland. Schooling was a low priority among the hard working parents. The first schools were built of logs and taught by anyone who could read, write, and do arithmetic. The school year lasted for only a few months. The first school buildings with frame construction were built in the 1860s, and a high school was built in 1871. The schools remained largely at the same level for the next thirty years with poor facilities and low salaries for teachers. The slow increase in the number of months designated for the school year was reduced from nine to seven and a half in 1911 to save money. A county institute for teachers was established in 1873. Between 1918 and 1926 the district schools were still staffed by underpaid, poorly educated, "incompetent, and inexperienced" teachers. Types of "ineffective teachers" were described as those who were "capable neither in intelligence nor training [and who also] tended to shift from place to place." The children were "rowdy and ill mannered and obviously formed habits of slovenliness and indolence." Another type of teacher was "not stupid" but was merely "putting in time." One teacher was described as "bored," and her classrooms consisted of routine with "no inspiration" to the pupils.[35] The researchers basically complained that there were "no progressive tendencies" in the Homeland District. Manual training and domestic science classes were voted down twenty-two to one in 1916 by the school board. Between 1913 and 1927 eighty-seven percent of the eighteen to twenty-two year olds completed the eighth grade, but only fifty-six percent went on to high school and of those forty-one percent were graduated and eighteen percent went on to college. Only thirty-one percent of the parents thought that high school was important and five percent believed it was reasonable for their children to go to school as "far as they wished." The Homeland situation appeared hopeless to the research team for the parents, teachers, schools, and community organizations did not want outside help and were suspicious of the researchers and their project. Parent education and other intervention mechanisms appeared to be necessary but next to impossible to introduce and implement.

Cedar Creek Childhood: A Study of Potential in a Rural Setting

The other district, Cedar Creek, while lagging behind the urban child, in the researchers' view, offered hope that with intervention rural communities could become progressive. Cedar Creek was settled slightly earlier than Homeland and by a different ethnic population. The ethnic and cultural differences between the two communities were cited as a possible explanation for the dramatic differences that the researchers found.[36] The dramatic difference in the interpretation of the two populations may also be an indicator of the underlying biases of the researchers. Cedar Creek was dominated by a Danish population divided between two groups of Friends (Quakers), one more conservative than the other, and two Protestant sects. In spite of their religious differences, the groups got along well and cooperated with each. The churches were not only places of worship but also served as community centers that encouraged family gatherings among neighbors and, according to the researchers, enlisted the energy and enthusiasm of the young. The plentiful social groups and recreation activities organized by the churches left little time for prolonged conflicts and jealousies. Children were likely to be supplied with toys and equipment deemed appropriate by the research team. Community recreation included movies, plays, and pageants. Even if not at the same rate as urban areas, the Cedar Creek community built public parks with sand piles and slides for children. Toys and other educational apparatus were not plentiful in the home, but the children benefited from their rural setting and often kept pets and found other rural sources of amusement.

Some children tested below normal educationally and in intelligence, but most tested as normal; and some had superior scores on standardized tests. The below normal children were described as from families that suffered from poverty, the death of a parent, or isolation from the community's religious and social life. Families that used the community's resources prospered compared to Homeland families but not as well as families from urban areas. That confirmed the researchers' preconceived expectations. For example, Hannah, a nine-year old girl from a family with a large number of social contacts in the community through clubs and the church, had an IQ of 100 and an educational score of ninety-eight. Her "physical defects" included "swollen glands, carious teeth, and speech defects." Yet, she wanted to attend college to become a teacher and "see things." Her thirteen-year old sister, Nell, had similar "defects" but managed to score slightly higher on the intelligence and educational tests. Nell was described as "alert, capable ... and equally willing and efficient." She "owned a pony, a calf, and some chickens" and could "milk cows, sew, ride horseback, and play basketball." This family had some advantages over other families in Cedar Creek. The father had returned for a visit to Denmark and brought Nell with him. In spite of this advantage and experience, Nell's ambitions were low. She wanted to "finish high school" but her only desire was to "become a housemaid." A few farm children from religious, hardworking families where education was valued were described as having superior intelligence and aptitude for education. Faith and Lewis, at twelve and thirteen respectively, had IQ scores of 130 and 131. Except for poor teeth, they suffered from no physical. The family was unique in that the father had a year of college and took a keen interest in civil and social affairs in the community. He kept a library of two hundred books and received one weekly and three daily newspapers. The children were given opportunities to listen to the phonograph and radio. This family was used as evidence that rural children can prosper if given stimulation and if their parents were willing to seek "broader educational opportunities than the [local schools and communities] afforded."[37]

Cedar Creek schools could not match the sophistication of urban schools but in their quality of curriculum, content and history were far superior to Homeland schools. The Friends built a private scripture school in the 1850s and upgraded it to a brick structure ten years later. They later transferred to the public. In 1867 a two-story seminary was added, and a second seminary was built in 1890. The elementary school and the high school were originally housed in the same building, but in 1920 a separate six-room high school was built. It was not then unusual for consolidated schools to consist of two buildings that contained a library, laboratories for domestic science and physics, a gymnasium, and an auditorium. While Homeland complained of spending $900 on a building and only reluctantly added schools, Cedar Creek had forty-four consolidated school buildings, two of which cost $2000 each. There was strong support for schools. Ninety-seven percent of the eighteen to twenty-two year olds completed the eighth grade. Eighty-eight percent entered high school, and eighty-two percent were graduated. Thirty-eight percent went on to attend college. Five percent of Homeland's parents felt that children should "go as far as they want in school," and twenty percent of Cedar Creek's parents felt the same way. Seventy of the Cedar Creek residents felt that limiting a child's access to high school was not acceptable.

Parent Education Research: Popularizing Findings

Baldwin wanted to find ways to disseminate the team's research on rural children. As early as 1923, he suggested that funds be secured to develop a "Syllabus of Child Welfare and Child Development for Parent Teacher Associations."[38] The syllabus concept was not immediately acted on, for the research on the rural family was at the top of the Stations agenda. Clearly, the logical next step in the Memorial's work was figuring out how to reach out to parents and to change their habits and lifestyle to conform to the ideals identified by the researchers. Parent education became a focus that paralleled research into child development, family life, school and home contexts. Lawrence K. Frank began parent education by interviewing key figures and officers of organizations likely to cooperate with Memorial efforts to disseminate information and to regularize the services that the Iowa Station's rural study provided. Frank talked to the superintendents of education, kindergarten supervisors, and the superintendent of the public health nurses association. He included the presidents and officers of the American Association of University Women (AAUW), Parent Teachers Association (PTA), and the Child Welfare Division of the Women's Christian Temperance Union. He argued that it was important to use non-university personnel as point people in setting up mechanisms to disseminate child welfare research to the public through parent education programs. "We want cities to feel this is a city project to be adopted by the city as soon as possible and that it must not be advertised as a university project," he declared.[39]

Notwithstanding Frank's views, the university-based Child Welfare Research Station maintained considerable supervisory control over parent training projects. By July 1925 it had nineteen study centers in the state. Enrollment in the centers was not limited to Iowans. The Iowa centers trained people from fifteen states, Canada, and forty-seven other universities.[40] The university researchers communicated their progress on their rural child research to Ruml and Frank. A Laboratory for Child Development and Parent Training was built at the university in 1925. There the researches studied the problems of parent training and also provided instruction in the "best methods for the care and training of young children."[41] In 1925, the University Extension Division in cooperation with the Station began to promote the study of children by parents. In this endeavor, the Station and the Extension presented "simple, scientific" facts and procedures to parents "of the whole life of a little child...then the problems which parents may bring." In 1926, meetings were organized to integrate the State Council for Child Study with Parent Education Institutions. A major objective of the meetings was to have the state support the university's budget for parent education and to increase the cooperation and coordination among the various groups interested in and responsible for disseminating parent education knowledge to the public. Dissemination included the creation of exhibits at state and with other related organizations such as the American Home Congress and Farmers Institutes. It was hoped that these groups would exchange speakers, study outlines, and other materials for conferences and short courses.[42]

The Laura Spelman Rockefeller Memorial awarded the State University of Iowa a total of $646,000 for child study and parent training. That support enabled the Child Welfare Research Station to enter its second decade.[43] The research on the rural child, child development, and parent education produced an enormous amount of material that eventually resulted in major publications. The final report for the study of rural children was published after Baldwin's death.[44] It was written by Baldwin's colleagues, Eva Fillmore and Lora Hadly under the auspices of the Memorial. Fillmore was responsible for the material on the mental and educational testing; and Hadly was responsible for the material on the clinic and the fieldwork. It was published as, *Farm Children: An Investigation of Rural Child Life in Selected Areas of Iowa*, in 1930.[45]

Studying the Urban Child and Cultural Lag

One of the earliest projects studied by Ruml and Frank and subsequently supported by the Memorial over three years with $124,000 was the Federation for Child Study (later changed to the Child Study Association of America). Originally organized in 1888 by Felix Adler with five women including his wife, by 1923 it had 1,500 members. Two-thirds of the members lived in New York; the other third came from other cities in the United States and Canada. Unlike the Monmouth County Organization for Social Service, it concentrated on urban problems and urban children. Organized into chapters, the Federation's purpose was to "provide an opportunity for parents to study the mental, physical, and psychological needs of children; and to teach parents to utilize this knowledge in bringing up their children." The rationalization of parenting included improving the mother's ability to substitute: "impulse and inertia for purpose; uncritical opinion for enlightened opinion and knowledge, and friction and antagonism for sympathy."[46] Parents taught other parents and the older groups assumed leadership responsibilities for the training. Subjects of study included: "emotional aspects of discipline; emotional aspects of habit formation; sex differences in education; motherhood and other activities; customs versus standards; religion and the life of a child; behavior problems in relation to personality; and, the arts in the life of a child."[47] The Federation, as part of the early child study movement, crossed between charitable voluntary work and the growing field of professionals. Mrs. Howard Gans (Bird Stein Gans) and Mrs. Sidonie M. Gruenberg, president and director respectively, became well-known authorities. The advisory board included academics such as John Dewey, psychologists Edward L. Thorndike and Patty Smith Hill, and sociologist Frank Giddens. The Memorial followed four paths in building on the work of the Federation. First, the "materials for child study groups," that had been developed by the Federation were to be "syndicated and furnished to all [relevant] magazines and journals,"as well as other organizations such as the American Association of University Women, American Child Health Association, the bulletins of the National Congress of Mothers, Parent Teachers Associations, and National Federation of Day Nurseries. Second, plans were developed for undergraduate and post-graduate as a semi-professional course to prepare participants to serve to serve as consultants. Teachers College, Columbia University in New York was chosen as the location for the degree programs, and Dean James E. Russell agreed to assist in developing the programs. Third, institutes were planned for the intensive training of leaders. Fourth, consulting and advisory services were developed to assist and cooperate with other organizations affiliated with Lawrence K. Frank and the Memorial's child study and parent education network.[48]

Urban Child Research at Teachers College, Columbia University

Between 1922-1923, Beardsley Ruml corresponded with Otis W. Caldwell, director of Teacher College's Lincoln School. Ruml was interested in Caldwell's investigation of children and parents and the relation between home life and school that was conducted with the Parents Association. Edward L. Thorndike joined the project and administered psychological tests to the students at Lincoln School and the Horace Mann School that was also affiliated with Teachers College.[49] A research proposal to study the "effectiveness of the school, home, and community relationships which contribute to the welfare of children in a certain type of community" was submitted. The research question was "whether [urban] children generally were getting an even break, or whether they were failing in school, losing health, turning delinquent, and otherwise being handicapped because neither the school, home, nor community generally were really helping them."[50] The study was designed to provide information about the "problem of child welfare" in a large urban center and to determine the degree to which urban children were or were not held back by inner city conditions just as rural children were held back by the conditions in isolated communities. On April 4, 1923, an initial grant of $6,750 to begin the research for a fifteen-month period was awarded to Teachers College.[51]

The final report indicated that the lives of inner city children were indeed breaking down. Over four hundred homes in the Upper West Side of Manhattan around Harlem as well as schools and community agencies were visited. The final analysis cited "physical defects, over agedness or school retardation" and the absence of any purpose or real ambition in the lives of the children. The children's "extremely limited knowledge of intellectual and other interests" was cited as the primary cause of their subnormal academic performance. The second factor for backwardness was cited as the character of the homes. The report identified "broken homes" as a source of dysfunction.[52] Without specifically acknowledging the role of social class or ethnicity, menial occupations such as janitorial services were singled out as troublesome for a child's progress. "Broken homes," it was stated, did not provide proper supervision and lacked the "essentials for wholesome living." When tested, the "children of janitors" were found to be mentally abnormal. The children of twenty-nine out of thirty-five families headed by janitors scored below average on standardized intelligence tests. The report cited as the third factor, the lack of community support facilities for either recreation or basic services for health. Finally, the report cited the lack of integrated services in the community.[53]

The Memorial's officers, Beardsley Ruml, Lawrence K. Frank, and new officer Arthur Woods, were not pleased with the report. Their displeasure was not because the research found cultural lag among the urban poor, but because the study did not correlate the four causal factors it identified with individual personality and performance differences. Ruml, Frank, and Wood believed that the report neither contributed to child development research nor considered the application of such research to parent education or teacher training. The "child and his personality, which embraces his health and emotional make up, his mental capacity, his range of interests and so on" were not addressed properly. According to Arthur Woods: "If children came to the schools in health, with wholesome personalities and with a general capacity for carrying on the work expected of them, then it is probable that the school situation and its influence on the lives of the children would be considerably different.... But just because children come physically handicapped, with distorted and warped personalities and with varying mental abilities" tells little of the sources of such warping. The answer, Woods offered, was in the obsolescent parenting traditions that created personality distress that was reflected in dysfunctional institutions both in the family and community. Poor inner city families were in trouble because their personalities had not kept pace with the rapid change of modern urban life. If such parents had been able to meet the "new and shifting economic and social conditions," they would not be poor janitors with dysfunctional children. The issue the report and its critics sidestepped with their individualistic therapeutic orientation was the social structural effects a changing economy had on personality and one's rather life chances. Woods concluded that: "The traditional methods of living and child caring are plainly breaking down in city life." The problem faced by investigators was that "the home cannot do the things which are expected of it in the way of care and guidance of children because the parents themselves are baffled by the task of child care and too much preoccupied with the difficulties of living in a big city to know what they should do for children."[54]

A second study was undertaken under Caldwell's direction. Two groups of forty-eight boys from the seventh and eighth grades were compared for intelligence, school accomplishment, school retardation, out of school activities, reading, movies, occupations of the parents, financial status, social status, family size, and parental attitudes toward strictness and school success. The boys were divided between those who participated in school organizations and a random sample. Little difference was found between the groups. It was concluded that children with established habits that fit into the school's expectations did well and children whose habits did not fit were at odds with the school. These sociological, rather than psychological, conclusions related more to needed structural changes in the organization of schools to accommodate unmotivated children from different backgrounds through the adjustment of classrooms and creation of different types of clubs. Memorial staff were displeased and dismissed the conclusions as obvious to anyone "in general acquaintance with the school situation in New York and the social life among children." The main disappointment was that the study again failed to explore the sources of personality differences that caused subnormal performance. The parental data that were gathered were inadequate. They neither provided an answer as to how differences in parenting habits contributed to dysfunctional personality formation nor did they identify the sources of normal personality formation.[55] Additional funds were not granted to the study series because it did not conform to the individualistic mental hygiene approach to social problem solving that employed a model of disease and health that maintained that prevention and cure had a psychobiological foundation. Research suggested alternative causation for social and school problems with inner city children, but Memorial officers held on to the original premise that a great need existed for research in personality and culture in the inner city.

PARENT EDUCATION AND THE INSTITUTE FOR CHILD WELFARE

The Memorial staff was prepared to provide funds to support major research within the boundaries of their own understanding of what it meant to conduct educational research that was useful and pointed to practical solutions. In 1924, the Memorial awarded $830,000 for parent education research carried out by the Federation for Child Study, Monmouth County Social Services, the Cooperative Education Association of Virginia, the Maternity Center Association of Brooklyn, *Better Homes* (that later became *Better Homes and Gardens*), the American Association of University Women, and Teachers College, Columbia University.[56]

On February 2, 1924, Frank wrote a memorandum that explained the need for an Institute of Child Research at Teachers College. It was to centralize records, provide a continuous study and investigation of the work of child welfare organizations, and study what gave "rise to such studies and the trends in child life." Child behavior would be studied through experimental studies in the laboratory and through fieldwork. The proposed Institute's work would be different from those concerned with child welfare activities. Demonstrations of best practices were to provide a laboratory setting for the "collection, review, and adjustment of literature on child life including the collection of experimental results and other materials needed for the parent training program and for any future periodical for parents." The project should be "pushed this spring as rapidly as possible," Frank concluded.[57] A short time later the Memorial awarded a five-year $250,000 grant for a "Special Study of Child Welfare in a Typical Community in New York." To establish an Institute of Child Welfare at Teachers College, a board of scientific directors was chosen to meet with Teachers College Dean James Russell. The board consisted of New York philanthropic child organization and academic elites: Mary Arnold, the executive secretary of the Children's Welfare Federation; Bess V. Cunningham, secretary of Child Welfare Research at Teachers College; Ella Crandall, associate general executive of the American Child Health Association; Charles DeForest, secretary for Moral Education of the National Child Welfare Association; Maurice Bigelow, director of the School of Practical Arts at Teachers College; Professor Frederick Bonser in Elementary and Practical Arts at Teachers College; and Otis Caldwell, director of Lincoln School. Edward L. Thorndike was "closely connected with the new research" and was expected to carry on with his previous measurement work with students at Lincoln School and in the Horace Mann School.[58] An additional $14,500 was devoted to fellowships to "bring promising young women to Teachers College for a year's training in methods of child care and parent education." An additional $10,000 was provided for a community study by Teachers College. Hope Farm, a residential "child caring institution," was awarded a five-year $57,000 grant so that its facilities would be available to Teachers College for research purposes. This created the "hands on" social laboratory educational researchers needed if they were to acquire a knowledge base on personality and culture that would be useful in parent training. The Federation for Child Study was to cooperate with the Teachers College Institute in collecting, editing, and rewriting publications and case studies bearing on child growth and personality development. Funds invested in

Teachers College for all these purposes related to child-study and parent education totaled $1,160,000.[59]

Funding for the Institute for Child Welfare was approved in June 1925. Plans for studies of preschool children and non-academic phases of school life were immediately undertaken. An educational clinic for gathering research material was opened in cooperation with the Manhattanville Day Nursery. By October, two nursery schools were opened in Speyer Hall. Under the direction of Lois Hayden Meek, the Institute for Child Welfare Research (the name was later changed to the Child Development Institute in 1929) became the major center for research on the family and childhood, the preparation of professionals for parent education, and, the preparation of materials for national and international distribution. Facilities for research, service, and instruction were organized and coordinated with city agencies. The Institute emphasized observational and participatory research in accordance with the idea that the social scientist must be in contact with the subject matter.[60] The laboratory for child development research and parent training was in the nursery school. Demonstrations were held at the Hope Farm's residential facilities as well as in laboratories and clinical settings where mental testing, studies of "emotions, tests of problem solving, imagination, and other aspects of mental development," were pursued and where anthropomorphic measurements on growth and health, and other statistic on nutrition, and respiration were collected.[61] The gathering of material for parent education was a goal that went back to the request from the Federation for Child Study. From the earliest discussions of the Institute mention was made of the need to establish a magazine for parents that would grow "naturally out of this juvenile research." In the effort to develop knowledge through educational research the Memorial program was closely associated with the parallel effort to establish other applied social science disciplines, especially those related to psychology and sociology as well as teacher training. The National Research Council and the Social Science Research Council were supported and used by Rockefeller related philanthropies to monitor the progress of disciplines associated with parent education. They also monitored the dissemination of literature.

The common purpose of the various studies was to identify methods of child rearing that would promote normal and superior development. The laboratory school settings allowed for both experimental methods and methods of controlled observation of spontaneous behaviors in children. This was adapted so that quantitative measures could be made on such elusive data as the growth of a children's concepts, information, imagination, make-believe, reasoning as revealed in play and their choice of play objects. Language patterns were also investigated. Emotional development was investigated by training parents to keep home records of child behaviors and through preschool experimental procedures. Interviews were conducted with parents and older siblings in an effort to make comprehensive studies of children's likes and dislikes, fears and hopes. Studies were conducted on laughter and crying, anger, jealousy, affection, and sympathy. These basic studies of individual children led to conclusions about social development that were universalized. Presumably, knowing the child thoroughly provided clues as to the source of normal adjustment and how to prepare children for productive lives. These studies attempted to trace the characteristics of children's behavior toward other children and adults. Observational data were collected on the how children initiated social contact and how they cooperated, or did not cooperate with each other and adults. They wanted to know how parents and teachers should respond if resistance and aggression overlapped with personal character traits and reactions.

The primary reason for attending to parent-child relationships was the desire to identify interventions that promised to be successful. That objective could not be effectively pursued unless researchers could secure the participation and cooperation of other agencies and voluntary groups that would provide the researchers access to homes that could be used as laboratories to study the outcome of various parental practices and techniques for dealing with children and how those practices were related to children's behavior and the subsequent development of their personalities. School practices and their effects on children were also studied.[62] To establish the most effective parental and pedagogical methods it was necessary to determine what the processes of normal development were at the various developmental stages. What skills should be most profoundly cultivated at what age levels? Are there premium ages that facilitate learning of various types such as the learning of language, music, and artistic ability? What was the relative importance of maturation, training, and the opportunity to learn? Was it possible that the lack of opportunity at certain maturational levels would limit future development? Answers to these question issued from the interest in and concern with cultural lag.

The assumption of virtually all the research questions was that there was a strong relationship among mental development, physical development, and social development. The need for data on parental practices related to children's health and growth produced detailed descriptions of feeding, digestion, and bowel movements, as well as the relationships among nutrition and behavior, disease and ability, and responses to external conditions such as the weather and temperature. Researchers did not overlook the architecture of buildings and homes and home furnishings. Their observations and analyses of the factors that appeared to enhance sound or normal physical development and mental development led them to make recommendations about various types of furniture, play materials, equipment, and clothing they saw as appropriate. What they learned from their studies of families was disseminated to inform practice through the classes they taught and their publications.

In 1932, a Family Consultation Bureau was established to offer a wide range of services to businesses in the attempt to improve child oriented merchandise before it reached the market. The Bureau produced a bulletin for both general and specialized audiences. Schools and child-care institutions were advised on how to introduce the most "modern methods of child guidance." This was done through lectures and a series of short courses. The Family Consultation Bureau received inquiries on a variety of subjects. Most were related to home management, housing, purchasing furniture, food, clothing, and household help. The second largest category of inquiries was related to child guidance, mental testing, special teachers, school and play groups, camps, and boarding facilities. The third largest category of inquiries was related to health, medical services, physical examinations, and nutrition. Family relationships and adult adjustments, family finance, and legal services were also subjects of the 930 consultations the Bureau managed during its first year. According to Frank, the Bureau was established "as a method whereby the Institute could study the problems of the home and family life with particular reference to child development, and could begin to train personnel for education with a fuller understanding of what home education and parent-child relationships mean to the growing personality."[63]

Institute records indicate that most of its students were professionals, but there were also a small number of homemakers. The Institute specialized in training professionals who would move on to other settings and train others. It also provided demonstrations for parents whose children were in the Institute nursery school programs. These parents were also offered individual consultations. Staff also met with parents in group meetings; and parents were allowed to participate as aids in the classroom. During the Great Depression, the tuition at the Institute—$150 to $400 depending on the program—is a clear indicator that the parents and children who participated in Institute programs were not from the lower classes.[64]

Courses in child development and parent education were offered for advanced graduate students. Many students were on fellowships from the Rockefeller philanthropies that assumed responsibility for the work of the Memorial when it was collapsed into the Rockefeller Foundation, General Education Board, and Spelman Fund of New York in 1929. Lawrence K. Frank followed Memorial projects into the Spelman Fund and subsequently into the General Education Board in the 1930s. The Spelman Fund of New York was established during the reorganization of the philanthropies. Its mission was to foster the development of the social sciences related to administration and professional training. Students enrolled in the Teachers College graduate program at the Institute could major in parent education and work either with parent groups or with individual parents in cooperation with the nursery schools or the Family Consultation Bureau. Additionally, the United Parents Association, Child Study Association, East Harlem Nursing and Health Center and other clinics in the New York area provided settings for clinical experience. Students whose fields were outside child development and parent education were also welcome. Relevant related fields included psychology, nutrition, sociology, education, teacher training, and supervision.[65]

Students enrolled in courses included medical students, historians, social workers, and students whose majors were as diverse as religious studies, modern language, and mathematics.[66] Graduates entered a wide variety of fields. The majority went into nursery school or primary school teaching, but there was a variety of educators who specialized in school administration, high school education, and rural education. Others pursued careers in nursing, home economics, child welfare work, mental hygiene, journalism, and mental measurements. Of the ninety-nine graduates surveyed in 1934, only fourteen were homemakers.[67]

CONCLUSIONS

As the annual assessments of the child development and parent education research projects supported by the Laura Spelman Rockefeller Memorial begun in the 1920s and continued by other Rockefeller philanthropies in 1930s researchers noted, even as the funding changed in the 1930s "there was no real beginning and no discernible end to the basic problems that revolved around the health, growth, behavior, and character of children." Progress was not achieved in any absolute sense. Yet, the need to assess the impact of educational research in this area, while important, is problematic. The Iowa Child Welfare Research Station estimated that it distributed 42,756 technical monographs, 898,738 popular bulletins and pamphlets, and 1,534,062 standards and test materials as of December 15, 1938. Director George D. Stoddard observed:

> It is difficult to appraise the effectiveness of the dissemination of information, or in the immediate service rendered in behalf of children. We have evidence of the need of families ... but we can think of no good way to evaluate the service.... We can only say in somewhat circular fashion that if our discoveries are real and our insights valuable, then to the extent that we can make them known to persons responsible for guiding the new generation, we shall have performed a credible service.

The researchers and pioneers affirmed their faith in progress through science by declaring: "I have more faith in our future than I have had at any period during the past ten years." Yet, they also recognized that the basic problems remained in that "the influence of home life upon the child is deep and sustained … many adults suffer disturbances of the personality that had beginnings in the impoverishments and frustrations of early home life." Cultural lag remained and the American dilemma remained. Problems were "inherent in any culture, they are of prime concern in a democracy that places high value upon self-realization and personal responsibility. The American child has to grow into his emotional and social stature; he cannot rely upon taboo, tradition, or the dictatorial word."[68] Speaking on the eve of World War II, Stoddard, in his expression of his belief in the future and the dilemmas of democracy and individual freedom established the ground work for a new transformation of modernism to so called post-modernism in the after World War II. Then research and the tensions between progress and the perceived forces of decadence were given expression in the post-war elaboration of adolescent culture.

Cultural lag, while no longer a common term today, remains a central concept in social criticism, popular rhetoric, and in the tacit frameworks used in educational research for purposes of accountability, standardization, social control, and legislation, for example, consider No Child Left Behind. The subjects given attention in the various forms of popular media—the breakdown of the American family, family values, the plight of poor and culturally different youth whether rural or urban, and the expressed questioning of the value and utility of traditional science, technology, and quantitative data—are grounded in the early attention given to cultural lag and, if not addressed, its possible consequences for the future of traditional American culture.

NOTES

1. Leonard Ayres. *Laggards in Our Schools: A Study of Retardation and Elimination in City School Systems* (New York: Charities Publications Committee, Russell Sage Foundation, 1909); Walter Hinds Page, *The Rebuilding of Old Commonwealths, Being Essays Toward the Training of the Forgotten Man in the Southern States.* (New York: Doubleday, Page Co., 1902).

2. Lawrence K. Frank,"Social Change and the Family," *Annual, American Academy of Political Science*, Vol. 160 (1932), pp. 94-102; Lawrence K. Frank "Discussion" in *Problems of Infancy and Childhood, Transactions of the Third Conference, March 7-8, 1949, New York* ed. Milton J. Senn (New York: Josiah Macy Jr. Foundation Publication, 1950); Lawrence K. Frank. *The Conduct of Sex: Biology and Ethics of Sex, Parenthood in Modern Life* (New York: William Morrow, 1961); Lawrence K. Frank. "Memorandum on Social Progress,"

January 16, 1924, L. K. Frank papers, Box 8, Folder "Leisure Time and Social Progress," Rockefeller Archive Center.

3. Beardsley Ruml. "Social Science" in *Director's Report, 1924-1925*, Laura Spelman Rockefeller Memorial (LSRM) II, Box 2, Folder 15, Rockefeller Archive Center.

4. *Ibid.*

5. *Ibid.*; Donald Fisher. *The Fundamental Development of the Social Sciences: Rockefeller Philanthropy and the Social Science Research Council* (Ann Arbor, Michigan: University of Michigan, 1996).

6. Beardsley Ruml. "Professional and Technical Training," *Director's Report, 1924-1925.*

7. Beardsley Ruml. "Child Study" *Director's Report. 1924-1925..*

8. Raymond B. Fosdick, Ernest M. Hopkins, and Arthur Woods. "Principles Governing the Memorial's Program in the Social Sciences" (Reference to a meeting appointing a committee to review the Memorial's program in social science and social technology, November 22, 1927) LSRM, III, Series 6, Box 63, Folder 678, Rockefeller Archive Center.

9. Hettie Harris to Lawrence K. Frank. December 4, 1924, Federation for Child Study Projects, 1924-1925, LSRM III, Series 5, Box 27, Folder 284 and 285. Rockefeller Archive Center.

10. See LSRM III, Series 5, Box 27, Folder 285. Rockefeller Archive Center.

11. Vernon Kellogg to Max Mason. November 21, 1929, LSRM III, Box 36, Folder 377. Rockefeller Archive Center.

12. *Ibid;* Ruml, "Special Committees," *Directors Report.*

13. Robert S. Woodsworth. December 30, 1924, "National Research Council Committee on Child Development;" "Announcement of National Fellowships in Child Development," circa 1926 for 1927-1928, LSRM III, Box 30, Folder 320; Committee on Child Development, September 1927, LSRM III, Box 30, Folder 321. Rockefeller Archive Center.

14. Harold Odum to Syndor H. Walker,.June 16, 1926. "The County Unit as a Basis for Social Work and Public Welfare in North Carolina," LSRM III, Series 3, Box 75, Folder 786. Rockefeller Archive Center.

15. *Ibid.*

16. George D. Stoddard to Lawrence K. Frank. April 13, 1933; Frank to Stoddard. April 21, 1933, General Education Board 930, Series 1, Subseries 3, Box 373, Folder 3893, Rockefeller Center Archives.

17. Alice B. Smuts. Science in the Service of Children, 1893-1935. (New Haven: Yale 2006; Alice B. Smuts, "The National Research Council on Child Development and the Founding of the Society for Research on Child Development" in eds. A. B. Smuts and H. W. Hagen, *History and Research in Child Development.* Monographs of the S.R.C.D., Serial No. 211, Nos. 4-5 (1985)).

18. Viviana Zelizer. *Pricing the Priceless Child: The Changing Social Value of Children* (New York: Basic Books, 1985).

19. *Ibid.*

20. Michael B. Katz. *In the Shadow of the Poor House: A Social History of Welfare in America* (New York: Basic, 1986), pp. 113-145.

21. Memorandum, "Confidential to Col. Woods on Activities of Seven Organizations assisted by the LSRM," March 1, 1926 LSRM III, Series 6, Box 63, Folder 678, Rockefeller Archive Center.

22. Ginalie Swaim. "Cory Bussey Hillis: Women of Vision," *The Palimpsest*, Vol. 60, No. 6 (1979); Henry L. Minton. "The Iowa Child Welfare Research Station and the 1940 Debate on Intelligence: Carrying on the Legacy of a Concerned Mother," *Journal of the History of Behavioral Sciences* Vol. 20 (April 1984), pp. 160-175; George D. Stoddard and Dorothy E. Bradbury. *Pioneering in Child Welfare: A History of the Iowa Child Welfare Research Station, 1917-1933* (Iowa City: University of Iowa Press, 1933); Hamilton Cravens. *Before Head Start* (Chapel Hill: University of North Carolina Press, 1993); Theresa R. Richardson. *The Century of the Child: The Mental Hygiene Movement and Social Policy in the United States and Canada* (Albany, New York: State University Press of New York, 1989), pp. 132-136.

23. State of Iowa, "Chapter 282. Iowa Child Welfare Research Station: An Act to Establish and Maintain the Iowa Child Welfare Research Station and Making An Appropriation Therefore," *Acts & Joint Resolutions Passed as the Regular Session Thirty-Seventh General Assembly of the State of Iowa*.

24. George D. Stoddard. *The Second Decade: A Review of the Activities of the Iowa Child Welfare Research Station, 1928-1938*, (University of Iowa Studies, New Series No. 366, February 1, 1939). Includes quotations from Stoddard and Bradbury, *Pioneering in Child Welfare* on Cory Bussey Hillis.

25. Bird T. Baldwin to Mr. Richardson, officer in the LSRM,"Memorandum on the need for expansion of the Iowa Child Welfare Research Station," LSRM Series 3, Box 40, folder 416, December 8, 1920, Rockefeller Archive Center.

26. *Ibid.*

27. Cravens, *Before Head Start.*

28. Bird T. Baldwin to Beardsley Ruml. May 2, 1923, LSRM Series 3, Box 40, Folder 417, Rockefeller Archive Center.

29. "Memorandum to Beardsley Ruml from Bird T. Baldwin," June 5, 1923; Beardsley Ruml to Bird T. Balddwin, June 9, 1923; Bird T. Baldwin to Beardsley Ruml, June 16, 1923, LSRM Series 3, Box 40, Folder 417, Rockefeller Archive Center.

30. Bird T. Baldwin, Eva Abigail Fillmore, and Lora Hadley. *Farm Children: An Investigation of Rural Life in Selected Areas of Iowa* (New York: Arno Press, 1972, original D. Appleton, 1930). The final report was published after Bird T. Baldwin's death, written by his colleagues under the auspices of the Memorial. Fillmore had headed the mental and educational testing and Hadley coordinated the clinics and fieldwork for the original study. "Memorandum on Rural Study," December 10, 1929, LSRM Series 3, Box 40, Folder 424. Rockefeller Archive Center.

31. *Ibid.*, p. 187

32. *Ibid.*, p. 137

33. *Ibid.*, pp. 128-129.

34. *Ibid.*

35. *Ibid.*, pp. 98-99

36. *Ibid.*, pp. 138-139.

37. *Ibid.*, pp. 132-133.
38. Bird T. Baldwin to Beardsley Ruml. June 5, 1923; Cory Bussey Hillis and Mrs. Isaac Lea, National Congress of Mothers and Parent Teachers Associations, to Bird T. Baldwin. June 6, 1923; Ruml to Baldwin. June 9, 1923, LSRM Series 3, Box 40, Folder 417. Rockefeller Archive Center.
39. L. K. Frank. "Memorandum of Interview, Child Study Work." March 2, 1925, LSRM Series 3, Box 40, Folder 418. Rockefeller Archive Center.
40. Ruth Haefner to Beardsley Ruml and L. K. Frank January 31, 1925; L. K. Frank to Bird T. Baldwin. November 11, 1925, LSRM Series 3, Box 40, Folder 418. Rockefeller Archive Center.
41. "Memorandum to the Laura Spelman Rockefeller Memorial, Subject: Laboratory for Child Development and Parent Training." January 29, 1925, LSRM Series 3, Box 40, Folder 418. Rockefeller Archive Center.
42. Bird T. Baldwin to L. K. Frank. December 28, 1926, LSRM Series 3, Box 40, Folder 419; "Significant Development in the State," April 1927, LSRM Series 3, Box 40, Folder 420. Rockefeller Archive Center.
43. University of Iowa, Extracts from the Report of the Work in Child Development and Parent Education of the Iowa Child Welfare Research Station submitted by Bird T. Baldwin for 1926-1927, LSRM Series 3, Box 40, Folder 422. Rockefeller Archive Center.
44. "Memorandum on Rural Study." December 10, 1929, LSRM Series 3, Box 40, Folder 424. Rockefeller Archive Center.
45. Bird T. Baldwin, Eva Abigail Fillmore and Lora Hadley. *Farm Children: An Investigation of Rural Child Life in Selected Areas of Iowa* (New York: D. Appleton,1930; Arno Reprint, 1972. Similar work resulting from Howard Odum's research was published by Nora Miller. *The Girl in the Rural Family* (Chapel Hill: University of North Carolina Press, 1935).
46. "Child Study and Parent Training, 1924, p. 5, LSRM Series 3, Box 30, Folder 315. Rockefeller Archive Center.
47. "Report, Federation for Child Study. April 18, 1923," LSRM Series 3, Box 28, Folder 289. Rockefeller Archive Center.
48. Lawrence K. Frank. "Memorandum of an Interview with Sidonie M. Gruenberg. November 27, 1923,' LSRM Series 3, Box 28, Folder 289. Rockefeller Archive Center.
49. Edward L. Thorndike to Beardsley Ruml. March 19, 1923; Ruml to Thorndike. March 21, 1923; Otis Caldwell to Arthur Woods. March 19, 1923; LSRM Series 3, Box 42, Folder 440; "Released by the Bureau of Educational Services." July 16, 1924, LSRM Series 3, Box 42, Folder 434. Rockefeller Archive Center.
50. "Comments on Mrs. Mossman's Report." February 1, 1925, LSRM Series 3, Box 42, Folder 440. Rockefeller Archive Center.
51. Beardsley Ruml to Otis Caldwell,.April 4, 1923, LSRM Series 3, Box 42, Folder 440. Rockefeller Center Archives.
52. The term "broken homes" at that time did not necessarily refer to divorce but indicated dysfunctional relationships that could be a result of the death, unemployability or under employability of family members.
53. Arthur Woods to Beardsley Ruml. "Memorandum for Mr. Ruml." February 25, 1925; Arthur Woods to Ruml, copy to Lawrence K. Frank, February 25,

1925; "Comments on Mrs. Mossman's Report," LSRM Series 3, Box 42, Folder 440. Rockefeller Archive Center.

54. *Ibid.*

55. "Memorandum on a Study of Children's Purposes," LSRM Series 3, Box 42, Folder 440. Rockefeller Archive Center.

56. Lawrence K. Frank."Memorandum, Institute of Child Research." February 2, 1924, LSRM Series 3, Box 42, Folder 434. Rockefeller Archive Center.

57. *Ibid.*

58. "Released by the Bureau of Social Services." July 16, 1924, LSRM Series 3, Box 42, Folder 434. Rockefeller Archive Center.

59. *Ibid.*

60. Lawrence K. Frank. "Memorandum of an Interview with Dean Russell." February 19, 1923, LSRM Series 3, Box 42, Folder 434. Rockefeller Center Archives.

61. "Child Development Institute, Teachers College, Columbia University." GEB Series 1, Subseries 3, Box 374, Folder 3905. Rockefeller Archive Center.

62. *Ibid.*

63. Lawrence K. Frank. "Interviews," October 25, 1932,. GEB 930, Series 1, Subseries 3, Box 374, Folder 3904. Rockefeller Archive Center.

64. Nursery Education in the Child Development Institute." GEB 930, Series 1, Subseries 3, Box 734, Folder 3904. Rockefeller Archive Center.

65. *Ibid.*

66. "Analysis of Students Enrolled in Major Courses." GEB 930, Series 1, Subseries 3, Box 734, Folder 3904. Rockefeller Archive Center.

67. "Analysis of Types of Positions Now Held by Previous Major Course Students." GEB 930, Series 1, Subseries 3, Box 734, Folder 3904. Rockefeller Archive Center.

68. George D. Stoddard. *"The Second Decade, A Review of the Activities of the Iowa Child Welfare Research Station, 1928-1938." University of Iowa Studies*, New Series, No. 366, (February 1, 1939).

PART V

THE POST-WORLD WAR II ERA

CHAPTER 13

EDUCATIONAL REFORM AND EDUCATIONAL RESEARCH IN THE POST-WORLD WAR II ERA

In the Post-World War II Era public education and the theories and practices on which it and the training of teachers were based came under scrutiny as the nation explored how to prosecute the Cold War. The longstanding question of how education and educational research related to the social science disciplines was renewed and vigorously considered. Psychologists who focused on the structure of knowledge and how knowledge was acquired briefly overshadowed those of an earlier time who had focused on either growth—on the mental, emotional, and physical growth and health of the child—or how knowledge of the laws of learning would improve teaching and student learning. Practitioners of the traditional academic disciplines were called upon to provide and to structure curriculum, the knowledge that was to be acquired by students. By the end of the 1950s, it was accepted that better, meaning pure or discipline-based, research was needed to improve public education.

Educational Research, the National Agenda, and Educational Reform:
A History, pp. 359–388
359

NEW MANDATES FOR PUBLIC EDUCATION

In the Post-World War II Era the nation's leaders realized that education and educational research were explicitly linked to many of the nation's objectives: national defense, civil rights, elimination of poverty, what was then characterized as the nation's race relations problem, and even economic recovery and development. As World War II was ending, public education was seen as having an importance it did not previously have. Public education was explicitly linked to the national interest, especially defense. After World War II and noticeably after *Sputnik*, public education was not merely a local concern but a national concern. Leaders such as James B. Conant then argued that the nation needed to identify and cultivate talented youth.[1]

When the Soviet Union launched *Sputnik* in October 1957, the Soviet's success in space rocketry was attributed to its superior educational system, and the apparent second place status of the United States in the space race was attributed to public schools that had strayed too far from the study of the academic disciplines. *Sputnik* gave instant credibility to those who had been complaining about the nation's schools. It convinced many leaders that the time had come to reform the nation's public schools so the nation could take the lead in the space race. Reform meant returning to a condition and set of practices critics believed existed when. Before the onset of the Great Depression, high school education was for the chosen few and before the influx of working class children. Educators were now directed to shift their focus from the programs they developed for first-generation students who a few decades earlier would not have been in high school to programs based on the academic disciplines for capable students so that they could advance to college and master advanced disciplines relevant to defense.

The federal government quickly adopted several measures to improve education and provided funds for their implementation. Traditional objections to federal involvement and support for public education became irrelevant[2] as the Congress enacted the National Defense Education Act (1958). Scholars from a variety of academic disciplines outside of education were recruited to revise and update curricula. Educators were given a new mission: excellence in education. For almost a decade, educational discussions focused on how to implement the recommendations for the comprehensive high school James B. Conant proposed in the *American High School Today* (1959) and how to revise curricula to emphasize the structure of knowledge that Jerome S. Bruner claimed was so essential in *The Process of Education* (1961). The claims of those who had earlier endorsed the Prosser Resolution—that the traditional high school was inappropriate for over half the nation's youth—were forgotten.[3]

SCHOOL EXPANSION

After World War II, youth had little choice but to attend high school. As Morris Janowitz so accurately observed, "the transformation and organization of the labor market under advanced industrialization restricted opportunities for youth and assigned a new role to the public schools." Before the Great Depression, "the socialization of youngsters from European immigrant families and of migrants from rural areas was in good measure accomplished through work experiences—part time and full time." After World War II, however, "high school graduation or its equivalent—not only in terms of social attitude, interpersonal competence, and maturity—[was] defined as a desirable and required goal, even for the lowest income groups."[4] After World War II, "actual work requirements, changed standards of employment and trade unions, [and] new legislation about minimum wages" required public schools to "accept responsibility for all youngsters who are not college bound until they develop levels of personal maturity sufficient for them to enter the labor market."

Educators had welcomed the consequent expansion of public education, for it seemed a true extension of equality of educational opportunity and what was tantamount to enforced compulsory attendance. The difficulty was that there was no widespread recognition that the schools were serving students who often were very different from those who had traditionally attended high school. According to Lawrence A. Cremin:

> ... compulsory attendance marked a new era in the history of American education. The crippled, the blind, the deaf, the sick, the slow-witted, and the needy arrived in growing numbers. Thousands of recalcitrants and incorrigibles who in former times might have dropped out of school now became public charges for a minimum period. And as the school-leaving age moved progressively upward, every problem was aggravated as youngsters, became bigger, stronger, more resourceful.[5]

Those who had previously dropped out of school to take jobs were all but forced to remain in school because there was no other place for them. What had once been a population seeking and exercising opportunity became, in large measure, a captive population. That captive population lost its opportunity to be independent (students do constitute a dependent class) and it often rebelled against its guardians. The social-economic structure and the social dynamics of public schooling were radically transformed. What was once opportunity became obligation. What was once choice became compulsory. There should be little wonder that attempts at school reform have been so unsatisfactory, for insufficient attention has been paid to how that transformation changed both the expectations of students, their parents, and teachers. As Cremin observed, "the dreams of the democratic idealists may have resided in compulsory-attendance laws, but so did the makings of the blackboard jungle."[6]

POVERTY

In the 1960s even before the United States demonstrated its scientific and technological capacities by landing a man on the moon, eradication of poverty was high on the national agenda. While educators were still attending conferences to discuss the importance and implications of the structure of knowledge for curriculum improvement and publishing new texts on curriculum that emphasized either the structure of knowledge[7] or the possibility of having both democracy and excellence in education,[8] President John F. Kennedy was developing an interest in poverty. The nation's concern about the welfare of children, especially those labeled as "disadvantaged," "was accompanied by an unprecedented expansion in government support of social service programs and social and behavioral science research in general and addressed to child development in particular."[9] Soon after Kennedy's assassination, his successor Lyndon B. Johnson, declared a "War on Poverty." To aid him, Congress passed the Economic Opportunity Act (1964) that led to the establishment of Head Start (originally known as the Comprehensive Child Development Program), based on the premises and conclusions of research on children and youth in the inter-war years. Congress then passed the Elementary and Secondary Education Act (1965). By the mid-1960s, education had a new mission. Public education was to end poverty, and "the new nationally recognized goal was to enhance the development of the total child." The National Institute of Child Health and Human Development (1963) soon began to address the "psychological aspects" as well as its original focus on the "largely biomedical" aspects of child development."[10]

It fell upon educational researchers to either revise or invent educational strategies and programs to qualify the poor and the culturally disadvantaged for jobs that would enable them to break the vicious cycle of poverty. Educators and educational researchers were directed to shift their emphasis from identifying talented youth for "social exploitation" and introduction to academic disciplines at an early age to assisting the poor in doing well in school. As Harry S. Broudy observed:

Overnight the new math and the new biology and the new physics and the new language labs were pushed into the background. The research funds began to flow into schemes in which elitist subjects and activities were "put down" so that poor children would be "turned on."[11]

CIVIL RIGHTS

Less than two weeks before the launching of *Sputnik*, President Eisenhower sent troops to Little Rock to uphold an order of a federal court and to protect the nine students who were selected to integrate the high school in Little Rock. The launching of *Sputnik* in 1957 overshadowed the significance of the Supreme Court Ruling, *Brown v. the Board of Education of Topeka Kansas* in 1954 that ruled public school segregation unconstitutional. Interpretations of *Brown II* (1955) and Judge John Parker's ruling that came to be known as the "Briggs dictum" allowed many states and communities to resist with considerable success the Supreme Court's ruling. Desegregation of public schools proceeded very slowly.[12] The *Brown* decision could be put off but it could not be denied. The nation had to determine whether equality of educational opportunity was as important as national defense issues. To answer the question, the United States Commissioner of Education, as directed by the United States Congress when it passed the 1964 Civil Rights Act, commissioned a study, now commonly known as the *Coleman Report* (1966), to determine progress toward equality of educational opportunity ten years after the *Brown* decision. The Educational Testing Service administered tests to students, and James S. Coleman and his associates analyzed the data. This significant report and its importance are taken up in the next chapter.

As demonstrated by the enactment of the Cooperative Research Act (Public Law 83-531)[13] in 1954, the National Defense Education Act (NDEA) in 1958, the federal government's publication of *A Nation at Risk* (1983) and the passage of the No Child Left Behind Act in 2002, public education has been and continues to be an agency designed to address the nation's economic, social, and political agenda. As priorities on the nation's agenda appear and disappear, so are the expectations placed on public school officials and educational researchers, sometimes quite suddenly.

THE ELEVATED SIGNIFICANCE OF EDUCATION

Since the end of World War II when there was recognition among national leaders that the nation was entering an era that required a workforce better educated than ever before, tests were selected as the device to identify, in what was believed to be a fair and objective manner, those who would be allowed to enter the best colleges and universities and thus the most lucrative and prestigious positions in society. While schools always had social, economic and political purposes to fulfill, their importance for the welfare of the nation state was dramatically increased in the Post-World War II Era. Recognition of that increased importance and the response to that recognition mark an important turning point in the history of educational research, for it was then that federal support for educational research was authorized with the Cooperative Research Act of 1954. Funds for such were appropriated in 1957.

Educational researchers saw the need to improve educational research and were directed to establish stronger, if not new, relationships with the academic disciplines. Public education was severely criticized for having abandoned the traditional school subjects, or disciplines, and all who were responsible for conducting schooling, training personnel for public education, and those responsible for conducting educational research felt the pressure to base their work on a traditional discipline.

WAR AND TECHNOLOGICAL CHANGE

The scientific and technological developments of the World War II Era were even more powerful than those that appeared after the Civil War. The transition from atomic to nuclear physics—a transition that began early in the century—was completed. It was as though Prometheus returned and gave humankind a new fire—nuclear energy. The development of nuclear energy radically transformed how war and peace were discussed. The requirements for maintaining the peace and waging war made education more important than ever before. Nuclear energy, the computer and television are the three developments of the World War II Era that signal the beginning of the post-industrial era, the information age, the electronic age, or the technetronic society as never before seen. The Post-World War II Era marks the beginning of a new cultural order. Post-war developments demonstrated to the nation's leaders that education was indeed essential for the nation's welfare whether the focus was on domestic tranquility, national defense, or the geo-political considerations brought about by the Cold War.

The politics of civil rights movements and concern over or denial of the persistence of social and educational inequalities gained center stage as full enrollment was achieved from the elementary grades through high school. Full enrollment dramatically transformed the nature of the teaching process and gave teachers a new population, a population that earlier did not attend school, especially high school. Teachers faced first-genera-tion students, and neither teachers nor students knew what to expect from the other. The social dynamics of schooling changed dramatically. By the mid-1950s, Hollywood produced *The Blackboard Jungle*, and moviegoers were given a portrayal of the new social dynamics. In the 1960s, a variety of labels were assigned to the new population: the poor, the socially disad-vantaged, the culturally deprived and social dynamite. The new popula-tion proved not to be docile. It was heard very quickly, and the politics and the priorities of American society were rearranged. In the 1970s, then Senator Birch Bayh related that during his six-year tenure as chair of the Senate Subcommittee to Investigate Juvenile Delinquency, he "became increasingly concerned with reports from educators and others over the rising level of violence and vandalism in our Nation's Schools."[14] Those who did not know how to meet the school's expectations were seen as delinquent. Eventually, educational researchers constructed behaviors and expectations and attached them to specific groups, and educators accepted and acted on them. The disparities were also studied and recorded. The achievement gap between traditional middle class, "white" students and their unconventional peers raised serious questions about the efficacy and quality of public schools.

Full enrollment marked an important turning point in the history of public education in the United States. The Progressive Era system of pub-lic education as a product of the Industrial Revolution in the common school tradition prepared youth for adult roles in an industrial society. Schools with the help of educational researchers and their standardized tests that measured intelligence as well as achievement could sort youth and prepare students either for labor or for management positions. Increasingly, in the second half of the twentieth century schools were required to select and to prepare those who would join a new technical elite. The task was to serve a clientele it never really had to serve previ-ously. The nation had reached a point in its economic development where it was no longer possible to rely on the workplace to complete the job of socialization and elementary job training for those who either found the schools uncomfortable or not suited to their interests. The custodial func-tion of the public school was greatly expanded. Schools were expected to retain more students for more time than ever before. Moreover, the stu-dents, in terms of interests, abilities and social and cultural backgrounds, were more diverse than ever before. The resulting imbalance and the solutions to redress inequities continue to challenge educational research-ers and policymakers.

Recognition of the increased importance of education and the responses to that recognition mark an important turning point in the his-tory of educational research and its diversification in response to criticism both of school practices and policy as well as the quality and conduct of educational research. While psychology continued and continues to dominate educational research theoretically and methodologically, researchers from other disciplines—sociologists, historians, philosophers, and other social researchers and social critics—turned to education broadly conceived as well as public schooling. Some sought to answer the critics of schools and provide research on which better school practices could be built; others were the voices of dissent and criticism.

CRITICISM OF PUBLIC EDUCATION

Criticism of public education began as World War II was being concluded. Years before the Soviet Union placed *Sputnik* in orbit, the criticism of public education was noticeable and of concern to professional educators. C. Winfield Scott and Clyde M. Hill reported that criticisms of public education then "mushroomed to alarming proportions."[15] The revelations during World War II that many men and women of draft age were educationally deficient, the claims that the schools were obviously at fault, and the counterclaims that the schools "deserved much credit for the success achieved by our military forces" were, they claimed, "only a harbinger of the deluge to come." To ascertain the actual amount of criticism that was then being directed at public education, Scott and Hill examined the entries in the *Education Index*. They discovered that in 1942 a new heading, Public Schools—*Criticism* was introduced. That introduction, they argued, meant "that the current wave of criticism was then a large enough ripple to attract serious attention." Between 1942 and 1950, the average number of entries under the new heading was nearly eight per year. After 1950, however, the increases were dramatic. There were thirty-five entries in 1951, nearly three times as many as in 1950. There were forty-nine entries in 1953, more than four times as many as there were in 1950.

In assembling their own collection of complaints about public schooling, Scott and Hill found significant statements in the popular media: articles by Dorothy Thompson in the *Ladies Home Journal*; an article by Walter Biddle Saul, a senior partner in one of Philadelphia's prestigious law firms, in the *Saturday Evening Post*; an article by historian Henry Steele Commager in the *Reader's Digest*, as well as articles in *Scientific Monthly*, *Life*, *New Republic*, the *Rotarian*, *Time*, *Parade*, the *American Legion Magazine*, the *Saturday Review of Literature*, and several other professional and lay magazines. The volume of material found in lay magazines allowed them to "conclude that both pro and con criticism must reflect to an important extent the opinions of laymen and must represent things they try to verbalize and often try to put into action in their own circles." Editors of such magazines, they concluded, certainly would not devote so much attention to criticisms of public education unless it was "good grist for their mill."[16] Such grist seems to have been just what the first wave of new Post-World War II parents and grandparents wanted to read. Editors do not persist in publishing material their readers do not want to read.

John Gunther's *Inside Russia Today* afforded Americans an opportunity to compare their public schools to those of the Soviet Union (Russia and the Soviet Union were then often and incorrectly considered to be one and the same). Children in the United States attended school five days a week, but Soviet children attended six. The Soviet school year was thirty-three days longer than the U.S.A.'s. Soviet students completed a curriculum that included ten years of mathematics, four years of chemistry, five years of physics and six years of biology. Soviet students studied English, but American students did not study Russian. Compared with Soviet students, American children clearly knew very little science. Only half of the American students enrolled in a one-year physics course. Almost two-thirds enrolled in chemistry, but it too was but a one-year course.

In *Educational Wastelands* (1955) Arthur E. Bestor, a professor of history at the University of Illinois who had earlier proposed that the nation's scholars assume responsibility for watching over the nation's public schools charged that the nation's public schools had been taken over by professional educators who lacked respect for the intellectual disciplines. In *The Restoration of Learning* (1956) he called for a return to the traditional school subjects (science, mathematics, history, English, and foreign languages). Those subjects, he claimed, constituted the only true foundation for "contemporary life." To understand their world, students needed not "the simple minded conception of mathematics as primarily a matter of making change and figuring out how many cups of punch can be dipped from a gallon bowl" but algebra, trigonometry, and calculus. To understand developments encountered in their daily social and economic lives and the products they used in their daily lives students needed to know the academic disciplines. Advanced physics would enable students to understand television, a device that then could be found in half the nation's homes. Use of antibiotics and vitamins required knowledge of biochemistry. Use of plastics and detergents required study of chemistry.[17] Bestor presented statistics to support his claim that enrollments in high school mathematics and science courses had declined significantly. Between the beginning and the middle of the twentieth century, enrollment in science courses fell from 83.9 percent to 53.8 percent. The decline in mathematics courses was nearly the same. The decline in enrollment in foreign language courses was even greater, from 72.2 percent to 21.8 percent.[18] Bester did not, however, note that a greater percent of the high school-age population was in school in the 1950s than were enrolled in the Pre-World War I Era.

CONFERENCES AND MEETINGS ON THE STATE OF EDUCATION

The Woods Hole Conference

In September 1959, about a month before the first anniversary of *Sputnik I*, thirty-five scientists, scholars, and educators met for ten days at Woods Hole on Cape Cod "to discuss how education in science might be improved in our primary and secondary schools." The meeting was called by the Education Committee of the National Academy of Sciences and was financed by the National Science Foundation (NSF), the United States Air Force, and the Rand Corporation. The assembled scholars believed that many significant advances made in the various disciplines during the previous half century had not yet reached the elementary and secondary schools. They had recently begun work on new curricula to remedy that situation and were now meeting to explore ways to impart to students "a sense of the substance and method of science."[19] It was now necessary to direct attention to the structure of the disciplines because while the scholars had been making great strides in their disciplines, psychology had turned away from "its earlier concern with the nature of the learning." According to the conference's chair, Jerome S. Bruner:

> The psychology of learning tended to become involved with the precise details of learning in highly simplified short-term situations and thereby lost much of its contact with the long-term educational effects of learning. For their part, educational psychologists turned their attention with great effect to the study of aptitude and achievement to social and motivational aspects of education, but did not concern themselves directly with the intellectual structure of class activities.[20]

Bruner further explained that as high school enrollments steadily grew during the twentieth century, the proper balance "between instruction in the useful skills and in disciplined understanding" became increasingly difficult to maintain. James Bryant Conant's "plea for the comprehensive high school" was, according to Bruner, an attempt to redress the imbalance."[21] The Woods Hole Conference was an attempt by many scholars and scientists to redress the imbalance by considering "anew the nature of the learning process."[22] Other educational objectives were not necessarily "less important," but it was necessary to ask: "Are we producing enough scholars, scientists, poets, lawmakers, to meet the demands of our times?"[23]

To redress the imbalance and to improve the schools' curriculum it was necessary to emphasize the *structure* of the disciplines. As Bruner later observed:

> The prevailing notion was that if you understood the structure of knowledge, that understanding would then permit you to go ahead on your own; you did not need to encounter everything in nature in order to know nature, but by understanding some deep principles, you could extrapolate to the particulars as needed. Knowing was a canny strategy whereby you could know a great deal about a lot of things while keeping very little in mind.[24]

Those who advocated pursuing what the "structure of knowledge" approach entailed believed in four claims. The first was that "understanding makes a subject more comprehensible." Application of this principle dictated that students be taught that knowledge of principles would allow them to understand the significance of facts. For example, if students were taught that nations needed trade to exist they would then understand the significance of the Triangular Trade of the colonial Americans, involving molasses, sugar cane, rum, and slaves. Similarly, if students were taught that Herman Melville was writing about the theme of good and evil in *Moby Dick* and that the number of "human plights" about which authors could write was limited, then they would understand the novel "more deeply."[25] The second claim was that the details of any subject were soon forgotten unless they were "placed into a structured pattern." Scientists did not commit details to memory. They did not memorize times and distances about various falling bodies but only the formula ($s = gt^2$), which allowed them to make appropriate calculations when they were needed. The third claim related to the psychological problem of "transfer of training." It maintained that understanding something as an instance of a more general principle enabled one to develop models of understanding similar phenomena. Thus the proper understanding of the "weariness of Europe at the close of the Hundred Years' War and how it created the conditions for a workable but not ideologically absolute Treaty of Westphalia" would enhance one's ability "to think about the ideological struggle of East and West." The fourth claim was that a constant scrutiny of the "fundamental character" of what was taught in the elementary and the secondary schools would serve to lessen the gap between the lower grades of the public schools and the discoveries of the best scholars at universities.[26]

According to Bruner, the public school curriculum was to be organized neither by the interests of students nor by practical applications of knowledge but by "the most fundamental understanding that can be achieved of the underlying principles that give structure to that subject."[27] To ensure that the "underlying structure" of a discipline was given proper attention, it was necessary "that the best minds in any particular discipline ... be put to work on the task."[28] Experts in a field were the only ones qualified to decide what was to be taught. Besides having scholars determine the content of the school curriculum, he urged that the style or attitude of the scholars be communicated to students. He suggested that there might be "certain general attitudes or approaches toward science or literature that can be taught in earlier grades that would have considerable relevance for later learning." He speculated that: "The attitude that things are connected and not isolated is a case in point." Students were somehow to learn how scholars thought about their work. There was a body of literature "about the forms of sensibility that make for literary taste and vigor," and historians had written about how they approached their work, gathered information, and made and defended generalizations. Mathematicians even had a name for such considerations—"heuristics." The task was to determine "what attitudes or heuristic devices are most pervasive and useful" so that "rudimentary versions" could be taught to students. This seemed an appropriate approach for the Woods Hole participants believed "that there is a continuity between what a scholar does on the forefront of his discipline and what a child does in approaching it for the first time."[29]

The Woods Hole participants began with "the hypothesis that any subject can be taught effectively in some intellectually honest form to any child at any stage of development."[30] That hypothesis allowed the scholars to propose any subject matter they wished for the curriculum. All educators needed to do was present the material in a form and manner consistent with the child's stage of development. During each grade of school, or at each developmental state, students would study the same subject. At each state, however, the sophistication of the subjects was to be increased as students progressed from the state of concrete operations to formal operations. Bruner explained that the criterion for selection of material was quite simple:

> We might ask, as a criterion for any subject taught in primary school, whether, when fully developed, it is worth an adult's knowing, and whether having known it as a child makes a person a better adult. If the answer to both questions is negative or ambiguous, then the material is cluttering the curriculum.[31]

Bruner's criterion was consistent with the belief that the purpose of secondary education was to prepare students for college, that college was to prepare students for professional careers or graduate school, and that the purpose of the elementary school was to prepare students for high school.

The Woods Hole participants assumed—an assumption not supported by research—that students wanted to learn. To construct a successful school program, little other than the states of intellectual development needed to be known. Even within the complex social setting of the school, that often included anti-intellectual forces, there was "the subtle attraction of the subjects in school that a child finds interesting."[32] Undoubtedly such interests could be cultivated. Bruner later admitted that belief in the students' interest was a "formula of faith." "Their motivation," he admitted, "was taken for granted."[33]

BRUNER'S RECEPTION

The Process of Education was widely noted, highly praised, and used to defend many educational strategies and programs. By 1971, it had been translated into twenty-one languages. The Soviets were the first to translate it. Educational reformers under Premier Nikita Khruschev seemed to believe that it supported their claim that students had to be led to discover the virtues of "socialist realism" rather than simply have it presented to them. In Italy, it was "used in a battle by the moderate Left, against doctrinaire Marxist educators on the one side and against traditionalists on the other who wanted to maintain a classical curriculum."[34] In the United States, Frank G. Jennings likened Bruner's endeavors at synthesizing the views of the Woods Hole participants to an "alchemist's efforts." Bruner, Jennings enthusiastically claimed, had "transmuted the inquiry of specialists into a declaration of the intellectual rights, duties, and desires of all who would teach and learn, not only in science but in the whole range of knowledge and experience."[35] G. J. Sullivan described it as "an epochal book" that gave "accurate expression to the current ferment in educational though in the country." He further suggested that it would lay "to rest the ghosts of some outmoded approaches" and offered "an exciting discussion of the direction educational theory and research should take."[36] While Paul Goodman suggested that Bruner did not fully "appreciate the moral and ideological obstacles that are put in the way of teaching children fundamental real ideas in the study of man," he nonetheless claimed that *The Process of Education* would be a classic, "comparable for its philosophical centrality and humane concreteness to some of the essays of Dewey."[37]

THE NEA SEMINAR

After the appearance of *The Process of Education* educators quickly turned their attention to the academic disciplines, to the structure of knowledge, and to the uses of knowledge. The National Education Association's

Project on Instruction sponsored a Seminar on the Disciplines that "was called to facilitate study and effective use of the disciplines by (a) focusing upon those fundamental ideas and methods of inquiry from selected fields of study which should be in the mainstream of the instructional program of the public schools, and (b) exploring frontier thinking and research in the nature of knowledge and ways of knowing."[38] The NEA was then sponsoring a seminar designed not to lead the nation toward a new plan for education but one designed to follow a lead that had already been provide by the scholars. The title of the seminar's report—*The Scholars Look at the Schools*—and the report's organization clearly reflect the interest in academic disciplines that then prevailed. Three divisions were used to organize the seventeen subject matter areas that were then considered: (1) the humanities, which included art, music, English, foreign languages, philosophy, and religion; (2) the physical and biological sciences and mathematics, which included mathematics, chemistry, biology, and physics; and (3) the social sciences, which included sociology, communication, geography, economics, history, political science, and psychology.

Joseph J. Schwab, who offered the opening presentation at the seminar, objected to the charge that the school curriculum placed too much emphasis on the learners and their social milieu. Besides wanting to maintain a proper balance among the four elements of curriculum construction—the learner, the social situation, the subject matter, and the teacher—he wanted to resist any emphasis on subject matter that assumed that the bodies of knowledge to be mastered were clearly defined and fixed. Such an emphasis incorrectly assumed that there was only "one grand genus of knowing" (he believed there were three genera) and led "to abdication of responsibility by the social scientists, the psychologist, and the educator in favor of the subject-matter specialists."[39]

While Schwab feared that too much emphasis would be placed on the disciplines, he presented a position that was discipline centered. For Schwab, it was necessary to distinguish among "three great genera of disciplines: the investigative (natural sciences), the appreciative (arts), and the decisive (social sciences)." It was also essential to note that all ideas, because of their human origins, were necessarily limited and tentative. The structures of the disciplines were always undergoing modification and correction. While some conclusions were abandoned, new ones were invented or discovered. A good curriculum was made by following three guidelines: First, the aim of education was expressed so that it encompassed "the best fruits of the disciplines." Second, the "best fruits" were taught not as immutable truths but in a manner that allowed students to understand "the extent and the sense in which they are true." Third, students had to be given "an awareness of the structure of inquiry" that produced the conclusions—the "best fruits"—so they could determine for themselves how true and durable they were."[40]

Schwab had two reactions upon contemplating the "riches of the disciplines." One was the realization that the curriculum had become "flaccid, especially for these demanding times," and the "hope that concern for the conceptual structure of the disciplines and for the rigor, precision, and thoroughness that characterizes the disciplines will repair this evil." The other was the fear that the then current curriculum reforms would "take an easy and indefensible course" and proceed "to ignore the disciplines."[41]

To take the easy course was to risk two undesirable results. First was the possibility of setting loose a competition among the disciplines for time and prominence in the curriculum. That would result in curriculum variations from place to place that would reflect the interests of the most powerful people in those places. Second was the possibility that educators would try to create a synthesis of the disciplines to meet the many social, personal, cultural, political, and economic aspirations of the diverse school clientele. Such an attempt at a synthesis could easily violate the integrity of the disciplines, because the differences among disciplines were neither arbitrary distinctions nor historical accidents but rather reflections of the different methods scholars had developed to handle the diverse questions posed by the many disciplines. Schwab believed that educators should follow the relationships the scholars made among the disciplines but not be so presumptuous as to create the connections before the experts did.

To avoid the difficulties of the easy course, the scholars at the NEA seminar recommended that curriculum be seen as having two parts: the nuclear and the cortical. That strategy, it was argued, would allow educators to reconcile the conflicting demands of the disciplines and the requirements of society. The nuclear component would include materials selected from the disciplines "to fulfill those objectives of education which are determined primarily from the needs of the developing child and the aims imposed by our culture and society." The cortical component would include representative materials from the disciplines that "would display the more important conceptual frames of each discipline, its techniques of discovery and verification, and the variety of problems to which it addresses itself."[42] When more than one discipline would meet such an objective, it would be possible to choose those which "also served present and recognized individual-social needs, provided the "criterion of representativeness of the discipline remained the paramount consideration." While the ratio of nuclear to cortical components could not be determined without detailed study, there was speculation that it would vary according to grade level. In the early grades it could "be as small as 80-90 percent."[43] An advantage of the nuclear-cortical approach was that it was "followed by many colleges and capable of adaptation to the elementary and secondary schools."[44] The participants in the NEA seminar agreed that each level of schooling from top to bottom, from the elementary school to the graduate school, should reflect the organization and purposes of the one above it.

THE MILWAUKEE CONFERENCE

Shortly after the NEA seminar the University of Wisconsin—Milwaukee School of Education used funds granted by the Uhrig Foundation to sponsor an invitational conference on "The Nature of Knowledge." The conference participants discussed an agenda clearly influenced by Bruner's *Process of Education*: the need for knowing, ways of knowing, knowledge and the structure of the disciplines, conceptions of knowledge and their significance for the curriculum, knowledge about knowledge for teachers, the structure of knowledge and the interrelationship of ideas, and the relationships among knowledge, schooling, and the preparation of teachers. The proceedings of this conference, like the report of the NEA seminar, reveal that it is one thing to proclaim that public schools should focus their attention on the disciplines and their structures and quite another to select disciplines and identify their structures so they can be effectively organized for use in public schools.

J. Martin Klotsche, the provost of the University of Wisconsin—Milwaukee, began the conference by pointing out that while society through its schools had an obligation to create opportunities for "those so inclined by talent and desire, wherever they may stand on the social and economic ladder of society, to extend the frontiers of knowledge into new and unexplored regions," it also had an obligation "to provide understanding on the part of all of the people so that knowledge discovered by the few will in the course of events become the means of improving the quality of our entire citizenry." The difficulty in satisfying those obligations was compounded by the knowledge explosion and the increased access scholars had to knowledge. Ironically, the problem was not a scarcity but a surfeit of knowledge. Scholars could neither know all there was to know nor even be certain that the utility of what they knew would endure as long as they would. In 1960, two million scientific and technical articles were published in nearly 1,000 journals in more than sixty languages. New journals were appearing daily. In 1960, the Chemical Abstract Services abstracted and indexed 150,000 articles and patents, "filling 22 issues containing as many words as the *Encyclopedia Britannica*."[45] In just three months, the weather satellite, *Tiros I*, transmitted 22,000 pictures of the earth's cloud cover.

The capability to store and retrieve new knowledge was truly astounding. In just half an hour the Western Reserve Center for Documentation and Communications Research could scan over 50,000 abstracts and select appropriate titles for a metallurgist who wanted to know about "the impact of forming metals at high speeds." Such capabilities underscored Margaret Mead's observation "that no one will live all of his life in the world in which he was born."[46] All changes, however, were not scientific and technical. Our relationships to other places on the planet and their relative importance had changed so much that it was necessary to question the scope and utility of traditional courses. As Klotsche noted:

> It used to be fashionable to teach courses in Western Civilization but new knowledge has made such a focus too narrow. Peiping and Cairo are as important to us today as London and Paris. The emergence of Africa further illustrates this point. There are more people on the African continent today than in the United States. Yet only three out of one hundred persons in Africa today are of European descent. At the end of World War II only four African nations were independent. Today two-thirds of the people of that continent have independent status.[47]

Perhaps the most useful and insightful discussion of the discipline issue was Arthur W. Foshay's examination of Bruner's claim that educators should use the structure of the disciplines to shape their conceptions of subjects as well as to determine how they should be taught and learned. Foshay, the executive officer of the Horace Mann-Lincoln Institute of School Experimentation at Teachers College, Columbia University, effectively showed that by following the call of the scholars to use the structure of the disciplines as the basis of the school curriculum, they were actually trying to bring about a revolution in American pedagogy. He also showed that, to be successful in the revolutionary effort, it was necessary "to make a desirable distinction between the term *discipline* and the term *school subject*."

For Foshay the common sense notion of a discipline as "a branch of knowledge involving research" was not as useful a notion as the one that specified that a discipline was "a way of learning, a way of knowing." For a discipline to exist, several conditions had to be satisfied. First, there had to be "agreement on the field of phenomena in question."[48] For example, physicists generally agreed on the kinds of questions appropriate for investigation. Second, the practitioners of a discipline had to "agree upon a set of rules which are to apply to the scholar's attempt to create knowledge within the field of his inquiry." The rules of one discipline differed from those of others. Foshay indicated that: "It is hard to understand that one's discipline cannot deal with all fields of human knowledge." Application of one discipline's rules to another's produced either nonsense or "a kind of scholarly monstrosity." The application of the disciplines had to have "a certain arbitrary quality which arises in part from their histories, and in part from the nature of the agreements on domain and rules that characterize them." Each discipline had a history that defined its domain and rules. All practitioners were obliged to adhere to the discipline's traditions. Modifications of rules did occur, but such modifications were not made by the individual scholar but "only in terms of agreements by members of the disciplines—that is, by practicing scholars."[49]

The educators' role was not to decide upon modifications in the disciplines but to "translate the disciplines into school subjects." In performing that role, they had to be aware that the practice of calling disciplines and school subjects by the same name "tended to obscure the necessary distinction between the subject and its underlying discipline." "If a discipline is a way of knowing its particular body of knowledge in its appropriate way," Foshay explained, "then a school subject can be thought of as a pattern of learning activities, worked out by an educationist (a teacher, if you please) which has as its purpose the introduction of students into the discipline."[50] The purpose of a school subject was to make disciplines available to students. Foshay claimed that "if a school subject is a teacher's attempt to translate a discipline into learning activities, then the success depends on the degree to which the students learn how knowledge is made or discovered in each of the branches of knowledge being studied."[51] Because the disciplines were defined by their distinctive modes of inquiry, school subjects had to be organized in accordance with those modes. Such translations required new conceptions both of what was taught and of the student, for traditional school practices were indeed contrary to the new emphasis on the disciplines. As Foshay explained:

> When we try to consider school subjects as modes of inquiry, it is important that we recognize we are at war with our own tradition. Nor does the pedagogical tradition tolerate students as inquirers happily. The pedagogical tradition calls for transmittal of he "given." It is a tradition of the transmittal of certainty, not of doubt. But doubt is precisely the quality of the scholar. The scholar, taken as an intellectual is one "who makes the given problematic." Our pedagogical tradition does not deal with problematic material. If we obey our tradition, we take what is problematic and make it into sets of certainties, which we then call upon the students to "master."[52]

If school subjects were to be taught as modes of inquiry, even educators would have to break with their own traditions. Most educators, Foshay observed, were not taught to see their fields as modes of inquiry but "were educated in accordance with the pedagogical tradition that implied that knowledge is a given and taught that love of learning consists primarily of passive listening." Foshay illustrated his point with examples from three disciplines: chemistry, history, and poetry. He also indicated how the teaching of their corresponding school subjects would have to change if they were to be used as suitable introductions to the disciplines. For example, if the objective of the chemistry course was to introduce students to how chemists think and what they try to achieve, then the student would have to spend more time in the laboratory "where he would try to learn to observe, to analyze, to predict; where he would also try to learn to formulate hypotheses, to take steps (at least) toward the development of theory and law" and less time "listening to the results of experiments, which he was to master."[53] Teachers would have to become more concerned with how well students learned to use the rules of chemistry and less concerned with how much specific content they had learned or how neatly they copied "results" into their lab manuals.

History differed from chemistry. History was part art and part science. For various historians the ratio of art to science varied, and thus they agreed less on how to conduct their inquiries than did chemists. However, significant agreements existed among them. They agreed that they dealt with the chronology of evens and the records of the past. Some were willing "to go very far from the immediate evidence they are dealing with," and others were not. Historians did agree on what they were trying to produce—"periodization." They tried to define and characterize historical periods, to explain why, for example, a certain period should be characterized as the "Age of Franklin" rather than the "Age of the American and French Revolutions." When historians made such a claim, they had to state their point of view and indicate which records they used to support their claim so others could inspect and criticize their conclusions. There was also a division of labor among historians, some were economic or cultural historians, and still others adopted a political, military, intellectual, or diplomatic interest. If students were to be introduced properly to the discipline of history, teachers could not be allowed to assign them lessons from standard textbooks, for that approach did not afford students the opportunity "to live with the ambiguity that the historian faces and with the subjectivity of history." Better than the conventional textbook was the "documentary approach to the teaching of history." It allowed the student, like the historian, "to understand that he never reads about what happened, but reads someone's interpretation of the records that happen to remain from the past."[54]

The teaching of poetry undoubtedly need to be improved. According to Foshay, "our approach to the teaching of poetry in the school is so far removed from the art itself that almost any application of the poet's approach to poetry that we would attempt would be an improvement."[55]

While it was difficult to state the rules of poetry or to find clear agreement about the rules, there were "canons of criticism, according to which at least gross distinctions can be made between good and bad poetry." It was also possible to specify that "the output of poetry as an art is *humanitas*—a deepened realization of the nature of man."[56] Meter and rhyme schemes—the focus of so many school lessons on poetry—were not unimportant to the study of poetry but they were neither its essence nor the proper focus for teaching it well. Meter and rhyme were simply elements poets used to fashion their statements about humanity. If students were to be taught to understand the discipline of poetry, teachers would have to assign them problems that could "be solved by the writing of poetry." Through comparison of their efforts with the efforts of others, students could begin to learn about the care and precision poets applied to their use of language to craft their distinctive statements.

For Foshay, a curriculum based on the disciplines was not contrary to the interests of those who believed that students should be encouraged to be creative. Creativity, he pointed out, did not occur in a "vacuum." Students had to have something with which to be creative. Proper translation of the disciplines into school subjects would provide students "both the materials and the means of intellectual life—which is to say, creativity."[57]

THE STRUCTURE OF KNOWLEDGE IN THE ARTS

In 1963, Phi Delta Kappa devoted its annual Symposium on Educational Research to a consideration of how several educators viewed the relationship between the structure of knowledge and the process of schooling. Particularly significant in an era when the fashion was to construe the disciplines to mean more work in mathematics and science was Harry S. Broudy's presentation, "The Structure of Knowledge in the Arts." For Broudy, there was no question that knowledge in the arts could and should be systematically taught. Art could be taught without insisting that students become artists. There were "definitions, rules, and procedures in art that can be identified, pointed to, and stated." That meant, Broudy explained, "that there can be systematic instruction in or, at least, about art, and that it need not be confided to apprentice training in art production."[58] It was possible to specify and classify the types of knowledge used making statements about the content of an art work, the technique used by the artists in creating the work, and the judgments made about the work. In part, the study of art entailed the study of its history and, Broudy pointed out, there was "no insuperable difficulty in classifying the cognitive activity involved in making historical statements about art and artists, about periods, styles and developments."[59]

Art, according to Broudy, did not produce meaningful statements in the say way other disciplines did, but it did express meanings. Works of art did not make precise descriptive statements about the nature of reality that could be verified in conventional ways. However, artistic expressions were "clues from which inferences that are assertions can be made." For example,

> While Beethoven's Ninth Symphony is not a set of statements about the exaltation of creation, the sounds are images of that complex of mood, idea, feeling, and action. Hearing it, one could infer that this is what creation feels like and that it is all very impressive and important. From the clues in some works of art one can make immediate inferences about the nature of love, of death, of war, of ideals, of every divagation of human experience, actual and possible.[60]

While the aesthetic experience needed no justification beyond itself, art nonetheless had a practical justification. As Broudy explained, "just as science is society's defense against distortions of the intellect by prejudice and special interests, so high cultivation in art is society's defense against undisciplined feeling swayed by parochial interests and limited experience."[61]

AUSUBEL AND PSYCHOLOGICAL STRUCTURES

Also of significance was David P. Ausubel's "Some Psychological Aspects of the Structure of Knowledge," for it demonstrated that educators were turning to new conceptions of how students learned as well as to new conceptions of what they should learn. It was basically a move away from Edward L. Thorndike's views on the laws of learning that dominated for most of the first half of the twentieth century. Ausubel maintained that too little attention had been paid to the formulation and testing of "theories of learning that are relevant for the kinds of meaningful ideational learning that takes place in school and similar learning environments." While he did not challenge the emphasis that was then being placed on the disciplines, he did warn that educators needed to recognize the distinction between how subject matter was logically expressed in textbooks and how it was actually organized "in the memory structures of particular individuals."[62] If educators were to enhance students' learning of the disciplines, they had to acquire knowledge of the structure of the disciplines *and* knowledge of psychological cognitive structures. Ausubel was effectively claiming that that the control of the school curriculum had to be shared by those who knew subject matter and those who claimed to know how people learned. To a large extent he was making a claim for what many now know as constructivism. He was also overlooking that that was no one proven theory of learning but that there were many learning theories.

To understand how students learned and organized what they learned, it was necessary to understand the principle of subsumption, that is, how information and ideas fell under comprehensive organizing principles. The structure of the human nervous system, according to Ausubel, was analogous to "a data process and storing mechanism." Its structure was such that "new ideas and information can be meaningfully learned and retained only to the extent that more inclusive and appropriately relevant conceptions are already available in cognitive structure to serve a subsuming roll or to provide ideational anchorage."[63] He offered a view very much like that earlier presented by Herbart and the Herbartians. Knowledge was not a collection of discrete and isolated facts or ideas. It was the acquisition *and* the relating of new ideas to what was already known by the learner. Students made sense of new material and experiences by relating the new to what they already knew. As students made such relationships, that is, learned, they developed hierarchical structures that comprised "the most inclusive concepts" at the top of their cognitive structures and the least inclusive at is base.

Because of the available knowledge on cognition and nervous system function, Ausubel claimed that it was possible to state how teaching should be organized and administered to facilitate learning. For the sake of organizing and integrating material, educators had to use "those unifying concepts and propositions in a given discipline that have the widest explanatory power, inclusiveness, generalizability, and relatability to the subject-matter content of that discipline" and that in the actual presentation of material to students teachers had to pay special attention to order, sequence, and the internal logic of the material they were teaching.[64]

Several principles were applicable to the design of instruction. The principle of progressive differentiation dictated that details were to be presented after the presentation of an "advanced organizer." By presenting students with a synthesis that included the general and inclusive ideas of a lesson, retention would be enhanced and rote learning would not be necessary. The principle of consolidation required that teachers present material in the proper sequence and that students master each step of lesson progressively. Mastery was also important because it allowed one to learn how to discriminate in acquiring new material. Ausubel explained that research showed that students with "greater knowledge of Christianity" were better able to learn about Buddhism than students with "less knowledge of Christianity"[65] New material could be placed into the cognitive structure according to either its similarity or dissimilarity to existing concepts.

The principle of integrative reconciliation required explicit efforts to determine similarities and differences and "to reconcile real or apparent inconsistencies."[66] Adherence to the principle of integrative reconciliation in organizing material for instruction would, Ausubel explained, require a drastic revision in how textbooks were organized. The common practice of grouping all seemingly similar and overlapping ideas into one chapter frequently obscured "significant differences between apparently similar concepts." The practice "of compartmentalizing and segregating particular ideas or topics within their respective chapters or sub-chapters" so that each was presented in only one of several possible places where inclusion was relevant and warranted was, Ausubel suggested, "perhaps logically valid, but certainly psychologically untenable."[67] Violation of this principle effectively created situations in which students had to learn without benefit of subsumable referents. In such situations learning was simply by rote.

Ausubel's emphasis on cognitive structure and the steps he outlined for educators to follow so that their instruction would be consistent with the contours of that structure was, as Arno Bellack observed, reminiscent of the late nineteenth century Herbartian psychology.[68] Ausubel and the Herbartians focused on a rational model of learning to determine how learning in school could be facilitated. While the Herbartians spoke of the necessity of attaching new ideas to the existing apperceptive mass, Ausubel spoke of cognitive structure. Each agreed, however, that teachers had a responsibility to determine what students knew and to relate new material to what they already knew. Teachers also needed to know how students learned. The nature of the process did not assign greater importance to either subject matter or method.

Ausubel may not have subscribed to the claim that teachers had to know and tend to the needs of the "whole child," but he did not subscribe to the claim that teachers only needed to be experts in subject matter. Like other educators, he demonstrated that education was more than a collection of the right disciplines. Unlike many others, he showed that the problem of public education was more complicated than finding ways to increase the intellectual rigor of public schooling.

IMPLEMENTATION PROBLEMS

Some school conventions seem to survive all reformers' and all researchers' assaults upon them. One such convention is the prominent position the textbook has in the instructional process. In large measure, the textbook defines the activities of both teacher and student, and, as Geraldine Joncich Clifford remarked about reforms aimed at giving the disciplines increased attention, "textbooks continued to eclipse both the laboratory inquiries and teaching machines of the latter-day reformers and the discussion groups and field trips of the earlier movement—as they always had."[69]

In his reconsideration of *The Process of Education*, Bruner admitted that making new curricula was not as easy as the scholars had believed it would be. "Something a bit strained would happen," he related, "when one caused to work together a most gifted and experienced teacher and an equally gifted and experienced scientist, historian, or scholar." Each side had a great deal to learn from the other. Moreover, the academic reformers learned that introduction of new materials entailed a process quite different from designing and producing them. They had not anticipated the public school bureaucracies and the complicated procedures for adopting and distributing new materials in school systems. They were also unaware of "the genuinely puzzling questions of teacher recruitment, training, and supervision."[70] They learned that public schools were something more than and different from colleges and universities.

Some educators tried to give the disciplines more attention without surrendering earlier held convictions about the necessity of relating school work to the world of human affairs and the interests of students. Some agreed that the disciplines were important and needed more attention but saw that the issue was more complicated than simply proclaiming that the student who was learning physics was no different from a physicists. For them, learning a new field and its rules was different from practicing or building on what one had mastered during a long period of study. Some, however, were not happy about the new curricula. They had reason to celebrate when educators were given a new direction to follow. For example, in a lecture delivered in 1970 at the meeting of the Association for Supervision and Curriculum Development—an organization which according to Clifford, "most represents latter-day 'establishment' progressivism."[71]—Fred T. Wilhelms announced that the "silly season" of "prestigious academicians" had ended. Their emphasis on "the pure disciplines" endured only "until the facts of life caught up with them." The new "battle cry," he proclaimed, was "relevance," and it was being heard "from coast to coast." Happily, "the great humane values which have been our chief concern are once more being forced upon those who sought to ignore them."[72]

Even Bruner seemed to turn to the relevance theme. By 1970, he was explaining that in the early 1960s there was a concern for "self direction of the intellect in the use of modern knowledge," and that in the second half of the decade it seemed appropriate to ask: "Did revision of curriculum suffice, or was a more fundamental restructuring of the entire educational system in order?"[73]

THE DISCIPLINES REDUX

The emphasis on and enthusiasm for the disciplines faded but did not disappear. A report ordered by President Carter and prepared by the National Science Foundation and the U.S. Department of Education claimed that the rigor of mathematics and science programs in the nation's public schools was less than that in the schools in the Soviet Union, Japan, and Germany. According to the report, "the number of young people who graduate from high school and college with only the most rudimentary notions of science, mathematics and technology portends trouble in the decades ahead." Unless "the current trend toward virtual scientific and technological illiteracy" is reversed, the report warned, many will be making important decisions in the future "on the basis of ignorance and misunderstanding."[74]

That President Carter ordered the study and that his successor's administration—the Reagan administration—also issued a report (A Nation at Risk) on public education are significant events. They show that, since World War II, public education has entered the arena of national politics and that public education has been high on the national agenda. Public education had become a national interest that began before the Sputnik era and has endured long after the Sputnik era. Traditional concerns about federal involvement in public education seem less important than before World War II. As President Kennedy told Congress in 1963, "we can no longer afford the luxury of endless debate over all the complicated and sensitive questions raised by each new proposal on Federal participation in education." The question was not whether there would be federal participation but how much participation there would be. President' Carter's establishment of a Department of Education with cabinet status was still another sign that education was high on the national agenda. President Reagan's promise to disestablish that Department and his support for tuition tax credits for parents who send their children to private schools were signs that all were not willing to end "debate over all the complicated and sensitive questions raised by each new proposal on federal participation in education.[75]

In 1961 President Kennedy indicated to Congress that the defense and the prosperity of the nation depended on education. Education, he maintained, was a good national investment. He told Congress:

> The human mind is our fundamental resource. A balanced federal program must go well beyond incentives for investment in plant and equipment. It must include equally determined measures to invest in human beings—both in their basic education and training and in their more advanced preparation for professional work. Without such measures, the federal government

will not be carrying out its responsibilities for expanding the base of our economic and military strength.[76]

In this 1963 message to Congress, Kennedy emphasized that failure to invest in education was bad economic policy. Education was inexpensive and it was a good investment. Education, it was assumed, equipped people to secure and hold jobs. The income lost during a year of unemployment was the equivalent to the cost of twelve years of schooling.

While Kennedy claimed that his proposals for aid to education were based on considerations other than the Cold War," he did nonetheless remind Congress of the Soviet Union's commitment to education. He indicated that:

> ... it is worthwhile noting that the Soviet Union recognizes that educational effort in the 1960s will have a major effect on a nation's power, progress, and status in the 1970s and 1980s. According to a recent report prepared for the National Science Foundation, Soviet institutions of higher education are graduating three times as many engineers and four times as many physicians as the United States. While trailing behind this country in aggregate annual numbers of higher education graduates, the Soviets are maintaining an annual flow of scientific and technical professional manpower more than twice as large as our own.[77]

When President Johnson called upon Congress to enact the Elementary and Secondary Education in 1965, he maintained that federal control of public education was not the issue. He reminded the Congress that even the late Senator Robert Taft, the conservative Senator from Ohio, had agreed that "in the field of education, as in the fields of health, relief, and medical care, the Federal Government has a secondary obligation see that there is a basic floor under those essential services for all adults and children in the United States."[78]

What may seem like a steady stream of continual criticism of public education did not begin in 1983 with the publication of A Nation at Risk. For some A Nation at Risk and the several other "national reports"[79] sounded like echoes from a recent past. As Charles Strickland observed shortly after its appearance:

> The recent avalanche of reports on education in these United States will leave anyone aged more than fifty with a sense of deja vu. After nearly thirty years the schools and their problems are moving once again to the center of the nation's consciousness. Once again we hear the litany about the mediocrity of the schools, followed by demands for excellence. Once again we hear a call for a tightening of standards and a toughening of discipline. Once again, the focus of concern is on the neglect of those subjects that promise technological superiority.[80]

Once again, school subjects, those that were offered, those in which students enrolled or did not enroll, how well students mastered the traditional school subjects, and suggestions for removing some subjects and adding others framed the debate, criticism and discussion about the nation's schools.

NOTES

1. Charles Burgess and Merle E. Borrowman. *What Doctrines to Embrace: Studies in the History of Education* (Glenview, Illinois: Scott, Foresman and Co. 1969), p. 131.

2. Historically, proposals for federal support for public education failed to overcome the resistance presented by one or more of what Diane Ravitch has described as the three R's. Religion became an issue that could not be resolved, for some in the Congress insisted upon aid to Catholic schools, and others objected. Race was an issue because some members wanted to insure that those that schools served mainly African-Americans would be treated fairly, and others invoked the doctrine of states' rights. Still others argued that federal support would entail federal regulation, and that federal regulation would be a move toward totalitarianism, and totalitarianism, was, of course, communism. These arguments disappeared in the Sputnik's wake. See: Diane Ravitch. *The Troubled Crusade: American Education 1945-1980* (New York: Basic Books, 1893), pp. 5-6.

3. On June 1, 1945 at a meeting of vocational educators that was called by the U.S. Office of Education's Division of Vocational Education. Charles A. Prosser expressed the belief that the sixty percent of second school students ere not receiving "the life adjustment training they need and to which they are entitled." Subsequently, "life adjustment education" was adopted in many schools and was soon the object of criticism. See: Ravitch. *Troubled Crusade*, pp. 64-67.

4. Morris Janowitz. *Institution Building in Urban Education* (Russell Sage Foundation, 1969), p. 9

5. Lawrence A. Cremin. *The Transformation of the School: Progressivism in American Education, 1876-1957* (New York: Alfred A. Knopf, 1962), pp. 127-128.

6. *Ibid.*, p. 128.

7. For example, see: Philip H. Phenix. *Realms of Meaning: A Philosophy of the Curriculum for General Education* (New York: McGraw Hill, 1964).

8. For example, see: Harry S. Broudy, B. Othanel Smith and Joe R. Burnett. *Democracy and Excellence in Secondary Education* (Chicago: Rand McNally, 1964).

9. Luis M. Laosa. "Social Policies toward Children of Diverse Ethnic, Racial, and Language Groups in the United States" in Harold W. Stevenson and Alberta E. Siegel (eds.). *Child Development Research and Social Policy* (Chicago: University of Chicago Press, 1984), p. 40.

10. *Ibid*

11. Harry S. Broudy. *The Real World of the Public Schools* (New York: Harcourt Brace Jovanovich, 1972), p. 36.

12.   Theresa R. Richardson and Erwin V. Johanningmeier. *Race, Ethnicity, and Education: What is Taught in Schools* (Greenwich, Connecticut: Information Age Publishing, 2003), pp, 205, 212.

13.   For an early discussion of this act see: Herold C. Hunt. "Educational Research and National Education Policy," *Journal of Educational Research*, Vol. XLIX, No. 9 (May 1956). Hunt, then the Under Secretary of Health, Education, and Welfare explained that the cooperative program was designed to focus on three major areas: "conservation and development of … human resources," "staffing and housing [the] Nation's schools and colleges," and "expanding technology and economy." p. 643.

14.   Birch Bayh. "School Violence and Vandalism: Problems and Solutions." *Journal of Research and Development in Education*, Vol. 2 (Winter 1978), p. 4.

15.   C. Winfield Scott and Clyde M. Hill. (eds.). *Public Education under Criticism* (Engelwood Cliffs, New Jersey: Prentice-Hall, 1954), p. 3.

16.   *Ibid.*, p. 4.

17.   Arthur E. Bestor. *The Restoration of Learning* (New York: Alfred A. Knopf, 1956), pp. 40-41.

18.   *Ibid.*, pp. 42-43.

19.   Jerome S. Bruner. *The Process of Education* (Cambridge, Massachusetts: Harvard University Press, 1961), p. vii.

20.   *Ibid.*, p. 4.

21.   *Ibid.*, p. 5.

22.   *Ibid.*, p. 2.

23.   *Ibid.*, p. 9.

24.   Jerome S. Bruner. *"The Process of Education Reconsidered"* in Glen Hass (ed.). *Curriculum Planning: A New Approach* (Boston: Allyn & Bacon, 1977), p. 195.

25.   Bruner. *Process of Education*, pp. 23-24.

26.   *Ibid.*, pp. 24-26.

27.   *Ibid.*, p. 39.

28.   *Ibid.*, p. 19.

29.   *Ibid.*, pp. 27-28.

30.   *Ibid.*, p. 33.

31.   *Ibid.*, p. 52.

32.   *Ibid.*, p. 63.

33.   Bruner. *"The Process of Education Reconsidered"* in Hass (ed.). Curriculum Planning, p. 195.

34.   *Ibid.*, p. 198.

35.   Frank G. Jennings, "A Friend of he Learning Child," *Saturday Review*, Vol. 43 (October 15, 1960), p. 94.

36.   G. J. Sullivan. "The Natural Approach to Learning," *Commonwealth*, Vol. 74 (June 23, 1961), p. 94.

37.   Paul Goodman. *New York Herald Tribune Lively Arts* (December 25, 1960), p. 28.

38.   *The Scholars Look at the Schools: A Report of the Disciplines Seminar* (Washington, D.C.: National Education Association, 1962), p. 2.

39. *Ibid.*, p. 3.

40. *Ibid.*, pp. 3- 4.

41. *Ibid.*, p. 50

42. *Ibid.*, pp. 50-51.

43. *Ibid.*, p. 52.

44. *Ibid.*, p. 51.

45. J. Martin Klotsche. "The Need for Knowing," in William A. Jenkins (ed.). *The Nature of Knowledge: Implications for the Education of Teachers* (Milwaukee: University of Wisconsin—Milwaukee. 1961), pp. 8-9.

46. *Ibid.*, p. 11.

47. *Ibid.*, pp. 10-11.

48. Arthur W. Foshay, "Knowledge and the Structure of the Disciplines" in Jenkins (ed.). *The Nature of Knowledge*, pp. 28-29.

49. *Ibid.*, pp. 30-31.

50. *Ibid.*, pp. 28-29.

51. *Ibid.*, p. 32.

52. *Ibid.*, p.. 32-33.

53. *Ibid.*, pp. 35-36.

54. *Ibid.*, p. 38.

55. *Ibid.*, pp. 39-40.

56. *Ibid.*, pp. 38-39.

57. *Ibid.*, p. 40.

58. Harrry S. Broudy. "The Structure of Knowledge in the Arts" in Stanley Elam (ed.). *Education and the Structure of Knowledge: Fifth Annual Phi Delta Kappa Symposium on Educational Research* (Chicago: Rand McNally, 1964), p. 99.

59. *Ibid.*, p. 105.

60. *Ibid.*, pp. 105-106.

61. *Ibid.*, p. 104.

62. David P. Ausubel. "Some Psychological Aspects of the Structure of Knowledge" in Elam (ed.). *Education and the Structure of Knowledge*, p. 222.

63. *Ibid.*, p. 229.

64. *Ibid.*, p. 239.

65. *Ibid.*, p. 242.

66. *Ibid.*, p. 245.

67. *Ibid.*, p. 244.

68. Arno Bellack. "Knowledge Structure and the Curriculum," in Elam (ed.). *Education and the Structure of Knowledge*, p. 277.

69. Geraldine Joncich Clifford. *The Shape of American Education* (Englewood Cliffs, New Jersey: Prentice-Hall, 1975), p. 151.

70. Bruner, *"The Process of Education Reconsidered"* in Hass (ed.). *Curriculum Planning*, p. 197.

71. Clifford, *Shape of American Education*, p. 150.

72. Fred T. Wilhelms. "Realignments for Teacher Education: The Eleventh Charles W. Hunt Lecture" quoted in Clifford. *Shape of American Education,* p. 150.

73. Jerome S. Bruner. *The Relevance of Education* (New York: W. W. Norton, 1971), p. x.

74. National Science Foundation and the Department of Education. *Science and Engineering Education for the 1980s and Beyond* (Washington, D. C.: U. S. Government Printing Office, 1980), p. 3.

75. John F. Kennedy. "Special Message to the Congress on Education, January 29, 1963" in Sol Cohen (ed.). *Education in the United States: A Documentary History* (New York: Random House, 1974), p. 3352.

76. John F. Kennedy. "Special Message to the Congress on Education, February 20, 1961" in Cohen (ed.). *Education in the United States,* p. 3348.

77. Kennedy. "Special Message to the Congress on Education, January 29, 1963" in Cohen (ed.). *Education in the United States,* pp. 3357-3358.

78. President Lyndon Johnson's Call upon Congress to Pass [the] Elementary and Secondary Education Act" in Cohen (ed.). *Education in the United States,* p. 3373

79. Almost all lists of the national reports include *A Nation at Risk* and the following: Ernest L. Boyer. *High School: A Report on Secondary Education in America* (New York: Harper & Row, 1983); College Board. *Academic Preparation for College: What Students Need to Know and Be Able to Do* (New York: College Entrance Examination Board, 1983); Philip A. Cusick. *The Egalitarian Ideal and the American High School* (New York: Longman, 1983); Linda Darling-Hammond. *Beyond the Commission Reports: The Coming Crisis in Teaching* (Washington, D. C.: Rand, 1984); John I. Goodlad. *A Place Called School: Prospects for the Future* (New York: McGraw-Hill, 1984); Sara Lawrence Lightfoot. *The Good High School: Portraits of Character and Culture* (New York: Basic Books, 1983); The National Science Board's Commission on Precollege Education in Mathematics, Science and Technology. *Educating Americans for the Twenty-first Century* (Washington, D. C.: National Science Board, 1983); Task Force on Education for Economic Growth. *Action for Excellence: A Comprehensive Plan to Improve Our Nation's Schools* (Washington, D. C.: Education Commission of the States, 1983); Task Force on Federal Elementary and Secondary Education Policy. *Making the Grade* (New York: Twentieth Century Fund, 1983; and Theodore Sizer. *Horace's Compromise: The Dilemma of the American High School* (Boston: Houghton Mifflin, 1984). The following are also included at times in the lists of the national reports: Mortimer Adler. *The Paidea Proposal: An Educational Manifesto* (New York: Macmillan, 1982) and *Paidea Problems and Possibilities: A Consideration of Questions Raised by the Paidea Proposal* (New York: Macmillan, 1983).

80. Charles Strickland. "Sputnik Reform Revisited," *Educational Studies,* Vol. 16 (Spring 1985), p. 15

CHAPTER 14

THE ACHIEVEMENT GAP

The *Coleman Report* and its Legacy in No Child Left Behind

After World War II and especially after the Supreme Court ruling in *Brown v. the Board of Education of Topeka Kansas* in 1954, and the appearance of *Equality of Educational Opportunity*, (commonly known as the *Coleman Report*) in 1966, it became clear that structural inconsistencies in the provision of equally effective public schooling for all children had to be faced. The nation could no longer afford vast discrepancies in access to education on the basis of race and class whether by law, *de jure*, or in fact, *de facto*. What constituted equality of educational opportunity and how to determine or measure the extent to which it did or did not exist, challenged and continues to challenge educational researchers just as it continues to engage those responsible for educational policy today.

This chapter takes up these vital questions as they have shaped public education, policy and practice for more than fifty years. They have challenged educational researchers and their impact has been enormous, at once elevating the use of objective research to determine educational policy, and also bringing such research into question as the problems continued to exist, defying the belief that objective research provides answers and that answers lead to permanent solutions. Whether researchers were

*Educational Research, the National Agenda, and Educational Reform:
A History,* pp. 389–411
Copyright © 2008 by Information Age Publishing
All rights of reproduction in any form reserved.

trying to develop an effective educational policy or trying to determine the most important index of equality of educational opportunity, they had to choose among the variables that promised to answer their questions. They had to choose among different data sets and the relationships among them: school resources (inputs); academic achievement (outputs or outcomes); and the extent to which schools were racially or otherwise integrated. How questions are framed affects conclusions. Acting on conclusions, even based on the best data and analysis, can have unexpected consequences when used to settle upon educational policies. At the beginning of the twenty-first century, elimination of the achievement gap was placed high on the national agenda and high on educational researchers' agenda when President George W. Bush signed the No Child Left Behind Act in 2002. If educators claim that they have either closed or made significant progress toward closing the achievement gap, they must produce scores on standardized tests to support their claims. That requirement among others specified in No Child Left Behind has clearly favored some forms of research.

EDUCATIONAL OPPORTUNITY AND THE NATIONAL AGENDA

In early 1945, when World War II was near its end, the United States Senate Committee on Education and Labor held hearings on a proposal to provide federal support for public education. The proposal for federal aid failed, as had earlier proposals. However, the hearings were significant. They constituted a sign that public education was high on the national agenda and that what Diane Ravitch identified as the "major theme" of the hearings—"the lack of equal opportunity in American education"[1]—would also be an item high on the national agenda for the remainder of the twentieth century and beyond. The testimony presented to the committee documented the disparities in support for schools, especially the differences in how schools in the North were supported as opposed to those in the South and how the schools to which African Americans were assigned where not nearly as well supported as those to which whites were assigned. The differences between the African American schools and the white schools in the North as well as in the South had recently been reported in Gunnar Myrdal's report for the Carnegie Corporation, *An American Dilemma* (1944). Underlying all the documentation of the gross disparities in how schools for various populations and in schools in different parts of the nation were supported was the belief that resources made a difference. Reduced to its simplest terms that meant that equal investments or expenditures would produce equal results, that students who attended equally supported schools would benefit equally.

To benefit equally, would eventually mean, of course, that scores on standardized achievement tests would not show consistent differences between the achievement level of those classified as members of the dominant or majority group and those classified as members of a minority group, or between disadvantaged students and those not so classified.

When the United States Supreme Court announced its *Brown* decision, it effectively introduced another way to measure equality of educational opportunity. It ruled in favor of the plaintiffs not because the schools to which African Americans were assigned were not as well supported as the schools to which others were assigned. In fact, the attorney for the Kansas plaintiffs, Robert Carter, acknowledged that the facilities provided for African American children in Topeka were in fact equal to those used by whites. Carter and the other Legal Defense Fund attorneys argued that the quality (or equality of schooling) depended on intangible considerations as well as tangible facilities. The Supreme Court accepted what the Chief Justice described as "academic evidence" and ruled that racial segregation in public schools constituted inequality and was therefore unconstitutional. In the future, school segregation would become another measure of equality of educational opportunity.

The ruling that separate but equal in public education was unequal and therefore unconstitutional was a modest beginning toward resolving the problem—"the lack of equal opportunity in American education." The Court did not then explicitly state that the federal government had an interest in public education, but it did report that it was necessary to "consider public education in the light of its full development and its present place in American life throughout the Nation." The Court further observed that: "compulsory school laws and the great expenditures for education both demonstrate our recognition of the importance of education to our democratic society." Education was the "foundation of good citizenship," and "required for the performance of our most basic public responsibilities, even service in the armed forces." The Court was suggesting what would soon be explicitly expressed, that is, the national defense required educated citizens. The Court further explained that citizens could not be "expected to succeed in life" if they were "denied the opportunity of an education."[2] In the Post-World War II Era—the Cold War era—education was necessary not only for the welfare of the nation but also the welfare of its individual citizens. What the Court was suggesting was confirmed by the United States Congress in 1954 when besides passing the Cooperative Research Act (Public Law 83-531) that authorized cooperative arrangements with universities, colleges, and state educational agencies for educational research, it also created the National Advisory Committee on Education (Public Law 83-532) the purpose of which was to identify needed studies of national interest in the field of education and to recommend appropriate action indicated by the identified studies.

WHITE HOUSE CONFERENCE ON EDUCATION

What was suggested in the *Brown* decision was made explicit two years later when the 1955 White House Conference on Education issued its Report. The Committee for the White Conference reported that "one fundamental fact" had emerged: the schools' importance for the "welfare" of the nation was then "more important than ever before" and that importance had been "dangerously underestimated for a long time." The report saw a connection between educational opportunity and economic opportunity, or social mobility. Schools prevented "rigid class barriers" from developing once the frontier closed. The availability of schools ensured that "a man is not frozen at any level of our economy, nor is his son."[3] It also recognized what the nation needed to prosecute the Cold War, or what the committee described as "this era of international stress." In addition to the "unusual demands for good scientists and engineers ... and other specialists," there was a demand for citizens who knew the "meaning of citizenship" and "who know something of other nations and are equipped to understand their own Nation's role in international affairs,"[4] circumstances not unlike the present.

The White House Conference recognized that: "Nowadays equality of opportunity for adults means little without equality of educational opportunity for children."[5] What was known but not fully addressed was that equality of educational opportunity had not been and was not being extended to all the nation's children. The *Brown* decision was a clear statement that equality of educational opportunity had not and was not being extended to all the nation's children. In between the *Brown* decision and the White House Conference on Education what has come to be known as *Brown II* was handed down by the Supreme Court. The Court did direct the defendants to "make a full and reasonable start toward full compliance" with the 1954 decision. However, it also acknowledged that once the start was underway, "additional time" may be required to carry out the Court's order.[6] Progress toward extending equality of opportunity—toward truly dismantling "separate but equal"—was delayed. Whatever pubic interest there may have been in implementing *Brown I* and *Brown II* was overshadowed on October 5, 1957 when Americans learned that the Soviet Union had successfully placed *Sputnik* in orbit. Those who had been criticizing the nation's public schools for not placing sufficient emphasis on standards and the traditional academic disciplines were given instantaneous credibility and were no longer seen as anti-democratic enemies of public education. The space race was on, and schools were to prepare the scientists and engineers that the White House Conference identified as needed.

JAMES S. COLEMEN AND THE RESEARCH CONDUCTED FOR EQUALITY OF EDUCATIONAL OPPORTUNITY

It is clear that the *Brown* decision did not immediately end racial segregation in the nation's public schools. However, it did set in motion a movement that culminated in the 1964 Civil Rights Act. To determine whether equality of educational opportunity was available to all the nation's children the United States Commissioner of Education was ordered by Title IV, Section 402 of the Civil Rights Act "to conduct a survey and make a report to the President and the Congress, within two years ... concerning the lack of availability of equal educational opportunities for individuals by reason of race, color, religion, or national origin in public educational institutions at all levels in the United States, its territories and possessions, and the District of Columbia."[7] Alex M. Mood, the Assistant Commissioner for Educational Statistics, assigned the task of conducting the survey to James S. Coleman from the Johns Hopkins University and Ernest Q. Campbell from Vanderbilt University. Mood agreed that the researchers could collect data that would allow them to investigate the relationships among students' family backgrounds, schools' resources, and students' academic achievement.[8]

The Coleman Report is arguably the most-well known and the most comprehensive study of American education. The $1.5 million the researchers had at their disposal enabled them to collect data from 570,000 students, 60,000 teachers, and 4,000 elementary and secondary schools. The Educational Testing Service administered standardized tests to students, and James S. Coleman and his associates analyzed the data.

Notwithstanding the cost and the magnitude of the study, its release was initially met with "deafening silence." In part that may have been because it was released just before the July 4, 1966 weekend. In part that may have been because the projects' advisory panel "refused to sign off on it, citing methodological concerns." Subsequently, others would express methodological concerns and there soon developed a cottage industry devoted to questioning, examining, and analyzing the methods and the conclusions of *The Coleman Report*.[9] *The Coleman Report* did eventually receive and continued to receive attention as evidenced by the claim in the June 21, 2006 issue of *Education Week* that *The Coleman Report's* "influence" was "felt 40 years latter." Perhaps the first significant attention given *The Coleman Report* was that given by Christopher Jencks in October

1966 in the *New Republic*. For Jencks, it was "the most important piece of educational research in recent years."[10] The title of Jencks' review—"Education: The Racial Gap"—was significant and certainly not misleading, for it clearly demonstrated that members of minority groups tended not to perform as well in school as their majority-group counterparts.

Subsequent to *The Coleman Report* educators and educational researchers had to attend to how school practices and instruments for the measurement of school achievement affected populations that had previously been neglected. Most importantly, a new measure for determining equality of educational opportunity was established. It was no longer sufficient to demonstrate that those who had been denied access to equal schools now had access to good schools. At the beginning of the twenty-first century, educators had to break the long established relationship between social-economic status and academic achievement as indicated by one's performance on standardized tests.

Equality of educational opportunity or lack thereof had become an important topic on the researchers' agenda as well as an important consideration on the national agenda. Determining whether there exists equality of educational opportunity in public schools turned out to not be a simple undertaking. Researchers had to deal with three measures of equality of educational opportunity: resources (input); the extent to which schools were desegregated or integrated; and student achievement (outcomes or output).

Coleman and his associates examined the educational opportunities available to six racial and ethnic groups: "Negroes, American Indians, Oriental Americans, Puerto Ricans living in the continental United States, Mexican Americans, and whites other than Mexican Americans and Puerto Ricans often called 'majority' or simply 'white.'"[11] They collected data to answer questions in four areas:

1. They attempted to determine how much segregation existed among the various racial and ethnic groups in the nation's public schools.

2. They attempted to determine whether all public schools offered equal educational opportunity by collecting information on laboratory facilities; textbooks; libraries; curricula; teacher characteristic, such as training and education, experience, salaries, attitudes, and verbal ability; and several student characteristics, such as socioeconomic status, parents' education, academic goals, and other attitudinal measures.

3. They measured student learning by examining their performances on standardized tests.

4. They tried to determine whether student achievement was related to the characteristics of the schools they attended.

Before *Equality of Educational Opportunity* was completed Coleman clearly believed the study would reveal "striking" differences between schools attended by African Americans and those attended by whites. He predicted that:

> ... the study will show the difference in the quality of schools that the average Negro child and the average white child are exposed to. You know yourself that the difference is going to be striking. And even though everybody knows there is a lot of difference between suburban and inner city schools, once the statistics are there in black and white, they will have a lot more impact.[12]

When Coleman and his associates began their study, they were effectively accepting a measure of equality of educational opportunity determined by inputs or resources. If, for example, the facilities, materials, teachers, and per pupil expenditures between and among schools were equal, then, according to this measure, equality of educational opportunity obtained. However, they did not find all that they expected to find.

The Coleman Report established that ten years after the Supreme Court ruled that the longstanding notion of "separate but equal" was not equal and therefore unconstitutional, the nation's schools were still mostly racially segregated. Therefore, inequality obtained, for the Supreme Court had effectively created a measure or determinant of equality of educational opportunity that was not directly related to either resources or student performance. The Court provided a stipulated definition of equality. Segregated schools were not and could not be equal. If the measure of equality was integration, then inequality persisted. Most of the nation's children were still attending schools that had not been desegregated. Nearly two thirds of African American first graders attended schools that were between ninety and one hundred percent African American and nearly fifty percent of African American twelfth graders attended schools in which half or more of the students were African American. Of all groups, white children were the most segregated. Eighty percent of the white students in both the first and the twelfth grades attended schools that were between ninety and one hundred percent white. According to this definition, a vast majority of American students—African Americans as well as whites—were being denied equality of educational opportunity.

That *The Coleman Report* documented the extent to which so many white students had successfully avoided desegregated schools is, in retrospect, not surprising, for *The Coleman Report* was based on information gathered in an era when the "Briggs dictum" prevailed.[13]

What was surprising was the failure of the investigators to find meaningful and significant differences between African American and white schools. That the survey was ordered and Coleman's remarks as it was getting underway constitute an indication that there was a prevailing belief that the quality of African American schools differed markedly from that of white schools. It was also expected that the study would "establish that Southern states systematically discriminated against African Americans in the provision of school facilities," but "the tabulated data do not support the presumption of gross discrimination in the provision of school facilities in the South."[14] The pattern of gross discrimination in the provision of resources for educational facilities and materials so evident in the South even as late as the mid-1940s had been effectively remedied.

Differences between minority and majority schools were not as great as they once were or believed to have been but differences had not been completely eliminated. The researchers did find that:

> There are fewer physics laboratories, there are fewer books per student in libraries, texts are less often in sufficient supply, schools are less often accredited, students who fail a subject are less likely to repeat a grade, they are less often schools with intensive testing, academically related extracurricular activities are less, the curriculum less often is built around an academic program.[15]

Such differences, however, were not as "striking" or as "significant" as had been expected. It was concluded that: "these differences in facilities and programs must not be overemphasized," for in many instances they were "not large." Moreover, it was also determined that "regional differences between schools are usually considerably greater than minority-majority differences."[16]

What was significant was the difference in achievement between minority and majority students. The difference between African Americans and whites was found to be "progressively greater for the minority pupils at progressively higher grade levels."[17] At age six, the "grade level gap" in achievement was 1.6 years. By the time students entered high school, grade nine, it was 2.4 years. At the end of school, grade twelve, it was up to 3.3 years. Minority students were at a disadvantage when the entered school and that disadvantage was still there when they left school.

The achievement differences could not be explained by the inequalities between the schools the students attended. As Coleman noted, "it appears that variations in the facilities and curriculum of the schools account for relatively little variation in pupil achievement insofar as this is measured by standard tests."[18] It seemed clear that "Whatever may be the combination of nonschool factors—poverty, community attitudes, low educational level of parents—which put minority students at a disadvantage in verbal and nonverbal skills when they enter the first grade, the fact is the schools have not overcome it."[19] Coleman's findings seemed to demonstrate that differences between and among schools were clearly not great enough to explain the differences in student achievement. One clear implication was that the schools were not totally responsible for the achievement differences in the groups that were studied, but Coleman was not willing to relieve schools for the responsibility for effecting academic achievement for all students.

COLEMAN ON THE COLEMAN REPORT FINDINGS

Coleman offered virtually no discussion of the significance of the findings reported in *Equality of Educational Opportunity*. However, he soon wrote in *The Public Interest* that while it may have seemed "flat," it was "not as uncontroversial as it appears" and suggested that: "Some of its findings, though cautiously presented, have sharp implications."[20] Coleman's discussions of *Equality of Educational Opportunity* reveal not only that the implications were "sharp" but also that he was proposing a revolutionary change in how equality of educational opportunity was defined and measured. Its "principal focus of attention was not on what resources go into education, but on what product comes out." To have equality of educational opportunity meant not just that schools were equal "in some formal sense" but that all children would leave school with the skills they needed to compete successfully either in the job market or in college, "that is, verbal and reading skills, and analytical and mathematical skills." To achieve equality of opportunity, the consistent and predictable relationship between social class and educational achievement had to be overcome. As Coleman explained: "Equality of educational opportunity implies, not merely 'equal' schools, but equally effective schools, whose influences will overcome the differences in the starting point of children from different social groups."[21] In a subsequent discussion of *Equality of Educational Opportunity*, Coleman admitted that "not just to offer, in a passive way, equal access to educational resources, but to provide an educational environment that will free a child's potentialities for learning from the inequalities imposed upon him by the accident of birth into one or another home and social environment" was "a task far more ambitious than has even been attempted by any society."[22]

The grade-level gap that grew progressively worse as students progressed from one grade to the next was, according to Coleman, "*obviously in part a result of the school.*"[23] Coleman did recognize and did admit that the source of the problem was not totally in the school. He explained that: "*The sources of inequality of educational opportunity appear to lie first in the home itself and the cultural influences immediately surrounding the home; then they lie in the school's ineffectiveness to free achievement from the impact of the home, and in the schools' cultural homogeneity which perpetuates the social influences of the home and its environs.*"[24] To allocate additional resources to schools to maintain the status quo in organization and operation would not improve matters, for "*per pupil expenditures, books in the library, and a host of other facilities and curricular measures show virtually no relation to achievement if the 'social' environment of the school—the educational backgrounds of other students and teachers—is held constant.*"[25] The solution was not in doing more of the same, but in adopting what Coleman described as "a modest, yet radical proposal."

Coleman's Proposal for Educational Reform

Coleman's "modest, yet radical proposal" challenged conventional school practice. The first of its three major points was essentially a restatement of a claim that educators and social theorists had been making since the end of the nineteenth century: the family did not have access to the resources necessary for preparing children for the requirements of a complex technological society, and the school was the institution qualified and prepared to teach children the values, knowledge, and skills necessary for competing successfully in a complex and impersonal social order. He pointed out that traditionally the school was "a supplement to the family in bringing a child into his place in adult society" and argued that: "The conditions imposed by technological change and by our post-industrial society, require a far more primary role for the school, if society's children are to be equipped for adulthood."[26] If children were to be properly equipped for adulthood in school, it was necessary to lessen the influence of the family and increase the influence of the school "by starting school at an earlier age, and by having a school which begins very early in the day and ends very late."[27] That recommendation was an endorsement of Project Head Start and Title I of the Elementary and Secondary Education Act (1965) that provided billions of dollars for schools that served disadvantaged students.[28]

Coleman's second point effectively raised questions about the public's attachment to the "neighborhood school." Adherence to the neighborhood school ensured that "the social and racial homogeneity of the school environment," that was strongly related to the differential achievement that he wanted to eliminate, would persist. For some, the way to overcome that "homogeneity" was to bus students, but Coleman opposed bussing. He claimed that an "incidental effect" of bussing "would be to increase the segregation within schools, through an increase in tracking."[29] Any increase in segregation would, according to the measures of equality of educational opportunity, including that decreed in *Brown*, increase inequality.

Coleman's third point was a recommendation for "new kinds of educational institutions, with a vast increase in expenditures for education—not merely for the disadvantaged, but for all children." While he did not offer any specific suggestions for new kinds of education until he described "open schools" in 1967, he did suggest that new forms of schooling worthy of consideration "might be in the form of educational parks, or in the form of private schools paid by tuition grants (with Federal regulations to insure racial heterogeneity), public (or publicly subsidized) boarding schools (like the North Carolina Advancement School), or still other innovations."[30] Better teaching methods had to be found so tracking could be avoided. Tracking was then necessary because current teaching methods were suited only to a narrow range of students. Better methods would allow teachers to teach a greater range of students effectively and thereby "make possible the informal learning that other students of higher educational levels can provide."[31]

Coleman's plan for "open schools" was designed to capitalize on the effects that students had on each other in school. In *Equality of Educational Opportunity* it was reported that:

> ... it appears that a pupil's achievement is strongly related to the educational backgrounds and aspirations of the other students in the school...Analysis indicates ... that children from a given family background, when put in schools of different social composition, will achieve at quite different levels. This effect is again less for white pupils than for any minority group other than Orientals. Thus, if a white pupil from a home that is strongly and effectively supportive of education is put in a school where most pupils do not come from such homes, his achievement will be little different than if he were in a school composed of others like himself. But if a minority pupil from a home without much educational strength is put with schoolmates with strong educational backgrounds, his achievement is likely to increase.[32]

In his discussion of the implications of his report, Coleman clearly stated that one finding of the study was that:

> ... students do better when they are in schools where their fellow students come from backgrounds strong in educational motivation and resources.... This effect appears to be particularly great for students who themselves come from educationally deprived backgrounds. For example, it is about twice as great for Negroes as for whites.[33]

For Coleman, equality of educational opportunity could only be achieved through "a more intense reconstruction of the child's social environment than that provided by school integration." It could be accomplished in a variety of ways—"through other children, through tutorial programs, through artificial environments created by computer consoles,"—but it had to be done."[34] One way to reconstruct the child's social environment was to open the schools. Opening schools entailed thinking of the school "not as a building into which a child vanishes in the morning and from which he emerges in the afternoon, but as a 'home base' that carries out some teaching functions but which serves principally to coordinate his activities and to perform guidance and testing functions."[35]

At the elementary school level, Coleman suggested that the teaching of reading and arithmetic—two important subjects that schools frequently failed to teach to lower class children and thereby handicapped them for life—"be opened up to entrepreneurs outside the school."[36] Entrepreneurs would have to agree to standards that would disallow discrimination on the basis of race, class, or educational level. They would be "paid on the basis of increased performance by the child on standardized tests."[37]

Coleman also suggested that the high school could also be opened up to "outside entrepreneurs." There "private contractors" would do teaching of "core subjects" in many instances. Thus, at both the elementary and the secondary levels, parents could choose to have their children attend "programs outside the school" or they could decide to leave their children in school for all subjects. The introduction of competition between the public school and the private contractors, Coleman suggested, would encourage schools to improve their programs.

Besides opening schools to equalize achievement, Coleman urged that schools be opened up to address "the problem of racial and class integration." While it was "almost impossible" to integrate (eliminate racial isolation) schools, especially those in large urban areas, it was, he maintained, possible to use schools to effect social integration. All students would have their own "home-base schools" but would have to attend other schools for some of their classes. "Thus," Coleman reasoned, "rather than having classes scheduled in the school throughout the year, some classes would be scheduled with children from other schools, sometimes in their own school, sometimes in the other—but deliberately designed to establish continuing relationships between children across racial and social class lines." Extracurricular activities could be organized and scheduled to coincide with class schedules so students "from different home base schools would not be competing against each other, but would be members of the *same* team or club." Organizations outside the school would be allowed to serve as contractors for extracurricular activities. "Community organizations," he suggested, "could design specific cultural enrichment activities or community action programs involving students from several schools of different racial or class composition, with students engaging in such programs by their own or parent's choice."[38] Students with different backgrounds would learn "to work together and to aid the community." He assumed that outside agencies would be better at conducting community improvement programs than would the public schools.

Coleman also claimed that his plan for open schools would settle other educational disputes. He noted that "the issue of parental control versus control by the educational bureaucracy" has always been an issue and had recently become an "intense" issue in New York City (an apparent reference to controversy over a decentralization plan in Brooklyn known as the Oceanhill-Brownsville affair). As long as parents and students had no choices about schooling, public schooling remained a monopoly and the only way "consumers" had to express their interest in the activities of the monopoly was through "organized power." The introduction of choice through contracts with outside entrepreneurs would eliminate the need for "organized power" and presumably the strategy of confrontational politics that community groups had to employ to get the attention of their public school officials. Open schools would extend to public school users some choice comparable to that enjoyed by "those who could afford to buy education outside the public schools."[39]

THE EDUCATION ESTABLISHMENT RESPONDS

The Coleman Report marked a turning point in what educational researchers studied and how they conducted their studies. Before its publication, "there had been relatively little observational research that examined schooling in America." However, after its publication there was "a flurry of input-output studies" that examined the relationship between "school resources" and "student outcomes," as measured by student performance on standardized tests. Significantly, those studies supported the conclusions of *The Coleman Report*, for those studies failed to show "any consistent relationship between resources and student outcomes."[40] Some used the conclusions of *The Coleman Report* and subsequent input-out studies to argue that there was little reason to study schooling "because the effects of schooling on student achievement are minor at best."[41]

However, by the mid-1980s, it was claimed that research on school effectiveness that focused on school processes demonstrated that schools could make a difference. That research showed that some schools employed processes that produced more student achievement (output) than comparable schools with similar resources (inputs) and that "some [school] processes consistently characterize more and less successful schools."[42]

The education establishment was not very happy with a report that "in effect declared that professional practice in a major social institution was not nearly so efficacious as had been thought."[43] *The Coleman Report* was "startling and corrosive," for it undermined what professionals believed schools could accomplish.[44] It undermined the belief that more resources would improve schools and overcome the effects of a poor family background. That basically caused a reexamination of the late eighteenth century decision to move the responsibility for education from the family to the school. However, educators and education researchers who had an interest in public education were not willing to accept that public schools were not capable of overcoming the social structures and practices that privileged some students and disadvantaged others.

The Coleman Report brought "school outputs out into the open as the chief focus for both schools and research."[45] Consequently and subsequently, educational researchers sought to identify schools and teachers that appeared to work—schools that produced academic achievement. Their efforts constituted a sign that the belief in the schools' ability to be the chief educational institution persisted. Some wanted to believe that schools and teachers could make a difference. What is most significant, however, is that little attention appears to have been given to understanding why some children begin school at a disadvantage. Educational researchers did not in any significant way ask about the structure and practices of a society that systematically privileged some and disadvantaged others. That some reply that such inquiries are social and not educational inquiries demonstrates that educational research is basically research about one educational agency—the school. Its agenda reflects and responds to the national agenda. It rarely challenges or questions it.

It was clearly stated in *The Coleman Report* that "it should be noted that many characteristics of teachers were not measured in this survey; therefore, the results are not at all conclusive regarding the specific characteristics of teachers that are important."[46] Yet, *The Coleman Report* was generally interpreted to mean that neither schools nor teachers were strongly related to student achievement. It was widely and correctly interpreted as explaining student achievement or lack thereof in terms of sociological factors—social status or family background—as opposed to the quality of either schools or teachers. Researchers and those responsible for formulating educational policy who were not prepared to accept the claim of *The Coleman Report* that "teachers, or more accurately variations among teachers, do not make a difference in school achievement" pointed out that Coleman's conclusions "were based on a classic input-output production function analysis of schools" and included no data on what actually transpired in the classroom.[47] Coleman's conclusions "were based on school measures, data available from school records, and averages across classrooms."[48] Subsequently, a number of researchers "scrambled to refute overinterpretations and overreactions to the negative findings from the school effects research exemplified by *The Coleman Report*."[49] That prompted a number of researchers to embark on what is now known as the process-product research, research that sought to determine whether there were teacher behaviors or practices that were significantly related to student achievement. That research demonstrated that "variations in teacher behavior [processes] were found to be systematically related to variations in student achievement [products or outcomes]."[50]

In 1986 when the third *Handbook of Research on Teaching* appeared, it was clear that education researchers were still dealing with issues framed by *The Coleman Report* and trying to show that schools and teachers, especially teachers, were important, that they did make a difference. Some believed there just had to be good teachers and good schools, and they needed to be identified so others could see "what works." In the 1970s, especially the period between 1972 and 1978, "research on teaching simply took on new meaning and emphasis as classroom researchers scrambled to refute overinterpretations and overreactions to the negative findings from the school effects research exemplified by *The Coleman Report*."[51] There may have been overinterpretations and overreactions, but there is no denying that *The Coleman Report* and other input-output research gave many good reason to argue that that schooling had minimal effect on student achievement.[52] Some argued that: "Much research in the late 1960s and early 1970s suggests that differences in school resources and practices do not relate to variations in student achievement as measured by standardized achievement tests." Others argued that and that "there could be some unusually effective individual schools" and that some unusually *ineffective schools* can also be masked when data are reported only in *group averages*."[53]

By 1986, researchers confidently observed that: "Pupils spend most of their time in school in classrooms, and evidence is now overwhelming that teaching makes a difference." To understand fully the difference that teaching makes and how it is related to other "potent variables in the environments of pupils" researchers needed to embark on longitudinal studies. That such studies have not been undertaken may be explained by the training of educational researchers." Most have been trained "as educational psychologists and feel more comfortable with experimental design and the analysis of variance than with longitudinal design and regression techniques."[54]

THE CONTEMPORATY LEGACY OF THE COLEMAN REPORT: NO CHILD LEFT BEHIND

At the beginning of the twenty-first century, Congress passed the No Child Left Behind Act, an Act designed to overcome what Coleman and his associates documented in the mid-1960s. *The Coleman Report* documented what is now commonly known as the "achievement gap" or what Christopher Jencks described as the "racial gap." Christopher Jencks claimed that the "racial gap" could not be overcome without massive federal interference in public education that many persisted in claiming was the prerogative of state and local authorities.

It is not possible to compare achievement between two groups until those groups are identified. Race and ethnicity are lived experiences. However, they are also primarily social designation. The idea of race was reified in the United States by misapplying Darwinian theories on evolution and speciation. However, there is only one human race and divisions based on extraneous physical attributes such as hair, skin, or eye color do not represent different species arranged in a hierarchy. Ethnicity is also problematic even though one's background is inherited from one's parents. It is possible to be descended from a particular group but to have virtually nothing in common with the culture, language, or shared experiences, or vice versa.

The minority groups Coleman identified—"Negroes, American Indians, Oriental Americans, Puerto Ricans living in the continental United States, Mexican Americans"—did not, as groups, perform as well in school, as the dominant group—"whites other than Mexican Americans and Puerto Ricans often called 'majority' or simply 'white.' "[55] What Coleman identified as a major inequality—the lack of academic achievement among minority groups—implicitly raised questions about the classifications and labels that are assigned to various groups in the United States. In 1973, less than a decade after *The Coleman Report*, Casper Weinberger, then the secretary of United States Department of Health, Education, and Welfare, and directed the Federal Interagency on Education "to develop consistent rules for classifying Americans by ethnicity and race." That led to the Office of Management and Budget's issuance of "Directive No. 15: Race and Ethnic Standards for Federal Statistics and Administrative Reporting" in 1977.[56] While the groups Coleman identified are not those—American Indian or Alaskan Native, Asian or Pacific Islander, Hispanic, White, Black—later officially designated by Statistical Directive No. 15, there is a remarkable similarity. The means used to assess students on a periodic basis—various forms of "objective" or standardized tests—to determine whether the achievement gap is being closed are part of the legacy from the Progressive Era when psychologists and educational researchers developed those tests.

Coleman found that as groups they did not perform as well in school as the dominant amorphous collection of "whites." Coleman's identification of the lack of academic achievement among minority groups is specifically addressed in the No Child Left Behind Act. A difference is that Coleman's argument that the social environment of many students contributes to unequal achievement and needed to be addressed in terms of social class is not recognized in No Child Left Behind. The No Child Left Behind Act specifically recognized that students identified as being members of minority groups consistently perform less well in school than their counterparts from the dominant classes and states as its purpose the elimination of the differences among the groups—the achievement gap. No Child Left Behind can be interpreted as an attempt to remedy the inequalities documented in *The Coleman Report*. The means now being used to assess students on a periodic basis—various forms of standardized achievement tests are the means developed during the Progressive Era by psychologists and educational researchers who wanted efficient procedures to ensure proper assignment of students to appropriate courses of study. The means used by Coleman to claim that equality of educational opportunity did not exist were not seen as relevant.

Once *The Coleman Report* was fully understood, those responsible for public education realized that they had to do more than simply find ways to "turn on" students so they would remain in school. Public education was soon to be accountable according to a new definition of equality of educational opportunity. To the extent that social class, race or ethnicity was associated with poor performance equality of educational opportunity did not obtain. Social class, race and ethnicity were often once used to explain poor or lack of academic achievement but now educators were assigned the responsibility for finding ways to eliminate their predictive power. What may have been only implicit in *The Coleman Report* became explicit in No Child Left Behind.

In terms of remediation in specific subjects, a full generation after Coleman's suggestion on reading and arithmetic, No Child Left Behind was designed to address the same inequality or differential achievement that Coleman identified and tried to address. No Child Left Behind appears to have no explicit provision for employing entrepreneurs to teaching arithmetic and reading, but districts receiving Title I funds are required to use reading programs that are supported by scientifically based research and the current climate celebrates entrepreneurship and its employment by school districts.

No Child Left Behind rewards schools whose students achieve satisfactorily with additional resources and allows parents of "failing" schools to remove their children from the failing school. For example, schools that fail to show annual yearly progress for two consecutive years are required to offer students' parents the opportunity to transfer to another school provided that state law does not prohibit school choice. Those schools are then required to use up to five percent of their Title I funds to pay for students' transportation to another school. Schools that fail to demonstrate annual yearly progress for three consecutive are allowed to use an additional ten percent of their Title I funds for either transportation to another school or for supplemental instructional services—tutoring, after school classes, and summer school—for low achieving disadvantaged students. The provision of supplemental services is not limited to public schools. Faith-based organizations are allowed to provide such services. Districts with schools that fail to show annual yearly progress for four consecutive years are required to implement an improvement plan. Districts with schools that fail to show annual yearly progress for five consecutive years are required to develop and implement plans that would change how the school is administered, allow the state to take control of the school, hire a private entity to administer the school, restructure the school's staff, or convert it to a charter school. All failing schools are required to provide supplemental instructional services and provide parents the opportunity to transfer their children to another school.

As noted earlier, Coleman wanted to introduce competition between the public school and the private contractors. Coleman felt this would encourage or force schools to improve their programs. Moreover, schools would then be able to adopt programs and innovations that worked in the private sector. No Child Left Behind is structured to do precisely this. Schools are assigned grades and thus competition is introduced not only between public and private but also between and among schools within a district. Coleman advocated the introduction of choice through contracts with outside entrepreneurs. Contract schools would extend to public school users some choice comparable to that enjoyed by the wealthy and middle classes who can afford to pay for education outside the public schools. A generation later, No Child Left Behind was designed to allow those who ordinarily could not afford to purchase education in the private sector the power to do so.

Coleman was not the only one to urge that the public school monopoly be broken. Kenneth Clark also urged that the "monopoly" be broken and replaced with a variety of alternative public school systems.[57] Charter schools have become popular in some quarters and can be seen as an alternative to public schools. They are supported with public funds and operate under standards set by the public. Writing in 1967, as were Clark and Coleman, Fred M. Newman and Donald W, Oliver also expressed concern about the public school monopoly that "fundamentally altered the nature of childhood and adolescence in American" and "destroyed to a large extent the opportunities for random, exploratory work and play outside of a formal educational setting."[58]

No Child Left Behind can be seen as having been designed to resolve either what is essentially a social justice issue or a concern over the future need for the human resources that is on the nation's agenda; and the desired political outcome determined the method that was to be favored. There is some belief that pursuit of what No Child Left Behind requires has effectively "reshaped much of the conscious paradigm regarding American education research." According to James W. Guthrie, the federal "Institute of Education Sciences, along with the National Institute for Child Health and Development and the National Science Foundation, is supporting research initiatives using rigorous randomized experiments to evaluate educational products and practices."[59] Presumably, such research will enable schools to eliminate what has come to be known as the "achievement gap."

No Child Left Behind may appear to have been designed to resolve what is essentially a social justice issue—the strong relationship that is consistently found between social class and school success—that has been an issue on the nation's agenda ever since, if not before, the appearance of *The Coleman Report*. No Child Left Behind requires that school districts disaggregate students' performances on standardized tests so it can be shown whether adequate yearly progress has been achieved by all students. That means districts must show the scores for each group: Students who are classified as belonging to one of the major racial ethnic groups; economically disadvantaged students; students with disabilities; and students whose English proficiency is limited. The desired political outcome determined how test results were to be analyzed and reported.

The What Works Clearinghouse received significant funding ($15 million) in 2002 from the Institute of Educational Sciences. Officials in the What Works Clearinghouse are attempting to identify effective instructional interventions by "using meta-analysis to aggregate the findings of different studies of the effectiveness of different instructional interventions."[60] The What Works Clearinghouse apparently found or had so little that actually worked, that is met its rigorous criteria, that there was concern that its Web site would not be useful to policymakers and practitioners in education. To enhance its usefulness the What Works Clearinghouse changed the format it uses and introduced a new category, "potentially positive," to report on studies.[61]

The support provided for scientifically based research by the Institute of Educational Sciences merits consideration because it is an effective way to basically control the questions that researchers will investigate. As

Catherine Cornbleth has observed: "The most harmful threat to the public interest stemming from the current push for scientific research in education and the scientific research procedures debate ... lies in the diversion of attention and other resources from issues and research questions that simply do not fit the referred procedures and the "what works (best)" question."[62] The questions Cornbleth believes should be asked— questions about cultural influences, the effects of racism and sexism—are clearly not the questions that interest the Institute of Education Sciences. The research priorities of the Department of Education published in the June 16, 2005 *Federal Register* concentrated "on studying conditions that are under the control of the education system: curriculum, instruction, assessment, the quality of teachers and administrators, accountability systems, and school choice."[63]

The current move to support only educational research that promises to demonstrate "what works" began with Congress' reauthorization of Title I of the Elementary and Secondary Education Action, now known as the No Child Left Behind Act. The essence of No Child Left Behind is that the school and teachers are solely responsible for student achievement. Now, of course, educators wish to emphasize the social context. They are returning to what *Equality of Educational Opportunity* was generally believed to demonstrate, that student achievement is more closely related to socioeconomic factors than to the quality of schools. In their discussion of the "Relation of achievement to school characteristics," the authors of *Equality of Educational Opportunity* reported:

> The first finding is that the schools are remarkably similar in the way they relate to the achievement of their pupils when the socioeconomic background of the students is taken into account. It is known that socioeconomic factors bear a strong relation to academic achievement. When these factors are statistically controlled, however, it appears that differences between schools account for only a small fraction of differences in pupil achievement.[64]

Clearly, those who want to place all responsibility for student achievement on schools and teachers and ignore and what *Equality of Educational Opportunity* claimed only need to return to what came to be known as the process-product research or continue to look for cause-and-effect relationships so they can tell teachers "what works." They do indeed want to ignore that "studies of school practices have consistently discovered powerful effects of family background on educational outcomes, much more powerful than the influence of schooling resources."[65]

NOTES

1. Diane Ravitch. *The Troubled Crusade: American Education, 9145-1980* (New York: Basic Books, Inc., 1983), p.5.

2. *Brown et al. v. Board of Education of Topeka et al.* 347 I/S/ 483 (1954) in Sol Cohen (ed.). *Education in the United States: A Documentary History*, Vol. 5 (New York: Random House, 1974), p. 3105.

3. *A Report to the President: The Committee for the White House Conference on Education, Full Report. April 1956* (Washington, D. C., 1956) in Cohen (ed.). *Education in the United States*, p. 3342.

4. *Ibid.*, p. 3345.

5. *Ibid.*, pp. 3344-3345.

6. *Brown v. Board of Education*, 349, U. S. 294 in Cohen (ed.). *Education in the United States: A Documentary History*, p. 3107.

7. James S. Coleman, Ernest Q, Campbell, Carol J. Hobson, James McPartland, Alexandar M. Mood, Frederic D. Weinfeld, and Robert L. York. *Equality of Educational Opportunity* (Washington, D. C,: U. S. Government Printing Office, 1966), p. iii.

8. David K. Cohen and Carol A. Barnes. "Research and the Purposes of Education" in Ellen Conliffe Lagemann and Lee S. Schulman (eds.). *Issues in Education Research: Problems and Possibilities* (San Francisco: Jossey-Bass Publishers, 1999), p. 23.

9. See, for example: William G. Spady. "The Impact of School Resources on Students" in Fred N. Kerlinger (ed.). *Review of Research in Education 1* (Itasca, Illinois: F. E. Peacock Publishers, Inc. (A publication of the American Educational Research Association), 1973), pp. 135-177.

10. Christopher Jencks. "Education: The Racial Gap," *New Republic*, (October 1966)

11. *Ibid.*

12. Quoted in Frederick Mosteller and Daniel P. Moynihan (eds.). *On Equality of Educational Opportunity* (New York: Vintage Books, 1972), p. 8.

13. The "Briggs dictum" was a 1955 ruling of a federal district court in South Carolina that maintained that public school officials were not constitutionally required to integrate schools and that school officials were only required not to discriminate. By holding that only governmentally required and enforced segregation was unlawful and holding that all students had the right to choose the school they wanted to attend the court provided a legal foundation for free-choice plans. Adoption of free-choice plans did not lead to any significant integration. It did, however, effectively sanction voluntary segregation. The "Briggs dictum" was overturned by a series of judicial decisions: *Jefferson* (1966); *Green* (1968); and *Swann* (1971).

14. Quoted in Mosteller and Moynihan (eds.). *On Equality of Educational Opportunity* , p. 10.

15. Coleman. *Equality of Educational Opportunity*, pp. 121-122.

16. *Ibid.*, p. 122.

17. *Ibid.*, p. 21

18. *Ibid.*, p.22.

19.   *Ibid.*, p. 21.

20.   James S. Coleman. "Equal Schools or Equal Students?" *The Public Interest,* No. 4 (Summer, 1966), p. 71.

21.   *Ibid.*, p. 72

22.   James S. Coleman. "Toward Open Schools." *The Public Interest,* No. 9 (Fall 1967), p. 21.

23.   Coleman. "Equal Schools," p. 73. Coleman's emphasis.

24.   *Ibid.*, pp. 73-74. Coleman's emphasis.

25.   *Ibid.* Coleman's emphasis.

26.   *Ibid.*, p. 75.

27.   *Ibid.*, p. 74.

28.   Title I on the Elementary and Secondary Education Act provided founds for school districts that served educationally disadvantaged students. It was the most important title, for most of the nation's school districts were eligible to receive funds and approximately three-fourths of the appropriated funds were in Title I. When Congress reauthorized ESEA in 1966 it authorized an expenditure of twelve billion dollars. That meant that the nation's public schools were eligible for a portion of the nine billion dollars to improve the education of poor children.

29.   Coleman. "Equal Schools," p. 74.

30.   *Ibid.*

31.   *Ibid.*, p. 75.

32.   Coleman. *Equality of Educational Opportunity*, p.22.

33.   Coleman, "Toward Open Schools," p. 21.

34.   *Ibid.*, p. 23.

35.   *Ibid.* p. 24.

36.   *Ibid.*

37.   *Ibid.*, p. 25.

38.   *Ibid.*, p. 26.

39.   *Ibid.*, p. 27.

40.   Thomas L. Good and Jere E. Brophy. "School Effects" in Merlin C. Wittrock (ed.). *Handbook of Research OonTeaching,* 3rd ed. (New York: Macmillan Co., 1986), pp. 597-598.

41.   *Ibid.*, p. 571.

42.   *Ibid.*, p. 598.

43.   Daniel P. Moynihan, "Sources of Resistance to the Coleman Report," *Harvard Educational Review,* Vol. 38, No. 1 (Winter 1968) p. 25.

44.   David K. Cohen and Carol A. Barnes. "Research and the Purposes of Education" in Lagemann and Schulman (eds.). *Issues in Education Research,* p. 23.

45.   *Ibid.*, p. 30.

46.   Coleman, *Equality of Educational Opportunity*, p. 22.

47.   Lee S. Schulman "Paradigms and Research Programs in the Study of Teaching" in Wittrock (ed.). *Handbook of Research OonTeaching,* 3rd. ed., p. 10.

48. Carolyn M. Evertson and Judith L. Green. "Observation as Inquiry and Method" in Wittrock (ed.). *Handbook of Research on Teaching*, 3rd ed., p. 191.

49. Richard J. Shavelson, Noreen M. Webb, and Leigh Burstein "Measurement of Teaching" in Wittrock (ed.), *Handbook of Research on Teaching*, 3rd. ed., p. 51.

50. Lee S. Schulman. "Paradigms and Research Programs in the Study of Teaching" in Wittrock (ed.). *Handbook of Research OonTeaching*, 3rd ed., p. 10.

51. Shavelson, Webb, and Burstein. "Measurement of Teaching," in Wittrock (ed.).*Handbook of Research on Teaching*, 3rd ed., 51.

52. Good and Brophy, "School Effects," p. 571.

53. *Ibid.,* p. 572.

54. Bruce J. Biddle and Donald S. Anderson. "Theory, Methods, Knowledge, and Research on Teaching" in Wittrock (ed.). *Handbook of Research on Teaching* 3rd. ed., p. 244.

55. Coleman, *Equality of Educational Opportunity*, p. iii.

56. Michael Lind. *The Next American Nation: The New Nationalism and the Fourth American Nation* (New York: Free Press, 1996) p. 119

57. Kenneth Clark, "Alternative Public School Systems," *Harvard Educational Review*, Vol, 38, No, 1 (Winter 1968).

58. Fred M. Newman and Donald W. Oliver. "Education and Community." *Harvard Educational Review*, Vol. 37 (Winter 1967), p. 81.

59. James W. Guthrie. "'For Want of a Nail... '" *Education Week*, Vol. 24, No. 34 (May 4, 2005), p. 48.

60. Debra Viadero. 'What Works' Rates Programs' Effectiveness. *Education Week*, Vol. 25, No. 37 (May 17, 2006), pp. 24, 26.

61. *Ibid.,* p. 25.

62. Cathernine Cornbleth. "Curriculum and Students: Diverting the Public Interest," in *Education Research in the Public Interest: Social Justice, Action, and Policy* (eds.) Gloria Ladson-Billings and William F. Tate (New York: Teachers College Press, 2006), 202.

63. Debra Viadero. "Learning by At-Risk Students Tops List of Proposed Research Priorities," *Education Week*, Vol. 24, No. 41 (July 13, 2005), p. 30.

64. Coleman, *et al. Equality of Educational Opportunity*, pp. 20-21.

65. William F. Tate. "In the Public Interest," in Ladson-Billings and Tate (eds.). *Education Research in the Public Interest*, 251.

CHAPTER 15

THE HISTORY OF EDUCATION AS EDUCATIONAL RESEARCH

The National Agenda and a Discipline

Educational researchers, including historians of education, since the beginning of the Post-World War II era and especially since *Sputnik*, have responded to criticisms of the nation's public schools with investigations of their own. A consideration of the work of four educational historians' writing what was called "revisionist history"—Lawrence A. Cremin, Raymond E. Callahan, David B. Tyack, and Jurgen Herbst[1]—show that historians of education often accept the claims as well as the recommendations embedded in the criticisms; at other times they do not. Some historians of education, as other educational researchers, may be described as communicants and can be counted among the faithful in support of institutions and practices; others are heretics and critics with their own calls for reform. This final chapter addresses the role and example of historians of education, who like other educational researchers, must consider whether and how to select and frame their research questions, methods, results, and analyses as priorities on the national agenda are rearranged.

This chapter addresses a question that has grown ever more important and ever more interesting as educational research has developed. Should educational research be objective and disinterested in its quest for truth

Educational Research, the National Agenda, and Educational Reform: A History, pp. 413–431

or should it be actively and consciously engaged in critical events and deliberately address and even challenge the national agenda? The quest for a scientifically based educational research has been an attempt to provide knowledge to inform decisions about schools and students independent of ideological or metaphysical considerations. Educational research was to contribute to a world of universal truths and laws so that such truths could be objectively applied to educational practices for the good of the nation and its citizens. However, public schools as engaged with children and youth exist within the context of their eras and evolve with and in response to social change. Research has also responded to external developments. The purposes and objectives of researchers as well as the subjects of their investigations have changed as researchers have been presented with new questions, questions often found either implicitly or explicitly on the national agenda. The history of education, as a form of educational research, not surprisingly, has also responded to changes on the national agenda. It can and has, as other forms of educational research, participated in the expansion of education and the attempt to answer questions on how schools should or could be reformed. It can and has also attempted to be a body of knowledge that objectively answers questions about what happened in the past and how and why. A consistent theme in criticisms of public education since World War II that has affected both the course of educational research and the history of education as a distinct and professional undertaking is the place of education as a field of study in the larger context of the content areas in the sciences, social sciences, and humanities known as the disciplines. Those who have addressed this theme have addressed important questions: Who should conduct educational research and how should they be trained for their work? Who should record the history of education and how should they be trained for their work? Who should be responsible for policy decisions based on research?

THE DISCIPLINES

Early in R. Freeman Butts' *A Cultural History of Education: Reassessing Our Educational Traditions* (1947) one encounters a discussion of good and evil, namely the Athenians and the Spartans. Athenians were portrayed as democrats and Spartans as fascists. Throughout the text various educators and educational systems were described either as Athenian or as Spartan. Clearly, one can only speculate what kind of text Butts would have written had there not been national concern about anti-democratic movements in Europe led by Franco, Hitler, and Mussolini. Butts took sides on an important political issue that was on the national agenda. The message was clear: Democracy was preferable to fascism. The western world was at a crossroads. It would go down or be taken down the road of either totalitarianism or democracy. That possibility informed and framed his test and its revision in 1955. In each edition, he was clearly interest in evaluating how well public education contributed to the maintenance of democratic traditions.[2]

Butts admitted in his first edition that his aim was not to "emphasize new research in the history of education." However, his successors, especially those now reviewed, were interested in developing new research and they did so. A review of Post-World War II criticism of education and a review of selected and important histories of education demonstrate that histories can be a reflection of what is on the national agenda just as Butts' texts were. Even those committed to sound historical scholarship, as Raymond E. Callahan, Lawrence A. Cremin, David B. Tyack, Jurgen Herbst and others have been, have not been able to avoid responding to the national agenda.

Critics of Public Education and Educators

As World War II was nearing its end, critics of public education in the United States subjected it to intensive and extensive scrutiny. According to a report prepared by the Committee on the Teaching Profession of the American Academy of Arts and Sciences submitted in 1954, "the criticism of our public schools and our institutions for the training of teachers has assumed a degree of vehemence which, whether justified or not, reveals dangerous schisms in the cultural life of the nation."[3] Post-World War II critics complained that "soft pedagogy" and a disregard for intellectual rigor characterized the public schools. They rejected the child-centered school, for "the idea of the 'child-centered' school has caused many educators to forget that the verb teaching has two accusatives, namely teaching (1) children (2) something."[4] Critics wanted a return to an earlier era when, they believed, students studied recognizable school subjects, the academic disciplines. The critics did not want life adjustment education; they wanted excellence. Educators were then interested, or told to be interested, in excellence. Those who had committed their professional lives to the study of public education and to the preparation of teachers were keenly interested in educational reform. Reform meant restoring rigorous study of the traditional academic disciplines to the schools' curricula. Those who wanted to pursue a career in education were encouraged to study the traditional academic disciplines and the social and behavioral sciences, history, philosophy or perhaps even business administration. As T. R. McConnell earlier advised:

> Competent educational research cannot be conducted without thorough knowledge of relevant phases of the basic disciplines which provide the foundations for a given field of educational activity. Problems in financing of education are obviously related to the whole field of public finance. Educational administration is one of several forms of public administration. It is difficult to see how research in educational finance and administration could be intelligently planned or executed without an understanding of the related portions of economics and political science. Almost every field of educational activity and research is, in like manner, tied with other fields of knowledge and investigation.[5]

There was widespread belief that the study and practice of education and the training of teachers for the nation's schools could not be reformed unless they were firmly rooted in some discipline, the legitimacy of which was recognized by those who worked in the traditional disciplines, by the officers of philanthropic foundations who supported the traditional disciplines, and officials in governmental agencies, especially at the national level.

Society's decision makers were then soliciting and following the advice not of professional educators but the advice freely offered by those with credentials in the disciplines, disciplines that were typically found not in schools or colleges of education but in arts and sciences colleges. For example, in 1955 Arthur E. Bestor, a professor of history at the University of Illinois who had earlier proposed that the nation's scholars assume responsibility for watching over the nation's public schools, published *Educational Wastelands*. He charged that the nation's public schools had been taken over by professional educators who lacked respect for the intellectual disciplines. In *The Restoration of Learning* (1956) he called for a return to the traditional school subjects (science, mathematics, history, English, and foreign languages). Those subjects, he claimed, constituted the only true foundation for "contemporary life." To understand their world, students needed not "the simple minded conception of mathematics as primarily a matter of making change and figuring out how many cups of punch can be dipped from a gallon bowl" but algebra, trigonometry, and calculus. To understand developments encountered in their daily social and economic lives and the products they used in their daily lives students needed to know the academic disciplines. Advanced physics would enable students to understand television, a device that then could be found in half the nation's homes. Use of antibiotics and vitamins required knowledge of biochemistry. Use of plastics and detergents required study of chemistry.[6] Bestor presented statistics to support his claim that enrollments in high school mathematics and science courses had declined significantly. Between the beginning and the middle of the twentieth century, enrollment in science courses fell from 83.9% to 53.8%. The decline in mathematics courses was nearly the same. The decline in enrollment in foreign language courses was even greater, from 72.2% to 21.8%.[7] Bester did not, however, note that a greater percent of the high school aged population was in school in the 1950s than were enrolled in the Pre-World War I Era.

It was assumed that psychologists knew about learning so they could tell teachers how to teach what the scholars said should be taught and how it should be taught. As we have seen, at the end of the 1950s, The Education Committee of the National Academy of Sciences called a meeting— and the National Science Foundation, the United States Office of Education, the United States Air Force, and the Rand Corporation financed it— to enable thirty-five scientists, scholars and educators to meet for ten days at Woods Hole "to discuss how education might be improved in our primary and secondary schools."[8] After the meeting, Jerome S. Bruner proclaimed that any student could learn anything at any age if educators would only attend to the structure of the disciplines. Educators generally tried to do what he said should be done, for Bruner was a proper psychologist and was reporting what a distinguished group of scholars just knew had to be so. His was a strong and a popular voice, but not the only voice, telling educators how important the scholarly disciplines were. After the appearance of *The Process of Education,* educators quickly turned their attention to the disciplines, to the structure of knowledge, and to the uses of knowledge. The National Education Association's Project on Instruction sponsored a Seminar on the Disciplines that "was called to facilitate student and effective use of the disciplines by (a) focusing on those fundamental ideas and methods of inquiry from selected fields of study which should be in the mainstream of the instructional program of the public schools and (b) exploring frontier thinking and research in the nature of knowledge and the ways of knowing."[9] The NEA was sponsoring a seminar designed not to lead the nation toward a new plan for education but one designed to follow the lead that had already been provided by the scholars. Shortly after the NEA Seminar, the School of Education at the University of Wisconsin—Milwaukee sponsored an invitational conference on "The Nature of Knowledge." The participants discussed the need for knowing, ways of knowing, knowledge and the structure of the disciplines, conceptions of knowledge and their significance for the curriculum, knowledge about knowledge for teachers, the structure of knowledge and the interrelationship of ideas, the relationships among knowledge, schooling and the preparation of teachers.[10]

EDUCATIONAL REFORM AND EDUCATIONAL RESEARCH

After World War II it was argued that education needed sound and rigorous theory, a theory based on the disciplines. Students did not know what they should know, so it was claimed, because neither educational theory nor educational practice was supported by theories from the disciplines. Social Foundations of Education was all but disassembled and gave way to specialized work based on a discipline.[11] Anthropology of Education, Sociology of Education, Economics of Education were obviously better than a course the foundation of which consisted of a little from many disciplines and not very much from any one of them. Educational research was needed if public education and the field of education were to be effectively reformed; and educational research was basically research done by practitioners of the disciplines. In the fourth edition of the *Encyclopedia of Educational Research* (1969) an excellent source for the views that prevailed in the 1960s, Fred M. Kerlinger offered a definition of educational research that emphasized how similar to, if not identical to, educational research was to the basic disciplines. Educational research, he wrote:

> is social scientific research, for a simple reason: an overwhelming majority of its variables are psychological, sociological, or social-psychological. Consider some of them: achievement, aptitude, motivation, intelligence, teacher characteristics, reinforcement, level of aspiration, class atmosphere, discipline, social class, race. All of these but the last two are psychological constructs. If the large portion of the variables are [sic] psychological, sociological, or social-psychological, then the conceptual and methodological problems of educational research are very similar to the problems of psychological and sociological research.[12]

For Kerlinger, educational research that was neither historical nor social scientific was simply "not as important as" that which was.

The History of Education and the National Agenda

In the late 1950s and early 1960s, there was some confidence that our understanding of school-society relationships would be enhanced if the methods of the academic disciplines were applied to analyses of public education. As Sol Cohen reported, "In 1954, under the personal direction of its president, Clarence Faust, the Fund [for the Advancement of Education established by the Foundation in 1951] held a conference to explore with a group of leading American historians the possibility of encouraging historical investigation of the role of education in the development of American society.[13] This new emphasis brought new vitality to inquiries and a desire to examine critically the public schools and how well they functioned. Eventually, pursuit of this emphasis brought needed attention to the difference between education and schooling. "Schooling," as David Hamilton has so ably and clearly explained, "has emerged as a malleable instrument of the political state—an agency charged with the transformation of immature human beings into appropriately-socialized adult citizens."[14] Some all but abandoned public schooling, and investigated the various ways in which culture is transmitted from one generation to the next. Note, for example, Lawrence Cremin's three-volume history of education—an undertaking initiated by W. Stull Holt, then secretary of the American Historical Association and supported by a "generous grant" from the Carnegie Corporation[15]—that virtually ignored formal education or "the time-honored tale of the genesis, rise, and triumph of the public school [which then] seemed flat and inadequate."[16] Cremin's three-volume history was closer to general American histories, in this instance to Daniel Boorstin's three-volume history (*The Americans*) than to earlier histories of American education. As Lawrence Veysey observed n his review of Cremin's third volume, *American Education: The Metropolitan Experience 1876-1980,* "Cremin has been deeply influenced by Daniel J. Boorstin, in the subtitles of his volumes and in his emphasis on variety rather than conflict." The subtitles of Boorstin's histories were: *The Colonial Experience, The National Experience,* and *The Democratic Experience.* The subtitles of Cremin's first two volumes were: *The Colonial Experience 1607-1783* and *The National Experience 1783-1876.*[17] Ellen Lagemann's work on the history of educational research, supported by the Spencer Foundation, is in the same vein. While acknowledging that Dewey lost and Thorndike won, she nonetheless suggested that a history of educational research should emphasize those who lost, those who were more likely than not practitioners of the disciplines.[18]

In their "attempt to inject a more rational note into the debate" about schooling and the training of teachers, the American Council of Learned Societies' Committee on the Teaching Profession, made it clear that a closer relationship between those who attended to education in schools and colleges of education and scholars in the liberal arts was desirable, if not imperative:

> The enormous increase in the literature on education should not lead us to deny that in the earlier years of American education there was a greater emphasis on humanistic and historical sources and studies than seems to be the case today. One lives too much on secondary materials. At some institutions the Doctor of Education degree has lost even the pretense of scholarship. Often schools of education have just "muddled along," or though that courses and changes in 'methods of teaching' would be sufficient for the enormous task of understanding and improving the role of mass education

in a modern democracy. If vigorous discussion, depth, and quality had more
generally gone along with the expansion, there would perhaps have been
more interest on the part of scholarly communities and thoughtful people
in the United States, as well as more effective financial support.[19]

The same committee also complained about the quality of history of
education texts and the lack of good material in the history of education:

An immense amount of work is to be done in the fields that connect education with the humanities. We possess no modern and scholarly monographies [sic] on the great educators from Comenius up to our modern time,
and there are no good editions of the works that have had a decisive influence on Western education. Neither such monographies nor such new editions would be accepted by publishers, while there is an abundance of
mediocre textbooks. In spite of a large number of "Histories of Education"
there exists no history of American education which would live up to modern historical standards. Consequently, young scholars do not feel encouraged to engage in the kind of patient and devoted study which is the
requisite of scholarly progress.[20]

The committee's call, issued in 1954, was soon answered. In 1957, the
first number in The Teacher's College Classics in Education Series was
published with Lawrence Cremins edited volume: *The Republic and the
School: Horace Mann on the Education of Free Men.* Cremin was also general
editor of the series. By 1987, this series made over fifty collections of
edited materials available to historians of education, educators, and policymakers.

The Response of Historians of Education

The philosophers of education and the historians of education heard
the critics and responded accordingly. They turned to the "parent" disciplines. Philosophers of education endeavored to become more philosophical than they had been[21] by strengthening their relationships to "pure"
or "straight" philosophy. For example, in 1955 the National Society for
the Study of Education devoted one of its yearbooks to the philosophy of
education. Like the earlier yearbook (the *Forty-First*), it was organized
according to the now almost out of fashion "isms," but the explicators of
the "isms" were not philosophers of education. As Harry S. Broudy
observed in the third *NSSE Yearbook* devoted to the philosophy of education, "it entrusted the writing of the chapters to 'real' philosophers." Each
real philosopher was assigned "a philosopher of education to keep him
[sic] relevant, so to speak, to problems of education."[22] Broudy further

observed that "the decision to have the chapters written by philosophers rather than by philosophers of education or educators reflected an awareness on the part of some of the prominent figures in the Philosophy of Education Society that philosophy of Education needed more philosophy."[23]

Philosophy of Education needed more philosophy, and the History of Education needed more history. On October 16-17, 1959, Bernard Bailyn presented his interpretative essay on "Education in the forming of American Society"[24] to "twenty invited scholars and historians" whose attendance at his presentation was made possible by "a grant from the Fund for the Advancement of Education, through its Committee on the Role of Education in American History."[25] Historians of education had a historiographical essay prepared for them by a proper historian. Soon thereafter, in *The Transformation of the School* (1961) Cremin explained to the post-war critics of public schools why the schools were as the critics claimed. His explanation was that the best educational theory—progressive education—had run amuck because it lost touch with the sound social, psychological, and philosophical theories that supported it in its early years.[26] Cremin's work, methods, conclusions, and his subsequent historiographical essay, originally sponsored by the Committee on the Role of Education in American History,[27] in which he exorcised the ghosts of early historians Ellwood P. Cubberley and Robert Herbert Quick[28] were difficult to ignore, for *The Transformation* earned him the Bancroft prize.

Cremin had also recently (1958) assumed leadership of the Social and Philosophical Foundations Department at Teachers College, for its previous leader, R. Freeman Butts was "getting more and more interested in international education." In 1964 the name of the department was changed to Philosophy and Social Sciences. According to Butts, this was done "to signalize" the redirection of the department that had already moved toward "stressing the scholarly disciplines rather than professional actions, research rather than service, and training the specialist in foundations rather than the generalist."[29] Butts was not very enthusiastic about these changes.

In *Education and the Cult of Efficiency* (1962), Raymond E. Callahan studied most of the same period Cremin studied but had a different focus—school administrators, those whom David Tyack would later name "administrative progressives," and concluded that the schools had gone soft because school administrators had embraced notions of scientific management spawned by Frederick W. Taylor and had not studied the appropriate disciplines, the social and behavioral sciences. According to Callahan, "the most effective educational research" conducted in the Progressive Era was done by Edward L. Thorndike, William C. Bagley, Charles H. Judd, and George S. Counts. He emphasized that each of them was trained in a discipline, Counts in sociology and the other three in psychology.[30]

Because the education and training of school administrators had not been in the social sciences, they lost touch with sound educational theory and sound educational values. Consequently, they allowed schools to abandon traditional school subjects. Cremin wanted educational theory to be rooted in the disciplines across the street from Teachers College, and Callahan effectively agreed that would be good for school administrators too.[31] Cremin made his position about the importance of the liberal arts—the humanistic studies and the social sciences—in his review of Callahan's *Cult*. He also expressed his agreement with the claim that educators should not have ignored the liberal arts. He contended that:

> They [the educators] have cut themselves off from the humanistic traditions that must ultimately provide the bases for their educational judgments, and have remained content to concentrate on the narrowest technical and political concerns. Thus alienated, they have fallen victim to tech new changing fashion in pedagogical ideas, grimly acting out Santayana's prophesy that those who forget history are condemned to repeat it. The need for fundamental reform is crucial, and one can only applaud Professor Callahan's call for a new professional education that emphasizes serious and sustained study of the humanities and social sciences.[32]

THE HISTORY OF EDUCATION AS EDUCATIONAL RESEARCH

Callahan and Cremin effectively endorsed a notion of schooling laid down by the Committee of Ten (1893) that was chaired by Harvard's Charles W. Eliot and effectively agreed with the critics that somehow public education had to return to where the critics believed the schools had been. It was where James B. Conant, in a study financed by the Carnegie Corporation, had recently told public school officials to take the schools.[33] As Richard Hofstadter remarked in 1963 in his discussion of the Committee of Ten, "the contemporary reader will notice the close similarity between [Eliot's] program and that recently recommended by James Bryant Conant, in his survey of the high schools."[34] The subtext of both Cremin and Callahan was clear: Had the "last picture show" high school not been abandoned in favor of life adjustment education, the Soviet Union may not have been first in space and the threat to democratic ways would not be as serious as it was.

Both *The Transformation* and *The Cult* may be considered nothing short of seminal works. Upon the publication of *The Cult* Ryland W. Crary urged that: "like Lawrence Cremin's *Transformation of the School*, Callahan's book warrants more than reviewing; both works deserve the focus of a continuing symposium."[35] His suggestion was accepted. For a full generation after their initial publication, they were still in print, still being assigned, read, and discussed. Yet, consideration of what was occurring as they were being written shows how rooted they are in the critics' calls, claims, and recommendations of the late 1940s and the 1950s. Teachers are conspicuous by their absence. Perhaps, that is additional evidence for Jurgen Herbst's later claim that education was professionalized but that teaching was not.[36] The *Brown* decision (1954) appears in the index of neither *The Transformation* nor *The Cult*. While race is conspicuous by its absence, so is gender. Betty Friedan's *The Feminine Mystique* (1963) did not appear until two years after *The Transformation* and one year after *The Cult*. However, it was, as Stephanie Coontz reported, "a product of the 1950s," a decade during which "the *Ladies' Home Journal* devoted an issue to "The Plight of the Young Mother" and "*McCall's* ran an article entitled *The Mother Who Ran Away*" which "set a new record for readership."[37] Such concerns were then overshadowed by the need to select and prepare talented youth for social exploitation. Excellence dominated the agenda. Equality and equity were to wait. Another way to state the point is to say that Cremin and Callahan were, wittingly or unwittingly, like Butts, working to preserve democracy while, it should be acknowledged, as Sol Cohen has recorded, working to blaze a new trail in the history of education.[38] Cremin and Callahan were among the first to follow that new trail.

New Agendas for the Nation

The nation's leadership soon turned away from excellence. Even before the nation landed a man on the moon, poverty and what was soon identified as an "urban crisis" were moving to the top of the nation's agenda. While educators were still attending conferences to discuss the importance and implications of the structure of knowledge for curriculum improvement and publishing new texts on curriculum that emphasized either the structure of knowledge or the possibility of having both democracy and excellence in education, President Kennedy was developing an interest in poverty. His successor, Lyndon B. Johnson soon declared a War on Poverty. Society directed educators to shift their emphasis from identifying talented youth for "social exploitation" and introduction to the academic disciplines at an early age to assisting the poor to do well in school. It quickly fell upon educational researchers to invent educational strategies and programs to qualify the poor, the culturally disadvantaged, for jobs that would enable them to break the vicious cycle of poverty.

The urban crisis was also a crisis in urban education, or as Charles E. Silberman, the former editor of *Fortune* who had the support of the Carnegie Corporation discovered, a *Crisis in the Classroom* (1970). *In The One Best System* (1974) a work supported by the Carnegie Corporation and the United States Office of Education, Tyack, studying the same period Cremin and Callahan studied—the Progressive Era—acknowledged the crisis. Like Cremin and Callahan, he accepted the charges of the critics and responded to what was high on the national agenda and explained how the schools came to be as the critics claimed they were. While claiming that: "urban schools did not create the injustices of American urban life," he did not deny that "they had a systematic part in perpetuating them."[39] He addressed his work "not only to specialists but also to citizens curious and concerned about how we arrived at the present crisis in urban education." Perhaps not forgetting the early admonitions to turn to the disciplines, he drew "heavily on the work of sociologists and political scientists" to explain how "institutional systems called schools ... often reinforced injustice for some at the same time that they offered opportunity to others."[40]

In *And Sadly Teach*[41] (1989) Jurgen Herbst, like Cremin, Callahan, and Tyack before him, attended to the critics' concerns. In this instance, Herbst's focus was on teachers. Unlike so many others who wrote about what had to be done to or for teachers, Herbst, after examining the history of teacher education, offered a new view. Rather than stating what teachers needed to do to become professionals or what would have to be done to teachers by way of imposing new demands upon them and placing them under even more stringent supervision, he showed how education—those who administered and supervised public education—had become professionalized but that teaching had not been professionalized. Callahan's *Cult* was, it should be noted, an account of that professionalization. In his discussion of the reports, many of which had been commissioned by philanthropies, that offered recommendations for how teachers could be made to perform better, Herbst pointed out that "there is not a single active classroom active classroom teacher among the signers of either the Holmes or the Carnegie report" and observed that "once more they [teachers] have been confined in their role as objects rather than subjects."[42]

In *The Once and Future School* (1996)[43] the subject of which is the comprehensive high school, Herbst once again offered an unconventional conclusion. It was a response to the same call Cremin and Callahan answered as well as the claims that restructuring of public education and parental choice are the means whereby education will be reformed in a way that will further enable the nation to compete effectively in the global economy. In the first lines of the preface, he recalled that: "In the decades following World War II Americans have called for the reform of public secondary education. They have protested what they have held to be the excesses of progressive education and the 'treason' of 'life adjustment.' "[44] Herbst's history of secondary education in the United States and in the colonies that preceded the formation of the new nation is essentially a history of the contest between advocates of the traditional academic course as is best exemplified by the recommendations of the Committee of Ten and those who advocated practical or even vocational education. Time after time, the advocates of the traditional academic course won the contest. Alternatives to the traditional course were assigned to the comprehensive high school, and during times of financial crisis when programs had to be eliminated, the traditional course more often than survived.

Herbst pointed out that questions about whether the high school should emphasized the academic or the practical are also questions about who should control the education—the education not just the schooling—of the nation's youth. A case can be made that educators, those who are identified as the "schoolmen" (and their relationship to Tyack's "administrative progressives" should not be overlooked) and those who support them and direct their inquiries wanted hegemony over the nation's youth. The "schoolmen's" objection to the War Department's control of educational programs in the Civilian Conservation Corps in the 1930s illustrates both their desire to control the education of youth and their preference for the academic as opposed to the practical course.

Callahan and Cremin effectively endorsed a conception of schooling set forth by Eliot's Committee of Ten, tacitly agreeing with the critics that somehow schools had to return to where the critics believed they once were. Herbst opted for neither the vision set forth by the Committee of Ten nor that set forth by the Commission on the Reorganization of Secondary Education (1917), but found in history the foundation for a third alternative. He reached back to the nineteenth century and proposed "up-to-date versions of the people's college."[45] That he proposed not a version but "versions" is significant, for it was recognition of the nation's diversity—a diversity that was but scarcely recognized in the 1950s.

Herbst agreed that public education needed to be restructured. However, while many want the governance of schools to be restructured so that students score better on tests that measure achievement in traditional school subjects and so that teachers can be held strictly accountable if they do not, Herbst recognizing that "When one institution fails to live up to the demand set before it, another will take up the challenge,"[46] argued that the education of youth—not just their schooling—needed to be restructured. In a proposal that is reminiscent of Cremin's extended account of the educational configuration,[47] Herbst argued that educators "will have to share the educational task with many other institutions within a framework that allows room for choice and banishes custodial compulsion." For those who want to hold on to the comprehensive high school, he had some words of solace: It will not "disappear," but it will have to give up its claim to monopolistic control over youth of senior high school age.[48]

When compared to works that responded to the claims of the Post-World War II critics, Herbst's works show how different the history of education is from what it was in the 1950s and early 1960s. That difference may be explained by the attention given to the need to ensure equality of educational opportunity after the appearance of *Equality of Educational Opportunity* (1966). In large measure, attention is now paid to equality and equity as they relate to groups who were overlooked as the schools were directed to rake Jefferson's "rubbish heap" so that talented youth could be selected for exploitation. Beyond that, and perhaps more important, there is some recognition that reforming—which usually means restoring existing institutions to what they were imagined to have been, as appealing as such restorations may be—will not satisfy present requirements. Herbst demonstrated the value and the utility of paying less attention to the solutions embedded in critics' calls and more attention to the historical record. Historians can confirm the existing policies of those who have the means to ensure that their "voices" are heard through their selective support of scholars or they can propose alternative viable policies.

CONCLUSIONS

The history of educational research provides an overview of the history of the nation and the forces and tensions upon which it has been built. We have called this the national agenda. The history of educational research reveals that the purposes, methods, and ideological underpinnings of educational research have evolved and changed over time. Educational research has been a humanitarian quest and a scientific quest. It has been directly involved in educational expansion and reform at all levels. Educational research has recorded the progress of reform movements. It has contributed to the initiation of reforms, guided them, and ended or institutionalized them with critical evidence of their failure or success.

It has been argued that modern educational research, as we have known it in the twentieth century, was largely a product of the Progressive Era. Three developments contributed to the creation of educational research as a relatively coherent enterprise: (1) the development of the common school as an institution recognized as important for the prosperity of the nation; (2) the legitimation of schools and school children as subjects that could be properly studied and the popular belief that the study of schools and students would result in better and more efficient schools; and finally, (3) the elevation of the idea of differences among children, groups, and other populations that could be either innate or learned, and that the study and measurement of these variations could lead to improved performance and the elimination of inequalities in educational progress that negatively affects the nation. Once in place, schools grew to become one of the most vital, expensive, and criticized institutions in the nation. Supported by the dynamics of the Progressive Era, educational researchers prospered, and their influence grew considerably in the twentieth century. Their work influenced practice, sometimes with astonishing ease, as they changed the way teachers taught, what subjects were advanced, how learning was assessed, and where and how students were placed. At other times, they were the target of critics and alternately contributed to the criticisms of public schools. As education became increasingly recognized as critical to the health and future of the nation, research on education took on an increasing variety of forms. Its practices, efficiency, and progress were scrutinized in detail and they were also examined by historians as an important part of the history of the nation, a battleground over national values and the attainment of national ideals for civil rights and equal educational opportunity for all children.

It should be clear to those who closely attend to history that the past, in point of fact, is not past. The past is not over; it is embedded in the present in policies and practices. Research, whether using the scientific method or historical methods, is not static. Each new advancement reveals an important insight for the time in which it is discovered, may later be found to not be important at a later time. Histories themselves are testaments to the nature of historical change and the times in which they are written. What is accepted as true today may be proven wrong in the future, such is the nature of scientific research. Whether educational research should be objective and disinterested in its quest for truth or actively and consciously engaged in critical events and whether it should attempt to shape the national agenda is a question we have clearly raised and one that merits a response. Our answer is that it cannot avoid doing both, for that is the very nature of social research of any kind. Social research is embedded in the human condition and thus embedded in history. Education, as the history of educational research shows, is a vital part of and reflection of the national agenda.

As a history of educational research, this book has attempted to place research on education within the framework of the history of the United States in a way that does justice to the historical record and provides useful knowledge about significant developments that have set the stage for ongoing issues. Sol Cohen once reminded us that the "progressive historians, like James Harvey Robinson, Fredrick Jackson Turner, Vernon

Parrington, Carl Becker, and Charles Beard ... attempted to create a 'usable history' that would contribute directly to the solution of contemporary problems; they subordinated the past to the present by selecting and emphasizing those aspects of the past that were most relevant to present problems."[49] The story of educational research told here is not deliberately subordinated either to the past or to the present. Rather than asking whether historians can or should abandon contemporary problems and risk becoming antiquarians, it may be equally, if not more profitable to ask how useful the history of educational research is to the present. Historians can serve as communicants and endorse the claims and recommendations embedded in those who have the means to construct and publicize the contemporary problems or they can serve as heretics and use their knowledge and craft to propose alternative viable policies by attending to the historical record. Useful history is not necessarily history that subordinates the past to the present. How we understand our past is, nonetheless, a critical part of understanding the present just as our concern about the present influences how we study our past. How useful our history is a judgment the reader must make.

NOTES

1. Lawrence A. Cremin. *The Transformation of the School: Progressivism in American Education, 1876-1957* (New York: Knopf, 1961); Raymond E. Callahan, (*Education and the Cult of Efficiency: A Study of the Social Forces That Have Shaped the Administration of Public Schools* (Chicago: University of Chicago Press, 1962); David B. Tyack, *The One Best System: A History of American Urban Education* (Cambridge, Massachusetts, 1974), and Jurgen Herbst, *And Sadly Teach: Teacher Education and Professionalization in American Culture* (Madison, Wisconsin: University of Wisonsin Press, 1989), *and The Once and Future School: Three Hundred and Fifty Years of American Secondary Education* (New York: Routledge, 1996).

2. R. Freeman Butts. *A Cultural History of Education: Reassessing Our Educational Traditions* (New York: McGraw-Hill Co., 19476), p. vi and *A Cultural History of Education: Its Social and Intellectual Foundations* (New York: McGraw-Hill Co., 1955), p. vii.

3. Howard Mumford Jones, Francis Keppel, and Robert Ulich *On the Conflict Between the "Liberal Arts" and the Schools of Education," American Council of Learned Societies Newsletter,* Vol. V, No. 2 (1954), p. 17.

4. *Ibid.,* p. 29.

5. T. R. McConnell, *The Nature of Educational Research*, *The Conceptual Structure of Educational Research: A Symposium Held in Connection with the Fiftieth Anniversary of the University of Chicago. Supplementary Educational Monographs* published in conjunction with *The School Review and The Elementary School Journal,* No. 55 (May 1942), p. 4.

6.   Arthur E. Bestor. *The Restoration of Learning* (New York: Knopf, 1956), pp. 40-41.

7.   *Ibid.*, pp. 42-43.

8.   Jerome S. Bruner. *The Process of Education* (Cambridge, Massachusetts: Harvard University Press, 1961), p. vii.

9.   *The Scholars Look at the Schools: A Report of the Disciplines Seminar* (Washington, D. C.: National Education Association, 1962), p. 2.

10.   William A. Jenkins (ed.). *The Nature of Knowledge: Implications for the Education of Teachers* (Milwaukee: University of Wisconsin-Milwaukee, 1961).

11.   That many such courses were but a hodgepodge of snippets from some instructors' favorite authors is doubtlessly so. For example, consider the text William Heard Kilpatrick assembled for the course at Teachers College, Columbia University. *Source Book in the Philosophy of Education* (1923) contained 557 selections in 339 pages. It served as the model for the two-volume *Readings in the Foundations of Education* (1941) prepared by the foundations faculty. Volume II contained 557 selections in its 339 pages. For further discussion of the difficulties practitioners of Social Foundations created and faced see: Erwin V. Johanningmeier, "Through the Disarray of Social Foundations: Some Notes Toward a New Social Foundations," *Educational Foundations*, Vol. 5, No. 4 (Fall 1991), pp. 5-39.

12.   Fred M. Kerlinger. "Research in Education" in Robert. L. Ebel (ed.). *Encyclopedia of Educational Research*, 4th ed. (Toronto: Collier-Macmillan, 1969), p.1127.

13.   Sol Cohen. "The History of the History of American Education, 1900-1976: The Uses of the Past," *Harvard Educational Review*, Vol. 46, No. 3 (August 1976), p. 299.

14.   David Hamilton. *Towards a Theory of Schooling* (London: The Falmer Press, 1989), p. vii.

15.   Lawrence A. Cremin. *American Education: The Colonial Experience, 1607-1783* (New York: Harper & Row, 1970), p. xii.

16.   *Ibid.*, p. ix.

17.   Lawrence Veysey. *"Review of Lawrence A. Cremin's American Education: The Metropolitan Experience, 1876-1980,"* in *The American Historical Review*, Vol. 95, No. 1 (February 1990), p. 285.

18.   Ellen Condliffe Lagemann "The Plural Worlds of Educational Research," *History of Education Quarterly*, Vol. 29, No. 2 (Summer 1989). Also see: Ellen Condliffe Lagemann. "Contested Terrain: A History of Educational Research in the United States, 1890-1950," *Educational Researcher*, Vol. 26, No. 9 (December 1997).

19.   Jones, Keppel and Ulich. "On the Conflict Between the "Liberal Arts" and the "Schools of Education," p. 29.

20.   *Ibid.*, p. 37.

21.   Nathaniel Champlin, *et. al.* "The Distinctive Nature of the Philosophy of Education," *Educational Theory* , Vol. IV. No. 1 (January 1954).

22.   Harry S. Broudy, "Between the Yearbooks" in Kenneth J. Rehage (ed.). *Eightieth Yearbook of the National Society for the Study of Education: Part I, Philosophy and Education* (Chicago: University of Chicago Press, 1981), p. 20.

23.   *Ibid.*

24. Bernard Bailyn. *Education in the Forming of American Society: Needs and Opportunities for Study* (New York: Vintage Books, n.d.). Originally published in 1960 by the University of North Carolina Press for the Institute of Early American History and Culture, Williamsburg, Virginia.

25. *Ibid.*, p. vi.

26. This claim is accepted and elaborated upon by Diane Ravitch in *The Troubled Crusade: American Education, 1945-1980.* (New York: Basic Books, 1983), pp. 45-46.

27. Lawrence A. Cremin, *The Wonderful World of Ellwood Patterson Cubberley: An Essay on the Historiography of American Education* (New York: Bureau of Publications, Teachers College, Columbia University, 1965.

28. Why he did not consider those who had recently dominated the field of the history of education has only been addressed by Cohen in "The History of the History of American Education, 1900-1976."

29. R. Freeman Butts. *In the First Person Singular: The Foundations of Education.* (San Francisco, California: Caddo Gap Press, 1993), pp. 29, 31.

30. Callahan. *Education and the Cult of Efficiency,* pp. 247-248.

31. Those responsible for the training of school administrators did attend to Callahan. In their history of educational administration, Roland F. Campbell, Thomas Fleming, L. Jackson Newell, and John W. Bennion clearly show the extent to which school administrators attended to Callahan. Callahan is cited on the first page of their text and is cited four times as frequently as Cremin. See: *A History of Thought and Practice in Educational Administration* (New York: Teachers College Press, Teachers College, Columbia University, 1987), pp. 1, 23, 32-34, 39-40, 103, 126, 128, 130, 131.

32. Lawrence A. Cremin, Review of Rayond E. Callahan. *Education and the Cult of Efficency. Teachers College Record,* Vol. 65, No. 2 (November 1963), p. 185.

33. James B. Conant. *The American High School Today: A First Report to Interested Citizens* (New York: McGraw-Hill, 1959).

34. Richard Hofstadter. *Anti-Intellectualism in American Life.* (New York: Knopf, 1963), p. 330.

35. Ryland W. Crary, "Perspective," *History of Education Quarterly,* Vol. III, No. 1 (March 1963), p. 2.

36. Jurgen Herbst *And Sadly Teach,* pp. 161, 188.

37. Stephanie Coontz. *The Way We Never Were: American Families and the Nostalgia Trap* (New York: Basic Books, 1991), p. 37.

38. Cohen. "The History of the History of American Education, 1900-1976."

39. Tyack, *The One Best System,* p. 12.

40. *Ibid,* p. 4

41. Herbst reported that he received support from the German Academic Exchange Service, the American Philosophical Society, the Spencer Foundation, and the Research Committee of the Graduate School of the University of Wisconsin-Madison for this work.

42. Herbst. *And Sadly Teach,* p. 9.

43. Herbst reported that he received support from the University of Wisconsin Graduate School and the Spencer Foundation.

44. *Ibid.*, p. xiii.
45. Jurgen Herbst. *The Once and Future School*, p. xv.
46. *Ibid.*, p. 167.
47. Lawrence A. Cremin. *American Education: The Metropolitan Experience 1876-1980* (New York: Harper & Row, 1988).
48. Herbst. *Once and Future School*, p. 213.
49. Cohen. "The History of the History of American Education, 1900-1976." p. 309.

REFERENCES

Adelman, Nancy E. "Sphere of Influence: Factors in the Educational Development of Three New Jersey Communities in the Progressive Era" in eds. Ronald K. Goodenow and Dian Ravitch. *Schools in Cities*. New York: Holmes and Meier, 1983.

Adler. Mortimer. *Paidea Problems and Possibilities: A Consideration of Questions Raised by the Paidea Proposal*. New York: Macmillan, 1983.

Adler, Mortimer. *The Paidea Proposal: An Educational Manifesto*. New York: Macmillan, 1982.

Alexander, Carter. *Educational Research: Suggestions and Sources of Data with Reference to Administration*. New York: Bureau of Publications, Teachers College, Columbia University, 1927.

Allen, William H. *Efficient Democracy*. New York: Dodd, Mead and Co., 1908.

American Psychiatric Association. *Diagnostic and Statistical Manual of Mental Disorders*. 4th ed. DSM-IV Text Revision. Washington, D.C.: American Psychiatric Association, 1994, 2000.

Anderson, John E. *The Unconscious: A Symposium*. New York: Knopf, 1927.

Anderson, John E. "The Clientele of a Parental Education Program," *School and Society*, Vol. 26 (August 26, 1927).

Anderson, V. V. *Psychiatry and Education*. New York: Harper and Bros., 1932.

Angell, James Rowland. "The Doctrine of Formal Discipline in the Light of the Principles of General Psychology." *Educational Review*, Vol. XXXVI (June 1908).

Anyon, Jean. "What Should Count as Educational Research: Notes Toward a New Paradigm" in eds. Gloria Ladson-Billings and William Tate. *Education Research in the Public Interest: Social Justice, Action, and Policy*. New York: Teachers College Press, 2006.

Arnett, Jeffrey Jensen and Cravens, Hamilton. "G. Stanley Hall's *Adolescence*: A Centennial Reappraisal," *History of Psychology*, Vol. 9, No 3 (August 2006).

433

Ary, Donald, Jacobs, Lucy Cheser, and Razavieh, Asghar. *Introduction to Research in Education*. New York: Holt, Rinehart and Winston, 1979.

Asher, Willaim J. "The Rose to Prominence: Educational Psychology, 1920-1960 in eds. Barry J. Zimmerman and Dale H. Schunk. *Educational Psychology: A Century of Contributions*. Mahwah, New Jersey: Lawrence Erlbaum Associates, 2003.

Ausubell, David P. "Some Psychological Aspects of the Structure of Knowledge" in ed. Stanley Elam. *Education and the Structure of Knowledge: Fifth Annual Phi Delta Kappa Symposium on Educational Research*. Chicago: Rand McNallly, 1964.

Ayres, Leonard P.. "History and Present Status of Educational Measurements" in ed. Guy M. Whipple. *The Seventeenth Yearbook of the National Society for the Study of Education: Part II The Measurement of Educational Products*. Bloomington, Illinois: Public School Publishing Co., 1918.

Ayres, Leonard P. *Laggards in Our Schools: A Study of Retardation and Elimination in City School Systems*. New York: Charities Publications Committee, Russell Sage Foundation, 1909.

Bagley, William C. *Education, Crime and Social Progress*. New York: The Macmillan Co., 1931.

Bagley, William C. *Education and Emergent Man*. New York: Thomas Nelson and Sons, 1934.

Bagley, William C. *Educational Values*. New York: The Macmillan Co., 1911.

Bagley, William C. "Ideals Versus Generalized Habits," *School and Home Education*, Vol. XXIV, No. 3 (November 1904).

Bagley, William C. "A Plea for the Scientific Study of Educational Problems," *Kansas School Magazine*, Vol.. 1, No. 2 (February 1912).

Bagley William. C. "Professor Terman's Determinism," *Journal of Educational Research* (1922).

Bagley, William C. "The School's Responsibility for Developing the Controls of Conduct," *The Elementary School Teacher*, Vol. 8, No. 7 (March 1908).

Bagley, William C., Bell, W. C., Seashore, C. E., and Whipple, Guy M. "Editorial," *Journal of Educational Psychology*, Vol., 1, No. 1 (1910).

Bailyn, Bernard. *Education in the Forming of American Society: Needs and Opportunities for Study*. Chapel Hill, North Carolina: University of North Carolina Press, 1960.

Baird, J. W. *The psychology of Learning*. New York: Appleton, 1913.

Baker, S. Josephine. *Child Hygiene*. New York: Harper and Bros., 1925.

Baldwin, Bird T. "Principles of Education: The Present Status of Education as a Science," Papers presented for discussion at the meeting of the National Society of College Teachers of Education in St. Louis, Missouri, February 27-29, 1912. *School Review Monographs Number II*. Chicago: University of Chicago Press, 1912.

Baldwin, Bird T. "William James' Contributions to Educational Psychology," *Journal of Educational Psychology*, Vol. II (1911).

Baldwin, Bird T., Fillmore, Eva Abigail, and Hadley, Lora. *Farm Children: An Investigation of Rural Life in Selected Areas of Iowa*. New York: D. Appleton, 1930.

Baldwin, James Mark. *Darwin and the Humanities*. Baltimore: Review Publishing Co., 1909.

Bannister, Robert C. *Social Darwinism: Science and Myth in Anglo-American Social Thought.* Philadelphia, Pennsylvania: Temple University Press, 1979.

Barr, A. S. "Research Methods" in ed. Chester W. Harris. *Encyclopedia of Educational Research*, 3rd ed. New York: The Macmillan Co., 1960.

Bayh, Birch. "School Violence and Vandalism: Problems and Solutions," *Journal of Research and Development in Education*, Vol. 2 (Winter 1978).

Becker, Carl. *The Heavenly City of the Eighteenth-Century Philosophers.* New Haven, Connecticut: Yale University Press, 1932.

Beecher, R. A. "Research into Practice" in eds. W. B. Dockrell and David Hamilton. *Rethinking Educational Research.* London: Hodder and Stoughton, 1980.

Beers, Clifford. *A Mind that Found Itself.* New York: Longmans Green, 1907.

Bell, Daniel. *The Coming of Post-Industrial Society.* New York: Basic Books, 1973.

Bellack, Arno. "Knowledge Structure and the Curriculum" in ed. Stanley Elam. *Education and the Structure of Knowledge: Fifth Annual Phi Delta Kappa Symposium on Educational Research.* Chicago: Rand McNallly, 1964.

Benjamin, Jr., Ludy T. ed. *A History of Psychology: Original Sources and Contemporary Research.* New York: McGraw-Hill Book Co., 1998.

Bestor, Arthur E. *The Restoration of Learning.* New York: Alfred A. Knopf, 1956.

Biddle, Bruce J. and Anderson, Donald S. "Theory, Methods, Knowledge, and Research on Teaching" in ed. Merlin C. Wittrock. *Handbook of Research on Teaching.* 3rd ed. New York: Macmillan Publishing Co., 1986.

Biddle, Bruce and Saha, Lawrence J. *The Untested Accusation: Principals, Research Knowledge, and Policy Making in Schools.* Westport, Connecticut: Ablex Publishing, 2002.

Biesta, Gert J. J. and Burbules, Nicholas C. *Pragmatism and Educational Research.* Lanham, Maryland: Rowman & Littlefield Publishers, 2003.

Binet, Alfred. *La Suggestibilité.* Paris: Schleicher Frères, 1900.

Binet, Alfred. *Les Idées Modernes sur l'Enfants.* Paris: Flammarion, 1909.

Binet, Alfred and Simon, Theophile. *The Development of Intelligence in Children* tr. Elizabeth S. Kite in ed. Henry H. Goddard. *The Development of Intelligence in Children: The Binet-Simon Scale.* Baltimore: Williams and Wilkes, 1916.

Binet, Alfred and Simon, Theophile. *Mentally Defective Children* tr. B. Drummon. London: E. Arnold, 1907.

Blanton, Smiley D. and Blanton, M. G. *Child Guidance.* New York: Century, 1927.

Blau, Joseph L. *Men and Movements in American Philosophy.* New York: Prentice-Hall, Inc. 1952.

Bledstein, Burton J. *The Culture of Professionalism: The Middle Class and the Development of Higher Education in America.* New York: W. W. Norton & Co., 1976.

Block, Ned and Dworkin, Gerald. eds. *The IQ Controversy: Critical Readings.* London: Quartet Books, 1977.

Blos, Peter. "The Adolescent Personality" in ed. V. T. Thayer *et al. Reorganizing the Secondary School Curriculum.* New York: Appleton-Century, 1940.

Bode, Boyd. *How We Learn.* Boston: D.C. Heath and Co., 1940.

Boorstin, Daniel J. *The Americans: The Democratic Experience.* New York: Vintage Books, 1973.

Boorstin, Daniel J. *The Image: A Guide to Pseudo-Evens in America.* New York: Atheneum, 1977.

Borden, Neil H. "Daniel Starch," *The Journal of Marketing*, Vol. XXI, No. 3 (January 1952).

Borg, Walter and Call, Meredith D. *Educational Research: an Introduction*. 4th ed. New York: Longman, 1983.

Boring, Edwin G. *A History of Experimental Psychology*, 2nd ed. New York: Appleton-Century Crofts, 1950.

Borrowman, Merle L., "Liberal Education and Professional Preparation of Teachers" in ed. Merle L. Borrowman. *Teacher Education in America: A Documentary History*. New York; Teachers College Press, 1965.

Bouchard, T. J. "The Hereditarian Research Program: Triumphs and Tribulations" in eds. S. Modgil and C. Modgil. *Arthur Jensen: Consensus and Controversy*. New York: Falmer Press, 1987.

Bowly, John. *Mental Health and Maternal Love*. New York: Columbia University Press, 1951.

Boyer, Ernest L. *High School: A Report on Secondary Education in America*. New York: Harper & Row, 1983.

Boynton, Paul L. "Intelligence and Intelligence Testing" in ed. Walter S. Monroe. *Encyclopedia of Educational Research*. New York: The Macmillan Co., 1941.

Bradbury, Dorothy E. *Pioneering in Child Welfare: A History of the Iowa Child Welfare Research Station, 1917-1933*. Iowa City: University of Iowa Press, 1933.

Brauner, Charles J. *American Educational Theory*. Englewwod Cliffs, New Jersey: Prentice-Hall, Inc., 1964.

Bredo, Eric and Feinberg, Walter. "Introduction: Competing Modes of Social and Educational Research" in eds. Eric Bredo and Walter Feinberg. *Knowledge and Values in Social and Educational Research*. Philadelphia: Temple University Press, 1982.

Bremner, Robert H., Barnard, John, Hareven, Tamara K. and Mennel, Robert M. eds. *Children and Youth in America: A Documentary History, Volume II: 1866-1932*. Cambridge, Massachusetts: Harvard University Press, 1971.

Briggs, T. H. "Needed Research in Secondary Education," *Fifteenth Yearbook of the National Society of College Teachers of Education*. Chicago: University of Chicago Press, 1926.

Broudy, Harry S. "Between the Yearbooks" in ed. Kenneth J. Rehage. *Eightieth Yearbook of the National Society for the Study of Education: Part I, Philosophy and Education*. Chicago: University of Chicago Press, 1981.

Broudy, Harry S. *The Real World of the Public Schools*. New York: Harcourt Brace Jovanovich, 1972.

Broudy, Harry S. "The Structure of Knowledge in the Arts" in ed. Stanley Elam. *Education and the Structure of Knowledge: Fifth Annual Phi Delta Kappa Symposium on Educational Research*. Chicago: Rand McNallly, 1964.

Broudy, Harry S., Ennis, Robert H., and Krimerman, Leonard I. eds. *Philosophy of Educational Research*. New York: John Wiley and Sons, 1973.

Broudy, Harry S., Smith, B. Othanel, and Burnett, Joe R. *Democracy and Excellence in Secondary Education*. Chicago: Rand McNally, 1964.

Brown et al. v. Board of Education of Topeka et al. 347 I/S 483 (1954) in ed. Sol Cohen. *Education in the United States: A Documentary History*, Vol. 5. New York: Random House, 1974.

Brown, Richard E. *Rockefeller Medicine Men: Medicine and Capital in America*. Berkeley: University of California Press, 1960.

Broyler, C. R., Thorndike, Edward L., and Woodward, Ella. "A Second Study of Mental Discipline in High School Studies, Journal of Educational Psychology," Vol. 18 (1927).

Brubacher, John S. *A History of the Problems of Education*. New York: The McGraw-Hill Book Co., 1966.

Bruner, Jerome S. *The Process of Education*. Cambridge, Massachusetts: Harvard University Press, 1961.

Bruner, Jerome S. "*The Process of Education* Reconsidered" in ed. Glen Hass. *Curriculum Planning: A New Approach*. Boston: Allyn & Bacon, 1977.

Bruner, Jerome S. *The Relevance of Education*. New York: W. W. Norton, 1971.

Bryner, Edna, "A Selected Bibliography of Certain Phases of Educational Measurement" in ed. Guy M. Whipple. *The Seventeenth Yearbook of the National Society for the Study of Education: Part II, The Measurement of Educational Products*. Bloomington, Illinois: Public School Publishing Co., 1918.

Buckingham, B. R. *Research for Teachers*. New York: Silver, Burdett and Co., 1923.

Buckingham, B. R., Doherty, Margaret, and MacLatchy, Josephine. *Bibliography of Educational and Psychological Tests and Measurements*. U. S. Bureau of Education Bulletin, No. 55. Washington, D.C., 1924.

Burgess, Charles and Borrowman, Merle L. *What Doctrines to Embrace: Studies in the History of American Education*. Glenview, Illinois: Scott, Foresman and Co., 1969.

Burnett, Joe R. "On Professor McMurray's 'Autonomous Discipline of Education'," *Educational Theory, Vol. VI, No, 1 (January 1956)*.

Burnham, John C. *Paths to American Culture: Psychology, Medicine and Morals*. Philadelphia: Temple University Press, 1988.

Butts, R. Freeman. *In The First Person Singular: The Foundations of Education*. San Francisco, California, 1993.

Butts, R. Freeman. *A Cultural History of Education: Reassessing Our Educational Traditions*. New York: McGraw-Hill Co., 1947.

Butts, R. Freemn. *A Cultural History of Education: Its Social and Intellectual Foundations*. New York: McGraw-Hill, 1955.

Calhoun, Daniel. ed. *Educating the Americans: A Documentary History*, Boston: Houghton Mifflin, 1969.

Callahan, Raymond E. *Education and the Cult of Efficiency: A Study of the Social Forces That Have Shaped the Administration of Public Schools*. Chicago: University of Chicago Press, 1962.

Cameron, Edward H. "Experimental Pedagogy" in ed. Paul Monroe. *Cyclopedia of Education*, Vol. II. New York: Macmillan, 1911.

Campbell, Roland F., Fleming, Thomas, Newell, L., Jackson, and Bennion, John W. *A History of Thought and Practice in Educational Administration*. New York: Teachers College Press, Teachers College, Columbia University, 1987.

Carnevale, Anthony B. "Discounting Education's Value," *Chronicle of Higher Education*, Vol. LIII, No, 5 (September 22, 2006),

Carolan, Brian V. and Natriello, Gary. "Data-Mining Journals and Books: Using the Science of Networks to Uncover the Structure of he Educational Research Community," *Educational Researcher*, Vol. 34, No. 3 (April 2005).

Carrier, James. *Learning Disabilities, Social Class, and the Construction of Inequality in American Education*. Westport, Connecticut: Greenwood Press, 1986.

Carter, James G. *Essays Upon Education Containing a Particular Examination of the Schools of Massachusetts, and an Outline of an Institution for the Education of Teachers*, Boston: Bowles and Darborn, 1826.

Castel, Robert, Castel, Francoise, and Lovell, Anne. *The Psychiatric Society* tr. Arthur Goldhammer. New York: Columbia University Press, 1982.

Cattell, James McKeen. "Mental Tests and Measurement," *Mind*, Vol. 15 (1890).

Cavanagh, Sean, "Some Conditions May Apply," *Education Week*, Vol. 44 (August 9, 2006).

Champlin, Nathaniel. "The Distinctive Nature of the Philosophy of Education," *Educational Theory*, Vol. IV, No. 1 (January 1954).

Chapman, H. B. *Research in Education*. Ohio State University Studies, Bureau of Educational Research Monographs, No. 7. Columbus, Ohio: The Ohio State University Press, 1927.

Chapman, P. D. *Schools as Sorters: Lewis M. Terman, Applied Psychology and the Intelligence Testing Movement*. New York: New York University Press, 1988.

Chekki, Dan A. *American Sociological Hegemony: Transnational Explorations*. New York: University Press of America, 1987.

Church, Robert L. and Sedlack, Michael W. *Education in the United States: An Interpretive History*. New York: The Free Press, 1976.

Clark, Kenneth B. "Alternative Public School Systems," *Harvard Educational Review*, Vol. 38, No. 1 (Winter 1968).

Clifford, Geraldine Joncich. *Edward L. Thorndike: The Sane Positivist*. Middletown, Connecticut: Wesleyan University Press, 1984.

Clifford, Geraldine Joncich. A History of the Impact of Research on Teaching" in ed. Robert M. W. Travers. *Second Handbook of Research on Teaching* (Chicago: RandMcNally, 1973).

Clifford, Geraldine Joncich. *The Shape of American Education*. Englewood, Cliffs, New Jersey: Prentice-Hall , 1975.

Cohen, David K and Barnes, Carol A. "Research and the Purposes of Education" in eds. Ellen Condliffe Lagemann and Lee S.. Schulman. *Issues in Education Research: Problems and Possibilities*. San Francisco: Josey-Bass Publications, 1999.

Cohen, Sol. ed. *Education in the United States: A Documentary History*, Vol. I–V. New York: Random House, 1974.

Cohen, Sol. "The History of the History of American Education, 1900-1976: The Uses of the Past," *Harvard Educational Review*, Vol. 46, No. 3 (August 1976).

Cohen, Sol. "The Mental Hygiene Movement, the Development of Personality, and the School, *History of Education Quarterly*, Vol. 23, No. 2 (Summer 1983).

Cohen, Sol. "The Mental Hygiene Movement: The Medicalization of American Education" in ed. Gerald Benjamin. *Private Philanthropy and Public Elementary and Secondary Education: Proceedings of the Rockefeller Archive Center held on June 8, 1979*. Tarrytown, New York: Rockefeller Archive Center Publication, 1979.

Cohen, Sol. "The School and Personality Development: Intellectual History" in ed. John Best. *Historical Inquiry in Education: A Research Agenda*. Washington, D.C.: American Educational Research Association, 1983.

Coffman, Louts Delta. *The Social Composition of the Teaching Population*. New York: Teachers College, Columbia University, 1911.

Cole, Percival R. "Herbart" in ed. Paul Monroe. *Cyclopedia of Education*, Vol. 3. New York: The Macmillan Co., 1909.

Cole, Percival R. *Herbart and Froebel: An Attempt at Synthesis*. Columbia University Contributions to Education, Teachers College Series No. 14. New York: Teachers College, Columbia University, 1907.

Coleman, James S. "Equal Schools or Equal Students?" *The Public Interest*, No. 4 (Summer 1966).

Coleman, James S. "Toward Open Schools," *The Public Interest*, No. 9 (Fall 1967).

Coleman, James S., Campbell, Ernest Q., Hobson, Carol J., McPartland, James, Mood, Alexander M., Weinfeld, Frederic D., and York. Robert L. *Equality of Educational Opportunity*. Washington, D.C.: U. S. Government Printing Office, 1966.

College Board. *Academic Preparation for College: What Students Need to Know and Be Able to Do*. New York: College Entrance Examination Board, 1983.

Commonwealth Fund. *Annual Report for 1923*. New York: Commonwealth Fund, 1923.

Commonwealth Fund. *Annual Report for 1924*. New York: Commonwealth Fund, 1924.

Commonwealth Fund *Annual Report for 1926*. New York: Commonwealth Fund, 1926.

Conant, James B. *The American High School Today: A First Report to Interest Citizens*. New York: McGraw-Hill, 1959

"Contents of Children's Minds on Entering School at the Age of 6 Years," *Report of the Commissioner of Education for the Year 1900-01*, Washington, D.C.: U. S. Government Printing Office, 1902.

Coontz, Stephanie. *The Way We Never Were: American Families and the Nostalgia Trap*. New York: Basic Books, 1991.

Cornbleth, Catherine. "Curriculum and Students: Diverting the Public" in ed. Gloria Ladson-Billings and William F. Tate. *Education Research in the Public Interest: Social Justice, Action, and Policy*. New York. Teachers College Press. 2006.

Counts, George S. *Arithmetic Tests and Studies in the Psychology of Arithmetic*. Supplementary Educational Monographs, Vol. 1. Chicago: University of Chicago Press, 1917.

Courtis, Stuart A. "Contributions of Research to the Individualization of Instruction" in ed. Guy M. Whipple. *Thirty-Seventh Yearbook of the National Society for the Study of Education: Part II, The Scientific Movement in Education*. Bloomington, Illinois, Public School Publishing Co., 1938.

Courtis, Stuart A. "Debunking the I.Q.," *The Nation's Schools*, Vol. 45, No. 2 (February 1950).

Courtis, Stuart A. "Courtis Tests in Arithmetic: Value to Superintendents and Teachers" in ed. Guy M. Whipple. *Fifteenth Yearbook of the National Society for* the *Study of Education: Part I, Standards and Tests for the Measurement of the Efficiency of Schools and School Systems*. Bloomington, Illinois: Public School Publishing, Co., 1916.

Courtis, Stuart A. "Fact and Fancy in Educational Measurement," *Bulletin of the University of Indiana School of Education*, Vol. XVIII. Bloomington, Indiana, 1942.

Courtis, Stuart A. "Forty Years of Educational Measurement: An Appraisal and a Prophecy," *National Elementary Principal*, Vol. 25 (February 1946).

Courtis, Stuart A. "Let's Stop This Worship of Tests and Scales, *The Nation's Schools*, Vol. 31, No.. 3 (March 1943).

Courtis, Stuart A. "Maturation Units for the Measurement of Growth," *School and Society*. Vol. XXX (November 16, 1929).

Courtis, Stuart A. "Personalized Statistics in Education," *School and Society*, Vol. LXXX (May 1955).

Courtis, Stuart A. *Philosophy of Education*. Ann Arbor, Michigan: Brumfield and Brumfield, 1939.

Courtis, Stuart A. "The Rate of Growth Makes a Difference," *Phi Delta Kappan*, Vol. 30 (April 1949).

Courtis, Stuart A. "Research Work in Arithmetic," *Educational Administration and Supervision*, Vol. 3, No. 2 (February 1917).

Courtis, Stuart A. and Packer, P. C. "Educational Research," *Journal of Educational Research*, Vol. 1, No. 1 (January 1920).

Crary, Ryland W. "Perspective," *History of Education Quarterly*, Vol. III, No. 1 (March 1963).

Cravens, Hamilton. *Before Head Start: The Iowa Station and America's Children*. Chapedl Hill, North Carolina: University of North Carolina Press, 1993.

Cremin, Lawrence A. *American Education: The Metropolitan Experience, 1876-1980*, New York: Harper and Row, 1988.

Cremin, Lawrence A. *The Genius of American Education*. New York: Vintage Books, 1965.

Cremin, Lawrence A. "Review of Raymond E. Callahan. *Education and the Cult of Efficiency*," *Teachers College Record*, Vol. 65, No. 2 (November 1963).

Cremin, Lawrence A., "The Revolution in American Secondary Education, 1893-1918," *Teachers College Record*, Vol. LVI, No. 6 (March 1955).

Cremin, Lawrence A. *The Transformation of the School: Progressivism in American Education, 1876-1957*. New York: Knopf, 1962.

Cremin, Lawrence A. *The World of Ellwood Patterson Cubberley: An Essay on the Historiography of American Education*. New York: Bureau of Publications, Teachers College, Columbia University, 1965.

Cremin, Lawerence A. ed. *The Republic and the School: Horace Mann on the Education of Free Men*. New York: Teachers College Press, 1961.

Cronbach, Lee J. "Five Decades of Public Controversy Over Mental Testing," *American Psychologist*, Vol. 30, No. 1 (January 1975).

Cronbach, Lee J. and Suppes, Patrick eds. *Research for Tomorrow's Schools: Disciplined Inquiry for Education*. Toronto: The Macmillan Co., 1969.

Crow, Lester D. and Crow, Alice. *Mental Hygiene in School and Home Life*. New York: McGraw-Hill, 1942.

Crunden, Robert M. *Ministers of Reform: The Progressives' Achievement in American Civilization, 1899-1920.* New York: Basic Books, 1982.

Cubberley, Elwood P. *An Introduction to the Study of Education and to Teaching.* Boston: Houghton Mifflin Co., 1925.

Cubberley, Elwood P. *Public Education in the United States: A Study and Interpretation of American Educational History.* Boston: Houghton Mifflin Co., 1919.

Cubberley, Elwood P. *Public Education in the United States: A Study and Interpretation of American Educational History,* rev. ed. Boston: Houghton Mifflin Co., 1934.

Cubberley, Elwood P. *Public School Administration.* Boston: Houghton Mifflin Co., 1919.

Curti, Merle E. "America at the World's Fairs, 1851-1893," *American Historical Review,* Vol. 55 (1950).

Curti, Merle E. *Human Nature in American Thought.* Madison, Wisconsin: University of Wisconsin Press, 1980.

Curti, Merle E. *The Social Ideas of American Educators,* rev. ed. Totowa, New Jersey: Littlefield, Adams & Co., 1971.

Cusick, Philip A. *The Egalitarian Ideal and the American High School.* New York: Longman, 1983.

Dain, Norman. *Clifford Beers: Advocate for he Insane.* Pittsburg: University of Pittsburg Press, 1980.

Daniels, George H. *Science in American Society: A Social History.* New York: Alfred A. Knopf, 1971.

Darling-Hammond, Linda. *Beyond the Commission Reports: The Coming Crisis in Teaching.* Washington, D.C.: Rand, 1984.

Darroch, Alexander. *Herbart and the Herbartian Theory of Education: A Criticism.* London:Longmans, Green and Co., 1903.

Darwin, Charles. "A Biographical Sketch of an Infant" in ed. Wayne Dennis. *Readings in Child Psychology.* Englewood Cliffs, New Jersey: Prentice-Hall, Inc., 1951.

Darwin, Charles. *The Expression of he Emotions in Man and Animals* in ed. Wayne Dennis. *Historical Readings in Developmental Psychology.* New York: Appleton-Century-Crofts, 1972.

Davidson, Jr., Emily S. and Benjamin, Ludy T. "A History of the Child Study Movement in America" in ed. John A. Glover and Royce R. Ronning. *Historical Foundations of Educational Psychology.* New York: Plenum Press, 11987.

DeGarmo, Charles. *Herbart and the Herbartians.* New York: Charles Scribner's Sons, 1895.

DeGarmo, Charles. "Most Pressing Problems: Concerning the Elementary Course of Study" in ed. Charles A. McMurry. *The First Yearbook of the Herbart Society for the Scientific Study of Teaching* [1895]. New York: Arno Press and New York Times, 1969.

Degler, Carl. *In Search of Human Nature: The Decline and Revival of Darwinsm in American Social Thought.* New York: Oxford, 1991.

Dennis, Wayne ed. *Historical Readings in Developmental Psychology.* New York: Appleton-Century Crofts, 1972.

Dennis, Wayne ed. *Readings in Child Psychology,* Englewood Cliffs, New Jersey: Prentice-Hall, Inc. 1951.

deMarrais, Kathleen B. and LeComte, Margaret. *The Way Schools Work: A Sociological Analysis*, 2nd ed. New York: Longmans, 1995.

De Tocqueville, Alexis, *Democracy in America* in eds. Merle E. Curti and Carolos Baker. *American Issues: The Social Record*, Vol. 1, rev. ed. New York: Lippincott, 1955.

Detroit Public Schools, University of Michigan and Wayne University. *Educational Contributions of Stuart A. Courtis: Listings and Summaries of Published Articles, Books and Tests through June 1944*. Detroit Public Schools, University of Michigan and Wayne University, 1944.

Dewey, John. "Body and Mind," *Mental Hygiene*, Vol. XII (1928).

Dewey, John. "Current Tendencies in Education," *The Dial*, Vol. LXII, No. 739 (April 5, 1917).

Dewey, John. *Democracy and Education*. New York: Macmillan, 1916.

Dewey, John. *How We Think*. Boston: D.C. Heath & Co., 1910.

Dewey, John. *The Influence of Darwinism on Philosophy and Other Essays in Contemporary Thought*. New York: Peter Smith, 1951.

Dewey, John. *Psychology*, 3rd rev. ed. New York: Harper and Brothers, 1984

Dewey, John. *The School and Society and The Child and the Curriculum*. Chicago: University of Chicago Press, ([1900, 1902] 1990.

Dewey, John. *The Sources of a Science of Education* (New York: Horace Liveright, 1929).

Dickenson, Virgil E. *Mental Tests and the Classroom Teacher*. Yonkers-on-Hudson, New York: World Book Co., 1923.

Dickenson, Virgil E. and Terman, Lewis M.. "Tests and Classification in the Primary Grades" in *The Classroom Teacher*, Vol. 11. Chicago: The Classroom Teacher, Inc., 1927-1928.

Dockrell, W. B. and Hamilton, David. eds. *Rethinking Educational Research*. London: Hodder and Stoughton, 1980.

Donzelot, Jacques. *The Policing of Families* tr. Robert Hurley. New York: Pantheon, 1979.

Douglas, O. B. "The Present Status of he Introductory course in Educational Psychology in American Institutions of Learning. *Journal of Educational Psychology*, Vol. 16 (1925).

Drummond, W. B. *An Introduction to Child Study*. London: Edward Arnold, 1908.

Dunkel, Harold. *Herbart and Education*, New York: Random House, 1969.

Dunkel, Harold. *Herbart and Herbartianism: An Educational Ghost Story*. Chicago: University of Chicago Press, 1970.

Dunkel, Harold. "Wanted: New Paradigms and a Normative Base for Research" in ed. Lawrence G. Thomas. *Twenty-Seventh Yearbook of the National Society for the Study of Education: Philosophical Redirection of Educational Research*. Chicago: University of Chicago Press, 1972.

Ebel, Robert L. "Some Limitations of Basic Research in Education," *Phi Delta Kappan* (October 1967) in ed. Harry s. Broudy, Robert H. Ennis and Leonard I. Krimerman. *Philosophy of Educational Research*. New York: John Wiley and Sons, 1973.

Educational Testing Service. *Conference on Testing*, Princeton, New Jersey: Princenton University Press, 1958.

Edwards, Newton and Richey, Herman G. *The School in the American Social Order.* 2nd ed. Boston: Houghton Mifflin, 1963.

Eighth Annual Report of the Board of Education of the City of Oswego (1861) in ed. Sol. Cohen. *Education in the United States: A Documentary History,* Vol. 3 (New York: Random House, 1974).

Eisenhart, Margaret and Towne, Lisa. "Contestation and Change in National Policy on 'Scientifically Based' Education Research," *Educational Researcher,* Vol. 32, No. 7 (October 2003).

Elam, Stanley. ed. *Education and the Structure of Knowledge: Fifth Annual Phi Delta Kappa Symposium on Educational Research.* Chicago: Rand McNallly, 1964.

Elder, Glen. *Children of the Great Depression.* Chicago: University of Chicago Press, 1947.

Engelhart, Max D. *Educational Research.* Chicago: Rand-McNally, 1972.

Engelhart, Max D. "Examinations" in ed. Walter S. Monroe. *Encyclopedia of Educational Research.* New York: The Macmillan Co., 1941.

Engelhart, Max D. and Macklin, Thomas. "Rice as the Inventor of the Comparative Test," *Journal of Educational Measurement,* Vol. 3, No. 2 (Summer 1966).

Erickan, Kadriye and Roth, Wolff-Michael, "What Good Is Polarizing Research Into Qualitative and Quantitative?" *Educational Researcher,* Vol. 35 (June/July 2006).

Erickson, Erik H. *Childhood and Society.* New York: W. W. Norton, 1950.

Evertson, Carolyn M. and Green, Judith L. "Observation as Inquiry and Method" in ed. Merlin C. Wittrock. *Handbook of Research on Teaching.* 3rd ed. New York: Macmillan Publishing Co. 1986.

Fagan, Thomas K. "Compulsory Schooling, Child Study, Clinical Psychology, and Special Education," *American Psychologist,* Vol. 47, No. 2 (February 1992).

Farley, Frank H. "The Future of Educational Research," *Educational Researcher,* Vol. 11, No. 8 (October 1982) and Vol.11, No. 9 (November 1982).

Felkai, Laszo. "The Influence of Herbart's and Ziller's Theory in Hungary" in ed. Sandor Komlosi. *Conference Papers for the 9th Session of the International Standing Conference for the History of Education: History of International Relations,* Vol. 1. Pecs, Hungary: Jannus Pannonous University, 1987.

Felix, Robert. *Mental Illness, Progress and Prospects.* New York: Columbia University Press, 1951.

Fenton, Norman. *The Counselor's Approach to the Home, School Case Work Manuals.* Stanford, California: Stanford University Press, 1943-1040.

Fenton, Norman. *The Counselor's Interview with the Student, School Case Work Manuals.* Stanford, California: Stanford University Press, 1943-1949.

Fenton, Norman. "Mental Hygiene and Its Administration in High School," *Junior-Senior Clearing House,* Vol. 6 (1932).

Fenton, Norman. *Organizing a Mental Hygiene Program Through the Child Guidance Conference.* Bulletin No. 9, New Series. Sacramento, California: State pringing Office, 1933.

Fenton, Norman. "A Survey of Clinical and Descriptive Instructions in Child Guidance in Superior Medical Schools," *Journal of Juvenile Research,* Vol. 13 (1929).

Fisher, Donald. *The Fundamental Development of the Social Sciences: Rockefeller Philanthropy and the Social Science Research Council*. Ann Arbor, Michigan: University of Michigan Press, 1996.

Fleming, Charlotte M. *Research and the Basic Curriculum*. London: University of London Press, 1946.

Flexner, Simon and Flexner, James Thomas. *William Henry Welch and the Heroic Age of American Medicine*. New York: Viking Press, 1941.

Fosdick, Raymond B. *The Story of the Rockefeller Foundation*. New York: Harper and Bros., 1952.

Foshay, Arthur W. "Knowledge and he Structure of the Disciplines" in ed. William A. Jenkins. *The Nature of Knowledge: Implications for the Education of Teachers*. Milwaukee, Wisconsin: University of Wisconsin—Milwaukee, 1961.

Foster, J. C. and Anderson, J. E. *The Young Child and His Parents: A Study of One Hundred Cases*. Minneapolis: University of Minnesota Press, 1927.

Frank, Lawrence K. *The Conduct of Sex: Biology and Ethics of Sex, Parenthood in Modern Life*. New York: William Morrow, 1961.

Frank, Lawrence K. "Discussion" in ed. Milton J. Senn. *Problems of Infancy and Childhood, Transactions of the Third Conference, March 7-8, 1949, New York*. New York: Josiah Macy Jr. Foundation, 1950.

Frank, Lawrence K. "Social Change and the Family," *Annual, American Academy of Political Science*, Vol. 169 (1932).

Freeman, Frank N. "Review of [Daniel Starch's] *Experiments in Educational Psychology*," *School Review*, Vol. XX, No. 3 (March 1912).

French, Lois Meredith. *Psychiatric Social Work*. New York: Commonwealth Fund, 1940.

Fry, Margaret. ed. *Child Care and the Growth of Love*. New York: Penguin, 1953.

Gage, N. L. ed. *Handbook of Research on Teaching*. Chicago: Rand McNally, 1963.

Gault, Robert H. "A History of the Questionnaire Method of Research in Psychology," *Pedagogical Seminary*, Vol. 14, No. 3 (September 1907).

Gay, Peter. *The Enlightenment: The Rise of Modern Paganism*. New York: Alfred A. Knopf, 1966.

Gesell, Arnold, *The Normal Child and Primary Education*. Boston, 1912. In eds. Robert H., Barnard, John, Hareven, Tamara K. and Mennel, Robert M. eds. Bremner *Children and Youth in America: A Documentary History, Volume II: 1866-1932*. Cambridge, Massachusetts: Harvard University Press, 1971.

Gesell, Arnold, *et al. The First Five Years of Life*. New York: Harper and Brothers, 1940.

Gilllispie, Charles Coulston. *The Edge of Objectivity: An Essay in the History of Scientific Ideas*. Princeton, New Jersey: Princeton University Press, 1960.

Gilman, Sander L. "The Struggle of Psychiatry with Psychoanalysis. Who Won?" *Critical Inquiry*, Vol. 13, No. 2 (Winter 1987).

Gleim, Sophia C. "The Visiting Teacher," *U.S. Bureau of Education*, Bulletin No. 10. Washington, D.C.: U. S. Government Printing Office, 1921.

Glenn, David,. "No Classroom Left Unstudied," *The Chronicle of Higher Education* (May 28, 2004).

Goddard, Henry H. "Editors Introduction," *The Development of Intelligence in Children*. Publications of the Training School at Vineland, New Jersey, Department of Research, No. 11, May 1916. Baltimore: Williams and Wilkins Co., 1916.

Good, Carter V., Barr, A. S., and Scates Douglas E. *The Methodology of Educational Research.* New York: Appleton-Century-Crofts, Inc., 1941.

Good, Thomas L. and Brophy, Jere E. "School Effects" in ed. Merlin C. Wittrock. *Handbook of Research on Teaching.* 3rd ed. New York: Macmillan Publishing Co. 1986.

Goodenough, Florence. *Anger in Young Children.* Minneapolis: University of Minneapolis Press, 1931.

Goodenough, Florence. *Developmental Psychology.* New York: D. Appleton, 1934.

Goodenough, Florence. *The Kuhlman-Binet Tests for Children of Preschool Age: A Critical Study and Evaluation.* Westport: Connecticut: Greenwood, 1928, 1973.

Goodenow, Ronald K. and Ravitch, Diane eds. *Schools in Cities.* New York: Holmes and Meier, 1983.

Goodlad, John I. *The Dynamics of Educational Change.* New York: McGraw-Hill, 1975.

Goodlad, John I. *A Place Called School: Prospects for the Future.* New York: McGraw-Hill, 1984.

Goodman, Paul. *New York Herald Tribune Lively Arts* (December 25, 1960).

Gould Stephen J. *The Mismeasure of Man.* New York: W. Norton & Co., 1981.

Gould, Stephen J. *The Mismeasure of Man,* rev. ed. New York: W. Norton & Co., 1996.

Gowin, D. Bob, "Is Educational Research Distinctive?" in ed. Lawrence G. Thomas. *The Seventy-First Yearbook of the National Society for the Study of Education: Part I, Philosophical Redirection of Educational Research.* Chicago: University of Chicago Press, 1972.

Graham, Patricia Albjerg, "Joseph Mayer Rice as a Founder of the Progressive Education Movement," *Journal of Educational Measurement,* Vol. 3, No. 2 (Summer 1966).

Greenfield, Thomas B., Griffiths, D., Stout, R. and Forsyth, P. eds. *Leaders for America's Schools,* Berkeley, California: McCutchan, 1988.

Grinder, Robert E. "Epologue: Two Models for the Study of Youth—1944 versus 1975, in ed. Robert J. Havighurst and Philip H. Dreyer. *The Seventy-Fourth Yearbook of the National Society for the Study of Education: Part I, Youth.* Chicago: University of Chicago Press, 1975.

Grinder, Robert E. *A History of Genetic Psychology: The First Science of Human Development.* New York: John Wiley and Sons, Inc., 1967.

Grund, Francis. *The Americans, In Their Moral Social, and Political Relations.* Boston, 1837 in ed. Sol Cohen. *Education in the United States: A Documentary History.* New York: Random House, 1974.

Groos, Karl. *Die Spiele der Tiere.* Jena: Fischer, 1896.

Groos, Karl. *Die Spiele des Menschen.* Jena: Eischer, 1899.

Guthrie, James W. "For Want of a Nail... ," *Education Week,* Vol. 24, No. 34 (May 4, 2005).

Haber, Samuel. *Efficiency and Uplift: Scientific Management in the Progressive Era, 1890-1920.* Chicago: University of Chicago Press, 1973.

Hall, G. Stanley. *Adolescence* in eds. Charles Strickland and Charles Burgess. *Health, Growth, and Heredity: G. Stanley Hall on Natural Education*. New York: Teachers College Press, 1965.

Hall, G. Stanley. "Child-Study and Its Relation to Education," *The Forum*, Vol. XXIX (1901) in ed. Sol Cohen. *Education in the United States: A Documentary History*, Vol. 3. New York: Random House, 1974.

Hall, G. Stanley. "Christianity and Physical Culture," *The Pedagogical Seminary*, Vol. 9 (September 1902) in eds. Charles Strickland and Charles Burgess. *Health, Growth, and Heredity: G. Stanley Hall on Natural Education*. New York: Teachers College Press, 1965.

Hall G. Stanley. "The Ideal School as Based on Child Study," National Education Association, *Journal of Addresses and Proceedings, 1901*. Washington, D.C., 1901 in ed. Sol Cohen. *Education in the United States: A Documentary History*, Vol. 3. New York: Random House, 1974.

Hall, G. Stanley. "The Needs and Methods of Education Young People in the Hygiene of Sex," *The Pedagogical Seminary*, Vol. 15 (March 1908) in eds. Charles Strickland and Charles Burgess. *Health, Growth, and Heredity: G. Stanley Hall on Natural Education*. New York: Teachers College Press, 1965.

Hall, Vernon C, "Educational Psychology from 1890 to 1920" in eds. Barry J. Zimmerman and Dale H. Schunk. *Educational Psychology: A Century of Contributions*. Mahwah, New Jersey: Lawrence Erlbaum Associates, 2003.

Haller, Mark H. *Eugenics: Hereditarian Attitudes in American Thought*. New Brunswick, New Jersey: Rutgers University Press, 1963.

Hallinan, M.T., Garmoran,A., Kubitschek, A., and Loveless, T. eds. *Stability and Change in American Education*. New York: Werner Publications. 2003.

Hamilton, David. "Bread and Circuses: Some Challenges to Educational Research in the 1980s." Presidential address delivered at the Conference of he British Educational Research Association, Lancaster, England, August 30 – September 2, 1984.

Hamilton, David. "Educational Research and the Shadows of Francis Galton and Ronald Fisher" in eds. W. B. Dockrell and David Hamilton. *Rethinking Educational Research*. London: Hodder and Stoughton, 1980.

Hamilton. David, *Towards a Theory of Schooling*, London: Falmer Press, 1989.

Hansen, Oscar Allen. *Liberalism and American Education in the Eighteenth Century*, New York: The Macmillan Co., 1926.

Harris, Chester. ed. *Encyclopedia of Educational Research*. New York: The Macmillan Co. 1960.

Harris, William Torrey. "Preface," *Journal of Speculative Philosophy*, Vol. 1, No. 1 (1867).

Haskell, Thomas L. *The Emergence of Professional Social Science: The American Social Science Association and the Nineteenth Century Crisis of Authority*. Baltimore: Johns Hopkins University Press, 2000.

Havighurst, Robert J. ed. *The Seventieth Yearbook of he National Society for the Study of Education: Part II Leaders in American Education*. Chicago: University of Chicago Press, 1971.

Hays, Samuel P. *The Response to Industrialism, 1885-1914*. Chicago: University of Chicago Press, 1963.

Heath, Shirley Brice, "Discipline and Disciplines in Education Research: Elusive Goals?" in eds. Ellen Condliffe and Lee S. Schulman. *Issues in Education Research*. San Francisco: Josey-Bass Publishers, 1999.

Hendon, Ursula Stendel. "Herbart's Concept of Morality in Education and Its Role in America," Ph.D. Dissertation, University of Alabama, 1980.

Hendrickson, Gordon, "Educational Psychology" in ed. Walter S. Monroe. *Encyclopedia of Educational Research*. New York: Macmillan, 1941.

Herbart, Johann Friedrich. *The Science of Education: Its General Principles Deduced from Its Aims and the Aesthetic Revelation of the World*, tr. Henry M. and Emmie Felkin, Boston: D. C. Heath and Co., 1896.

Herbst, Jurgen. *And Sadly Teach: Teacher Education and Professionalization in American Culture*. Madison, Wisconsin: University of Wisconsin Press, 1989.

Herbst, Jurgen. *The Once and Future School: Three Hundred and Fifty Years of American Secondary Education*. New York: Routledge, 1996.

Herrnstein, Richard and Murray, Charles. *The Bell Curve: Intelligence and Class Structure in the United States*. New York: Free Press, 1996.

Higham, J. *Strangers in the Land: Patterns of American Nativism, 1860-1925*. New York: Atheneum, 1965.

Hildreth, Gertude Howell. *A Bibliography of Mental Tests and Rating Scales*. New York: Psychological Corporation, 1933.

Hilgard, Ernest R. *Theories of Learning*. New York: Appleton-Century-Crofts, Inc., 1949.

Hilgard, Ernest R. *Psychology in America: A Historical Survey*. San Diego: Harcourt Brace Jovanovich, 1987.

Hinsdale, B. A. *History of the University of Michigan* in eds. Edgar W. Knight and Clifton L. Hall. *Readings in American Educational History*. New York: Appleton-Century-Crofts, 1951.

"History of the Movement in Preschool and Parental Education" in ed. Gut M. Whipple. *The Twenty-Eighth Yearbook of the National Society for the Study of Education: Part I, Preschool and Parental Education*. Bloomington, Illinois: Public School Publishing Co., 1929.

Hobbes, Nicolas ed. *Issues in the Classification of Children*. San Francisco: Jossey-Bass, 1975.

Hoffman, B. *The Tyranny of Testing*. New York: Crowell-Collier, 1962.

Hofstadter, Richard. *Anti-Intellectualism in American Life*. New York: Knopf, 1963.

Hofstadter, Richard. *Social Darwinism in American Thought*, rev. ed. Boston: The Beacon Press, 1955.

Hollingsworth, Leta S. *The Psychology of Adolescence*. New York: D. Appleton Century, 1925.

Horne, Margo. *Before It's Too Late: The Child Guidance Movement*. Philadelphia: Temple University Press, 1989.

Horne, Margo. "The Moral Message of Child Guidance, 1925-1945," *Journal of Social History* (September 1948).

House, Ernest R. "Three Perspectives on Innovation" in eds. Rolf Lehming and Michael Kane. *Improving Schools: Using What We Know*. Beverly Hills, California: Sage Publications, 1981.

Hughes, Robert. *The Shock of the New*, New York: Alfred A. Knopf, 1981.

Hunt, Herold C. "Educational Research and National Education Policy, *Journal of Education Research*, Vol. XLIX, No, 9 (May 1956).

Iran-Nejad and Pearson, P. David eds. *Review of Research in Education 24*. Washington, D.C.: American Educational Research Association. 1999.

Iowa, State of. "Chapter 282. Iowa Child Welfare Research Station: An Act to Establish and Maintain the Iowa Child Welfare Research Station and Making An Appropriation Therefore," *Acts & Joint Resolutions Passed at the Regular Session Thirty-Seventh General Assembly of the State of Iowa*.

James, William. *Talks to Teachers*, New York: Dover, 1962.

Janowitz, Morris. *Institution Building in Urban Education*, Russell Sage Foundation, 1969.

Jarvin, Linda and Sternberg, Robert J. "Alfred Binet's Contribution to Educational Psychology" in eds. Barry J. Zimmerman and Dale H. Schunk. *Educational Psychology: A Century of Contributions*. Mahwah, New Jersey: Lawrence Erlbaum Associates, 2003.

Jastrow, Joseph and Moorhouse, G.W. "Some Anthropometric and Psychological Tests of College Students," *American Journal of Psychology*, Vol. 4 (April 1892).

Jefferson, Thomas. "A Bill for the More General Diffusion of Knowledge" in ed. Gordon C. Lee. *Crusade Against Ignorance*. New York: Teachers College Press, 1961.

Jefferson, Thomas. *Notes on the State of Virginia* in ed. Gordon C. Lee. *Crusade Against Ignorance*. New York: Teachers College Press, 1961.

Jencks, Christopher. *Inequality: A Reassessment of the Effects of Family and School in America*. New York: Basic Books, 1972.

Jencks, Christopher. "Education: The Racial Gap," *The New Republic* (October 1966).

Jenkins, William A. ed. *The Nature of Knowledge: Implications for the Education of Teachers*. Milwaukee: University of Wisconins-Milwaukee, 1961.

Jensen, Arthur. *Straight Talk About Mental Tests: Their Uses and Abuses in No-Nonsense Terms by the World's Foremost Authority*. New York: The Free Press, 1981.

Jennings, Frank G. "A Friend of he Learning Child," *Saturday Review*, Vol. 43 (October 15, 1960).

Johanningmeier, Erwin V. *Americans and Their Schools*. Boston: Houghton Mifflin, 1980.

Johanningmeier, Erwin V. "Dunkel's Herbart Revisited: The Milieu in which He Worked," *Journal of the Midwest History of Education Society*, Vol. 17 (1989).

Johanningmeier, Erwin V. "It Was More Than a Thirty Years' War But Instruction Finally Won: The Demise of Education in the Industrial Society" in eds. Kathryn M. Borman and Nancy P. Greenman. *Changing American Education: Recapturing the Past or Inventing the Future?* New York: State University of New York Press, 1994.

Johanningmeier, Erwin V. "Through the Disarray of Social Foundations: Some Notes Towards a New Social Foundations," *Educational Foundations*, Vol. 5, No. 4 (Fall 1991).

Johanningmeier, Erwin V. and Johnson, Henry C. "Charles DeGarmo, Where Are You—Now That We Need You?" *Philosophy of Education 1969: Proceedings of the*

Twenty-Fifth Annual Meeting of the Philosophy of Education Society. Carbondale, Illinois, 1969.

Johnson, Henry C. and Johanningmeier, Erwin V. *Teachers for the Prairie: The University of Illinois and the Schools, 1868-1945.* Urbana, Illinois: University of Illinois Press, 1972.

Johnson, M. Clemens. *A Review of Research Methods in Education.* Chicago: Rand-McNally Co., 1972

Joncich, Geraldine M. ed. *Psychology and the Science of Education: Selected Writings of Edward L. Thorndike.* New York: Teachers College Press, 1962.

Jones, A. J. "An Outline of Methods of Research and Suggestions for Teachers," *U. S. Bureau of Education*, Bulletin No. 26. Washington, D. C.: U. S. Government Printing Office, 1926.

Jones, Howard Mumford, Keppel, Francis, and Ulich, Robert. "On the Conflict Between the "Liberal Arts" and the Schools of Education," *American Council of Learned Societies Newsletter*, Vol. V, No. 2 (1954).

Judd, Charles H. "Contributions of School Surveys" in ed. Guy M. Whipple. *The Thirty-Seventieth of the National Society for the Study of Education: Part II The Scientific Movement in Education.* Bloomington, Illinois: Public School Publishing Co., 1938.

Judd, Charles H. *Introduction to the Scientific Study of Education.* Boston: Ginn and Co., 1918.

Kaestle, Carl. "The Awful Reputation of Educational Research," *Educational Researcher*,Vol. 22 (January-February 1993).

Kaestle, Carl. *Pillars of the Republic.* New York: Hill and Wang, 1983.

Kallen. Horace. "Functionalism," *Encyclopedia of he Social Sciences*, Vol. 6, New York: Macmillan, 1931.

Kamin, L. J. *The Science and Politics of IQ.* Potomac, Maryland: Erlbaum Associates, 1974.

Kanner, Leo. *Child Psychiatry.* Springfield, Illinois: Charles C. Thomas, 1935, 1957.

Karier, Clarence J. *Scientists of the Mind: Intellectual Founders of Modern Psychology.* Urbana, Illinois. University of Illinois Press, 1986.

Karier, Clarence J. ed. *Shaping the American Educational State.* New York: The Free Press, 1975.

Katz, Michael B. "From Theory to Survey in Graduate Schools of Education," *Journal of Higher Education*, Vol. 37 (1966).

Katz, Michael B. *In the Shadow of the Poor House: A Social History of Welfare in America.* New York: Basic Books, 1986.

Kawin. Ethel. "Records and Reports: Observations, Tests, and Measurements" in ed. Nelson B. Henry. *The Forty-Sixth Yearbook of the National Society for the Study of Education: Part II, Early Childhood Education.* Chicago, Illinois: University of Chicago Press, 1956.

Keliher, Alice V. *Life and Growth.* New York: Appleton-Century, 1938.

Kerlinger, Fred N. "Research in Education in ed. Robert L. Ebel. *Encyclopedia of Educational Research.* Toronto: Collier-Macmillan, 1969.

Kevles, Daniel J. *In the Name of Eugenics: Genetics and the Uses of Human Heredity.* New York: Knopf, 1985.

Key, Ellen K. S. *Barnets århundrade.* Stockholm: A. Bonnier, 1900.

Key, Ellen K. S. *The Century of the Child*. New York: G. Putman's Sons, 1909.

King, Irving. *Education for Social Efficiency: A Study in the Social Relations of Education*. New York: D. Appleton, 1913.

Kimmins, C, W. *The Mental and Physical Welfare of the Child*. London: Partridge, 1927.

Klemm, L. R. *European Schools, or What I Saw in the Schools of Germany, France, Austria and Switzerland*. New York: D. Appleton and Co., 1897.

Klotsche, Martin J. "The Need for Knowing" in ed. William A. Jenkins. *The Nature of Knowledge: Implications for the Education of Teachers*. Milwaukee, Wisconsin: University of Wisconsin—Milwaukee, 1961.

Knox, H. M. "The Progressive Development of J. F. Herbart's Educational Thought," *British Journal of Educational Studies*, Vol. XXIII, No. 3 (October 1975).

Knox, Samuel. "An Essay on the Best System of Liberal Education, Adapted to the Genius of the Government of the United States" in ed. Frederick Rudolph. *Essays on Education in the Early Republic*, Cambridge, Massachusetts: Harvard University Press, 1965.

Kohn, Alfie. *The Case Against Standardized Testing: Raising the Scores, Ruining the Schools*. Portsmouth, New Hampshire: Heinemann, 2000.

Kolb, Charles. "The Cracks in Our Education Pipeline," *Education Week*, Vol. 25, No, 42 (July 12, 2006).

Kolesnik, Walter B. *Mental Discipline in Modern Education*. Madison, Wisconsin: University of Wisconsin Press, 1966.

Krug, Edward A. *The Shaping of the American High School*. New York: Harper and Row, 1964.

Kuhlman, Frederick. *Experimental Studies in Mental Deficiency*. Worchester, Massachusetts: Clark University, 1904.

Kuhlman, Frederick. *A Revision of the Binet-Simon System for Measuring the Intelligence of Children*. Faribault: Minnesota School for Feebeminded and Colony for Epileptics, 1912.

Labaree, David F. "The Peculiar Problems of Preparing Educational Researchers," *Educational Researcher*, Vol. 32, No. 4 (May 2003).

Labaree, David F.. "Power, Knowledge, and the Rationalization of Teaching: A Genealogy of the Movement to Professionalize Teaching, *Harvard Educational Review*, Vol. 62, No, 2 (Summer 1992).

Ladson-Billings, Gloria and Tate, William F. *Education Research in the Public Interest: Social Justice, Action, and Policy*. New York: Teachers College Press. 2006.

Lagemann, Ellen Condliffe. "Contested Terrain: A History of Educational Research in the United States, 1890-1950," *Educational Researcher*, Vol. 26, No. 9 (December 1997).

Lagemann, Ellen Condliffe, "Does History Matter in Education Research? A Brief for Humanities in an Age of Science," *Harvard Educational Review*, Vol. 75, No. 1 (2005).

Lagemann, Ellen Condliffe. *An Elusive Science: The Troubling History of Educational Research*. Chicago: University of Chicago Press, 2000.

Lagemann, Ellen Confliffe, "The Plural Worlds of Educational Research," *History of Education Quarterly*, Vol. 29, No. 2 (Summer 1989).

Lagemann, Ellen Condliffe and Shulman, Lee S. "Introduction: The Improvement of Education Research: A Complex, Continuing Quest" in eds. Ellen Condliffe and Lee S. Schulman. *Issues in Education Research.* San Francisco: Josey-Bass Publishers, 1999.

Laitsch, Daniel, Heilman, Elizabeth E., and Shaker, Paul. "Teacher Education, Pro Market Policy and Advocacy Research," *Teaching Education.* Vol. 13, No. 3 (2002), p. 254.

Landis, Paul H. *Rural Life in Process.* New York: Mc-Graw Hill, 1940.

Lane, Michael A. *The Level of Social Motion: An Inquiry into the Future Conditions of Human Society.* New York: Macmillan, 1902.

Laosa, Luis M. "Social Policies toward Children of Diverse Ethnic, Racial, and Language Groups in the United States" in eds. Harold W. Stevenson and Alberta E. Siegel. *Child Development Research and Social Policy.* Chicago: University of Chicago Press, 1984.

Lascarides, V. Celia and Hinitz, Blythe F. *History of Early Childhood Education.* New York: Falmer Press, 2000.

Latisch, Daniel A., Heilman, Elizabeth E., and Shaker, Paul, "Teacher Education, Pro-Market Policy and Advocacy Research," *Teaching Education,* Vol. 13, No. 3 (2002).

Lay, Wilhelm. *Experimentelle Didaktik.* Wiesbaden, 1903.

Lay, Wilhelm. *Experimentelle Pädagogik.* Leipzig: Taubner, 1908.

Lay, Wilhelm. *Die Tatschule.* Leipzig: Zickfeldt, 1911.

Lee, Carol D. "Why We Need to Re-Think Race and Ethnicity in Educational Research," *Educational Researcher,* Vol. 32, No. 5 (June/July 2003).

Lee, Godrin C. ed. *Crusade Against Ignorance.* New York: Teachers College Press, 1961.

Lehming, Rolf and Kane, Michael. eds. *Improving Schools: Using What We Know.* Beverly Hills, California: Sage Publications, 1981.

Leiby, James.. *A History of Social Welfare and Social Work in the United States.* New York: Columbia University Press, 1978.

Lemann, Nicholas. *The Big Test: The Secret History of the American Meritocracy,* New York: Farrar, Straus and Giroux, 1999.

Lenroot, Katharine F. and Lundberg, Emma O. *Juvenile Courts at Work: A Study of the Organization and Methods of en Courts.* U. S. Department of Labor, Children's Bureau Publication No. 141. Washington, D.C.: U..S. Government Printing Office, 1925.

Levinger, Leah and Murphy, Lois Barclay. "Implications of the Social Scene for the Education of Young Children" in ed. Nelson B. Henry. *The Forth-Sixth Yearbook of the National Society for the Study of Education: Part II, Early Childhood Education.* Chicago: University of Chicago Press, 1956.

Licht, W. *Industrializing America in the Nineteenth Century.* Baltimore: Johns Hopkins Press, 1995.

Lightfoot, Sara Lawrence. *The Good High School: Portraits of Character and Culture.* New York: Basic Books, 1983.

Lind, Michael. *The Next American Nation: The New Nationalism and the Fourth American Revolution.* New York: Free Press, 1996.

Lippman, Walter. *Drift and Mastery*. Englewood Cliffs, New Jersey: Spectrum Books, 1962.

Liu, B. *Educational Research in Major American Cities*. New York: Kings Crown Press, 1945.

Loveless, Tom. "The Use and Misuse of Research in Educational Reform" in ed. Diane Ravitch. *Brookings Papers on Education 1998*. Washington, D.C.: Brookings Institution Press, 1998.

Lomax, Elizabeth M. R. *Science and Patterns of Child Care*. San Francisco: W. H. Freeman and Co., 1978.

Lowenberg, Bert James, "Darwinism Comes to America, 1859-1900," *Mississippi Valley Historical Review*, Vol. 28 (June 1941- March 1942).

Lowenberg, Bert James. "The Reaction of American Scientists to Darwin," *American Historical Review*, Vol. 38 (1938).

Lowrey, Lawson. "Psychiatry for Children," *American Journal of Psychiatry* (November 1944).

Lubove, Roy. *The Professional Altruist: The Emergence of Social Work as a Career, 1880-1930*. Cambridge, Massachusetts, Harvard University Press, 1965.

Ludy, Benjamin T. *A History of Psychology: Original Sources and Contemporary Research*. New York: McGraw-Hill Book Co., 1998.

MacDonald, Arthur, "Child Study in the United States," *Report of the Commissioner of Education for the Year 1897-987*, Vol. 2,Whole Number 258. Washington, D.C.: U. S. Government Printing Office, 1899.

Mann, Horace. *Twelfth Annual Report* in ed. Lawrence A. Cremin. *The Republic and the School: Horace Mann on the Education of Free Men*. New York: Teachers College Press, 1957.

Marro, Antonia. *La Puberta*. Torino: Bocca, 1897.

Maxwell, Joseph. A. "Causal Explanation, Qualitative Research, and Scientific Inquiry in Education," *Educational Researcher*, Vol. 33, No. 2 (March 2004).

Mayer, Richard E. "E. L. Thorndike's Enduring Contributions to Educational Psychology" in eds. Barry J. Zimmerman and Dale H. Schunk. *Educational Psychology: A Century of Contributions*. Mahwah, New Jersey: Lawrence Erlbaum Associates, 2003.

McLaren, Angus. *Our Master Race: Eugenics in Canada, 1885-1945*. Toronto: McClelland & Stewart, 1990.

McClintock, Robert. "Toward a Place for Study in a World of Instruction," *Teachers College Record*, Vol. 73 (1971).

McConnell, T. R. *The Nature of Educational Research, The Conceptual Structure of Educational Research: A Symposium Held in /connection with the Fiftieth Anniversary of the University of Chicago. Supplementary Educational Monographs*, (published in conjunction with *The School Review* and *The Elementary School Journal*), No. 55 (May 1942).

McMurray, Foster. "Preface to an Autonomous Discipline of Education," *Educational Theory*, Vol. 3 (1955).

McMurry, Charles A. and McMurry, Frank M. *The Method of he Recitation*. New York: The Macmillan Co., 1897.

McMurry, Dorothy. *Herbartian Contributions to History Instruction in American Elementary Schools*. Columbia University Contributions to Education, Teachers

College ?Series, No. 920. New York: Bureau of Publications, Teachers College, Columbia University, 1946.

Meek, Lois Hayden, *et al. The Personal Development of Boys and Girls*. New York: Progressive Education Association, 1940.

Mercer, Jane R. *Labeling the Mentally Retarded*. Berkeley, California: University of California Press, 1977.

Meyer, Adolphe E. *An Educational History of the Western World*. New York: McGraw-Hill, 1965.

Meumann, Ernst. *Vorlesungen zur Einfurung in die Experimentelle Pädagogik*. Leipzig: Engleman, 1907-1908.

Miller, Nora. *The Girl in the Rural Family*. Chapel Hill, North Carolina: University of North Carolina Press, 1935.

Minton, Henry L. "The Iowa Child Welfare Research Station and the 1940 Debate on Intelligence: Carrying on the Legacy of a Concerned Mother," *Journal of the History of the Behavioral Sciences*, Vol. 20 (April 1984).

Minton, Henry, L. *Lewis M. Terman: Pioneer in Psychological Testing*. New York: New York University Press, 1988.

Mitchell, Theodore R. and Haro, Analee," Poles Apart: Reconciling the Dichotomies in Educational Research" in eds. Ellen Condliffe Lagemann and Lee S. Schulman. *Issues in Education Research*. San Francisco: Jossey-Bass Publishers, 1999.

Moehlman, Arthur B. "Stuart Appleton Courtis: Master Teacher," *The Nation's Schools*, Vol. 33 No. 2 (June 1944).

Mohan, Raj P. and Wilke, Arthur S. eds. *International Handbook of Contemporary Developments in Sociology*. Westport, Connecticut: Greenwood, 1994.

Monroe, Paul. *A Brief Course in the History of Education*. New York: The Macmillan Co., 1927.

Monroe, Paul. *Cyclopedia of Education*. New York: The Macmillan Co., 1911.

Monroe, Walter S., "Educational Measurement in 1920 and 1945," *Journal of Educational Measurement*, Vol. 38, No. 5 (January 1945).

Monroe, Walter S., "Existing Tests and Standards" in ed. Guy M. Whipple. *The Seventeenth Yearbook of the National Society for the Study of Education: Part II The Measurement of Educational Products*. Bloomington, Illinois: Public School Publishing Co., 1918.

Monroe Walter S. *Ten Years of Educational Research, 1919-1927. University of Illinois Bureau of Educational Research Bulletin No. 42, University of Illinois Bulletin*, Vol. 25, No. 51 (1928).

Monroe, Walter s. and Englehart, Max D. *The Scientific Study of Educational Problems*. New York: The Macmillan Co., 1936.

Moore, Harold E., Russell, John, and Ferguson, Donald G. *The Doctorate in Education: Volume II—The Institutions*. Washington, D.C.: The American Association of Colleges for Teacher Education, 1969.

Morison, Samuel Eliot. *The Oxford History of the American People*, Vol. I. New York: New American Library, 1972.

Morphett and Washburn, Carleton, "When Should Children Begin to Read?" *Elementary School Journal*, Vol. 31 (1931) in ed. Wayne Dennis. *Readings in Child Psychology*. Englewood Cliffs, New Jersey: Prentice-Hall, Inc., 1951.

Mosteller, Frederick and Moynihan, Daniel P. eds. *On Equality of Educational Opportunity.* New York: Vintage Books, 1972.

Moynihan, Daniel P. "Sources of Resistance to the Coleman Report," *Harvard Educational Review,* Vol. 38, No. 1 (Winter 1968).

The National Science Board's Commission on Precollege Education in Mathematics, Science and Technology. *Educating Americans for the Twenty-First Century.* Washington, D.C.: National Science Board, 1983.

National Science Foundation and the Department of Education. *Science and Engineering Education for the 1980s and Beyond.* Washington, D.C.: U.S. Government Printing Office, 1980.

Newlon, J. H. "What Research Can Do for the Superintendent," *Journal of Educational Research,* Vol. 8 (September 1923).

Nisbet, John, "Educational Research: The State of the Art" in ed. W. B. Dockrell and David Hamilton, *Rethinking Educational Research.* London: Hodder and Stoughton, 1980.

Oakes, Jeannie. *Keeping Track: How Schools Structure Equality.* New Haven: Yale University Press, 1985.

Odencrantz, Louise C. *The Social Worker: In Family, Medical and Psychiatric Social Work ,Volume I Job Analysis Series American Association of Social Workers.* New York: Harper and Row, 1929.

Odgers, Merle M. "Education and the American Philosophical Society," *Proceedings of he American Philosophical Society,* Vol. 87, No. 1 (July 1943).

O'Donnell, John M. *The Origins of Behaviorism: American Psychology, 1870-1920.* New York: New York University Press, 1985.

Office of Education, U. S. Department of Health, Education and Welfare. *Educational Research and Development in the United States,* Washington, D.C.: U.S. Government Printing Office, 1970.

Ogg, F. A. *Research in the Humanistic and Social Sciences.* New York: The Century Co., 1928.

Ohles, John F. "Courtis, Stuart A." in ed. John F. Ohles. *Biographical Dictionary of American Educators.* Westport, Connecticut: Greenwood Press, 1978.

Oppenheimer, J. J. *The Visiting Teacher.* New York: Progressive Education Association, 1924.

Orata, Pedro. *The Theory of Identical Elements.* Columbus, Ohio: The Ohio State University Press, 1928.

Orfield, Gary and Kornhaber, Mindy L. eds. *Raising Standards or Raising Barriers? Inequality and High-Stakes Testing in Public Education.* New York: The Century Foundation Press, 2001.

Osgood, C. E. *Method and Theory in Experimental Psychology.* New York: Oxford University Press, 1953.

Page, Walter Hines. *The Rebuilding of Old Commonwealths, Being Essays Toward the Training of the Forgotten Man in the Southern States.* New York: Doubleday, Page, Co., 1902.

Persons, Stow ed. *Evolutionary Thought in America.* New Haven, Connecticut: Yale University Press, 1950.

Petrina, Stephen, "Luella Cole, Sidney Press, and Educational Psychoanalysis, 1921-11931," *History of Education Quarterly,* Vol. 44, No. 4 (Winter 2004).

Phenix, Philip H. *Realms of Meaning: A Philosophy of the Curriculum for General Education.* New York: McGraw Hill, 1964.

Phillips, D. C. *Philosophy, Science, and Social Inquiry: Contemporary Methodological Controversies in Social Science and Related Applied Fields of Research.* Oxford: Pergamon Press, 1987.

Phillips, D. C., "Post-Kuhnian Reflections of Educational Research" in ed. Jonas F. Soltis. *The Eightieth Yearbook of he National Society for the Study of Education: Part I Philosophy and Education.* Chicago: University of Chicago Press, 1981.

Pickens, Donald T. *Eugenics and Progressives.* Nashville, Tennessee: Vanderbilt University Press, 1968.

Popkewitz, Thomas S. *Paradigm and Ideology in Educational Research: The Social Function of the Intellectual.* London: The Falmer Press, 1984.

Porter, Theodore M. *Karl Pearson: The Scientific Life in a Statistical Age.* Princeton, New Jersey: Princeton University Press, 2004.

Powell, Arthur G. *The Uncertain Profession: Harvard and the Search for Educational Authority.* Cambridge, Massachusetts: Harvard University Press, 1980.

Prescott, Daniel A. *Emotion and the Educative Process.* Washington, D.C.: American Council on Education, 1938.

Prewett. Clinton R. "The Development of the Unit Method of Teaching from the Herbartian Movement to the Present" Ph.D. dissertation, University of North Carolina at Chapel Hill, 1950.

Public Education Association of the City of New York. *The Visiting Teacher in the United States.* 2nd ed. New York: Progressive Education Association, 1923.

Randall, John Herman. "The Changing Impact of Darwin on Philosophy," *Journal of the History of Ideas*, Vol. XXII, No, 4 (October-December 1961).

Randels, George Basis. "The Doctrines of Herbart in the United States" Ph.D. thesis, University of Pennsylvania, 1911.

Ramsay, David. *The History of the American Revolution*, Vol. II [1789] ed. Lester H., Cohen. Indianapolis: Liberty Fund, 1989.

Ravitch, Diane. *The Troubled Crusade: American Education, 1945-1980.* New York: Basic Books, 1983.

Reese, William. J. "What History Teaches About the Impact of Educational Research on Practice' in eds. Asghar Iran-Nejad and P. David Parson. *Review of Research in Education 24.* Washington, D.C.: American Educational Research Association. 1999.

Remmers, H. H., and Knight, F. B. "The Teaching of Educational Psychology in the United States," *Journal of Educational Psychology*, Vol. 13 (1922).

Report of the Committee on Secondary School Studies Appointed at the Meeting of the National Education Association, July 9, 1982 with the Reports of the Conference Arranged by the Committee and Held December 28-30, 1892. Washington, D.C.: U. S. Government Printing Office, 1893.

A Report to the President: The Committee for the White House Conference on Education. Full Report. April 1956 (Washington, D.C., 1956) in ed. Sol Cohen. *Education in the United States: A Documentary History*, Vol. 5. New York: Random House, 1974.

Rice, Joseph Mayer. "The Futility of the Spelling Grind," *The Forum*, Vol. 23 (April 1897 and June 1897).

Rice, Joseph Mayer. *The Public-School System of he United States* [1893]. New York: Arno Press and New York Times, 1969.

Rice, Joseph Mayer. *Scientific Management in Education* [1914]. New York: Arno Press and New York Times, 1969.

Richardson, John T. E. "Howard Andrew Knox and the Origins of Performance Testing on Ellis Island, 1912-1916, *History of Psychology*, Vol. 6, No. 2 (May 2003).

Richardson, Theresa R. *The Century of the Child: The Mental Hygiene Movement and Social Policy in the U. S. and Canada*. Albany, New York: State University of New York Press, 1989,

Richardson, Theresa R. and Johanningmeier, Erwin V. "Intelligence Testing: The Legitimation of a Meritocratic Educational Science," *International Journal of Educational Research*, Vol. 37, No. 8 (1997).

Rockefeller Foundation. *Annual Report, 1913-1914*. New York: Rockefeller Foundation, 1914.

Rockefeller Foundation. *Annual Report, 1921*. New York: Rockefeller Foundation, 1922.

Roback, A. A. *History of American Psychology*. New York: Library Publishers, 1952.

Robarts, James R. "The Rise of Educational Science in America." Unpublished Ph.D. dissertation. University of Illinois. 1963.

Rockefeller Archive Center. Sleepy Hollow, New York.

Rose, Lowell C. and Gallup, Alec M. "The 38th Annual phi Delta Kappan/Gallup Pool of the Public's Attitudes Toward the Public Schools," *Phi Delta Kappan*, Vol. 88, No. 1 (Septemebr 2006).

Rosen, George. *Preventive Medicine in the United States, 1900-1975*. New York: Science History Publications, 1975.

Rosenberg, Charles E. *No Other Gods: Science and American Thought*. Baltimore: Johns Hopkins University Press, 1976).

Rosenberg, Emily S. *Spreading the American Dream: American Economic and Cultural Expansion, 1890-1945*. New York: Hill and Wang, 1982.

Ross. Dorothy. G. *Stanley Hall: The Psychologist as Prophet*. Chicago: University of Chicago Press, 1972.

Ross, Dorothy. *The Origins of American Social Science*. New York: Cambridge, 1991.

Ruchin, J. "Does School Crime Need the Attention of Policeman or Educators?" *Teachers College Record*, Vol. 79 (1977).

Rudolph, Frederick. *The American College and University.*, New York: Alfred A. Knopf, 1962.

Rudolph, Frederick. ed. *Essays on Education in the New Republic*. Cambridge: Belknap Press of Harvard University Press, 1965.

Rudy, Willis. *Schools in an Age of Mass Culture: An Exploration of Selected Themes in the History of Twentieth Century American Education*. Englewood Cliffs, New Jersey: Prentice Hall, 1965.

Rugg, Harold O. "Three Decades of Mental Discipline: Curriculum Making *via* National Committees" in Guy M. Whipple. *The Twenty-Sixth Yearbook of the National Society for the Study of Education: The Foundations and Technique of Curriculum Construction*. Bloomington, Illinois: The Public School Publishing Co., 1926.

Rush, Benjamin. "Plan for the Establishment of Public Schools" in ed. Frederick Rudolph. *Essays on Education in the Early Republic*, Cambridge, Massachusetts: Harvard University Press, 1965.

Russett, Cynthia Eagle. *Darwin in America: The Intellectual Response, 1865-1912*. San Francisco: W. H. Freeman and Co., 1976.

Ryan, Carson W. "History of Mental Hygiene in Schools," *American Journal of Insanity*, (1944).

Sacks, Peter. *Standardized Minds: The High Price of American's Testing Culture and What We Can Do to Change It*. Cambridge, Massachusetts: Perseus Publishing, 1999.

Sandiford Peter. "Transfer of Learning" in ed. Walter S. Monroe. *Encyclopedia of Educational Research*, rev. ed. New York: The Macmillan Co., 1950.

Samelson, Franz. "World War I Intelligence Testing and the Development of Psychology," *Journal of History of the Behavioral Sciences*, Vol. 13, No. 3 (July 1977).

Scates, Douglas E. "Fifty Years of Objective Measurement and Research in Education," *Journal of Educational Research*, Vol. 41, No. 4 (December 1947).

Scates, Douglas E. "Organized Research in Education, National, State, City, and University Bureaus of Educational Research," *Review of Educational Research*, Vol. 9 (1939).

Scates, Douglas E., "Research and Progress in Educational Administration, *Journal of Educational Research*, Vol. 38, No. 5 (January 1945).

Schneider, B. "Sociology of Education; An Overview of the Field at the Turn of the Century" in eds. M. T. Hallinan, A. Garmoran, A. Kubitschek and T. Loveless. *Stability and Change in American Education*. New York: Werner Publications. 2003.

The Scholars Look at the Schools: A Report of the Disciplines Seminar. Washington, D.C.: National Education Association, 1962.

Scoon, Robert. "The Rise and Impact of Evolutionary Ideas" in ed. Stow Persons. *Evolutionary Thought in America.*. New Haven, Connecticut: Yale University Press, 1950.

Scott, Winfield C. and Hill, Clyde M. *Public Education Under Criticism*. Englewood, Cliffs, New Jersey: Prentice-Hall, 1954,

Shavelson, Richard J., Webb, Noreen M., and Burstein, Leigh. "Measurement of Teaching" in ed. Merlin C. Wittrock. *Handbook of Research on Teaching*. 3rd ed. New York: Macmillan Publishing Co., 1986.

Sherman, Mandel. "Contributions to Education of Scientific Knowledge in Mental Hygiene" in ed. Guy M. Whipple. *Thirty-Seventh Yearbook of the National Society for the Study of Education: Part II: The Scientific Movement in Education*. Bloomington, Illinois, Public School Publishing Co., 1938.

Shinn, Millicent W. *The Biography of a Baby*. Boston: Houghton Mifflin Co., 1900.

Shinn, Millicent W. "Notes on the Development of a Child, I," *University of California Publications in Education*. Berkeley: University of California, 1893-1899.

Shinn, Millicent W. "Notes on the Development of a Child, II, The Development of the Senses in the First Three Years," *University of California Publications in Education*. Berkeley: University of California, 1904.

Shirley, Mary M. *The First Two Years*, Vol. 3 in ed. Wayne Dennis. *Readings in Child Psychology*. Englewood Cliffs, New Jersey: Prentice-Hall, Inc., 1951.

Shulman, Lee S. "Knowledge and Teaching: Foundations of the New Reform," *Harvard Educational Review*, Vol. 57 (1987).

Shulman, Lee S., "Paradigms and Research Programs in the Study of Teaching: A Contemporary Perspective" in ed. Merlin C. Wittorck. *Handbook of Research on Teaching*, 3rd ed. New York: Macmillan, 1986.

Siegel, Harvey, "Epistemological Diversity and Education Research: Much Ado About Nothing," *Educational Researcher*, (March 2006).

Simon, Brian. "Education and Social Change" paper delivered at meeting of American Educational Research Association, Washington, D.C. (April 2, 1975).

Simon, Brian. *Intelligence, Psychology and Education*. London: Lawrence and Wishart, 1971.

Singham, Mano. *The Achievement Gap in U. S. Education: Canaries in the Mine*. Lanham, Maryland: Rowman & Littlefield, 2005.

Singer, Judith D. and Butler, John A. "The Education for All Handicapped Children Act: Schools as Agents of Social Reform," *Harvard Educational Review*, Vol. 57, No. 2 (May 1987).

Sizer, Theodore. *Horace's Compromise: The Dilemma of the American High School*. Boston: Houghton Mifflin, 1984.

Slavin, Robert E. *Educational Research in an Age of Accountability*. Baltimore: Johns Hopkins University Press, 2007.

Smedley, Frederick W. "A Report on the Measurement of the Sensory and Motor Abilities of the Pupils of the Chicago University Primary School land the Pedagogical Value of Such Measurements," *Transactions of the Illinois Society for Child Study*, Vol. II, No. 2 (1896-97).

Smith, Anna C. and Dobbin, John E. ""Marks and Marking Systems" in ed. Chester W. Harris. *Encyclopedia of Educational Research*, 3rd ed. New York: The Macmillan Co., 1960.

Smith, Barry C. "Report of the General Director, November 1921, Child Welfare Program for the Prevention of Delinquency," Laura Spelman Rockefeller Memorial Archive (LSRM) 3,111,1113, Rockefeller Archive Center (RAC) Sleepy Hollow New York.

Smith, Frank. *Further Essays into Education*. Portsmouth, New Hampshire: Heineman, 1988.

Smith, James V. and Hamilton, David eds. *The Meritocratic Intellect: Studies in the History of Educational Research*. Aberdeen: Aberdeen University Press, 1980.

Smith, Samuel Harrison. "Remarks on Education: Illustrating the Close Connection Between Virtue and Wisdom." in ed. Frederick Rudolph. *Essays on Education in the Early Republic*, Cambridge, Massachusetts: Harvard University Press, 1965.

Smuts, Alice B. "The National Research Council on Child Development and the Founding of the Society for Research on Child Development" in eds. Alice B. Smuts, and J. W. Hagen. *History and Research in Child Development*. Monographs of the S.R.C.D., Serial No. 211, Nos. 4-5 (1985).

Smuts, Alice B. *Science in the Service of Children, 1893-1935*. New Haven: Yale University Press, 2006.

Solomon, Richard L. "An Extension of Control Group Design," *Psychological Bulletin*, Vol. XLIX (1949).

Spady, William G. "The Impact of School Resources on Students" in ed. Fred N. Kerlinger. *Review of Research in Education I*, Itasca, Illinois: F. E. Peacock Publishers, Inc., 1973.

Stafford P. L. and Stafford, E. J. *A History of Childhood and Disability*. New York: Teachers College, Columbia University, 1966.

Stallings, Jane A. and Stipek, Debrorah. "Research on Early Childhood and Elementary School Teaching Programs" in ed. Merlin C. Wittrock. *Handbook of Research on Teaching* 3rd ed. (New York: Macmillan Publishing Co., 1986).

Stanley, Julian C., "Rice as a Pioneer Educational Researcher," *Journal of Educational Measurement*, Vol. 3, No. 2 (Summer 1966).

Starch, Daniel. *Educational Measurements*. New York: The Macmillan Co., 1917.

Starch, Daniel. *Educational Psychology*. New York: The Macmillan Co., 1919.

Starch, Daniel. *Educational Psychology*, rev. ed. New York: The Macmillan Co., 1927.

Starch, Daniel. "The Measurement of Efficiency in Reading," *Journal of Educational Psychology*, Vol. VI, No. 1 (January 1915).

Starch, Daniel. "A Test in Latin," *Journal of Educational Psychology*, Vol. X, No. 10 (December 1919).

Starch, Daniel and Elliot, E. C. "The Reliability of Grading High School Work in English," *School Review*, Vol. XX (1912).

Starch, Daniel and Elliott, E.C. "The Reliability of Grading Work in Mathematics," *School Review*, Vol. XXI (1913).

Starch, Daniel and Elliott, E. C. "The Reliability of Grading Work in History," *School Review*, Vol. XX1 (1913).

Stern, Clara and Stern, W. *Die Kindersprache*. Leipzig: Barth, 1907.

Stern, W. *Psychologie der Frühen Kindheit*. Leipzig: Quelle and Mayer, 1914.

Stevenson, George S. "Child Guidance and the National Committee" in eds. Lawson Lowrey and Victoria Sloan. *Orthopsychiatry, 1923-1948: Retrospect and Prospect*. Menasha, Wisconsin: George Banta Publishing for American Orthopsychiatric Association, 1948.

Stevenson, George S. and Smith, Geddes. *Child Guidance: A Quarter Century of Development*. New York: Commonwealth Fund, 1934.

Stoddard. George D. "An Evaluation of the Yearbook" in Nelson B. Henry. *The Forth-Third Yearbook of the National Society for the Study of Education, Part I, Adolescence*. Chicago: University of Chicago Press, 1944.

Stoddard, George D. *Pioneering in Child Welfare: A History of the Iowa Child Welfare Research Station, 1917-1933*. Iowa City: University of Iowa, Press, 1933.

Stoddard, George D. *The Second Decade: A Review of the Activities of the Iowa Child Welfare Research Station, 1928-1938*. University of Iowa Studies, New Series No. 366, Iowa City: University of Iowa Press (February 1, 1939).

Stolurow, Lawrence M. *Psychological and Educational Factors in Transfer of Training*, Section 1, Final Report. Urbana, Illinois: Training Research Laboratory, 1966.

Strickland, Charles E. "Sputnik Reform Revisited," *Educational Studies*, Vol. 16 (Spring 1985).

Strickland, Charles E. and Burgess, Charles eds. *Health, Growth, and Heredity: G. Stanley Hall on Natural Education*. New York: Teachers College Press, 1965.

Strong, Jr., Edward R. "Psychological Methods as Applied to Advertising," *Journal of Educational Psychology*, Vol. IV, No. 7 (September 1913).

Sullivan, G. J. "The Natural Approach to Learning," *Commonweal*, Vol. 74 (June 23, 1961).

Sully, James. *Studies in Childhood*. London: Longmans Green, 1895.

Suppes, Patrick. ed. *Impact of Research on Education: Some Case Studies*. Washington, D.C.: National Academy of Education, 1978.

Swaim, Ginalie. "Cory Bussey Hilllis. "Women of Vision" *The Palimpest*, Vol. 60, No. 6 (1979).

Task Force on Education for Economic Growth. *Action for Excellence: A Comprehensive Plan to Improve Our Nation's Schools*. Washington, D.C.: Education Commission of the States, 1983.

Task Force on Elementary and Secondary Education Policy. *Making the Grade*. New York: Twentieth Century Fund, 1983.

Tate, William F. "In the Public Interest" in ed. Gloria Ladson-Billings and William F. Tate. *Education Research in the Public Interest: Social Justice, Action, and Policy*. New York. Teachers College Press. 2006.

Taylor, Lloyd C. *The Medical Profession and Social Reform, 1885-1945*. New York. St. Martin's Press, 1974.

Terman, Lewis M. "The Conservation of Talent," *School and Society* (March 1942).

Terman, Lewis M. *The Intelligence of School Children: How Children Differ in Ability, the Use of Mental Tests in School Grading and the Proper Education of Exceptional Children*. Boston: Houghton Mifflin, Co., 1919 in eds.. Robert H. Bremner, John Barnard, Tamara K. Hareven, and Robert M. Mennel. *Children and Youth in America: A Documentary History, Volume II: 1866-1932, Parts Seven and Eight*. Cambridge, Massachusetts: Harvard University Press, 1971.

Terman, Lewis M. *Intelligence Tests and School Reorganization*. Yonkers-on-Hudson, New York: Word Book Publishing Co., 1922.

Terman, Lewis M. "The Intelligence Quotient of Francis Galton in Childhood," *American Journal of Psychology*, Vol. 28 (1917) in ed. Wayne Dennis. *Readings in Child Psychology*. Englewood Cliffs, New Jersey: Prentice-Hall, Inc., 1951.

Terman, Lewis M. *The Measurement of Intelligence: An Explanation of and a Complete Guide for the Use of the Stanford Revision and the Extension of the Binet-Simon Intelligence Scale*. Boston: Houghton Mifflin Co., 1916.

Terman, Lewis M. "The Mental Test as a Psychological Method," *Psychological Review*,Vol. 31 (March 1924).

Termn, Lewis M. *National Intelligence Tests, With Manual of Directions*. Yonkers-on-Hudson, New York: World Publishing, Co., 1920.

Terman, Lewis M. *The Stanford Revision of the Binet-Simon Scale*. Boston: Houghton Mifflin, 1916.

Thomas, Lawrence G. *Twenty-Seventh Yearbook of the National Society for the Study of Education: Philosophical Redirection of Educational Research*. Chicago: University of Chicago Press, 1972.

Thomas. W. I. and Thomas, Dorothy Swaine. *The Child in America: Behavior Problems and Programs*. New York: Alfred A. Knopf, 1928.

Thorndike, Edward L. *Animal Intelligence, Psychological Review Monograph Supplements*, No 8 (1898) in ed. Wayne Dennis. *Readings in the History of Psychology*. New York: Appleton-Century-Crofts, Inc., 1948.

Thorndike, Edward L. "Autobiography" in ed.. Geraldine M. Joncich. *Psychology and the Science of Education: Selected Writings of Edward L. Thorndike*. New York: Teachers College Press, 1962.

Thorndike, Edward L. "Darwin's Contribution to Psychology," *University of California Chronicle*, Vol. 12 (1909) in ed.. Geraldine M. Joncich. *Psychology and the Science of Education: Selected Writings of Edward L. Thorndike*. New York: Teaches College Press, 1962.

Thorndike, Edward L. "Do Animals Reason?" *Popular Science Monthly* (1899) in ed. Wayne Dennis. *Readings in General Psychology*. New York: Prentice-Hall, Inc., 1949.

Thorndike, Edward L. "Eugenics: With Special Reference to Intellect and Character," *Popular Science Monthly*, Vol. LXXXIII (April 1913).

Thorndike, Edward L. "Evolution of the Human Intellect, *Popular Science Monthly*, Vol. 69, No. 5 (November 1901).

Thorndike, Edward L. *Introduction to the Theory of Mental and Social Measurements*. New York: Science Press, 1904.

Thorndike, Edward L. "Measurement in Education" in ed. Guy M. Whipple *The Twenty-First Yearbook of the National Society for the Study of Education: Intelligence Tests and Their Use*. Bloomington, Illinois: The Public School Publishing Co., 1922.

Thorndike, Edward L. "Mental Discipline in High School Studies," *Journal of Educational Psychology*, Vol. 15 (1924),

Thorndike, Edward L. "The Nature, Purposes, and General Methods of Measurements of Educational Products" in Guy M. Whipple. *The Seventeenth Yearbook of the National Society for the Study of Education: Part II The Measurement of Educational Products*. Bloomington, Illinois: Public School Publishing Co., 1918.

Thorndike, Edward L. *The Principles of Teaching Based on Psychology*. New York: G. Seller, 1906 in ed. Geraldine M. Joncich. *Psychology and the Science of Education: Selected Writings of Edward L. Thorndike*. New York: Teachers College Press, 1967.

Thorndike, Edward L. *The Psychology of Arithmetic*. New York: The Macmillan Co., 1922 in ed. Geraldine M. Joncich. *Psychology and the Science of Education: Selected Writings of Edward L. Thorndike*. New York: Teachers College Press, 1967.

Thorndike, Edward L. "Quantitative Investigations in Education: With Special Reference to Co-operation Within this Association," *School Review Monograph No. 2: National Society of College Teachers of Education Yearbook*, Chicago: University of Chicago Press, 1912.

Thorndike, Edward L. *Notes on Child Study*. New York: The Macmillan Co., 1901.

Thorndike, Edward L. and Woodworth, Robert S. "I. The Influence of Improvement in One Mental Function upon the Efficiency of other Functions;" "II. The Estimation of Magnitudes;' and "III. Functions Involving Attention, Observation and Discrimination." *Psychological Review*, Vol. VIII (May, July and November 1901).

Travers, Robert M. W. *How Research Has Changed American Schools.* Kalamazoo, Michigan: Mythos Press, 1983.

Travers, Robert M. W. ed. *Second Handbook of Research on Teaching.* Chicago: Rand McNally, 1973.

Tuddenham, R. D. "Intelligence Measurement" in *Encyclopedia of Educational Research*, 5th ed. New York: Macmillan, 1969.

Turner, Frederick Jackson. *The Frontier in American History,* New York: Holt, Rinehart and Winston, 1962.

Tyack, David B. *The One Best System: A History of American Urban Education.* Cambridge, Massachusetts: Harvard University Press, 1974.

Tyack, David B. and Hansot, Elisabeth. "From Social Movement to Professional Management: An Inquiry into the Changing Character of Leadership in Public Education," *American Journal of Education* (1980).

Tyack, David B. and Hansot, Elisabeth. *Managers of Virtue: Public School Leadership in America, 1820-1980.* New York: Basic Books, 1982.

Umbeck, Nelda. *State Legislation on School Attendance.* Washington, D.C.: U. S. Government Printing Office, 1960.

Van Waters, Miriam. "The Socialization of Juvenile Court Procedure" in ed. Ernest B. Hoag and Edward H. Williams. *Crime, Abnormal Minds and the Law.* Indianapolis: Bobbs-Merril Co., 1923.

Veysey, Lawrence. Review of Lawrence Cremin's *American Education: The Metropolitan Experience* in *The American Historical Review,* Vol. 95, No. 9 (December 1997).

Viadero, Debra. "AERA Sessions Run Gamut from NCLB to Instant Messages," *Education Week,* Vol. 25, No. 32 (April 19, 2006).

Viadero, Debra. "Learning by At-Risk Students Tops List of Proposed Research Priorities," *Education Week,* Vol. 24, No. 42 (July 13, 2005).

Viadero, Debra.. "'What Works' Rates Programs Effectiveness," *Education Week,* Vol. 25, No. 37 (May 17, 2006).

Vincent, George. *President's Annual Review.* New York: Rockefeller Foundation, 1922.

Vinovskis, Maris A. "The Changing Role of the Federal Government in Educational Research," *History of Education Quarterly,* Vol. 36 (Summer 1996).

Washington Research Project. *Children Out of School.* Washington, D.C.: Children's Defense Fund, 1974.

Watson, R. I. "A Brief History of Clinical Psychology" in ed. R. B. Brozek. *R. I. Watson's Selected Papers on the History of Psychology.* New Hampshire: University Press of New England, 1977.

Weil, A. and Schawartz, E. K. trans. *Experimental Psychology.* New York: Prentice-Hall, 1936.

Welter, Rush. *Popular Education and Democratic Thought in America.* New York: Columbia University Press, 1965.

Westfall, Barry F. "German Educational Thought Adapted to American Schools: Herbartian Influence on American Teacher Education Through Selected Publications of Charles DeGarmo and Charles and Frank McMurry." Ph.D. dissertation, Northern Illinois University. 1987.

Whipple, Guy M. ed. *The Thirty-Seventh Yearbook of the National Society for the Study of Education: The Scientific Movement in Education.* Bloomington, Illinois: The Public School Publishing Co., 1938.

Whipple, Guy M. ed. *The Seventeenth Yearbook of the National Society for the Study of Education: Part II The Measurement of Educational Products.* Bloomington, Illinois: Public School Publishing Co., 1918.

Whipple, Guy M. *The Twenty-First Yearbook of the National Society for the Study of Education: Part II, The Administrative Use of Intelligence Tests.* Bloomington, Illinois: Public School Publishing Co., 1922.

Whipple, Guy M. *The Twenty-Eighth Yearbook of the National Society for the Study of Education: Part I, Preschool and Parent Education Orgaization and Development.* Bloomington, Illinois, 1929.

White, Richard Grant. "The Public-School Failure," *North American Review,* Vol. CXXXI (1980) in ed. Daniel Calhoun. *The Educating of Americans: A Documentary History,* Boston: Houghton Mifflin Co., 1969.

White, William A. *The Mental Hygiene of Childhood.* Boston: Little, Brown, and Co., 1919.

Wiebe, Robert H. *The Search for Order, 1977-1920.* New York: Hill and Wang, 1967.

Wilson, R. J. ed. *Darwinism and he American Intellectual.* Homewood, Illinois: The Dorsey Press, 1967.

Winder, Paul H. *Minimal Brain Dysfunction in Children.* New York: John Wiley, 1971.

Winship, A. E. "The Herbartian System," *Journal of Education,* Vol. XXVIII, No. 7 (August 23, 1888).

Wittrock, Merlin ed. *Handbook of Research on Teaching,* 3rd ed. (New York: The Macmillan Publishing Co., 1986).

Wolf, Theta. *Alfred Binet.* Chicago: University of Chicago Press, 1973.

Worcester, Dean A. "The Wide Diversities of Practice in First Courses in Educational Psychology, *Journal of Educational Psychology,* Vol. XXVIII (1927).

World Health Organization. *Manual of the International Classification of Diseases, Injuries, and Causes of Death,* 9th ed. Geneva, Switzerland: Department of Mental Health and Substance Abuse, 2003.

Wuthnow, Robert. *Meaning and Moral Order: Explorations in Cultural Analysis.* Berkeley: University of California Press, 1987.

Yerkes, Robert M. *Psychological Examinations in the U.S. Army,* Vol. 15. Washington, D.C.: National Academy of Science, 1921.

Young, Michael D. *The Rise of the Meritocracy.* New Brunswick, New Jersey, Transaction, 1994.

Zachry, Caroline. "Emotion and Conduct in Adolescence" in ed. V. T. Thayer *et al. Reorganizing the Secondary School Curriculum.* New York: Appleton-Century, 1940.

Zelizer, Viviana. *Pricing the Priceless Child: The Changing Social Value of Children.* New York: Basic Books, 1985.

Zimmerman, Barry J. and Schunk, Dale H. eds. *Educational Psychology: A Century of Contributions.* Mahwah, New Jersey: Lawrence Erlbaum Associates, 2003.

Znaniecki, Florian, "The Scientific Function of Sociology of Education," *Educational Theory,* Vol. 1, No. 2 (August 1951).

INDEX

Bowditch, Henry Pickering, 181, 185
Borrowman, Merle, ix, 21
Brass instrument psychology, 169
Brauner, Charles, 40
Briggs dictum, 95, 363
Briggs, T. H., on educational research,
   60
Brookings Institute Graduate School,
   329
Brooklyn, 401
Broudy, Harry S., 362
   on philosophy of education, 420
   on structure of knowledge in the arts,
   378-379
Brown, Elmer, E., 139
Brown, George P., 139
Brown v. Board of Education, xii, 317,
   363, 389, 391-393, 399, 423
Brown II, 363, 392
Bruner, Jerome S., 360, 374, 382, 417
   on curriculum, 369-370
   on high school enrollments, 368
   on learning, 368
   reception of, 371
   on structure of knowledge, 369
Bryant, Ernest, 199
Bryner, Edna, 13, 265
Brzoska, H, G., 135
Buckingham, B. R., 233
   on psychology and education, 59
Buddhism, 380
Bureau of Census, U. S., 219
Bureau of Child Guidance, 279
Bureau of Education, U. S., 106, 181,
   314
Bureau of Educational Experiments,
   179
Bureau of Juvenile Research, 282
Bureau for the Eradication of Hook-
   worm Disease, 332
Bureau of Social Hygiene, 332
Bureaucracy, 110
   and public schools, 4
Burgess, Charles, ix
Burt, Cyril, 307
Bush, George W., 72, 390
Business administration, 416

Bussing, 398
Butler, Nicholas Murray, 139
Butts. R. Freeman, 414-415, 421, 423

Caldwell, Otis, W., 343, 345-346
Calhoun, Daniel, 106
California, 34
   Bureau of Juvenile Research, 282
   child guidance, 281
   legislature, 283
   schools, 283
Callahan, Raymond E., 215, 413, 415,
   421-422, 424-425
Calvinistic dogma, 171
Cambridge, 154, 187
Campbell, Ernest Q., 393
Canadian National Committee for
   Mental Hygiene, 274
Cape Cod, 368
Cardinal principles, 8
*Caring for Children and Adolescents with
   Mental Disorders*, 288
Carnegie Corporation, 390, 419, 422,
   424
Carter, James G., 104, 160, 383
   on common school, 105
   on teaching, 105
Carter, Robert, 391
Catholic University of America, 35
Cattell, James McKeen, 21, 216, 251,
   254, 313
   laboratory, 304
   studies in Wundt's laboratory, 39
Cedar Creek, 338-340
Census Bureau, U.S., 193
Center for Collaboration and Docu-
   mentation, 286
Central Bureau of Planning and Statis-
   tics for the War Industries Board,
   217
Central Normal College, 198
Certificate systems, 34
Certification standards, 111
Chamberlain, Alexander Francis, 157
Chance research results, 171
Change as an object of inquiry, 161,
   165, 168, 170

Fleming, Charlotte, 37, 43
Flexner, Abraham, 310
Ford, Henry, 5
The "Forgotten man," 327
Formalen Stufen, 138
Fortune, 424
Forum, 30-31
Foshay, Arthur W.
   on curriculum, 378
   on school subjects, 376-377
   on structure of disciplines, 375-376
Fourier, 93
France, 36
Franco, 414
Frank, Lawrence K., 276, 327, 333, 335
   340-344, 349
Franklin, Benjamin, 96
Frederick Academy, 96
Freeman, Frank N. 219-220
   on Starch, 219
French Revolution, 93
Freud, Sigmund, 37
Frick, Otto, 134-135
Friedan, Betty, 423
Froebel, Friedrich, 180, 187-188
The frontier, 3-4, 108
Frontier Thesis, 139
Full enrollment, 113, 364-365
Full inclusion, 319
Functionalists, 165
Fund for the Advancement of Education, 418, 421

Gage, N. L., 20
Galton, Sir Francis, 38, 68, 156, 171,
   199, 216, 223, 254, 303-304,
   315-316
   opens laboratory, 304
Gans, Bird Stein, 342
Gary Indiana Survey, 232
Gay, Peter, 92
Gedney Farms Conference, 275
General Classification Test, 314
General Education Board, 3, 202, 278,
   285-287, 310, 326, 331-332, 349
   support for mental hygiene studies,
   286

General Methods, 136
Genetics, 155
   methods, 163
   and psychology, 163, 188
   research, 315
   "g" factor, 315-316
Gifted children, 198-199
George Peabody School for Teachers,
   139
Germany, 118, 124, 383
Gesell, Arnold, xvii, 15-16, 131, 182,
   197, 274
   use of cameras, 184
   on child development, 195
   on evolutionary theory, 195
   medical degree, 195
   on mental hygiene, 196
   norms for children, 197
   on reading instruction, 196-197
   on schools, 195
   on stages of development, 15, 194
Giddens, Frank, 342
Gillispie, Charles Coulston, 156
Global economy, x, 58, 424
Glueck, Bernard, 279
Goddard, Henry, H., 36, 200, 304, 307-
   309, 316
   hereditarian theories, 312
   and Binet-Simon tests, 306
Godwin, Parke, 93-94
Goldilocks, 56
Gompertz formula, equation, 236 also
   see Stuart A. Courtis
   law, 237
Good, Carter V., 60-61
Good stock, 325
Goodenough, Florence, 279
Goodlad, John, 6
Goodman, Paul, 371
Göttingen, 126, 135
Gould, Steven J., 307
Gowin, D. Bob, on educational
   research, 67
The Grammar of Science, 6, 46
Gray, Asa, 159
Grade-level gap, 397
Graduate programs in education, 35

Reagan, Ronald, administration of, 383
on Department of Education, 383
Recapitulation, 108, 183
Recitation methods, 140
Rein, Wilhelm, 30, 134-135, 138, 140-141
Remmers, H. H., 71, 223-224
Renaissance, 92
Republican government, principles of, 100
Republican Party, 3
Research Notes on Educational Effectiveness, 74
Research
on intelligence, 302
on child development, 333, 341
child guidance, 290
design, 9
discipline-based, 359
genetic, 315
on human subjects, 272
on intelligence, 313
mental hygiene, 290
on teaching, 117, 136
paradigms, xiii, 58
on parent education, 341
philosophical, 62
on the rural child, 341
on teaching, 136
Researchers on research, 58-59
The Restoration of Learning, 367, 416
Review of Research Methods in Education, 61
Revisionist history, 413
Reyna, Valerie, 72
Rice, Isaac, 30
Rice, Joseph Mayer, 29-30, 40, 63, 68, 235, 271
conducts national survey, 31
on education discourse, 30
on educational reform, 32
on new education, 31
on old education, 31
pilot test, 33
on psychology, 32
spelling tests, 33
studies in Germany, 30

on time, 33
Ritalin, 289
Rockefeller, Sr., John D., 3, 325-326
Rockefeller Foundation, 217, 275, 288, 332, 349
officers, 288
support of psychiatric research, 287
Medical Division, 288
Rockefeller, Laura Spelman 325
Rockefeller philanthropic boards, 278
Rockefeller philanthropies, 275, 284, 320, 332, 347, 350
Rockefeller philanthropy, xvii, 3, 16, 262, 276, 283, 285, 310
agenda, 326
campaign for expansion of public schooling, 275
guided by Ruml and Frank, 327
support for child research, 327,330
support for educational research, 326
support for mental hygiene movement, 326
Robins, James Harvey, 427
Rosenkranz, 128, 136
Ross, Dorothy, 187
Roosevelt, Franklin D., 190
Roosevelt, Theodore, 275
Rotarian, 366
Rousseau, Jean-Jacques, 97, 129, 181-182, 191
Rugg, Harold O., 171, 222, 257-258
Ruml, Beardsley, 286, 327-329, 317, 333, 335, 341, 342-344
Rural children, 335
problems of, 333
research on, 341
Rush, Benjamin, 98
on diversity, 99
on education, 99
Russell James E., 343, 346
Russell Sage Foundation, 13, 217, 333
Russett, Cynthia Eagle, 159

Salmon, Thomas W., 274-275, 279
Sandiford, Peter, 258
Samoa, 4

DATE DUE

Demco, Inc. 38-293

Printed in the United States
145757LV00001B/4/P

9 781593 117306